A Schoenberg Reader

A Schoenberg Reader
Documents of a Life

Joseph Auner

Yale University Press
New Haven & London

For Edie

Published with assistance from the fund established in memory of Philip Hamilton McMillan of the Class of 1894, Yale College.

Designed by Mary Valencia.
Set in Veljovic type by Keystone Typesetting, Inc.

Printed in the United States of America by Sheridan Books.

Library of Congress Cataloging-in-Publication Data
Auner, Joseph Henry, 1959–
A Schoenberg reader : documents of a life / Joseph Auner.
p. cm.
Includes bibliographical references (p.   ) and index.
ISBN 0-300-09540-6 (cloth : alk. paper)
1. Schoenberg, Arnold, 1874–1951. 2. Composers—Austria—Vienna—Biography.
I. Title.
ML410.S283 A97 2003
780′.92—dc21   2002154114

A catalogue record for this book is available from the British Library.

The paper in this book meets the guidelines for permanence and durability of the Committee on Production Guidelines for Book Longevity of the Council on Library Resources.

10 9 8 7 6 5 4 3 2 1

Contents

Acknowledgments

In putting together this project I have benefited enormously from the archival, bibliographic, and editorial work of the many scholars who have concerned themselves with Schoenberg's music and writings, in particular: Walter Bailey, Antony Beaumont, Mark Benson, Jack Boss, Juliane Brand, Reinhold Brinkmann, Patricia Carpenter, Roy E. Carter, Michael Cherlin, Jean Christensen, John Covach, John Crawford, Alexander Dümling, Murray Dineen, Egbert Ennulat, Allen Forte, Gerold Gruber, Jelana Hahl-Koch, Christopher Hailey, Martha Hyde, Jane Kallir, Ulrich Krämer, Eberhardt Klemm, Moshe Lazar, Jan Maegaard, Scott Messing, Severine Neff, Dika Newlin, Alexander Ringer, Willi Reich, Josef Rufer, Ullrich Scheideler, Barbara Z. Schoenberg, Joan Allen Smith, Claudio Spies, Leonard Stein, Hans Heinz Stuckenschmidt, Ivan Vojtech, Horst Weber, and Rudolf Stephan and all those involved with the *Arnold Schönberg Sämtliche Werke*.

Special mention and warm thanks go to Nuria Schoenberg-Nono, whose *Arnold Schoenberg: Self Portrait* and *Lebensgeschichte in Begegnungen* were invaluable resources for this book. For specific commentary and many useful suggestions during the writing of this book, I am indebted in particular to Charlotte Cross, Steven Cahn, Ethan Haimo, Elizabeth Keathley, Walter Frisch, Severine Neff, Jennifer Shaw, Bryan Simms, and Leonard Stein. Heartfelt thanks to Klaus Kropfinger and Helga von Kügelgen for all their help navigating Berlin archives, for matters of translation, and for many insights into Schoenberg's thought. For additional assistance pertaining to German archival sources and questions of translation, I am grateful to Hermann Danuser, Albrecht Riethmüller, Annagret Janda, Joy Calico, Sabine Feisst, and Isabella Goldschmidt. Otto Bohlmann suggested countless improvements to the text. My deep appreciation goes to two people who have been closely involved with this project from the beginning: Harry Haskell, music editor of Yale University Press, who invited me to undertake it, and Robert Morgan, my adviser, mentor, and friend. Whatever merits this book may have are due in large part to their tireless and patient support, and their wise and thoughtful counsel on every aspect of the organization and presentation of the material. For remaining errors, omissions, and points of obscurity, I take full responsibility.

All scholars of Schoenberg's music have been enormously fortunate to have had access to the riches of Schoenberg's Nachlaß at the Arnold Schoenberg Institute in Los Angeles, under the directorship of Leonard Stein, and now in its splendid new home at the Arnold Schönberg Center in Vienna, under the directorship of Christian Meyer. Wayne Shoaf, archivist of the Arnold Schoenberg Institute during the genesis of this project, was an endless source of information, assistance, and mountains of photocopies. The staff of the Arnold Schoenberg Institute, including Camille Crittenden, Nora Henry, Heidi Lesemann, Anita Lüginbühl, Marilyn McCoy, and Maja Reid produced countless transcriptions, translations, and bibliographic resources that have greatly facilitated my work. Therese Muxeneder, archivist of the Arnold Schönberg Center, has continued this tradition of exemplary service, now aided by the technological resources of the internet. I am also grateful to the staff and directors of the music divisions of the Library of Congress, the Pierpont Morgan Library, the University of Pennsylvania Library, the University of Wisconsin Library, the Staatsbibliothek zu Berlin, the Geheimes Staatsarchiv Preussicher Kulturbesitz, Berlin, and the Akademie der Künste, Berlin.

My warmest thanks go to Lawrence and Anne Schoenberg, Nuria Schoenberg-Nono, and Ronald and Barbara Schoenberg for their permission to publish all the archival materials, letters, photographs, and paintings included here, as well as for their support and encouragement over many years. I am grateful to Belmont Music Publishers for permission to include excerpts and translations of Schoenberg's song and choral texts, libretti, and literary works. Thanks to the *Journal of the Arnold Schoenberg Institute* for permission to quote from materials originally published in its pages. For permission to use translations and transcriptions, I am grateful to Walter Bailey, Jean Christensen, Charlotte Cross, Moshe Lazar, and Severine Neff. Permission has been granted for items previously published by Columbia University Press, Faber and Faber, Scarecrow Press, University of California Press, University of Nebraska Press, and W. W. Norton.

Warm thanks to my wonderfully supportive colleagues in the Department of Music at Stony Brook, in particular, Sarah Fuller, Perry Goldstein, Bonnie Gordon, Gilbert Kalish, Maiko Kawabata, David Lawton, Judith Lochhead, Timothy Mount, Daria Semegen, Sheila Silver, Jane Sugarman, Dan Weymouth, and Peter Winkler, and former colleagues Richard Kramer and Bryan Hyer. Thanks as well to staff members Theresa Berndt, Marie Coen, Robin Pouler-McGrath, and Joan Vogelle. I was helped in many ways by the staff of the Music Library, Gisele Glover, Susan Opisso, Erik Robinson, and Joan Signorelli. I have benefited greatly from the opportunity to work with many outstanding graduate students, all of whom have left their mark on this project, in particular those noted above, Steven Cahn, Elizabeth Keathley, and Jennifer Shaw, along with Lisa Barg, Mark Berry, Murat Eyuboglu, Oksana

Ezhokina, Deborah Heckert, Sonya Hofer, Stefan Litwin, Brian Locke, Margaret Martin, Katie Schlaikjer, and Kirsten Yri. Special thanks to Theo Cateforis and Christine Fena, who were substantially involved with the project as my research assistants while the project was just taking shape and in the final stages. Stefan Eckert expended enormous energy and time over several years as my German tutor, translation adviser, and Finale expert. Few pages in the text have not benefited from his help.

Finally, my warmest thanks to my family for all their unwavering support and encouragement over the many years this book has been in progress; to my mother and late father, Ruth Ann and Cecil Auner, to Henry and Nancy Lowe, to my children Eric and Mary, and above all to Edith Lowe Auner, who has been beside me every step of the way.

Introduction

Arnold Schoenberg and his music have been objects of celebration, controversy, and vilification for more than a century, from the time of his first
performances to the present day. Not surprisingly, in accounts of his life and
works by both his champions and his critics the adjective *Schoenbergian* has
come to mean so many things as to be almost meaningless. Schoenberg has
been interpreted variously as the standard-bearer of a revolutionary modernism, the guardian of the evolutionary path of musical tradition, a reactionary
Romantic who did not realize the implications of his own discoveries, an
isolated and misunderstood prophet, the founder of a school of composition
whose hegemony has only recently been challenged, an irrational expressionist, and the chief instigator of a cerebral sonic mathematics that has remade
modern music in the image of science.

Although there may be a grain of truth in each of these representations, all
of these "Schoenbergs" are based on partial, one-sided, and ahistorical accounts of his music and thought.[1] Works, writings, and activities that do not fit
within the various explanatory models are de-emphasized or omitted. Inconsistencies and contradictions in his views from different stages of his life are
smoothed over. Statements that were intended to be exploratory or provisional
are regarded as categorical. Through the separation of Schoenberg's writings
from their broader intellectual and cultural context the meaning and significance of his words have been too easily misinterpreted or misunderstood.

By bringing together a wide range of writings and materials, including many previously unpublished or untranslated documents, *A Schoenberg
Reader* reconstructs a balanced and multifaceted image of the composer, his
interaction with contemporary cultural and intellectual trends, and the continuities and disruptions in his creative output over the course of his long life
from turn-of-the-century Vienna, to Weimar Berlin, to 1950s Los Angeles.

Organization

The *Reader* is organized chronologically to give a sense of the development of
Schoenberg's thought and music. In addition to clarifying the biographical and

historical placement of the documents, the chronological presentation is in-tended to counterbalance the frequent reliance on Schoenberg's own very influential accounts in the retrospective essays from the final decade of his life, such as "Composition with Twelve Tones" (1941) and "My Evolution" (1949).[2] In these and many other writings by Schoenberg and his circle, an explicit goal was to demonstrate the historical necessity and inevitability of twelve-tone composition. This teleological framework shaped many aspects of his thought, as is clear in a late fragment entitled "My Way":

> It seems to me at present possible to examine the manner of my musical writings from the start on from the viewpoint of what it resulted into.
>
> I mean: I hope I can show how in numerous phases of my career little features always showed up, that is, little peculiarities of the technique which had to be developed gradually until the universal instrument was finished which enabled me to formulate my ideas in a manner adequate to their contents.
>
> Becoming aware of the consequence and logic in such a development suggests strongly the belief that there operates a power directly and unerr-ingly toward a preconceived goal: even the deviation from a straight line and the lapses of time between phases of a certain similarity can be under-stood as actions of a definite will, of a definite purpose and intention.[3]

In the documents assembled here there are indeed many striking examples of the kinds of premonitions and anticipations Schoenberg describes, as for ex-ample in the close relationship between one of the earliest selections, the fragmentary opera libretto *Superstition* (see section 1.12 below) dating from around 1900, and the sixth of the *Modern Psalms* (7.31), written shortly before his death, which includes the line, "What truly moves us in superstition is the faith of the superstitious, his faith in mysteries."

At the same time, however, it is often the case that the Schoenberg of the 1940s and 1950s has been allowed to overpower—and at times to silence—his voice from the preceding decades. In the essay "Gustav Mahler," Schoenberg recounts examining photographs of the composer from various stages in his life. Referring to the portrait of the fifty-year-old Mahler, Schoenberg writes: "It shows almost no resemblance to the youthful pictures. The development from within has given it a form which, I might say, has swallowed up all the previous phases."[4] But along with the significant ideological and aesthetic continuities, the chronological organization of the documents shows that there were also profound changes in Schoenberg's music, aesthetic ideals, sense of tradition, ideas of expression, attitudes toward teaching and the role of theory, and many other aspects of his thought in response to the equally profound changes in the world he experienced so intensely.[5]

Rather than regarding the inconsistencies and contradictions as a weakness in his thinking, we might view his willingness to confront ambiguities and compulsion toward constant self-questioning and reassessment as arguably the most characteristic and engaging aspects of his personality and intellect. As the documents presented here show, this trait is evident at every stage, in his readiness to challenge earlier statements in later writings, his practice of revising essays over many years before publishing them, and the care he took in the formulation of an individual idea. In a 1928 statement on Stravinsky's *Oedipus Rex*, for example, Schoenberg begins with a number of sarcastic comments on the piece, such as "the orchestra sounds like a Stravinsky-imitation by Krenek." But he then continues in a very different tone: "My remarks about Stravinsky now strike me not only as less witty than they did a few hours ago, but as something almost equally bad: rather philistine."[6] In the preface to the *Theory of Harmony*, a book for which he prepared a substantially revised edition (see 2.16, 4.11), he places doubt at the center of his project: "The teacher must have the courage to admit his own mistakes. He does not have to pose as infallible, as one who knows all and never errs; he must rather be tireless, constantly searching, perhaps sometimes finding. Why pose as a demigod? Why not be, rather, fully human?"[7]

To trace these continuities and transformations, the *Reader* consists of seven chapters, which are coordinated with the major turning points in Schoenberg's life and works. The opening section, "Autobiographical Documents and Reminiscences," provides an overall chronology of his life and works, along with his recollection of his childhood and musical education. The rest of Chapter 1 concerns the early years in Vienna and Berlin through the First String Quartet, Op. 7. Chapter 2 starts with the composition of the First Chamber Symphony, Op. 9, in 1906, charts the subsequent breakthrough to atonality, and concludes with his second move to Berlin in 1911. Chapter 3 encompasses the years leading up to and including the First World War, 1911 to 1918, a time that saw particularly significant transformations in his thought. Chapter 4, covering 1918 to 1925, traces the formation of the method of composing with twelve-tones and the wide range of his teaching activities at the time he was living in the Viennese suburb of Mödling. Chapter 5, spanning 1926 to 1933, deals with the period of Schoenberg's return to Berlin as a professor at the Prussian Academy of the Arts and concludes with the collapse of the Weimar Republic. Chapter 6, ranging from 1933 to 1943, covers his emigration from Germany to the United States, where after a very difficult year on the East Coast he settled in Los Angeles. Chapter 7 spans 1944 to 1951 and includes Schoenberg's amazingly prolific final years, starting with his retirement from teaching to his death.

Although not intended as a complete biographical account, the selection of items does provide an overview of the main formative events in

Schoenberg's life as well as an introduction to many of his most important works. Each chapter includes facsimiles of compositional sketches and manuscripts to illuminate Schoenberg's approach to the compositional process at various phases in his career. Along with photographs corresponding to the time period, most chapters also include one of the many self-portraits Schoenberg painted throughout his life; they illustrate his shifting self-perception and the range and development of his graphic technique—which is closely related to his compositional evolution.

Within each chapter, the selections are presented chronologically, except for a few instances where documents related to a specific topic are grouped together. The annotations, however, often include exerpts from later writings, as in the case of the letter to David Joseph Bach (July 25, 1895) concerning Schoenberg's early interest in socialism (1.9), the annotation to which cites "My Attitude Towards Politics" from 1950. Rather than explaining or clarifying the earlier statements, such later commentaries are intended to allow alternative, and sometimes contradictory, viewpoints to emerge. The most substantial departure from the chronology of the writings is in the placement of exerpts from Schoenberg's analyses, program notes, and lectures on individual works, most of which were written in the latter part of his life.[8] In order to provide a clearer account of his compositional development, these are placed, in most cases, according to the completion date of the compositions discussed.

Selection

A *Schoenberg Reader* brings together diverse documents representing all aspects of the composer's creative, intellectual, and personal life. These include completed and fragmentary essays on aesthetics, theory, analysis, performance, teaching, politics, and religion, as well as biographical items and personal correspondence, literary writings, aphorisms, musical sketches, paintings, and photographs. This approach was inspired most directly by two publications edited by Nuria Schoenberg-Nono: *Arnold Schoenberg: Self-Portrait* (*SP*), which included most of Schoenberg's commentaries on his music along with letters and other writings, and the *Lebensgeschichte in Begegnungen* (*LB*) (Life story in encounters), a collection of facsimiles and transcriptions from the huge range of archival material in Schoenberg's *Nachlaß*.[9] The diversity and richness of these publications provide vivid testimony to Schoenberg's incredibly energetic and wide-ranging intellect.

Something of the extent of the topics that concerned him is evident in the list of categories he devised to organize his writings, including: Aesthetics, divided into music (Mus) and all others arts (Kü); Interpretation (Deut), divided into theories, interpretations, explanations, discoveries, recommendations, improvements; Monuments (Denk), portraits, experiences, adventures, pillories; Mixed ideas (Verm), political, economic, social; Nature (Nat), nature, physics, animals; Linguistics (Sprach), including glosses; Aphorisms (Aph), jokes, witticisms, satires, glosses, polemics, without theoretical significance; Anecdotes (An), experiences; Moral (Mor), philosophy of life, world-view, philosophical wisdom; Biography (Bio), including the origins of works.[10]

The miscellany assembled in the *Reader* might appear peculiar from the perspective of present-day disciplinary boundaries and in light of critical approaches that would separate the works from the author. Yet it is precisely through the juxtaposition of these seemingly different kinds of documents that a clearer picture of Schoenberg's thought and music can be formed. Schoenberg's writings are best known in English through the 1975 collection *Style and Idea* (*SI*), edited by Leonard Stein, a much expanded version of the original publication (*SI* [1950]), edited by Dika Newlin, which first appeared in 1950. The most complete collection in German is also entitled *Stil und Gedanke*, edited by Ivan Vojtech (*GS*).[11] Although the original *Style and Idea*, and still more so its two successors, contain an astonishing range of material, Schoenberg intended it only as a first volume of a "complete" edition of his literary works that would include "theory, aesthetics, poetry, and many other subjects." As he wrote to Reba Sparr, who was editor of the Philosophical Library, which published *Style and Idea*: "It seems to me the purpose of such a book should not only be to offer ideas, but it should also deliver a 'portrait' of the man, of his compass, of his inclinations and dislikes. It is of course also the positive value of the ideas and theories brought about; but behind the writing of an artist, his personality should not remain entirely in the background."[12]

If anything typifies Schoenberg, it is that he left the stamp of his personality on everything and everyone he encountered. Central to his personality was his conviction that emotional, moral, and spiritual concerns were not separable from artistic issues. Accordingly, many of his most important aesthetic pronouncements can be found in documents that would not typically be included in a corpus of musical writings, such as letters, literary works, and autobiographical materials. In his most personal writings, such as "Draft of a Will" (2.2), written in a period of despair in 1908, Schoenberg considered his own emotional traumas in the same language, and often in the same breath, as broader aesthetic questions that would occupy him intensively over the coming years. Moreover, even his most personal writings appear to have been written with one eye on posterity. As a result, for the reader of these documents there is rarely a sense of eavesdropping or prying into something that was intended to remain private. On the contrary, Schoenberg's private writings often give the impression that he was directly addressing some future reader.

Selections from the thousands of letters Schoenberg wrote and received throughout his life are a particularly valuable resource.[13] At every stage of his life Schoenberg was in close contact with important figures in music, literature, art, and other intellectual endeavors. In addition to the information they offer about the events they chronicle and his personal and professional relationships, Schoenberg's letters contain some of the most detailed and extensive statements of his aesthetic goals. The correspondence also reveals a great deal about the different aspects of Schoenberg's personality in the range of styles and tones he adopts, depending on the recipient and subject under consideration. Discussions of Schoenberg often stress his irascibility and quickness to take offense; indeed, he was aware that he did not always make things easy for those around him. In a 1924 letter to the critic Paul Bekker he wrote: "If only we could manage to be wise enough to put people on probation instead of condeming them, if we could only give proven friends such extended credit!—I am speaking of my own defects, knowing very well why I have often been more lonely than could well be pleasant."[14] Yet along with his undeniably problematic personal traits, Schoenberg's letters show him capable of extraordinary generosity, insight, and warmth.

Arguably the least known and least studied segments of Schoenberg's creative output are his literary works. From the turn-of-the-century libretto fragments given in chapter 1, to the *Modern Psalms* he was working on at the time of his death, Schoenberg was active as a writer throughout his life. He wrote many texts for musical settings, including the librettos for *Die glückliche Hand* and *Moses und Aron*, as well as many shorter texts, especially for chorus. In addition to the texts for music there are a large number of aphorisms, several poems, and the formative work from the period of his reconversion to Judaism, the play *The Biblical Way*. Schoenberg's own texts have not been always favorably received, and readers will no doubt disagree on the literary quality of the examples included here. But it is clear that he did consider them as having a value that would allow them to be considered independently from their musical settings. In 1926 Universal Edition published the collection *Texts*, which included *Die glückliche Hand*, the *Death-Dance of Principles*, the *Requiem*, and *Die Jakobsleiter*. Schoenberg commented in his foreword,

> These are texts: that means, they only yield something complete together with the music. However, that is not said in order to ask more indulgence for them than is granted my music. For the quality of the finished product which one envisages is surely not dependent on the quality of the component parts, since each of these parts needs only to be as good at any given time as circumstances demand: that good, and good in that particular way! But one who has looked upon the whole also sees it in the smallest component and could not let anything pass muster as suitable if it were not so in every respect.

Just as little as one can expect a reader to form an idea of music which is unknown to him, can one expect from an author that he write music which corresponds to such a conception. The author of the text must save space on the surface for music to occupy, since music's aim is to penetrate the depths. The incompleteness then shows itself as imperfection on the most exposed flank, and this is no doubt the reason why an artist in several art-forms has seldom had the experience of achieving more recognition than had been his due from one art. On the contrary: people always conclude from the one achievement which they find slight that the other one is slighter still.[15]

Editorial Procedure

A considerable number of the writings included in the *Reader* are drafts, outlines, and fragments of projects that were never completed or published. Notwithstanding the enormous amount of work that Schoenberg did finish, a much larger number of compositions and writings were abandoned throughout his life. Commenting on his tendency to compose very rapidly in an unpublished statement entitled "Creative Agonies" (5.9), he acknowledged: "I have often, mostly for external reasons, had to interrupt a work for some time and have then found it difficult to resume." But there were clearly internal reasons as well for the large number of fragmentary works in his output. In a letter to Berg dated September 17, 1933, he wrote: "It is strange that all my larger works (beginning with *Gurrelieder*) have been in danger of remaining torsos: *Jakobsleiter, Der biblischer Weg, Moses und Aron*, the counterpoint book, and the other theoretical works."[16] Indeed, a central pillar of Schoenberg's thought was the inevitable gap between an "idea" and its realization. If it is a subject of debate that the incomplete state of works like *Moses und Aron* is intrinsic to their meaning, there is no question that Schoenberg placed a very high value on these fragments and torsos. This is evident in the great care he took to preserve and catalog the tremendous amount of material in his *Nachlaß*, and even more so in his frequent references to his unfinished projects in his writings. And while there is no doubt that Schoenberg would have brought many of the fragments and drafts presented here to a more polished state before publication, their relative incompletion offers opportunities to observe his creative processes from the earliest stages to the final formulations.

Because Schoenberg often used graphic means for clarifying the organization of his ideas, I have preserved the layout and appearance of the originals where possible. Where lines of text have been combined, as in the long lists of names from "Notes for an Autobiography" and some of the literary works, I have indicated the original line breaks with a slash mark. The versions of the texts presented here are not, however, intended as diplomatic transcriptions, and in the case of multiple readings only the final layer of revision is indicated. Editorial additions are indicated by square brackets.

I have attempted where possible to allow the documents themselves to carry the narrative of Schoenberg's life and work. Thus, for example, I begin the first chapter with a résumé he prepared near the end of his life to provide an initial overview of the main biographical events and compositional activities (1.1). Similarly, as I noted above, the annotations frequently draw on Schoenberg's own commentaries about the topic under consideration. These often include excerpts from his better-known essays from *Style and Idea*, and they thus also serve to direct the reader to further writings.

It is not my intent to impose a single interpretation on the documents included here, beyond what is implicit in the selection and organization. Many central themes in Schoenberg's life and thought do emerge over the course of the seven chapters, such as the tension between idea and presentation, his shifting attitudes toward the roles of the intellect and intuition in the creative act, the nature of order and comprehensibility in the artwork, program versus absolute music, revolution versus evolution in the arts, his stance toward mass culture and popular music, his ambivalent relationship to the audience, ideas about concert life and performance, the importance of his students and pedagogical activities, the evolution of his beliefs about the interactions of art and politics, and his relationship to religion, his Jewish identity in particular. Yet in the annotations I have chosen to cross-reference only some of the many connections between the documents; many more can be traced by means of the index. It is my hope that each reader will discover new paths through the material.

Together with the usual problems of translation, Schoenberg's German poses special challenges due to his life-long fascination with language, along with the conviction he shared with his Viennese contemporary Karl Kraus that language, as the "mother of thought," was a moral issue.[17] As he wrote to Dika Newlin (February 4, 1949) concerning her translations for *Style and Idea* (1950): "I am really astonished how well you understood my German. It is quite clear you did not understand all the stylistic finesses of my German style. My German style is really unusually difficult to understand. I mean, among ten highly educated Germans there might be only two or three who understand every point of mine."[18] While striving for readability and clarity, I have attempted in the translations to preserve the character and structure of Schoenberg's formulations as well as, to the degree possible, his often dense wordplay.

Soon after arriving in the United States in 1933, Schoenberg began writing in English and made rapid progress in his new language. Many of the items in the final two chapters, as well as the program notes and analyses of individual works that appear throughout the book, were written in English. Yet, as is evident in writings quoted above, his English retained many aspects of his native German, along with his own idiosyncrasies. In my editorial approach I have followed Schoenberg's instructions in another letter to Newlin, from January 25, 1949, concerning her editorial work on his English writings:

> The task to be editor of the articles in my own English of this book, is a self-sacrifice: you must entirely forget your own personality, your own ideas, your own style of presenting them. Because I do not plan to hide the fact that I am not born in this language and I do not want to parade adorned by stylistic merits of another person. I think, if my ideas are not strong enough to conquer my misrepresentation of them, then the book should not be published at all. But if they are worthwhile, they can counterbalance some of my shortcomings. [. . .]
>
> Your self-sacrifice: I ask you to act here like a school teacher; correcting here only errors of grammar and idiom. If you find some of my mistakes correctable, ask me. It happens sometimes that I can improve them.
>
> I am sorry to ask such degrading work in this part of the book. But don't forget, that when you translate my German articles, you can reveal all your art.[19]

The bibliography of sources provides detailed information about each of the items, including an indication of the language in which it was written, German (G.o.) or English (E.o), publication and/or archival information, and, where relevant, notes on the translation.[20] Where no translation is provided for German originals, the translations are my own; translations indicated as "adapted from" have been substantially reworked, drawing on one or more sources. Where possible, I have consulted the original manuscripts to check transcriptions and translations. Biographical information for the many figures who appear throughout the text has been compiled from Stuckenschmidt, Reich, Ringer, Joan Allen Smith's *Schoenberg and His Circle*, "A Preliminary Inventory of Correspondence to and from Arnold Schoenberg," and *The New Grove Dictionary of Music and Musicians* (2001).

Abbreviations

ASI: Arnold Schoenberg Institute. University of Southern California, Los Angeles. Repository of the Schoenberg *Nachlaß*, 1977–1997.

ASC: Arnold Schönberg Center. Vienna. Repository of the Schoenberg *Nachlaß*, 1998–.

ASL: Schoenberg, Arnold. *Arnold Schoenberg Letters.* Edited by Erwin Stein. Translated by Eithne Wilkins and Ernst Kaiser. Berkeley and Los Angeles: University of California Press, 1987.

Bailey: Bailey, Walter B. "Schoenberg's Published Articles: A List of Titles, Sources, and Translations." *Journal of the Arnold Schoenberg Institute* 4, no. 2 (1980): 156–191.

Bailey, *Programmatic Elements:* Bailey, Walter B. *Programmatic Elements in the Works of Arnold Schoenberg.* Studies in Musicology, no. 74. Ann Arbor: UMI Research Press, 1984.

BSC: Brand, Juliane, Christopher Hailey, and Donald Harris, eds. *The Berg-Schoenberg Correspondence: Selected Letters.* New York: Norton, 1988.

Beaumont, *Busoni: Selected Letters:* Beaumont, Antony, ed. and trans. *Ferruccio Busoni: Selected Letters.* New York: Columbia University Press, 1987.

C: Christensen, Jean, and Jesper Christensen. *From Arnold Schoenberg's Literary Legacy: A Catalog of Neglected Items.* Warren, Mich.: Harmonie Press, 1988.

E.o. English original.

G.o. German original.

GS: Schönberg, Arnold. *Stil und Gedanke. Aufsätze zur Musik, Gesammelte Schriften 1.* Edited by Ivan Vojtech. Frankfurt am Main: Propyläen Verlag, 1976.

H: Schoenberg, Arnold. *Theory of Harmony.* Translated by Roy E. Carter. Berkeley and Los Angeles: University of California Press, 1978.

JASI: Journal of the Arnold Schoenberg Institute. Edited by Leonard Stein and Paul Zukofsky. University of Southern California: Los Angeles, 1976–1996.

LB: Schoenberg-Nono, Nuria, ed. *Arnold Schönberg 1874-1951: Lebensgeschichte in Begegnungen.* Klagenfurt: Ritter, 1992.

LC: Library of Congress.

M: Maegaard, Jan. *Studien zur Entwicklung des dodekaphonen Satzes bei Arnold Schönberg.* 2 vols. and supplement. Copenhagen: Wilhelm Hansen, 1972.

Messing: Messing, Scott. *Neoclassicism in Music: From the Genesis of the Concept Through the Schoenberg-Stravinsky Polemic.* Studies in Musicology, no. 101. Ann Arbor: UMI Research Press, 1988.

PM: Pierpont Morgan Library.

PNM: Perspectives of New Music

R: Rauchhaupt, Ursula. *Schoenberg/Berg/Webern: The String Quartets: A Documentary Study.* Hamburg: Deutsche Grammophon, 1971.

Reich, *Schoenberg:* Reich, Willi. *Schoenberg: A Critical Biography.* Translated by Leo Black. New York and Washington: Praeger, 1971.

Ringer: Ringer, Alexander L. *Arnold Schoenberg: The Composer as Jew.* Oxford and New York: Oxford University Press, 1993.

Rufer: Rufer, Josef. *The Works of Arnold Schoenberg: A Catalogue of His Compositions, Writings, and Paintings.* Translated by Dika Newlin. London: Faber and Faber, 1962.

SI: Schoenberg, Arnold. *Style and Idea: Selected Writings of Arnold Schoenberg.* Edited by Leonard Stein. Translated by Leo Black. Berkeley and Los Angeles: University of California Press, 1984.

SI (1950): Schoenberg, Arnold. *Style and Idea.* Edited by Dika Newlin. New York: Philosophical Library, 1950.

SK: Hahl-Koch, Jelena, ed. *Arnold Schoenberg, Wassily Kandinsky: Letters, Pictures, and Documents.* Translated by John Crawford. Boston: Faber and Faber, 1984.

SP: Schoenberg-Nono, Nuria, ed. *Arnold Schoenberg: Self-Portrait.* Pacific Palisades: Belmont, 1988.

Stuckenschmidt: Stuckenschmidt, H. H. *Arnold Schoenberg: His Life, World, and Work.* Translated by Humphrey Searle. New York: Schirmer, 1978.

SW: Arnold Schönberg Sämtliche Werke. Rudolf Stephan, general editor. Mainz: Schott; Wien: Universal Edition. Individual volumes as indicated.

1   Early Years in Vienna and Berlin: 1874–1906

Autobiographical Documents and Reminiscences

Schoenberg's Résumé, c. 1944

1.1 "Arnold Schoenberg, composer, teacher of musical composition."

*Prepared around 1944, following his retirement from UCLA, this version of Schoen-
berg's résumé includes biographical events up to 1941, publications up 1942, and
works up to 1943; the addenda of later writings was added c. 1950. Perhaps most
striking about this account of Schoenberg's first seventy years is the list of works
still to come before his death in 1951, including: Prelude to the Genesis Suite, Op.
44 (1945); String Trio, Op. 45 (1946); A Survivor from Warsaw, Op. 46 (1947);
Three Folksongs, for Mixed Chorus, Op. 49 (1948); Phantasy for Violin with
Piano Accompaniment, Op. 47 (1949); Three Songs for Low Voice, Op. 48 (composed 1933, published 1952); Dreimal tausend Jahre, Op. 50A (1949); De profundis, Psalm 130, Op. 50B (1950); and the Modern Psalm No. 1, Op. 50C (1950).
Editorial additions and corrections to the dates are indicated in brackets.*

Arnold Schoenberg, composer, teacher of musical composition.

Professor *emeritus* of Music at the University of California at Los Angeles.

Residence: 116 N. Rockingham Avenue, Los Angeles 24, California.

Date and Place of Birth: Vienna (Austria), September 13, 1874.

Parents: Samuel Schoenberg (d. 1890) Pauline Nachod (d. 1921).

Education: Volkschule and Realschule in Vienna.

In music at first autodidact; later 1895/96 studied with Alexander von
Zemlinsky.

Married first [in 1901] to Mathilde von Zemlinsky (died 1923); children, Gertrud Greissle (1902), Georg Schoenberg (1906)

1924: second marriage: Gertrud Kolisch (1898); children: Dorothea Nuria
(1932), Rudolf Ronald (1937), Lawrence Adam (1941).

Started composing at the age of eight years; started musical career as a cellist
and teacher of composition.

Photo previous page: Schoenberg, c. 1900. Arnold Schönberg Center, Vienna.

1902 [1901–1902]: conductor at Wolzogen's "Buntes Theater" in Berlin;[1] taught musical theory at Sternsches Konservatorium.

1904: returned to Vienna [1903], private teaching of composition. Pupils among them: Anton von Webern, Alban Berg (composer of *Wozzeck*) and many others.[2]

1911–1915: in Berlin, private teaching, conducting own works in Amsterdam, Berlin, St. Petersburg, Leipzig, Dresden, Vienna, etc. Touring with *Pierrot Lunaire*, composed 1912, conducting *Gurrelieder* in Leipzig, lecturing about Gustav Mahler in Prague, Stettin, Vienna and many other places.

1915 [1915–1916, 1917]: Austrian Army.

1919: Vienna, teaching; founded *Verein für Musikalische Privataufführungen Moderner Musik* [Society for Private Musical Performances]. Pupils at this time: Rudolf Kolisch, primarius of the Kolisch Quartet, Eduard Steuermann, concert pianist, Hanns Eisler, composer, Karl Rankl, conductor, director of the opera in Graz, later in the same position in Prague.

1920: in Holland; conducting ten concerts with own works and teaching.

1926–1933: in Berlin, appointed Professor of Musical Composition at the Akademie der Künste zu Berlin.

1933: October: Malkin Conservatory in Boston, Mass.

1934: Hollywood, private teaching, conducting, also conducting in New York, Boston, Mass., and Chicago, Ill.

1935/6: conducting also in Los Angeles.

Lecturing: Princeton, 1934; Chicago, 1934; Los Angeles, 1935; Denver, 1937; Kansas City, 1939.

1935: Professor of Music at the University of Southern California.

1936: Professor of Music at the University of California at Los Angeles.

1940 [1941]: Annual Research Lecture on "Composition with Twelve Tones" at the University of California at Los Angeles.

Member of: Music Teachers National Association; American Society for Aesthetics, American Society of Composers (ASCAP).

Honorary member of the Academy Santa Cecilia at Rome, Italy; of the Music Teachers Association of California; formerly of several musical and artistic societies in Germany.

Published books: *Harmonielehre* (out of print)	Universal Edition 1911[3]
Texte (a collection of poems on which my compositions are based)	Universal Edition 1926
Die Jakobsleiter, Oratorio.	Universal Edition 1917
Models for Beginners in Composition	G. Schirmer Inc. New York, 1942

Unpublished: *Moses and Aaron,* an opera.
   Der Biblische Weg, a drama.

Published in magazines and newspapers a great number of essays, mostly on
   musical and theoretical subjects.
Unpublished a great number of lectures, also on musical subjects. A collection
   of them will be published sometime.
I am writing at present a textbook on counterpoint, three volumes: I. Preliminary Exercises; II. Multiple Counterpoint; III. Counterpoint in 19th and
   20th Century Music.[4] Besides a textbook *Fundamentals of Musical Composition* (unfinished).[5]

A Partial List of my Musical Works
A) Symphonic and other Orchestral Works

	composed	1st performance	published
Gurrelieder	1899+1902[6]	1913	1912
Pelleas and Melisande	1902 [1903]	1905	1920 [1911]
Five Orchestral Pieces	1908 [1909]	1914 [1912]	1913 [1912]
Variations for Orchestra	1928	1928	1929
Lichtspielmusik[7]	1930	1930	1930
Concerto for Violoncello and Orch. (Monn)	1932 [1933]	1936 [1935]	1935
Concerto for String Quartet and Orch. (Handel)	1933	1937 [1934]	1935
Suite for String Orchestra	1934	1935	1935
Violin Concerto	1936	1941 [1940]	1939
Piano Concerto	1942	1944	1943 [1944]
Chamber Symphony, No. 1, Version for Orch.		1937	
Second Chamber Symphony	1940 [1939][8]	1940	

Transcriptions of Bach, Preludes and Prelude and Fugue in E flat
Transcriptions of Brahms Piano Quartet and others.

B) Operas

Erwartung, Monodrama, Op. 17	1909	1924	1916 [1917]
Die glückliche Hand, Op. 18	1913	1924	1924 [1917]
Von heute auf morgen, Op. 32	1929	1930	1930

Moses and Aaron, unfinished, second act finished in 1932

(Under A) by mistake these works have been omitted:
Ode to Napoleon Buonaparte   1942 (version for String Orchestra)

Variations for Wind Band   1943 [1942]
The same, Version for Full Orchestra   1943 [1942]

C) Chamber Music

String Quartets, Op. 7 (1904) [1905], Op. 10 (1907) [1908], Op. 30 (1930) [1927], Op. 37 (1939) [1936]

String Sextet *Verklärte Nacht* (1899), I. Chamber Symphony, Op. 9 (1906) *Pierrot Lunaire,* Melodramas, (1912); Serenade (1923); Wind Quintet (1924); Septet Suite (1927) [1926]; *Herzgewächse* (1915) [1911]; *Ode to Napoleon Buonaparte,* recitation with piano quintet (1942)

D) Piano Solo: Op. 11, Op. 19, Op. 23, Op. 25, Op. 33 A/B[9]

E) Songs with Orchestra: Op. 8 (1904); Op. 22 (1914–1915) [1913–1916]

F) Choral Works: *Peace on Earth,* Op. 13 (1907); Four Pieces for Mixed Choir, Op. 27 (1926) [1925]; Three Satires for Mixed Choir, Op. 28 (1926) [1925]; Six Pieces for Male Choir, Op. 35 (1930); Three German Folk Songs, transcriptions for mixed choir [1928]; *Kol Nidre,* with choir and orchestra (1938)

G) Songs with piano: Op. 1, 2, 3, 6, 12, 14, 15: Four German Folk Songs (transcriptions)

ADDENDA

Structural Functions of the Harmony [1948]

Models for Orchestra[10]

Collection of Essays under the Title of *Style and Idea* (Philosophical Library) [1950]

Key Terms of a Life

1.2 Notes Toward a Biography (c. 1949)

A biographical summary of selected events in Schoenberg's life up to his seventy-fifth birthday, probably dictated to his wife Gertrud.

vaccination certificate
grade cards from school
milkman downstairs
his first love: a horse
water outside only
bathtub on Saturday evenings
playing funerals with a violin case

big impression of the French teacher: such as telling him that a nice boy
   should not part his hair in the middle

"Last Rose of Summer": heard it once, and could remember it all[11]

He was on either the top or the bottom in the scale of school grades[12]

Fighting: (1) hole in the knees of his pants a sign of victory

(2) winning a fight

(3) drinking his coffee with the spoon in it

German grammar teacher: first one who made him realize the inadequacy of
   his home surroundings—such as how they talked in his home

His friends: D. J. Bach, Zemlinsky, Adler

His bank experience: he was told that his brother was much better than he;
   gave all he earned to his mother

His father's death: influenza, for which the doctor gave the wrong prescription
   on Dec. 31; the next day his father died. The doctor asked to have the
   prescription back, saying he would take care of the children.

Ringtheater fire: 2 cousins brought to stay with them

Mother's pension

Engaged to Bach's sister; Zemlinsky's sister was engaged to a man who left
   her, and she always took out her spite on Schoenberg.

Schoenberg married Zemlinsky's sister, who said she would kill herself if he
   would not marry her. She was a friend of Schoenberg's sister.

Schoenberg's sister admired his work very much and really loved him. She
   showed his work to a composer of light opera in Vienna; Schoenberg stood
   for a long time waiting to meet this man, who told him that he was talented but should study longer.

Schoenberg left the bank, which later went broke. He said he did not do
   anything there but write notes all of the time.

When he married Zemlinsky's sister, three different men refused to be the
   best man. His friends everywhere were not happy about his marriage.

He and his wife went to Berlin where R. Strauss helped him to obtain a teaching position at the Stern Conservatory. Trudie was born there. After he
   made some money, they had a comfortable place to live.

Von Gütersloh, a writer, became a good friend of his at Überbrettl. (Check with
   Alma for the letter from Strauss; look also in Schoenberg's letters why he
   did not write a birthday letter to Strauss.)

Prater his first love.

His birthdays in the country with his pupils: Klammer, Tönkirchen, München

When he went to his wife in the country and Trude told him that his friend, a
   painter, was going around with his wife. The friend killed himself afterward. His sister was also involved in this. Later at Berg's house Schoenberg's wife had an affair with someone else.

Invited to Switzerland for the *Gurrelieder;* wished a peace treaty, wrote to
   Busoni, and his coming was canceled.

Sued for money; return of money for performing *Gurrelieder.*

Crazy neighbor who wanted to kill him, forcing him to move.

Malkin did not renew the contract.

No affidavit, first papers for citizenship

Asked Heifetz for $3000; same thing happened with Stravinsky in Italy

When he and his family came to this country on the Ile de France, Bodanzky
   was on the ship with them. The ship line gave Mr. S 1/2 fare, Mrs. S 1/4
   fare, and let Nuria come without charge; only the dog was charged full
   fare.

Kreisler met the family at customs when they arrived in America, but his wife
   did not let him talk with the Schoenbergs. (When Kreisler's wife said that
   he had no Jewish blood, someone said "How anemic!")

Story about the ranger and bringing furniture here

Story about the synagogue in Paris: Einstein, what took place (Kreisler in N.Y.)

Wedding bells not ringing

medical papers

Letters to (1) Berlin Akademie (2) UCLA

75th Birthday letter

envelope of "Biography letters"

Paris: (1) Jewish society (2) E. Toch (3) Kreisler (4) Furtwängler (5) pupil of
   Schoenberg (6) [the document breaks off here.]

A Life Story in Encounters

1.3 From "Notes for an Autobiography" (1944–1945)

*This collection of miscellaneous materials, ranging from lists of names and frag-
mentary notes to extended essays, grew out of an idea for an autobiography
in 1924: "I have for a long time been planning to write my autobiography in such
a way that I, to the best of my memory, will present all persons with whom I
have been in contact, in so far as their relationship to me is of some interest; I will describe them as they have shown themselves to me and characterize
the relationship between them and me. Of course, this is not primarily an act
of revenge; rather it is merely a system which I expect will help my memory. As
I proceed, the links between different persons and separate events should emerge,
and I thus should be able to be as truthful as possible; while I surely would
fail if I attempted to write a chronological representation."[13] In 1932 Schoenberg returned to the project, adding the title "Life Story in Encounters." It is
likely that the following outline on the first page of the notebook was written at
this time:*

How I became a Musician
How I became a Christian
How I became a Brahmsian
How I became a Wagnerian
Encounters and relationships with: Mahler, Strauss, Reger, Ravel, Debussy, Stravinsky, Mann, Werfel, Loos, Kandinsky, Kokoschka, Kraus.[14]

When he again took up the project in 1944, he began with the same plan, but in a much-expanded form and with some noteworthy differences, as for example with the inclusion of the line "How I became a Jew *again." Additional materials from the "Notes for an Autobiography" are given in 7.2.*

How I became a *Musician*
How I became a *Christian*
How I became a *Jew* again
How I became a *Wagnerian*
How I became a *Brahmsian*

————

My friendships: Oscar Adler / David Bach / Alexander Zemlinsky • / Anton von Webern • / Alban Berg / Adolf Loos / Gustav Mahler / Alma Mahler-Werfel / Steuermann • / Erwin Stein • / Ratz, Weiss • / Dr. Emil Lemberger / Polnauer, Riesenfeld / Jalowetz, Bodanzky / Eisler / Rankl

Publishers: Hertzka, Kalmus, Winter / Rothe, Marschalk, Engel / Hinrichsen, Bote & Bock (30,000 RM), Heinrichshofen / Marschalk: Dreililien, Tischer & Jagenberg

My relatives: My brother, Görgi / father, mother, sister, Trudi / Olga, Mela, Arnold / Hans Nachod, Herman / Rudolf Kolisch, Uncle Fritz / Artur Schoenberg / Rudolf de Pascotini

Musicians, Painters, Poets, Writers: Mahler, Zemlinsky / Strauss, Reger, Pfitzner / Busoni, Schillings, Hindemith, Schreker / Krenek, Toch, Stravinsky / Milhaud, Ravel, Honneger / Koechlin, Florent Schmitt, G. Schumann / Gärtner, Schenker, Violin, Oscar Strauss / Godowski, Lehar, Casella, Malipiero / Hoffmann, Bloch, Mandyczewski, Grädener / Schnabel, Bruckner, Franz Schmidt / Casals, Posa, Korngold, Weigl / Kreisler, Kokoschka, Oppenheimer / Heifetz, Moll, Klimt, Loos / Achron, Kandinsky, Liebermann / Gruenberg, Heu / Th. Mann, H. Mann, Werfel / Altenberg, Karl Kraus / Dehmel, Schnitzler, Hofmannsthal / Wassermann, Hermann Bahr / Bernard Shaw (?) / Giraud / Kahane, Harndl, Reinhardt

Music critics and theorists: Karpath, Hirschfeld, Hanslick, Kalbeck / Korngold, Graf, Stefan, Konta, Specht / Leopold Schmidt, Einstein, Strobel / Wallaschek, Stauber, Springer, Marschalk/Reitler, Bienenfeld/Schenker, Hauer, Reich/Kallenbach-Greller/Cort van der Linden/Haba

Conductors: Mahler, Nikisch, Schuch, Klemperer/Walter, Mengelberg, Koussevitzky/Furtwängler, Kleiber, Clemens Krauss/Schalk, Loewe, Stiedry, Siloti/Wood, Szell, Rosbaud, Steinberg/Scherchen, Zemlinsky, Bodanzky/Herz, Stock, Muck, Toscanini (!)/Ormandy/Stokoswki, Boult/Rabbi Wise, Sonderling, etc.

University:
Scientists: Einstein, Knudsen, Reichenbach/Eichberg

Thiefs: Hull . . . , Reti, Hauer, etc.

Rascals: Rubsamen, Milenkovič, Wellesz, Levant/Neuer (Contract)

Mäcene: Karl Redlich, v. Fränkel, Lieser, "Ein Jude 1919"/Henry Clay Shriver, Elizabeth Sprague Coolidge/Dr. Emil Lemberger

Students: Webern, Berg, Krüger, Jalowetz, E. Stein/Polnauer, Weirich, Neumann, Linke/??Wellesz??, Seligmann/Steuermann, Clark, Zweig

Rudi Kolisch, Eisler, Rankl, Deutsch/Novakovič, Bachrich, Pisk, Travnicek

Leonard Stein, Strang, Halma, Estep/Newlin/Zillig, Hannenheim, Skalkottas/Schacht, Goehr, Weiss, Dannenberg/Levant

Orchestras: Wiener Philharmoniker, Konzert-Verein/Wiener Tonkünstler Orch. (The trombonist), Conertgebouw Orch./BBC, Cologne, Barcelona, Boston, New York/Radio: Vienna, Berlin, Frankfurt Opera

Performers: Zehme, Erica Wagner-Stiedry, Steuermann, Khuner/Gutheil-Schoder, Maliniak, Kindler/Essberger, De Vries, Van Leuwen, Rosé/Fitzner, Kolisch Quartet, Pro Arte Quartet/Fleury, Winternitz-Dorda/Wunderer, Marya Freund, Winkler, Polatschek/Feuermann, Schnabel, Buhlig, Serkin/Drill Orridge[?], Hans Nachod,—, Lehner, Nusbaum

On Schoenberg's Home Life and Musicality among His Relatives

1.4 Letter to Leopold Moll, November 28, 1931

In this letter Schoenberg talks about his early family life in Leopoldstadt in Vienna's Second District, an area where more than 40 percent of the Jewish population of the city resided.[15] The letter was written from Barcelona, where he was staying on one of his extended absences from Berlin during his years at the Prussian Academy of the Arts. Leopold Moll was connected with the State Institute for Mother and Infant Care in Vienna.

Dear Mr. Counselor.

To answer your questions exactly and without poeticizing is not so easy. I shall give it a try, but I doubt that much with regard to traits will come out of it.

Neither my father nor my mother was artistically active in any way. Both had no more than an "average musicality," though they certainly enjoyed music, particularly singing, and my father was in a singing society when he was young; but in no way would I say that this surpassed what every Austrian possesses who is not actually hostile to music. I can say, however, that my musical aptitude found unusually little support in my home, although I had already started composing when I was eight. While I have no specific recollection of it, there may have been some talk around our house that I had a knack for music, for it is striking to me that I read a Mozart biography quite early on, leading me from the start to write my compositions without the aid of an instrument.

My grandparents also seem not to have been especially musical. On the other hand, there were many fine singers among all the relatives on my mother's side; a great-uncle was supposed to have had a magnificent tenor voice. My brother and sister are both singers, one of my cousins even had a not inconsiderable success for a while as an operatic tenor (his father, who was my favorite uncle, wrote lyric poetry of a rather "effusive" bent, was a highly enthusiastic liberal, and perhaps had some influence on me up to at most my tenth year); four other cousins had beautiful tenor voices but remained amateurs.[16]

There is little that stands out in the biographies of my parents. My father was born in 1838, when he was fourteen he came to Vienna, where he became an apprentice in a business, and then had his own small business. He married when he was thirty-two; I was the second child, born when he was thirty-six.[17] He died of pulmonary influenza in the influenza epidemic of 1890 (on New Year's Eve) when he was fifty-two. I was then sixteen and thus knew relatively little from my own observations.

My parents' marriage seems to have gone along smoothly and to have been quite normal, troubled at most by financial concerns. I don't know any more about it.

My mother was born in 1848 in Prague. When she was young, she came with her father's family to Vienna.[18] She lived to be seventy-four. She was a clever woman who slaved away with three of her own children, two foster children, and later with the cousins. She was very self-sacrificing, unselfish, selfless, modest, and I may perhaps have inherited from her a certain industriousness and a sense of duty. I don't know if she suffered under the hostilities to which I was certainly exposed for a long time; in any case she had great joy when I later had success. In spite of that, her life was not exactly pleasant, for with my father's death she was left with her own three and two foster children without any means of survival, and so had a lot to struggle through.

I have certainly been much too detailed here, and that is because I have nothing more interesting to say: such things would have gone more quickly.

It would please me very much if something I have written is of use to you.

I will close, dear Mr. Counselor, with the expression of my greatest respect,

humbly,

On His Early Musical Life and Friendships

1.5 From "My Evolution," 1949

Of the seventy-five years of my life I have devoted almost ninety percent to music. I began studying violin at the age of eight and almost immediately started composing. One might accordingly assume that I had acquired very early a great skill in composing. My uncle Fritz, who was a poet, the father of Hans Nachod, had taught me French very early; there was not, as has happened in many child-prodigy-producing families, any music enthusiast in mine. All my compositions up to about my seventeenth year were no more than imitations of such music as I had been able to become acquainted with—violin duets and duet-arrangements of operas and the repertory of military bands that played in public parks.[19] One must not forget that at this time printed music was extremely expensive, that there were not yet records or radios, and that Vienna had only one opera theater and one yearly cycle of eight Philharmonic concerts.

Only after I had met three young men of about my own age and had won their friendship did my musical and literary education start. The first was Oscar Adler, whose talent as a musician was as great as his capabilities in science.[20] Through him I learned of the existence of a theory of music, and he directed my first steps therein. He also stimulated my interest in poetry and philosophy and all my acquaintance with classical music derived from playing quartets with him, for even then he was already an excellent first violinist.

My second friend at that time was David Bach.[21] A linguist, a philosopher, a connoisseur of literature, and a mathematician, he was also a good musician. He greatly influenced the development of my character by furnishing it with the ethical and moral power needed to withstand vulgarity and commonplace popularity.

The third friend is the one to whom I owe most of my knowledge of the technique and problems of composing: Alexander von Zemlinsky.[22] I have always thought and still believe that he was a great composer. Maybe his time will come earlier than we think. One thing is beyond doubt, in my opinion: I do not know one composer after Wagner who could satisfy the demands of the theater with better musical substance than he. His ideas, his forms, his sonorities, and every turn of the music sprang directly from the action, from the scenery, and from the singers' voices with a naturalness and distinction of supreme quality.

I had been a "Brahmsian" when I met Zemlinsky. His love embraced both Brahms and Wagner and soon thereafter I became an equally confirmed addict. No wonder that the music I composed at that time mirrored the influence of both these masters, to which a flavour of Liszt, Bruckner, and perhaps also Hugo Wolf was added. [. . .]

True, at this time I had already become an admirer of Richard Strauss, but not yet of Gustav Mahler, whom I began to understand only much later, at a time when his symphonic style could no longer exert its influence on me. But it is still possible that his strongly tonal structure and his more sustained harmony influenced me. [. . .]

On His Beginnings as a Composer

1.6 From "Preface to the Four String Quartets," c. 1949

In a letter from 1943 Schoenberg writes, "I grew up practically with chamber music." He goes on to emphasize the importance of both composing and performing chamber music for his early musical life: "Chamber music, all combinations of it, from duo or trio to string quartet, piano sonatas, trios, etc., offer a student the opportunity to become acquainted with the greatest treasures of our musical culture in a manner which is much superior to mere listening to performances. What you play yourself will be anchored more deeply in your memory than what you hear, and besides, you will like to repeat it and will by that know it still better." Commenting on the large number of duets, trios, and quartets he wrote to play with his friends, he points out that he "continued writing chamber music at a time when all contemporary composers except Max Reger would only compose for orchestra."[23]

The four string quartets I have published had at least five or six predecessors. The habit of composing so many string quartets had gradually arisen. As a child of less than nine years, I had started composing little and, later, larger pieces for two violins, in imitation of such music as I used to play with my teacher or with a cousin of mine. When I could play violin duets of Viotti, Pleyel and others, I imitated their style. Thus I progressed in composing in the measure I progressed in playing. After all, I came so far as to compose once a kind of symphonic poem, after Friedrich von Schiller's drama "Die Räuber," that is, "The Robbers," which I called "Die Räuber-Phantasie."

Decisive progress took place when, a few years later, I found a classmate who possessed a viola and could play it. At once I started writing Trios for two violins and viola, though there was no model for imitation available. Next, with money I had earned for teaching German to a Greek, I bought, second hand, a few scores of Beethoven: the third and fourth symphonies, two Rasoumovsky string quartets and the Great Fugue for string quartet, Op. 133. From this minute, I was possessed by an urge to write string quartets.

Yet this desire did not find satisfaction until I had acquired a friend, Oscar Adler, who was to play a great role in my evolution. I am obliged to him for a great many matters he taught me. Not only did he teach me elementary harmony, he also stimulated me in the direction of exercising my ear in order to strengthen my memory of pitches. Besides, our repertory of trios was augmented by his arrangements of violin sonatas for this ensemble.

We wanted to play quartets of Mozart and Beethoven, so Adler procured a large viola, furnished with zither strings, which produced the pitch and compass of the cello. This instrument I was to play, which, knowing no better, I played by using the fingering of the viola. Soon thereafter I purchased a cello, and this also I played with the same fingering with which I had played the violin, viola and the (as I called it) violincello. This went on for quite a time, until Adler had been told by a real cellist that the fingering on the cello is different. The rest I had to find out myself.

At once, of course, I started writing string quartets. In the meantime, "Meyers Konversations Lexikon" (an encyclopedia, which we bought on installments) had reached the long-hoped-for letter "S," enabling me to learn under "Sonate" how a first movement of a string quartet should be constructed. At the time I was about 18 years old, but had not obtained any other instruction than that which Oscar Adler had given me.

However, studying the "Lexikon" more and more, and becoming acquainted with a few more musician students of composition in the "Wiener Konservatorium"—helped me to expand my knowledge. Thus I became able to write also for other instruments and ensembles, and I even tried a first movement of a symphony, the main theme of which I still remember.

Sketch for an early symphony.

Mozart, Brahms, Beethoven and Dvorak were my models at this time.

Nevertheless, it still required quite a number of years before I could write a string quartet in D major, good enough for a public performance in the Wiener Tonkünstler Verein, half a year after Brahms, its honorary president, had died.[24] While this work was strongly under the influence of Brahms and Dvorak, an almost sudden turn toward a more "progressive" manner of composing occurred. Mahler and Strauss had appeared on the musical scene, and so fascinating was their advent, that every musician was immediately forced to take sides, pro or contra. Being then only 23 years of age, I was easily to catch fire, and to begin composing symphonic poems of one uninterrupted movement, the size of the models given by Mahler and Strauss. One, which I did not finish, was "Hans im Glück" (a Grimm fairytale). Climaxing this period were "Transfigured Night," Op. 4, and "Pelleas and Melisande," Op. 5.

Documents: 1891–1906

On Essence and Appearance

1.7 "If upon your life's journey," c. 1891

Schoenberg wrote this poem for Malvina Goldschmied, a first cousin on his mother's side, who was born in 1877. With the death of his father Samuel Schoenberg on New Year's Eve at the start of 1890, Schoenberg left the Realschule and began to work as an apprentice in a bank in Vienna.[25] A letter to Malvina from May 19, 1891, already indicates the life-long pattern of periods of exhilarating productivity followed by extended dry spells: "Would it be any interest to you that yesterday, after a long break, I finally composed something new again—a song without words, and that I hope that from now on a new epoch of joyful creativity will dawn?"[26]

> *If upon your life's journey*
> *Some harm should befall you:*
> *Look upon it not with somber eyes,*
> *But be always full of hope.*
> *For you must not be guided by*
> *What appears to be; self-assured,*
> *You must bring out the core,*
> *And not give in to mere outward appearance.*
> > *From your cousin*
> > *Arnold Schoenberg*

Concerning the Bible and the Modern World

1.8 From a Letter to Malvina Goldschmied, May 25, 1891

Schoenberg's interpretation here of the Bible in present-day terms reflects the language of Reform Judaism with its emphasis on the basic idea or essence of Judaism unfolding through a process of historical development.[27] The tension between an unchanging, eternal, and ultimately unrepresentable "idea" and the manner of its development, presentation, and "style" lies at the heart of Schoenberg's thought. He returned specifically to the question of reconciling biblical laws and a "contemporary point of view" in his play The Biblical Way *(5.8).*

Ma chère cousine!

Your letter did not satisfy me in any way. You say for example that I have rejoiced too early that you are not going to amuse yourself.—Now that is a nice phrase, but badly used here. For, firstly, so far as I remember, I wrote that out of malice it would be nicer for me if you did not amuse yourself too much; secondly, I have not rejoiced at all. You go on to say that you have only disputed the amount of nonsense that is in the Bible; now I must oppose you, as an unbeliever myself, by saying that nowhere in the Bible is there any nonsense. For in it all the most difficult questions concerning Morals, Law-making, Industry and Medical Science are re-solved in the most simple way, often treated from a contemporary point of view; in general the Bible really gives us the foundation of all our state institutions (except the telephone and the railway).

On Socialism and Aesthetics

1.9 Letter to David Joseph Bach, July 25, 1895

Shortly after leaving his job as a bank clerk in 1895 Schoenberg began conducting and composing for several suburban workers' choirs.[28] It is not exactly clear how long he was involved in these activities, but it is likely that they continued up to the time of his first move to Berlin in 1901. In 1950, as the House Committee on Un-American Activities was holding hearings, he drafted a short statement, "My Attitude Towards Politics," discussing his early political development: "In my early twenties, I had friends who introduced me to Marxian theories. When I thereafter had jobs as Chormeister—*director of men's choruses—they called me "Genosse"—comrade, and at this time, when the Social Democrats fought for an extension of the right of suffrage, I was strongly in sympathy with some of their aims.*

"But before I was twenty-five, I had already discovered the difference between me and a laborer; I then found out that I was a bourgeois *and turned away from all political contacts."[29]*

Dear Dunjo!

Before I begin, I would like to bow down obsequiously, as you requested. I don't quite know why exactly; for if I'm not mistaken you have the honor of speaking reasonably to a reasonable man. But that doesn't matter, if you ask me, I'll do it. You certainly know that I am so good-natured that it makes it hard to say "no" if someone else says "yes." Therefore it also won't be easy to withhold your letter from your people, particularly because I have already promised here and there to read it. I will simply share with them what is incontestable and also make exerpts of certain other parts. What is contestable—and to this belongs, doesn't it, what you cite in order to prove that you are no lyricist (and to make a terrible transition)—is that nature must enter into an active relationship with the poet, certainly a very nice thing. But I believe that you've taken the concept of the modern lyricist too narrowly if you demand that he is supposed to take his associations solely from nature. It may have been the business of the Romantics to find correspondences to their inner life and emotions in nature. But we who live under the banner of the recognition of social conditions have somewhat distanced ourselves from these feelings. Certainly we're still in the position of empathizing with the Romantics' feeling toward nature, but for self-creation empathy is obviously not sufficient. One must differentiate between the feelings received from nature and those taken from one's own life. For self-creation the former can no longer suffice, and you are also mistaken if you look there for a test of your talents. But the latter certainly can suffice. It alone can offer the foundation for an individual and contemporary creativity. In our lives the recognition of social struggles also plays the decisive role.—Yet nothing is gained by the one-sided rejection of the earlier conception. But precisely as the movement of social relations is the product of the struggle of the classes, the aesthetic must present itself as the product of the struggle of the idealistic with the materialistic worldview, and art must show the marks of the battle of the artistic feelings from these two conceptions.— What nature is to us and to the Romantics are two different things. Our task, etc., is to strive so that what we have won from these experiences should also really be art.

I doubt that you will be able to gather what I really mean from these scribblings. The deftness of expression is lacking. Discussion will have to clarify the rest.

I also got your postcard. The necessary steps are already taken. We can talk about it when we are together. That will be Sunday the 28th at 1:41. I shall come on the same train as you and shall follow your instructions.

With warm greetings,

Your Arnold Schoenberg.

In the future don't write to the office, but to
II. Leopoldgasse 9.

On the Imitation of Nature and Stylization

1.10 "Some Ideas for the Establishment of a Modern Theory of Composition" (c. 1900)

From a group of early writings Schoenberg bound together with the title "Seven Fragments—First Literary Attempts." In the catalogue of his manuscripts he described the collection as written "around or before 1900."

The theory of composition accepts the theme, and at best the motive, as the sole reason for creating a musical composition. This appears to me to be more than doubtful. In two respects: I assume the reason lies elsewhere, and I understand the purpose of the motive to be for a different effect.

I wish to tell someone a story, with which I hope to win his interest, his sympathy. Assuming that certain events have an effect almost without artistic ornamentation, I can never for a moment neglect a concern for the purely material effect of my story. Thus with simple events, joyous or sad occurrences as everyone experiences them, the purely historical account of facts is sufficient, mostly even the mere citing of the facts alone, as with births, engagements, deaths, and the like.

I only have to make other demands on my presentation if the event to be reported is unusual or complicated, or if it is my intention to achieve still other effects with my narration that are independent of the material. For example: to awaken interest in myself, or to create unusual or strange moods, or to reveal perspectives of a didactic or philosophical content. Here the questions regarding the best, most effective arrangement and structure become most important, demanding consideration alongside the material, if not even priority. At this point, I am obliged to depart to a certain degree from the pure truth; I can no longer content myself with representing things and events as they are, as they happened; I have to change the sequence of events; must color light things darker, shade the dark things lighter; I must present insignificant matters more modestly; and grant what is essential more room, a position of priority, and the external attributes of a more important occurrence. I must often separate and dissociate where my story is in reality connected; but there I must strive to bring together what is necessary for my special effect. Thus I distance myself from facts, ignore them, and place myself—the narrator—above them. I renounce their effects and aim at achieving special ones that are of a different quality. This first step away from the imitation of nature is the first step into art, and that is stylization.

Fragment of an Opera Libretto

1.11 From Odoakar, *c. 1900*

Schoenberg did not complete his first opera until Erwartung *of 1909, based on a text by Marie Pappenheim. Two of his largest works from the preceding decade might be seen as redirection of the operatic impulse to other genres. The* Gurrelieder *(1900–1901, 1911), using texts by Jens Peter Jacobsen, clearly shows Schoenberg grappling with the Wagnerian musico-dramatic legacy, first in the form of a song cycle and then as a massive choral cantata. His symphonic poem* Pelleas und Melisande, *completed in 1903, grew out of plans in 1901 and 1902 for an opera on Maeterlinck's symbolist drama. Yet Schoenberg did work on several operas during this period, as if to try out the various operatic genres.*[30] *Of special significance in light of Schoenberg's later preference to set his own texts are three projects from these years that were to be on libretti that he himself wrote:* Die Schildbürger, *a comic opera based on German folktales (an extensive libretto fragment is dated July 28, 1901), and the two texts excerpted here,* Odoakar *and* Superstition *[Aberglaube].*[31]

Odoakar shows even more strongly than the Gurrelieder *the influence of Wagner, and in particular* The Ring of the Nibelung, *in its characters, plot, and alliterative verse form. The title character was based on the historical figure Odoacer, who became the first barbarian ruler of Italy in 476, unseating the emperor Romulus Augustulus.*[32] *He ruled for thirteen years before being betrayed by Theodoric the Ostrogoth. Schoenberg may have been attracted to the character as a man who achieved greatness despite coming from a humble background. Odoaker's jesting, ironic tone no doubt reflects something of Schoenberg's love of wordplay, puns, and paradoxes (see Alma Mahler's description of his manner of speech in 1.16, and his letter to her, 2.14).*

Act I

Scene 1

When the curtain rises, the stage is completely dark. Odoakar is lying asleep in a great gothic hall. Suddenly, a glaring light flares up, illuminating a sword floating in the air, while at the same time the piercing sound of a horn can be heard. After a few moments the sword breaks in two with a loud noise and falls to the floor; but the horn continues to sound. Then very soon it becomes lighter with the dawn, so that in a short time the stage and Odoakar are visible. It grows continuously brighter until it is full daylight. Shortly after the sword breaks, but only when it is already rather light, he suddenly awakens.

ODOAKAR: (*agitatedly he springs to his feet, looking about for his sword.*)

My sword! (*he finds it next to his bed*)

There it is!

Whole and unbroken!

Taunting vision, / How do I interpret you?

It was like this: / In a circle of mildly agitated men / A fierce argument
    arose;

My horn rang out.

The sword in my right hand, / The horn still at my lips,

Effortlessly I withstood the strongest among them.

But suddenly, unforeseen, / A weak little man creeps up,

Gray and of hideous appearance; / With a light stroke he hits my sword,

It falls in pieces from my right hand, / As if it were merely wood.

To throttle the repulsive worm, / I let loose the horn in my left hand.

But miraculously, free from my lips, / It continues to sound out in warning.

A bright fire flares up: / I awaken!

Taunting vision, / From what dark impulse do you arise?

———

But of course, / Who would be able to have sweet dreams,

Who could enjoy enticing sleep, / With bitter feelings in his heart,

Resentful rage in his mind, / Thinking of the honor of his people

That he loves more than his life?!

Troubles can kindle only rage, / And hatred against all who scorn;

And blazing hatred shall explode upon those / Whose ravenous minds

Undermine the strength of the empire.

Cheating each other, / Robbing each other, / Falling from one ecstasy

Into the next, / Coveting each other's lives and property;

The house is already undermined, / They do not notice the weakened
    edifice,

Which their greed has robbed of its supports.

If it falls, it will bury you too.

But I do not lament you!—

I lament only the powerful Hun / Who is strong enough to destroy on the
    battlefield

The Romans in their empire,

Or the worm-eaten tree, / Without the strength to kill

The enemy in its own body, / And dies from it.

Sleep peacefully, those who can!

I am haunted even in my dreams.

———

But who might be the one / For whom sleep brings peace?

Certainly not the weakling, / He feels always threatened;

The strong even less, / His mind is set on pillaging.

Perhaps it is the one whom/A woman tenderly lulls to sleep

Scattering the cares from his mind,/With kisses putting great joys in their place;

Might that lucky one dream sweetly?

Whether I would be able,/I do not know!

(*Pause*)

(*Amused, strongly*): Taunting web of dreams,/You won't trouble me for long.

I leave dreams for the women,/And their interpretation no less.

My sword is whole and unbroken!

And my horn rings out!

But only if I sound it;/And I shall sound it!

(*He blows the horn loudly. Awakened by the sound, Adelrich comes quickly to the stage.*)

Scene 2

ADELRICH (*lively*): You are not calling to the hunt!

So, does an enemy threaten us;/Or are you only making a jest?

ODOAKAR (*merry*): I did indeed call you to the hunt,/And an enemy too threatens us, But I am also jesting!

ADELRICH (*adopting the same tone*): Now I doubt no longer/That you are only jesting.

It would be funny indeed,/If we wanted to hunt,

Where we wait for the enemy to strike.

ODOAKAR: That's the way it should be:/Merry and funny!

What's the use of seriousness,/Of dignity and defiance.

Let us be merry/And enjoy pleasure!

ADELRICH (*more seriously*): What? Do I grasp the pleasure that drives you to

Make a mockery of serious things?

ODOAKAR: If only your serious things/Were worthy of mockery,

Then they might be useful for something more serious.

Even for the enemy they are too wretched.

ADELRICH: But who is the enemy,/Tell me now;

And what's this about hunting?

Make an end to your jests.

ODOAKAR: I spoke of the enemy last,/Which should explain what I mean by hunting;

But the jest (*suddenly becoming very serious*)/Should perish with us,

And we with it, and our pleasures with both!

Man only jests twice!

First as an innocent child, / Who only sees everything in a rosy hue,

To whom every change seems only an improvement, / If he even notices.

But the second time, it is as a defiant man,

Who futilely squanders by worthless exertions

The sacred seriousness, the productive force,

Unable to hinder the course of commonness!

And then he madly bursts into laughter, / The sacred and worthy around him seem twisted,

Hardly worthy of the scorn soaked with gall / That powerfully bursts out as a joke.

Are you surprised by my wrath?

Now mark well, / If the one who makes the joke can explain it.

When our tribe, crowned with honors and laden with booty,

Conquered this land in a peace-shattering campaign,

There was a king, wise and gentle, / Who distributed property and honors

Through only shrewd judgment of merit.

Then from his noble understanding he gave laws and teachings

To the people he had led to victory, / So to control their war-frenzied senses.

It was Geiserich,[33] your ancestor; / so long as he lived, the ways of our tribe and our honor

Were safeguarded by custom and discipline.

Not oppressed, but little loved / And respected even less,

The defeated and soft enemy / Was a stranger in our midst

On the land that had been taken from them, / Forced into peace by respect.

But Geiserich died, and after him / Followed no one as wise.

Believing it had to be the eldest, / The wisest of the lineage, he decreed

This man should be king.[34]

Experience and wisdom, however,

Can never be regarded as equal in merit.

One is acquired by age, / It knows of counsel others would laugh at.

The second, a gift of the gods, / Finds help even where the first fails.

For new troubles, it knows new counsels, / For new sufferings, it knows new remedies.

And the counsel was of trouble and remedy, / For the suffering that tormented us was new.

A fierce enemy / Gnawed us to the marrow.

To simple customs and manly virtue / Our people owed victory and possession.

The enemy was lecherous and decadent / As he withdrew before our attacks.

Too cowardly and weak for open war,/He knows how to take his
    revenge.
Into our heritage he mixes the poison that brought him defeat:
Sensuality fells our strength.
Those who should rule in wisdom,/Using their power for good
And honored custom,/Stagger, falling lecherously
Into the malicious enemy's revenge.
They only use their power/For their own pleasure,
It is tempting, therefore, to be king.
Yet no one is certain of their rule,/For their next successor
Covets their life and throne.
Here help is needed,/If the empire is not to crumble,
Succumbing to the enemies/Who hard at the border already threaten—
If the tribe is not to go under,/Succumbing to the enemy
Churning up within its own body;
He who honestly and fervently loves his own people/Must help as
    he can.
That is the enemy/Whom I want to hunt down—
Can you now appreciate my jest?
ADELRICH (*moved*): What you have told me hurts deeply,
Long have I felt the burning wound,/That you have now made clear
    to me.
Though I did not recognize the roots of the malady,/I have always pon-
    dered a cure,
But whatever I thought,/I did not find the remedy
For what caused the suffering.
How gladly I used my arm;/How gladly for the good of the realm
Did I swing my sword high!
ODOAKAR (*enthusiastically*): It is your sword!
With your sword in your fist, you brought us/Victory and honor
In campaigns that smashed empires;/Now steel shall be the physician
Saving our honor in need!/We only have it to thank for our power,
What we give, it gives back a thousand fold;
It alone brings well-being,/If we hold to the sacred and noble,
It returns our well-being a thousand fold;/That which resists it,
Should be called worthy;/That which falls before it,
Should be despised.
That shall be the solution! (*more cheerfully*):/I hope we soon endure
The test of whether this suffices.
And if we perish,/Let it be by the sword,
And not from lethargy and weakness. (*exits*)

Draft of an Opera Libretto

1.12 From Superstition, *c. 1901*

In marked contrast to the Wagnerian Odoakar, *Schoenberg's draft for the libretto of* Superstition *suggests the fusion of naturalistic and mystical erotic elements in a modern setting typical of the poetry of Richard Dehmel, whose writings served as the source for a large number of songs from these years as well as for the programmatic string sextet* Verklärte Nacht *(see 1.13). The extended libretto offers insights into Schoenberg's thinking on many topics, including the relationship of the sexes, personal morality as opposed to social morality, religion, and superstition—notably Schoenberg's lifelong obsession with the number 13.*[35] *The Christian references in the text may reflect his Lutheran conversion in March 1898 (he did not formally reconvert until 1933).*

Much of the libretto is taken up by conversations between the two main characters, Maria and Konrad, who are part of a circle of artists and university students. In one of the "Seven Fragments" from around 1900, Schoenberg relates the act of conversation to the issue of the listener's role in the reception of music, a topic that would concern him throughout his life.

Whoever speaks wishes to find attention, yes, even interest. Perhaps one would have to grant even to someone who only wants to "make conversation" that he wishes to have a listener in the person sitting opposite to him. But certainly for whoever speaks because he is moved, the polite listener is not enough. He wishes to arouse interest, sympathy. Sympathy, perhaps even compassion, or even shared joy, shared feelings: his listener should remain under his spell at least for the duration of his speech. The effect will be achieved without effort if the event in itself has enough human significance to arouse interest. Few people will withhold their sympathy from the effect of an obituary notice, and only the worst enemy does not share one's joy.[36]

With its mixture of fully written-out speeches and dialogue, along with other sections where the action and dialogue are only described, it is not immediately apparent how the text would have been adapted to music. However, the proselike form of the libretto is comparable to the dramatic texts that were set directly in contemporary works, such as Debussy's Pelléas et Mélisande *(1902) and Strauss's* Salome *(1905).*

Dramatis Personae
MARIA, a student
KONRAD, a student
FERDINAND, an artist
HEDWIG, a student
AUGUST, a musician
BERTHA, a musician

Friends and colleagues of Hedwig and Maria

    KARL, OTTO, THEODOR, FRANZ, WALTER, students

    JOHANNA, EMMA, SOPHIE, students

Act I

Scene 1

MARIA's living room. Table, chairs, sofa, piano, bookshelves, some pictures (etchings, reproductions), etc. MARIA is at home alone; when the curtain goes up, we see her putting some things in the room in order (silent scene.)

Sketch for **Superstition,** *act 1, scene 1.*

Then she takes a book from the bookshelf and sits down on the sofa in a half-sitting, half-lying position. At some points silent acting in which she expresses her delight about some sentences in the book.—The doorbell rings; she puts the book on the sofa and comes back in with FERDINAND. A not very friendly, almost frosty welcome on the part of MARIA;—FERDINAND notices the book and asks her about it. (He does not know the book or the author.) She tells him he would not like it. He would not have any understanding of such books. FERDINAND is hurt by this remark and responds sharply with an attack on the probably eccentric author of the book that was unknown to him.

MARIA replies: "Eccentric! Naturally, what he would call eccentric! Artists who touch the most tender and secret feelings of highly complicated people, who are able to hear the faintest vibrations of sensitive souls, would be strange, eccentric to him. How else could it be. He would not be able to understand such people, and in consequence not such writings either."

FERDINAND tauntingly asks her if she thinks of herself as such a person.—There is no answer.—FERDINAND continues: He would understand her very well; better than she thought. Even if she did not think so at all. He had known her since she had come to town to attend the university. So he had probably had enough opportunity to get to know her. Of course, then she had also been slightly different toward him. In those days when she was without any acquaintances, when he was the only one who took care of her; who spared her from loneliness and was helpful to her whenever he could be, in those days she had also had a great interest in his art. Naturally, today, as she had many acquaintances, and now especially, as she would be going away in a few days, he had become superfluous. Didn't she perhaps have a vague notion that she might be under an obligation of gratitude to him?

MARIA: "You want gratitude? Someone who demands gratitude for something has forfeited his right to gratitude. If you did anybody a favor, and while doing it had even only the faintest thought that that person would have to be grateful to you, you actually intended to do good to *yourself,* but never to *that person.* No matter if the single deed meant more or less effort for you, gave more or less pleasure to the other person.—*But let me tell you* why I can't be grateful to you besides this. Now it has to be said, since now I know precisely how highly I should think of you. When I first came here, you really were the only one who would take care of me. It is true: you very much went out of your way for me. And now I can tell you: your pains, your apparent selflessness assured you a strong influence over me, perhaps in a roundabout way via my feeling of gratitude—which for me was then still of decisive importance. But how did you take advantage of it? I have realized this lately. You had always striven to convert me to the commonness of your views. Weak and uneducated in those days, I did not listen to the slight reluctance of my heart. Your former superiority in so many things gave you a halo that made me think that almost everything you said was right. I regretted that I was not able to see and feel everything like you. And where I could not follow you, I tried to push myself. But I was not able to make myself follow in every respect; and so I came to self-examination and found myself again. And I saw: you would have made me not what I am but only that which *I* could have been. But I would have become what you are. And what are you? A man like all the others. Someone who demands gratitude for those deeds that should only have happened for their own sake. And what makes my ingratitude? The fear of suffocating in a garment that confines my own shape, binds my chest, hinders me from breathing freely. And for this reason I want you away from me. I cannot bear being with you any longer. I can hardly hear a word from you anymore, no matter how trivial, that does not make the blood pound in my temples."

FERDINAND is upset. He had no idea how far the argument could go and still does not realize that he really is supposed to go. He tries to make up. But MARIA clearly and sharply points out to him that he should go. The doorbell rings.

Scene 2

HEDWIG arrives. FERDINAND tires to compose himself, while MARIA, still under the effect of her irritation, welcomes HEDWIG a little stiffly. HEDWIG's greeting is friendly. She realizes at once that something has happened here. She does not mention it, however, but gives expression to her happiness at finding FERDINAND here, as she can now invite him personally: for a little gathering tomorrow at her place; in a few days she is going away for the summer and wants to see her friends again before she leaves. FERDINAND accepts thankfully. MARIA says she does not know yet if she'll attend. She feels a little sick, perhaps she will come anyway; she could not promise it definitely. HEDWIG urges her. The doorbell rings again.

Scene 3

KONRAD enters. He is welcomed by MARIA and HEDWIG in a very friendly manner. FERDINAND greets him a little stiffly, unfriendly; whereas KONRAD greets everybody equally cordially. He immediately turns to HEDWIG, thanking her for the invitation he has just received in the mail. Of course he will come. HEDWIG asks him if perhaps he would like to read from his work at her gathering. She had already heard so much about his talent. KONRAD is surprised: somebody had heard of his talent? He had been here only for a short time and had only read something to one person, and he would certainly not read to this person again. And also, he was only a beginner. He would rather read them something by the great N (the same person who wrote the book mentioned at the beginning.)[37] Why didn't he do both, HEDWIG suggests, read something by N and something by himself. KONRAD replies that he does not particularly enjoy reading to people. Afterwards he always had a feeling of remose. But it depends on his mood. Tomorrow perhaps he would be just in the mood; in that case he would bring something. HEDWIG contents herself with this and wants to leave. FERDINAND, who during this conversation has not said a single word and has given KONRAD and MARIA suspicious glances, exits with HEDWIG. She urges MARIA to come at any rate. MARIA sees them to the door.—Then she returns.

Scene 4

KONRAD and MARIA alone. MARIA comes back into the room saying, "I shall not go to Hedwig's tomorrow." KONRAD asks her if she had had an incident with FERDINAND. Yes, she had, she says; finally an open argument with him, something she had wished for a long time. A little quarrel had suddenly turned into a major argument. KONRAD asks her if she would have wanted to go to Hedwig's.—Certainly! she would have liked to go very much, especially as she would be separated from her friend soon.
KONRAD: "Can this, then, be a reason for you not to go where you wanted to go, only because there will be an unpleasant person there?"

MARIA: "Of course this is important to me. I can't bear to hear another word from this person, I can't bear to know he is near me.[38] He who wanted to press me into the narrowness of his mind dares to demand gratitude for it. As if the efforts he made for my sake would give him a right to my gratitude. And even if they gave him a right, he has forfeited it now by demanding it."

KONRAD: "The gardener plants and nurtures a flower. He expects it to bloom as a result, to bloom for him; he counts on it, since he only plants and nurtures it so that it will bloom for him. And the flower? What does it care if the gardener expects it to bloom or not? One day it will bloom for its own joy. And in blooming it is doubtlessly showing its gratitude to the gardener. (Nature is grateful.)"

MARIA: "That is true, but the gardener that nurtures a flower has to know it. If he grows a plant that needs open air and sunlight in a greenhouse, the plant won't thank him by blooming. It will die, and its blood will be on his hands."

KONRAD: "It dies for its own sake, not for him. One never dies for one's friend or enemy. Its last breath is meant for its fading life. It surrounds its last sigh with fragrance, intending even in death to bring to life the last of its remaining beauty—only in order to be more beautiful. That can't be revenge. (Nature does not know revenge.)"

MARIA: "It does not think of revenge, but also neither of gratitude."

KONRAD: "It does not think of gratitude, but it does not refuse it either. The one whose part it is by nature to give, gives. Such a person gives limitlessly, whether he is the one to receive gratitude (a creditor), or to give thanks (a debtor). He gives because he has to give. Merely because he is rich. Only because he wants to rid himself of his abundance. God is like this, as is the sun, the earth, and so is the artist and the artistic human being; and above all, love is like this. It is always the stronger person that gives to the weaker. The one who can give the most is the stronger person, not the one who can take the most. The great and powerful forces of nature are like that, and so too are great people. Of course the small, poor ones that always have to be given things, always calculate taking from the next smaller and sometimes even from the greater. Everywhere they scrounge.—God made men to be the stronger, women to be the weaker beings. In consequence man should give, the woman should receive. But what does reality look like for our small, pitiable humans? So long as he does not own the woman, he dances around her, acts like her protector, saves her from all trouble, every pain. And why? So that she will give him the greatest thing that a child of mankind is able to give; so that she will give him her love. But how often merely so that she will give him her body. In other words, an exchange, a business; a business in which the man demands the purchase price in advance in the form of humility, subservience, readiness to be of service, etc. God did not want love to be like that. It was supposed to be like his love; like the love of Christ. To give, to sacrifice oneself, to suffer pains—

only for love. And if love were like this, then it would be as fertile as Christ's love, whose fruit means eternal salvation for those in need."

MARIA has been listening to KONRAD with growing delight. When he is finished, she remains silent a little while longer. Then she says, half hesitatingly, a little shyly, quietly: "What you are saying sounds so new to me, and yet I feel as if I had heard it all once before. Or perhaps I only thought it myself? Maybe not so clearly, so forcefully; perhaps it was only a feeling that told me that it had to be like this. I wonder if there is a person who is like this? I think there was a person once with whom I had this feeling."

KONRAD: "That can only have been your mother. Only the mother, who sees in her daughter her reincarnated youth, gives her everything she has."

MARIA: "Yes, mother, it was you; you, the only being whose gifts of love I was always allowed to accept without having to fear regretting it later. Your gifts of love were capable of giving happiness. Happy the woman to whom you gave presents. If only I had the power to become like you. You who saw inside me so totally, because I was your exact likeness. You would have made me what you are.—And I had to leave her so early that people like Ferdinand were able to win influence over me; so it was possible to make me believe in duties I do not have in order to suppress those needs that I do have. This is how it happened that I could lose myself, that I could possibly sit in a room with Ferdinand and these people for hours and days through the years and discuss things that were far from me, that were totally foreign to my inner being. I who languish with the desire for luxury, art, colors, sounds, was sitting together with these people and mortifying myself through conversation about abstract things.

"Instead of going out into the woods, of taking a clear, fresh sip of water at the spring, of becoming absorbed in the worship of nature; instead of intoxicating myself with colors and sounds, with rhythms; instead of pursuing my true needs, I sat in a room and talked about dead objects—while life, blooming life, was so close. Only now I feel what I lost in this time, what I always missed. Now I know why I felt so empty.—And I have to tell you that I know I owe all this knowledge to you. I think I was an eager pupil."

KONRAD: "Yes, you were an eager pupil. I saw it immediately; where I dropped only a slight, gentle hint, you understood at once. I think I didn't have to teach; I only had to rouse you and you yourself woke up; I only had to clear away the debris, and your soul lay there bright and radiant. I did not change you. I only helped you to become clear about yourself. I am infinitely happy to see you like this."

Pause—both are lost in deep thought, after a while KONRAD walks over to the piano and plays a few quiet chords; MARIA listens dreamily—the doorbell rings; MARIA rises somewhat reluctantly from the sofa in order to open the door. KONRAD leaves the piano.[39]

Sketch for Superstition, *act 1, scene 4.*

Scene 5

[HEDWIG returns on FERDINAND's behalf and entreats MARIA to come to the party. MARIA at first angrily rejects the offer, complaining that FERDINAND did not even have the courage to ask her himself, but she ultimately agrees to come.]

Scene 6

KONRAD and MARIA alone again. MARIA asks KONRAD whether he heard. KONRAD says he didn't hear everything; he had tried not to listen but had not been totally successful.

MARIA: "Well, what do you think of Ferdinand now?"

KONRAD makes a calming gesture that expresses something like: why do you upset yourself about the poor creature!—MARIA tells him that she confirmed with HEDWIG that she would attend; KONRAD is glad about it.—MARIA asks KONRAD to read to them tomorrow from his works.—KONRAD replies that he does not like to read to people, it really makes him uneasy. To bother so many good and dear people, it is unlikely that they will understand him. Why stir them out of their peace of mind.

MARIA: "Then read for me, only for me."

KONRAD: "In that case I will, to you alone."

MARIA: "Yes, but I want you to read to me alone during this social gathering. We shall then be among so many people, and yet alone. From you to me, from me to you, worlds will emanate, vibrations of ether will transmit the movements of our souls."

KONRAD, holds out his hand to her: "I will read."

Long, blissful silence. Then MARIA says: "And to me alone!"

Curtain. End of Act I

Act II

Scene 1

[A description of a spacious room at HEDWIG's home that is set up to receive the guests, who include: HEDWIG, FERDINAND, KARL, OTTO, THEODOR, FRANZ, WALTER, JOHANNA, EMMA, SOPHIE, and, shortly thereafter, AUGUST and BERTHA. OTTO announces that he must leave to meet his uncle.]

Scene 2

HEDWIG asks if she might offer him a cup of tea, which OTTO accepts. In the meantime AUGUST has looked around the room and says: "We really are a large gathering today." He counts: "We are twelve." Then the bell rings and KONRAD enters. "There is the thirteenth person. Oh, that is a bad omen."

EMMA, anxiously: "But you don't believe in such things, do you?"

AUGUST: "Well, you never know."

HEDWIG, calmingly: "But two people are not here yet, Maria and Anton. Besides, Otto is unfortunately going to leave in a minute. So we are actually only twelve."

OTTO has finished his tea and says: "So, in order to put some minds at rest I shall sacrifice myself and leave as quickly as possible." He quickly says goodbye and leaves.

HEDWIG urges him once again to return later if possible. He promises to. HEDWIG, who saw him out, returns and says: "Where can Maria be?"

In the room AUGUST has in the meantime started to introduce KONRAD, who is not acquainted with the larger part of the gathering. EMMA says that she is very pleased to meet KONRAD. HEDWIG has told her that he would read from his work.

KONRAD answers: "Now it would appear to him, since he had arrived as the 13th person, that he would read something to them. The reader in a gathering would always be the 13th person."

THEODOR asks: "You also believe in such things? That is certainly strange, one should think that only uneducated people, etc."

The conversation about superstition is continued here. One can hear single phrases from it and one sees KONRAD involved in a conversation with the male and female students. Meanwhile FERDINAND takes HEDWIG aside and whispers with her. He had told HEDWIG he didn't think that MARIA would come.

HEDWIG: "But I saw her and she told me she would definitely come."

FERDINAND: "But she will not come; she only told you that in order to get rid of you."

HEDWIG: "On no, I know Maria better; from the way she assured me, I know for certain she will come."

Almost at the same time as these words are spoken, one can hear EMMA say from the other side of the room: "But I have already had enough of this superstition; besides, we are only twelve." One hears these two comments almost simultaneously. Immediately afterwards the bell rings and HEDWIG goes to the entrace hall and joins FERDINAND: "You see, here she comes." At the same time a voice in the group says: "The thirteenth person." A short moment of embarrassingly expectant silence.

Scene 3

[HEDWIG enters with MARIA. AUGUST and BERTHA announce that they will be departing the following day. With a cancellation from ANTON, the party will remain at thirteen.]

KONRAD counts too and notices the number thirteen. By now everybody has sat down again. In the first group MARIA talks with AUGUST and BERTHA about their wedding. In the second group FERDINAND talks about the poet from whose works KONRAD is supposed to read something; he also makes a few derogatory remarks about KONRAD. HEDWIG and a few others contradict him, others agree with him, parts of the conversation are held quietly. In the third group people are going on from the conversation about superstition to talk about God. THEODOR and EMMA are atheists. KONRAD polemicizes against atheism. The conversations are held in such a way that one alternately hears one group and then the other. Finally one listens to the group around KONRAD, who is just saying: "The belief in God leads to culture and art. Unbelief, however, deprives man of any relationship to imagination, and thus of every basis for art."

AUGUST and BERTHA sing a love song as a duet, with AUGUST accompanying at the piano. MARIA remains silent, thoughtful. KONRAD turns to MARIA: "How well they know singing of love. This is because they sing of their own love. Naturally happy and unaffected, a passionate and sweet sensuality streams out from their hearts."

MARIA: "If one could only love like them. Without doubts, without demanding anything from each other, without asking.—That is also what their song

sounded like: free, heartfelt, passionate, and yet simple, unaffected, a volun-
tary proof of their genuine naturalness."

HEDWIG goes up to KONRAD again and asks him to read. KONRAD hesitates,
but MARIA requests with a glance that he read. He would first like to read
something by the poet, N.N., but he is asked to let them hear something from
his own writings, and he reads them a poem. It conveys an atmospheric
picture. (Melodramatic music in the orchestra.) Content (the poem is in the
first person):

> A restless urge takes hold of me; a longing toward something of which I
> know nothing, of which I don't want to know anything. A feeling that
> wants to dominate me, that bends my will, trying to make it submit to a
> stronger one. I do not yield; I cannot obey and do not want to; I want to be
> free; free like God—not a slave. Should I plead and beg, try to catch a
> glance, try to win favor, to beg for requited love? To beg for love?—I who
> have so much to give. No, I want to give myself with all my love, I want to
> give myself to *her,* and if she gives me her love then I shall give it back
> threefold and a hundredfold and thousandfold—then I shall equal God.

When he has finished talking there is an embarrassed silence in the room;
nobody present (except for BERTHA and AUGUST) liked the poem. Nobody
stirs. During the reading MARIA has been sitting opposite KONRAD (who had
sat down in the center) and has listened to him with the greatest enthusiasm,
her gaze constantly resting on him. When he has finished she sits as if entranced.—HEDWIG wants to end the silence, she goes up to KONRAD and
thanks him; AUGUST also goes up to him and says: "Well, this is certainly not
for love." During the reading FERDINAND has been standing behind MARIA.
While HEDWIG is talking to KONRAD, he says, standing behind MARIA, softly
but still audibly to her: "What hair-raising rubbish: totally muddled stuff."

MARIA flinches, turns around, and sees FERDINAND: "Of course, you," she
bursts out, "who else could it be. Certainly the most shallow, most empty,
most rigid person in the whole gathering; it can only be someone who is too
thick-skinned to be reached by a poem like that."

FERDINAND turns pale: "Maria, control yourself, you insult me."

MARIA: "Insult you? Isn't your sense of honor bound in thick pig skin just like
your soul? Does it react at all? I'd already assumed that it didn't respond to
anything anymore. I already told you yesterday never to talk to me again. And
you! Wherever I go you follow me; you pursue me everywhere. Our paths
separate and yet you follow my trail. Please, once and for all, stop bothering
me. You are unbearable to me."

Now FERDINAND too bursts out: "You are saying this to me? You dare say this
in earnest to the one to whom you owe so much? Now you want to push me

away because somebody else has been pressing himself on you and putting all sorts of crazy things into your head. Someone who is crazy himself and turns you into a crazy person?" As the argument gets louder it attracts attention, and HEDWIG goes up to settle the argument. KONRAD, who knows immediately what it is about, approaches them as well. When FERDINAND notices him, he stops talking to HEDWIG and addresses KONRAD in an impudent tone: "Say, does that poet idol of yours also write such obviously crazy stuff?"

KONRAD answers him calmly: "Call my writing crazy if you want to. I did not ask to read, and therefore I'm not responsible if it throws someone off balance."

FERDINAND, smiling ironically: "Oh, that couldn't knock anyone out of balance, since it doesn't have any effect."

KONRAD: "Well, then you cannot hold it against me. Everybody is able to hide away deep within themselves surrounded by an impenetrable shield of indifference."

FERDINAND: "Well, you know it is not really a matter of indifference when one hears such things presented as art."

KONRAD: "If I were really you and acted consistently, then the whole matter would be totally indifferent to me."

FERDINAND: "Would you explain to me what you mean by that?"

KONRAD: "Only what I have told you already, if something does not affect you, then you shouldn't be affected if it matters to somebody else."

FERDINAND: "Yes, this would be true if only one person were concerned, the one who made this thing; naturally not. But we know from experience that it is not enough for the author to be crazy himself; he has to find soul mates. And if he does not find someone totally kindred, he makes do with any weak creature and talks to her until she becomes a kindred soul—I think this is harmful and I shall always fight against it."

KONRAD: "If it is your intention to remedy such craziness, I must confess that your methods don't seem quite right to me."

MARIA, who has been listening the whole time with increasing exasperation, interrupts KONRAD: "You call that 'not quite right'—those brutalities merely 'not quite right'? I implore you, don't talk to this person; don't talk to him."

FERDINAND comes up and makes a violent gesture in MARIA's direction as if he wanted to attack her. KONRAD interferes, holds him by the arms, and says: "You ought to be ashamed of yourself." HEDWIG also quickly moves toward KONRAD and drags him away. MARIA has jumped up from her seat and is standing, her face pale but contemptuous. Then she says quietly to HEDWIG: "I am going. Konrad, surely you will accompany me?" KONRAD nods. MARIA does not say good-bye to every guest, she only says to AUGUST and BERTHA: "I'll see you at my place tomorrow before you leave."

HEDWIG sees both out, then she returns and says to FERDINAND, whose mood in the meantime has changed to desperation: "Now you have lost her forever."

Curtain. Change of set.

Scene 4
KONRAD and MARIA

A street lined by old houses. Moonlit night. Quiet. The street constantly changes (panorama), so that one gets the impression of KONRAD and MARIA walking down the street. The street is crooked, deserted. Every so often there is passer-by. KONRAD and MARIA walk for a while silently side by side. Finally KONRAD says: "You are very upset; take my arm."

MARIA: "Yes, but let's not talk about it any more; he is dead to me. I am so happy finally to be alone with you. Earlier, when you were reading, I was alone with you too; then I knew you were only reading for me. Your marvelous poetry—only for me. You must read me other things. Why haven't you come to see me in the past few days?"

KONRAD: "Perhaps I was petty. You never told me to come back, and so I had to swallow my pride every time I visited you. I only came if I could think of a pretext: once I thought I had forgotten a book. A book I never had—because otherwise it might have occurred to you that I had it at home. Once I came in order to ask if August might perhaps be with you. I didn't want to appear obtrusive."

MARIA: "I don't understand you. I didn't think I had to tell you that you should come. That is something I say to people who are only allowed to come when I give them permission. But with you I feel so safe; I know you won't do me any harm or be dangerous to me. I don't first have to tell you—the one to whom I talk about the things that move me the most deeply—that you may come."

KONRAD: "I think you are right. But I also thought that I have only known you for such an incredibly short time; if I came so often anyway, your friends might tease you. And I also didn't know if you would like having male visitors that often—people talk—and now you see it for yourself—Ferdinand!"

MARIA: "Don't talk to me of Ferdinand. As regards people's gossip, you must know what I think about it."

KONRAD: "Yes, I know what you think about, but not whether I would be allowed to take advantage of the freedom of your views for myself. So long as they are considering something only in principle, people often *think* totally differently from how they *feel* when they are confronted with a certain situation in reality. Are principles capable of helping in situations where our emotions trick our principles to feel differently? I think only the battle with my pride made these ideas come to me. But I still don't think that any man of flesh and blood can subordinate his actions to principles."

MARIA: "You are wrong. This is not only a principle. I am really totally indifferent to what other people think about how I conduct my life. But now you know that you are supposed to come. Do come as often as you like."

KONRAD, agitated with happiness: "No, I shall not come quite as often as I like, that could get too much for you. I shall only come as often as you like."

MARIA, quickly, with a private, almost enraptured expression: "You cannot possibly come that often."

Pause

During this conversation MARIA and KONRAD have been walking slowly, now and then still more slowly, perhaps also stopping for a moment. During their walk the street has changed, so that toward the end of their conversation the scene changes, so that finally one sees the entrance to a park. Winding pergolas, alleyways with flower beds, lawn, some benches. The scene is lit by bright moonlight, here and there a slight cloud.

KONRAD, after a pause: "Wouldn't you like to go into the park for a while?"

MARIA: "It's already late, but let's go." They enter the park. For a while they continue walking slowly in silence. Then KONRAD asks if perhaps they should sit down. MARIA gives her consent. They sit down on a bench.

KONRAD: "It is a pity that August and Bertha are leaving, so that we have to miss our moonlit boat trip together."

MARIA: "Yes, it would have been wonderful; it's hard for me to do without it."

KONRAD: "But I don't think we have to do without it. If August and Bertha cannot come, then the two of us could go alone."

MARIA: "We could ask Hedwig to join us; I think she would definitely like to come."

KONRAD: "No, please don't ask Hedwig. I do like your friend, but she does not fit into my picture of a boat trip on a moonlit lake. There could be just two together there. Two souls that are one—then the bodies become weightless and the boat glides over the water as if it were immaterial. Everything immaterial: the light, the air, the souls, the whole atmosphere—inconceivable, intangible, and yet intense and penetrating. Please not Hedwig, only the two of us."

MARIA: "The two of us alone?"

KONRAD: "Yes."

MARIA: "No, that's impossible."

KONRAD: somewhat negatively, "Oh, was I right then when I feared that you minded the gossip of your friends and neighbors?"

MARIA: "Please, Konrad, you must not think that. I am going to be here for exactly one more week. The day before my departure I shall go on this boat trip with you."

KONRAD: "But tell me, why don't you want to go the day after tomorrow as we had planned? If it is possible in seven days from today, then it should be possible in two days. The reasons certainly don't change. Or did you have something else planned that day?"

MARIA: "No, that's not the reason. But please stop questioning me. In seven days I am going on the trip with you.—I would rather you tell me when you wrote the poem you read today."

KONRAD, a little annoyed: "A few days ago."

MARIA, tonelessly: "So!"—Pause—KONRAD is disgruntled, MARIA is thoughtful, a little restless. After a while she says: "Do you know what Hedwig said to me when she saw me out? She tried to make excuses for Ferdinand: he was jealous of you because he loves me. She asked me to forgive him."

KONRAD: "That poor man, that pitiful man." Pause—then KONRAD again: "I have to ask you again, why don't you want to go on the boat trip with me the day after tomorrow? I can't understand that."

MARIA, hesitates at first, then becomes determined with a scarcely noticeable sharpness: "I'm afraid of you!"

KONRAD: "You are afraid? Of me?—"

MARIA: "Yes, I'm afraid you could be dangerous to me; you could hurt me."

KONRAD: "I don't understand you; why could I be dangerous to you? You said earlier you felt so secure with me."

MARIA: "Yes, that's what I said. But now I have this feeling that you could hurt me."

KONRAD, overcome by doubts, self-consciously: "And if I had to hurt you?"

MARIA: "That's just what I'm afraid of."

KONRAD, even more self-conscious, quietly with an extreme, scarcely controllable, excitement: "I'm afraid I shall have to hurt you."

MARIA: "If you know that what you want to do is going to hurt me, then why do it?"

KONRAD: "I believe I shall not be able to do any differently." With the highest agitation, quickly, "No, it must be; Maria—"

MARIA, interrupts him: "I beg you—"

KONRAD: "I can't help myself: Maria . . . I love you!"

MARIA, shocked at first, then coolly and sharply: "Why do you tell me that?"

KONRAD, baffled, but then in despairing defiance: "Why do I tell you? Because I want to know—if you love me too."

MARIA: "And why do you want to know?"

KONRAD, determined to do anything, agitated: "I cannot love contently otherwise."

MARIA, jumps up from the bench. Coldly and sharply: "Now I know why I had the feeling earlier that I had to be afraid of you. You are just like all the others."

KONRAD, broken down, desperately: "I knew that I had to hurt you." Pause—

MARIA, a little more calmly and gently; always a short pause after each sentence, as if new thoughts came to her after each sentence: "If you love me,

why did you have to tell me?" KONRAD does not answer. "I don't know, perhaps I love you, but I believe the man I love is totally different from what you
are like now." KONRAD sits in a dull, expectant silence, his head in his hands.
"Just an hour ago I would not have dared to hope that you love me. But I would
certainly never have thought that you would expect your love to be returned.
Why can't you love contentedly? Why can't you be happy about your love;
become great through it, like God. What was that you said before? Love
shouldn't be a business. God wanted love to be like his own love. Love should
be like Christ's love.—And now it is you, especially you who had this beautiful
thought, who is the first to strike me." Pause—a little hesitantly: "Tell me, how
would it have been had I told you that I loved you?"

KONRAD, softly: "Then that would have been love."

MARIA, sharply: "Yes, love! What you call love!"

KONRAD, flares up: "Yes! That is what I call love—what a man of flesh and
blood calls love."

MARIA, with scorn: " . . . men of flesh and blood—ordinary people."

KONRAD: "Have I so quickly become a different person to you that I am now
just 'ordinary'?"

MARIA: "I believe . . . "—Pause—

KONRAD: "In that case, I shall probably have to go, just like Ferdinand."

MARIA: "Do what you want."

KONRAD: "Maria, do you think that we'll still be able to see each other? Do I
have to lose you forever just because I lost control of myself for a moment?"

MARIA: "I don't know."

KONRAD: "Don't you think it could still change? That I could be to you what I
was before. Maria, I am able to change; I can be what I want to be when I see an
error and I make amends. I can better myself, change, reform, as long and as
much as it takes until I'm the person I want to be. Maria, I know I disappointed
you terribly earlier. I am not yet ready for my own views. I have to suppress, to
eradicate the bad that comes up. Maria, I have the strength to do it; give me
time. Give me hope. I want to become again what I was to you before."

MARIA, after a pause: "I think that I can never believe you again. You could
deceive me a second time. Even if I wanted to believe you, as much as I would
like to, I know for sure I wouldn't be able to."

KONRAD: "Does that mean you don't give me any hope at all?"—MARIA does
not answer. "Does that mean I have to leave you?"—There is no answer—
"That I shall never visit you again?"

MARIA: "You know now what I think about you, do what you think."

KONRAD, bursting out in utmost desperation: "Maria, I cannot do without you,
cannot live without you."

MARIA: "You'll have to, I am only one person."—Pause—"I would like to go
home now."

KONRAD: "May I at least see you home?"

MARIA: "No! I shall go alone. I have to be alone now."

KONRAD: "Maria, please, at least give me your hand to say goodbye."

MARIA, without a word, gives him her hand. She sighs deeply and gets up quickly.

KONRAD, who has also risen from the bench, breaks down, sobbing loudly, when she leaves, and falls back onto the bench.

Curtain. End of Act II.

Act III

Scene 1

About an hour after act II. An old street in a modern town (lengthwise across the whole stage; it is crossed by a side alley.) Maria's apartment is in the foreground, in the second house to the left on the second floor. The night is bright. But there is a restless feeling. From time to time some clouds pass the moon. As the curtain rises there is nobody on stage. Then one of the windows of Maria's apartment is opened. MARIA looks out of the window. Then she leaves the window, after closing one casement and leaving the other slightly open.—Immediately after this one can see KONRAD coming from the side alley. He walks slowly to the front up to Maria's window, his head bent, hands behind his back. He lifts his head and sadly looks up to her window for a long time. Then he says, his voice trembling: "Oh God! . . . that I had to say it . . . oh, if only I had kept quiet . . . just a few hours ago I was so happy . . . but now? . . . "

Someone comes from the left side of the side alley. KONRAD notices him and walks a little farther to the front and waits until the man, who crosses the street and vanishes into the side alley to the right, is gone. Then he slowly walks back, hesitating for a moment in front of Maria's window; he then walks farther up to the left side alley, halts there a while, then turns and walks back to the front, crossing the street to the right side, where he finally remains standing, leaning on the wall of a house opposite Maria's window.

[The text breaks off at this point.]

On Program Music and *Transfigured Night*

1.13 *From the Program Notes to* Verklärte Nacht, *Op. 4 (1899),* August 26, 1950

The couple strolling through the park in Superstition *are very much a part of the same world as the two characters represented in the programmatic string sextet* Verklärte Nacht *(Transfigured Night), which was composed in 1899 and first performed in 1902.* Verklärte Nacht *is part of a series of works based on the poetry of Richard Dehmel (1863–1925), in particular on poems from the collection* Weib und Welt *(1896). Dehmel's poetry was controversial for its mixture of, in the words of the critic Julius Hart in 1896, "archaism, symbolism and allegory, everyday-realistic naturalism, with elements of sexuality, immorality and Satanism, and the Nietzschean superman."*[40] *Although the two men did not meet until the end of 1912 (see 3.9), Dehmel's poetry played an important role in Schoenberg's early development, a fact attested to both by the quantity of settings (at least eighteen works begun between 1897 and 1915, eight of which were completed), as well as directly by Schoenberg, who wrote to the poet: "You, far more than any musical example, were what determined our group's purpose . . . from you we learned the ability to listen to our inner selves. . . . "*[41] *The version of the program notes given here omits the music examples (with the location in the score indicated) following the format of the original manuscript.*[42] *For more on* Verklärte Nacht, *see 6.22. See fig. 1-1 for an example of his songs from this period.*

At the end of the 19th century the foremost representatives of the "Zeitgeist" in poetry have been Detlev von Liliencron, Hugo von Hofmannsthal and Richard Dehmel. But in music, after Brahms' death, many young composers followed the model of Richard Strauss by composing program music. This explains the origin of *Verklärte Nacht:* it is program music, illustrating and expressing the poem of Richard Dehmel.[43]

My composition was perhaps somehow different from other illustrative compositions, firstly by not being for orchestra, but for a chamber group; secondly because it does not illustrate any action or drama, but was restricted to portraying nature and expressing human feelings. It seems that due to this attitude my composition has gained qualities which can also satisfy if one does not know what it illustrates, or in other words, it offers the possibility to be appreciated as "pure" music. Thus it can perhaps make you forget the poem which many a person today might call rather repulsive.

Nevertheless, much of the poem deserves appreciation because of its highly poetic presentation of the emotions provoked by the beauty of nature, and for the distinguished moral attitude in dealing with a staggeringly difficult human problem.

Promenading in a park, Ex. 1 [mm. 1–4], in a clear, cold moonlit night, Ex. 2 and 3 [RA, 1–2; RB, 1–2], the wife confesses a tragedy to the man in a dramatic outburst, Ex. 4 [RC, 1–4]. She had married a man whom she did not love. She was unhappy and lonely in this marriage, Ex. 5 [RD-5, 1], but forced herself to remain faithful, Ex. 6 [RE+12, 1–2], and finally obeying the maternal instinct, she is now with child from a man she does not love. She even had considered herself praiseworthy for fulfilling her duty toward the demands of nature, Ex. 7 [RF-10, 1–11]. A climactic ascension, elaborating the motif Ex. 8 [RG-5, 1–2], expresses her self-accusation of her great sin.

In desperation she walks now beside the man, Ex. 9 [RK+14, 1–4], with whom she has fallen in love, fearing his sentence will destroy her. But "the voice of a man speaks," a man whose generosity is as sublime as his love, Ex. 10 [RL+13, 1–11].

The preceding first half of the composition ends in E-flat minor, (a), of which, as a transition, only B-flat, (b), remains, in order to connect with the extreme contrast in D-major, (c).

Harmonics, Ex. 11a [RM+9, 1–2], adorned by muted runs, b, express the beauty of the moonlight and introduce above a glittering accompaniment, Ex. 12 [RN-4, 1–2], a secondary theme, Ex. 13 [RN, 1–4], which soon changes into a duet between Violin and Cello, Ex. 14 [RN+4, 1–2]. This section reflects the mood of a man whose love, in harmony with the splendor and radiance of nature, is capable of ignoring the tragic situation: "The child you bear must not be a burden to your soul."

Having reached a climax, this duet is connected by a transition with a new theme, Ex. 15 [RO-4, 1–3]. Its melody, expressing the "warmth that flows from one of us into the other," the warmth of love, is followed by repetitions and elaborations of preceding themes. It leads finally to another new theme, Ex. 16 [RR, 1–3], which corresponds to the man's dignified resolution: this warmth "will transfigure your child," so as to become "my own." An ascension leads to the climax, a repetition of the man's theme, Ex. 10c, of the second part.

A long coda section concludes the work. Its material consists of themes of the preceding parts, all of them modified anew, so as to glorify the miracles of nature, that have changed this night of tragedy into a transfigured night.

It shall not be forgotten that this work, at its first performance in Vienna, was hissed and caused riots and fist fights. But very soon it became very successful.

Two Statements on *Pelleas und Melisande,* Op. 5, 1903

1.14 *"Foreword to a Broadcast of* Pelleas and Melisande," *February 17, 1950, and from the "Analysis of* Pelleas und Melisande," *December 1949*

The symphonic poem Pelleas und Melisande *was composed in 1902 and 1903, and it was first performed, with Schoenberg conducting, on January 26, 1905, at a concert of the Society for Creative Musicians (see 1.15). The version of the "Analysis of* Pelleas und Melisande" *given here omits the music examples (with their location in the score indicated). On the sketch page, given in fig. 1–2, Schoenberg made a prose outline of the story indicating the main events, as well as musical motives.[44]*

It was around 1900 when Maurice Maeterlinck fascinated composers, stimulating them to create music to his dramatic poems. What attracted all was his art of dramatizing eternal problems of humanity in the form of fairy tales, lending them timelessness without adhering to imitation of ancient styles.

I had first planned to convert *Pelleas and Melisande* into an opera, but I gave up this plan, though I did not know that Debussy was working on his opera at the same time. I still regret that I did not carry out my initial intention. It would have differed from Debussy's. I might have missed the wonderful perfume of the poem; but I might have made my characters more singing.

On the other hand, the symphonic poem helped me, in that it taught me to express moods and characters in precisely formulated units, a technique that an opera would perhaps not have promoted so well.

Thus my fate evidently guided me with great foresight.

———

I composed the Symphonic Poem "Pelleas and Melisande" in 1902. It is inspired entirely by Maurice Maeterlinck's wonderful drama. I tried to mirror every detail of the work with only a few omissions and slight changes of the order of the scenes. Perhaps, as it happens frequently in music, there is more space devoted to the love scenes.

The three main characters are presented by themes in the manner of Wagnerian leitmotifs, except, that they are not as short. Melisande in her helplessness is pictured by Ex. 1 [R1, 1–2], which undergoes many changes in response to various moods. Golaud is pictured by a theme which first appears in the horns, Ex. 2 [R3, 1–4]. Later this is often transformed, for instance, Ex. 3 [R4, 1–3] or Ex. 4 [R5, 1–3]. Pelleas is contrasted distinctly by the youthful and knightly character of his motif, Ex. 5 [R9, 1–9]. The two harmonies starred (a) [R9, 4–5] and another short motif (b) Ex. 6 [m. 2, bass clarinet] of the very beginning are supposed to present the "destiny." This motif appears in many transformations.

Melisande's playing with the ring which falls to the bottom of the fountain is expressed in a scherzo section.

Golaud's jealousy is pictured, Ex. 7 [R23, 1–2].

The scene where Melisande lets her hair hang out the window is richly illustrated. The section begins with flutes and clarinets, closely imitating one another. Later, harps participate, solo violins play Melisande's motif and a solo cello plays Pelleas' theme. Divided high strings and harps continue.

When Golaud leads Pelleas to the frightening subterranean tombs, a musical sound is produced which is remarkable in many respects; especially, because here, for the first time in musical literature, is used a hitherto unknown effect: a glissando of the trombones [R30+6, 1–2].

The love scene begins with a long melody, Ex. 8 [R36, 1–8]. A new motif appears in the death scene, Ex. 9 [R50+1, 1–5]. The entrance of the servants as a premonition of the death of Melisande is mirrored by a choral like theme in trumpet and trombone combined with a countermelody in flutes and piccolos, Ex. 10 [R59, 1–7].

The first performance 26.I.1905 in Vienna under my own direction provoked great riots among the audience and even the critics. Reviews were unusually violent and one of the critics suggested to put me in an asylum and keep music paper out of my reach. Only six years later under Oscar Fried's direction it became a great success, and since that time did not cause the anger of the audiences.[45]

Reforming Concert Life

1.15 Prospectus for the Society of Creative Musicians, March 1904

In keeping with other attempts in Vienna to form groups to further the cause of modern art, with the Viennese Secession being the most prominent example in the visual arts, Schoenberg and Zemlinsky founded the Society of Creative Musicians in 1904. Mahler served as the honorary president; other members included the composer Karl Weigl (1881–1949) and the conductor Bruno Walter (1876–1962).[46] In the course of the single concert season the society survived (1904–1905), performances included—with Mahler conducting—Strauss's Symphonia Domestica, *Op. 53 (1903), Mahler's* Kindertotenlieder *(1904), songs from* Des Knaben Wunderhorn *(completed in 1898), and the premiere of* Pelleas und Melisande, *Op. 5 (1903), with Schoenberg conducting. While the authorship of the prospectus for the society is not known, and there is evidence that it may have been written by composer and conductor Oskar Posa (1873–1951),[47] the content is anticipated in Schoenberg's "The Opera- and Concert-Public and Its Leaders," from the "Seven Fragments," c. 1900. Among the "kinds of influence on the public" that restrain or support artists Schoenberg lists: "I. criticism; II. the artists themselves as critics; III. the dilettante; IV. program books." The document continues by acknowledging the great changes in literature and painting in the last quarter of the nineteenth century but notes that no single new or modern style had been defined, only a range of individual artistic directions. The fragment breaks off as Schoenberg poses the question of whether it would be better for the culture "to have one very great artist who swallows the weaker ones" or "a good average with low peaks."[48] The efforts of the Society of Creative Musicians were continued after World War I with the Society for Private Musical Performances (see 4.2).*

In Vienna's musical life, very little attention is given to the works of contemporary composers, especially Viennese ones. As a rule, new works are heard in Vienna only after doing the rounds of Germany's many musically active towns, great and small—and even then they usually meet with little interest, indeed, with hostility.

There is a crass contrast between this state of affairs and Vienna's musical past, when she used to set the tone; the usual explanation is that the public seems to feel an insuperable distaste for everything new. Vienna is not the place for novelties—that is the story, and the people who say so seem, at first glance, to be in the right if one disregards the operetta, a field in which our city does set the tone, beyond a doubt.

One thing, though: in musical life, since time immemorial, anything new has had to overcome greater and more passionate resistance than in other fields. Nearly all the works nowadays generally acclaimed—but particularly those one must regard as milestones in the development of music—met, when still new, with a cold or even hostile reception, and were felt to lack beauty, to be confused and incoherent. One need think only of Beethoven's *Eroica,* or Ninth Symphony, or late quartets; Bach's works, or those of Wagner and Brahms!

Now, this is not to say that every work received with indifference, or rejected, is of great and epoch-making importance. But a work does not have to be the Ninth Symphony in order to be misunderstood; the case of the Ninth Symphony proves that it is unsafe to base one's conclusions about a new work's artistic importance on first impressions, and that many a present-day work, rejected or laughed out of court at its first performance, *can* be liable, on closer acquaintance, to make one change one's mind completely.

After all, music of any kind can only make its effect if there is an inner relationship between the work and the listener; not only the work's qualities but the listener's too are of decisive importance in producing this. The listener's powers of musical thought and feeling must be able to rise to the demands imposed by the work, just as the work must meet all one's own demands, be everything one asks of an artistic work.

So the most pressing need, if the musical public is to establish a kind of relationship with present-day music, is the need for familiarity with this music's special qualities—just as it took familiarity with classical music to bring about a relationship between such music and the public. There is, indeed, a small selection of the public that is still completely uncultivated, so that for the moment its musical horizons stop short at light music; even today, it finds classical music boring.

All progress, all development, leads from the simple to the complex, and the latest developments in music are the very ones to increase all those difficulties and obstacles against which anything new in music has always had to battle; since this music is more complex, and its harmony and melody more concentrated, there are more obstacles, and they have increased in size, so that numerous, repeated, first-class performances are needed in order to overcome them, even assuming the listener to be receptive (and that is a matter both of ability and willingness). Such performances need preparation that must be extraordinarily exact, and strictly in accordance with the composer's intentions.

But this will remain impossible, so long as the programs of established concert promoters continue to include the occasional new work merely as a kind of curiosity or monstrosity. These works need an artistic setting that would deal *exclusively* with present-day works; *a permanent home where the new would be fostered.*

Only regular performances of new works can show whether interest in the output of the present day can be awakened and kept awake in musical circles; whether the Viennese musical public, like that of many German musical centers, great and small, will sympathize with—or perhaps even take pleasure in—new works, which so far have either remained completely unknown in Vienna, or else have been laid aside after a single performance.

There are, however, further factors, of a more outward nature, that have up to now prevented present-day music from being intensively cultivated in Vienna.

Music differs from the visual arts in that, to attract a public, the creative artist requires the performing artist as middleman; but performers and their associations choose programs primarily with their own artistic and material interests in mind, preferring for the most part to put on works of proven effectiveness, which the public has already taken to its heart; their sole guide, should they choose anything new, is their own insight, critical faculties, and—last but not least—goodwill. All this is understandable.

The possibilities of performing modern music are still further reduced because the existing concert agents and promoters, who are in most cases the middlemen between the artist and the public, likewise influence the choice of programs as much as they can, with an eye to their own financial advantage; everything that seems unlikely to offer them an almost certain box-office success they try to exclude. The free development of Viennese musical life finds its special enemies in such people; as a result of these "factors," with their identical and never-changing programs, the general public has already begun to stop being interested in music at all.

If all these outward obstacles to a free expansion of productive energies are to be removed, the people nearest to music—the creators—may not be permanently excluded from actual musical life. They must take steps to replace their indirect, distorted relationship with the public by one that will be *direct,* like the one the painters and sculptors long since achieved, to the great benefit of art.

And, just as in the latter case it took organization, collective action, to achieve what no one could ever have achieved on his own—emancipation from the art dealers—so, too, do composers need to close their ranks and act together.

The majority of the creative musicians in Vienna have therefore resolved to found a society that aims

> to create such a direct relationship between itself and the public; to give modern music a permanent home in Vienna, where it will be fostered; and to keep the public constantly informed about the current state of musical composition.

The society will pursue these aims by promoting public performances of artistically important new works, and of others which, it is convinced, Vienna has not yet assessed at their true value. It is to bear in mind Austrian and German composers in particular.

In choosing works to be performed, no trend or stylistic genre will be specially preferred; since a work's artistic stature has nothing to do with adherence to any movement or school, there will be performances of works from the classicist school and from the New German, and works of Apollonian, as of Dionysian, tendencies, insofar as they manifest *a powerful artistic personality, expressing itself in a manner that is formally above reproach.*

As for the public, let them judge the works presented to them, not by whether they are easier or harder to comprehend, nor by how suave, or otherwise, their language is, but solely and simply *by the degree of artistry manifest in them; by the magnitude of the artistic achievement these works record.*

On Program Music and Mahler's Third Symphony

1.16 Letter to Gustav Mahler, December 12, 1904

Schoenberg became acquainted with Mahler through Zemlinsky, who had previously introduced him to Alma Mahler.[49] She provides an account of Schoenberg's early relationship to Mahler in her diary notes for 1905: "I met Schoenberg again later. I was acquainted with Mahler by then [1901], although nobody knew it. I asked Schoenberg whether he was going to hear the performance of the Fourth Symphony. He answered me by one of those paradoxes he was so fond of: 'How can Mahler do anything with the Fourth when he has already failed to do anything with the First?' This was true 'Schoenberg.' Yet he was to be Mahler's greatest and most convinced follower. [. . .] Schoenberg [. . .] was inspired by a youthful rebelliousness against his elder, whom at the same time he revered. They used to come in the evening. After one of our devastatingly simple meals, all three went to the piano and talked shop—at first in all amity. Then Schoenberg let fall a word in youthful arrogance and Mahler corrected him with a shade of condescension—and the room was in an uproar. Schoenberg delighted in paradox of the most violent description. At least we thought so then; today I should listen with different ears. Mahler replied professorially. Schoenberg leapt to his feet and vanished with a curt good night. Zemlinsky followed, shaking his head.

"As soon as the door had shut behind them, Mahler said: 'Take good care you never invite that conceited puppy to the house again.' On the stairs Schoenberg spluttered: 'I shall never again cross that threshold.' But after a week or two Mahler said: 'By the way, what's become of those two?'"[50]

My dear Director,

I must not speak as a musician to a musician if I am to give any idea of the incredible impression your symphony made on me: I can speak only as one human being to another. For I saw your very soul, naked, stark naked. It was revealed to me as a stretch of wild and secret country, with eerie chasms and abysses neighbored by sunlit, smiling meadows, haunts of idyllic repose. I felt it as an event of nature, which after scourging us with its terrors puts a rainbow in the sky. What does it matter that what I was told afterwards of your "program" did not seem to correspond altogether with what I had felt? Whether I am a good or bad indicator of the feelings an experience arouses in me is not the point. Must I have a correct understanding of what I have lived and felt? And I believe I felt your symphony. I shared in the battling for illusion; I suffered the pangs of disillusionment; I saw the forces of evil and good wrestling with each other; I saw a man in torment struggling towards inward harmony; I divined a personality, a drama, and *truthfulness,* the most uncompromising truthfulness.

I had to let myself go. Forgive me. I cannot feel by halves. With me it is one thing or the other!

In all devotion,

Arnold Schoenberg

A Recollection of Mahler

1.17 "Bells over the Thury," July 21, 1932

Around 1903 to 1909 I lived in the Liechtensteinstrasse in Vienna and had a view from my study window over the Thury—the Liechten Valley—with a church right in the middle. The many lessons I gave at that time were usually fixed for the afternoon. But sometimes I had an afternoon free, and spent it composing. Well, from two o'clock onwards there was an unbroken succession of funerals in the church, so that the bells did not stop ringing for hours on end.

At the outset, absorbed in work, I hardly noticed them. After a while a certain fatigue, a depletion of imaginative reserves, set in, and in the end I had to give up working.

I told this to Mahler and complained about it.

It is strange how indifferent people can be if they have not experienced something themselves. One cannot really appreciate the sufferings of others.

This is why Mahler's answer was (and I would call that "pretty-rich," as I have committed the same fault hundreds of times):

"Surely it doesn't disturb you. Just compose the bells in!"

But even stranger—and again I have experienced it myself many times—is that one is *punished* for this sort of arrogance. (I grow fat when I mock fat people; I am treated unjustly after abusing others, . . . etc.). Mahler had a composing-house on the Wörther-See, built specially for him, a quarter of an hour up through the woods from his villa. In the stillness of the spot, the birds' singing disturbed him so much that he declared he could no longer compose there.

Did he remember then that he had advised me to include the bells in my composition?

On the First String Quartet, Op. 7, 1905

1.18 From "Prefaces to the Records of the Four String Quartets" (1937)

Schoenberg composed the First String Quartet in 1904 and 1905. The work was premiered in Vienna on February 5, 1907. The following comments were taken from the notes to a private 1937 recording of the four string quartets by the Kolisch Quartet.[51] The Kolisch Quartet had performed the quartets together with late Beethoven quartets in January 1937 in four concerts that were supported by Elizabeth Sprague Coolidge, who had also commissioned the last two quartets.[52] In "How One Becomes Lonely," Schoenberg wrote: "But I must admit that in 1905 the music sounded confusing to the ears of some of my contemporaries and that the score also offered enigmas. So when I showed the First String Quartet to Gustav Mahler, the great Austrian composer and conductor, at the time head of the Imperial Opera in Vienna, he said: 'I have conducted the most difficult scores of Wagner; I have written complicated music myself in scores of up to thirty staves and more; yet here is a score of not more than four staves, and I am unable to read them.'"[53]

There will not be many people today who would understand the opposition which this work provoked at its first performance in Vienna, February 5, 1907. Nevertheless, with a retrospective glance at the time in question it is comprehensible. First its unusual length. It is composed in one very long movement, without the conventional interruptions after each movement. Influenced by Beethoven's C-sharp Minor Quartet, by Liszt's Piano Sonata, Bruckner's and Gustav Mahler's symphonies, we young composers believed this to be the artistic way to compose. Secondly it is the very rich and unusual employment of the harmony and its influence on the construction of the melody which obstructed comprehension. It was and still is my belief that this very quick and partly new succession of harmony ought not to be an unrelated addition to the melody but should be produced by the melody itself: that it ought to be a result, a reaction, a consequence of the very nature of the melody, so express-ing vertically the contents in a manner corresponding to that in which the melody does the same horizontally. It took nearly twenty years before musi-cians and music lovers became able to follow such a complicated style of musical expression.

Today many of the difficulties are not any more in existence and so the listener will easily recognize the principal themes and their use, variation, and development. He will also recognize that there are to be found the four general types of themes, each representing a movement. That is, a group of themes representing the first movement of a sonata, another group represent-ing the Scherzo, a third representing the Adagio and finally a short Rondo. Besides, he will find transitions, recapitulations and a coda finale, but also two so-called developmental sections in which the themes are carried out: the first one before the Scherzo, the second before the recapitulation of the first theme.

He who can would do well to read the score while he listens, because that would help him to recognize the contrapuntal work, which I do not hesitate to call remarkable.

On Program Music and the First String Quartet

1.19 Schoenberg's "Private Program," for the First String Quartet (c. 1904)

In the "Preface to the Four String Quartets" (see 1.6), Schoenberg identified the First String Quartet as marking a turn away from programmatic compositions, such as Verklärte Nacht and Pelleas und Melisande: "Thereafter I abandoned program-music and turned in the direction that was much more my own than all the preceding. It was the First String Quartet, Op. 7, in which I combined all the achievements of my time (including my own) . . . "[54] But he also let drop hints that this work too had programmatic aspects. Dika Newlin noted in her diary on March 6, 1940, the following exchange between Schoenberg and Leonard Stein during a class at UCLA: "He said some of the extravagances of the form were because the piece was really a sort of 'symphonic poem,' and when Stein pressed him as to whether there was a definite program to it or not, he replied promptly, 'Oh yes, very definite—but private!' After that he whispered a few words to Stein, and while I didn't catch all he said, I understood him to reproach Stein for having asked such a question, and to say, 'One does not tell such things anymore!' "[55] A one-page text glued to the back cover of Schoenberg's 1904–1905 Sketchbook has subsequently been identified as this "private program."[56]

I. 1) a) Revolt, Defiance; b) Longing; c) Rapture.

  2) a) Dejection; Despair; Fear of being engulfed; unaccustomed
      feelings of love, desire to be wholly *absorbed.*

      b) Comfort, Relief (She and He)

      c) New outbreak: Dejection, Despair; and

      d) Transition to

  3) Struggle of all the motives with the determination to begin a
      new life.

      e) Mild disagreement

II. 1) "Feeling New Life"

      a) Aggressively joyful strength, fantasy development,
         animation.

      b) New love: tenderness, surrender, rapture, understanding,
         supreme sensual intoxication (Repeat part of II 1.a)

  2) a) Disappointment, (hangover), (brief).

  3) a) Return to dejected moods, despair, transition to

      b) The return of the first mood, I. 1.a

      c) Transition to gentler tones

III. 1) a) Increasing yearning for abandoned loved ones, transition to
         despair over the pain it has caused them.

      b) Onset of sleep. A *dream image* shows the abandoned ones,
         each mourning in his own way for that distant one, thinking
         of him, hoping for his return.

      c) Transition to the decision to return home; increasing
         yearning for peace and rest.

      d) Homecoming; joyful reception, quiet joy and the entrance
         of rest and harmony

2 "Air from Another Planet": Vienna, 1906–1911

A Style of Concision and Brevity

2.1 From "Program Notes for the First Chamber Symphony," Op. 9 (1906), 1949

Schoenberg started work on the First Chamber Symphony at the end of 1905, completing the autograph score on July 25, 1906. The work was premiered in Vienna on February 8, 1907. In "How One Becomes Lonely," he wrote of the piece:

> After having finished the composition of the *Kammersymphonie* it was not only the expectation of success which filled me with joy. It was another and a more important matter. I believed I had now found my own personal style of composing and that all problems which had previously troubled a young composer had been solved and that a way had been shown out of the perplexities in which we young composers had been involved through the harmonic, formal, orchestral and emotional innovations of Richard Wagner. I believed I had found ways of building and carrying out understandable, characteristic, original and expressive themes and melodies, in spite of the enriched harmony which we had inherited from Wagner. It was as lovely a dream as it was a disappointing illusion.[1]

The *Kammersymphonie,* composed in 1906, is the last work of my first period which consists of only one uninterrupted movement. It still has a certain similarity with my First String Quartet Op. 7, which also combines the four types of movements of the sonata form and in some respect with the symphonic poems "Verklärte Nacht" Op. 4 and "Pelléas and Mélisande" Op. 5, which, disregarding the conventional order of the movements, bring about types resembling the contrasting effect of independent movements. Opus 9 differs from the preceding works, however, in its duration. While Opus 4 lasts about 30 minutes, Opus 5 and Opus 7 last 45 minutes, Opus 9 lasts around 22 to 25 minutes.

The length of the earlier compositions was one of the features that linked me with the style of my predecessors, Bruckner and Mahler, whose symphonies often exceed an hour, and Strauss, whose symphonic poems last a half hour. I had become tired—not as a listener—but as a composer of writing

---

Photo opposite page: Schoenberg, 1911. Arnold Schönberg Center, Vienna.

Included in the background are several photographs and paintings of Gustav Mahler.

music of such length. The cause of this is probably to be ascribed to the fact that much of this extension in my own works was the result of a desire, common to all my predecessors and contemporaries, to express every character and mood in a broad manner. That meant, that every idea had to be developed and elaborated by derivatives and repetitions which were mostly bare of variation—in order not to hide the connection.

Students of my works will recognize how in my career the tendency to condense has gradually changed my entire style of composition; how, by renouncing repetitions, sequences and elaboration, I finally arrived at a style of concision and brevity, in which every technical or structural necessity was carried out without unnecessary extension, in which every single unit is supposed to be functional.

In the *Kammersymphonie* I was only at the beginning of this slowly growing process. However, while there is still much elaboration, there is certainly already less unvaried repetition, and a smaller amount of sequences. Besides, while in the First String Quartet there are two large sections of *Durchführung,* that is elaboration (or development) here is only one, and it is much shorter.

If this work is a real turning-point of my career in this respect, it is that even more in that it presents a first attempt at creating a chamber orchestra. The advent of radio was perhaps already to be foreseen and a chamber orchestra would then be capable of filling a living-room with a sufficient amount of sound. There was perhaps the possibility in prospect that one could rehearse a small group at lesser costs more thoroughly, avoiding the forbidding expenses of our mammoth orchestras. History has disappointed me in this respect—the size of the orchestras continued to grow, and in spite of a great number of compositions for small orchestras, I had also to write again for the large orchestra.

The *Kammersymphonie* occupies 15 instruments, all solo: Flute, Oboe, English Horn, Clarinet in E♭, Clarinet, Bass Clarinet, Bassoon, Contrabassoon, 2 Horns, 1st and 2nd Violin, Viola, Violoncello, and Double Bass.

It consists of five divisions:

I. Sonata-Allegro	beginning to number 38[2]
II. Scherzo	number 38–60
III. Durchführung (elaboration)	number 60–77
IV. Adagio	number 77–90
V. Recapitulation and Finale	number 90–100

A Marital Crisis: The Gerstl Affair

2.2 Draft of a Will ("Testaments-Entwurf"), c. 1908

This remarkable document, which contains some of Schoenberg's strongest statements about the gulf between idea and realization and between internal and

external realities, was written in the summer of 1908 when Mathilde had tempo-
rarily left Schoenberg for the painter Richard Gerstl. Gerstl (1883–1908), who had
studied at the Vienna Academy of Arts, lived near Schoenberg on Liechtenstein-
strasse.[3] *With a strong interest in music, Gerstl attempted first to enter into the*
circle around Mahler; he then became friends with Schoenberg and Zemlinsky
around 1907. Both Schoenberg and his wife began painting under Gerstl's tu-
telage; Gerstl's surviving works include portraits of Schoenberg, Mathilde, and
their family (see further 2.12). During the 1908 summer holiday in Gmunden,
while Schoenberg was involved in the composition of the Second String Quartet, an
ongoing affair between Mathilde and the painter intensified to the point that she
left Schoenberg and her children.[4] *Only through the mediation of Webern and*
others was she persuaded to return a short time later. The following November,
after destroying what he was able to of his documents and works, Gerstl com-
mitted suicide. Although the question is far from settled, some scholars have
linked the quartet to the traumatic affair, especially its scherzo movement with its
quotation of the children's song "Ach, Du lieber Augustin" and the associated text
"alles ist hin" (all is lost), which has been interpreted as referring to Schoenberg's
personal situation as well as to the incipient break with tonality in the final two
movements. The selection of the Stefan George poems set in these movements may
also reflect Schoenberg's emotional turmoil from this period, in particular the
third movement, "Litany," which concludes, "Kill every longing, close my heart's
wound, / Take from me love, and grant me thy peace!"

I, who have been hindered so long in the exertion of my will, find it necessary, as a preliminary exercise for some acts of will that I now intend, to record my *Last Will.* I am also urged on by the realization that, with my energy gone and my vitality at its end, it is very likely that I shall soon follow the path, find the resolution, that at long last might be the highest culmination of all human actions. It could well be that I shall have to shake off the many sorrows that I have had to endure until now. Whether it be my body that will give way or my soul—I don't feel the difference, but I foresee the separation.

Here I shall now, while I have time, put some of the external circum-stances of my life in order. As little as these things I have to speak about seem worth the fuss that I have made over them, it nevertheless seems necessary to attend to them.

True, I would have liked to have seen what I shall leave behind be richer. Richer in the number of works and deeds, more richly developed and more profound in what they mean and in their intent. I would have still liked to have brought one or another idea into the world, and still more to have stood up for it, spoken for it, and fought for it. I would have liked to have done for myself what my disciples will do. I would have also liked—I cannot deny it—to have won the glory for it. Now I suppose I must do without all that, and content myself with what is really there, with all that I have borne, whose paternity will undeniably be granted to me, and not begrudge recalling ideas, undoubtedly brought forth by my creative will, that will now be adopted by others. Unfortunately, I know only too well how disciples differ from the prophet. How what was free and agile, perhaps even seemingly full of contradictions, now becomes rigid, pedantic, orthodox, exaggerated, but uniform—for the talented, all that is great, like nature, is full of contradictions because they don't see the real connections, and thus the essential eludes them. This damned uniformity! He who has a feeling for diversity laughs at the constricted mind that stakes out a territory to be able to survey it; that wants to bring order into things which are ordered on laws very different from what the Philistine's sense of order can imagine; that applies laws, without realizing that already in the word law is the limitation that men can impose on each other if they have power to do so, but which men can never impose on things that lie outside human power. He who recognizes all these facts is talented.

To be talented is the ability to utilize things. But the ability to utilize things is to exploit. The capacity for exploitation comes only to those for whom everything has only a momentary value, who hastily put everything to momentary uses.

With regard to my deeds and ideas that I leave undone or unlegitimated, I thus see myself as dependent on the talented. There will soon thus be a weak, diluted rehash of my ideas being turned to a concrete profit. Godparents will be promoted to fathers, and will bring up children, who should have become giants, to be well-bred men who know how to get on in life.

Ideas, whose fulfillment perhaps would have never been permitted, ideas that mankind must have always had in mind as the scarcely-to-be-attained purpose of its existence, will now be brought to that simplified form that makes their realization possible. That damned realism of those talented disciples and bloodsuckers would not even shrink back from approaching the ideal of mankind: to be God, to become immortal and infallible, but in an inexpensive and tastefully designed popular edition, if the idea had even a chance of realization. An airship with electric wiring, an airship carried by a balloon, is that what seems to the competent and talented to be an acceptable substitute for the idea of floating in space, of abolishing distance to attain proximity, proximity to God? To get from one place to another through the air by hanging on a wire, or to fly with a body lighter than air around a pole—but in a circle!

These are deeds that fill the world with enthusiasm. And he who knows how to get on in life knows why he chooses this path and not another.

But it is different: facts prove nothing. He who sticks with facts will never get beyond them to the essence of things. I deny facts. All of them, without exception. They have no value to me for I elude them before they can pull me down. I deny the fact that my wife betrayed me. She did not betray me, for my imagination had already pictured everything that she has done. My capacity for premonition had always seen through her lies and expected her crimes long before she herself had thought to commit them. And I only trusted her because I saw what she presented as facts to be lies, and thus considered them from the standpoint of a higher level of credibility and verifiability.

The fact that she betrayed me is thus of no importance to me. But there are, however, some things worth noting here.

She lied—I believed her. For had I not believed her would she have been with me for so long? Wrong! She did not lie to me. For *my* wife does not lie. The soul of *my* wife is so at one with my soul that I know everything about her. Therefore she didn't lie; but she was not my wife. That's how it is. The soul of my wife was so foreign to mine that I could not have entered into either a truthful or a deceitful relationship with her. We have never even really spoken to each other, that is, communicated, we only talked.

And now I know what was going on.

She did not lie to me. Because one does not tell me lies. I only hear what sounds in *me,* thus only the truth. To anything else I'm deaf; it reaches me perhaps somewhere on the outside, but it does not get through to me. How would I have been able to hear her then? She may perhaps have spoken, but I did not hear. Thus I absolutely don't know that she lied.

Now, it can't be denied that subjectively she consciously lied. For she presented to me the opposite of what she believed to be the truth. It is possible that she subjectively lied. But I don't actually know anything about it. I must have slept through it or have forgotten it, perhaps I didn't notice it at all. If I sing a pure note A into my piano, then all the strings that contain A also ring. But if I sing a wrong note, higher or lower, the reverberation is much weaker. Obviously only some distant overtones resonate—musically wrong, useless—but I believe that the well-tempered piano really doesn't know anything about them; it can forget them; they don't penetrate into its harmonic musical nature.[5]

She maintained that she was faithful to me. I asked her about it. How would I have been able to ask her if I hadn't known that she is unfaithful to me? Can someone who is faithful also be unfaithful? My wife can only be faithful. Therefore she was not my wife, or the question was superfluous. That's how it is: the question was superfluous. If I asked her, then I knew it. If I knew it, then I knew that she was true to me. How could I have been able to presume faithfulness when I believed only in unfaithfulness. Therefore I did not ask. I received no answer. But: I knew everything.

Now, it certainly cannot be denied that I am extremely unhappy about her breach of faith. I have cried, have behaved like someone in despair, have made decisions and then rejected them, have had thoughts of suicide and almost carried them out, have plunged from one madness into another—in a word, I am totally broken. Is this fact not also proof? No, for I am only despairing because I don't believe the facts. I cannot believe. I don't regard it as possible that I can have a wife who deceives me. Then I never really had one, then she was never really even my wife, and I was perhaps never married. The whole thing was only a dream, and only the logical succession of events speaks against this assumption. Because a dream, thank God, is not logical, and that's why disciples and the talented don't dream. Or if they do, then they at least attempt to interpret the dream, to make it more logical in order to bring it at once nearer to their little brains. So if it is no dream, then it is just a fact. And I cannot believe in facts: they do not exist for me.

This thing therefore didn't happen to me, but to some kind of monstrosity out of the imagination of a woman. It was the man she took me for that my wife lied to and betrayed. He was her creation; she could do what she wanted with him. He had believed her too, trusted, mistrusted, was jealous; had begged her for the truth; had cried and whined in front of her; had begged her to stay with him; despaired when she would not stay; went to her when she called him back; wanted to take her back, defiled, as they both were, but then at the last moment reconsidered and let her go. This filthy swine was not me. No, and a thousand times no. And if a thousand witnesses swear it, it is not true. She could not betray me. Not me—but someone else who was her creation, her intellectual property, her equal or counterpart—but not me.

I was distant from her. She never saw me and I never saw her. We never knew each other. I don't even know what she looks like. I can't even summon up an image of her. Perhaps she doesn't even exist. She lives only in my imagination. Perhaps she is only my invention. A device, a vessel, a frame or something similar that is suitable to take in and embody everything that is horrible and repulsive to me. Perhaps she is just a fact or some other

[The document breaks off here.]

Notes on the Second String Quartet in F-sharp Minor, Op. 10, 1908

2.3 From "Prefaces to the Records of the Four String Quartets," 1937

Schoenberg composed the Second String Quartet in 1907 and 1908. He described the return to a multimovement form as "one of the first symptoms that the period of greatly expanded forms, which had been inaugurated by Beethoven's C♯ Minor Quartet, was passing and that a new period aimed for rather shorter forms, in size and content, and also in expression."[6] In "My Evolution," he wrote: "My Two Ballads, Op. 12, were the immediate predecessors of the Second String Quartet, Op. 10, which marks the transition to my second period. In this period I renounced a tonal center—a procedure incorrectly called 'atonality.'[7] In the first and second movements there are many sections in which the individual parts proceed regardless of whether or not their meeting results in codified harmonies. Still, here, and also in the third and fourth movements, the key is presented distinctly at all the main dividing-points of the formal organization. Yet the overwhelming multitude of dissonances cannot be counterbalanced any longer by occasional returns to such tonal triads as represent a key. It seemed inadequate to force a movement into the Procrustean bed of a tonality without supporting it by harmonic progressions that pertain to it. This dilemma was my concern, and it should have occupied the minds of all my contemporaries also. That I was the first to venture this decisive step will not be considered universally a merit—a fact I regret but have to ignore."[8] In the final movement, "Entrückung," or "Transport," an extraordinary instrumental introduction with harmonies that seem to float free of tonal gravity, leads to the famous opening line, "I feel the air of another planet" (see fig. 2–3).

My second string quartet caused at its first performance in Vienna, December 1908, riots which surpassed every previous and subsequent happening of this kind. Although there were also some personal enemies of mine, who used the occasion to annoy me—a fact which can today be proven true—I have to admit, that these riots were justified without the hatred of my enemies, because they were a natural reaction of a conservatively educated audience to a new kind of music.

Astonishingly the first movement passed without any reaction, neither for nor against. But after the first measures of the second movement the greater part of the audience started to laugh and did not cease to disturb the performance during the third movement "Litanei" (in the form of variations) and the fourth movement "Entrückung." It was very embarrassing for the Rosé-Quartet and the singer, the great Mme. Marie Gutheil-Schoder.[9] But at the end of this fourth movement a remarkable thing happened. After the singer ceases there comes a long coda played by the string quartet alone. While, as before mentioned, the audience failed to respect even a singing lady, this coda was accepted without any audible disturbance. Perhaps even my enemies and adversaries might have felt something here?

On Modern Music, Audiences, and Critics

2.4 "With Arnold Schoenberg: An Interview by Paul Wilhelm," January 10, 1909

This article was published in the Neues Wiener Journal *in the shadow of the scandalous premiere of the Second String Quartet on December 21, 1908. It initiated a series of challenges to the Viennese critical and academic musical establishment in some of Schoenberg's earliest published writings, including the "Open Letter to Ludwig Karpath" (see 2.6) and "About Music Criticism," published in* Der Merker, *October 1909.[10] The interview is preceded by Wilhelm's account of his visit to Schoenberg's Liechtensteinstrasse apartment (and see the photograph at the beginning of this chapter):*

> Pleasant rooms, with a plain, tastefully decorated simplicity. A few pictures adorning the walls divulge that the artist also wields a paintbrush—and indeed with an odd talent in a broad impressionistic manner with canvases that make a strong effect. A small head, an interesting attempt at self-portrait, was striking in the artful way Schoenberg managed to capture the strange, wild, and at times darting glance of his eyes. In a corner is a characteristically rendered bust of Schoenberg by the masterful hand of Josef Heus. Above his desk hang two pictures with warm dedications by Gustav Mahler; a portrait of Zemlinsky looks out from the side of the central pillar. That is the plain, unassuming decoration of his rooms, of his world; small, but comprehended with deep feeling. His manner is plain and unpretentious, but full of vigor and energy with every artistic remark. While speaking he paces back and forth nervously through the room. His round, beardless face, despite its strangely still, nearly pastoral expression, reacts first. A slight frown, a flaring of the eyes, betrays the activity of his thoughts.

I ask about the decisive factors in his artistic development, and Schoenberg says: The most meaningful factor is no doubt the inner necessity of one's own development. One does not develop intentionally and consciously. The musical environment doubtlessly exerts certain influences. First I became a Wagnerian—then the subsequent development came rather quickly. Today all artistic evolutions take place in very rapid succession. I could analyze my development very precisely, though not theoretically, but retrospectively. It is an interesting observation that the thing that had initiated a development mostly brings about its opposite; that as soon as one has digested it, it is also the first thing that we find repellent, so that development always means a reaction against the thing that caused it. . . . And I believe, if I contemplate my own development, that I can in effect describe the development of the last ten or twelve years of music—much in me coincides with Reger, Strauss, Mahler, Debussy, and others.

I speak about Wagner's influence on the development of modern music, and Schoenberg answers:
Wagner—most importantly, insofar as the modern development is considered—bequeathed to us three things: first, rich harmony; second, the short motive with its possibility of adapting the phrase [*Satz*] as quickly and often as required to the smallest details of the mood; and third, at the same time, the art of building large-scale structures and the prospect of developing this art still further.—All these seem to have developed in succession, and then to

have led to their opposites. The first thing that began to ferment seems to have been the harmony of expression.[11] With that, the short motives next led to a symbolization of technique. A consequence of the mostly sequential continuations was the loss of formal refinement. The first reaction to that was an overgrowth of the form and the striving for long melodies, as for example with Richard Strauss in *Ein Heldenleben*.

Do you regard melody, in the sense in which it is usually understood, as a thing of the past?
One could find the answer by looking at my recent works. They are still melodic throughout. Only I believe that melody has taken another form. Moreover, I believe that there is a lack of clarity about the concept of melody. Normally melody is understood to be what someone can whistle back to you. But what a musician and what a nonmusician can whistle back are already two very different things. In general, melody seems to be understood as the most concise formation of a musical idea with a lyrical character, arranged to be as clear as possible. But along with this simplicity that makes a melody captivating, however, comes the other side of the coin: primitiveness. It follows that our simplicity is different from that of our predecessors, that it is more complex, but also that even this complexity will in turn be regarded one day as primitive.

Do you believe that the masses show an understanding for this form of development?
It is not surprising that a time does not understand or appreciate the immediately preceding stage of development, since it is the reaction to it. So it was certainly no accident that ten years ago the Wagnerians began to discover Mozart and Beethoven—though they did not really discover them, but rather they lost Wagner. I feel that with such a development a similar occurrence takes place as happens in medicine with heredity. But in the other direction. In going back the reaction usually skips over the closest link in the chain of development.

Do you believe that the public would be capable of following this development? After all, I think that the broad masses will always adhere to certain musical forms.
I believe that the level of the average education must be raised substantially, or art will again become, as it was before, a concern of a select group of the most cultivated people of the time. But I hope, to be sincere, for the opposite.

My question now goes to whether the public's taste influences the artist, and Schoenberg replies:
No! Never the *real* artist, for he is never in the position to create anything other than what he is urged to by his nature and development. Unfortunately, here and there some believe themselves able to adapt to the public, but the betrayal

is definitely avenged later. For those who do not bear within themselves in some way the nature of the public will not succeed in pleasing it entirely. One soon notices the falsehood, so the betrayal is mostly pointless anyway.

We come to speak of the stance of the artist toward the public, and I ask Schoenberg whether success or failure enhances his self-esteem or deepens his doubt; he answers with an ironic laugh:

The public and critics nowadays have so taken leave of their artistic senses that they can in no way serve as a measure. Today one can't even gain self-confidence through a failure. The public and the critics don't recognize their own taste veiled in an artistic form so that they occasionally themselves bring about the failure of a work that should have actually appealed to them. They don't recognize their own intellectual progeny any more.

Schoenberg speaks about the Viennese critics in particular with sharp disapproval, from which one can sense the extent of his bitterness, but also his deep inner isolation. And with it he also fights passionately for his goal. But the honest courage with which he expresses his convictions is also somewhat sympathetic. To my question, "Do you believe that in our time an artist is capable of prevailing against the opinion of the critics and the public?" he replies:

I will only be able to judge that at the end of my days.

Concerning Music Critics

2.5 Letter to Karl Kraus (c. January–February, 1909)

The Viennese social critic, journalist, and poet Karl Kraus (1874–1936) founded the journal Die Fackel *(The torch) in 1899, first as editor and eventually as the sole author for many years until the final issue in 1936. He was greatly revered, and also feared, by all those in the Schoenberg circle for his extremely high linguistic standards, which he viewed as one and the same with high moral standards. Schoenberg's close friend, the painter Oskar Kokoschka (1886–1980), wrote of Kraus: "He was absolutely intolerant with everybody, and he gave permission to see him in the café at a certain time in the evening when he ate his dinner. He ate a sausage, a very sharp sausage. . . . And then there were three or four men—always Adolf Loos and always Altenberg. . . . Kraus was very intolerant so everybody had to stand his test when he had read the new edition of the* Fackel *that he could explain every phrase, even the comma, whether it's in the right place."[12] In this letter, Schoenberg discusses the interview from the* Neues Wiener Journal, *given above in 2.4, as well as the "Open Letter to Mr. Ludwig Karpath" in 2.6.*

Dear Mr. Kraus,

You were sent a copy of my "Open Letter to Mr. Karpath." I have just read it—because it was urgent, I dictated the letter—and find some ridiculous grammatical errors, apparently "corrections" by the secretary. Please do not make any "allowances" for me in this regard; I deserve it to be better. I have had a very rough time this year, and everything has come out so lopsided that if I write an "open" letter it would no doubt have been better to keep it "closed." It doesn't please me at all.

I must still apologize on account of my interview in the *Neues Wiener Journal!* Really apologize—I still feel answerable to a few people in Vienna.

I only did this thing on account of the two closing sentences, and they were left out!

I give them to you to use as you like:

"The Viennese music critics, with very few exceptions, are of such incompetence and ignorance that one can now evaluate them only on the basis of the extent or lack of the damage they cause. Moreover, most of them actually understand their trade in this sense: producing advertising for a popular artist or stirring up opinion against an unpopular one."

But in addition, almost everything I said is garbled, distorted, and toned down! Through corrections, omissions, wrong words ("symbolization" instead of "simplification," "harmony of expression" instead of "harmony as expression") and similar suitable methods.

I was in complete despair—or to the degree that I had not already been rather stunned by the many mishaps. And I still had the fear of losing the respect of the few people to whom I mean something.

Certainly, I could also live without this respect. But so much recognition is denied to me, and I have to rely so much on what I think of myself, that it would not be easy. And I have my convictions: of my talent and of my absolute purity. But all the same . . . you, who have no doubt also not become a recluse willfully, certainly understand this the best!

Incidentally: I must still say what I have wanted to write for so long.

About your "personal matters."

I have experienced something similar recently—is that a consolation?

It was for me when I read something similar soon after in the *Bluebook:* "Der Vampyr," "Der Kleber," "Zinnobers Anatomie," etc.[13]

And your "personal matters" were thus also very upsetting and very moving to me.

Perhaps this kind of impact will please you a little.

With warm greetings,

Yours truly,

Arnold Schoenberg

A Challenge to a Critic

2.6 "Open Letter to Mr. Ludwig Karpath," February 15, 1909

Kraus prefaced Schoenberg's "open letter" in Die Fackel *with a short introduction that included Karpath's review of the performance of the Second String Quartet as published in the Berlin journal* Signale *(January 6, 1909). There Karpath wrote:*

> I shall confine myself to the statement that it resulted in an unholy scandal, the likes of which we have never before experienced in a Viennese concert hall. Right in the middle of the movements there was persistent and uproarious laughter, and in the middle of the last movement people shouted at the top of their voices: "Stop! Enough! We will not be treated like fools!" And I must confess to my sorrow that I, too, let myself be driven to similar outbursts. It is true that a critic should not express his disapproval in the concert hall. If I nevertheless abandoned my customary reserve, I only proved by it that I suffered physical pain, and as one cruelly abused, despite all good intentions to endure even the worst, I still had to cry out. By publicly reprimanding myself here, I have also won the right to smile about my attackers. These, numbering about a dozen, maintained that the Schoenberg quartet was a work of art, that the rest of us did not understand it, that we didn't even know the nature of sonata form. Now for my part, I am quite willing to stand for an examination in harmony, form, and all other musical disciplines before any Areopagus. Admittedly, I have still studied on the model of the "ancients" and could therefore only pass my exam by compliance with the "old system." If the dozen say, "That doesn't count!"—that's fine too.[14]

Following Schoenberg's letter, Kraus pointed out that while the challenge to Karpath had been ignored, it was still not too late for the critic to take the exam and so to put an end to the "old mistrust" and earn for the office of music critic a "certificate of qualifications."

> I don't belong to the dozen who say "That doesn't count," and shall prove that to you by accepting any "Areopagus" you put together according to the "new" or the "old system." On the contrary, I recommend for this Areopagus the following gentlemen, who are one hopes ready to assume this office: Professor Robert Fuchs, Professor Eusebius Mandyczewski, Professor Richard Heuberger, Professor Hermann Grädener, and Professor Josef Labor.[15] On the basis of your declaration, I challenge you to stand for your exam before this Areopagus "in harmony, form, and all other musical disciplines" under the conditions to which you have declared yourself ready. If you wish—as you can see, I also leave the choice of weapons to you—the exam can be done only on the "old system" which you have studied, and I leave to you to name for yourself the theorists who shall serve as the basis for the questions. I request only the following

requirements: the exam shall be public, and I myself shall put the questions to you. The gentlemen of the Areopagus will judge whether you have succeeded. You now have the opportunity to prove what you have claimed. If you withdraw from this exam for any reason you will confirm the evidence that you have something to fear.

"Great art must proceed to precision and brevity"

2.7 Aphorisms from Die Musik, 1909

The large number of aphorisms that Schoenberg wrote throughout his life reflect his love of language and wordplay, but they also include some of his most important statements on a whole range of topics.[16] Though aphorisms were a broadly popular literary genre in turn-of-the-century Vienna, his early aphorisms are most closely related in style and topic to the many that Kraus published in Die Fackel.[17] *Schoenberg's attraction to aphorisms can be linked to some of his most deeply held beliefs about art, as is evident in the essay "Brahms the Progressive" (1947): "Great art must proceed to precision and brevity [. . .] lending to every sentence the full pregnancy of meaning of a maxim, of a proverb, of an aphorism. This is what musical prose should be—a direct and straightforward presentation of ideas, without any patchwork, without mere padding and empty repetitions."[18]*

In the years leading up to the First World War the aphoristic form of expression took on a special significance as Schoenberg, along with Berg and Webern, wrote a series of very short pieces, including Schoenberg's Six Little Piano Pieces, *Op. 19 (1911), Webern's* Five Pieces for String Quartet, *Op. 5 (1909), and Berg's* Five Orchestral Songs on Picture-Postcard Texts of Peter Altenberg, *Op. 4 (1912). Later he described "the extreme short forms" as teaching him "to formulate ideas in an aphoristic manner, which did not require continuations out of formal reasons . . . [and] to link ideas together without the use of formal connectives, merely by juxtaposition."[19]*

In some of the longer aphorisms given below, it is evident that the urge toward brevity ran up against Schoenberg's natural volubility. In other cases, the aphorisms are closely related to more extended formulations in his other writings. For example, the sentence "Talent is the capacity to learn, genius the capacity to develop oneself" reappears in the 1912 essay on Gustav Mahler in a more developed form: "Talent is the capacity to learn, genius the capacity to develop oneself. Talent grows by acquiring capacities which already existed outside of itself; it assimilates these, and finally even possesses them. Genius already possesses all its future faculties from the very beginning. It only develops them; it merely unwinds, unrolls, unfolds them."[20]

This set of aphorisms appeared in the German periodical Die Musik, *which covered all aspects of musical life in Germany and Austria, and which published several of Schoenberg's early writings.*

Art is the cry of distress uttered by those who experience firsthand the fate of mankind. Who are not reconciled to it, but come to grips with it. Who do not apathetically serve the motor of "dark forces," but hurl themselves in among the moving wheels, to understand how it all works. Who do not turn their eyes away, to shield themselves from emotions, but open them wide, so as to tackle what must be tackled. Who do, however, often close their eyes, in order to perceive things incommunicable by the senses, to envision within themselves the process that only seems to be in the world outside. And within, inside them, is the movement of the world, what bursts out is merely the echo: the work of art.[21]

Talent is the capacity to learn, genius the capacity to develop oneself.

Something that is called "worth the sweat of the noble" is worth absolutely nothing, for the noble don't sweat; the strength that tirelessly pours forth from a creator couldn't be squeezed out by the ignoble even if they summoned all their forces.

My inclinations developed more rapidly from the moment that I started to become clearly conscious of my aversions.

Melody is the most primitive form of expression in music. Its goal is to present a musical idea through many repetitions (motivic work) and the slowest possible development (variation) so that even the dense can follow it. It treats the listener the way a grown-up treats a child or a sensible person treats an idiot. For the swift intellect this is an insulting presumption, but that's the reason our grown-ups make it the essence of music.

Compositional child prodigies are those who already in their earliest youth compose as badly as others do only in ripe old age.

The artwork is a labyrinth, in which at every point the expert knows the entrance and exit, without a red thread guiding him. The more intricate and winding the passages, the more surely he glides along every path to the goal. The wrong paths, if there were any in the artwork, would show him the right way, and each digression would orient him toward the direction of the essential content. Thus meaningful through and through is God's greatest creation: the artwork brought forth by man. It may be that this clarity is what the pseudo-artists have in mind when they weave threads through their tendentious creations, dragging their little thoughts and their fake tangles along; the straws without which they would drown; the crutches of an intellectuality without whose support they would never get off the ground. Only for a short while can the imitation persuade the expert, soon he will notice that the labyrinth is marked; he sees through the intention that imagines making the goal seem appealing by clumsily hiding it; he recognizes that they only want to play hide and seek but are afraid they won't be found: something they could not survive. The expert sees the clarity that these signposts provide as a crafty expedient. This petty arithmetic has nothing in common with the work of art except the formulas. But while these formulas are only incidental to the creation of genius, for the nongenius it is as if they were there from the start. Calmly the expert turns away and sees the revenge of a higher justice revealed: the miscalculation.

Only if the unnatural—the abnormal and the supernatural—becomes a habit is it disagreeable: then it is natural again.

If someone takes a trip in order to have a story to tell, then he certainly should not go as the crow flies.

Composition is so easy that one could become megalomaniacal about it. Publishing is so difficult that one can barely escape a persecution mania. But to have to associate with publishers must definitely result in a maniacal rage.

The purpose of a woman's large hat is not only to overshadow her rivals but still more to hide them.

With the first thought [*Gedanke*] emerges the first error.

There are presentiments, but no pre-thoughts, and prejudice is a presentiment; that's why it's almost never mistaken.[22]

I have often not known immediately if something I have written is beautiful, only that it was necessary. "And God saw that it was good," but only after he had finished creating.

It is no disgrace for a man of importance if someone makes a fool of him, or if he is duped. The things that he can be persuaded to believe true although they are false are such that are only permitted outside his sphere of observation. If, for example, I make a deal with a businessman, then I'm going to be cheated, for it is beneath me to inquire into what he is really thinking, while he is saying something else. It would be immaterial in relationship to the transaction. I must assume that is why he also would be businesslike, although I know that he is in fact otherwise personable, in his own way. For if I had the ability to think the way he does, then I would also have the inclination. And if I have the inclination, then I am like him. The ocean that separates us could be filled by a single unbefitting thought, and the opposite shorelines would run together.

Through self-discipline conquer self-obsession.[23]

Why are ugly women mostly shortsighted as well?

So that he won't have to survive it, the artist gives his pain immortality through the artwork.

Comparisons must obviously be awkward if one expects that the things compared can be brought into complete congruence in every situation; for to compare is not to equate ($=$) but to posit a similarity ($\sim$). Statements of congruence should not be employed, but rather statements of similarity. But the painter can freely equate a portrait he has created to the model, even if there is no similarity; and the dramatist can freely posit a similarity between the people through whom he translates himself and those who are like them. Comparisons, then, must obviously be awkward; in particular, those through which the public want to bring themselves closer to the artwork.

It must be difficult to hinder those unoriginal people whose temperament compels them to offer their "that is my opinion"—namely, what is everyone's opinion—and, if possible, to offer it to one whose fertile originality especially provokes the cud-chewing mechanism that regulates their impotence.

A disheartening fact: cleanliness is just an extremely diluted uncleanliness. These are all certainly only approximate values; $0 = x - x$ or $\sim - \sim$ or even $x/\sim$, and if one only takes it rather materially, there is always a remainder that forces us to confess: the smallest compromise is the utmost that we are able to achieve.

The man is what he experiences; the artist experiences only what he is.

Whenever banality and triviality discover their homogeneity the nationalistic idea arises.

I am certain that the second half of this century will spoil by overestimation whatever good the first half allowed to me through underestimation.[24]

I certainly don't want to be flattered when I deserve it, only to be praised when I don't deserve it.

If the Oriental wants to honor his friend he uses self-deprecation as the most effective means. "Your slave, your servant; I am not worthy of loosening the laces of your shoe"—when a servant says this to a prince, it is not particularly flattering, since it is true. But if a prince says it to a prince, then it means: "You know who I am, and how highly I am regarded. Now observe, I place you even higher than myself. I step down so that you can be better seen. Notice from that how important you are to me." Only the superior one who is certain that he is not in the position to diminish his own importance is capable of such unreserved praise.

Biblical translation: "I shall plague you with scorpions," that means, "I have created publishers of every shape and kind, that they may multiply and enrich themselves."

Science is a woman who needs whole men. No wonder: only half-men dedicate themselves to her.

The art lover: "If I'm really supposed to pay 200 crowns for a painting by Kokoschka, then it must be so good that everyone I tell it cost 5,000 crowns will think it dirt cheap—and it should only cost me 150."

Self-observation is the only true path to learning. But how does one now prevent the student from acquiring out of his own intuition those false ideas that the pedagogues would have imparted in a much shorter time?

The apostle begins as the pioneer of a new idea and ends as the defender of one that has become old. Thus he certainly takes an active part in the honor of victory, but hardly in the actual development. His route, so to speak, is like a spiral. The genius, however, makes leaps; always the shortest path, and he leaves it to the disciples to fill in the gaps as penance for unearned honor. But since it results from many experiments rather than instinct, the apostle's own motion has a certain torque. Thus the spiral.

Life in Vienna

2.8 From a Letter to Mathilde Schoenberg, June 23, 1909

Schoenberg's family preceded him to Steinakirchen am Forst for the summer holiday. In this letter, which offers a glimpse of his life in the Viennese café society, he mentions the artist Max Oppenheimer (1885–1954), who painted a well-known portrait of Schoenberg. Around this time, Oppenheimer also acted as an intermediary between Schoenberg and Oskar Kokoschka, leading to a correspondence in the fall about an unfortunately unrealized opera for which Kokoschka would write the libretto (following on the performance of his Murderer Hope of Womenkind *at the Kunstschau in Vienna in July 1909.)[25] When, in the summer of 1910, it appeared that* Erwartung *might be staged at the Vienna Volksoper, Schoenberg asked Oppenheimer to do the staging.[26]*

Dearest Mathilde,
　　　　so that you can get this on time, I am writing to you at the post office. Yesterday I really went out on the town—but I won't do it anymore. First I

spent three hours at the Gänsehäufel; then stayed through supper with Alex and Stein at the Pilsensetzer, then with the "above" and Berg at the Arkaden café, and finally—and this is the worst—until 1:00 A.M. at the American Bar, where we also met Oppenheimer and Frau von Eger.[27] But as I said, I won't do it anymore and shall live very frugally. . . . How are the children? Are they being good? Have they been a nuisance? . . . Yesterday I spent the night at the Zemlinskys. On the couch. Quite nice . . . I am looking forward very much to seeing you all soon. I am certain everything will go well with you. Be sure to eat plenty and stay indoors less.[28] Kisses and hugs to you, Trudi, and Görgi.

Arnold

Wednesday morning 10:30 at the post office.

A New Style of Expression

2.9 Introduction to the Three Pieces for Piano, Op. 11, July 27, 1949

The Three Pieces for Piano, written between February and August 1909, and published the following year by Universal Edition, were the first atonal pieces to be published and to become widely known. In a 1949 letter, Schoenberg wrote to the pianist Eduard Steuermann (mentioned below), who was hesitating to release a recording of the complete piano music: "You virtuosi always think you are the main factor, and you forget that I who had to wait fifty years have a greater right to be impatient than you. [. . .] There exists no perfection among human beings, and I myself had also to renounce perfection. Why should you have the privilege?"[29]

The Three Pieces for Piano, Op. 11 (1909), were not my first step toward a new style of expression in music. They were preceded by parts of my Second String Quartet, and by some of my Fifteen Songs after Stefan George, Op. 15. But they were the first publication of music of this kind, and they accordingly provoked a great sensation.

I must confess that I was startled about the public reaction. To me, the difference between this music and the third and fourth movements of my Second String Quartet did not seem unsurpassable. The latter, at its first performance, had met with great resistance; but the next performance, a few weeks later, was much applauded. Why then so much excitement?

I was furiously attacked in newspapers and in the musical press of most of Europe. It was not very pleasant. I was suddenly quite isolated. Even such friends who, in spite of my preceding scandals, had remained friendly toward me, abandoned me now. I was blamed and scorned by the best musicians of the time, and even a Massenet did not hesitate to speak up against me.

Despair might not have destroyed me—it seems, on the contrary, that I was destined to survive. I had found mighty support in the faithfulness of my pupils: Anton von Webern, Alban Berg, Heinrich Jalowetz, and, last but not least, Erwin Stein.[30] And I had acquired the interest and support of one singularly great musician: Ferruccio Busoni. A great creator and fighter for innovations, he had taken my side in a highly courageous and generous manner. I will never forget that.

The first to perform the Three Pieces for Piano publicly was Richard Buhlig.[31]

But thereafter came Eduard Steuermann, who since then has remained my ambassador at the piano.

On Variegation, Expression, and Illogicality

2.10 From Two Letters to Ferruccio Busoni, c. August 18 and August 24, 1909

The Italian composer, pianist, and conductor Ferruccio Busoni (1866–1924) was a major figure in the musical life of Berlin from the turn of the century until his death. It was his position at the Prussian Academy of the Arts that Schoenberg took over at the end of 1925 (see 5.1). Schoenberg had first corresponded with him in 1903, attempting unsuccessfully to arrange for the premiere performance of Pelleas und Melisande. *Busoni did, however, conduct Schoenberg's orchestration of Heinrich Schenker's* Syrian Dances *in November 1903.*

Their correspondence resumed in 1909 in connection with a planned performance of the First Chamber Symphony. Although this also did not come to fruition, Schoenberg sent Busoni the first two movements of what would become the Three Piano Pieces, Op. 11, touching off in the process an exchange of letters that include some of the most fully worked-out statements of his aesthetic stance at the time he was writing his atonal masterpieces. The first letter was written shortly before he completed the third movement of the piano pieces (see fig. 2-4) and during the composition of the Five Orchestral Pieces, Op. 16. By the time of the second letter, he had completed Op. 11 and Op. 16 and was preparing to start work on the opera Erwartung, *Op. 17, collaborating closely with the poet and physician Marie Pappenheim (1882–1966), who was also spending the summer in Steinakirchen.[32]* Erwartung, *with its extreme reduction of traditional structural features, is arguably the most far-reaching of Schoenberg's attempts to write the kind of music he describes in these letters to Busoni: music that captures the constantly changing and irrational flow of unconscious sensations.*

Busoni responded favorably to the first two movements of Op. 11 but expressed reservations about Schoenberg's manner of writing for the piano. Much of the second letter concerns Schoenberg's reaction to Busoni's confession in a letter of August 2, 1909, to having "rescored" the second movement. This "Concert Interpretation" of the second movement was published by Universal Edition at the same time as Op. 11 in the fall of 1910.[33]

Letter of c. August 18

[···]

To close, I must add that I was overjoyed to hear that you already like the one piece. And I really hope that you will later come to like the other one. Earlier I had also preferred the 12/8 one (which I composed second) to the first. But recently I looked at the first one again: I almost believe that what I had conceived in terms of freedom and variegation of expression, of unshackled flexibility of form uninhibited by "logic," is much more evident in the first than the second.

What I had visualized has been attained in neither. Perhaps, indeed definitely also not in the third, which will soon be finished. In a few orchestral pieces which I wrote very recently, I have in certain respects come closer, but again in others have turned far from what I considered already achieved.

Perhaps this is not yet graspable. It will perhaps take a long time before I can write the music I feel urged to, of which I have had an inkling for several years, but which, for the time being, I cannot express.

I am writing in such detail because I want to declare my intentions (encouraged by your comment: my music affects you because you envisage something of the kind as the goal of our immediate developments).

I strive for: complete liberation from all forms
from all symbols
of cohesion and
of logic.
   Thus:
away with "motivic working out."
Away with harmony as
cement or bricks of a building.
Harmony is *expression*
and nothing else.
   Then:
Away with Pathos!
Away with protracted ten-ton scores, from erected or constructed
towers, rocks and other massive claptrap.
My music must be
brief.
Concise! In two notes: not built, but *"expressed"*!!
And the results I wish for:
no stylized and sterile protracted emotion.
People are not like that:
it is *impossible* for a person to have only *one* sensation at a time.

One has *thousands* simultaneously. And these thousands can no more readily be added together than an apple and a pear. They go their own ways.

And this variegation, this multifariousness, this *illogicality* which our senses demonstrate, the illogicality presented by their interactions, set forth by some mounting rush of blood, by some reaction of the senses or the nerves, this I should like to have in my music.

It should be an expression of feeling,[34] as our feelings, which bring us in contact with our subconscious, really are, and no false child of feelings and "conscious logic."

Now I have made my confession and they can burn me. You will not number amongst those who burn me: that I know.

[. . .]

Letter of August 24

Dear Mr. Busoni,

Above all, I must apologize for something which is only partly my fault and only my fault in a way that allows forgiveness.[35] While I was writing the first half of my previous letter, I had intended to ask you for your transcription, but then I forgot. Then I was going to do so in the postscript and forgot again. Finally I wanted to follow this long letter with a postcard—but I forgot for a third time. Can you forgive forgetfulness? I am banking on it, for it continually brings me into conflict. I trust that you will look upon the matter more from this angle, and that your ill-feeling on this account will evaporate.

But now I beg you to send me your transcription as soon as possible; I am truly anxious to get acquainted with the "motivic report" of your proposals for improvement.

Further, I must thank you kindly for your suggestion of printing the one piece together with its paraphrase, which, considering your entirely justified ill-feeling, is truly magnanimous. But here new difficulties arise, and I really do not know if we would be able to come to an agreement over the new problems. Firstly a purely material consideration, the publication would have to be so arranged that my rights to republish the piece would not be encroached upon, otherwise my "opus" would be split up. I would also require authorization from my publisher, but this would in fact be easy to obtain. Then it would prey on my mind if I accepted the entire fee, when your transcription should also have a right to it.

But for me the most important and decisive factor is the artistic question. And will we find a solution here . . . ? . . . ?

You must consider the following: it is impossible for me to publish my piece together with a transcription which shows how I could have done it *better.* Which thus indicates that my piece is *imperfect.* And it is impossible to try to make the public believe that my piece is *good,* if I simultaneously indicate that it is *not good.*

I could not do this—out of my instinct for self-preservation—even if I believed in it. In this case I would either have to destroy my piece or *rework it myself.*

But now—please forgive my unrestrained frankness, just as I do not take yours amiss—*I simply don't believe it.* I firmly believe you are making the same mistake as every *imaginative critic:* you do not wish to put yourself in the writer's place but seek rather, in the work of another, yourself, *only yourself.* And that just isn't possible. An art which is at one and the same time its creator's and its appraiser's cannot exist. One of these has to give way, and I believe this must be the appraiser.

And your reasoning seems to me quite unsound, when you say that I shall become different but no richer by pointlessly doing without what is already established.

I do not believe in putting *new wine* into old bottles. In the history of art I have the following antipodal observations:

Bach's contrapuntal art vanishes when Beethoven's melodic homophony begins.

Beethoven's formal art is abandoned when Wagner introduces his expressive art.

Unity of design, richness of coloring, working out of minutest details, painstaking formation, priming and varnishing, use of perspective and all the other constituents of older painting simply die out when the Impressionists begin to paint things as they *appear* and not as they *are.*

Yes indeed, when a new art seeks and finds new means of expression, almost all earlier techniques go hang: seemingly, at any rate; for actually they are retained; but in a different way. (To discuss this would lead me too far.)

And now: I must say that I actually dispensed with more than just piano sound when I began to follow my instincts and compose *such* music. I find that, when renouncing an *art of form,* the architecture of the leading voice, the polyphonic art that Brahms, Wagner and others brought to a high degree of perfection in the past decades—the little bit of piano sound seems a mere trifle. And I maintain: one must have grasped, admired and marveled at the mysterious wonders of our tonal harmony, the unbelievably delicate balance of its architectural values and its cabbalistic mathematics as *I* have, in order to feel, when one no longer has need of them, that one requires new means. Questions of sonority, whose attraction ranks scarcely so high amongst the eternal values, are by comparison trivial.

Nevertheless, I take a standpoint in this question from which it is absolutely unnecessary to consider me a renouncer, a loser. Were you to see my new orchestral pieces, you would be able to observe how clearly I turn away from the full "God and Superman" sound of the Wagner orchestra. How everything becomes sweeter, finer. How refracted shades of color replace the former brilliant hues. How my entire orchestral technique takes a path which seems to be leading in quite the opposite direction to anything previously taken. I find this to be the natural reaction. We have had enough of Wagner's full, lush sonorities, to the point of satiation: "Nun laßt uns andere Töne anstimmen . . . "[36]

And now I must add that I feel myself justified in believing (I must repeat this) that my piano writing is *novel.* Not only do my feelings tell me so. Friends and pupils express the opinion that the sonorities of my piano writing are completely novel.

For me the matter is as follows:

I do not consider my piano texture the result of any sort of incompetence, but rather the expression of *firm resolve, distinct preferences and palpably clear feelings.*

What it *does not* do is not what it *cannot,* rather what it *will* not.

What it does is not something which could have turned out differently, rather what it *had* to do.

Therefore it is distinctive, stylish and organic.

———

I fear that a transcription, on the other hand, would either

introduce what I avoid, either fundamentally or according to preferences;

add what I myself—within the limits of my personality—would never have devised, thus what is foreign or unattainable to me;

omit what I would find necessary, or

improve where I am, and must remain, imperfect.

Thus a transcription would be bound to do me violence: whether it helps or hinders my work.

In your pamphlet, which gives me uncommon pleasure and truly proves how the same thoughts can occur to different people at once, you write about transcription.[37] I particularly agree with your thesis that all notation is transcription. I argued similarly some years ago when Mahler was publicly attacked for changing Beethoven's orchestration. But again: whether one improves upon Beethoven's undoubtedly *old-fashioned* treatment of the instruments and orchestration on account of undoubtedly superior *newer* instrumental techniques, or whether one improves upon my piano style with older techniques or, at any rate, techniques whose greater appropriateness has today not been established, there is no doubt at all that these are two different matters.

I can at present say this without your having to take it as any harsh criticism, because I have not yet seen your transcription. After all, your arrangement could always prove that I am mistaken. But also, apart from that, I am sure you will not take my vehemence amiss, I am certain, because your opinion of my work was otherwise neither harsh nor un-favorable.

Another point occurs to me which seems a suitable argument against you.

Do you really set such infinite store by perfection? Do you really consider it attainable? Do you really think that works of art are, or should be, perfect?

I do not think so. I find even God's works of art, those of nature, highly imperfect.

But I find perfection only in the work of carpenters, gardeners, pastry-cooks and hairdressers. Only they produce that smoothness and symmetry which I have so often wished to the Devil. Only they fulfil every requirement one can expect of them, but otherwise nothing human or god-like in the world.

And if

Notation = Transcription = *Imperfection*

then also

Transcription = Notation = *Imperfection.*

For if $a = b$ and $b = c$, then also

$a = c$.

Why then replace one imperfection with another?

Why eliminate that which perhaps contributes to the appeal of a work and substitute something added by a foreign hand?

Don't the characteristics of a man's personality also include his de-fects? Do these not have an effect, even if unbeautiful, then at least as contrast, like the basic color upon which the other shades are super-imposed?

I have often thought that one should give Schumann's symphonies (which I believe you have greatly underestimated[38] and which I rate *far above* those of Brahms) a helping hand by improving the orchestration. The theoretical aspects were quite clear to me. This summer I spent a little time on this and—lost courage. For I can see exactly that wherever things misfire, something highly original was intended, and I lack the

courage to replace an *interesting idea*, which has not been quite successfully carried out, with a *"reliable"* sonority. And with a true work of art,
the imagination of an outsider can achieve no more than this!—

From a purely technical angle, I would like to ask you if you have
perhaps taken too slow a tempo. That could make a great difference. Or
too *little* rubato. I never stay in time! Never in tempo!—

Your *Outline of a New Aesthetic of Music* gave me uncommon pleasure,
above all on account of its audacity. Particularly at the beginning, there
are a few powerful sentences, of compulsive logic and superlative acute-
ness of observation. I have also thought a lot about your idea of thirds of
tones, though in a different way. But I have been thinking of quarter-
tones, am however now of the opinion that it will depend less on the
construction than on other things. Moreover, one of my pupils[39] calcu-
lated, at my suggestion, that the next division of the octave with similar
properties to our twelve semitone division would have to introduce 53
notes. If you adopt 18 thirds of tones, that would be approximately equal,
for $3 \times 18 = 54$. But then the semitones would disappear completely.

Earlier I thought out the following method of notating quarter-tones:

c-1/4   c   c+1/4

[A Quarter-Tone Notation.]

$<$ and $>$ are
mathematical symbols.

However, I scarcely think that such attempts at notation will catch
on; for I confidently hope that the notation of the future will be—how can
I say: "wirelesser."

I also think differently about tonality—my music shows that. I believe: everything one can do with 113 keys[40] can also be done with 2 or 3
or 4: major-minor, whole-tone and chromatic. Anyway, I have long been
occupied with the removal of all shackles of tonality. And my harmony
allows no chords or melodies with tonal implications any more.

Now to your questions.

To what extent I realize my intentions?[41] Not as far as I would like to.
Not one piece has yet satisfied me entirely. I would like to achieve even
greater variegation of motifs and figures without melodic character; I
would like to be freer and less constrained in rhythm and time-signature;

freer from repetition of motifs and spinning out of thoughts in the manner of a melody. This is my vision: this is how I imagine music before I notate = transcribe it. And I am unable to force this upon myself; I must wait until a piece comes out of its own accord in the way I have envisaged.

And thus I come to answer your other question: how much is intentional and how much instinctive.

My only intention is

to have *no* intentions!

No formal, architectural or other artistic intentions (except perhaps of capturing the mood of a poem), no aesthetic intentions—none of any kind; at most this:

to place nothing inhibiting in the stream of my unconscious sensations. To allow nothing to infiltrate which may be invoked either by intelligence or consciousness.[42]

If you knew how I have developed, you would have no doubts. But I have prepared myself for this question and am thus able to answer it. I knew one would question the naturalness of my intentions, precisely because they are natural. That one would find them formalized for the very reason that I avoid anything formal.

But when one sees how I have developed in stages, how I was long ago approaching a form of expression to which I now adhere freely and unreservedly, one would understand that nothing unorganic, no "schmock aestheticism" is involved, but that *compulsion* has produced these results.

As I am now fairly clear about the theoretical side, only those can scoff who imagine the unconsciously creating artist to be a sort of half-cretin; and who cannot grasp that after unconscious creativity follows a period of *quiet clearsightedness,* in which one renders account of one's situation.

As for the third piece, which you do not care for at present, as can be inferred from your caustic criticism, I find it goes a considerable way beyond what was successful in the other two.[43] At any rate, as far as the above-mentioned variegation is concerned. But also in the "harmony"—if one can speak so architecturally here—there seems to be something novel in it. In particular: something more slender, more linear. But I also consider it unjust to expect that one can revolutionize music in three *different* ways in 3 little piano pieces. Does it not seem permissible, to gather new strength, before one rushes on? And is it not unjust to describe laconicism as a mannerism? Is formalism just as much a manner as pointillism or impressionism? Must one build? Is music then a savings-bank? Does one get more when it is longer?

If I was wrong *there* to be brief, I have *amply* compensated for it in this *letter!* But there were indeed several things I wanted to say—that I could not express them more concisely can be blamed upon my technical shortcomings.

And finally: I hope my frankness does not annoy you, and that you maintain your interest in me.

Maybe you will find a formula, an explanation, through which I shall be able to publish my piece in your series.

Or perhaps you could publish all three and your paraphrase, with an explanation some other time??

In any case, I hope not to lose your goodwill if I now ask you to tell me whether you wish to play my pieces. For, clearly this would mean an enormous amount to me.[44]

One other curious thing, to close: before composing these piano pieces, I had wanted to contact you—knowing of your predilection for transcriptions—to ask if you would take one of my chamber or orchestral works into your repertoire, transcribed for piano solo.

Curious: now we come into contact again through a transcription! Was I misunderstanding a message from my subconscious, which made me think of you in the context of a transcription?

This has just occurred to me!

Breaking through Every Restriction of a Bygone Aesthetic

2.11 Program and Foreword to a Concert, January 14, 1910

In "How One Becomes Lonely" (1937), Schoenberg wrote: "I had started a second Kammersymphonie. But after having composed almost two movements, that is about half the whole work (see 3.18), I was inspired by poems of Stefan George, the German poet, to compose music to some of his poems and, surprisingly, without any expectation on my part, these songs showed a style quite different from every-thing I had written before. And this was only the first step on a new path, but one beset with thorns. It was the first step towards a style which has since been called the style of 'atonality.'"[45]

Ehrbar Hall, January 14, 1910, 7:30 P.M.

The Society for Art and Culture

New Compositions by Arnold Schoenberg

Soprano, Martha Winternitz-Dorda

Tenor, Hans Nachod

Etta Werndorf will play the Three Piano Pieces and accompany the George songs.

Kapellmeister Arnold Winternitz will accompany the *Gurrelieder* and the five individual songs.

Dr. Anton von Webern and Dr. Rudolf Weirich will join with the previously named for a two-piano, eight-hand setting of the prelude and interludes from the *Gurrelieder.*

FOREWORD

I started composing the *Gurrelieder* early in 1900, the George songs and the piano pieces in 1908 [1908–1909]. The time between perhaps justifies their great difference in style. Since it expresses in a striking way a particular intent, the combination of such heterogeneous works within the space of a single evening's performance perhaps requires justification as well.

With the George songs I have for the first time succeeded in approaching an ideal of expression and form that has been in my mind for years. Until then I lacked the strength and confidence to make it a reality. But now that I have set out along this path once and for all, I am conscious of having broken through every restriction of a bygone aesthetic; and though the goal toward which I am striving appears to me a certain one, I nonetheless already feel the resistance I shall have to overcome; I feel how hotly even the least of temperaments will rise in revolt, and suspect that even those who have so far believed in me will not want to acknowledge the necessity of this development.

So it seemed appropriate to point out, by performing the *Gurrelieder*— which eight years ago were friendless, but today have many—that I am being urged in this direction not from the lack of invention, or technical ability, or the knowledge of the other demands of the prevailing aesthetics, but that I am obeying an inner compulsion, which is stronger than my education; that I am obeying that formative process, which, being natural to me, is stronger than my artistic training.

On Painting, Technique, and Education

2.12 Letter to Carl Moll, June 16, 1910

Carl Moll (1861–1945), the stepfather of Alma Mahler, was a Secessionist painter in the circle around Gustav Klimt. Schoenberg had contacted Moll in hopes of arranging an exhibit of his works at the prestigious Galerie Miethke in Vienna. Schoenberg had started painting in 1907, coinciding with his friendship with Richard Gerstl, and continued to paint for most of his life, but from 1910 to 1912 painting became a central creative outlet. His comparative lack of technical training as a painter seems to have permitted a kind of spontaneity that increasingly eluded him in his compositions as he attempted to live up to the standard he spelled out to Busoni of placing "nothing inhibiting in the stream of my unconscious sensations" (see further, 3.2).[46] Financial concerns played a role as well. In a desperate letter of March 7, 1910, to Emil Hertzka (1869–1932), the director of Universal Edition, he asked for employment in any capacity, including a proposal that Hertzka locate patrons who would be willing to commission portraits by

Schoenberg: "Only you must not tell people that they will like my pictures. You must make them realize that they cannot but like my pictures, because they have been praised by authorities on painting; and above all that it is much more interesting to have one's portrait done by or to own a painting by a musician of my reputation than to be painted by some mere practitioner of painting whose name will be forgotten in 20 years, whereas even now my name belongs to the history of music."[47]

In October 1910 Schoenberg mounted a one-man exhibit of his works at the Heller Bookshop in Vienna (see 2.14 for more on the exhibit), and the following year his works were included in the first of Kandinsky's Blue Rider exhibitions. Contemporary discussions of Schoenberg, as seen already in the interview with Paul Wilhelm, frequently represented him as both a painter and a composer. The 1912 book in Schoenberg's honor, for example, included two articles on Schoenberg as a painter, as well as reproductions of a number of paintings (see 2.15).

The catalogue of Schoenberg's paintings lists more than 260 works, divided into self-portraits (the largest category, examples of which are included in the figures); what he called "visions" and "gazes" (ranging from the more explicitly expressionistic self-portraits to nearly abstract works); portraits (mostly of family and acquaintances); caricatures; landscapes; stage settings; and still lifes.[48] In a short essay from 1938 entitled "Painting Influences," Schoenberg began by disputing claims in the biography by Paul Stefan (Vienna, 1924) that he had been influenced as a painter by Kokoschka: "If one compares my pictures with those of Kokoschka one has to recognize forthwith their complete independence. I painted 'Gazes,' which I have already painted elsewhere. This is something which only I could have done, for it is out of my own nature and is completely contrary to the nature of a real painter. I never saw faces, but, because I looked into people's eyes, only their 'gazes.' This is the reason why I can imitate the gaze of a person. A painter, however, grasps with one look the whole person—I, only his soul." He then continued with a commentary on a "certain Mr. Gerstl": "When this person invaded my house he was a student of Keffler for whom he supposedly painted too radically. But it was not quite so radical, for at that time his ideal, his model, was Liebermann. In many conversations about art, music and sundry things I wasted many thoughts on him as on everybody else who wanted to listen. Probably this had confirmed him in his, at that time, rather tame radicalism to such a degree, that when he saw some quite miscarried attempts of mine, he took their miserable appearance to be intentional and exclaimed: 'Now I have learned from you how one has to paint.' I believe that Webern will be able to confirm this. Immediately afterwards he started to paint 'Modern.' I have today no judgment if these pictures are of any value. I never was very enthusiastic about them."[49]

Dear Mr. Moll:

I thank you again for the kind visit and for the very interesting conversation, which is still giving me much to think about. But when I look back on my own experiences of artistic struggles, I am pointed to an opposite path as the correct one. A youthful work of mine, imperfect both in what it attempted and what was achieved, is well received today, although it had previously failed. But with my other works, the more mature and artistic they are, the more perfectly they achieve what was attempted, and the more highly what they attempted is valued, the less of an impression they make. And now I believe that after a time my works will always reveal to me only their imperfection, their comparative—measured by me—failure; those works composed earlier will always be failures to me, while those recently composed will, for the time being, succeed. I could thus never come to publish something that I knew after a while would seem bad to me. Thus I think, provided that one has the feeling "Here I have expressed myself," it is almost unimportant at what stage of technical maturity one goes before the public. If one thing only is clear to me: *Have I expressed myself here? Have I said what I wanted to say?*, the "how" will be better as the "what" increases. But the main thing is the "what," the "who."

I am certain you are right if you measure my imperfect ability in the nature pieces at zero. I find all that very poor myself. But not, for instance, because I think it lacks originality, as you seem to believe. No, I find it poor on the whole in the same sense as you do; and I have always found it to be poor. Because I have *never* felt the familiar sense of satisfaction that I know from my musical works that says to me: *it is good!*

On the other hand, I have had this feeling with almost all the other paintings (the fantasy pieces) and therefore I must believe: *this is something.* At first glance, it must seem strange that I assume that someone who can do nothing is suddenly capable of doing something. However, I do not only consider this possible; it is in fact with me routinely the case. *I have always been able to do only that which is suited to me—absolutely, immediately* and almost without any *transition* or preparation. On the other hand, the things that *others can do*—that which passes for "education"—have always caused me difficulties.[50] I have also learned those things. But only later. Only after I struggled through to a certain security in my natural domain did I also acquire the power to do what the others could. And more often than not, since it was *earned* and not merely *learned,* to do it far better than the others could. I can and could never learn as others do. Some things I could always do on my own without any guidance. When it came to other things, no teacher in the world could have taught me.

And so, although I know that in my own artistic field I would speak to a student in the same way as you do to me, I have decided in spite of everything to exhibit in the coming year. For I have to be in the thick of things; I learn from it. Once these things are away from me and hostile eyes look at them, they will also become something different for me. Then it will come more easily for me to develop beyond them.

But also contributing to this decision in no small part is the intention to *sell* something. My life is so far from being a bed of roses that I would also like to take this path for bringing my income to an appropriate level. And I hope to find people to whom my works will say something and who want to give something back for them.

Thus please tell me if an exhibition at the Miethke would be possible. And if I may ask: as soon as possible. For I would now like to look into doing it at Heller's if it's not possible there.

Most respectfully yours,
Arnold Schoenberg

"Making Music with the Media of the Stage"

2.13 From Die glückliche Hand, *Op. 18 (Libretto Completed 1910, Music 1910–1913)*

Die glückliche Hand, *which Schoenberg called "a major drama compressed into about twenty minutes," is written for a large orchestra, a chorus of six men and six women, and a small offstage ensemble. There is one main singing character, called simply the Man, and two pantomimed characters, a Woman and a Gentleman. The libretto is another attempt to come to terms with the problem of the unrepresentable idea, here presented as the inevitable failure of attempts to realize personal and artistic aspirations in a hostile and uncomprehending material world. The work is in four scenes, identified in the score as "Bilder," or pictures. In the first and fourth scenes the twelve-voice chorus presents the central conflict between "the worldly" and the "otherworldly." The two central scenes trace the Man's hope, deceptive triumph, disillusionment, and despair, represented by his pursuit of the Woman, who betrays him for the Gentleman, the successful man of the world.*

The title Die glückliche Hand *has proven to be very difficult to translate, because the word* glückliche *has many possible meanings, such as lucky, happy, fortunate, or fateful, all of which Schoenberg is playing upon in the title. In a lecture given in Breslau on the occasion of the German premiere of* Die glückliche Hand *in 1928, Schoenberg commented on the title and the larger meaning of the work: "This title,* Die glückliche Hand, *is connected to the text at the end of the second scene, where it says: 'The man does not realize that she is gone. To him, she is there at his hand, which he gazes at uninterruptedly.' [. . .] It is a certain pessimism which I was compelled to give form to at that time: 'Fateful [glückliche] Hand, which tries to grasp that which can only slip away from you, if you hold it. Fateful Hand, which does not hold what it promises!'*[51]

While the plot of romantic betrayal in Die glückliche Hand *has obvious*

resonances with the Gerstl affair, it is better seen not as any sort of literal represen-
tation but rather as a reworking of autobiographical material filtered through
contemporary attitudes toward the relationship of the sexes expressed in the writ-
ings of August Strindberg, Otto Weininger, Kokoschka, and others.[52] *Indeed, the*
symbolism is problematic in autobiographical terms, with the worldly and dispas-
sionate Gentleman with his elegant overcoat and walking stick scarcely an appro-
priate representation of the struggling, mentally unstable Gerstl. Similarly, while
the Man in his torn clothes, bloodied and scarred, and with the wound of a nail
through his foot, certainly reflects aspects of Schoenberg's own self-image as an
artist, he also brings together characteristics of Christ, Siegfried, and Tristan. The
Woman, who begins by regarding the Man with "unspeakable pity" but soon turns
cold, is already prefigured in Maria from Superstition.

In the Breslau lecture Schoenberg described his vision of a new form of theater
in Die glückliche Hand *that he called "making music with the media of the*
stage." Like the Wagnerian Gesamtkunstwerk, *the goal was a synthesis of the arts,*
but it was to be a synthesis in the image of music: "It must be evident that ges-
tures, colors, and light are treated here similarly to the way tones are usually
treated—that music is made with them; that figures and shapes, so to speak, are
formed from individual light values and shades of color, which resemble the
forms, figures and motives of music."[53] *In keeping with this aim Schoenberg not*
only provided the music but also wrote his own libretto, his first completed literary
text. He precisely specified every aspect of the staging in the score, including the
elaborate colored lighting, all the movements and gestures of the characters, and
the scenery and costumes, for which he produced a large number of paintings and
drawings, some of which were included in the Heller exhibit.[54] *The most striking*
example of the idea of "making music with the media of the stage" is the famous
passage in the third scene where a rapidly shifting sequence of colors, combined
with a musical crescendo and a rising storm, depict the Man's pain over the
Woman's betrayal.

The libretto was first published, in a form with some significant differences
from the final version, in the Viennese journal of music and the arts Der Merker,
vol. 2, no. 17 (June 1911), and then in the 1926 collection Texts *(Vienna: Universal*
Edition).[55] *Schoenberg composed the music between September 1910 and Novem-*
ber 1913. The score was published in 1917; the first performance took place at the
Vienna Volksoper in 1924. Two pages from Schoenberg's Compositions-Vorlage, *a*
heavily revised copy of the libretto bound together with sheets of music paper, are
given in fig. 2-5 a and b.

1st Scene

(Left and right are from the spectators' point of view.)

The stage is almost completely dark. In front lies the MAN, face down. On
his back crouches a cat-like, fantastic animal (hyena with enormous, bat-like
wings) that seems to have sunk its teeth into his neck.

The visible portion of the stage is very small, somewhat round (or shallow curve). The rear stage is hidden by a dark violet curtain. There are slight gaps in this curtain from which green-lit faces peer: SIX MEN, SIX WOMEN.

The light is very weak. Only the eyes are clearly visible. The rest is swathed in soft red veiling, and this too reflects the greenish light.

THE SIX MEN AND THE SIX WOMEN: (spoken very softly, with deepest pity)

Be still, be silent: restless one! You know how it is, you knew how it is, and yet you remain blind. Will you never be at rest? So many times already! And once again? You know it is always the same thing again. Once again the same ending. Must you once again rush in? Will you not finally believe? Believe in reality: it is thus, thus it is, and not otherwise. Once again you trust in the dream; once again you fix your longing on the unattainable; once again you give yourself up to the temptations of your thoughts, thoughts that roam the cosmos, that are unworldly, but long for worldly happiness! Worldly happiness!—you poor fool—worldly happiness! You, who have the divine in you, and long for the worldly! And you cannot win out! You poor fool!

They disappear (the gaps in the curtain grow dark). The fantastic animal also disappears. For a while everything is still and motionless. Then long, black, shadows (veils) fall slowly across the MAN. Suddenly, *behind the scene, loud, commonly gay music* is heard, a joyous uproar of instruments. *The shrill, mocking laughter of a crowd of people* mingles with the final chord of the backstage music.

At the same moment the MAN springs powerfully to his feet. The dark curtains at the back are simultaneously rent asunder.

The MAN stands there, upright. He wears a dirty yellow-brown jacket of very coarse, thick material. The left leg of his black trousers comes down only to the knee; from there on it is in tatters. His shirt is half open, showing his chest. On his stockingless feet are badly torn shoes; one is so torn that his naked foot shows through, disclosing a large, open wound where it has been cut by a nail. His face and chest are in part bloody, in part covered with scars. His hair is shorn close.

Rising, he stands there for a moment with head sunk, then he says fervently:
THE MAN:

Yes, oh yes! (sung)
SCENE CHANGE

At the same instant, the stage becomes light, and now shows the following picture:

2nd Scene

A somewhat larger stage area, deeper and broader than the first. In the background, a soft blue, sky-like backdrop. Below, left, close to the bright brown earth, a circular cutout 1¹/₂ meters in diameter through which glaring, yellow sunlight spreads over the stage. No other lighting but this, and it must be very intense. The side curtains are of pleated, hanging material, soft yellow-green in color.

THE MAN: (singing)

The blossoming: oh, longing!

Behind him, left, a beautiful young WOMAN emerges from one of the folds of the side-hanging. She is clothed in a soft deep-violet garment, pleated and flowing; yellow and red roses in her hair; graceful figure. *The MAN trembles (without looking around). After a few small steps, the WOMAN pauses about a quarter of the way across the stage, and looks with unspeakable pity at the MAN.*

THE MAN:

O you blessed one! How beautiful you are! How sweet it is to see you, to speak with you, to listen to you. How you smile, how your eyes laugh! Ah, your lovely soul!

The WOMAN holds a goblet in her right hand and, stretching forth her right arm (the sleeve of her garment hangs down to her wrist), offers it the MAN. Violet light falls from above upon the goblet.

Rapturous pause.

Suddenly the MAN finds the goblet in his hand (although neither has stirred from their place and the MAN has never looked at her. (The MAN must never look at her; he always gazes ahead; she always remains behind him.) The MAN holds the goblet in his right hand, stretching out his arm. He contemplates the goblet with rapture. Suddenly he becomes deeply serious, almost dejected; reflects a moment; then his face brightens again and with a joyous resolution he puts the goblet to his lips and drains it slowly.

As he drinks, the WOMAN watches him with waning interest. A coldness takes possession of her face. With a rather ungraceful motion she gathers her dress to her, rearranges its folds, and hastens to the other side of the stage. She remains standing not far from the side curtain on the right (always behind him).

With the goblet still raised to his lips, the MAN takes several steps forward and to the left, so that he stands approximately at stage center.

When he lets his hand and the goblet sink, the WOMAN's face shows indifference, over which a hostile impulse sometimes slips. He stands deep in thought, moved, entranced.

THE MAN:

How beautiful you are! I am so glad when you are near me; I live again . . .

He stretches out both his arms, as if she stood before him.
THE MAN:

Oh, you are beautiful!—

Meanwhile she begins slowly to withdraw. When she has turned far enough so that she is looking directly at the side curtain on the right, her face lights up. At the same time a GENTLEMAN appears before this curtain, in a dark gray overcoat, walking stick in hand, elegantly dressed—a handsome, genteel figure. He stretches his hand to her; she goes smilingly to him; confidently, as to an old acquaintance. He takes her impetuously in his arms, and both disappear through the right-hand curtain.

As she begins to smile at the GENTLEMAN, the MAN becomes uneasy. He turns his head around by degrees, as if the back of his head perceived these things. He bends forward slightly. At the moment when the GENTLEMAN stretches his hand toward the WOMAN, the MAN's left hand stiffens convulsively; and as she rushes into the arms of the GENTLEMAN, the MAN groans:
THE MAN:

Oh . . .

He takes several steps forward and to the left, and then stands still in utter dejection.

But in a moment the WOMAN rushes from the side curtain on the left and kneels before him. The MAN listens to her without looking at her (his glance is directed upward). His face glows happily. Her face is full of humility and she seems to beg forgiveness.
THE MAN:

You are sweet, you are beautiful!

She gets slowly to her feet, and seeks his left hand in order to kiss it. He comes before her and sinks down on his knees and reaches toward her hands (without touching them, however). As she stands and he kneels, her face changes somewhat—takes on a slightly sarcastic expression. He looks blissfully up at her, raises his hand and touches hers lightly. While he continues to kneel, deeply stirred, directing his gaze at his own upraised hand, she quickly flees through the left curtain.

The MAN does not realize that she has gone. To him, she is there at his hand, which he gazes at uninterruptedly. After a while he rises by a colossal effort, stretching his arms high in the air, and remains standing giant-like on tip-toe.

THE MAN:

Now I possess you forever!

[The third scene takes place in a wild and rocky landscape. At the beginning of the scene, the Man outrages a group of artisans, who are laboring in "something between a machine shop and goldsmith's workshop," by forging a jeweled diadem with a single blow, while they must labor and toil to create, a clear depiction of Schoenberg's aesthetic ideal from this time of spontaneous and unmediated expression. The encounter with the workers is followed by the color crescendo, at the end of which the Woman appears with part of her dress torn away. At the end of the scene the Man pursues the Woman through the precipitous terrain.]

THE MAN:

You beauty—stay with me—!

Sliding on his knees, he tries to reach her, but she slips from him and hastens up the rock. He leaps after her and slides farther on his knees. She gains the top quickly and hurries to the man-sized stone near the ravine. At the moment when she had leapt from the grotto to the plateau, this stone had begun to glow (from within) with a dazzling green light. Now, its peak looks like a monstrous sneering mask, and the shape of the entire stone changes so that one might take it to be the fantastic animal of the first scene, standing upright. At this moment the MAN stands below and directly opposite the WOMAN, so that, when she gives the stone a slight push with her foot, it topples over and hurtles down upon him.

SCENE CHANGE

At the moment the stone buries the MAN it grows dark, and the loud music and mocking laughter of the first scene are heard again.

4th Scene

The stage is lighted again quickly.

The same as the first scene: the SIX MEN and the SIX WOMEN. Their faces are now lit by a gray-blue light, and the fantastic animal is once again gnawing the neck of the MAN, and he is lying on the ground in the same spot where the stone had been cast down on top of him (thereby strengthening the impression that the stone and the fantastic animal are one and the same).

THE SIX MEN AND THE SIX WOMEN: (accusingly, severe)

Did you have to live again what you have so often lived? Can you never renounce? Never at last resign yourself? Is there no peace within you? Still none? You seek to lay hold of what will only slip away from you when you grasp it. But what is in you, around you, wherever you may be, do you not feel it? Do you not hear it? Do you understand only what you hold? Do you feel only what you touch, the wounds only in your flesh, the pain only in your body?

And still you seek!

And torment yourself!

And are without rest!

(The gray-blue light that falls on their faces is somewhat tinted with red.)

You poor fool!

The stage grows slowly dark, and the curtain falls.

On *Die glückliche Hand*

2.14 Letter to Alma Mahler, October 7, 1910

Soon after completing the libretto, Schoenberg sent copies to several of his friends, including Alma Mahler, Webern, and Zemlinsky, as well as important figures in the theatrical world of Vienna, such as Hermann Bahr, and Rainer Simons of the Vienna Volksoper, who had expressed interest in staging the work. In a 1913 letter to Emil Hertzka of Universal Edition he discussed the possibility of a film realization, with scenes to be designed by Kokoschka, Kandinsky, or the prominent opera designer Alfred Roller. He wrote that he was interested in film not only because it offered technical solutions to the problems of staging but also because of its potential to create "the opposite of what the cinema generally aspires to . . . 'the utmost unreality!' The whole thing should have the effect (not of a dream) but of chords. Of music. It must never suggest symbols, or meaning, or thoughts, but simply the play of colors and forms. Just as music never drags a meaning around with it, at least not in the form in which it [music] manifests itself, even though meaning is inherent in its nature, so too this should simply be like sounds for the eye, and so far as I am concerned everyone is free to think or feel something similar to what he thinks or feels while hearing music."[56]

Dear Madam,

Thank you very much for your letter. That my work meant something to you even in this incomplete form is a great joy to me, since I hope that when you eventually see it as a whole, it will be able to say to you what I really wanted to express. As for thinking, or what is called "thinking," I actually thought *nothing at all* about it; but I certainly suspected that it could cause people to think many things. If I am to be honest and say something about my works (which I don't do willingly, since I actually write them in order to conceal myself thoroughly behind them, so that I shall not be seen), it could only be this: it is not meant symbolically, only envisioned and felt. Not thought at all. Colors, noises, lights, sounds, movements, looks, gestures—in short, the media that make up the material of the stage—are to be linked to one another in a varied way. Nothing more than that. It meant something to my emotions as I wrote it down. If the component parts, when they are put together, result in a similar picture, that is all right with me. If not, then that's even better. Because I don't want to be understood. I want to express myself—but I hope that I shall be misunderstood. It would be terrible if one could see through me. Therefore I prefer to say technical, aesthetic, or philosophical things about my works. Or this: certainly no symbolism is intended. It is all direct intuition. You will perhaps see what I mean by this most clearly if I tell you that I would most prefer to write for a magic theater. If tones, when they occur in any sort of order, can arouse feelings, then colors, gestures, and movements must also be able to do this. Even when they otherwise have no meaning recognizable to the mind. Music also doesn't have this meaning! What I mean is: this is music!

Again, many thanks.

And now: tomorrow (Saturday) my exhibition at Heller's will open.[57] Will you be able to go? The concert is Wednesday evening.[58] It would please me very much if you could be there.

I would also like to know how Herr Director liked it (the drama). Probably not much! But a little bit, one hopes, if it didn't seem ridiculous to him. At the moment I have absolutely no faith in myself.

I am looking forward very much to Saturday evening. If something unpleasantly adverse does not happen in the meantime, I will be there.

With many warm greetings,

Arnold Schoenberg

N.B. I am sending you my new piano pieces.[59]

Art and the Unconscious

2.15 Letter to Wassily Kandinsky, January 24, 1911

The correspondence between Schoenberg and Kandinsky began early in 1911, after the painter, together with Franz Marc and others, attended a concert in Munich that included the Second String Quartet and the Three Piano Pieces. Kandinsky responded to the experience at once with the paintings Impression III (Concert) *and* Romantic Landscape.[60] *He then wrote to Schoenberg on January 18, "In your works, you have realized what I, albeit in uncertain form, have so greatly longed for in music. The independent progress through their own destinies, the independent life of the individual voices in your compositions, is exactly what I am trying to find in my paintings."[61] With this letter began one of the most interesting artistic relationships of the twentieth century; a relationship marked initially by extraordinary parallels in their development and thought, and later by tensions resulting from the political and social crises over the following decades.*

*Schoenberg here presents one of the most categorical statements of his aesthetic of intuitive expression of unconscious sensations. Schoenberg's conception of the unconscious no doubt draws in part on what was generally known of Freud's writings (*The Interpretation of Dreams *was published in 1900), but Schoenberg himself said virtually nothing about Freud and does not appear to have read his books. With this silence, he may have been following in the rejection of psychoanalysis by Kraus and his circle. In addition to any possible Freudian influence, Schoenberg's idea of the unconscious brings together many currents of thought from turn-of-the-century psychology, literature, art, and music.[62]*

Schoenberg and Kandinsky first met face to face in September 1911 at the Starnberger See (located near Munich) and remained in frequent contact until the outbreak of the war. Kandinsky included paintings by Schoenberg in the first Blaue Reiter *exhibition (1911) and in the* Blaue Reiter Almanac *(1912), for which Schoenberg wrote "The Relationship to the Text," and which also included a facsimile of his setting of Maurice Maeterlinck's* Herzgewächse, *Op. 20. Kandinsky in turn wrote an essay on Schoenberg's paintings for the 1912 book in his honor,* Arnold Schönberg.[63] *Their relationship resumed after the war, though with considerable strains (see 4.8, 4.13).*

Dear Sir,

I thank you most warmly for your letter. It gave me extraordinary pleasure. For the present, there is no question of my works winning over the masses. All the more surely do they win the hearts of individuals— those really worthwhile individuals who alone matter to me. And I am particularly happy when it is an artist creating in another art from mine who finds points of contact with me. Certainly there are such unknown relationships and common ground among the best artists who are striving today, and I dare say they are not accidental. I am proud that I have most often met with such evidence of solidarity from the best artists.

First of all, my heartfelt thanks for the pictures. I liked the portfolio very much indeed. I understand it completely, and I am sure that our work has much in common—and indeed in the most important respects: In what you call the "unlogical" [*sic: Unlogische*] and I call the "elimination of the conscious will in art." I also agree with what you write about the constructive element. Every formal procedure which aspires to traditional effects is not completely free from conscious motivation. But art belongs to the *unconscious!* One must express *oneself!* Express oneself *directly!* Not one's taste, or one's upbringing, or one's intelligence, knowledge or skill. Not all these *acquired* characteristics, but that which is *inborn, instinctive.* And all form-making, all *conscious* form-making, is connected with some kind of mathematics, or geometry, or with the golden section or suchlike. But only unconscious form-making, which sets up the equation "form = outward shape," really creates forms; that alone brings forth prototypes which are imitated by unoriginal people and become "formulas." But whoever is capable of listening to himself, recognizing his own instincts, and also engrossing himself reflectively in every problem, will not need such crutches. One does not need to be a pioneer to create in this way, only a man who takes himself seriously—and thereby takes seriously that which is the true task of humanity in every intellectual or artistic field: to recognize, and to express what one has recognized!!! This is my belief!

Again, many thanks for the pictures. As I said, the portfolio pleased me *very, very* much. I understand the photographs [of the other pictures] less well, for the moment. One would have to see such things in color. For that reason, I hesitate to send you some photographs of my pictures. Perhaps you do not know that I also paint. But color is so important to me (not "beautiful" color, but color which is expressive in its relationships), that I am not sure whether a person would get anything out of looking at the reproductions. Friends of mine think so, but I have my doubts. However, if you are interested, I will send you some. Although I paint completely differently, you will nevertheless find points of contact—at least I find such points in the photographs; most of all, in that you seem to be objective only to a very small degree. I myself don't believe that painting must necessarily be objective. Indeed, I firmly believe the contrary. Nevertheless, when imagination suggests objective things to us, then, well and good—perhaps this is because our eyes perceive only objective things. The ear has an advantage in this regard! But when the artist reaches the point at which he desires only the expression of inner events and inner scenes in his rhythms and tones, then the "object in painting" has ceased to belong to the reproducing eye.

I am sorry that I was not in Munich. Perhaps then we could have gotten to know each other. In any case that will happen one day, either when I come Munich or you to Vienna. I think we would have a lot to say to each other. This thought gives me pleasure, and I hope to hear from you soon. Until then,

warmest regards,

Arnold Schoenberg

Quite right: I do not have the [concert] poster at hand, and can't find it.[64] Thus I myself don't know which sentences you mean—these sentences were put on the poster by the Gutmann concert agency *without my knowledge.* To me, such advertising is unwanted and distasteful, but I could do nothing about it except complain to the agency. I didn't even have the right to do that, since the concert was arranged by this agency at its own risk (for which I am otherwise *very* grateful). Thus I had no influence at all [on the wording of the announcement].

The sentences are taken from an article entitled "A Chapter from my Theory of Harmony," which appeared in the October issue of *Die Musik*.

On Order and Aesthetic Laws

2.16 From the Theory of Harmony [Harmonielehre], *First Edition, 1911; Third Edition, 1922*

The publication in 1911 of Schoenberg's massive Harmonielehre *marked the public emergence of what was to be a lifelong involvement with theoretical and pedagogical activities. Written at the request of Hertzka at Universal Edition, the theory book served many functions for Schoenberg, beyond the immediate much-needed financial reward. His March 1910 application for the position of* Privat-dozent *(an unpaid lecturer) at the Royal Academy of Music and Graphic Arts in Vienna stressed his "marked taste for theoretical research."[65] As he later remarked in "How One Becomes Lonely," "The* Harmonielehre *endowed me with the re-spect of my former adversaries who had hitherto considered me a wild man, a savage, an illegitimate intruder into musical culture"[66] At the same time, the book reflects his belief in the limitations of theory, which he wrote about in the 1911 essay "Problems of Teaching Art," where he argues that traditional artistic educa-tion based on the principle "you must be able to walk before you learn to dance" teaches the pupil only the easily mastered fundamentals of a craft. When it comes to the important aspects of aesthetics, however, the pupil is left to his own re-sources: "The pupil learns how to use something he must not use if he wants to be an artist."[67]*

The Harmonielehre *was first published in 1911 and then revised in 1921 in a third edition that appeared in 1922.[68] It is this later edition that serves as the source of the well-known translation by Roy E. Carter. Few pages of the* Harmo-nielehre *are unchanged in the later edition, and occasionally Schoenberg's emen-dations significantly change the meaning of a passage, reflecting the development of his thought from the time of the first atonal works, when the first edition was written, to the period of the first twelve-tone works, when the later edition was prepared.[69] To provide some sense of the extent and nature of the revisions, the excerpt below indicates passages that are essentially unchanged in the two edi-tions, with the revised passages given side by side. These pages are taken from chapter 4, "The Major Mode and the Diatonic Chords," where Schoenberg writes about tonality not as a structural necessity but as a law "established by custom," and thus subject to the same forces that caused the church modes to fall out of use. The discussion of the question of order relates to the problems raised in the "Testaments-Entwurf" (2.2) and in his letters to Busoni and Kandinsky about the relationship between the conscious and the irrational and illogical unconscious in composition. For additional passages from the* Harmonielehre, *see 4.11.*

It is nevertheless necessary, as I said before, that the pupil learns to ma-nipulate the devices that produce tonality. For music has not yet evolved so far that we can now speak of discarding tonality; moreover, the necessity for explaining its requirements arises also from the need to recognize its functions in the works of the past. Even if the present allows us to envision a future freed from the restrictive demands of this principle, it is still, even today, but much more in the past of our art, one of the most important musical techniques. It is one of the techniques that contribute most to the assurance of order in musical works—that order, consistent with the material, which so greatly facilitates the untroubled enjoyment of the essential beauties in the music. One of the foremost tasks of instruction is to awaken in the pupil a sense of the past and at the same time to open up to him prospects for the future. Thus instruction may proceed historically, by making connections between what was, what is, and what is likely to be. The historian can be productive if he sets forth, not merely historical data, but an understanding of history, if he does not confine himself simply to enumerating, but tries to read the future from the past.

Applied to our present concerns, that means: Let the pupil learn the laws and effects of tonality just as they still prevailed, but let him know of the tendencies that are leading toward their annulment. Let him know that the conditions leading to the dissolution of the system are inherent in the conditions upon which it is established. Let him know that every living thing has within it that which changes, develops, and destroys it. Life and death are both equally present in the embryo. What lies between is time. Nothing intrinsic, that is; merely a dimension, which is, however, necessarily consummated. Let the pupil learn by this example to recognize what is eternal: change, and what is temporal: being [*das Bestehen*]. Thus he will come to the conclusion that much of what has been considered aesthetically fundamental, that is, necessary to beauty, is by no means always rooted in the nature of things, that the imperfection of our senses drives us to those compromises through which we achieve order. For order is not demanded by the object, but by the subject. [The pupil will conclude], moreover, that the many laws that purport to be natural laws actually spring from the struggle of the craftsman to shape the material correctly; and that the adaptation of what the artist really wants to present, its reduction to fit within the boundaries of form, of artistic form, is necessary only because of our inability to grasp the undefined and unordered. The order we call artistic form is not an end in itself, but an expedient. As such by all means justified, but to be rejected absolutely wherever it claims to be more, to be aesthetics.

| [First edition] It should not be said that order, clarity, and comprehensibility can impair beauty, but they | [Third edition] This is not to say that some future work of art may do without order, clarity, and comprehen- |

are not a necessary factor without which there would be no beauty; they are merely an accidental factor. For nature is also beautiful even when we do not understand her, and where she seems to us unordered. Once we are cured of the delusion that the artist's aim is to create beauty and have recognized that only the *necessity to produce* compels him to bring forth what will perhaps afterwards be recognized as beauty, then we will also understand that comprehensibility and clarity are not conditions that the artist is obliged to impose on his work, but conditions that the observer wishes to find fulfilled. The fact that all masterworks seem comprehensible and ordered does not speak against what is offered here, for comprehensibility can also come about through the adaptation of the observer.

sibility, but that not merely what we conceive as such deserves these names. For nature is also beautiful even when we do not understand her, and where she seems to us unordered. Once we are cured of the delusion that the artist's aim is to create beauty and once we have recognized that only the *necessity to produce* compels him to bring forth what will perhaps afterwards be designated as beauty, then we will also understand that comprehensibility and clarity are not conditions that the artist is obliged to impose on his work, but conditions that the observer wishes to find fulfilled. Even the untrained observer finds these conditions in works he has known for some time, for example, in all the older masterworks; here he has had time to adapt. With newer works, at first strange, he must be allowed more time.

But whereas the distance between the onrushing, brilliant insight of the genius and the ordinary insight of his contemporaries is relatively vast, in an absolute sense, that is, viewed within the whole evolution of the human spirit, the advance of his insight is quite small. Consequently, the connection that gives access to what was once incomprehensible is always finally made. Whenever one has understood, one looks for reasons, finds order, sees clarity. [Order, clarity] are there by chance, not by law, not by necessity; and what we claim to perceive as laws [defining order and clarity] may perhaps only be laws governing our perception, without therefore being the laws a work of art must obey. And that we think we see [laws, order] in the work of art can be analogous to our thinking we see ourselves in the mirror, although we are of course not there. The work of art is capable of mirroring what we project into it. The conditions our perceptual power imposes, a mirror image of our own nature [*Beschaffenheit*], may be observed in the work. This mirror image does not, however, reveal the plan upon which the work itself is oriented, but rather the way we orient ourselves to the work. Now if the work bears the same relation to its author, if it mirrors what he projects into it, then the laws *he* thinks he perceives may also be just such as were present in his imagination, but not such as are inherent in his work. And what he has to say about his formal purposes could be relatively inconsequential. It is perhaps subjectively, but not necessarily objectively, correct. One has only to look in the mirror from another point of view; then one can believe that mirror image, too, is the image of the work itself, although that image, too, is actually projected by the observer, only this time the image is different.

The investigation into the presumed bases of artistic effects therefore results more in a picture of the psychological state of the observer than it really explains the causes of the effects. And even this presentation would go too far, since because of the interaction of the object and subject, the psychological state of the observer is in fact also dependent on certain, if also misunderstood, essential characteristics of the artwork, it thus follows that the order is not in the artwork but in us. But as already explained, we recognize in it the state of the observer.

Now even if one can assume with certainty that the observer will not see in the work of art something entirely different from what is actually in it—since the object and subject do indeed interact—even so the possibility of misapprehension is still too great to allow us to say with absolute confidence that the presumed order is not just that of the subject. All the same, the state of the observer can be ascertained from the order he sees.

It is, indeed, not to be maintained that compliance with such laws, which after all may correspond merely to the state of the observer, will assure the creation of a work of art. Moreover, these laws, even if they are valid, are not the only ones the work of art obeys. Yet, even if adherence to them does not help the pupil attain clarity, intelligibility, and beauty, they will at least make it possible for him to avoid obscurity, unintelligibility, and ugliness. The positive gain of a work of art depends on conditions other than those expressed by the laws and is not to be reached by way of the laws. But even what is negative is gain, since through avoiding such particulars as presumably hinder the realization of artistic values the pupil can lay a foundation. Not one that promotes creativity, but one that can regulate it, if it will allow itself to be regulated! Instruction that proceeds this way accomplishes something else, as well. It leads the pupil through all those errors that the [historical] struggle for knowledge has brought with it; it leads through, it leads past errors, perhaps past truths as well. Nevertheless it teaches him to know how the search was carried on, the methods of thinking, the kinds of errors, the way little truths of locally limited probability became, by being stretched out into a system, absolutely untrue. In a word, he is taught all that which makes up the way we think. Such instruction can thus bring the pupil to love even the errors, if only they have stimulated thought, turnover and renewal of intellectual stock. And he learns to love the work of his forebears, even if he cannot apply it directly to his own life, even if he has to translate it in order to put it to very different use. He learns to love it, be it truth or error, because he finds in it necessity. And he sees beauty in that everlasting struggle for truth; he recognizes that fulfillment is always the goal one yearns for, but that it could easily be the end of beauty. He understands that harmony—balance—does not mean fixity of inactive factors, but equilibrium of the most intense energies. Into life itself, where there are such energies, such struggles—that is the direction instruction should take. To represent life in art, life, with its flexibility, its possibilities for change, its necessities; to acknowledge as the sole eternal law evolution and change—this way has to be more fruitful than the other, where one assumes an end of evolution because one can thus round off the system.

On Mahler's Final Illness

2.17 From a Letter to Alma Mahler, March 27, 1911

Between 1907 and 1911 Mahler conducted the New York Philharmonic, returning to Austria for the summers. After Mahler became ill in the spring of 1911, he returned to Europe in April, going first to Paris, and then to Vienna shortly before his death on May 18, 1911. When Schoenberg had been facing a disastrous financial situation in the summer of 1910, Mahler had given him a substantial loan. Alma Mahler reported that during his last days "his thoughts often went anxiously to Schoenberg. 'If I go, he will have nobody left.' I promised him to do everything in my power."[70]

Schoenberg later wrote that the final movement of the Six Little Piano Pieces, dated June 17, 1911 (the other five movements are dated February 19, 1911), was written in response to Mahler's death. He also painted a windswept grave-yard scene depicting the burial of Mahler, dated May 22, 1911. The first edition of the Harmonielehre *was published with a dedication "to the memory of Gustav Mahler":*

> The dedication was intended, while he yet lived, to give him a little pleasure. It was to express veneration for his work, his immortal compositions. And it was to bear witness to the fact that his work, which the educated musicians pass over with a superior shrug of the shoulders, even with contempt, is adored by one who perhaps understands a thing or two.
>
> Gustav Mahler had to do without pleasures greater than that which this dedication intended for him. This martyr, this saint passed away before he had established his work well enough even to be able to entrust its future to his friends.
>
> I should have been content just to give him a little pleasure. But now that he is dead, it is my wish this book bring me such recognition that no one can pass over my words lightly when I say: "He was an altogether great man."[71]

My very dear Madam,

> I read in the newspaper that the Director is sick and that your return journey had to be postponed as a result. That is very painful to me. But I hope that the matter isn't so serious that you won't be able to be here again soon. I have looked forward to your return for so long. Now when he should be here so that from time to time we could be together, every day that delays it further is a loss. Since you perhaps have too much to do with all your concerns, I shall not expect you to write to me but shall inquire in Vienna. One hopes I shall hear soon that he is healthy again and on his way. [. . .]
>
> I have thought about the Director so much (oh, that one must speak so stiffly!—but in any case I don't want to be disrespectful). My wife and I have played his songs *very often*. Nowadays my wife sings them by heart. That's the right way! I like them more and more!! Actually I liked them enormously from the start. Then at the *Merker* concert I heard your songs, which I liked very much.[72] You really have a great deal of talent. It is a shame that you have not continued working. That would have amounted to something. But now I must get to work. I am getting my *Harmonielehre* ready to print, and that is an enormous nuisance. But I believe the work is something! I am absolutely certain. I hope that it will be worthy of the dedication. You know to whom it is dedicated—if it will only please him. So please: make him well in a hurry. We need him in Vienna. I don't even feel that there is a Vienna anymore. For me it was always only a city in which this or that personality lived. But when Mahler is not in Vienna, then it is hardly Vienna any longer.

Concerning an Essay on Mahler

2.18 Letter to Kraus (c. summer 1911)

Schoenberg's first essay on Mahler was published in the March 1, 1912, Mahler commemorative issue of Der Merker. *A much longer essay was given as a lecture in Prague on March 25, 1912, and then subsequently in Berlin and Vienna, but it was only published in a revised version from 1948 in* Style and Idea *(1950).*[73] *This letter to Kraus is marked by the despondent tone that resurfaces in other correspondence from the fall and winter of 1911 (see further, 3.2). For example, in a letter to Berg from December 21, 1911, after Schoenberg's move to Berlin, he writes: "I am unusually depressed. Perhaps it's because of the revolting news I hear from Vienna about my works, etc. But perhaps only because I'm not composing anything at all right now. At any rate: I've lost interest in my works. I'm not satisfied with anything any more. I see mistakes and inadequacies in everything. Enough of that, I can't begin to tell you how I feel at such times. It's not ambition. Otherwise I would be satisfied that there are some people who think better of it than I do."*[74]

Dear Mr. Kraus,

Unfortunately, I cannot carry out my intention of writing an essay about Mahler for *Die Fackel*. Above all, I am at the moment so depressed on account of many disappointments and many other troubles that there is absolutely nothing I feel like doing. But I have so much to do, partly things that are necessary, partly things I am committed to, that even if I were in the mood, nothing would come of it.

And then it is so terribly difficult to write a short essay about Mahler. A book would certainly work—as you say, a book is always easier—but I don't know how I should stop once I started. I can't organize the material and I don't see how to limit it.

But I definitely hope later on to succeed in writing it. And perhaps you will then also still be so kind as to accept it.

I would very much have liked to call on you, but it was scarcely possible. And also at the moment I am really too distracted, too little collected, to be permitted to seek out company in which one is supposed to be focused.

With warm regards,
respectfully yours,
Arnold Schoenberg

3   "War Clouds":
Berlin and Vienna, 1911–1918

The Move to Berlin; Publication Plans

3.1 Letter to C. F. Peters Publishing House, October 19, 1911

Mounting financial pressures, an unpleasant episode with a neighbor that threatened to turn violent, and the possibility of professional advancement persuaded Schoenberg to move with his family back to Berlin. They left Vienna on August 4, 1911, traveling first to Munich before settling in Berlin in October. Schoenberg's financial troubles became particularly acute at this time, and in September Berg sent out an appeal for help: "Arnold Schoenberg's friends and pupils consider it their duty to bring his extremity to the notice of the public. Shame prevents him from doing so himself; that is why we take the initiative and cry for help over his head. Our mouths are opened by the thought of this artist coming to grief for lack of the common necessities of life. Catastrophe has overtaken him with unexpected speed, and help from a distant source would be too late."[1] Forty-eight people responded, and on September 29, 1911, Schoenberg wrote to Berg of receiving 424 marks: "I am really happy to have such friends. Yet it is curious: I should feel very important as a result of these things. But, instead of raising my self-esteem, it lowers it. I can't stop wondering whether I am worth all this. And though while I'm working my ego says 'yes,' this here is something else. I'm happy, but depressed. I'm pleased and worried—whether I am the person I thought I was and would have to be, to deserve so much effort."[2]

In Berlin, while his financial worries continued, his living conditions improved dramatically. No doubt with some exaggeration, Schoenberg wrote to his publisher Hertzka on October 31, 1911: "You cannot imagine how famous I am here. I am almost too embarrassed to mention it. I am known to everyone. I am recognized from my photographs. People know my 'biography,' all about me, all about the 'scenes' I have occasioned, indeed know almost more than I, who forget such things quickly. So if you would lend a bit of a hand, we should see some results soon. Everybody banks on you in this respect. You, personally, are very well spoken of here and are regarded as being different from the general run of Viennese. I too have sung your praises. Now please print my work!!! I'm certain it's good!!!"[3]

A newspaper clipping entitled "Arnold Schoenberg's Newest Compositions," from the March 2, 1912, Berliner Zeitung am Mittag, commented on the "hotly

---

Photo opposite page: Schoenberg, 1912. Arnold Schönberg Center, Vienna.

This photograph was taken in Prague in November 1912, at the time of his lecture on Gustav Mahler (see 3.10).

contested success" of a performance of Pelleas *in Prague, his most recent composition* Erwartung, *and his current work on* Die glückliche Hand. *In response to the question why he had left Vienna, Schoenberg responded: "Vienna did me little good. And yet, how hard it is for a Viennese to get used to the very different ways of the Berliners! But Berlin has what Vienna lacked: respect for honest work and the self-assurance of those who are genuinely and seriously interested in the new."[4]*

In the letter given here to Henri Hinrichsen of the C. F. Peters publishing house Schoenberg is responding to an inquiry about publishing some of his works. Of the works discussed, only the Five Pieces for Orchestra were ultimately published by Peters (see further 3.4). The letter provides an important reminder of the considerable delays Schoenberg faced in getting his works before the public.

Dear Sir,

please excuse that I am only today answering your letter, which brought me so much pleasure. I have been so preoccupied with my move to Berlin that I didn't get around to it.

I am currently under contract to Universal Edition and therefore cannot yet freely dispose of my works. But I do have hopes of getting some works released. First, because Universal Edition must decide by the end of December which works to acquire of those now available to them. Second, so many works are in question, some of which are substantial, that I myself scarcely think it possible that Universal Ed., though it is now publishing some of my things, can acquire them all. But third, based on the personal kindness of Director Hertzka, I hope that he would release some works to me sooner. And so accordingly, I believe the following works should come into consideration:

1. Chamber Symphony for 15 solo instruments (possibly with multiple string parts, thus a small orchestra). Around 100 score pages.[5]

2. George Lieder for voice and piano. Around 35 pages.[6]

3. Orchestra Pieces (five short), around 60 pages.

If need be also (but the latter less probable):

1 volume of songs[7]

2 Ballades[8] and

6 short piano pieces.[9]

But now I must ask you something. You perhaps do not know that my music appears so unusual on the page that even the best musicians are unable to form any idea of the sound and the effect. Even Gustav Mahler said of my Second Quartet that "he was unable to read these *four* staves."—Naturally, the young musicians can already sight-read my things now.—With this long explanation I only wanted to say to you (and please do not take this as arrogance; I am only acknowledging a fact), that one must just accept my things without looking at them, simply out of trust in the man who speaks to you in them, because in this case the judgments of musicians usually fail. Very simply: few have the courage, as Mahler did, to admit that they don't have the ability to read the score, and thus condemn a work which they absolutely do not know.

I am naturally ready to send you the works in question to look over. I only wanted to prevent some "fine musician" from unnecessarily cracking a tooth on them, without reaching the core.

A rejection of my work by you would hurt me with Universal Edition, which has certainly done things for me, but which unfortunately is somewhat timid. Therefore, I want perhaps first to send you the music, and then approach Universal Edition and attempt to be released.

I ask you now to let me know:

I. should I send you the first three works indicated above?

II. should I then attempt to be released by Universal Edition at once, or

III. wait until you have seen the pieces and have declared yourself in principle for one or the other pieces, or

IV. should I just wait until January 1, when some of them will certainly be free, and keep your kind interest to myself until then?[10]

Looking forward to your early reply,

Respectfully yours,

Arnold Schoenberg

On Theory and Painting

3.2 Letter to Kandinsky, December 14, 1911

After the explosively creative period in 1908 and 1909, Schoenberg found composition increasingly difficult. In 1910 he set aside Die glückliche Hand *after making a few isolated sketches; other pieces like the posthumously published Three Pieces for Chamber Orchestra, from February 1910, were left as fragments. In November 1911 Schoenberg completed the scoring of* Gurrelieder, *and he briefly took up the composition of the Second Chamber Symphony, Op. 38. The only completed works from 1911 were the Six Little Piano Pieces, Op. 19, and* Herzgewächse, *Op. 20, for high soprano and chamber ensemble, completed on December 9. This was the work that, after repeated requests from Kandinsky and the painter Gabriele Münter (1877–1962), who lived with Kandinsky in Murnau, Schoenberg submitted in February 1912 for the* Blaue Reiter Almanac.

At the time of this letter Schoenberg was in his second month of a series of lectures on aesthetics and composition at the Stern Conservatory in Berlin, where he had previously taught harmony during his first Berlin sojourn from 1901 to 1903.[11] In a letter of December 5 he wrote to Berg about the tension between composing and his teaching and theoretical work, including the Harmonielehre:

I don't get around to writing very often because I'm very absorbed in my lectures. Even though I don't spend all my time preparing, in fact, postpone preparation until the last days so as not to tire myself, I nonetheless continually catch myself thinking about it. Or at other times I'm burdened by the thought that I ought to be dealing with it. It is rather inconvenient, but gives me pleasure nonetheless. And I believe it's turning out to be worthwhile. I find it rather useful to have to present in an organized form all these things I've thought about for so long. Otherwise I would have continued just to think them instead of ever writing them down. I think I'll begin a book when I've finished the series.

On the other hand, I'd rather compose just now. But working with so much theoretical material makes it impossible for me to open up there. I'll have to take a long break from it soon. Otherwise it might spell the end of my composing. Perhaps that's why at present I feel no inclination to paint, either.

From the fact that, though inwardly very preoccupied, I am at present not working on anything—at least to the extent that one considers that to mean deskwork—it's clear to me how very much I am a musician and how much less satisfying I find theories than composing.[12]

Together with the loss of confidence in himself and his ability to live up to the demands of his aesthetic ideals, Schoenberg also began to question the value of his paintings. In a letter to Kandinsky dated March 8, 1912, Schoenberg responded to an invitation to have his paintings included in a Blaue Reiter *show in Berlin sponsored by Herwarth Walden and* Der Sturm: *"I do not believe that it is advantageous for me to exhibit in the company of professional painters. I am surely an 'outsider,' an amateur, a dilettante. Whether I should exhibit at all is almost already a question. Whether I should exhibit with a group of painters is almost no longer a question. In any case, it seems disadvantageous to me if I exhibit paintings other than the ones in which [I] believe!"[13]*

Dear Mr. Kandinsky,

I have still not read all of your book, only two thirds of it.[14] Nevertheless, I must already write to you now that I like it extraordinarily. You are certainly right about so many things, particularly what you say about color in comparison to musical timbre. That is in accord with my own perceptions. Your theory of forms is most interesting to me. I am very curious about the "Theory" chapter. I am not in complete agreement with some of the details. In particular, I do not agree when you write, if I understand you correctly, that you would have preferred to present an exact theory. I do not think that is necessary at present. We search on and on (as you yourself say) with our feelings. Let us endeavor *never* to lose these feelings to a theory.

Now, I must write to you about your pictures. Well: I liked them very much indeed. I went immediately, on the day after I got your letter.[15] "Romantic Landscape" pleased me the most. The other pictures are not hung very advantageously. There is something that I cannot reconcile myself to: the format, the size.[16] I also have a theoretical objection: since it is only a question of proportions, for example

black 24 : white 120

by red 12 : yellow 84

it cannot possibly depend on the format, because I can certainly say the same thing if I reduce it, for example by 12:

black 2 : white 10

by red 1 : yellow 7

I believe it easier to grasp this equation if it is reduced.

Practically expressed: I feel these color-weights less, because they disappear too much from my field of vision. (A few escape me entirely.) I had to stand far away, *and then of course the picture is smaller, the equation "reduced."*

Perhaps I have for this reason less of an impression of the very large pictures, because I could not take them in as a whole.

Now to Miss Münter's pictures: although I did not immediately remember them, they attracted my attention at once as I entered the room: They are really extremely original and of salutary simplicity. Absolute naturalness. An austere undertone, which is certainly a characteristic feature, behind which goodness and love are hidden. I enjoyed the pictures very much.

Mr. Marc's pictures also pleased me very much. There is a curious gentleness in this "giant." I was actually surprised by this, but I soon managed to bring it into harmony with the impression I had of Marc. Very likeable, in any event. Otherwise, not much pleased me in the exhibition. Best of all a Mr. Nolde, whom I then met, but I did not like him personally very much. Then from Prague: Kubista.[17] He is affected, but has talent and courage!! The Berliners will turn their hand to anything. Especially to what is the "latest modern." I guessed immediately that there must be a Frenchman who painted "Bathing Women." These you will find five or six times in the room. Exactly like Cézanne. On the other hand, I would be glad to find out which Frenchman provided the original for the many "circus people!"[18]

I am very sorry that you don't like my pictures very much. Also, the most important ones were not sent to you in every case. But nevertheless in large part.

Now to the *Blaue Reiter,* I believe I can after all give you some of my music for reproduction. How long may it be? May it be four or five pages? Or shorter? Write to me about this at once! On the other hand, I have still not written anything for you. My lectures at the Stern Conservatory take up so many of my thoughts. Perhaps it will still come!

Now something else:

I am to send my pictures to Budapest for an exhibition. I have been allotted a whole room for twenty-four paintings.[19]

Now I have no idea which ones you have. Could you notify me? And: would you be willing to send the pictures directly to Budapest? That is, those that I specify to you (charges to be collected on delivery!). The others come to me. That is to say, I am exhibiting no portraits or such, but only those paintings which I call "Impressions" or "Fantasies." I believe you have eight paintings there, but there are certainly portraits (finger exercises, scales) among them. Please write to me immediately about this. And you will be so good, won't you, as to send on the pictures as soon as I write you.

I recommended to the painter Gütersloh that he get in touch with you.[20]

Adolf Loos, the *most outstanding architect,* has also written to you at my suggestion. Also concerning Kokoschka! What have you arranged with him?

I hope you can read my letters more easily than I yours.

I have sent you my *Theory of Harmony.* You will be astonished at how much I say that is closely similar to you.

Today I am at last sending you my photo.

Please greet Miss Münter most warmly for me. I will write separately to her soon. Then also Mr. Marc and the others whom I found on your card.

Many kind regards to you. In sincere friendship,

Your Arnold Schoenberg

On the Artist's Relationship to the World

3.3 Selected Aphorisms, 1911–1912

These aphorisms were published in the Gutmann Concert Calendar *for the 1911–1912 season and in* Der Ruf *(February 1912), a publication of the Academic Society for Literature and Music (see 3.10).*

That one who murders for money finds the sex murderer incomprehensible is comparable to the business traveler's lack of understanding for one who travels for pleasure.[21]

Women are ambitious, but they also understand how to be content. In their striving for the best they are prepared to sacrifice everything, to give up everything. But if their goal is unattainable, they can achieve the same bliss quickly making do with the next person that comes along—if only he will court her.

My subject is my person; whoever neglects the former insults the latter; but whoever gets close to the latter is estranged from the former.

The artist can present much less, the dilettante much more, than he is able to imagine.

Many are called to the lucrative positions in art who are less chosen than I.[22]

People, who come calling in order to get to know me, often weary me with lectures about their opinions, impressions, and views. They thus seem to be less curious about what I would say to them than what they would say to me. That is annoying and simply wrong. I shall gladly enlighten anyone who asks, but if someone wants to talk to me, he should keep his mouth shut.

One can recognize the nature of the difference between talent and genius in that there is the expression "a talent for mimicry."[23]

Instead of saying "talent," I now prefer saying only "a talent for mimicry."

He then gave me a meaningful look, but I understood: nothing.

The portrait need not resemble the model, only the artist.

The artist never has a relationship with the world but rather always against it; he turns his back on it, just as it deserves. But his most fervent wish is to be so independent, that he can proudly call out to it: *Elemia, Elem-ia!*[24]

A poor devil must be careful not to spend more on a thing than it's worth. That's why those who are as economical with their tastes and opinions as they are with their money fear nothing so much as the possibility of overrating someone.

What difference is there between a journalist and a human!
(That is no riddle. It is not even a question. Only a pronouncement.)

Dramatic music: I find it more trouble than it's worth to immerse myself in the inner motivation of people indifferent to me, in order to portray them through their actions.

I love her very much, but I can't keep her—here I don't mean by this a woman, but order [*die Ordnung*], which apparently is also a woman.

On His Life, Works, and Relationships in Berlin

3.4 *From the* Berlin Diary

Schoenberg made regular entries in this diary between January and March 1912. Many of the entries concern preparations for two concerts. The first of these, given on February 4 at the Harmonium-Saal in Berlin, included the Songs, Op. 6, The Book of the Hanging Gardens, *the Six Little Piano Pieces,* Herzgewächse, *and a two-piano, eight-hand performance of three movements of the Five Pieces for Orchestra. Later in the month Schoenberg traveled to Prague, where he conducted the Prague Philharmonic in a February 29 performance of* Pelleas und Melisande *and Mahler's orchestration of a Bach Suite (in the concert, Zemlinsky also conducted two concertos featuring cellist Pablo Casals, the Saint-Saëns in A minor, and the Haydn in D major). In a letter to Kandinsky of March 8, 1912, he wrote of the concert: "Subjectively, I believe the performance was very good. The audience response was remarkably excited. More than twenty minutes of the loudest hissing and applause! It was exactly the same on 5 March in Berlin with Rosé, who performed my First String Quartet. Here I am engaged in a violent feud with the Berlin critics, brought about by two articles which I published in* Pan *against Leopold Schmidt (on 20 and 27 February). The rest of the critics are taking revenge on me on behalf of their pope!!"*[25]

Several entries also concern the commission from the singer and actress Albertine Zehme (1857–1946) to compose settings of Albert Giraud's Pierrot lunaire *poems, in the translation by Otto Erich Hartleben. The beginning of the composition of* Pierrot *on March 12, 1912, marked the end of a long creative dry spell. Significantly, the next day marked Schoenberg's last entry in the* Berlin Diary, *with the exception of two later brief notations. Brinkmann says of the coincidence of the conclusion of the diary with the beginning of work on* Pierrot lunaire: *"One would like to think that the act of writing music had now replaced the act of writing words."*[26] *The final movement of* Pierrot *was completed on July 9, 1912.*

January 20, 1912: Finally started. Had intended to for so long already. However, I could not rid myself of the idea that I first had to note down things that occurred to me about my earlier life. That is why I let ten or more years slip by. But it will work now. Because I have resolved to deceive myself by persuading myself that everyday I shall only write down very short remarks for which I can find the time.

[. . .]

January 21 (Sunday): Pleasant news by mail today (the first in a long time): Peters accepts Pieces for Orchestra. Low fee! However, Peters Edition! That is decisive. And printed! Marschalk presents himself again.[27] He has hidden motives! He obviously discussed my *and* his affairs with Hertzka. Have asked Hertzka regarding the printing of the five available works for the last time. At the same time, asked Tischer und Jagenberg whether they wanted to have them. I don't think I am doing anything wrong in that, since it is not my intention to get one to outbid the other. Rather, on the contrary: I have demanded less from Hertzka, yet despite that I shall give the things to him without waiting for T. und J. So it is only to gain time.

In the morning, unpleasant news: Mrs. Simon-Herlitz will not play the harmonium part in my concert. Recommends Kämpf. Bad thing to have to look for someone at the last moment. By the way, still no assent from Winternitz. Then, in the afternoon, more unpleasant things! Webern will not be in Berlin on March 5 for Rosé's performance here of my 1st Quartet. I am sorry, because he's the only friend who knows the work, the only one who regards it with warmth. He is going to Vienna to hear Mahler's VIIIth Symphony. Would like to do that myself. This shows, however, that he is not as exclusively attached to me as he would like to make one believe. Discussion about that in the evening with Mathilde. Result: we are partially upset with each other. Of course she goes way too far; since for certain reasons, (G),[28] she has the urge to settle a score with him. I reproached her by saying that I often did not conduct myself any better toward Mahler; that parents behave badly toward children as do children toward parents. That goodness is something abstract, not something absolute. Therefore, that absolutely good people beyond any reproach do not exist. And I do not want to forget on how many other occasions Webern behaves extremely well toward me. But she does not want to see. She stubbornly sticks by her allegations and barely listens.

January 22: Had rehearsal with [Egon] Petri. He will probably play the pieces excellently. At least pianistically. On the whole, he took everything too fast; or rather, too hastily. I said to Webern: for *my* music one has to have time. It is not a thing for people who have other things to do. Yet it is quite a pleasure to hear one's things performed by someone who completely masters them technically. It seems that the concert will be quite beautiful. I expect the best from my Pieces for Orchestra for eight hands![29] I was a quarter-hour late for the lecture.[30] Busoni present with wife and son. [. . .] Spoke at the lecture without any preparation. On the whole, not really half bad. Though I seriously lost my train of thought several times because of the bad night I had spent when Görgi had been crying due to chilblains. But despite that, I managed to present and substantiate my ideas on the "obligatory recitative"[31] (for some strange reason I forgot to mention this term) rather clearly. But not completely. The idea goes deeper: the unutterable is said in a free form (= recitative). In this it comes close to nature, which likewise cannot be completely grasped, but which is effective nonetheless. Webern was with me. Did not especially like him today. When he noticed I was upset, he had a (somewhat) suppressed air of disdain about him.

Tomorrow, rehearsal with the three piano virtuosos. Webern asked me not to make a fool of him with my reprimands! As if I had ever done anything like that. Had to refuse to be quiet about those things that are important for execution. Strange. Such a minor irritation, which does not want to go away. But I do not feel like letting myself become prejudiced against Webern. I *do* believe that he has done something incorrect here for once; but other than that, he only wants what is best!! And that is what counts!

[. . .]

January 28: On the 24th, Winternitz-Dorda canceled the concert! Change of repertory. She is singing on Sunday afternoon. Great embarassment. Petri is leaving for London on the 29th for five weeks. Therefore have to find another pianist for the piano pieces, George, and older songs. [. . .] proposition to compose a cycle *Pierrot lunaire* for Dr. Zehme's intended recital. Holds out the prospect of a large fee (1,000 marks). Have read the preface, looked at the poems, am enthusiastic. Brilliant idea, absolutely to my liking. Would want to do this even without a fee. That is why I made another proposition: instead of a fee, royalties from performances. More acceptable to me, since I am not able to work on command anyway. This way, however: if I succeed in writing these melodramas, then she should perform them and pay me the agreed-upon royalties for twenty to thirty evenings. Quite likely to be accepted.

25th, afternoon, held rehearsal despite the cancellation. Is not going especially well. Grünberg without rhythm; Closson quite musical, but dry. Asked Closson whether he wanted to substitute for Petri. He declined. Impossible in such a short time. Turns out that the evening performance has to be on February 4 since Grünberg and Closson will otherwise be gone as well. Decide to ask Winternitz. Gutmann, despite my vigorous protest, had written a very harsh letter to her.[32] Winternitz replaced indignantly. Reproaches me with everything she has ever done for me. Silly goose! Forgets that it is through my concerts that she was able to emerge from complete obscurity. Simply do not pay attention to these stupidities. Mainly in order to force a clear answer out of her as to whether she wants to participate or not. But does not seem attainable. As little intelligent as this female may otherwise be, in this respect she is cunning. Besides: all females lie better than men tell the truth. [. . .]

On the 27th. Nothing in particular is happening. Kept busy with the corrections of the continuo for Prof. Guido Adler.[33] Did not get very far.

On the 28th. Correction of the aphorisms for the Academic Society in Vienna. Letter from Peters, who is giving me an appointment in Berlin for Wednesday in order to get to know me personally. Wants titles for the Pieces for Orchestra; on the grounds of "technicalities of publishing." Might possibly give in, since I found titles that are at least feasible. Do not altogether like the idea. Since music is fascinating in that one can say everything in such a way that the knowledgeable will understand it all, and yet one has not given away his secrets, the secrets one does not even admit to oneself. Titles, however, give away. Besides: whatever there was to say, the music has said it. Why the word in addition. If words were necessary, they would be in there. But the music does say more than words. The titles, which I perhaps will assign, will not give anything away now, partially because they are quite obscure, partially because they indicate technical things. Namely: I. "Premonitions" (everyone has those), II. "Yesteryears" (everyone has those as well), III. "Chord colorations" (technical), IV. "Peripeteia" (is quite likely general enough), V. "The Obligatory (maybe better the 'worked-out' or the 'endless') Recitative." In any case with a note indicating that it has to do with the publishing technicalities and not with "poetic content." In the afternoon there should have been a rehearsal; however, due to a misunderstanding Steuermann and Grünberg did not come. But Closson wants to play the piano pieces.

On the 27th Steuermann was with me. Played his compositions for me. Very talented! Wants to study with me. I assign him to take on the piano pieces and the accompaniment of the songs for the concert. He is looking at them. Now he has to hand over the piano pieces to Closson. But most likely will do the accompaniments. If he is going to study with me, and in case [Fritz] Zweig comes, I could already be earning 200 marks a month. And above all: I have students once more. Told Steuermann that I would even teach him for free. He does not know yet if, and how much, he could pay me.

On the 28th, in the *Berliner Tageblatt:* Strindberg's thank-you for birthday wishes. Could have been written by me. Exactly my sentiments and experiences: the devotion and humility versus a compliment one does not feel worthy of; on the other hand the arrogance and the indignation when deserved recognition has been withdrawn. [. . .]

February 9: Once again did not find time for a whole week. First the concert, then having to catch up with neglected things and backlogs caused by it: correspondence, a whole mountain of it! [. . .]

Sunday, February 4. Morning, 10 o'clock rehearsal with Winternitz. She is somewhat embarrassed in front of me, which she tries to conceal with a lot of talk. I could not help being somewhat cool. I really cannot forgive that quickly. At the rehearsal I am once more amazed at how musical she is. And her voice sounds very beautiful as well. Despite the fact that it is actually hoarse. During the concert, however, she sang the older songs and especially the George Lieder much too dramatically (somewhat vulgarly), shaping everything according to the text rather than according to the music. In a word, in the currently fashionable manner. Because of this, only one of the George Lieder completely impressed me; whereas many other things became utterly incomprehensible to me. Closson played the piano pieces much too fast. Had forgotten everything I had told him. And especially: no breaks at all between the separate pieces. So that no one knew that there were six piano pieces. [. . .]

February 18 (Sunday): On February 16 (Friday), extremely unpleasant letter from Hertzka. With reproaches that are too silly to be taken as criminal acts, and too criminal to be taken as silliness. In my initial anger I wrote a rather harsh letter. Following Mathilde's advice, however, I tore it up and decided not to reply. (The copy of the letter is in the copy book.) Maybe our being together in Prague and with him seeing the great success, he will find himself obliged to behave more decently. And I cannot risk anything at this time since he now has the larger portion of the things I have written after having come to an agreement with the Dreililien-Verlag regarding my works.

During the past few days, a strong decline in general in all the things that looked so promising up until now. Strange: ever since I canceled the Mahler lecture [see 3.10]. Am I supposed to have committed an injustice in this for which I am being punished? Not to my knowledge. I believed in having to act this way. At first and in reality I had acted contrary to the example set for me by Mahler, who stayed away from Vienna whenever he could possibly do so after he had been driven out. I realized that he was right after all and canceled. Maybe I should have put this duty before the other. But, at least, I did not want to withdraw from the duty: that is exactly why I announced my lecture for Prague. And I am certain I shall repeat it in other places.

17th (Saturday). Find out from Gutmann that Dr. Zehme is hesitant about accepting my conditions. Quite unpleasant, since I was really counting very much on that money. Yet at the same time I feel somewhat relieved, because I had felt quite depressed about having to compose something I actually didn't feel compelled to do. It seems as if my fate wants to keep me from even the most minor artistic sin. Since the one time I do not have the courage to decline a sum of money offered to me and which I need sorely, nothing comes out of the negotiations. This way I shall always remain clean and shall only have committed a sin in my thoughts. Is that not bad enough? Anyway it depresses me, and I feel very despondent.

[. . .]

March 11, 1912: I am in danger of not continuing this diary. In any case, it is hardly a diary anymore. The journey to Prague and many other occupations kept me from it. Whether I still even know the most important of the factual things is already doubtful. Actually I would have liked to jot down the other things, the things that have nothing to do with facts. I shall try to say whatever still occurs to me.

[. . .]

Sunday, February 25 [. . .] Evening, large party at the Zemlinskys. Quite nice. Above all I am surprised by Ida [Zemlinsky], who really is very attentive, quite obviously is very pleased by our visit, and is doing everything with cordiality. Alex is not quite as nice. Above all he denies me any word of praise almost out of principle. He seems to think that I am too highly praised within my circle and obviously wants to prevent me from behaving like a mega-lomaniac. The only thing he forgets, though, is just how much I am despised in other circles! I do not believe that envy plays a part in this. But quite likely a little bit of irritation or bitterness over the fact that he, who really is a person of great merit, is given so very little recognition. I can understand that very well. Taking the lack of judgment of people into consideration, he had to fear that as a reward for his noble-mindedness, namely, providing me with this opportunity to conduct, his circle, and even the audience, would prefer me to him, if I were lucky. Fortunately this did not happen. I myself would have felt this to be an outrageous injustice. For the same reason he might, in addition, have been upset about the book about me, which my students published.[34] I feel I am being talked about in really much too effusive a way. I am too young for this kind of praise, have accomplished too little and too little that is perfect. My present accomplishment, I can still only regard as a hope for the future, as a promise that I may keep; but not as anything more. And I have to say, were I not spoiling the joy of my students by doing so, I might possibly have rejected the book. On the other hand, however, I was so overwhelmed by the great love which shows in all this, that I really had been happy, insofar as something like this can provide happiness. And I was proud as well: I find everything, almost everything, written so well and with such beautiful words, that I really should have a high opinion of a group of human beings like these. Above all, of course, Webern! He is a wonderful human being. How moved he was when he handed the book to me. Solemn and yet so unpretentious. Almost like a schoolboy; but like the one who only prepared something so as not to be overwhelmed. I have resolved to drink to brotherhood with him at the first opportunity. Then Berg, and [Karl] Linke and Jalowetz. Yes, even [Karl] Horwitz. And: Kandinsky. A magnificent essay.

But I was embarrassed in front of Alex. He is somewhat skeptical. I know he does not like to believe. And though he thinks much of me—I almost feel he would like it best if he alone thought highly of me! Strangely enough, he does not trust or believe in the enthusiasm of others. Despite the fact that he himself is capable of so much genuine enthusiasm! Why? [. . .]

March 12: In the morning was very much in the mood to compose. After a very long time! I had already considered the possibility that I may not ever compose again at all. There seemed to be many reasons for it. The persistence with which my students nip at my heels, intending to surpass what I offer, this puts me in danger of becoming their imitator, and keeps me from calmly building on the stage that I have just reached. They always bring in everything raised to the tenth power. And it makes sense! It is really good. But I do not know whether it is necessary. At least not whether it is necessary for me. That is why I am now forced to distinguish even more carefully whether I must write than earlier. Since I do not care all that much about originality; however, sometimes it does give me pleasure, and in any case I like it better than unoriginality. Then came the preoccupation with theoretical matters. Doing that very definitely dries one out. And maybe this is the reason why I suddenly, for about two years, no longer feel as young. I have become strangely calm! This is also evident when I conduct. I am missing the aggressive in myself. The spontaneous leaving of all constraints behind oneself and attacking, taking over. Maybe this will change for the better since I am now composing once more anyway. Or could it be that this is better. I remember having written a poem ten to twelve years ago where I wished to grow old and undemanding, calm. Now, as I suddenly see the earlier possibilities of unrest again, I almost have a yearning for them. Or are they already here again?

[March 13]. I should actually work out my lecture on Mahler that I shall be giving in Prague on the 25th. However, for the next few days I would rather be composing. Yesterday, the 12th, I wrote the first of the *Pierrot lunaire* melodramas.[35] I believe it turned out very well. This provides much stimulation. And I am, I sense it, definitely moving toward a new way of expression. The sounds here truly become an almost animalistically immediate expression of sensual and psychological emotions. Almost as if everything were transmitted directly. I am anxious to see how this is going to continue. But, by the way, I do know what is causing it: Spring!!! Always my best time. I can already sense motion inside myself again. In this I am almost like a plant. Each year the same. In the spring I almost always have composed something.

On Vienna, Composition, and "Construction"

3.5 Letter to Kandinsky, August 19, 1912

In June 1912 Schoenberg was offered a position teaching composition, harmony, and counterpoint at the Academy of Music in Vienna. In a letter to the president of the academy, Karl Wiener, he declined the position citing the salary, the requirement to teach harmony and counterpoint "to all eternity, until the arteries are quite hardened," and above all, "his dislike of Vienna."[36] In a letter to Guido Adler of August 20, 1912, he remarked on his rejection of the position: " . . . my aversion toward the 'City of Songs by Murdered Artists' was too great for me to overcome."[37]

Dear Mr. Kandinsky,

I was sorry to learn that you have been ill and had to be operated on. What actually was the matter? You don't mention that at all. Was it something dangerous? And above all, are you well now, unlikely to have a recurrence? I imagine it was your appendix. I hope that was it. That at least is no cause for concern.

I do not have very much to report. You know that I was to go to the Vienna Academy as professor and that I declined. But not, as I would have liked, in order to "devote myself completely to composition," for I have unfortunately not yet reached that point. But rather because I considered it unsuitable that I, who left Vienna for a reason of primary importance, should go back for a reason of secondary importance. And what was offered to me was not of more than secondary importance. A pensionable post and a steady income, to be sure, and that is something I need very much. But a relatively limited field of activity, since Schreker was engaged at the same time as myself, and Novak also was supposed to come.[38]—I have been living the whole summer in Carlshagen on the Baltic. Very beautiful. For once completely without thoughts, purely in tranquil mindlessness. Thus actually less beautiful than restful. But it seems that's what I needed. I had been very irritable and tired lately.—I have written a [. . .][39] Perhaps no heartfelt necessity as regards its theme, its content (Giraud's *Pierrot lunaire*), but certainly as regards its form. In any case, remarkable for me as a preparatory study for another work, which I now wish to begin: Balzac's *Seraphita*.[40] Do you know it? Perhaps the most glorious work in existence. I want to do it scenically. Not so much as theater, at least not in the old sense. In any case, not "dramatic." But rather: oratorio that becomes visible and audible. Philosophy, religion that are perceived with the artistic senses.—Now I am working on my *Glückliche Hand* without making real progress. Soon it will be three years old and it is still not composed. That is very rare with me. Perhaps I shall have to lay it aside once more, although I am very content with what is finished up to the present.

I must also speak to you about your contribution to the *Blaue Reiter*—thus: your stage composition pleases me extremely. Also the preface to it. I am completely in agreement. But how does this all stand in relation to "construction"?[41] It seems to me to be the opposite. It seems to me that he who constructs must weigh and test. Calculate the load capacity, the relationships, etc. *Der gelbe Klang,* however, is not construction, but simply the rendering of an inner vision.

There is the following difference:

An inner vision is a whole that has component parts, but these are linked, already integrated.

Something that is constructed consists of parts that try to imitate a whole.

But there is no guarantee in this case that the most important parts are not missing and that the binding agent of these missing parts is: the soul.

I am sure that this is only a quarrel over words and that we agree completely about essentials. But "construction," though it is only a word, is nevertheless the word of yours with which I do not agree. Even though it is the only one. But as I said, *Der gelbe Klang* pleases me extraordinarily. It is exactly the same as what I have striven for in my *Glückliche Hand,* only you go still farther than I in the renunciation of any conscious thought, any conventional plot. That is naturally a great advantage. We must become conscious that there are puzzles around us. And we must find the courage to look these puzzles in the eye without timidly asking about the "solution." It is important that our creation of such puzzles mirror the puzzles with which we are surrounded, so that our soul may endeavor—not to solve them—but to decipher them. What we gain thereby should be not the solution but a new method of coding or decoding. The material, worthless in itself, serves in the creation of new puzzles. For the puzzles are an image of the ungraspable. And imperfect, that is, a human image. But if we can only learn from them to consider the ungraspable as possible, we get nearer to God, because we no longer demand to understand him. Because then we no longer measure him with our intelligence, criticize him, deny him, because we cannot reduce him to that human inadequacy which is our clarity.—Therefore I rejoice in *Der gelbe Klang*, and imagine that it would make a tremendous impression on me when performed.

I would have been glad to hear what you think of my *Theory of Harmony*. Have you read it? Then also my article in the *B[laue] R[eiter]*. There are also many things in it that are very close to what you say in your preface to *Der gelbe Klang*.

I hope to hear something from you soon. How is Miss Münter? I owe her an answer to her very delightful letter. It should follow soon. Although: in just a few days I shall be having rehearsals for *Pierrot lunaire*, which will be performed by Mrs. Albertine Zehme on a big tour. But after that, I shall find time for it. So for today, once again: warmest regards to both of you, from my wife as well.

Your Arnold Schoenberg

What about your visit to us in Berlin???

On Vienna and Teaching

3.6 Letter to Guido Adler, September 7, 1912

Guido Adler (1855–1941), succeeded Eduard Hanslick as professor of musicology at the University of Vienna, 1897–1927, where he taught Webern, Rudolf Kolisch, and others who became important in Schoenberg's circle. At Schoenberg's request in 1910, Adler had invited him to prepare continuo realizations and cadenzas for several works for one of the volumes of the Denkmäler der Tonkunst in Österreich *[Monuments of Austrian music], which he edited.*[42] *In a letter to Adler from August 20, 1912, Schoenberg described his struggle to earn a livelihood in Berlin, and in addition to asking Adler for additional assignments for the DTÖ, requested that he bring the* Harmonielehre *to the attention of Hermann Kretzschmar, director of the Hochschule für Musik in Berlin.*

Esteemed Professor:

I thank you most cordially for your kind letter and your promise. Unfortunately, it is not easy for me to "swallow my resentment" towards Vienna as you desire, for it is too long-lived. I must say, however, that apart from this, I would not consider it a good thing to return to Vienna any time soon. I do not at all overestimate the measure of enthusiasm for me now, but even that would be detrimental for me. At present I have to come to terms with myself, and I could not really cope with such overt praise about which I hear on occasion from Vienna. I do not wish to be lulled to sleep, but to remain alert. I want to clarify for myself whether I do amount to something, and who I really am. And thus I would rather hear censure than praise. Not that I would prefer censure, but I am more used to it and know that I need not concern myself with it. By means of it I am able to find myself, and that is what I need at present.

I thank you also heartily for your intention to call Privy Councillor Kretzschmar's attention towards me. I only hope that your remark that you had recommended me at one time especially for harmony and counterpoint does not mean that you will recommend me only for these subjects. The reason is this: that, as I truly hope, my real calling is as a composer; hence I ought to be most suited for teaching composition. N.B. which modern composer (with the possible exception of Strauss and Pfitzner) would be more suitable than I, who, to vary a remark by O. J. David (an "educated German-Bohemian"), am an educated Brahmsian, Beethovenian, or Mozartian? But I think, if you would be willing to read the chapter in my *Harmonielehre* on choral harmonization (it is quite short), you could easily conclude that I have considerable insight on questions of form. It would please me very much if you would be willing to make this little effort.

Again, I thank you with all my heart, and ask you to remember me to your family.

With cordial regards,

Your Arnold Schoenberg

On Life in Berlin and *Pierrot*

3.7 *Letter to Berg, October 3, 1912*

Dear friend,

I am very busy with rehearsals for *Pierrot lunaire.* In addition, I'm reading proofs for the full score of the Chamber Symphony and have to revise my Mahler lecture, which I'm giving in Berlin on the 13th (on the occasion of *Lied von der Erde*).[43] In between I have orchestrated four

Schubert songs for Frau Culp,[44] some of which were fairly long. And then there are so many people who come by. I usually have more visitors here in a week than in Vienna in 3 months. Truly! There are far more people interested in me here than in Vienna.—The *Pierrot* rehearsals are almost over (20 so far!). The last are on the 5th, 7th, and 8th; on the 9th there is an open dress rehearsal (to which I also invited your sister, who just wrote to me). Then there are at most another one or two rehearsals for the 2nd set of performers. Then the performance on the 16th, which I hope will be excellent. Then comes the tour. I myself will participate in the following cities: Hamburg 19/X, Dresden 24/X, Stettin 25/X, Breslau 31/X, Vienna 2/XI, Leipzig 23/XI. In addition there are Danzig, Munich, Stuttgart, Karlsruhe, Mannheim, Frankfurt, and Graz![45] (For the present!) Those will be conducted by Herr Scherchen. I'll be away a lot for other reasons, too. On 28 and 30 November I'm conducting *Pelleas* in Amsterdam and The Hague, on 21 December in Petersburg. (Bodanzky is doing it in Mannheim and Mengelberg in Frankfurt).[46] On top of that, Specht wants to do *Pelleas* or the Chamber Symphony in Vienna.[47] But I don't know what's happening with my chamber music this year. For the moment it seems to be in hibernation. Likewise the songs. Strange, that no quartet other than Rosé has played both of my quartets. Apparently they are too difficult for everyone.—I already have a few students here, too. On the whole, I'm not at all dissatisfied.—

Now let me hear some time what you're up to! Do you already have students! Do you have any other work? I hear you had a falling out with Hertzka about the Schreker piano score. Unfortunately that is the fate of all piano scores: the first are always too difficult. A few years later, when it is easier to prepare a less difficult one, no one minds any more. I had the same experience with the piano scores I did for Zemlinsky. And Zemlinsky got an unusable (?) one from Bodanzky, after which Zemlinsky prepared an unusable (?) one for himself. Cheer up, dear Berg! Your score really is too difficult. You remember I warned you. The *Gurrelieder* score is also too difficult. But that doesn't matter. You'll make a simpler one next time.—A pity though that you yourself don't offer to prepare the simplified score for Schreker. But that's no great misfortune. Hertzka will give you other jobs.—

What about your compositions? Have you finished anything? Wouldn't you like to show it to me? Wouldn't you like to come visit me with it?—I was horrified at your wife's misfortune this summer. Stupidly enough, I kept forgetting to ask how she was. I hope she has completely recovered by now.—I'm not working—that is to say, composing—at all. I probably won't get to it this winter. It seems that my intention to conduct more frequently is to become a reality. I hope so! But don't spread it around!!—Wouldn't you like to get back to composing? Have you ever thought of writing something for the theater? I sometimes think you would be good at that! In any case it could be very stimulating for you. Just see that you don't take the *Dream Plays* away from me, for I'm considering them myself. But some other Strindberg work! I consider that very feasible! Let me hear from you soon and warmest regards to your wife.—

From your Arnold Schoenberg

Warm regards also from my wife!

N.B.: are you absolutely sure you can't come to Berlin for the 14th? *Das Lied von der Erde* is on the 18th. You and your wife could stay with us, as well as the Weberns and Jalowetz. We have plenty of room!

N.B. Another thing: I've long been wanting to ask you, since I can't remember: don't I have another 500 kronen "coming" from this *Kommerzialrat* Redlich? Or from Frau Mauthner?[48] If so, then surely this would be the time to "sue for it"!! I could use it. Perhaps you'll take care of it right away—

Warm regards

Schoenberg

On the Performance of *Sprechstimme*

3.8 Preface to the Score of Pierrot lunaire

The half-sung, half-spoken vocal technique of Sprechstimme *had been developed at the end of the nineteenth century in melodramas by Engelbert Humperdinck and others.*[49] *In addition to* Pierrot, *Schoenberg used it in the melodrama in* Gurrelieder, *the choral scenes of* Die glückliche Hand, *and later works, including* Moses und Aron *and the* Ode to Napoleon.[50] *That the ongoing controversy about the proper performance of* Sprechstimme *admits no simple solution is suggested by the carefully nuanced performance indications Schoenberg adds in the scores of* Pierrot *and* Die glückliche Hand. *In the first section of "Der Dandy," Op. 21, No. 3, for example, the following instructions to the "Rezitation" appear: "spoken," "whispered tonelessly," "spoken with tone," "sung," "almost sung, with some tone."*

In the 1949 essay "This is My Fault," Schoenberg returned to his closing remarks in this preface concerning the performer's role in interpreting the text:

In the Preface to *Pierrot lunaire,* I had demanded that performers ought not to add illustrations and moods of their own derived from the text. In the epoch after the First World War, it was customary for composers to surpass me radically even if they did not like my music. Thus when I had asked not to add external expression and illustration, they understood that expression and illustration were out, and that there should be no relation whatsoever to the text. There were now composed songs, ballets, operas and oratorios in which the achievement of the composer consisted in strict aversion against all that his text presented.

What nonsense![51]

The melody given in the *Sprechstimme* by means of notes is not, except for isolated exceptions that are specially marked, intended for singing. The task of the performer is to transform it into a speech-melody, taking into account the given pitch. This is achieved by:

I. Keeping very closely to the rhythm as if you were singing, i.e. with no more freedom than would be allowed with a singing melody;

II. Becoming aware of the difference between singing tone and speaking tone: the singing unalterably stays on the pitch, whereas the speaking tone gives the pitch but immediately leaves it again by falling or rising. However, the performer has to be very careful not to adopt a *singsong* way of speaking. That is not intended at all. In no way should one strive for realistic, natural speech. Quite on the contrary, the difference between ordinary speaking and the kind of speaking involved in a musical form should become obvious. But at the same time it must never be reminiscent of singing.

Incidentally, I would like to make the following comment on the performance:

It is never the task of the performers to recreate the mood and character of the individual pieces on the basis of the meaning of the words, but solely on the basis of the music. To the extent that the tone-painting-like rendering of the events and feelings given in the text was important to the author, it is found in the music anyway. Where the performer finds it is lacking, he should abstain from presenting something that was not intended by the author. Otherwise he would be detracting rather than adding.

On Modern Man and Religion

3.9 Letter to Richard Dehmel, December 13, 1912

Schoenberg is responding here to an appreciative letter Dehmel had written after hearing a performance of Verklärte Nacht. *The spiritual and religious concerns that emerge in this letter became increasingly central for Schoenberg over the next decade, evident especially in a series of unfinished works, including the setting of Balzac's* Seraphita, *a Choral Symphony, and* Die Jakobsleiter *(see especially 3.13, 3.16, 3.22). Rather than preparing a new oratorio text as Schoenberg requested in the letter, Dehmel sent a poem that was later used in the symphony fragment.*

Dear Mr. Dehmel,

I cannot tell you how glad I am to be directly in touch with you at last. For your poems have had a decisive influence on my development as a composer. They were what first made me try to find a new tone in the lyrical mood. Or rather, I found it even without looking, simply by reflecting in music what your poems stirred up in me. People who know my music can bear witness to the fact that my first attempts to compose settings for your poems contain more of what has subsequently developed in my work than there is in many a much later composition. So you will understand that the regard in which I hold you is therefore both cordial and—above all—*grateful.* And now I have had the pleasure of meeting you in Hamburg, where your great kindness at once made me feel at home though I was a stranger in that city.[52] And here now is your very kind letter, which at last gives me courage to ask you a question that has long been in my mind. It is this. For a long time I have been wanting to write an oratorio on the following subject: modern man, having passed through materialism, socialism, and anarchy and, despite having been an atheist, still having in him some residue of ancient faith (in the form of superstition), wrestles with God (see also Strindberg's *Jacob Wrestling*) and finally succeeds in finding God and becoming religious. Learning to pray! It is *not* through any action, any blows of fate, least of all through any love of woman, that this change of heart is to come about. Or at least these should be no more than hints in the background, giving the initial impulse. And above all: the mode of speech, the mode of thought, the mode of expression, should be that of modern man; the problems treated should be those that harass us. For those who wrestle with God in the Bible also express themselves as men of their own time, speaking of their own affairs, remaining within their own social and intellectual limits. That is why, though they are artistically impressive, they do not offer a subject for a modern composer who fulfills his obligations.

Originally I intended to write the words myself. But I no longer think myself equal to it. Then I thought of adapting Strindberg's *Jacob Wrestling.* Finally I came to the idea of beginning with positive religious belief and intended adapting the final chapter, "The Ascent into Heaven," from Balzac's *Seraphita.* But I could never shake off the thought of "Modern Man's Prayer," and I often thought: If only Dehmel . . . !

Is there any chance of your taking an interest in something of this kind? Let me say at once: if you should think it possible, it would not be merely superfluous but actually a mistake to write the text with any thought of the music in mind. It should be as free as if there had never been any question of its being set to music. For a work by Dehmel is something that I—being in such profound sympathy with every word— can set to music just as it stands. There would have to be only one limitation: considering the average speed of my music I do not think that the words for a full-length work should much exceed the equivalent of 50 or, at most, 60 printed pages. On the contrary, that would almost be too much. I dare say that is a great difficulty. But is it an insuperable one?

I should be very grateful if you would write and tell me what you think. I really do not know whether I am not asking too much. But my excuse is: I must write this music! For this is something I have to say.

Now let me once more thank you most warmly for your very kind letter and above all for the wonderful poem that you appended to it. May I add one more request? Can I have a photograph of you?

I remain, with most cordial esteem and regard,

yours very sincerely,

Arnold Schoenberg

Preparations for a Concert ("Skandalkonzert")

3.10 Letter to the Academic Society for Literature and Music in Vienna, March 10, 1913

Since its formation in 1908, the Academic Society for Literature and Music in Vienna had presented concerts and lectures by such figures as Adolf Loos, Oskar Kokoschka, and the novelists Stefan Zweig and Thomas Mann.[53] In November 1912 the society had sponsored Schoenberg's lecture on Gustav Mahler, along with a concert that included the premiere of the Six Little Piano Pieces, Op. 19, played by Rudolf Réti. A photograph of Schoenberg taken in Prague on this trip is given at the beginning of this chapter. This letter concerns plans for a concert on March 31, 1913, since known as the "Skandalkonzert," due to the altercations that broke out during Webern's Six Pieces for Orchestra, Op. 6, and intensified during songs two and three of Berg's Altenberg Lieder. *In reaction to the widely reported event, Berg wrote to Schoenberg: "Of the latest insults, the following is of interest and almost gratifying: Reitler (the 2nd music critic of the* Neue Freie Presse)[54] *said 'that Korngold and he had decided not to attend any concerts that include the names Schönberg—Webern and Berg!' Thank Heavens!! (That reminds me of a scene in the concert: after my first song someone shouted into the uproar: 'Quiet, here comes the 2nd picture postcard!' And after the words 'plötzlich ist alles aus!' [suddenly it is all over!] someone else shouted loudly: 'Thank Heavens!') By the way, it's interesting that the ushers sided with those who where hissing and laughing. Someone from the audience wanted to evict my student Kassowitz, who was applauding heartily, and two ushers were actually about to do it! Many people threw small change at the people applauding in the standing room section—as payment for the claqueurs—Yes, that's Vienna! You are so right, dear Herr Schön-*

*berg! Your revulsion against Vienna has always been justified and I see—unfortu-
nately too late—how wrong I was to have tried to reconcile you to Vienna, dear
Herr Schönberg. It's true! One can't hate this 'city of song' enough!!"*[55] *The concert
came only a week after the triumphant premiere of* Gurrelieder, *on March 23,
under Franz Schreker.*

Erhard Buschbeck (1889–1960), who had been in charge of the literature
section of the society since 1911, had also taken an active interest in the Schoenberg circle. The "Skandalkonzert" marked the end of his involvement with the
society, which was disbanded the following spring. Buschbeck was forced to appear in court and pay a fine for striking a member of the audience.[56]

Dear Mr. Buschbeck:

here is the program and the order:
I. Webern: 6 Pieces for Orchestra
II. Berg: 2 Orchestral Songs (Herr Boruttau)
III. Schönberg: Chamber Symphony Op. 9
IV. Zemlinsky: 4 Orchestral Songs[57]
V. Mahler: *Kindertotenlieder*
The following reasons were decisive for the order:
1. the first three numbers in the program are relatively dangerous.
Webern is the most dangerous, the Chamber Symphony relatively the
least dangerous. Therefore it is good if the public—while it is still fresh
and patient at the beginning—must swallow the Webern first: the bitterest
pill in this concert. Berg will have a milder effect; the Chamber Symphony will certainly not be a success, but they will behave decently out of
respect. The Zemlinsky should be very effective, and the *Kindertotenlieder*
are a sure thing.

Thus, in any case, it is the most practical.

For artistic reasons I would have liked to have placed some things
differently: Webern more in the middle, the Chamber Symphony at the
end. But it is preferable to me to send the concert audience away under
the impression of the *Kindertotenlieder;* and besides, a different placement
of the *Kindertotenlieder* would hardly have been possible without doing
harm to the Berg and Zemlinsky. But in the end: artistic reasons are not a
consideration with such a mixed program since it is a potpourri, and thus
such artistic concerns must give way.

I believe that they are all quite well placed.

Berg will be helpful with the exact titles of the pieces by Berg,
Webern, and Zemlinsky.

Take care that Webern's Orchestra Pieces are available at the box
office. Perhaps you can also manage to have some music stores put them

on display. In any case, they must definitely be available that evening to the public (for 1 mark). Possibly someone from your society should take care of the sales. That's what Wymetal did once with my First Quartet.

Why did you publicize the *Tristan* Prelude? I had certainly already said that I couldn't do it!! Thus the cancellation is still doing damage!

I shall be in Vienna early Wednesday at the latest. Perhaps Tuesday evening.

Saturday (the 22nd) I shall travel to Prague, staying with Zemlinsky (Prague II. Hawliczekgasse 9)

Warm regards,

Schoenberg

On Repetition, Art, and Kitsch

3.11 "Why New Melodies Are Difficult to Understand," October 10, 1913

This short essay was published in Die Konzertwoche *(1914) in Vienna, where it came to the attention of the music theorist Heinrich Schenker, who in turn attacked Schoenberg in a published commentary from 1915 on Beethoven's Piano Sonata, Op. 111: "Never once in his unspeakable miserable incompetence does he recognize the repetitions in the works of our masters; there he flails at all those who cannot or will not sink as rapidly with him into the depths of his ignorance. . . . What do such musicians know of 'progress,' musicians who are still comparable to unborn children? Let them only peddle their so-called 'modernity' like shopkeepers; but, finally, they should leave undisturbed our masters' eternal modernity."[58]*

Every melody results from the repetition of a more or less varied basic motive. The more primitive, the more artless the melody is, then the more modest the variation and more numerous the repetitions. The lower the demands which may be put upon the capacity for comprehension, the quicker the tempo of repetitions, then the more inferior must be its inner organization. Since indeed every genuinely new melody, as a premise of its newness, must deal with the preexistent lower organisms, the melody uses either hardly new basic motives in fewer or more artful variations, therefore developing itself more quickly, or it uses entirely new motives, which it develops slowly in perhaps many variations. It cannot be within the interest of art to go forward systematically, i.e. always first presenting the very simplest usable motive in the broadest acceptable manner and only then, when all the simpler things are settled, turning to new motives or to quicker methods of development. Art is content with typical cases: it leaves the rest to kitsch and popular tunes; it passes over some steps in the process, and, seemingly abruptly, places new forms beside old ones. Its characteristics, always in relation to what came before, are the following: something known is assumed to be known and is therefore no longer mentioned; the characteristics of the new stipulate new forms of variation (whose methods also wear out); less is conceded to the need to a give a visible and slowly pursuable image to the affinity of the cohesion-shaping elements. It can be assumed that a perceived cohesion holds, even if the manner of connection is not compositionally explicit. One saves space and expresses not with ten words what can be said with two.

Such "brevity" is disagreeable to him who wants to enjoy his comfort. But why should the privileges of those who think too slowly be preserved?

Plans for a Symphony, Relations with Universal Edition

3.12 From a Letter to Alma Mahler, April 1, 1914

In one of his later essays on the origin of twelve-tone composition, Schoenberg described as an important first step his "plans for a great symphony of which Die Jakobsleiter *should be the last movement. I had sketched many themes, among them one for a scherzo which consisted of all the twelve tones. An historian will probably one day find in the exchange of letters between Webern and me how enthusiastic we were about this."[59] A page from the symphony showing the twelve-tone theme is given in fig. 3-1. The outline given below in 3.13 shows Schoenberg's first conception for this massive choral symphony, a work that occupied him between 1914 and 1915, before it gradually evolved into the oratorio* Die Jakobsleiter. *A considerable number of musical and textual sketches and drafts survive, one of the earliest being the scherzo fragment dated May 27, 1914.*

[. . .]

I am very pleased that next year I shall be conducting *Gurrelieder* in Amsterdam. And Wood (London), who also was the first to perform Mahler in London and who just recently performed and repeated (!!) *Das Lied von der Erde* (the G-major song even had to be repeated in the concert!), wants to perform the *Gurrelieder.*[60]

I am now also on a better footing with Hertzka. We have fashioned a new contract that is essentially more favorable than the old one, and Hertzka is now really very nice to me. By the way, my music is now finally appearing. Still to come this year: *Pierrot, George-Lieder,* Monodrama [*Erwartung*], Harmonium-Celesta-Lied [*Herzgewächse*], and next year the rest: *Glückliche Hand,* "Seraphita Lied" [first movement of the Four Orchestral Songs, Op. 22, No. 1, dated October 6, 1913], and other songs.

It is now my intention after a long time once again to write a large work. A kind of symphony. I have already felt it; I can see it already, now perhaps this summer it will come to something. For a long time I have been yearning for a style for large forms. My most recent development had denied this to me. Now I feel it again and I believe it will be something completely new, more than that, something that will say a great deal. There will be choirs and solo voices; that is certainly nothing new. Today that is already allowed to us. But what I can feel of the content (this is not yet completely clear to me) is perhaps new in our time: here I shall manage to give personal things an objective, general form, behind which the author as person may withdraw.

Perhaps it will be different! Perhaps I am talking about it too much, before it is completely clear to me. One hopes that won't harm me. I believe I shouldn't do it. Thus I shall stop.

I hope you are well and wish to have the pleasure of seeing you soon. With the greatest respect and devotion

Yours,

Arnold Schoenberg

A Choral Symphony

3.13 Plan for a Symphony (1914–1915)

All the movements but the first of the projected symphony were intended to include chorus and soloists. In addition to Schoenberg's texts for the "Death Dance of Principles" (see 3.17) and Die Jakobsleiter *(see 3.22), the movements included excerpts (referred to by page numbers in the sketch) from Richard Dehmel,* Schöne wilde Welt *(Berlin: S. Fischer, 1913), the Indian writer Rabindranath Tagore's* Gitanjali *(Leipzig: Wolff, 1914), and the Bible (Berlin: Britische une Auslandische Bibelgesellschaft, 1907).*

Part I

1st Movement		Change of Life (looking backward, looking to the future; gloomy, defiant, withdrawn). All motives that later become important are presented.
2nd Movement		(Scherzo) Joy of Life
I.	Part	Scherzo with 2 Trios
II.	Part	Reprise in its entirety with voices
	a)	Dehmel, *Schöne wilde Welt,* p. 10, "Call of Joy"
	b)	Dehmel, *Schöne wilde Welt,* p. 70, "Marriage of the Gods"
	c)	Dehmel, *Schöne wilde Welt,* p. 117, "Aeonic Hour"
3rd Movement		("Allegretto") "Bourgeois God": Dehmel Cantata, *Schöne wilde Welt,* Oratorium natale "Celebration of Creation," p. 61. Orchestra: all flutes, clarinets, violas, and harps.

4th Movement	"Interlude"
1)	Unsatisfied: The Bourgeois God does not suffice.
2)	Tagore No. 86, "Death of the Servant"
	No. 88, "Deity of the Ruined Temple" (solo vocal quartet!!)
	No. 92, "I Know a Day Will Come"
	No. 100, "I Dive Down into the Depth of the Ocean"
5th Movement	Psalm: Biblical[61]

Part II

6th Movement	"Death-Dance of Principles" (basic ideas)
1)	Burial
2)	Funeral oration (quasi) short sketch of intervening events with *offstage orchestra* from "Call of Joy" (See No. 2 above).
3)	Death-Dance
	Tagore No. 88
	Close: Prayer

	Isaiah	58	p. 711
		66	718
	Jeremiah	7	726
		17	737

| V. Movement[62] | The faith of the "disillusioned one." The union of objective skeptical consciousness of reality with faith. In the simple is concealed the mystical. |

Reactions to the War

3.14 From a Letter to Alma Mahler, August 28, 1914

Like many of his contemporaries, Schoenberg was initially extremely enthusiastic about the war. In a collection of materials he later labeled "My War Psychosis (1914) and That of the Others," he assembled newspaper items about the conduct of the war by the hostile nations—including accounts of the use of dumdum bullets, designed to cause severe wounds, and a Russian attack on a hospital train— along with many clippings concerning the political implications of the war. He wrote an essay, dated September 14, 1914, about the importance of training all citizens for combat, starting with their entry into school, so that they would be ready to defend the nation. As in his letter to Alma Mahler below, many of the fragmentary jottings in "My War Psychosis" discuss the war in cultural and artistic terms: "I can understand that the governments of our enemies find it necessary to transform their unpopular war into a war of peoples through which they stir up hatreds. But can it really be that intellectuals from neutral countries are labeling as barbarian the land of Goethe, Kant, Wagner, Schopenhauer, Beethoven, Bach (to cite only six personages who could not be surpassed in any foreign country)? Don't they find this situation intolerable?"[63]

Meanwhile, you have certainly already heard of the glorious victory of the Germans against France, England, and Belgium. It is among the most wonderful things that have happened. But it does not surprise me: it is not any different from the war of the Greeks against the Persians. And I'm certain our Austria is approaching a new, more beautiful future as well, if the auspicious start of the first battle against the Russians meets with an equally auspicious continuation. Then we shall possess what we have fundamentally lacked: self-confidence, and with it the ability to value the seriousness and dignity of our achievements; and also to defend them! One hopes all will continue to go well. What was at first harder for me to endure, and what I found astonishingly shocking, was England's attitude. But now, when Japan (and perhaps also America) have shown their true face as our enemy in a less whitewashed manner, my eyes are opened about so many of my earlier feelings that I had against foreigners. My friends know it, I have often said to them, I never had any use for *all* foreign music. It always seemed to me stale, empty, disgusting, cloying, false, and awkward. Without exception. Now I know who the French, English, Russians, Belgians, Americans, and Serbians are: barbarians! The music said that to me long ago. [. . .] For a long time this music has been a declaration of war, an attack on Germany. And if someone in a foreign country had to show apparent respect to us—since they must have sensed with each individual who was with them (even Strauss and Reger) that he was better than their whole shabby nation—there was nevertheless an element of arrogance along with it, which I have always felt, but which is only now consciously apparent to me. But now comes the reckoning. Now we shall send these mediocre purveyors of kitsch back into slavery, and they shall learn to honor the German spirit and to worship the German God. I would very much like to hear from you. How is your health? And how are things going with your child? Please write me a few lines. We are now all alone in Berlin; without acquaintances, without contacts. For my students have all enlisted, and I have no other contacts.

A "Belief in Higher Powers"

3.15 From the War-Clouds Diary, 1914–1915

Schoenberg began this diary on September 24, 1914, and over the next three months, though with decreasing regularity, made daily observations on the weather, sometimes adding colored-pencil drawings of cloud formations. After dropping the project for several months, he made a few more entries the following spring. The importance Schoenberg places on direct, intuitive impressions of the meteoric conditions is closely related to the creative aesthetic he expressed to Busoni and Kandinsky, but it also demonstrates the connection between Schoenberg's compositional ideals and his superstitious and mystical leanings, evident as well in his lifelong numerological concerns. But in a letter of June 15, 1915, he responded to Berg's concerns about the bad numerological omens associated with his enlistment (in connection with Berg's own fateful number, 23): "Everyone has a number like that, but it doesn't necessarily have to be unlucky, it's simply one of the numbers that come into question. In connection with other numbers I'm sure it can have other and more favorable meanings. [. . .] In any case you must see that you become less dependent on these lucky and unlucky numbers by doing your best to ignore them!"[64]

War-Clouds Diary; started September 24, 1914

Many people, like myself today, will have tried to interpret the events of the war by the sky, since finally the belief in higher powers and also in God has returned. Unfortunately only now the thought occurred to me to put down my impressions in writing. But I shall do so from now on and hope to find some coincidences once more accurate reports are available, since so far a number of war events could be premonitioned by the "mood" of the sky.

Repeatedly I noticed that "golden glitter," "victory wind," a "deep-blue sky," "bloody clouds" (at sunset) always preceded victorious German events.

Likewise, heavy deterioration of the weather with storm and rain, deep black clouds of eerie impression anticipated bad turns at the Austro-Russian front. The storm lasting two days, which coincided with the retreat of the right wing of the German Army, should also be mentioned here.

I must note, however, that a bloody sky does not always create the impression of unfavorable events. Therefore, I intend to record in the *first* place the impression, secondly the actual condition, and thirdly, as often as possible, draw a little sketch.

Arnold Schoenberg

September 24: about 10:45 a.m.:
   icy-cold mood, *like in a circus before a very*
daring stunt: silence, tension, no wind;
impression of the sky is at first predominantly
clear, pure; only later I observe a slowly expanding cloud streak.
   Total impression: a daring operation, which began under
auspicious circumstances.
12:40 p.m. <u>uncertain</u>; very cool; still tense, the
clouds on the right larger; to the left still clear sky. Very little wind.
7:20 p.m. not unpleasant
Stars in the bright sky, clouds in the background.

9:30 p.m. *fair*
entirely clear sky. Stars.

September 25
11:45 a.m.
slightly hazy, but still sun. Faint light,
only like an immeasurably thin veil of haze.
Unfocused shadows. No impression
2:30 cloudy; overcast, no sun.
During the last days, it was unusually overcast at this time;
it even rained sometimes, and later usually turned fair again.
6:20 p.m.: not quite clear; to the right dazzling: like a radiant hope.
to the left gloomy: gray, with some red (evening glow) extending in
front
6:40 p.m.: the red-golden gleam by which I am always favorably impressed
between the two houses behind the branches of the tree.
7:40 p.m.: cloudless, stars: victory sky

[. . .]

April 11, 1915, about 6:30
I have discontinued these records because what I was afraid of happened: from the moment I wanted to make notes, I felt self-conscious and
therefore could not arrive at a convincing impression. Nevertheless, I was
able to observe every time that the exceedingly numerous, violent storms
of this year seemingly always coincided with unfavorable events.

Today I make notes because the day is as beautiful as those of last
autumn which I especially noticed. And because yesterday the sky was
especially peculiar.

—half an hour later it is raining! But very strangely; in the background it's still bright and in the foreground are very black rain clouds.

Concerns about the War; More on the Symphony

3.16 From a Letter to Zemlinsky, January 9, 1915

*Schoenberg is responding to a letter Zemlinsky had sent on December 31, 1914,
commenting on the bad war reports from France, Serbia, and Russia, and his
concern that the Czechs had welcomed news of German defeats and had looked
forward to the arrival of the Russians.[65] Along with the clear evidence of Schoenberg's growing disillusionment with the war, the letter is particularly important
for the remark he makes about the symphony as again being a " 'worked' [gear-
beitetes] piece." This marks a significant shift from his earlier rejection of construction, technique, and conscious intervention in the creative act, thus laying
the groundwork for the compositional developments of the war years and after.*

Now to other parts of your letter: although I am very pessimistic, I don't share your anxiety concerning the war situation. You are probably surrounded by many defeatists, and it is certainly understandable that, in Prague, one is anxious. There may well be many Czechs who think just as you describe. But I don't believe that such thoughts can be turned to action. Above all, I have a certain feeling that a decisive change will now come directly from *Austria.* I can't substantiate this; it is merely a matter of feeling. But I believe: *there is a brilliant commander among us,* who until now has been absent from *all warfare.* And now I hope he will show himself. I have never much liked Potiorek. I couldn't believe that he was appointed general music director of the city of Prague and I was very indignant about that. But I have the feeling that the casualties in Serbia, terrible as they are, do not mean much overall.

We spent Christmas Eve very pleasantly. The children are really very nice and give us a lot of joy with their happiness. Your presents arrived on time and pleased us all very much. The children should have written and thanked you themselves. But they were so lazy over the holidays that they have thoroughly forgotten to do it. So I'll heartily thank you here and now on their behalf—Of course I'll write straight away to Hertzka. Unfortunately he gives me absolutely nothing. It seems that he basically does the opposite of what I say to him.—We manage tolerably with what we have—but not entirely. Nevertheless, we cope. Do you know that Webern was retained for a medical reexamination? He is now taking an officers' course and is very much looking forward to being in service. One hopes, however, we'll have peace before that. I have a strong feeling that it will come soon.—Berg, Jalowetz, Stein, Linke were not retained.[66]

Hertzka has already sent me your songs, and we have also already sung through them. They are very nice; quite unique. You haven't changed anything in them? The key, though, struck me as odd.[67]

If Hertzka wants to play your quartet in the *Tonkünstlerverein* I'm of the opinion that it only makes sense if the Rosé Quartet performs it. Certainly no others. I would *in no way* permit that. In your position, I would rather rehearse the work in *Prague* with the rank and file from your orchestra and invite Hertzka to a performance. (Suggest this to him!) He won't want to hear it (or, at best, in order to read the score of my Second Quartet at the same time, while having trouble with the page turning), but he will see the kind of success it has. Presumably he has someone in Vienna, probably a rival of mine, to whose advice he listens. Intelligent as he is otherwise, and capable of being so nice, he is in that respect painfully stupid.

I am working only a little. For a time I set about all sorts of things, but at present everything has again been at a standstill for a long while. I worked on a theory of modern harmony then, for my symphony, I also began to write texts for the third and fifth movements. Two of my orchestral songs on Rilke are ready [see 3.19], but I think that I shall certainly return to work on my symphony in the near future. There are still major difficulties and a few preliminary studies before I can go right to the whole. It will again be a "worked" [gearbeitetes] piece, in contrast to my many purely impressionistic pieces of recent times.

Otherwise I occupy myself with hobbies: carpentry, wallpapering, book-binding, putting things in order. I've produced many useful things and in that way I kill some time productively. Have you read the last *Fackel?* He says: . . . . "In these great times, . . . , which I knew when they were *this* (!!) small. . . . "[68]

Now I have only one wish: Peace! It's high time for it. The war might well have cost so much already that the greatest victories would not be able to compensate for it. Since only a few of those waging war are motivated by pure, ideal reasons (which?), it must soon come to an end. That's why I believe that peace (perhaps one without decisive outcome?) is near.

Do you already have my George Lieder and the *Pierrot* score? If not, please write to me!! And another thing: many, many warm greetings to you and yours. How is Hansi? (We greet you all a thousand times.) And Ida? Yours

A Text from the Symphony

3.17 "Death Dance of Principles," January 15, 1915

The text given below corresponds to the outline for the sixth movement of the symphony plan (3.13.) In Fin-de-siècle Vienna, *Carl Schorske describes the symphony as a celebration of the death of the "Bourgeois God," with the movements based on the Dehmel texts associating "the Bourgeois God with nature in a Festival of Creation . . . in the spirit of the* fin de siècle *[as] . . . a kind of paean to nature parturient under the sign of Eros." Schorske interprets the "Death Dance" as marking a progression to a higher stage, with Schoenberg presenting the "dying bourgeois world as on the edge between surfeit and void": "Schoenberg had shared Dehmel's pan-naturistic vision in his early years. Now he assimilates it into his plan only to subvert it. In the fourth movement he introduces a contrary idea: 'The Bourgeois God does not suffice.' The symphony's whole second part, entitled 'Death-Dance of Principles,' dramatizes the burial of and funeral oration for the Bourgeois God. The death dance brings the slim hope that the death of meaning is only a dream, for 'man likes to live and believe; to be blind!' "[69]*

There is no evidence that Schoenberg composed any music for the text; he did, however, include it in the 1926 publication Texts. *While the "Death Dance of*

Principles" is most closely related to the text of Die Jakobsleiter, *it also shares features with* Die glückliche Hand, *including such specific events as the chorus of laughter, as well as the fundamental conflict of the "worldly" and "otherworldly." Yet, as suggested in his April 1, 1914, letter to Alma Mahler (3.12), the personal elements are now presented in a much more objective form.*

(*Orchestral prelude, short sketch of an event, in a hard dry tone, then burial, funeral oration, all very short, short pause, after this the toll of a steeple bell offstage, which becomes progressively louder and faster in the course of the following, turning gradually into frenzied pealing.*)

Twelve chimes—thirteen! fourteen—fifteen!—Oh! What does it mean? Sixteen, seventeen!—Shall it be midnight twice today? Or still more often? The midnight of midnight? The blackest? Darkest?—(*The ringing stops.*)

(*Pause*)

The darkest—it appears never to have been light. The darkness is eternal; it was, is, and will be. In the beginning there was darkness, it always was and always will be—that is the infinite, the unimaginable, because it does not stand out from a background: behind the darkness is more darkness. And the distance is not darker than the foreground. A sound! Without any distinction.—

(*Pause*)

Is something alive?—

(*Pause*)

Nothing!—

(*Pause*)

Yet—something—one hears it—everything—everything can be heard—too much; too much at the same time.—
Everything is alive; everything dead is living;
it races, rages, storms, roars,
it pricks, burns, pains,
gives pleasure and pain,
is indifferent and exciting,
true and invented,—
  it lives!
Too much—it is as unbearable as
the infinite light.

One hears too much!

Now one can make a distinction. One thing is louder than all the others. All the others are actually quite soft. Scarcely audible. The one swells up:

(Soft laughter)

Ha, ha, ha,—*(louder and louder).*

Ha, ha, ha,—*(turning into a mocking deafening noise).*

Ha, ha, ha. . . .

A sound of joy! *(roaring laughter).*

Ha, ha, ha. . . .

How warm and sunny it is, so pretty, playful and charming; *(parodying)* so complete and final. Some corner considers itself the world and thinks it is really something. And perceives. Perceives that that is joy, nothing else. But the world?—Who perceives it? As soon as we begin to make a distinction we stop seeing. The blind feel and are capable of joy.

The darkness becomes visible—!

Is it that the joy is in the right?

The darkness is really fairly bright—and in the background it is still brighter!

Or actually pale—.

Or is that not trite?

One can no longer distinguish sight, touch, and taste. One distinguishes too much!

The paleness also pierces; and cries and stinks.

Oh! it can also lie—

Oh; and it also looks like the truth—*(with ironic pathos; preaching.)*

We realize that it lives; by its paleness and flatness; in the abundance of its indistinctness; in the concealment of each sense; in the strong impression of pain and pleasure. *(Making a transition.)* The paleness and flatness now dissolving into colors and forms; one calls this unification . . . *(descriptively).* It crumbles more and more and is in motion. *(More devoutly.)* So many and each single thing seems important . . . *(warmer).* Now it sings; each sings something different thinking that it sings the same thing; and, in fact, sounds in one dimension together *(surprised)* in another diverse. In a third and fourth it sounds still otherwise, which one cannot express. It has countless dimensions and each one is perceivable *(increasing).* And all disappear to some place where they could be found. It would be easy to pursue them, for now one has their conception. . . .

It grows; actually, it turns. But that is the same. For in growing it does not get larger and in turning it seemingly always shows the same side.

One should truly be able to understand that, since one now has the conception!

Is it yet only a sound! Without any distinction.

A sound? Or is it no sound? Or are there many sounds? All? Is it infinite or nothing?

Impossible!

The multiplicity before was easier to understand than the oneness now. It is overwhelming. It is magnificent, because it is overwhelming. Each sings something different, thinking that it sings the same thing, but it actually sounds multi-voiced, five-, six-, or only three-voiced. Or are there more? (*Making a transition.*) Or fewer? Or nothing?—That is really laughable!—

One sees the threads! Everything runs on tracks. And comical—for they never emerge where they should. For the most part underneath. A few emerge on top—but that will make little sense either. The whole is frightfully ordered. And just as much disorder. If one demands sense. All is equally order and disorder. One cannot distinguish it, much less determine it.

It is perhaps overwhelming, but one has no image. One has that only if one blows away everything around the framework.

Now the colors fade away.

The forms wear out; in rank and file—here at least order; but senseless order—. Away with it; into paleness! No, that is not pale, but immaterial.

But neither is it the purpose, for it looks as if it is situated above the whole, under which is nothing. Nevertheless, it does not hover, but adheres to something that is not there.

It gets bigger—from inside out! How it becomes inflated—now it fills the entire space with its emptiness—as if it will burst.

No, it does not burst.

It appears to have no pressure—perhaps for this reason it is stable.

Yet not—it bursts!

But it is still there, even though it burst.

And nothing was seen or heard as it burst; no pressure, no movement, no change.

It is overwhelming perhaps because it produces no image. By no means is it especially attractive.

(*Precocious.*) That is also entirely unintelligible; inconsistent; the spiritual world collapses for no reason at all; or bursts. Seemingly without any reason. There are causes, but reasons? An event is no reason. There are enough events. Very nice ones even; so to say "sufficient ones." Enough to destroy a sensual world. But one believes one has to do justice to the spiritual world when one ignores it in a noble way. But why has the spiritual world exploded?

And this is this most ridiculous thing: that it is there again. Or, in the end, is it something else?

Something new?

Look closely! . . .

No! It is the same thing in another form: a sensual world in the form of a spiritual world. (*Preaching.*) Thus one sees how everything spiritual corresponds only with feelings.

Now the old magic begins again.

The preceding was still more amusing. But this wants to be taken seriously in a still different way from that; this demands spiritual devotion! (*Heightening; excited; reluctantly offering resistance.*) The only thing that one appears to be, although one does not know it for certain.

(*Energetic, strong.*) One is not willing to give that! Not at any price.

Let loose! Give freedom, independence!

Indifference! Laughter!

(*Large increase.*) You shall have nothing, nothing. You glutton; you insatiable one.

Ah! Oh! How it lashes, pierces, tortures, torments one.

(*Beginning anew.*) Without mercy.—With its morality, its ethics, its rules and regulations.

"You shall"—but I do not want to. I don't have to!

To the devil with it—that is the most loathsome of all; the most obtrusive. (*Increasing.*) It penetrates the body like a bad smell penetrates the nose. It will not be turned away.—It continually breaks out again of all pores like sweat—as if one produced it oneself. That cannot be!

Is it that this repulsive thing is within us?

Then it is also outside us! Then it is our inner and outer essence.

The protoplasm of which we are a part!

(*Long pause*)

Enough! This is intolerable. . . .

(*Orchestra disappears entirely.*)

All is gone!

(*Thirteen chimes are heard.*)

Thirteen.—Clearly not twelve, but at least a boundary in this emptiness! Remorse remains; but it explains nothing, for it does not name its cause. It is not without repentance, but without a visible image. The spiritual eye is blind to it, the will does not intend to bring it sacrifice.

It is not capable of inducing the smallest renunciation.

Everything that could be its cause, exercises greater allurement; for it is without image.

(Interlude)

A pale hope: one has just awoken, has cheerful or indifferent dream images behind one—actually no real hope; only: hopelessness is forgotten for a few moments; really only forgotten. Nevertheless it refreshes and gives strength: mankind likes to live and believe. Illusion or forgetfulness is enough for him; to be blind!

The darkness recedes—

But the sun is without power.

"A New Path Toward Salvation"

3.18 "Turning Point," Text for a Melodrama for the Second Chamber Symphony (c. 1916)

The following text—which shows Schoenberg's growing self-awareness of the major transformations in his compositional thinking, as well as the increasing importance to him of religion—was found in a sketchbook among materials for the Second Chamber Symphony. He had started composing the Second Chamber Symphony in 1906, shortly after completing the First Chamber Symphony, but only made isolated sketches over the next two years. He returned to the piece in 1911 and then again in 1916, when the melodrama text may have been written. Many years later, in 1939, he again took up the work, completing two movements, which were published as Op. 38. A third movement was left unfinished, and the melodrama text was not set.[70]

To continue on this path was not possible.
A ray of light had illuminated a mourning of both a general
as well as a particular nature. Depending not only on the whims
of its constitution but also on
the whims of outer coincidences, a soul cannot now behave
as unresponsively toward a stroke of luck
as formerly it did toward misery.
Suddenly the soul responds with joyous
exhilaration, then soars with a mighty upsurge,
dreams of blissful fulfillment, sees itself as victor,
storms on, feels its power growing, and
with the illusion of being able to possess a world that
it already imagines it holds, it gathers all its capabilities

to reach in one mighty effort a divine height.

What should have happened out of necessity is taken care of by chance:

when the amassed strength should burst forth, it falters;

a small but insidious event—a speck of dust in the clockwork—can impede its
    progress.

The breakdown is followed by mourning, first of a particular,

then of a general nature. Stemming from external

events, the soul seeks to a find a reason for this,

then seeks within its own constitution.

This is the actual culmination of the breakdown. But this

Does not mean the end; on the contrary, it is a beginning;

A new path toward salvation opens up—the only one, the eternal one.

To find this path was the goal of all former experience.

On Text and Music, Brevity, and Expressionism

3.19 From the "Analysis of the Four Orchestral Songs, Op. 22" (1913–1916), February 1932

Schoenberg composed the Four Orchestral Songs between 1913 and 1916, using texts by Ernest Dowson, for the first movement, and Rilke, for the remaining three.[71] The works were completed in Vienna, following his move back in September 1915 after the outbreak of the war. Although the complete set was published in 1917 by Universal Edition—in an innovative short-score format—the works were not performed until 1932, in a concert in Frankfurt under the direction of Hans Rosbaud with soprano Hertha Reinecke. The analysis given below was prepared for a radio broadcast, accompanied by musical examples on piano and by the full orchestra. Since Schoenberg was unable to travel to Frankfurt because of illness, the lecture was read by Rosbaud for the February 21, 1932, broadcast.

    These remarks make up Schoenberg's only extended commentary on one of his atonal compositions. At the same time, they indicate some of his later strategies for explaining his atonal works from the perspective of his subsequent development, whereby brevity and the use of texts are viewed as temporary solutions to compositional problems solved only by the method of composition with twelve tones.

I composed the Orchestral Songs, Opus 22, in 1915. Their style may best be characterized if I briefly describe the development leading up to and beyond them. About 1908 I had taken the first steps—also with songs—into that domain of composition which is falsely called atonal, and whose distinguishing characteristic is the abandonment both of a tonal center and of the methods of dissonance-treatment that had been customary up to that time. It was this latter feature, as I subsequently ascertained, that occurred if the perception of a dissonance could be ideally equated to that of a consonance.

Yet, indeed, only ideally!—since, in fact, the conscious and unconscious inhibitions in the perception of dissonance existed then and continue still, to a certain degree, to exist not only for the listener, but for the composer as well. Furthermore, while the use of consonances had fulfilled, as it were, the function of shaping form and context, their avoidance was bound to lead to stringent precautionary measures and to require a variety of safeguards.

One of the most important aids to comprehension is clarity of design. *Brevity* facilitates a grasp of the whole; it furthers clarity and it encourages comprehension. Unwittingly, I wrote *unusually short* pieces of music at that time.

Ladies and gentlemen, you have, no doubt, heard that I am a constructor; and I shall not contradict this, since it flatters me—at any rate, it flatters me more to be called a "brain musician" than if I were to be called a blockhead. For I have unwittingly done a number of other right things. There are, of course, various means of different value with which to produce formal cohesion within a piece of music. One of these means, tonal harmony, with its emphasis on tonal centers, guaranteed not only cohesion, but also made for clarity of design by articulating the constituent parts. By not using this device in the new direction that my music had taken, I was compelled, in the first place, to renounce not only the construction of larger forms, but to avoid the employment of larger melodies—as well as all formal musical elements dependent upon the frequent repetition of motifs. It seemed at first impossible to find pertinent substitutes for these through musical means. Unwittingly, and therefore rightly, I found help where music always finds it when it has reached a crucial point in its development. *This, and this alone,* is the origin of what is called Expressionism: a piece of music does not create its formal appearance out of the logic of its *own* material, but, guided by the feeling for internal and external processes, and in *bringing these to expression,* it supports itself on their logic and builds upon that.[72] No new procedure in the history of music!—at each renewal or increase of musical materials, it is assisted by feelings, insights, occurrences, impressions and the like, mainly in the form of poetry—whether it be in the period of the first operas, of the *lied,* or of program music.

At the time that I wrote these Songs, I had overcome the initial difficulties of the new style to a certain extent, even though it was only through composition with 12 tones that the formal possibilities of an absolute music were unleashed and broke through, freed from all admixture of extra-musical elements.

Still, I continued to prefer composing music for texts, and I was still dependent purely upon my feeling for form. And I had to say to myself—and was perhaps entitled to do so—that my feeling for form, modeled on the great masters, and my musical logic, which had been proved in so and so many cases, must guarantee that what I write is formally and logically correct, even if I do not realize it. This consideration, as well as one other, increases the difficulty in making a formal analysis of these Songs.

As always during the first decades of a new style of composing, music theory has in this case not progressed nearly far enough. The other consideration, however, is that compositions for texts are inclined to allow the poem to determine, at least outwardly, their form. To be sure, this tendency can generally be noted less in songs than in dramatic or choral music. Yet here, in my Opus 22, it appears conspicuously, for the abovementioned reasons.

[. . .]

[Schoenberg then goes through the opening theme showing the motivic cohension produced by a returning intervallic pattern in the main lines and in the accompaniment. He also points out in particular the accompaniment to the words "life's passionate sea" (*Lebens wilder See*), and "troublous and dark and stormy though my passage be" (*sei meine Fahrt auch voll von finster Sturm und Weh*).]

I hope I may not have in vain called your attention to a place in the text, for in this regard there are some not unimportant matters of principle to be adduced.

"Passionate sea," "passage," "dark storm," "woe"—: these are words whose representational impact hardly any composer from Bach to Strauss could have resisted—words which could not simply glide past without being reflected by some musical symbol. And yet this place affords a very telling example of a new way to deal with such images. I may say that I was the first to have proceeded in this new manner; the others who imitated it under a misapprehension have, for the most part, concealed this fact—yet, thanks to that very misunderstanding, I am pleased to acquiesce. . . . It had apparently been thought that I took no notice *whatever* of texts, since with me they no longer give rise to sounds like a storm or swords clashing or sardonic laughter. This impression was exaggerated to such a degree that music was composed to *no* text, or at best to a text *other* than the one which was actually being sung. My music, however, took representational words into account in the same way as abstract ones: it furthered the immediate, vivid rendering of the whole and of its parts, according to the measure of their meaning within the whole. Now, if a performer speaks of a passionate sea in a different tone of voice than he might use for a calm sea, my music does nothing else than to provide him with the opportunity to do so, and to support him. The music will not be as agitated as the sea, but it will be *differently* so, as, indeed, the performer will be. Even a painting does not reproduce its whole subject matter; it merely states a motionless condition. Likewise, a word describes an object and its state; a film reproduces it without color, and a color film would reproduce it without organic life. Only music, however, can bestow this last gift, and that is why music may impose a limit on its capacity to imitate—by *placing* the object and its being *before the mind's eye,* through performance.

[. . .]

The third and fourth songs afford their analysis far greater difficulties. I would not, however, want to act as if I were withholding this analysis from you merely because I cannot take for granted so thorough an acquaintance with technical notions as might be desirable. Yet, in fact, this *is* the case, as I will prove to you through an example. Nevertheless, the reason is not that—on the contrary, I believe I could almost be tempted to try to present this difficult matter to you in such a way as to allow it to be grasped readily. But in actual fact I cannot do so. I know that these songs do not dispense with logic—but I cannot prove it.

New Teaching Activities

3.20 Seminar for Composition, September 1, 1917

In the fall of 1917 Schoenberg conducted a series of lectures at the Schwarzwald School, a school primarily for girls, founded by Eugenie Schwarzwald (1873–1940), a long-time supporter of Schoenberg, Kokoschka, and others. According to a letter from Alban Berg to his wife Helene, about a hundred people attended the opening lecture on September 28, 1917.[73] *After an interruption due to Schoenberg's military service in the fall and winter, the courses continued at the school, as well as in more informal meetings at Schoenberg's house in the Viennese suburb of Mödling, where he lived from 1918 until his move to Berlin. The courses covered harmony, counterpoint, form, instrumentation, analysis, and other subjects. Students were asked to pay any amount they thought appropriate. Among the fifty-five students who signed up for the second year of the course (twenty-seven women and twenty-eight men), were Max Deutsch, Olga Novaković, Erwin Ratz, Josef Trauneck, and Viktor Ullmann.*[74] *Many of the concerts of the Society for Private Musical Performances were also held at the Schwarzwald School (see 4.2).*

One learns perfectly only those things for which one has an aptitude. In this case, no particular pedagogic discipline is needed: a model, provoking emulation, suffices; one learns whatever one was created for, without knowing how; one learns as much as one's inborn aptitudes allow.

This carefree way of learning has to be helped out by pedagogic means only because the number of things to be learned is ever on the increase, and the amount of time available correspondingly smaller.

Now, though it is astonishing how many people can in fact reach a "prescribed standard" in matters for which they have little aptitude, there is no denying that the results are but mediocre. This is particularly apparent in the artistic field. At one time, the difference between the very best amateur and the artist might lie not in their respective performances but merely in the fact that the amateur did not earn his daily bread through art; nowadays, there are all too many artists whose performance is amateurish, the only difference being that their sole concern is with breadwinning. The able amateur has, however, become relatively rare.

One main cause is teaching. It asks too much and too little of artist and amateur alike; too little, since in bringing him to the prescribed standard it gives him more than he needs, and so relieves him of the need to find within himself that superabundant energy through which his natural gifts can spread themselves and take on fullness; too much, since by the same token it gives him less than he needs, so paralyzing whatever energies he has, and preventing his becoming even the specialist his aptitude fits him to be.

In art there is but one true teacher: inclination. And this has but one usable assistant: imitation.

In order to pass on to the learner the fruits of these conclusions, reached after twenty years' teaching experience, I have decided to found a

Composition Seminar

at the Schwarzwald School, No. 9, Wallnerstrasse, Vienna I, and to formulate the conditions of admission in such a way that anyone, *rich or poor, artist or amateur, advanced student or beginner,* can take part.

I shall explain the nature of this new organization at a meeting (the date of which shall be announced by the school office). The following may be said provisionally: there shall be nothing omitted from this seminar that a student can learn from a teacher: he will by no means learn less, there will rather be more subjects. But apart from selecting them according to his inclination and his gifts, there shall occur here that which according to my experience in private teaching achieves the best results: constant and unconstrained communication between me and my students. I shall reserve certain regular hours to discuss with them questions they may put before me; we shall play, analyze, discuss, search, and find. They will come when they want and stay only as long as they wish; and it will be my concern to heighten their inclination and thereby to foster their gifts. They shall not feel that they are learning; they will perhaps work, perhaps even toil, but without noticing it. They shall be there as the painting students were once at home in the painter's studio, when through their inclination for this art and out of respect for the Master they endeavored to gain admission into his studio.

Please send the application to the school office before September 15, along with a self-addressed stamped envelope, in which the confirmation of the meeting will be returned.

Vienna, September 1, 1917   Arnold Schoenberg.

On Comprehensibility, Coherence, and the Audience

3.21 *From the treatise* Coherence, Counterpoint, Instrumentation, Instruction in Form, *1917*

After completing the Harmonielehre *in 1911, Schoenberg considered a number of other theoretical works, but he made little headway on any of them (see 2.16). In the spring of 1917, Schoenberg started work on a more encompassing project entitled* Coherence, Counterpoint, Instrumentation, Instruction in Form. *Though it remained unfinished, the manuscript indicates several developments in his thought that would be central for the formulation of twelve-tone composition, concerning in particular a new understanding of the relationship between comprehensibility and coherence. In a significant departure from his earlier claims of the irrelevance of the listener, such as in "Why New Melodies Are Difficult to Understand" (3.11), Schoenberg now considered comprehensibility in terms of the size of the desired audience: "The* more comprehensible *a form and a content, the* larger the circle *of those* affected *by it.* The more difficult to comprehend, the smaller." *Schoenberg continued to develop many of the concepts in the Gedanke manuscripts of the 1920s and 1930s (see 4.15).*

An attempt at a sequence of ideas for *coherence*

1st Part
- **I.** Simple, logical coherence
- **II.** The inverse of simple, logical coherence
- **III.** The stylistic principles of logical coherence
- **IV.** Metaphysical coherence
- **V.** Relation of metaphysical coherence to logical coherence (correspondence)
- **VI.** Psychological coherence
- **VII.** Correspondence of psychological to logical and metaphysical coherence

2nd Part
- **I.** The idea of a piece of music is
  - 1) in its conception
    - a) purely material
    - b) metaphysical
    - c) psychological
  - 2) in its presentation
    - a) logical
    - b) metaphysical
    - c) psychological
- **II.** The conception does not require logic
- **III.** The presentation requires logic
  - a) if it aims at general intelligibility

b) so long as the author does not himself have the necessary trust in his intention

c) as a perceptible (external) symptom of an internal logic

IV. The presentation can dispense with logic

a) if no general intelligibility is aimed for

b) if the author trusts his intuition

c) because the presence of external symptoms does not depend on internal logic, and internal logic does not depend on the external.

3rd Part

Relationship of coherence to the concept of beauty

4th Part

Musical technique and the various kinds of coherence

Sketch for Assembling a Sequence of the *Theory of Coherence*[75]

[. . .]

I. *Concept* of coherence: . . . Coherence is based on repetition . . .

II. Coherence is what binds individual phenomena into *forms.*

III. A form (form in appearance) is an *art form* if the recognizable *connections,* a few of whose individual components are connected, *are essential* in the same way *for the part as for the whole.*

IV. The artistic exploitation of *coherence* aims at *comprehensibility* . . .

V. *Comprehensibility* is a *requirement*

a) of *those in need of communication*

b) of *those whose perceptions are keen.*

7.[76] The *more comprehensible* a form and a content, the *larger the circle* of those *affected* by it.

The more difficult to comprehend, the *smaller*

8. The *degree of comprehensibility* depends on the type and number of connections used [. . .]

9. The limits of comprehensibility are not the limits of coherence, which can be present even where comprehensibility has ceased. For there are connections inaccessible to consciousness. Such connections possibly have an effect on those more experienced or trained.

[. . .]

Understanding = Recognition of Similarity

§ 1

To understand a thing, it is necessary to recognize that in many (or, if possible, in all) of its parts, it may be similar or even identical to things or parts that are familiar.

If I base this statement upon my ensuing observations, I do not mean that it states conclusively and completely what understanding is. Rather, it is as though:

A wardrobe is supposed to be opened, but the unknown key to it is not at hand. Before resorting to the locksmith, one gathers up all the keys in the house, since all locks require a key. A number of keys that are definitely much too large or much too small are immediately excluded, without even trying them out. The first that seems possible is too large, the next too small: yet all was not in vain, because one now has an approximate idea of the size. The next has a completely wrong shape. One tries a differently shaped fourth key. Finally, after many, one is found that, although it can be completely turned in the lock, still does not work. Now, however, one knows the lock somewhat, and has rejected so many keys that only a small number are left. Despite this effort it is usually necessary to wait for the locksmith, but now and then the right key can be found in this way, or one may learn how a similar key must be filed so it might lock.

There is no further purpose to my hypothesis: whether my key fits, whether it can be turned, or whether it will lock is not yet known.

All the same, I shall attempt it: perhaps one will become familiar with the lock.

§ 2

If a person is meant to understand what another is saying to him, the first presupposition is that:

the speaker uses such signs or means of expression as are known to the listener; for example, the words of a language familiar to him. And the first degree of understanding begins here as the listener recognizes familiar words. In addition, though, these words must succeed each other in such a sequence and context as usage requires. Yet the concepts and meanings of these words must be placed in relation to one another in familiar ways, too, otherwise deviations would have to be explained. (It would be inconceivable—the Dadaist may here be disregarded—to say that the table salt screams in high-swung wrinkles.) And so it continues up to the idea, which again can only be understood if it is recognizable that its individual parts are identical to or resemble what is familiar.

Text for an Oratorio

3.22 Jacob's Ladder, *from the Opening Scene, 1915–1917*

Die Jakobsleiter was first conceived as the final movement of the symphony in 1915 but was then recast as an independent oratorio. After composing a substantial section of the music in 1917, Schoenberg returned to the piece at several points through the rest of his life, but he never completed the score.[77] *The libretto was first published by Universal Edition in 1917, and then again in* Texts *(1926). At a concert of the Society for Private Musical Performances on May 22, 1921, held at the Schwarzwald School, the complete libretto was recited by the actor Wilhelm Klitsch in a performance coached by Schoenberg.*[78]

Of the various characters who appear before the archangel Gabriel to be judged on their worthiness to ascend to a higher stage of existence, the Chosen One would seem to be the closest to Schoenberg's own self-image, while the other characters could depict contemporaries, or conversely, different sides of his personality, as in Moses und Aron *(see 5.8, 5.11).*

GABRIEL: Right or left, forward or backward, uphill or downhill—you must go on. Do not ask what lies in front or behind. It must be hidden; you ought to forget, you must forget, so that you can fulfill your task!

CHOIR (*in many groups*): The unbearable pressure . . . !

    The heavy load . . . !

    What terrible pains . . . !

    Burning longing . . . !

    Hot desires . . . !

    Illusion of fulfillment . . . !

    Inconsolable loneliness . . . !

    Constraining formulae . . . !

    Destruction of the will . . . !

    Lies about happiness . . . !

    Murder, robbery, blood, wounds . . . !

    Possession, beauty, enjoyment . . . !

    Pleasure in conceit, self-love . . . !

    Secret hours, sweet contentment . . . !

    Joyful energy, successful undertakings. . . . !

    A work is achieved, a child was born, a woman kisses,

    a man rejoices . . . and becomes dull again . . .

    and sinks back;

    and starts to groan again;

    and dies,

    is buried,

    forgotten . . .

    —(Short rousing interlude)

(*Choir together, in the same rhythm*)

    Do not ask?

GABRIEL: Never mind! Go on!

[. . .]

GABRIEL: On! Don't stop! Come forward, you, who think that you have come closer because of what you have done.

THE CALLED ONE: I searched for beauty. I sacrificed everything for it; nothing was sacred, no means was obvious. Unbridled I stormed toward this goal, untried I pushed aside what was natural, without any hesitation I subordinated all meaning to form. Perhaps I would have done the same, if I had had to suffer for it. But I have not suffered. On the contrary: my life was full of luminous joy. I saw brightness everywhere I looked, without being blinded. The sun's rays smiled on me and warmed me, warmed me just like the warmth of life; made everything rose-colored and gilded the filth. I never suffered; no movement blocked my own! I saw only the sun, I felt the rhythm of beauty!

GABRIEL: You're still too pleased with yourself: your idol gives you easy satisfaction before you, like the seekers, enjoy the torments of longing. Self-containment—(too simple a solution; for any progress means suffering)—keeps you warm. You heathen, you have understood nothing.

A PROTESTOR (*passionately*): To obey commandments, which are just words, but to be deaf to instincts, which shake the whole being;

to think that it is good to have commandments, that expose the soul and make it suffer,

to think that it is bad to have instincts that incite the soul to desire happiness; which is enough happiness already—

it cannot be the same god,

who through our instincts shows us one way,

and through commandments shows us the other way!

How the god of instincts mocks the god of commandments,

as he lets the wolves

who possess, loot, steal,

bear false witness, and commit adultery, be happy!

How powerless, however, the lord of commandments is,

since he delivers up his sheep to the suffering and persecution,

created by themselves and inflicted by others.

GABRIEL: This Either and this Or, one and two, like shortsightedness and arrogance, one depending on the other, and consequently nothing but the lever for your indignation!

You can open your jowl in wonder, but not to contradict!

A STRUGGLING ONE: In spite of ancient wisdom—that which I've heard, read and seen myself—

which all seemed banal to me,

I searched naively for happiness.

When I failed to attain it, I strove for "painlessness" (Schopenhauer) through abnegation—which also failed.

A dim remembrance of past sufferings

enables me to bear easily present ones,

therefore I thought, that it is all the same
whatever one is unhappy about.

GABRIEL: You're wrong, the more inducements can make you unhappy, the
more sensitive you show yourself to be, the closer you are.

THE STRUGGLING ONE: I'm not complaining about that, I don't mind being
unhappy.
I know that in that way I expiate old guilt.
But how to avoid new ones?

    "You know the commandments:" (Luke 18:20)
    "Do not—!" I have never done it!
    "Do—!" I have always done it!
    "I have kept all these since I was a boy!" (Luke 18:21)
    Whatever I had to give—it wasn't much,
but still my best—I have always given.
I have taken from no-one, acquired almost nothing,
I followed it as well as I could.[79]

    But in the puzzling, ambiguous situations,
in which my destiny perpetually put me,
I suffered the absence of the guiding word,
saw myself sink and become unclean
and unable to distinguish right from wrong.

    Why were we given no sense,
to intuit unspoken laws,
no eye, to see,
no ear, to hear?

GABRIEL (*very radiantly*):
(*This speech of Gabriel's is accompanied ppp by choral singing, without text.*)

    A person is here— against his will and yours—who can guide you.
    Step closer, you on the middle level
who resembles, radiates like, one much higher;
related, like the fundamental to the distant overtone,
while others—lower ones—themselves almost fundamentals,
are far from him, who is like the bright rock crystal;
farther than coal is from diamonds.
    Step closer, so they can see you!

THE CHOSEN ONE: I shouldn't get closer, for it will degrade me.
But I have to get into the middle, it seems,
even though what I have to say then will not be understood.
Is it because they want it, am I driven
to being attached to them, because they resemble me?
    Am I the one who shows them the hour and the course of time,

who is at the same time the scourge and mirror, lyre and sword,
both their master and servant, their wise man and fool?
    Though close to a glorious, exalted sphere,
I am still subject to humiliation;
I try to flee from matter;
Disgust makes it easy for me,
hunger forces me back;
I might raise myself ever so high,
yet I never lose sight of them,
the best they have is mine, as well as their worst,
I rob it from them, steal, take it away,
despise what I have acquired, inherited,
gather it together, grab it, in order to get a hold of it:
Undoubtedly to prepare for something new, possibly for something higher.
    They are the theme, I am the variation.
Still, I am driven by a different motive.
I am driven toward a goal.
Which one? I must find out! Beyond!
My *word* I leave here,
Make what you can of it!
My *form* I take with me, but it will remain in front of you,
until it shows up in your midst
with new words—again the old ones—
to be misunderstood anew.

On the War and the Idea of Progress

3.23 "We knew we didn't live in Paradise . . . " (undated)

We knew we didn't live in Paradise, but many could hope that things were gradually turning out that way.

    Almost everything that had earlier been especially hard, ugly, and cruel, had—if it had not disappeared—at least been mitigated or suppressed.

    For everything ugly and evil, we had our publicly virtuous ones who never gave up pointing us in the right direction, and a great number of men showed a willingness to follow.

    Then came the war.

4   "The Path to the New Music":
Mödling, 1918–1925

After the War

4.1 From "What Is the Influence of the War on Composition?" (Undated)

Yes, what is the influence of the war on composition?
Perhaps at first: is there an influence at all?

During a war the muses are silent
    at least on the battlefield
        but:
    in the hinterland?

Today there are no horses anymore eager to fight at the sound of trumpets
    and
tanks, motorcars, cannons, are immune to these exciting sounds.
One might try loudspeakers so as not to endanger the trumpeters.

In 1914 Austrian troops marched against the Russian armies, preceded—
for a brief moment—by the regimental band; unfortunately for a brief moment only— the Russian cannons proved too strong.

Lützen
Theodor Körner:[1]
    Sword at my left; what means thy cheerful glittering?
    Perhaps in the battle of Lützen some of his comrades might have heard
him sing it.
    But would they hear him today?

Can a change occur in music itself?
It could hardly influence its rhythem, its harmony, its melody.
No composer needs a war to try something in rhythm, harmony, or melody which he would not have tried without a war.

Rather:
the *influence* of music on war.
Beethoven, Napoleon
    "If I were a general,—I would beat him."

Photo opposite page: Arnold and Gertrud Schoenberg in Vienna, c. 1924. Arnold Schönberg Center, Vienna.

What has been composed during a war?

It seems:
What can musicians do:
    the only thing is to do what army leaders find essential for winning the war:
If Socrates and Nietzsche esteemed their lives less important than the welfare of their country, why then should lesser geniuses consider themselves differently.

I have been through one war. I have been in the army and I know what a soldier is thinking and feeling—or at least when he is a musician and if he has time to think:
You think about your food, your uniform, your advancement, your superiors, your free time, your furlough—at least I refused to talk about art or music. You had no interest in mental affairs; you were concerned only with material problems.

Coda
But nevertheless there was one influence of the war.
But it showed only when the war was over.

The Society for Private Musical Performances

4.2 From the "Prospectus of the Society for Private Musical Performances," 1918

Schoenberg's long-standing interest in reforming concert life, evident already in his activities with the Society of Creative Musicians in 1904 (see 1.15), resurfaced after the war as part of his growing concern for the listener (see 3.21). The first manifestation was a series of ten open rehearsals for the Chamber Symphony held in June 1918. The music critic Heinrich von Kralik published an account of the series on July 4, 1918: "Along with Schoenberg and fifteen valiant musicians, a no less valiant adventurous flock of listeners tackled the vile beast. One cacophonous passage after another was tackled, and the muscular power of one's aural apparatus was steeled by the struggle with its sharp points, its hard surfaces, and its asperities. And, even before the day of the tenth and final rehearsal, the players were played-in, the listeners listened-in. The worst had been overcome. The terrifying apparitions looked less full of menace, their appearance had taken on a new mildness, their way of living a new accessibility. One began to feel thoroughly at home and cheerful in their company."[2]

A similar emphasis on extensive rehearsal and frequent repetitions of works to ensure a high level of performance and their greater familiarity for the audience were the central aims of the Society for Private Musical Performances, which was founded on November 23, 1918. From the time of the first performance on Decem-

*ber 29, 1918, to the last concert in December 1921, the society presented more than
a hundred concerts, with nearly 250 works, including compositions by Scriabin,
Debussy, Mahler, Reger, Strauss, Hauer, Pfitzner, Schreker, Bartok, Berg, Webern,
Busoni, Suk, Ravel, Satie, Zemlinsky, Stravinsky, Dukas, Mussorgsky, and many
others.[3] Schoenberg did not permit any of his own works to be performed until the
second season. There were 320 members in 1919; among the performers were
many who had a significant impact on musical life throughout the twentieth
century, including Rudolf Serkin, Rudolf Kolisch, and Eduard Steuermann. Financial pressures brought about by the extreme inflation, as well as Schoenberg's
desire to devote his time to teaching and composition, contributed to the end of the
society's activities in Vienna.*

*In the "Four-Point Program for Jewry" from 1938 Schoenberg wrote, "I was a
kind of dictator, 1920, in a musical society, created by myself in my ideas and on
the whole very successful."[4] The prospectus for the society was formulated by
Alban Berg.*

The Society was founded in November 1918, for the purpose of enabling
Arnold Schoenberg to carry out his plan to give artists and music lovers a real
and exact knowledge of modern music.

The attitude of the public toward modern music is affected to an immense
degree by the circumstance that the impression it receives from that music is
inevitably one of obscurity. Aim, tendency, intention, scope and manner of
expression, value, essence, and goal, all are obscure; most performances of it
lack clarity; and specially lacking in lucidity is the public's consciousness of
its own needs and wishes. All works are therefore valued, considered, judged,
and lauded, or else misjudged, attacked, and rejected, exclusively on the basis
of one effect which all convey equally—that of obscurity.

The situation can in the long run satisfy no one whose opinion is worthy
of consideration, neither the serious composer nor the thoughtful member of
an audience. To bring light into this darkness and thus fulfill a justifiable need
and desire was one of the motives that led Arnold Schoenberg to found this
Society.

To attain this goal, three things are necessary:

1. Clear, well-rehearsed performances.
2. Frequent repetitions.
3. The performances must be removed from the corrupting influence of
publicity; that is, they must not be directed toward the winning of
competitions and must be unaccompanied by applause, or
demonstrations of disapproval.

Herein lies the essential difference revealed by a comparison of the Society's aims with those of the everyday concert world, from which it is quite
distinct in principle. Although it may be possible in preparing a work for

performance, to get along with the strictly limited and always insufficient number of rehearsals hitherto available, for better or worse (usually the latter); yet for the Society the number of rehearsals allotted to works to be performed will be limited only by the attainment of the greatest possible clarity and by the fulfillment of all the composer's intentions as revealed in his work. And if the attainment of these minimum requirements for good performance should necessitate a number of rehearsals that cannot be afforded (as was the case, for example, with a symphony of Mahler, which received its first performance after twelve four-hour rehearsals and was repeated after two more), then the work concerned should not, and will not, be performed by the Society.

In the rehearsal of new works, the performers will be chosen preferably from among the younger and less well-known artists, who place themselves at the Society's disposal out of interest in the cause; artists of high-priced reputation will be used only so far as the music demands and permits; and moreover that kind of virtuosity will be shunned which makes of the work to be performed not the end in itself but merely a means to an end which is not the Society's, namely: the display of irrelevant virtuosity and individuality, and the attainment of a purely personal success. Such things will be rendered automatically impossible by the exclusion (already mentioned) of all demonstrations of applause, disapproval, and thanks. The only success that an artist can have here is that (which should be most important to him) of having made the work, and therewith its composer, intelligible.

While such thoroughly rehearsed performances are a guarantee that each work will be enabled to make itself rightly understood, an even more effective means to this end is given to the Society through the innovation of weekly meetings and by frequent repetitions of every work. Moreover, to ensure equal attendance at each meeting, the program will not be made known beforehand.

Only through the fulfillment of these two requirements—thorough preparation and frequent repetitions—can clarity take the place of the obscurity which used to be the only impression remaining after a solitary performance; only thus can an audience establish an attitude toward a modern work that bears any relation to its composer's intention, completely absorb its style and idiom, and achieve an intimacy that is to be gained only through direct study— an intimacy with which the concert-going public can be credited only with respect to the most frequently performed classics.

The third condition for the attainment of the aims of the Society is that the performances shall be in all respects private; that guests (foreign visitors excepted) shall not be admitted, and that members shall be obligated to abstain from giving any public report of the performances and other activities of the Society, and especially to write or inspire no criticisms, notices, or discussions of them in periodicals.

This rule, that the sessions shall not be publicized, is made necessary by the semi-pedagogic activities of the Society and is in harmony with its tendency to benefit musical works solely through good performances and thus simply through the good effect made by the music himself. Propaganda for works and their composers is not the aim of the Society.

For this reason no school shall receive preference and only the worthless shall be excluded; for the rest, all modern music—from that of Mahler and Strauss to the newest, which practically never, or at most rarely, is to be heard—will be performed.

An Opera Parody

4.3 From "Pfitzner: Three Acts of the Revenge of Palestrina" (c. 1919)

German composer and conducted Hans Pfitzner (1869–1949) taught at the Stern Conservatory in Berlin starting in 1897, followed by teaching and conducting positions in Munich and Strasbourg. From 1920 to 1929 he was at the Prussian Academy of the Arts in Berlin. This unfinished parody of Hans Pfitzner's opera Palestrina *was intended for a "lieder concert evening" of the Society for Private Musical Performances. Pfitzner's opera (composed to his own libretto between 1912 and 1915, and first performed in 1917), is set in 1563 at the time of the Council of Trent. The plot is based on the legends that depicted Palestrina as the savior of polyphonic church music with his* Missa Papae Marcelli. *The opera portrays Palestrina as caught between the dangerous new trends from Florence— where a "clique of amateurs" have "worked out artificial theories according to which music will be made"—and the intention of Pope Pius IV to ban polyphonic music from the Mass because it interferes with the comprehensibility of the text. Schoenberg's parody starts with act 1, scene 3, where Cardinal Borromeo comes from Rome to persuade Palestrina to write a mass that would convince the pope to moderate his stance. He then concentrates on scenes 4 to 6, which show Palestrina, despairing over his inability to compose after the death of his wife, falling asleep at his desk, and then being visited first by the spirits of past musical masters—all dressed in appropriate historical outfits—and finally by a chorus of angels who dictate the* Missa Papae Marcelli *to him during the night, with the last notes fading away at the dawn.*

A backdrop to the parody was Pfitzner's polemic with Busoni, whose 1907 treatise Draft of a New Aesthetic of Music *had been reprinted in 1916 and been critiqued by Pfitzner in his 1917 pamphlet* The Danger of Futurism *[Futurist-engefahr]. Heavily annotated copies of both publications were in Schoenberg's library. While the Pfitzner parody was never completed, Schoenberg took up many of the issues in his* Three Satires *(4.22, 4.23), a link that is made clear in a fragmentary essay dated November 29, 1923:*

An important difference between me and the polytonalists and folklorists and all others who manufacture folk melodies, dances, and so on in a homophonic manner—Stravinsky, Milhaud, the English, Americans, and everyone else—is that they seek the solution by means of a historical parallel, while I have found it from within, in which I merely obeyed the subject and followed my imagination and feeling for form.

They know, as I, that just now the old model of harmony could not be taken further. (I have even said so in my book; they know it from there!) They now obviously look upon the present to be a phenomenon parallel to Palestrina's time, which Pfitzner wanted to bring to life.[5]

Pfitzner
Three Acts of the Revenge of Palestrina

Act I: The Composer at the Crossroads (1919)[6] between Organ and Desk

Dramatis Personae: Hanserl, a Modern Composer
                      Bo & Romeo, Counselor of Commerce and
                      Publisher
     Appearances: The Modern Masters
                      Critical Poultry

Act II: Palestrina: Council of the Publishers and Concert Agents at Leipzig (1919)

Dramatis Personae: Publishers: The Biggest Modern—
                                     The Other Bigger—
                                     A Few Small—
                      Big and Small Concert Promoters

Act III: Pfitzner does not appear at all (1820)

Dramatis Personae: The Genius from Act I

ACT I

The Composer walks back and forth in deep thought. Suddenly he stops, lifts his finger and cries:
HANSERL: Aha!—*he stands still for a time, then shakes his head and says:*
No!—*he continues walking back and forth*
Aha?—
Again nothing!—*walks back and forth again.*
Aha!—
Now I've got it; I've not nothing!
If I write Wagnerian; it's too old,
If I write Verdian; it's not national,

Mascagni and Leoncavallo aren't a draw anymore either,
Puccini, however, wouldn't be bad,
since I am a writer/composer—that is, I can
write as well as I compose—but I am not allowed to
to have such an effective libretto, but must write one
that is awkward and without literary value—
but that makes up for this by being boring.
How shall I write?
It's better not to write operas at all,
It's still better not to write anything at all—
At this point Counselor of Commerce and Publisher Bo & Romeo enters and inter-
rupts Hanserl with the words:
BO & ROMEO: —but one has it printed immediately, in other words, if one
wants to write at all, one has it written with the new music-typewriter (Patent
Bo & Romeo). Something that is nicely printed or typed will be accepted by
the theaters immediately. Since they won't have so much trouble reading it,
they don't read it all but will accept it for its nice appearance, its nice print, its
pretty writing, and the reputation of the publisher. We modern publishers at
least know that for composers to write is totally superfluous work. The main
thing is that it is printed. That makes publicity, and publicity is everything.
Just now, for instance, I received a telegram with the following contents:
Sings: (Couplet, first stanza)
Everybody has a hard time getting used to new things
And that's because the things one is used to
are mostly already old, and not of much use anymore,
in that case the following publicity is useful,
for it seems so clever—
(Couplet, second stanza)
See that's what you've got to do,
For my new opera, which I want to write/publish,
you can already have the following printed:

   1st Item: M. M.[7] is on the point of taking his quill in hand, from which a new
musical work will flow.

   2nd Item: M. M. is making his way to the Court Library to choose the name
of the poet for his next item.

   3rd Item: M. M. has already found the name of the poet, but this will remain
a secret for the time being.

   4th Item: M. M. has already tried to find out whether the name of the poet
will go well with the title of his new work.

   5th Item: The title of the new work has not yet been decided upon.

   6th Item: Berlin is finished, Vienna is up and coming.

   7th–15th Items: I shall send you in three hours.

as the 16th Item, you can place the following in the meantime:
—used to put artistic goals above all else.

and as 17th Item:—as for the rest, I insist on fulfilling the contract forced upon me without neglecting the slightest detail. M. M.

You see, his sole artistic goal is success, and that he has, thanks to publicity.

[*he exits*]

HANSERL: It's easy for him to talk; nobody interrupts his lines;
Although he has no lines anyway; I had some, not for composing,
but just like someone talks; I just talked, about what I don't know,
where I talked in the 1st scene, before that fellow disturbed me.
Ah, I know; I said:
"It's better not to write operas at all."
And then I continued:
"It's still better not to write anything at all—"
And now I continue:
but to leave the whole business—no, not that,
not the business, but the whole work—to one's genius,
and thus for this purpose I go to bed.
For luck only comes in sleep.

He sits down at his desk and falls asleep.
Enter the Modern Masters: the (living) Strauss, Pfitzner, Ravel, Stravinsky,
Bittner, Schreker. They approach the desk, shout:

MODERN MASTERS: Hanserl!—Hans!—Hans—!
Ha—Ha, Ha, Ha— (*this turns to laughter*)
Ha, ha, ha, ha, hee, hee, hee, hee . . .

One: Right Hanserl! *Another:* what do you think you're doing? *A Third:* you want to create a printed work? What are you doing at your desk? *The First:* get right into bed so that your Genius can be shown to its advantage.

While they lift him, carry him to bed and put him down, the Genius appears,
walks a few steps toward the front, then turns around furiously,

GENIUS: Damn it, where are my two lighting technicians; have you ever seen a genius in the dark?

Exits; reenters with two lighting technicians. They constantly light him the
wrong way. He stands in the middle of the stage in a characteristic pose. While
parodies of their music are played, the Modern Masters approach the com-
poser one at a time, surrounding his bed, so that he looks like he is being
attacked; he moans, seems to be having nightmares. The Genius, on the other
hand, seems very bored by the music. The lighting technicians pull back in
order to seem despondent; the Genius calls them back indignantly.

ONE OF THE MODERN MASTERS: Your attention please, your attention please; not too much, otherwise he will wake up, and nothing will come of the whole masterpiece.

*As the Masters slowly draw back, the composer starts breathing more freely,
the Genius, however, yawns extremely loudly.*

HANSERL (*in his sleep calls out in answer*): Oh, I see it, I hear it, it's my sleepy
Genius;[8] I know it, that's the way it always is. *Continues sleeping.*

*The Critical Poultry enter, at first individually, from behind the organ, then
several from all sides. Performers playing ravens, with big black beaks, black
wings; one white one among them is ducked in the ink-bottle so that he is black
too.*

1st RAVEN: Not too many dissonances; modern, but not ultramodern!

2nd RAVEN: Very pleasant melody!

3rd RAVEN: A tenor who has already lost his veneer, but he has not given up
finishing his creation with a period.

4th RAVEN: Schumannesque; today Hoffmannesque; Brahmsesque; grotesque,
adjectivesque. A brown light from the original source of embraced, ennobled
tone-stitchers.

5th RAVEN: What is all this compared to my son. Woiferl, Woiferl, what a
genius you are compared to this.[9]

*While the critics keep talking to him persuasively, three female secretaries have
walked downstage, put down typewriters, sat down and started typing hastily.
In a short time, many pages are finished. They gather them and pile up the
whole lot with much commotion, and then leave with the Critics.*

It grows dark and then immediately afterward it is dawn.

*Hanserl awakes, stretches, rubs his eyes. He notices the book lying on the floor,
doesn't believe his eyes; jumps to his feet, takes the fat book in his hands:*

HANSERL: It's really true, printed, a whole work printed in one night. This is
really wonderfully convenient. I'm never going to write anything again.

Curtain

[For the other two acts only fragmentary notes survive.]

On Creativity and Compositional Developments

4.4 "Certainty," June 20, 1919

*This essay is one of many writings in which Schoenberg attempts to come to terms
with his own compositional development in the face of the sharp reduction in his
creative output over the war years (his last completed work was the Four Orchestral Songs from 1916), as well as the breakdown of his earlier ideal of intuitive,
unconscious expression as he explored new methods for ensuring comprehensibility and coherence.*

It is not at all difficult for the artist to say something about his work if he
simply observes inaccurately. Then, according to taste, everything is either
classically simple or romantically complicated; a clear path is followed, goals

are reached or in sight; mannerism is style, style is personality, personality is the Redeemer or Lucifer—according to taste; in any case, however, everything is so self-evident that the smoothest biographer could hardly write it more smoothly. It is possible that there are artists who carefully live up to their prescribed biographies, who are as loyal to broken laws as others are to the laws they have kept, who are able to make bonds out of liberty but unable to feel free in the knowledge of the bonds of their inner laws! If creators of this sort are artists, one may envy them for the blindness which allows them to see such a smooth path.

I am not so fortunate.

When, after an interruption in my creative work, I am thinking of future compositions, then my future direction lies so clearly before me that I—at least today—can be certain that it will be different from what I have imagined. That I am turning around—perhaps even whirling around—I might still be able to guess; where I am standing, where I stood—it can only be because of my blindness that I do not realize it. Only one circumstance soon appears: that the new seems as strange and incomprehensible to me as the old once did; that, as long as this condition obtains, the old appears more comprehensible to me, until finally the newest phase apparently becomes more familiar to me and I cease to understand how I was previously able to write otherwise.

Yes, when one observes carefully, these things gradually become unclear to one. One begins to understand that one is intended, not only not to guess the future (merely to represent it) but also to forget the past (which one has already represented). One gains a feeling that one has truly fulfilled one's duty only when (although one might wish it otherwise) one does not do what was sacred to one in the past and betrays what the future seemed to promise. Only then one begins quietly to enjoy one's blindness, with seeing eyes.

Very seldom, though; and very secretly; for that might betray a delicate secret—there have been moments when one has looked at the completed piece, and the piece still to be completed, and was satisfied.

I cannot say any more about my creative work.

It would be easier to say less; I, too, could proclaim an expressionistic program.

Better, however, one for others only. I am sure they would fulfil it, and thereby relieve me of any future obligations.

Perhaps I shall do it, one of these days.

But, in the meantime, just one more thing:

I cannot recommend anyone to let himself go this way. It is not supposed to be very advantageous, and ought not to be.

And that one makes oneself interesting by such means is, in the long run, not true either!

When one cannot do anything better, it may still, perhaps, be worthwhile. But woe to him who . . . !

Anti-Semitism on the Mattsee

4.5 Letter to Berg, July 16, 1921

On July 14, 1921, a short article entitled "Schoenberg, Mattsee, and Denomination" appeared in the Wiener Morgen-Zeitung: *"A reader writes to us: 'As to your report that the composer Arnold Schoenberg had abandoned his summer holiday on the Mattsee near Salzburg—where Jews are not welcome—although he is Protestant, one could counter that Mr. Schoenberg's Protestantism is not very old. He was actually born a Jew and was baptized when he was a young student. Since he thus is a non-Aryan, he preferred to leave the "Aryan" Mattsee to avoid further trouble. The baptismal certificate sometimes also lies.' "[10] Despite Schoenberg's ironic tone in this letter to Berg from not long after the event, it is clear that it had powerful repercussions on both his emerging Jewish identity (see 4.13) and his intensified claims to the German tradition (see 4.6). In a letter to Rabbi Stephen S. Wise of May 12, 1934, he referred to this incident, writing that he "was possibly one of the first Jews in Central Europe to become the victim of an actual expulsion."[11]*

Dearest friend,

We've been here since the 14th. Toward the end it got very ugly in Mattsee. The people there seemed to despise me as much as if they knew my music. Nothing happened to us beyond that. But it's just as unpleasant outside one's profession as within it—only there one has to accept it. Perhaps here too? I wouldn't know why.—Now I want to continue working here. I had already written the first ten pages of *Zusammenhang*.[12] I hope I can get back to it soon.—What are you doing? Don't despair if writing is difficult at first: you've probably set yourself higher standards and now have to attain this level.[13] I know how it is: it is a painful state, but one full of promise.

Many warm regards to you and your wife.

Your Arnold Schoenberg

On German Music

4.6 "When I think of music . . . ," 1921

It was against the backdrop of his firsthand experience of anti-Semitism that Schoenberg made his famous proclamation to his pupils about twelve-tone composition in the summer of 1921 at Traunkirchen: "I have made a discovery thanks to which the supremacy of German music is ensured for the next hundred years."[14]

Such German nationalist sentiments became increasingly common in his writings during his period. This short statement appeared in a publication entitled Faithful Eckart, *which, according to the preface, was dedicated to the economic and spiritual rebuilding of Germany after the war. The issue was devoted to "the meaning of music for German culture" and consisted of short responses from various composers. Schoenberg's contribution was prefaced by the following note: "Arnold Schoenberg, who as an artist belongs to the extreme left, expresses himself cautiously and in general terms. He has never made a secret of his international enthusiasms, and on the basis of his latest works can be regarded as an outspoken advocate of atonalism and anarchy in music. Nevertheless, he must concede to German music its preeminence over the music of other countries, acknowledging its idealistic charm, that with wordless power creates, builds, inspires, and acts as a vehicle of culture."*

When I think of music, the only type that comes to my mind—whether I want it to or not—is German music. He who is its enemy will often be guilty of starving others into submission before this insight has become second nature to him. German music, however, thrives even in times of hunger: scrimping and saving, its wordless power will create and fill stately mansions of the spirit into all eternity. And it will always reach for the heavens, while worldly superiority only boasts with artifice.

On the Music of Other Nations

4.7 "Ostinato," May 13, 1922

Schoenberg's appeals to the German tradition in the 1920s can also be seen as part of a reaction against the explosion of new movements and slogans after the war, associated with such terms as neoclassicism, polytonality, Gebrauchsmusik, *and* Neue Sachlichkeit *(see 5.10), as well as the direct challenges from Stravinsky, Milhaud, and the younger generation of German and Austrian composers, including Hindemith and Weill.[15] This unpublished aphorism anticipates the tone of writings like "National Music" (1931), in which he states, "Nobody has yet appreciated that my music, produced on German soil, without foreign influences, is a living example of an art able most effectively to oppose Latin and Slav hopes of hegemony and derived through and through from the traditions of German music." Tracing his lineage from Bach and Mozart, through Beethoven, Wagner, and Brahms, he concludes: "I venture to credit myself with having written truly new music, which being based on tradition, is destined to become tradition."[16]*

For me, the thing I first expect from a work of art—and which appears to be true for no one else—is: *richness!* Although it should be comical, this insufficiency in Latins, and their Russian, Hungarian, English, and American imitators, is instead always for me rather more ridiculous and painful. Their method—variation of the harmonies once in a while to produce something "clever," or until this asinine repetition itself turns out to be "witty," since it at least cannot possibly be taken seriously—recalls the humor of drunks, clowns, and blockheads (above all, ones that are offensive: falling down, fighting, mocking), or as much as I am able to glean from it. One certainly smiles to some degree every time from the novelty, but one always does so with little sympathy, and always particularly with little respect! On the other hand, there is a growing displeasure: a feeling of annoyance turning to disgust!

On Religion and Reactions to the War

4.8 Letter to Kandinsky, July 22, 1922

Kandinsky, who had returned to Russia in 1914 at the outbreak of the war, came back to Germany in 1921, spending time in Berlin before settling the next year in Weimar, where he was appointed professor at the Bauhaus. Founded in 1919 by Walter Gropius (1883–1969), the school brought together innovative architects, artists, scenic designers, and craftsmen, with an emphasis on integrating design and functionality.

My dear Kandinsky,

I'm very glad to have heard from you at long last. How often I've thought of you with anxiety during these eight years! And how many people I have asked about you, without ever getting any definite and reliable information. You must have been through a great deal!

I expect you know we've had our trials here too: famine! It really was pretty awful! But perhaps—for we Viennese seem to be a patient lot—perhaps the worst was after all the overturning of everything one has believed in. That was probably the most grievous thing of all.

When one's been used, where one's own work was concerned, to clearing away all obstacles often by means of one immense intellectual effort and in those 8 years found oneself constantly faced with new obstacles against which all thinking, all power of invention, all energy, all ideas, proved helpless, for a man for whom ideas have been everything it means nothing less than the total collapse of things, unless he has come to find support, in ever increasing measure, in belief in something higher, beyond. You would, I think, see what I mean best from my libretto *Jacob's Ladder* (an oratorio):[17] what I mean is—even though without any organizational fetters—religion. This was my one and only support during those years—here let this be said for the first time.

I can understand your being surprised by the artistic situation in Berlin. But are you also pleased about it? Personally, I haven't much taste for all these movements, but at least I don't have to worry that they'll irritate me for long. Nothing comes to a standstill sooner than these movements that are brought about by so many people.

For all the rest, all these people aren't peddling their own precious skins, but ours—yours and mine. I find it perfectly disgusting, at least in music; these atonalists! Damn it all, I did my composing without any "ism" in mind. What has it got to do with me?

I hope you'll soon be able to get down to work. I think it's precisely these movements that can do with your putting some hindrances in their way.—What are your plans?—How is your book *Das Geistige in der Kunst* getting on? I think of it because it appeared at the same time as my *Harmonielehre,* a much-revised new edition of which I am just sending to the printers (see 4.11).—It may interest you to know I am at present working on *Jacob's Ladder.* I began it several years ago, but had to break off work (at one of the most rapt passages) in order to join the army. Since then I've never got back into the mood to go on with it. It seems, however, that it is meant to go ahead this year. It will be a big work: choir, solo voices, orchestra. Apart from that I plan to write a smaller theoretical book, *Theory of Musical Unity* [*Lehre vom musikalischen Zusammenhang*], which has also been in my mind for several years and which is always being postponed—probably because it hasn't yet matured. For the rest: chamber music, etc. Further, I am thinking about a *Theory of Composition,* for which I've been making preliminary studies for years now (see 4.15).

Well, now I've gone jabbering on like a small child, which I actually stopped being some decades ago. But that's the way it is with letter writing: by the time one's warmed up, one is also worn out.

Will you be able to come to Austria one of these days? I'd very much like to see you.

In any case I hope to hear from you more often now; it does me a lot of good. I greet you most warmly [. . .] also your wife. Greetings as well from my wife and daughter, now Mrs. Gertrud Greissle (neé Schoenberg).[18] My boy is already an enthusiastic football player, who is making my name known in wider circles—I am the father of Georg Schoenberg, the well-known football player.

Many, many kind regards,
Arnold Schoenberg

N.B.: My *Theory of Harmony* has been out of print for three years (I have been working almost that long, with interruptions, on the new edition); that is why you can't buy it anywhere. I will send it to you as soon as it is published.

Illustrations

Figure 1-1. Draft for "Geübtes Herz" (Experienced heart). Text by Gottfried Keller. From the Six Songs, Op. 3 (1899–1903). Arnold Schönberg Center, Vienna.

Many of Schoenberg's early published works were songs, including Opp. 1, 2, 3, and 6, and there were many more songs that remained unpublished. This draft shows Schoenberg's practice in vocal music of composing the vocal line first and then adding the accompaniment. In the published version, which is a whole step lower, the vocal line is retained, but with a different accompaniment. The poem compares a lover's heart to a violin that a virtuoso has "long played upon in pleasure and pain." Just as a violin gains value by being played by a master, "thus many a skilled woman has played true soulfulness into my heart."

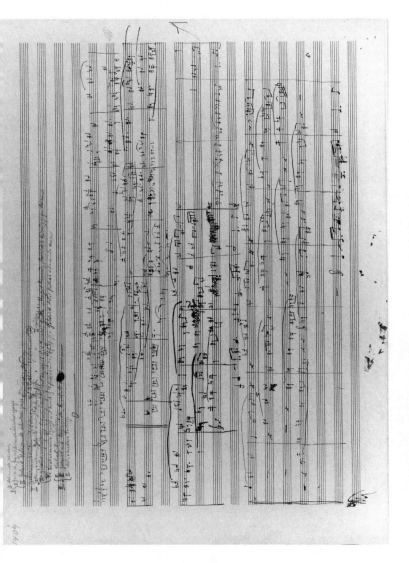

Figure 1-2. Sketch page for Pelleas und Melisande, Op. 5. Arnold Schönberg Center, Vienna.

At the top of the page is a programmatic overview of the entire work, showing the appearance of important motives in conjunction with the main events of the plot (see 1.14). The passage sketched here, mm. 18–35, includes the motives for Melisande and Golaud.

Figure 2-1. Self-Portrait, dated December 26, 1908. Brush, pen, and ink on paper. Arnold Schönberg Center, Vienna.

One of Schoenberg's earliest dated paintings.

Figure 2-2. Green Self-Portrait, dated October 23, 1910. Oil on wood. Arnold Schönberg Center, Vienna.

The painting represents an intermediate stage in the process of gradual dematerialization evident in his self-portraits and "gazes" until only the eyes remained.

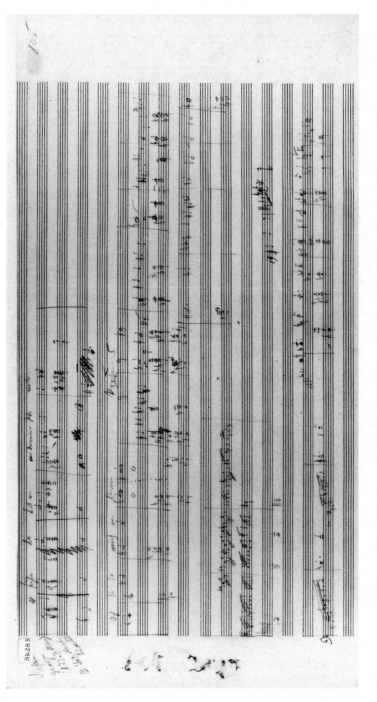

Figure 2-3. Sketchbook page for the Second String Quartet, Op. 10, fourth movement. Arnold Schönberg Center, Vienna.

The page includes sketches for the vocal line and accompaniment for the phrases from Stefan George's "Transport" ("Entrückung"): "I feel the air of another planet" (Ich fühle luft von anderem planeten), mm. 21–25, and "I am dissolved in swirling sound" (Ich löse mich in tönen, kreisend), mm. 52–66. At the bottom of the page are sketches for the instrumental introduction where Schoenberg leaves tonality behind (see 2.3.).

Figure 2-4. Autograph for the Three Piano Pieces, Op. 11, third movement. Arnold Schönberg Center, Vienna.

As with many works from the period 1909–1912, Schoenberg composed this movement very quickly and apparently without any preliminary sketches. The only significant change between this draft and the final version is the substantial deletion of a passage in the first three systems. This section may have been omitted because its repetitions were not in keeping with the character of constant change that marks the rest of the movement (see 2.10).

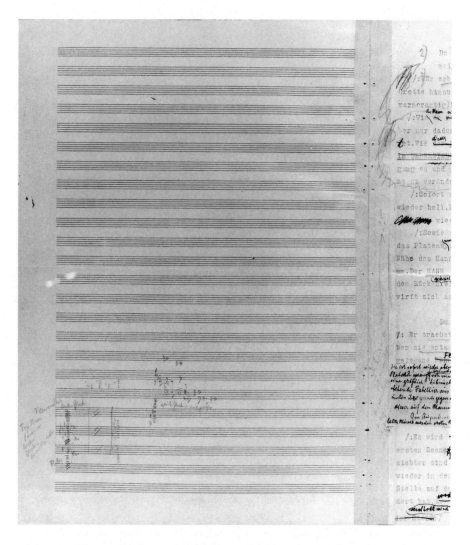

Figure 2-5, a and b. Facing pages from the Compositions-Vorlage (compositional copy) of the libretto of Die glückliche Hand, Op. 18. *Arnold Schönberg Center, Vienna.*

The heavily revised libretto shows the extent of changes Schoenberg made to the text during the composition, in particular at the transition to the fourth scene, shown here. As with many of his operatic works, he made sketches directly in the manuscript adjacent to various points in the text. The sketch at the lower left, corresponding to the scene change, includes two twelve-note chords, perhaps the earliest appearance of this idea in Schoenberg's works (see 2.13).

DER MANN (singt)

Du -----Du!Du bist mein ----!du warst

mein ----!sie war mein ----!

/:Er erhebt sich und macht verzweifelte Anstrengungen zur
Grotte hinauf zu klettern(die Wand ist vollständig glatt;
marmorartig)Es gelingt ihm nicht:/

/:Wie ...., bemerkt ihn der Herr .... ruhig auf ihn .....
ber nur dadurch kund ...., dass e....... ..... ruhig auf ihn ....
t.Wie ..... dann ...... versucht hinauf zu klettern,wirft der HERR
IM ÜBERKLEID ihm den Fetzen mit einer ruhigen,kalten,Bewe-
gung zu und geht mit höchster Gleichgültigkeit ohne die Mie-
ne zu verändern fort:/

/:Sofort wird die Bühne ganz finster und gleich nachher
wieder hell.Halbhell;fahles grünlich graues Licht.Die Grotte
.... wieder dunkel wie zu Anfang:/

/:Sowie es hell ist ...... das WEIB .... auf
das Plateau,den Kleiderfetzen zu suchen.Sie sieht ihn in der
Nähe des Mannes liegen, eilt hin,nimmt ihn auf und legt ihn
um.Der MANN hat den Kopf an die Wand gelehnt und ...... ihr
den Rück.Wie sie den Kleiderfetzen anlegt dreht er sich um,
wirft sich auf die Knie .. (singt, flehend)

MANN :

Du Schön------blieb bei mir -----

/: Er trachet auf den Knien rutschend an sie heranzukommen;a-
ber sie entschlüpft ihm indem ...... vom Plateau auf das vorn ....
gelegene ...... stück hinunter ...... .Er springt ihr nach.Sie ...
......

Verwandlung

/:Es wird .... sofort wieder hell.Das ...... Bild der
ersten Scene;die sechs Männer und die sechs Frauen. Deren Ge-
sichter sind nun graublau beleuchtet,das Fabeltier hat sich
wieder in den Nacken des Mannes verbissen,der an derselben
Stelle auf dem Boden liegt,auf die ihn der See ....
......

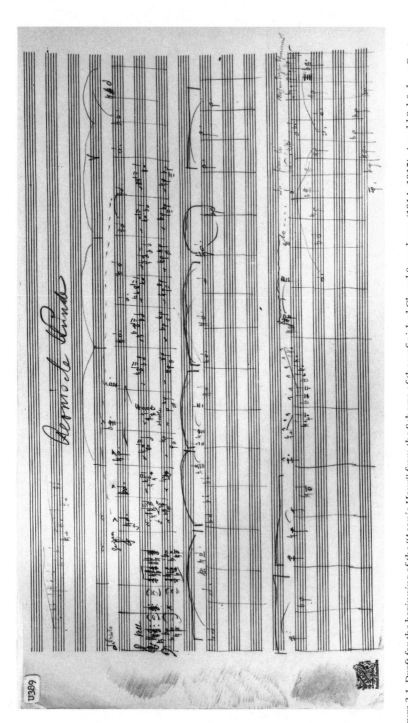

Figure 3-1. Draft for the beginning of the "Aeonic Hour" from the Scherzo of the unfinished Choral Symphony (1914–1915). Arnold Schönberg Center, Vienna.

The "Aeonic Hour" was to be a setting of a text by Richard Dehmel (see 3.13), which begins, "You heavenly reveler! / Still a drop of melancholy in my glass, / Still a tear glowed and glittered wildly in my heart, / yet you sang, you sang—" (Bailey, *Programmatic Elements*, p. 89). The canonic treatment of the opening violin theme of the "Aeonic Hour" in the final measures of the sketch, accompanying the entrance of the chorus, is typical of the more systematic compositional devices Schoenberg used throughout the symphony. On the top-left corner of the page he notated the twelve-tone theme he had

Figure 4-1. Self-Portrait, June 1919. Brush and ink on paper. Arnold Schönberg Center, Vienna.

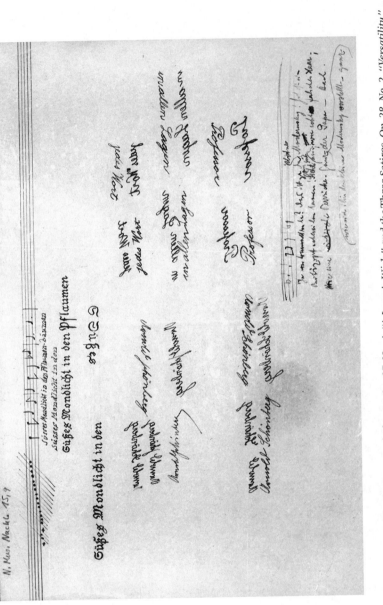

Figure 4-2. Sketch page for the Four Pieces for Mixed Chorus, Op. 27, No. 4, "A Lover's Wish," and the Three Satires, Op. 28, No. 2, "Versatility." Staatsbibliothek zu Berlin. Preußischer Kulturbesitz, Musikabteilung.

The fourth movement of Op. 27 is a twelve-tone piece, but as is evident in the sketch of the opening melodic line at the top of the page, the row is ordered so that the first and last five pitches are pentatonic (see 4.21). The sketch for Op. 28 includes what is probably the first attempt at the text poking fun at Stravinsky, along with a musical sketch that shows Schoenberg's original plan to make a more explicit reference to Bach by using the b-a-c-h motive (see 4.22 and 4.23). In the center of the page Schoenberg experiments with writing his name and various words, including what was to be his new title of "Professor," in the four mirror forms in which twelve-tone rows appear.

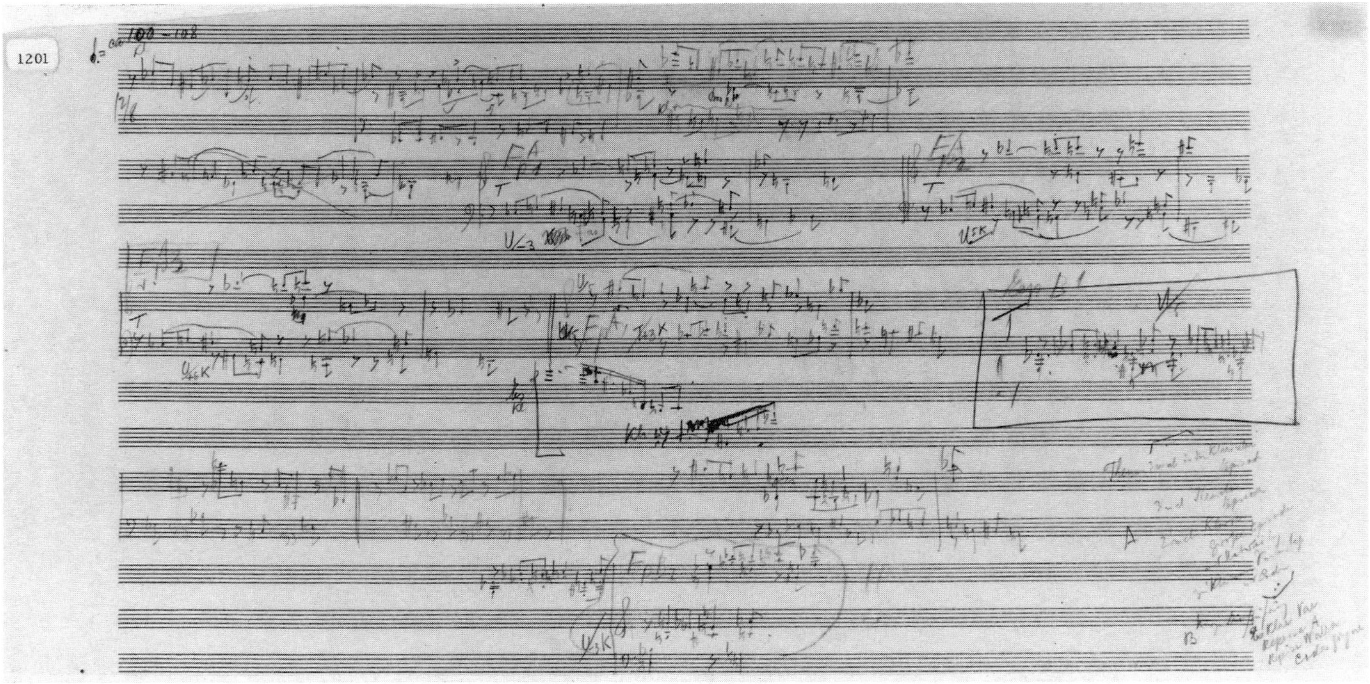

Figure 4-3. Sketch page for the Suite, Op. 29, Fourth Movement, "Gigue." Arnold Schönberg Center, Vienna.

The sketch page, which includes a draft of the beginning of the movement, shows Schoenberg's frequent practice in his manuscripts for the twelve-tone works of indicating the row forms and transpositional levels he was using. (T = Thema [basic set]; U = Umkehrung [inversion]; K = Krebs [retrograde]; UK = Krebs der Umkehrung [retrograde inversion].) The symbol U /-3 stands for the inversion starting a minor third beneath the first pitch of the basic set, thus on C-natural. Also included on the lower-right side of the page is a prose outline for the overall form of the movement (see further 4.20).

Figure 5-1. Self-Portrait, March 17, 1933. Pen and ink on paper. Arnold Schönberg Center, Vienna.

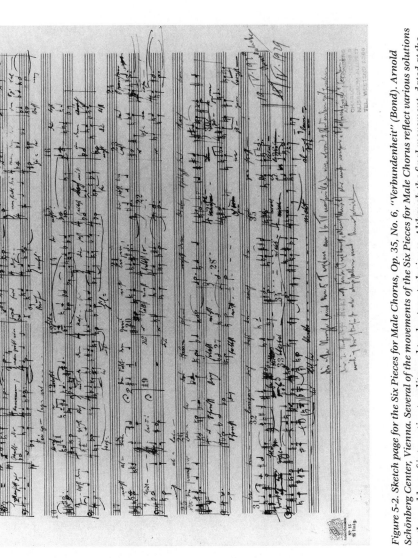

Figure 5-2. Sketch page for the Six Pieces for Male Chorus, Op. 35, No. 6, "Verbundenheit" (Bond). Arnold Schönberg Center, Vienna. Several of the movements of the Six Pieces for Male Chorus reflect various solutions to the problem of integrating tonality and twelve-tone techniques. Although the final movement, dated at the conclusion April 19, 1929, is tonal, it is designed so that the second half of the piece, shown here, is a strict inversion of the first half (see 5.15).

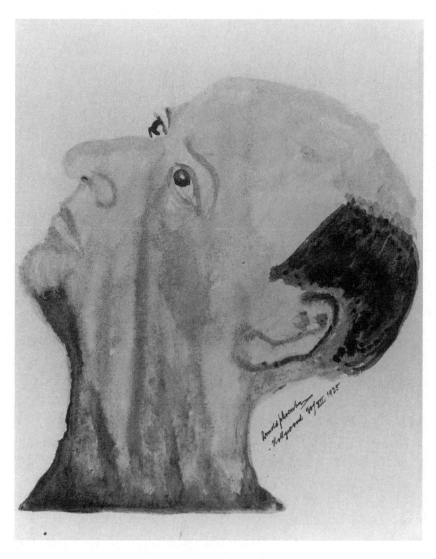

Figure 6-1. Self-Portrait, "Hollywood, December 30, 1935." Brush and ink on paper.
Arnold Schönberg Center, Vienna.

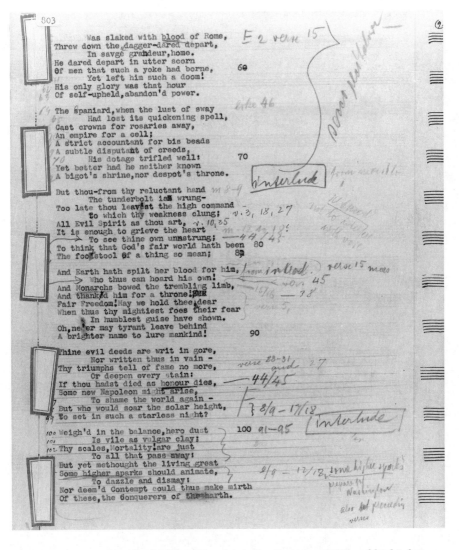

Figure 6-2. Annotated text for the Ode to Napoleon, *Op. 41, stanzas 1–6 Arnold Schönberg Center, Vienna.*

Schoenberg used this document during the planning and composition of the Ode to Napolean; *it shows thematic connections in the text, along with indications of musical characteristics and formal features of the setting (see 6.18).*

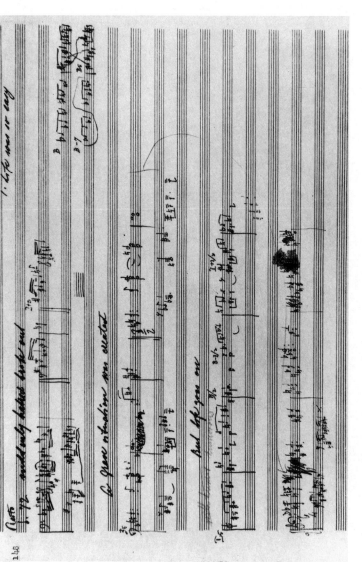

Figure 6-3. Sketch page for the Concerto for Piano and Orchestra, *Op. 42. Arnold Schönberg Center, Vienna.*

Schoenberg composed the piano concerto in 1942, on a commission from the pianist and film and radio personality Oscar Levant (1906–1972), who had studied composition with Schoenberg in 1936 and 1937. The sketch page contains Schoenberg's programmatic outline for the work, which suggests autobiographical parallels to his life over the previous decade: "Life was so easy; suddenly hatred broke out; a grave situation was created; but life goes on" (see Bailey, Programmatic Elements, pp. 136–151).

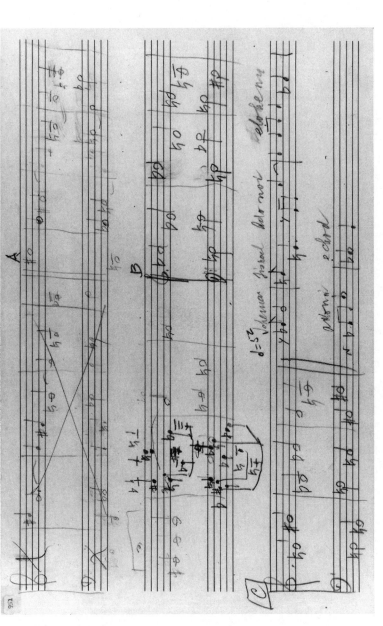

Figure 7-1. *Sketch page for A Survivor from Warsaw, Op. 46, Arnold Schönberg Center, Vienna.*

As with the Ode to Napoleon, in A Survivor from Warsaw Schoenberg worked more freely with ordered and unordered hexachords, rather than a single ordering the row. Some of these hexachords are shown in the sketch, which also includes a draft from the beginning of the Shema Yisrael (see 7.9).

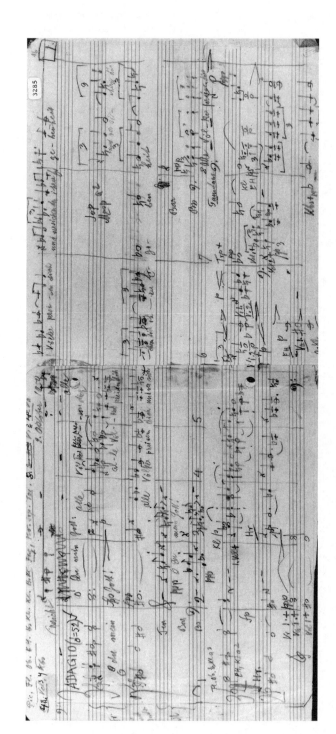

Figure 7-2. Draft for the Modern Psalm, No. 1, Op. 50c, 1950. Arnold Schönberg Center, Vienna.

On Intellect and Intuition

4.9 "Art Golem," August 15, 1922

Schoenberg's deliberate, legalistic language here perhaps indicates his awareness of how significant a departure this formulation of the creative process was from his earlier statements on the relationship between intellect and inspiration. That he compares the mechanically created work to the figure of the Golem, from the Jewish legends of an artificial creature fashioned from clay and magically brought to life, reflects his ambivalence. In various versions of the legend, the Golem was depicted as a servant, a protector, or a destructive, uncontrollable monster.

At the time he wrote "Art Golem," Schoenberg was involved with a series of works, including Die Jakobsleiter, *the Five Pieces for Piano, Op. 23, and the Serenade Op. 24 (see 4.12), which were structured according to the technique he later called "composing with tones" or "working with tones of the motif."[19] Although he noted in a letter to Nicolas Slonimsky that this was a "vague term," it entailed using a motive not in the "ordinary way" but "already almost in the manner of a 'basic set of twelve tones,'" to build "other motives and themes from it, and also accompaniments and other chords."[20] In "My Evolution," following the presentation of themes from* Die Jakobsleiter *based on an unordered collection of six pitch classes, Schoenberg illustrated his brief discussion of "working with tones" with examples from the first movement of the Five Piano Pieces and the "Tanzscene" from the* Serenade *showing collections recurring in different orderings, rhythms, and registral configurations.[21]*

Since everything that happens around us may be called a result of the interaction of specific forces that are related specifically to one another, and since the interaction of everything that happens around us is, in turn, related specifically to us, under the specific influence of our inner forces (laws, precepts); since, therefore, all external events, insofar as they act upon us, should, so to speak, be referred to a common denominator (ourselves), it is certain that external interactions brought about by us will be predisposed to adapt themselves to this common denominator in direct proportion to the internal forces brought to bear by us in creating those interactions.

I therefore conclude that if a thinker were to compose (without recourse to his imagination) an intellectually really good, *invented* piece of music which would take into account all the rules arising from a correct realization of its artistic stipulations, we should react to it with the same feeling as we might derive from such structures as are created through the purely intuitive use of the imagination. It is unlikely that such an Art/Golem could be created; yet, were it to be possible, then no objection to its artificial, dryly cerebral origins would hold.

Traunkirchen, August 15, 1922.

Concerning the Bach Orchestrations

4.10 From a Letter to Josef Stransky, August 23, 1922

In April 1923, Stransky (1872–1936), who was Mahler's successor at the New York Philharmonic, conducted the premieres of Schoenberg's orchestrations of two choral preludes by J. S. Bach, "Komm, Gott, Schöpfer, heiliger Geist," BWV 631, and "Schmücke dich, O liebe Seele," BWV 654, both completed in 1922. In a 1930 letter to the conductor Fritz Stiedry (1883–1968), Schoenberg justified his use of a large orchestra, describing the act of transcription as a "duty": "Our aural requirements do not aim at any 'full flavor' that comes of varied color; rather colors help to clarify the movements of the parts, and, in a contrapuntal texture, that is very important! Whether the Bach organ was capable of it, we do not know. Present-day organists are not: that I do know (and it is one of my starting points)."[22]

Dear Herr Kapellmeister Stransky,

What a pity I missed seeing you in Mödling!

So far I have arranged two Bach chorale preludes. These are No. 35 (Peters Edition), "Come, God, Creator, Holy Ghost," for large orchestra, and No. 49, "Adorn thyself, O my soul," for solo cello and large orchestra.

It is uncertain whether I shall do anything more of this kind in the immediate future, but it is not quite impossible.

I should be very pleased to let you have these pieces for performance and should therefore like to know: 1. if you care to have them. 2. if you are absolutely set on having the rights for the first performance (for since I did not hear from you, I have already more or less given my consent to Zemlinsky in Prague and Webern in Vienna, without however being bound by this, since neither of them insists on first-performance rights and both merely need to know the date). 3. In the event of your wishing to give the first performance, please inform me of the date of the concert [. . . .]

Would you not like to look at scores of works by Dr. Anton von Webern and Alban Berg, two real musicians—not Bolshevik illiterates, but men with a musically educated ear!

U. E. has published a Passacaglia of Webern's that has been repeatedly performed with unmitigated success and which is not yet such a "dangerous work" (also several series of orchestral pieces and orchestral songs). Among Berg's things there are three very interesting orchestral pieces: "Reigen" (Round Dances), approximating to the dance, but *quite* modern. They are unpublished and unperformed.

On Revolution and Evolution in Art

4.11 From the Theory of Harmony, *Third Edition, 1922*

Just as he attempted to separate Berg and Webern from any taint of "musical Bolshevism" in the letter to Stransky (4.10), in many writings from the period after the war Schoenberg sought to downplay the revolutionary aspects of his work and depict himself, as he stated in a letter to the patron Werner Reinhart from July 1923, as "a natural continuer of properly understood good old tradition!"[23] *An unfinished essay entitled "Art and Revolution" (c. 1920) discusses the Wagner essay of that title, in the context of a critique of the younger generation of composers who equated artistic and political revolution. Schoenberg writes:* "Art has nothing to do with revolution . . . only with evolution, development."[24]

As discussed above (2.16), in 1921 Schoenberg undertook a revision of the Harmonielehre *that was published the following year. A number of the revisions reflect a shift from the revolutionary aspects of his earlier formulations in favor of a more evolutionary model of history. In chapter 21, "Chords Constructed in Fourths," for example, Schoenberg writes of the emergence of the artist in the first edition, stressing inborn and internal factors leading to a break with tradition:*

> But the young artist does not know himself; he does not yet sense wherein he is different from the others, different above all from the literature. He still adheres to the precepts of his education and is not able to break through it everywhere in favor of his own inclinations. [. . .] *The artist who has courage submits wholly to his own inclinations. And he alone who submits to his own inclinations has courage, and he alone who has courage is an artist.* The literature is thrown out, the results of education are shaken off, the inclinations come forward, the obstacle turns the stream into a new course, the one hue that earlier was only a subordinate color in the total picture spreads out, a personage is born. A new man! This is a model for the development of the artist, for the development of art.[25]

In the third edition, however, Schoenberg followed this proclamation with a new paragraph that stresses continuity with the past.

That is called revolution; and artists, those who submit to such necessities and cherish them, are accused of all possible crimes that can be culled from the rubbish of the political vocabulary. At the same time, however, it is forgotten that one may call it revolution, if at all, only in a comparative sense, and that this comparison has to hold only with respect to the *points compared,* i.e. *points of similarity,* but not in every respect. An artist who has a good, new idea is not to be confused with a bomb thrower. Any similarity between the advent of the new in the spiritual and intellectual sphere and in political revolutions consists at most in this: the successful will prevail for a period of time, and in the light of this prospect, the older will feel under threat from what is new. But the fundamental distinctions are greater: the consequences, the spiritual and intellectual consequences of an idea endure, since they are spiritual and intellectual; but the consequences of revolutions that run their course in material matters are transient. Besides: it has never been the purpose and effect of new art to suppress the old, its predecessor, certainly not to destroy it. Quite the contrary: no one loves his predecessors more deeply, more fervently, more respectfully than the artist who gives us something truly new; for respect is awareness of one's station and love is a sense of community. Does anyone have to be reminded that Mendelssohn—even he was once new—unearthed Bach, that Schumann discovered Schubert, and that Wagner, with work, word, and deed, awakened the first real understanding of Beethoven? The appearance of the new can far better be compared with the flowering of a tree: it is the natural growth of the tree of life. But if there were trees that had an interest in preventing the flowering, then they would surely call it revolution. And conservatives of winter would fight against each spring, even if they had experienced it a hundred times and could affirm that it did become, after all, *their* spring too. Short memory and meager insight suffice to confuse growth with overthrow; they suffice for believing that when the new shoots emerge from what was once new the destruction of the old is at hand.

On His New Compositions

4.12 Letter to Emil Hertzka, Universal Edition, March 13, 1923

This letter concerns the end of Schoenberg's long compositional drought with the rapid completion of a set of works he had been occupied with for several years, including the first pieces composed using "the method of composing with twelve tones which are related only with one another." Schoenberg wrote to Zemlinsky on February 12, 1923, about the timing of his trip to Prague for the upcoming premiere of Erwartung. *He expressed concerns about breaking off work on several new compositions: "I shouldn't at all care to risk such an interruption for I have very often found it may be fatal to me (e.g., 'Jacob's Ladder') to lose the thread. In this case it is not only that I ought to get something finished again at long last after so many disturbances, but also a matter of a, for me, very large fee to be paid for two works that are only just begun. Now, Hertzka has waived his rights in this case solely on condition that I deliver him two works, which are, however, still further from completion. So I have to compose four works: two series of piano pieces, of which not much more than half is finished, the Serenade, with six-seven movements of which three are almost finished and three sketched out, or rather, begun, and a septet for strings or a violin concerto, both of which are only just begun. So there's a long road ahead of me, and I should be glad to get the money soon, so long as it still has any value at all."[26] The Five Pieces for Piano, Op. 23 (1920–1923), and the Serenade, Op. 24 (1920–1923), were published by Wilhelm Hansen in*

Copenhagen in 1923 and 1924, respectively. The twelve-tone Suite for Piano, Op. 25 (1921–1923), and Wind Quintet, Op. 26 (1923–1924), were published by Universal Edition in 1925. Only sketches survive for the violin concerto and the string septet.

Dear Director,

in today's *Neues Wiener Journal* is the following:

Arnold Schoenberg, the leader of the Expressionists in music, is now working on a violin concerto. It is noteworthy that Schoenberg, who has not produced anything new for years, has with this work abandoned his customary path, and wants to (! ! ! ! ! follow ! ! ! ! ! !) a somewhat more moderate style.

Apart from the many outrageous claims, this lying piece of tripe also includes one correct fact: that I am planning a violin concerto.

Since of my circle only Webern and Berg know of my intention, this publication can only have originated with Universal Edition. I must strongly request that you look into this matter energetically.

I have not taken care of my reputation for more than twenty years only to now allow myself to be mocked. I am not now some sort of Richard Strauss; neither according to his merits nor to his faults.

I am convinced that you take these matters as seriously as I do. And please, if someone with you really despises me as much as as this item indicates, and which certainly brings attention to what kind of opportunist I am, I ask you to see to it that he merely treats me with contempt, but doesn't shout out my shame from the rooftops.

Warm regards,

Schoenberg

p.s. I must come to see you one day to discuss some things. It will please you to hear that I am already working on the Serenade: that is, the two sets of piano pieces (11 movements) are already finished. In this time when I have "not produced anything new for years," one will soon observe with astonishment how much I nevertheless have composed, once I have completed everything that has been started.

Yours, Sch.

On Anti-Semitism and Politics

4.13 Two Letters to Kandinsky, April 19 and May 4, 1923

Kandinsky answered Schoenberg's letter of July 22, 1922 (4.8), almost ten months later on April 15, 1923, to approach him about coming to Weimar as director of the

Musikhochschule, writing: "How often I have said to myself: 'If only Schoenberg were here!' "[27] Schoenberg had in the meantime heard reports from Alma Mahler and others of "anti-Semitic tendencies" among some of the faculty at the Bauhaus, including Kandinsky.[28] In response to Schoenberg's first letter below, Kandinsky wrote: "I love you as an artist and a human being, or perhaps as a human being and an artist. In such cases I think least of all about nationality—it is a matter of the greatest indifference to me. Among my friends who have been tested through many years (the word 'friend' has a great meaning for me, so I seldom use it) are more Jews than Russians or Germans. [. . .] Why didn't you write to me at once when you heard of my remarks? You could have written to me that you objected to these remarks. You have a frightful picture of the 'Kandinsky of today': I reject you as a Jew, but nevertheless I write you a good letter and assure you that I would be so glad to have you here in order to work together!"[29]

April 19, 1923

Dear Mr. Kandinsky,

If I had received your letter a year ago I should have let all my principles go hang, should have renounced the prospect of at last being free to compose, and should have plunged headlong into the adventure. Indeed I confess: even today I wavered for a moment: so great is my taste for teaching, so easily is my enthusiasm still inflamed. But it cannot be.

For I have at last learnt the lesson that has been forced upon me during this year, and I shall not ever forget it. It is that I am not a German, not a European, indeed perhaps scarcely even a human being (at least, the Europeans prefer the worst of their race to me), but I am a Jew.

I am content that it should be so! Today I no longer wish to be an exception; I have no objection at all to being lumped together with all the rest. For I have seen that on the other side (which is otherwise no model so far as I'm concerned, far from it) everything is also just one lump. I have seen that someone with whom I thought myself on a level preferred to seek the community of the lump; I have heard that even a Kandinsky sees only evil in the actions of Jews and in their evil actions only the Jewishness, and at this point I give up hope of reaching any understanding. It was a dream. We are two kinds of people. Definitively!

So you will realize that I only do whatever is necessary to keep alive. Perhaps some day a later generation will be in a position to indulge in dreams. I wish it neither for them nor for myself. On the contrary, indeed, I would give much that it might be granted to me to bring about an awakening.

I should like the Kandinsky I knew in the past and the Kandinsky of today each to take his fair share of my cordial and respectful greetings.

May 4, 1923

Dear Kandinsky,

I address you so because you wrote that you were deeply moved by my letter. That was what I hoped of Kandinsky, although I have not yet said a hundredth part of what a Kandinsky's imagination must conjure up before his mind's eye if he is to be my Kandinsky! Because I have not yet said that for instance when I walk along the street and each person looks at me to see whether I'm a Jew or a Christian, I can't very well tell each of them that I'm the one that Kandinsky and some others make an exception of, although of course that man Hitler is not of their opinion. And then even this benevolent view of me wouldn't be much use to me, even if I were, like blind beggars, to write it on a piece of cardboard and hang it round my neck for everyone to read. Must not a Kandinsky bear that in mind? Must not a Kandinsky have an inkling of what really happened when I had to break off my first working summer for 5 years, leave the place I had sought out for peace to work in, and afterward couldn't regain the peace of mind to work at all. Because the Germans will not put up with Jews! Is it possible for a Kandinsky to be of more or less one mind with others instead of with me? But is it possible for him to have even a single thought in common with HUMAN BEINGS who are capable of disturbing the peace in which I want to work? Is it a thought at all that one can have in common with such people? And: can it be right? It seems to me: Kandinsky cannot possibly have even such a thing as geometry in common with them! That is not his position, or he does not stand where I stand!

I ask: Why do people say that Jews are like what their black-marketeers are like?

Do people also say that the Aryans are like their worst elements? Why is an Aryan judged by Goethe, Schopenhauer, and so forth? Why don't people say the Jews are like Mahler, Altenberg, Schoenberg, and many others?

Why, if you have a feeling for human beings, are you a politician? When a politician is, after all, someone who must not take any count of the human being but simply keep his eyes fixed on his party's aims?

What every Jew reveals by his hooked nose is not only his own guilt but also that of all those with hooked noses who don't happen to be there too. But if a hundred Aryan criminals are all together, all that anyone will be able to read from their noses is their taste for alcohol, while for the rest they will be considered respectable people.

And you join in that sort of thing and "reject me as a Jew." Did I ever offer myself to you? Do you think that someone like myself lets himself be rejected! Do you think that a man who knows his own value grants anyone the right to criticize even his most trivial qualities? Who might it be, anyway, who could have such a right? In what way would he be better? Yes, everyone is free to criticize me behind my back, there's plenty of room there. But if I come to hear of it he is liable to my retaliation, and no quarter given.

How can a Kandinsky approve of my being insulted; how can he associate himself with politics that aim at bringing about the possibility of excluding me from my natural sphere of action; how can he refrain from combating a view of the world whose aim is St. Bartholomew's nights in the darkness of which no one will be able to read the little placard saying that I'm exempt! I, myself, if I had any say in the matter, would, in a corresponding case, associate myself with a view of the world that maintains for the world the right view of the two-three Kandinskys that the world produces in a century—I should be of the opinion that only such a view of the world would do for me. And I should leave the pogroms to the others. That is, if I couldn't do anything to stop them!

You will call it a regrettable individual case if I too am affected by the results of the anti-Semitic movement. But why do people not see the bad Jews as a regrettable individual case, instead of as what's typical? In the small circle of my own pupils, immediately after the war, almost all the Aryans had not been on active service, but had got themselves cushy jobs. On the other hand, almost all the Jews had seen active service and been wounded. How about the individual cases there?

But it isn't an individual case, that is, it isn't merely accidental. On the contrary, it is all part of a plan that, after first not being respected on the ordinary conventional road, I now have to go the long way round through politics into the bargain. Of course: these people, to whom my music and my ideas were a nuisance, could only be delighted to find there is now one more chance of getting rid of me for the time being. My artistic success leaves me cold, you know that. But I won't let myself be insulted!

What have I to do with communism? I'm not one and never was one! What have I to do with the Elders of Zion? All that means to me is the title of a fairy-tale out of a Thousand and One Nights, but not one that refers to anything remotely as worthy of belief.

Wouldn't I too necessarily know something of the Elders of Zion? Or do you think that I owe my discoveries, my knowledge and skill, to Jewish machinations in high places? Or does Einstein owe his to a commission from the Elders of Zion?

I don't understand it. For all that won't stand up to serious examination. And didn't you have plenty of chance in the war to notice how much official lying is done, indeed that official talk is all lies. How our brain, in its attempt to be objective, shuts down on the prospect of truth forever. Didn't you know that or have you forgotten?

Have you also forgotten how much disaster can be evoked by a particular mode of feeling? Don't you know that in peacetime everyone was horrified by a railway-accident in which four people were killed, and that during the war one could hear people talking about 100,000 dead without even trying to picture the misery, the pain, the fear, and the consequences? Yes, and that there were people who were delighted to read about as many enemy dead as possible; the more, the more so! I am no pacifist; being against war is as pointless as being against death. Both are inevitable, both depend only to the very slightest degree on ourselves, and are among the human race's methods of regeneration that have been invented not by us, but by higher powers. In the same way the shift in the social structure that is now going on isn't to be lodged to the guilty account of any individual. It is written in the stars and is an inevitable process. The middle classes were all too intent on ideals, no longer capable of fighting for anything, and that is why the wretched but robust elements are rising up out of the abysses of humanity in order to generate another sort of middle class, fit to exist. It's one that will buy a beautiful book printed on bad paper, and starve. This is the way it must be, and not otherwise—can one fail to see that?

And all this is what you want to prevent. And that's what you want to hold the Jews responsible for? I don't understand it!

Are all Jews communists? You know as well as I do that that isn't so. I'm not one because I know there aren't enough of the things everyone wants to be shared out all round, but scarcely for a tenth. What there's enough of (misfortune, illness, beastliness, inefficiency and the like) is shared out anyway. Then, too, because I know that the subjective sense of happiness doesn't depend on possessions; it's a mysterious constitution that one either has or has not. And thirdly because this earth is a vale of tears and not a place of entertainment, because, in other words, it is neither in the Creator's plan that all should fare equally well, nor, perhaps, has it any deeper meaning at all.

Nowadays all one needs is to utter some nonsense in scientifico-journalistic jargon, and the cleverest people take it for a revelation. The Elders of Zion—of course; it's the very name for modern films, scientific works, operettas, cabarets, in fact everything that nowadays keeps the intellectual world going round.

The Jews do business, as businessmen. But if they are a nuisance to their competitors, they are attacked; only not as businessmen, but as Jews. As what then are they to defend themselves? But I am convinced that they defend themselves merely as businessmen, and that the defense as Jews is only an apparent one. I.e., that their Aryan attackers defend themselves when attacked in just the same way, even though in somewhat other words and by adopting other (more attractive???) forms of hypocrisy; and that the Jews are not in the least concerned with beating their Christian competitors, but only with beating *competitors!* and that the Aryan ones are in exactly the same way out to beat *any* competitors; and that any association is thinkable among them if it leads to the goal, and every other contradiction. Nowadays it is race; another time I don't know what. And a Kandinsky will join in that sort of thing?

The great American banks have given money for communism, not denying the fact. Do you know why? Mr. Ford will know that they aren't in a position to deny it: Perhaps if they did they would uncover some other fact much more inconvenient to them. For if it were true, someone would long ago have proved it is untrue.

WE KNOW ALL THAT! THAT'S THE VERY THING WE KNOW FROM OUR OWN EXPERIENCE! Trotsky and Lenin spilt rivers of blood (which, by the way, no revolution in the history of the world could ever avoid doing!), in order to turn a theory—false, it goes without saying (but which, like those of the philanthropists who brought about previous revolutions, was well meant)—into reality. It is a thing to be cursed and a thing that shall be punished, for he who sets his hand to such things must not make mistakes! But will people be better and happier if now, with the same fanaticism and just such streams of blood, other, though antagonistic, theories, which are nevertheless no more right (for they are of course all false, and only our belief endows them, from one instance to the next, with the shimmer of truth that suffices to delude us), are turned into reality?

But what is anti-Semitism to lead to if not to acts of violence? Is it so difficult to imagine that? You are perhaps satisfied with depriving Jews of their civil rights. Then certainly Einstein, Mahler, I and many others, will have been got rid of. But one thing is certain: they will not be able to exterminate those much tougher elements thanks to whose endurance Jewry has maintained itself unaided against the whole of mankind for 20 centuries. For these are evidently so constituted that they can accomplish the task that their God has imposed on them: To survive in exile, uncorrupted and unbroken, until the hour of salvation comes!

The anti-Semites are, after all, world-reforming busybodies with no more perspicacity and with just as little insight as the communists. The good people are Utopians, and the bad people: businessmen.

I must make an end, for my eyes are aching from all this typing. . . . I had to leave off for a few days and now see that morally and tactically speaking I made a very great mistake.

I was arguing! I was defending a position!

I forgot that it *is not a matter* of right and wrong, of truth and untruth, of understanding and blindness, but of power; and in such matters everyone seems to be blind, in hatred as blind as in love.

I forgot, it's no use arguing because of course I won't be listened to; because there is no will to understand, but only one not to hear what the other says.

If you will, read what I have written; but I do ask that you will not send me an argumentative answer. Don't make the same mistake as I made. I am trying to keep you from it by telling you:

I shall not understand you; I cannot understand you. Perhaps a few days ago I still hoped that my arguments might make some impression on you. Today I no longer believe that and feel it as almost undignified that I uttered any defense.

I wanted to answer your letter because I wanted to show you that for me, even in his new guise, Kandinsky is still there; and that I have not lost the respect for him that I once had. And if you would take it on yourself to convey greetings from me to my former friend Kandinsky, I should very much wish to charge you with some of my very warmest, but I should not be able to help adding this message:

We have not seen each other for a long time; who knows whether we shall ever see each other again; if it should, however, turn out that we do meet again, it would be sad if we had to be blind to each other. So please pass on my most cordial greetings.[30]

On Twelve-Tone Composition and Tonality

4.14 From "Composition with Twelve Tones," c. 1923

During the formative years of the twelve-tone method Schoenberg kept even his closest colleagues in the dark about the details of his compositional activities. In The Path to the New Music *Webern describes visiting Schoenberg in 1917 when he was composing* Die Jakobsleiter: *"He explained to me that he was 'on the way to something quite new.' He didn't tell me more at the time, and I racked my brains— 'For goodness' sake, whatever can it be?' "[31] Concerned to defend his claim to be the originator of twelve-tone composition, particularly against the Viennese composer Josef Hauer, who was also working with related techniques, on February 17, 1923, Schoenberg called his students and friends together to explain the method as he then understood it (for more on the relationship with Hauer, see 5.19, 7.21).[32] The excerpt below is from an unsigned and undated typescript entitled "Komposition mit zwölf Tönen," which was found in the Alban Berg Nachlaß, and which may represent a reconstruction of Schoenberg's presentation at the February 17 gathering by Erwin Stein or another of Schoenberg's pupils.[33] While there are*

many points of contact between formulations here and Schoenberg's writings per-
taining to twelve-tone composition, there are also differences (such as the em-
phasis on a three-voice texture, or his use of the term polytonal) *that may reflect*
errors or misunderstandings in the original document or aspects of the method
that Schoenberg later modified. It would be many years before he himself pub-
lished any detailed explanations of the method. Although he did give several
public presentations on some technical aspects, such as his 1931 radio lecture on
the Variations for Orchestra *(see 5.16), his first substantial publication was the*
essay "Composition with Twelve Tones," from Style and Idea *(1950).*[34]

One creates for oneself an ordering of the twelve tones not by chance (Hauer) but, rather, according to the following principle: a basic shape (Grundgestalt) is built, which must be of [such] a kind that a complementary form can be produced. From this form, the rest of the twelve tones are also to be worked out, so that a three-voice composition results. These forms can be used in every direction, partly as a horizontal voice, partly as chords. These are the motivic basis for all development.[35]

The twelve tones first presented themselves as a succession, from which a three-voiced composition then developed. The second voice functions as the complement of the first. The third voice acts as the rest, part completion, part absence that demands completion.

From these basic shapes all conceivable forms are constructed, following from the inversion, retrograde, and retrograde of the inversion. From this basic shape a dominant form is built, proceeding from the following idea: the dominant of a twelve-tone row lies in the middle, and is the same as the diminished fifth.

Through these transformations eight basic forms are generated, just like eight springs from which forms may flow. The subsequent use of the form can occur more freely.

It would seem that the progression of chords with six or more tones could be justified by the chromatic scale. For the most part, the chords are related so that the second chord contains as many such tones as possible that are chromatically raised from those in the preceding chord. But they seldom occur in the same voice. Then I have noticed that tone doublings, octaves, seldom occur. This is perhaps explained by the fact that the tone doubled would acquire predominance over the others and would thereby become a kind of root, which it should hardly be—but perhaps there is also an instinctive (possibly exaggerated) aversion to recalling even remotely the traditional chords. For the same reason, circumstances seem to dictate that the simple chords of the earlier harmony are not suited to this environment, but I think that there is another reason. I think they would sound too cold, too dry, and too expressionless. Or perhaps what I mentioned at an earlier opportunity applies here.

Namely, that these simple chords, which are imperfect imitations of nature, seem too primitive to us. The perfect consonance is to be handled with the same circumspection as dissonance was earlier. Naturally the occasional meeting on a dissonance could not have been avoided.

Nevertheless, there are still misgivings that the doubled tone will become predominant. Thus perhaps it would be no misfortune if we were to compose not "atonal" music but "polytonal" music. It would then be no surprise if this music, as with monotonal music, were to make felt the aftermath of tonality, in such a way that a tonality arose incidentally. Perhaps the striving to avoid tonality is merely one manifestation of a reaction.

The situation is reminiscent of circumstances in the time of the church modes. With the church modes, since one did not know the fundamental tone, one experimented with all of them. We, since we do not know [the fundamental tone], attempted it with none of them.

The chromatic scale allows *every* tone to be related as a fundamental. The harmonic relationships are so rich that a continuously changing fundamental could occur. Even without chords with five or more tones, a complete tonality would be possible.

The avoidance of tone repetitions and triads is not an eternal law but probably only one manifestation of a reaction. We compose according to our taste, and this has placed restrictions on us. Nevertheless, that we proceeded from this is not proof that we shall adhere to it. A new kind of tonality may be found again. Triads would once again probably be possible. (*Harmonielehre,* p. 70.)

Yet it is possible that a combination of perspectival and nonperspectival components is available in a work of art. In our case, a mixture of triads and chords with many tones occurred. The triad provisionally fulfils the purpose of better marking divisions and of better producing the feeling of beginnings and endings. In this sense it can certainly be employed now. Certainly "purity of style" comes very much into question. Nevertheless, whether there really is a "purity of style" is very doubtful.

As to the question of avoidance of tone repetitions, one must say that this prescription is also, of course, not an eternal law. To avoid tone repetitions completely is, of course, impossible, for then a piece would be ended after twelve tones. So repetition must be possible.

It also happens that certain intervallic steps are often not seen. Namely, the consonant steps. Yet, if one wanted to use "dissonant steps," there would generally be only three steps within the octave (diminished fifth, minor seventh, and major seventh). So the use of consonant steps also is altogether possible. Only the octave is dropped. Our intuition struggles against fifths and fourths probably for the reason that they play such a large role in old music, especially in beginning and ending turns of phrase.

The question of tone repetition should never be interpreted such that, after the twelve tones, the piece has come to an end, but, rather, the case is that after twelve tones another twelve must follow. Nevertheless, it is not the case, as Hauer claims, that after twelve tones the twelve tones are repeated. If one wanted to postpone the repetition of a tone as long as possible, one must then push apart *each* tone as far as possible. For if each tone is postponed at an equal distance, then all twelve tones will be repeated in the same row succession. Thus it follows that the distance of the repetition must be unequal. Tone repetition can occur in one voice, without the eleven other tones having been stated in the meantime. In general, one is to avoid repeating a tone in the same voice much too soon, because the danger might arise that the repeated tone could be perceived as a tonic. But perhaps that is not always to be avoided. (Also, thirds were repeated in monotonal music without a new tonic arising from them. Nevertheless, the danger is far greater in this case, for there is no declared fundamental tone to be opposed.)

On Science, Art, and the Idea

4.15 From the Gedanke *Manuscripts, August 19, 1923, and November 12, 1925*

Schoenberg's formulation of twelve-tone composition was closely bound up with the development of his theoretical thinking about the "musical idea." In the unfinished essay "Twelve-Tone Composition," also from 1923 and closely related to the document given in 4.14, Schoenberg attributed the avoidance of traditional tonal features to "the unconscious urge to try out the new resources independently, to wrest from them possibilities of constructing forms, to produce with them alone all the effects of a clear style, of a compact, lucid and comprehensive presentation of the musical idea."[36]

The short statement "On the Presentation of the Idea," dated August 19, 1923, is the first in the series of the twelve so-called Gedanke *[Idea] manuscripts from 1923 to c. 1940, which culminated in the unfinished treatise* The Musical Idea, and the Logic, Technique, and Art of its Presentation.[37] *The second statement is from a manuscript dated November 12, 1925. In "New Music, Outmoded Music, Style, and Idea," Schoenberg defined the "idea" as follows: "In its most common meaning, the term idea is used as a synonym for theme, melody, phrase or motive. I myself consider the totality of a piece as the* idea: *the idea which its creator wanted to present. [. . .] An idea can never perish."[38] Beyond its explicitly musical meanings, Schoenberg explored the metaphysical and spiritual dimensions of the "idea," in the* Requiem *(4.16),* The Biblical Way *(5.8), and* Moses und Aron *(5.11).*

Science aims to present its ideas exhaustively so that no question remains unanswered. Art, on the other hand, is content with a many-sided presentation from which the idea will emerge unambiguously, but without having to be stated directly. Consequently, in contrast, a window remains open through which, from the standpoint of knowledge, presentiment demands entry.

In counterpoint the issue is not so much the combination *per se* (i.e., it is not a goal in itself), as it is rather the many-sided presentation of the idea: the theme is so created that is already holds within itself all these many *Gestalten* through which this will be made possible.

Compositions executed tonally in every sense proceed so as to bring every recurring tone into a direct or indirect relationship to the fundamental tone, and their technique tries to express this relationship so that doubt about what the tone relates to can never last for an extended period. . . . Composition with 12 tones related only to one another (incorrectly called atonal composition) *presupposes the knowledge of these relationships,* does not perceive in them a problem still to be solved and worked out, and in this sense works with entire complexes similar to the way in which language works with comprehensive concepts whose range and meaning are assumed generally to be known.

The Death of Mathilde Schoenberg

4.16 From the Requiem (1923)

Mathilde, who had been in declining health for some time, died on October 18, 1923. Less than a month after her death, Schoenberg completed the Requiem, *noting on the typescript that he had written sections 2 to 12 on November 15, 1923, between 5:45 and 6:15 in the evening.[39] According to a letter to Zemlinsky dated January 5, 1924, he had written the first part of the text approximately two years before her death.[40] In an unpublished note from the same day he finished the poem, Schoenberg wrote: "Mathilde: I vowed to erect a memorial to you. Now I have begun to keep my word: the text of the* Requiem *is finished. It shall become a memorial so that in hundreds of years one will still say the name Mathilde with the admiration a woman deserves who is able to awaken such love as you did! All the world shall honor you. That shall be the thanks for what you have given me."[41] The* Requiem *was published in the 1926 collection* Texts. *Reich indicates that there were some musical annotations on the manuscript, but there is no additional evidence that a setting was undertaken. The* Requiem *consists of twelve sections; included here are the first section in its entirety, which focuses on a comparison of the spirit of the departed to an "idea," and the final six parts.*

I

Pain, rage till you are still,
Grief, lament till you are weary!
Compassion, open the inner eye:
Here lies life that has run its course,

that suffered while rejoicing,
and rejoiced in suffering:
Passed away!

Passed away—from whence it did not come
and where it will not stay,
to that which is always here and there:
A state:
that is more of the bearable,
less of the necessary,
nothing of reality,
effective, but more intense than this one.

Passed-away life,
Union of all opposites,
Of well-being and woe,
Mourning and joy,
Delight and pain,
Happiness and misery,
Virtue and vice,
Weakness and strength,
Desire and renunciation,
Cowardice and daring . . . !
Passed away, you are more there,
You are closer to us, than before.

Now we love you, dead one,
More than life;
now you are more mysterious to us,
than were your contradictions,
which we could rarely love, but mostly only hate,
because we were rarely capable of love, but mostly only hate,
because you seldom deserved love, but mostly only hate—
so far as we could understand.

Now we understand your contradictions,
Because the greater mystery knows its own.
How could you not be full of them?
How could we hate you?
How could we deny you love,
and leniency and pity?
How could we be cruel to you
and hard and indifferent?
To deny sympathy: gravest guilt!

And that is our everyday life, as it was yours.

Now shame and regret give us,
through compassion, grief, and pain,
the great human moment,
in which expatiating our guilt we feel:
    You can never pass away!

    You can never pass away,
for you have become an idea.
Now you live in memory,
that holds you not long, in its brevity,
you sink, it passes you on,
there to where all ideas reside
and the feelings that possess us:
in the treasure chamber of humanity,
which no key of the everyday can lock.

Thus are you now immortal:
You have become a soul,
whose immortality is our hope
and our certainty.
You must be immortal,
for the immortality of your soul
is our most fervent desire,
which like any true desire,
is not fulfilled in this life.

    Not in this life!
But in the one whose clarity
is the aim of all our striving.

    You can never pass away,
eternal certainty, eternal hope,
eternal longing, eternal pain,
eternal misery, eternal guilt—
Cry . . . !
Cry . . . !
Cry . . . !
And rejoice!
Rejoice,
be full of joy,
for you have just experienced
your great moment.

And from a full heart give thanks,
to the one passed on,
who leads you to the place,
where you find your soul,
your immortal soul.
[· · ·]

VII

Do the wanderers ever meet again?
In the realm of the directionless?
Of the timeless?
And yet on earth time passes!
And all directions diverge!
How is one to find anyone?

VIII

But: my ears hear nothing anymore,
The eyes do not see.
Yes: to sense! to hope! to imagine! . . .
The only reality is mourning.

IX

Should one wish to die?
What is mourning, to the soul,
When one is dead?
Is it still aware of the loved one?
Perhaps it stands so far above it all,
that even that is lost.
What has been gained in return?

X

Hopeless: perhaps we pass
each other by forever,
and never meet again.

XI

To the Lord, a thousand years are as a day.
Such a day, whenever they lose each other,

He gives to lovers,
to see each other again,
to find each other, ever and again.

XII

Be strong!
Reject all comfort:
it wants only to rob you
of what is worth preserving.
Reflect:
The beloved had to go from you uncomforted.
They, too, knew not whither.
They, too, knew nothing of all
You are asking.
Be worthy of them.
Go forth as bravely,
as they went forth.
If one can die—
and that is hard—
then one can also live.

Communications from the Other Side

4.17 From a Diary, November 28 and 29, 1923

Schoenberg made these short notes in a diary less than two weeks after he had completed the Requiem.

November 28, 1923, 10:00 a.m. Ten minutes ago, that is, 9:50 a.m., I suddenly heard three or four times (perhaps oftener) in my wife's voice (which in the beginning I took to be Görgi's): "Papa, Papa . . . ," called in a very intense whisper which made it sound similar to Görgi's. I was standing in the alcove next to the desk and was just thinking about how I could word a letter to Alderman Weber. When I turned around, no one was in the room. It is true that the maid was in the dining room. It is however equally precluded that the maid called out, as that I misunderstood the cry. The cries were, so to say, "*indeliberately fast*"; the first so fast that perhaps they were partly simultaneous, the last following (perhaps as a correction) substantially slower. It is obviously difficult for one from the other side to adapt to our way of doing things one after another. If only Mathilde would speak further! Did she want to warn me?

The expression of the voice, however, was not so, but rather joyful! At any rate, whether a conclusion is to be drawn from it, I do not know. For as she confused the tempo of this world, so perhaps she did the same with the expression and dynamics—for why did she call out in a whisper?

There was a reason? Or in order to ask something?

November 29. Perhaps it is possible for every deceased person to show themselves several times to their loved ones. In so doing, they must only then be able to make good use of these opportunities. Mathilde told that she saw her mother twice, soon after her death. Then never again. I can only remember the description which she once gave to me of it, and which, I want to say here, in one sense is identical to that which I felt.

Namely, Mathilde said (approximately):

"It was not *uncanny at all, but on the contrary, very beautiful.* Just think, I saw my mother as she looked when she was alive. It is there (it was in the kitchen) that she stood. She became gradually more distinct and then less distinct again."

She came out of the kitchen and told me that calmly and joyfully.

I would at this opportunity like to mention the feeling which I had as well. I was so pleasantly stimulated. Perhaps those from the other side have the power to affect our senses and nerves directly just as present bodies do. I would like to say: I had a general feeling as if something were flowing through me. That was something quite inconspicuous. So that I can only recall it with difficulty now. Perhaps they have been given the ability to become apparent to us while flying by (on some kind of planet). Perhaps it is also merely that they think about us? Hopefully it is at least that! I hope to find out more! If it only doesn't happen to me, like Mathilde, who only saw her mother two times. Maybe she should not have told it. I will not do that, for the present at any rate.

Maybe I also should not write anything about it. Since I know that many things should not be said![42]

The Serenade at Donaueschingen; On the Aristocracy

4.18 Letter to Prince Egon Fürstenberg, c. April 1924

Prince Egon Fürstenberg was the principal patron of the contemporary-music festivals in the German town of Donaueschingen, the first of which took place in 1921 under the musical directorship of Heinrich Burkhard, Joseph Haas, and Eduard Erdmann.[43] Schoenberg conducted the Serenade in Donaueschingen on July 20, 1924. As with other compositions from these years, Schoenberg worked on the Serenade *for several years, with the first sketches dating from 1920 and the fair copy completed in April 1923. The score was published by Wilhelm Hansen Verlag (Copenhagen) in 1924. In a letter to the critic and scholar Paul Bekker (1882–1937) of August 1, 1924, Schoenberg commented in similar terms to those below on his attitude toward the aristocracy: "Now I don't mind confessing that at our meeting I received a very pleasant impression of your personality and your ideas, and felt that you have indeed the capacity to behave respectfully to one who deserves respect. It seems to me that the only people who do this are those who respect themselves, and the real skeptics are above all those who do not believe in themselves. On the other hand, someone who believes in himself and respects himself is the one and only person capable of respecting and honoring merit. For this reason I also find association with the aristocracy very pleasant to one who thinks something of himself."*[44]

May it please Your Highness,

May I, first and foremost, most respectfully thank you from the bottom of my heart for the extremely gratifying words that Your Highness has had the goodness to address to me?

The splendid enterprise in Donaueschingen is something I have long admired: this enterprise that is reminiscent of the fairest, alas bygone, days of art when a prince stood as a protector before an artist, showing the rabble that art, a matter for princes, is beyond the judgment of common people. And only the authority of such personages, in that it permits the artist to participate in the distinctive position bestowed by a higher power, is able to demonstrate this demarcation in a sensuously tangible manner to all who are merely educated, who have merely worked their way up, and to make manifest the difference between those who have become what they are and those who were born what they are; between those who arrive at a position and occupation by indirect means and those who are directly born to it. If I may really be permitted to respond to this summons, it would, I must confess, be very much to my own liking to do so with my latest work, the Serenade and, in accordance with your wish, to conduct it myself. It must however be mentioned that this unfortunately cannot be actually a first performance, since the latter will take place—though privately, not in public—on the 2nd May, a performance for which we are just now having the final rehearsals.[45] Yet I will—if Your Highness attaches importance to it—do all that is in my power to secure my publisher's agreement that it shall be at least the first public performance in Germany.

Once more thanking Your Highness most respectfully for all your flattering and kind words, I remain, with deep veneration and respect,

Arnold Schoenberg

On Brevity and the Heathen

4.19 Foreword to Webern's Six Bagatelles for String Quartet, Op. 9, June 1924

Webern's aphoristic Six Bagatelles, *completed in 1913, were published in 1924 by Universal Edition, as part of a publication agreement dating from 1920. The 1920s saw a significant increase in performances of his music in Europe and abroad. Among his regular conducting positions, Webern took over the Workers' Symphony Orchestra and Chorus in Vienna from 1922 to 1934. In 1927 he conducted a concert for the Austrian radio, the first of twenty radio concerts over the next eight years.*

While the brevity of these pieces is their eloquent advocate, such brevity stands equally in need of advocacy. Think what self-denial it takes to cut a long story so short. A glance can always be spun out into a poem, a sigh into a novel. But to convey a novel through a single gesture, or felicity by a single catch of the breath: such concentration exists only when emotional self-indulgence is correspondingly absent.

These pieces will be understood only by someone who has faith in music as the expression of something that can be said only musically. They can no more withstand criticism than this faith can, or any other. If faith can move mountains, disbelief can refuse to admit they are there. Against such impotence, faith is impotent.

Does the performer now know how he is to play these pieces—the listener, how he is to take them? Can barriers remain between performer and listener, when both are men of faith? But how is one to deal with the heathen? With a fiery sword, they can be kept in check, bound over; but to be kept spellbound—that is only for the faithful. May they hear what this stillness offers!

Schoenberg Marries for a Second Time

4.20 From a Letter to Gertrud Kolisch, July 28, 1924

Gertrud Kolisch (1898–1967) was the sister of the violinist Rudolf Kolisch. In a biographical note from 1950 Schoenberg wrote: "I met Gertrud for the first time on New Year's Eve 1923/24 at a gathering at my house. Over the following six months I saw her at the most five or six times. I met her again on July 12, 1924, and on July 13 we became engaged."[46] They were married on August 28, 1924. Schoenberg's Suite (Septet), Op. 29, composed between 1924 and 1926, included several programmatic references to Gertrud and himself. A sketch for the movement titles included "Jo-Jo Foxtrott" (short for the Jolly-Joker), "Fl. Kschw. Walzer" (referring to Fräulein Kolisch), "Film Dva" (Film Diva), and "Tenn Ski" (referring to tennis and skiing.)[47] A sketch page for the Suite is given in fig. 4-3.

[. . .] is it also such a great joy to me? Oh yes! Constantly, when I am thinking about other things (necessities), something surges in me and conjures you up in my imagination, and I feel so happy and am so glad that I cannot express it. I haven't worked at all. I had so much correspondence that had to be dealt with. Then I had to write a commemoration for D. Bach's fiftieth birthday. Also a letter of condolence to Mrs. Busoni; his death has upset me greatly.[48] Yesterday I also hired a chambermaid. Dr. Stiedry, the director of the Volksoper, was here for dinner. *Die glückliche Hand* will be performed (on October 10) at the Volksoper.[49] This is very favorable!—Tomorrow I have to go into town to take care of some things: change money, buy the typewriter, go to Universal Edition, and also to your mother. In the afternoon I have appointments. Thus I shall hardly be able to start working before Thursday. But then I hope it will go well [. . . .]

"Not 'Thou shalt,' 'Thou must'"

4.21 From the Four Pieces for Mixed Chorus, Op. 27, September–December 1925

Although the final two movements for these choral works used texts adapted from Hans Bethge's Chinese Flute, *the source from which Mahler took the poems for* Das Lied von der Erde, *Schoenberg wrote his own poems for the first two pieces. These poems introduce themes that would be later developed in* The Biblical Way *(5.8) and* Moses und Aron *(5.11).[50] In a letter to Berg dated October 16, 1933, following his reconversion to Judaism, he cited the second movement, "Du sollst nicht, du musst," as evidence that his "return to the Jewish faith took place long ago" (see 6.1).[51] The Four Pieces were published by Universal Edition in 1926. A sketch page for the fourth movement of Op. 27 is given in fig. 4-2.*

1. *"No Escape"*

   Brave are they who accomplish deeds
   beyond the limits of their courage.
   They possess the strength to conceive of their mission,
   and the character not to be able to refuse.
   If a God was so unkind as to grant them insight into their condition,
   they are hardly to be envied.
   And that is why they suffer envy.

2. *"Not 'Thou shalt,' 'Thou must'"*

   Thou shalt make unto thyself no image!
   For an image restricts,
   limits, grasps

that which should remain unlimited and unimaginable.
An image demands a name:
Which you can only take from the small;
Thou shalt not worship the small!
Thou must believe in the spirit!
Immediately, unsentimentally,
and selflessly.
Thou must, Chosen One, must, if thou are to remain so!

On Contemporary Musical Trends

4.22 Foreword to Three Satires for Mixed Chorus, Op. 28 (1925–1926)

In a letter of May 13, 1949, to Amadeo de Filippi, Schoenberg said of the Three Satires, *"I wrote them when I was very much angered by attacks of some of my younger contemporaries at this time and I wanted to give them a warning that it is not good to attack me."[52] As is evident from the second piece in particular, Stravinsky ("kleine Modernsky") was a special target (see fig. 4-2). In June 1929 Schoenberg was asked by the editors of the Berlin journal of art and culture* Der Querschnitt *to comment on the current musical situation. In a sketch of a reply that was never sent, he wrote, "I want to hurry answering this question, otherwise I shall get there too late, as happened with the* Satires *that I wrote four years ago about what was then current: they had scarcely been printed when they became obsolete, faster than anything else by me. What had just been considered current didn't exist anymore."[53] Schoenberg did much of the composition of the* Three Satires *at the end of 1925, completing the final movement, along with three short canons that were published as an appendix, in early 1926 after his move to Berlin. The* Three Satires *were published by Universal Edition in 1926.*

This seems to me the greatest danger: that those at whom I have aimed these Satires might be in doubt about whether they should consider themselves attacked.

Let us thus, where text and music seem dark enough for those shunning the light to think they could hide, eliminate uncertainty with less veiled words.

1. I wanted to attack all those who seek their personal salvation by taking the middle road. For the middle road is the only one that does not lead to Rome. But it is the one taken by those who nibble at dissonances, wanting to pass for modern, but who are too cautious to draw the consequences; the consequences that result not only from the dissonances but even more so from the consonances. The same applies to those who make a tasteful selection from the dissonances, without being able to account for the reason why

their discords are allowed, while those of others should be forbidden; those who "don't go so far," without explaining why they go as far as they do. And then the quasi-tonalists who think they can take the liberty of doing anything that shatters tonality, just so long as they occasionally profess their faith in tonality by using a tonal triad, whether it is fitting or not. Who that listens can believe them? And who that possesses knowledge and awareness of form can overlook the fact that their longing for "form" and "architecture" cannot be fulfilled in this way, unless they knew to take precautions in doing so through other and more artistic means: something that is certainly possible.

2. I take aim at those who pretend to aspire "back to. . . . " Such a person should not attempt to make people believe that it is in his hands to decide how far back he will soon find himself; and or indeed that through this he is coming closer to one of the great masters (who "strives his hardest"), while he is actually stepping on his toes by quoting him. This backwards-rake, just now reborn, missed a lot in school and must therefore at once newly experience the tonic and the dominant. One would gladly help him out with a round-trip ticket through the styles. But it is superfluous to disclose the "rules of the game" to him (as the mediocre playfully put it), because his masterly ability consists in "corriger la fortune" and guarantees that he will help himself as usual by looking at his involuntary partner's cards.[54] Moreover, since many a loudly proclaimed "Renaissance" has soon turned out to be a discreet miscarriage, suffice it to say that such a person voluntarily writes as wretchedly as a poor conservatory student is forced to.

3. With pleasure I also attack the folklorists who—either because they have to (because they have no themes of their own at their disposal) or because they do not have to (since an existing musical culture and tradition could eventually bear them, too)—want to apply to the naturally primitive ideas of folk music a technique that only suits a complicated way of thinking. They are reminiscent of those who used the refined "die Schinke" or the folksy "oan Oadelwoass."[55]

4. Finally, all " . . . ists," in whom I can only see mannerists. Their music is enjoyed most by those who constantly think of the slogan, which is intended to prevent them from thinking of anything else.

I cannot judge whether it is nice of me (it will surely be no nicer than anything else by me) to make fun of certain things that were intended to be serious, show considerable talent, and are in part worthy of respect, knowing as I do that anything can be made fun of. About much sadder things. And in a much funnier way! In any case, I am excused since as usual I have done it only as well as I am able. May others be able to laugh about it more than I can; more than I, who am also able to take it seriously!

Perhaps it is this I was trying to hint at?

"At the Crossroads"

4.23 Three Satires for Mixed Chorus, *Op. 28 (1925–1926)*

I. *"At the Crossroads"*

> *Tonal or atonal?*
> *Just tell me*
> *In which stable*
> *In this case*
> *The greater number,*
> *So that one can cling,*
> *Can cling to the safe wall.*
> *Please, no regrets!*

II. *"Versatility"*[56]

> *But who's this beating the drum?*
> *Why, it's little Modernsky!*
> *He's had his hair cut in an old-fashioned queue,*
> *And it looks quite nice!*
> *Like real false hair!*
> *Like a wig!*
> *Just like (or so little Modernsky likes to think)*
> *Just like Papa Bach!*

III. *"The New Classicism"* (A Little Cantata)

> *Tenor:* I shall no longer be Romantic,
>   I hate Romantic;
> *Alto:* Ah . . . !
> *Tenor:* Starting tomorrow, I shall only write
>   The purest Classic!
> *Soprano:* Ah . . . !
> *Bass:* The power of time
>   Can no longer touch him,
> *Soprano* and *Alto:*—See Riemann!—[57]
> *Bass:* Who follows the laws of art
>   To the letter.
> *Soprano* and *Alto:* Letters? If you can master them!
> *Bass:* I'm surprised about the pace of change:
>   From one day until the next
>   You command the perfect form?
>   Can you borrow it?
> *Soprano* and *Alto:* . . . only borrow!

Choir: The main thing is the decision.
   But that is easily made.
   It's technique that irritates so many,
   Which is why so many hate it.
   They simply leave it aside,
   After all, perfection is the motto!
   It matures the idea in timely fashion,
   Even if only on paper.
(closing fugue)
   Classical perfection,
   Severe in every phrase,
   No matter where it may come from,
   That is not the question,
   No matter where it may go to:
   That is the new style.

An Invitation to Moscow

4.24 Letter to Alexander Weprik, May 11, 1925

Shortly before learning of the possibility of his going to Berlin to teach at the Prussian Academy of the Arts, Schoenberg received a letter on May 2, 1925, from the Russian musicologist and composer Alexander Weprik offering him a position at the Moscow Conservatory. Although the negotiations apparently broke off with the announcement of Schoenberg's move to Berlin, there was further correspondence in 1927. Schoenberg again considered a move to Russia in 1934, when Eisler contacted him about setting up a music school (see 6.4).

Dear Sir:

I am in principle possibly ready, as requested in your proposal, to move to Moscow to take over the entire division of musical composition at the conservatory.

I am, however, at present unable to make an offer for the salary, since I am completely uninformed about the cost of living in Moscow. Therefore, I ask conversely that you make a salary proposal to me and with it agree to the following requirements:

I. All the cost of the move would have to be paid, and a comfortable apartment placed at my disposal.

II. I must be given an appropriate assurance (with regard to the limited housing available here) for a possible move back at the dissolution or expiration of the contract.

III. Here I am used to a fairly comfortable standard of living, the cost of which I support without too much effort through composition lessons and in particular through concert tours to present my works. If I have to give up the many advantages of the western location of Vienna with such a move, I would thus require:

1. an appropriate financial arrangement;

2. sufficient vacation time so that I may regularly visit my friends and relatives, and so that I might maintain and renew my career through important concerts; and

3. I would particularly like to be in the position of undertaking an American tour in the 1925/26- or 1926/27-concert season.

I would like to take this opportunity to assure you again that such a position would bring me great satisfaction if I could influence young musicians and not only give them their money's worth through my passion for teaching but also be able to achieve a great many useful things.

In anticipation of your kind response, respectfully,

Arnold Schoenberg.

5 Prussian Academy of the Arts: Berlin, 1926–1933

The Berlin Master Class

5.1 "Requirements for Admission to the Master Class at the Prussian Academy of the Arts" (1925)

Leo Kestenberg (1882–1962), who was in charge of musical affairs for the Ministry of Science, Culture, and Education, and who had earlier appointed Franz Schreker as director of the Hochschule für Musik in Berlin, approached Schoenberg in the spring of 1925 about becoming Busoni's successor at the Prussian Academy of the Arts. On August 28, 1925, Schoenberg signed the contract to become director of one of three master classes in composition, joining on the faculty Hans Pfitzner and Georg Schumann (1866–1952).[1] Pupils came from Germany, Austria, England, the United States, Russia, Greece, and Spain, and included Josef Rufer, Winfried Zillig, Roberto Gerhard, Walter Goehr, Adolph Weiss, Marc Blitzstein, Niko Skalkottas, Norbert von Hannenheim, and Natalie Prawossudowitsch.[2] His position on the faculty brought with it the title of professor, a large salary, a requirement of only six months' teaching each year, professional recognition as a member of the Senate of the Academy, and "permanent" Prussian nationality.[3] The move to Berlin was delayed until the following January because of Schoenberg's travels in the fall, including a performance of the Serenade at the International Society for Contemporary Music in Venice, and surgery for appendicitis in November.

I.

One can only be accepted into the master class who

    1. has the intention and the aptitude to be a composer as his main occupation, and

    2. has completely learned everything of the craft (theory of harmony, counterpoint, theory of form, instrumentation) either in a school, privately, or through independent study, and is in a position to present samples of his talent and his ability in the form of completed works;

    3. as an exception, he who has not fully completed the above-mentioned studies—to the extent that the submitted works give evidence of an unusual

---

Photo previous page: Schoenberg, conducting for a radio broadcast in Berlin, c. 1929. Arnold Schönberg Center, Vienna.

talent and that the person concerned knows himself to be capable—must at least pass a strict examination in the areas of harmony and counterpoint in the form of an independent exam.

II.

The applicants must deposit the following in the office at the Academy of the Arts:

1. an abridged résumé (two pages at the most), which should include their personal information, and the course, success, and location of their studies;

2. if possible, recommendations by earlier teachers or musicians of note;

3. three to five of their works, regardless of instrumentation or size, but chosen according to the following points:

a) where possible, a solid contrapuntal student composition for the evaluation of his knowledge in this area;

b) one or two works written as a student under the guidance of the teacher from which it should be possible to gather the success of the instruction;

c) one or two recently written works that he regards as his most mature;

4. an addressed envelope for the written decision on the application.

Opera and Film

5.2 "Is There an Opera Crisis?" 1926

The Berliner Tageblatt *had solicited a group of commentaries from several prominent composers and opera directors on the widely debated question of the continuing relevance of opera. The* Musikblätter des Anbruch, *published by Universal Edition (and later edited by Theodor Adorno from 1928 to 1931), reprinted the statement by Schoenberg as "especially interesting." Schoenberg's compositional response to the "opera crisis" took very different forms with* Moses und Aron *(5.11) and* Von heute auf morgen *(5.14). For his further thoughts on film and film music, see 5.4.*

It would be a shame to renounce the many possibilities the stage offers through the union of solo and ensemble singing, orchestra, and dramatic action on a grand scale. The theater crisis has been brought about in part by film, and opera finds itself in the same situation: neither can compete with the realism it offers. Film has spoiled the eye of the viewer, one sees not only truth and reality but also every illusion that would have otherwise been reserved for the stage, and that was only intended as an illusion, now presents itself in a fantastic way as reality. In order to avoid the comparison with film, therefore, opera will probably turn away from realism or must otherwise find an appropriate path for itself.

Polemics Against Krenek

5.3 *"Krenek for Light Music: With Regard to Krenek's Article 'Music in the Present,'" February 26, 1926*

Ernst Krenek (1900–1991), a student of Franz Schreker, had followed the lead of Stravinsky and Milhaud in using elements of jazz in his opera Der sprung über den Schatten *(1923, premiered 1924). In a 1923 essay on the work, Schoenberg criticized both the text and music, but concluded, "Alongside all this condemnation, I must say that he is quite certainly someone who expresses himself as a musician. This language is his native language. Whether he says good or bad things, shallow or profound ones, the fact that he has to say them, and his ability to say them, are not open to doubt for him or for his listeners."[4] Krenek's jazz opera* Jonny spielt auf *(1925–1926, premiered in 1927), was one of the most successful pieces of the Weimar period.[5]*

Schoenberg's unpublished commentary on Krenek continues in a still sharper tone some of the topics addressed in the Three Satires. *The specific motivation was Krenek's essay "Music in the Present," printed in* 25 Jahre neue Musik *(Universal Edition, 1925) and based on a lecture delivered on October 19, 1925, at the Congress for Music Aesthetics in Karlsruhe. Schoenberg responds directly to a number of Krenek's arguments and formulations, in particular to a passage he took as an explicit criticism of twelve-tone composition. Krenek describes some present-day "absolute music" as a "game that is only interesting to those who know the rules. . . . Taken to its conclusion, it becomes the self-gratification of an individual who sits in his studio and invents rules according to which he then writes down his notes [literally: writes figures]. In transforming these notes by means of musical instruments into audible substance, none of this adherence to his rules will be passed on to the listeners unless they are prepared for it in the most exacting way."[6] Among the many puns and extensive wordplay in his commentary, Schoenberg concentrates on the various meanings of the word* leicht, *such as "lightweight," "easy," and "simple," along with its sexual connotations as "loose."*

Little Krenek is making propaganda for light music—are things going so badly for it that one must help it along? That's something I certainly hadn't heard. It has usually run like a well-oiled machine. Has the enterprise broken down? Or is it supposed to be getting jammed up? Must one make it easier for the music? Or for him? Or is it not easy enough? (I am afraid he will cause a traffic jam by this, though until now I have regarded him as talented: I have in fact my own rules of etiquette for traffic with such talents.) Or is he supposed to fit in better with this enterprise, since the other still hasn't yet achieved enough turnover for him? Where on earth does such a person want to force his way into, who already understands at such an early age how to get ahead?

Naturally, he has Bach on the tip of his tongue, where his mouth starts to water over the royalties the others earn:[7] today only the theater and dance music offer a composer the opportunity to write functional music. Functional music! What function? What an unbelievable stupidity and a careless toying with misunderstood values! Just because composers have written cantatas for the church means at most that they would be functional music for the church; but for the authors they would simply be music. It is a very stupid confusion to think that musicians have written functional music merely because they were badly paid for it by the church. In that case we also write functional music, because we're badly paid for it by publishers, or because we receive a percentage from the audience in the concert hall. Doesn't Mr. Krenek know very well that the Mahlers and Schoenbergs of church music have concerned themselves just as little with the function of church music as have the Mahlers and Schoenbergs of concert music? Doesn't Mr. Krenek know that Bach's music was so little concerned with the listener that it is still not understood today, and therefore that it was not often performed then (as today) because no one understood it. There were no critics at the time of this church music that many forward strivers would quickly like to elevate; therefore the absence of failures—as would have been the case had they been performed in concert halls—and also the greater failure: that this noise, that was not to disturb the service, only in rare cases aroused the need in anyone to submit to it more than once. This indifference, which is unparalleled, speaks well for the fact that Bach's functional music missed its function. But in Italian opera there were da capos and reprises because it was understood and pleasing. Because it achieved the purpose it had not striven for.

Must the stupid boy blather every platitude that the historians deceive him with? Therefore, then, that Bach's music edified the listener? As far as I know people, they cry out "da capo" if something pleases them. But Mr. Krenek, who approves of the life of warm hearts, enjoys other platitudes and apparently can't go by one without putting his leg up to mark the way that he has gone[8] (and will nevertheless not find his way back), seems to be satisfied with the royalties if they have fulfilled the unique, never-to-be-repeated purpose of making a theatergoer rise and call out "da capo!" for the royalties alone.

We thus have a Krenek operetta to look forward to. Oh God, that will be light; a thousand to a bushel. You make it easy for it! It makes it easy for you: art represents (see page 58) "absolutely nothing so important as we would always like to believe," and "Whoever places art at the beginning of his credo, according to his *modest* experience, *will succeed at nothing.*" The thing that, judging from my naturally thanks be to God modest experience with Mr. Krenek, is even more important to him than all the precepts of all creeds taken together is: *to succeed at something.*

Mr. Krenek imagines a man in his studio, the man writes figures (or sets down notes—one does not have to stay with the image, it's a composer [Ton-setzer] one way or another)—which transmitted in audible substance do not immediately flow over the listener. He regards it as self-gratification if one can't find any loose girl [leichte Dirne] who will hear and feel with him. And he who wishes for only whores as listeners and wants to impose on such light ones still lighter music, wants it to be a measure whether the music is passed on to the listener (thus outside the studio!!).

On Film and Art

5.4 "Draft for a Speech on the Theme of the Talking Film," February 1927

A marginal note reads: "Spoken as I was admitted to the first talking picture." Later, in the 1940 essay "Art and the Moving Pictures," Schoenberg wrote, "When Berlin's UFA made its first successful experiments with talking pictures, about 1928 or 1929, I was invited to record myself in picture and sound. The speech I delivered was an enthusiastic address of welcome to the new invention through which I expected a renaissance of the arts. [. . .] How wrong I had been!" Yet while bewailing the proliferation of "the lowest kind of entertainment," he goes on to describe his hope for film dramatizations of "Balzac's Seraphita, *or Strindberg's* To Damascus, *or the second part of Goethe's* Faust, *or even Wagner's* Parsifal." *The essay concludes with a proposal for the film industry to devote some of its resources to "pure art," on the basis of the argument that while the audience for such films would be small, just like the concert audience they would attend a film many times over many generations; "perhaps people might come to realize then that art is less expensive than amusement, and more profitable."[9] In 1930 Schoenberg composed his* Accompaniment to a Film Scene, *Op. 34, which was conceived independently of any specific film or scenario, beyond the sparse programmatic outline, "threatening danger, fear, catastrophe," indicated in the subtitle. The short orchestral work resulted from a commission to contribute to a special series for the Heinrichshofen publishing house, which specialized in scores for the still thriving German silent-film industry.*

One should not consider the talking film to be simply a coupling of picture, language, and music.

On the contrary, it is a completely new and independent instrument for innovative artistic expression.

In this sense it has a great future.

It is surely here through the force of the Idea that the word and art music will soon gain decisive influence.

Therefore the application of overall standards will become the rule, standards that up to now could only be reached by exceptionally gifted personalities like Chaplin.

Namely: standards of artistic value!

German film has previously been regarded as too burdened with ideas and emotions.

But now true artists will be able to grant to it true and deep ideas and emotions:

then marketability of broad mass appeal will certainly no longer alone determine production;

then German film will achieve the position that corresponds to the rank of its poets and musicians!

Two Statements on the Third String Quartet, Op. 30, 1927

5.5 From "Prefaces to the Records of the Four String Quartets," 1937, and from "Preface to the Four String Quartets, c. 1949

This string quartet was commissioned by Mrs. Elizabeth Sprague Coolidge and performed (1927) in Vienna on the occasion of one of the festivals of chamber music, which this great patron of the art of chamber music arranged in Vienna.[10]

Neither at this first performance, nor at some following performances in Prague and Berlin did it provoke any kind of riot, as my former two string quartets had done. This might make one think that now my music was understood and I finally had succeeded in convincing the public of my mission as a composer. But it would be a great error to assume this. Because when I read afterwards the criticisms I could realize there was now a different attitude towards my work than before. On account of the success of my "Gurrelieder" my reputation had changed and the public as well as critics believed in my sincerity and in my knowledge. But this new reputation was even worse than my former. Because while in spite of the riots, caused by part of the public, there were always a certain number of critics who stood by my work against the opposition, now there was a certain unanimity among these judges, saying that I might possess a remarkable musical knowledge and technique, but did not create instinctively, that I wrote without inspiration. I was called a constructor, a musical engineer, a mathematician.

This was caused by the fact that I had meanwhile begun to use the "Method of composing with twelve tones." According to the belief of the ordinary, everyday critics, the use of such a method could only be attempted in a scientific way, and a scientist seemed to them opposed to the concept of an inspired composer. Actually this method of composing was a serious difficulty to every composer whose inspiration was not strong enough to overcome such impediments, which I personally did not feel. However, I was now marked again and will have to wait another twenty years until music lovers will discover that this is music like other music and differs only in so far from other music as one personality is different from another.

[From the "Analysis of the Third String Quartet, First Movement"]

As a little boy I was tormented by a picture of a scene of a fairytale "Das Gespensterschiff" ("The Ghostship"), whose captain had been nailed through the head to the topmast by his rebellious crew. I am sure that this was not the "program" of the first movement of the third string quartet. But it might have been, subconsciously, a very gruesome premonition which caused me to write this work, because as often as I thought about this movement, that picture came to my mind. I am afraid a psychologist might use this story as a stepping-stone for premature conclusions. Being only an illustration of the emotional background of this movement, it will not furnish enlightenment of the structure. We must not forget, that a theory for teaching and judgment must be the goal of research, whether it is based on acoustics or on psychology—but it is not as easy as that.

Concerning Rehearsals for a Performance of the *Gurrelieder*

5.6 Letter to Edward Clark, February 24, 1927

Schoenberg was increasingly active as a conductor during his years in Berlin, particularly of his early works, including Pelleas und Melisande *and* Gurrelieder. *After its first performance in February 1913 and other performances the following year,* Gurrelieder *had not been heard again until 1920, when Schoenberg conducted the work with the Vienna Philharmonic at the State Opera. Thereafter, the work received a number of performances throughout Europe, including Amsterdam, Prague, and Duisberg in 1921; Vienna in 1923; Mannheim in 1930; and Nuremberg and Berlin in 1931. A* Christian Science Monitor *review of a January 27, 1928, London performance, the preparations for which are discussed below, included the following: "Not much of the 'Gurrelieder' had been heard at Queen's Hall before the greater part of the audience turned to its neighbor and whispered 'Wagner.' Yet the finest passages in the 'Gurrelieder' are wholly characteristic of their composer, and explain much that at first mystifies in his later works. It is not a pose when Schönberg vehemently denies he is a revolutionary, and refuses to admit that there is necessarily any change in fundamentals because composers now use more dissonances than they used to. Rather is he an ardent 'evolutionary.' [. . .] Schönberg himself came over to conduct the performance of the 'Gurrelieder' at Queen's Hall and was not only welcomed with exceptional warmth but received an ovation at the end."[11] Edward Clark (1888–1962), who served as Berlin correspondent for the* Musical Times, *became Schoenberg's pupil in 1912, after having assisted with his move to Berlin. From 1922 to 1936 he worked for the BBC as a conductor, administrator, and champion for new music.*

Dear Mr. Clark,

I was sick and still am; therefore the delay in my reply.

I am rather disappointed that I am supposed to do *Gurrelieder* with three rehearsals, when before I have always had at least ten. But I still hope that you will be able to provide me with at least a fourth. For with three it can scarcely be managed since the piece lasts two and a half hours! If, minus the breaks, I therefore have at my disposal at most around three times two and three-quarter hours—thus all together eight and one-quarter hours—then one could just play through it three times without a break, and I don't know how I am supposed to concentrate on the hard parts; and one must definitely rehearse the thing a little bit with the chorus! I have carefully thought about the situation: I can do it some-how, but it can hardly turn out to be a beautiful performance. I shall play all the easy parts only once, then somewhat more time will remain for the difficult parts. That will one hopes be sufficient; if I could at least also have a dress rehearsal, then things would go somewhat better.

So far as the personnel is concerned: the orchestra (150 players) is rather too large; between 130–135 is sufficient for me. The choir by com-parison is definitely too small. At least the male chorus for the "Wild Hunt" (namely the first) must be larger. That is a twelve-part choir, you know. Each part must be sung by at least twelve to fifteen men, so that must be a choir at least 120–150 strong. In the closing mixed chorus around 60 sopranos, 50 altos, 50 tenors, and 50 basses would be sufficient. I could also manage in the second male chorus with around 30 first tenors, 25 second tenors, 25 first basses, and 25 second basses. Only, as I said, the first male chorus must be more strongly filled in. One could possibly in this case, as I have already recommended elsewhere, rein-force the first tenors with some altos. The tenor parts are actually very demanding here on account of the high range.

In any case, it is urgently necessary to begin with the rehearsals at once. The most urgent are:

1. The male choruses
2. The speaker

Both of these *absolutely cannot begin too early to learn their parts!*

I would very much like to be there at least ten or so days before the concert. Then I shall personally hold the following rehearsals:

3–4 Orchestral rehearsals (9–12 hours)	9–12 hours
One each with each of the three male choruses	6 "
2 times with the first male chorus, all together	4 "
2 times with the second male chorus	4 "
1–2 times with the closing chorus	3 "
With each singer 1–2 times c. 1½ hours	8 "
With the speaker 4–5 times " "	7 "
together c.	45 hours

therefore I really need approximately eight days.

I ask that you lay out the rehearsals from the outset so that I can begin at once to work with the male choruses and the speaker.

Perhaps you could send me right away an approximate sketch of the rehearsal schedule. I can quite well rehearse up to nine hours a day on occasion. But one must break it up where possible so that it is not necessary too often. Please tell me also whether the choir rehearsals will be in the evenings or otherwise what time of day, and how long they can last.

I assume that the choirs will *already be prepared* before I come! Who will do that? Will you do that?

Naturally the singers must also have completely mastered their parts, for I would like to study only the diction with them.

One hopes you will provide for me a young musician to accompany the choral and solo rehearsals. For you know that I cannot play the piano!

Now something very important:

please have the English translation written into a piano score at once and send it to me. I must have this copied into my score and, where possible, learn it by heart!

If it is difficult for you to write to me in German, write in English; I understand it very well.

Now I think I have said everything and look forward to your prompt reply.

With many warm regards,

On National Styles

5.7 "Suggestion for the Foundation of an International School of Style," March 1927

In contrast to the combative tone of some of his other statements about the superiority of German music (see. 4.6, 4.7), Schoenberg proposes here a model of international exchange very much in keeping with the internationalist mood of the time. A note at the end of the documents adds, "Suggestion for the foundation of an international school of style, which I conceived around 1920 and recommended for the first time on the occasion of the establishment of the Mahler Fund in Holland."

The International School of Style should impart to students and teachers the knowledge of the compositional and performance styles of the leading musical nations.

It will accordingly aim to achieve the following:

I. To ensure that foreign works will always be understood and performed in the sense of their national characteristics.

II. It is to be expected (and striven for) that an exchange of ideas combined with practical exercises will stimulate the mutual acquisition of certain improvements or preferences.

This end shall be worked toward through practical and theoretical means.

Practically, by having masters of the various nations teach in the school for shorter or longer periods. Composers as well as instrumentalists, singers, conductors, choral conductors shall be available, whose responsibilities can be ranked and determined in accordance with their importance in providing a living example through their own performance, and in the direct guidance and suggestions that they offer when the students play or perform.

Theoretically, in that the teachers will provide, according to a plan I shall prepare, quite definite explanations (perhaps lectures) about their subjects, which shall assist both the teachers as well as the students in grasping and recognizing the greater or lesser merit of the various methods.

The foreign artists must by no means be limited to the performance of works from their own nations, for it is just as interesting to Germans how the French, Italians, and Russians conceive of Beethoven or Bach and why they do it that way, as it is for the others to know how we in Germany conceive of their works.

The students of this institution, which will probably be the first of its kind, could naturally be members of all nations.

They shall be able to study as many subjects as they wish. Just as they shall have completely free choice of teachers.

In general, it would be good to demand a certain preparatory training. But this should not be made into an absolute condition, because it would serve no purpose for such a school to be further vested with the same authority as other schools with regard to examinations and the issuing of certificates, etc. For a student would only come here who found such preparation necessary for themselves in order to increase their knowledge. The fulfillment of conditions of admission would only be necessary here insofar as it concerned the granting of scholarships, support, etc.

But obviously, the character of a school of higher education, which thus assumes adequate background, would be retained in all things.

(The restrictions above are aimed at ruling out bureaucratic pedantry, which would, for example, exclude a composer who is no piano virtuoso but who naturally must also know this style, from the class of a pianist.)

In general less weight will be placed on the theoretical instruction than on the practical. But obviously theoretical subjects will be added.

A Play About the Formation of a Jewish State

5.8 The Biblical Way, *1926–1927*

Following the Mattsee incident in 1921 (4.5), Schoenberg became increasingly interested in the Zionist movement.[12] *Already anticipating elements of the plot of* The Biblical Way, *in 1924 he wrote his "Position on Zionism," for the publication* Pro Zion!: *"The re-establishment of a Jewish State could come into being only in the way similar events have always occurred in history: not through words and morality, but through successful military might and a fortunate commonality of interests."*[13] *He worked extensively on the play between 1926 and 1927, with the final typewritten versions dated July 12, 1927. Materials for the staging and sketches for incidental music also survive. Schoenberg negotiated with Max Reinhardt and others for a performance, but the work was never performed in his lifetime.*

The play, which is closely linked to the libretto for Moses und Aron, *focuses on the problem of reconciling the Idea and its presentation, embodied in the main character, Max Aruns, who is described in the text as wanting to be "Moses and Aron in one and the same person!"*[14] *The first act takes place in Europe of the present day (1920s) and concerns Aruns' negotiations with the emperor of the fictional African state of Ammongaea for the establishment of New Palestine in his territory, and, still more centrally, Aruns' struggle to unify the various Jewish parties and interests, "orthodox and assimilationist, socialist and capitalist." The first act ends with a speech by Aruns, excerpted below, in a stadium in the Alps where many spectators have assembled to watch sporting contests. The second and third acts take place in New Palestine and chart the dissension and intrigues that bring the settlement to a crisis. Act 3, scene 3, given below, consists of a long dialogue between Aruns and David Asseino, the Orthodox religious leader of the settlement. At the conclusion of the third act, threatened by inner turmoil and external enemies, the inhabitants of the settlement riot, culminating in the murder of Aruns by the mob.*

Scene 9

(The bleachers, which had been sparsely occupied before, are now full. The young athletes occupy the greater part of the stage. The opponents of Aruns—GOLBAN, GADMAN, SETOURAS, etc.—stand in a group off to the side, without however being particularly conspicuous. Gadman's active interest in Aruns' address should nonetheless become clearly visible. As soon as ARUNS is seen on the balcony, the sound of a trumpet calls for silence, and the audience rises to its feet; the audience remains standing during Aruns' address.)

Scene 10

ARUNS: People of Israel!

What is this celebration?

Is it a sports festival? A parade? A political gathering? A popular rally?

Is this day not a day like any other?

No, it is not; it is one that shall survive forever among the Jewish people as a day of remembrance.

As on the eve of that day when the youngest son asks:

"Why do we sit reclining today?"

But here he will have to ask differently:

"Why do we all stand today?

Why did we all rise? Why don't we remain sitting, on the ground, humiliated, as on all other days before?"

We have risen to our feet, we have lifted and elevated ourselves to a greatness no one would have expected.

We have again straightened our crooked backs, that had become bent because they had to be ready to receive every beating that should have been dealt to others. We stand here again, as did that ancient, tenacious, defiant, stiff-necked people of the Bible; but unlike then, today we are not stiff-necked *against* our God but rather *for* Him, He who has elected us to be His people.

Brothers! Do you still know those humble, downtrodden, frail little Jew-boys—*Hep-Hep!*—who looked around intimidated whenever they found themselves among people not of our own; who were nonetheless considered presumptuous, and branded as "impertinent Jews" whenever they dared to make a move or even dared to refuse to swallow any insult; who were ranked as an inferior race even in the imagination of the lowest people of other races; who were always scorned and despised by all other nations, and most of all by those whose spiritual concepts could not have been shaped without ours?

Brothers! Do you still remember those humiliated, scorned, persecuted little Jew-boys who, as much as they were despised, still dared—one against ten—to muster enough courage not to let their race disappear, and who were too proud to intermingle with those who considered them by birth to be inferior aliens?

These cowardly Jews, who had the courage to accept being ridiculed as "cowards" as long as they could remain Jews, who made every sacrifice, suffered every persecution, put up with every curse and every wounding of their pride, because none of them for a moment ever ceased to feel that we had been chosen for such suffering; that these sorrows might bring forth future benefits to us; that only in sorrow is life brought forth; that we must suffer because we were chosen to maintain the Messianic Idea throughout the ages; the strict, unadulterated, relentless Idea; that there is only one, eternal, invisible and unimaginable God.

We are an ancient people.

What could a God mean to us, a God whom we could understand, whom we could represent in an image, whom we could influence?

We do not need miracles. Persecution and contempt have strengthened us, have built our tenacity and stamina, nourished and fortified our bodies, enhanced our ability to resist.

We are an ancient people.

As yet not every individual can fully grasp our concept of God, nor recognize that all that happens derives from a Supreme Being, whose laws we can sense and acknowledge, but about whose essence we must not inquire.

But as soon as every last man can grasp it:

then, the Messiah will have come.

The Messiah of inner equilibrium!

———

Dear young friends! Your teachers and leaders have planted this faith in you, developed your minds and trained your bodies.

Since you have understood that the knowledge of the true essence of God towers above all other knowledge and spiritual aspirations, and since you have learned to appreciate the value of your physical strength and to find pleasure in it, you were able in a short time to prove yourselves capable of accomplishing feats and enduring great efforts at which your physically weakened forefathers would have failed. In no way do you lag behind the nations amongst whom we have sojourned. You possess the strength, which in a few generations will be the strength of our entire people. Your vigor and health will regenerate that which is old and decayed in the trunk of Israel. You alone are capable of successfully reforming our nation, of transforming a nation of scholars, artists, merchants and money-changers into a healthy and strong nation, dedicated to leading a life worthy of a nation to whom God has granted a homeland.

You are now able to undertake our noble task!

You are gifted with flexibility, drive, enthusiasm, adaptability and readiness for sacrifice.

To you has been allotted the most difficult task.

For all our striving is oriented toward our youth.

The future is theirs to enjoy, a future in which no Jew will have to depend on being respected or despised by the people of other nations.

Therefore, the youth has to assume the decisive share of the task.

You, young people, you shall be the pioneers in the new land; you shall prepare the soil, and lay the foundation upon which the glorious edifice of the State will be erected.

This is the deeper meaning of today's celebration, and therefore it shall become a day of remembrance forever and ever.

Today, for the sake of your people, you sacrifice all your past striving for those intellectual pursuits that have been useful in the Diaspora. And today, through your strength, you proclaim that you are ready to serve a knowledge superior to common human wisdom: that you want to enable your people to *live* its concept of God to the end, to *dream* it to the end!

(*Collective rejoicing, in which Gadman's passionate expressions of enthusiasm are evident. After a while, trumpet blasts; thereafter, a moment of silence, followed by a hymn sung by all.*)

End of Act I

(*Curtain*)

[. . .]

Act III

Scene 3

ARUNS: Venerable man, I see it as a sign of God's grace that He sent you to me at this hour.

ASSEINO: May God preserve your enterprise and bestow His blessing upon you! May He be at your side, illuminate you and fill your heart with the spirit of His eternal and immutable laws.

May you be blessed, for you have put a new heart into our people and returned them to the belief in the sublimity of our religion.

You were on the right way when you anchored your enterprise in God's word; when you declared that God had elected this nation above all others in order to firmly believe in the one and only, unimaginable God; only this belief made us into a nation, destined to survive and to preserve this Idea through the centuries, until all mankind would be able to comprehend it.

God has so far blessed your enterprise, and will not cease to bless it, as long as you remain faithful to His word and put your trust only in His spiritual might.

ARUNS: I seem to hear in your words a certain reproach which astonishes me. I am not aware that I have done anything which did not flow spontaneously from my idea. After I became conscious of the fact that the Scriptures showed the way to liberation, everything else followed as a direct consequence. It became self-evident that we could not achieve our independence by depending on the good graces of other nations; that we would have to obtain it through our own power; that we would have to employ weapons adequate to our own times; once all resistance and all opposing factions had been identified, every subsequent idea, every action followed on its own.

ASSEINO: (*raising his voice*) Max Aruns, you want to be Moses and Aron in one and the same person! Moses, to whom God granted the Idea but from whom He withheld the gift of speech; and Aron, who could not grasp the Idea but had the ability to communicate it and to move the masses. Max Aruns, you who so well understood the art of interpreting God's word in contemporary terms, how could you fail to understand why God did not unite both powers in only one person?

ARUNS: I am flattered that you should use my interpretation to underscore your criticism, and that makes me hopeful that you may also accept some of my other contemporary interpretations of the divine word.

If I may contrast my opinion with yours, the problem you stated is solved as follows:

To me, Moses and Aron represent two activities of *one* man—a *statesman,* whose two souls ignore each other's existence. The purity of his Idea is not blurred by his public actions; and these actions are not weakened by his thoughtful consideration of yet unsolved problems that the Idea presents.

But you also unjustly accuse me of arrogance. I would never have wanted to be more than, at most, a kind of Aron, had there been time to wait until all of our people whose gifts qualified them to be a Moses agreed upon one, upon the leading one.[15] In the urgency of the situation, I had to step forward *alone,* and for this very reason I am presently speaking to you, for I recognize in you the only living man from whose spiritual, human and ethical greatness we may expect the wonder of a second revelation.

Asseino, God has revealed His will through the mouth of His prophets. You shall be a Moses, a Samuel, or an Elijah to us; give our nation a contemporary Law which would allow us to hold our own amongst all the competing nations, and do not constrain us to live according to laws which were valid five thousand years ago.

ASSEINO: You speak blasphemy!

Were I to be a spokesman for God, I would raise my voice only to proclaim forever and ever the eternity of His word.

ARUNS: In God's word only His spirit is eternal! The letter of the word is only its figurative appearance, adapted to a given time—namely, the circumstances of the wandering in the wilderness.

But a nation in our own time cannot afford, every Friday, to shut down its blast furnaces and close its electrical plants.

ASSEINO: Once again your materialism betrays your Idea.

ARUNS: You have reproached me for being a man of action. Very well: as a man of action I demand from you, man of the spirit, the new laws!

ASSEINO: What you demand from me is as if Aron had asked Moses to consent to and assist him in erecting the Golden Calf.

ARUNS: Not at all. I only demand your consent not to force our nation to strict observance of the letter of the law as articulated during the wandering in the wilderness, but to allow us to observe the living spirit of the law.

ASSEINO: We shall never understand each other.

Let us bring this debate to an end.

[. . .]

Scene 7

[. . .]

(*ARUNS lies on the floor, dying.*)

ARUNS: Lord, you have smitten me. Thus I have brought it upon myself. Thus Asseino was right, when he accused me of being presumptuous, of wanting to be both Moses and Aron in one person. Thus I have betrayed the Idea, relying upon a machine rather than upon the spirit.[16]

Lord, only now do I recognize it, and implore you: accept my blood as expiation.

But do not let these poor innocent people atone for my sins.

Lord, my God, save them! Give them a sign that you are castigating only me for my sins against the spirit, but that you will not let the Idea die with me.

Lord, my God, I have been vanquished, smitten, castigated.

I am dying, but I feel that you will allow the Idea to survive. And I shall die in peace, for I know that you will always provide our nation with men ready to offer their lives for this concept of the one and only, eternal, invisible and unimaginable God.

(*ARUNS dies*)

On His Creative Process

5.9 "Creative Agony," April 7, 1928

As Schoenberg noted in his remarks on the Third String Quartet (5.5), together with the dissemination of information about the twelve-tone method came the charge that he was "a constructor, a musical engineer, a mathematician." Adolf Weissmann's Problems of Modern Music *(1925) claimed that this "dialecticism, excess of cleverness constantly seeking expression," had fettered his creativity and crippled his imagination, with the result "that since 1913 Schönberg has given the world little music of value, but has nevertheless exercised a vast influence, increasing as his productivity lessens, through the fanatic devotion of his disciples."[17] Schoenberg returned to the question of the "Heart and Brain in Music" in many writings throughout the rest of his life.[18]*

"Creative agony" . . . an expression often to be seen in recent critiques about me.

To engage in polemics against such things, as I often do, can easily give the impression that one wanted to defend oneself. But it must at least be granted to me that I don't do it because I regard my position as weak; also not only for the joy of the attack; perhaps at best it is in pursuit of the truth; but probably I do it because I believe it to be valuable for future generations to show what the author himself had to say about this, regardless of what my future importance might be. That I cannot in the least influence the verdict on me through such polemics is clearer to no one more than myself. For I know that only what the works say, or what one senses in them, can determine my ultimate position, and also that in the end this could not be altered through a flood of various party principles.

Therefore: in general I write little, but *very quickly.* Let it be established here what I have often said:

1. The monodrama *Erwartung,* including the complete indication of instrumentation, was written in eleven to twelve working days within a fourteen-day period.

2. I composed the second and fourth movements of the Second String Quartet, after having already made sketches for the beginnings, in barely three days.

3. I composed the Third String Quartet, Op. 30, in a scant five weeks within a six-week period, during which I was sick for five or six days.

4. The entire first part of *Gurrelieder* was composed in three weeks. If I am not mistaken, I needed approximately five weeks for the second and third parts.

5. In the case of *Pierrot lunaire,* I often wrote two pieces in one day. Although I had already begun to rehearse the completed movements, the composition of the entire work lasted approximately from March until the beginning of June, except for one piece, which I finished in Carlshagen in July.[19]

—There are only a very few pieces that I composed slowly; when I have actually set myself to a task, it has gone quickly. But I have often, mostly for external reasons, had to interrupt a work for some time and have then found it difficult to resume.

Still to be mentioned is the first part of *Die Jakobsleiter:* I composed up to the ensemble "Soul, Gabriel . . . etc.," in an unbelievably short time. I believe in approximately—I can look it up! It states in the sketchbook: "started at the beginning of June, 1917," and with the last sketch, "reported for duty September 19, 1917!" Starting with June 19, 1917, that is thus three months!

I haven't noticed any "creative agony" along the way. Rightly or wrongly my works may displease, but for the most part they please me very well! In any case, I am not acquainted with this condition of "creative agony."

Usually when I am composing I am absolutely unaware that I am working—I am very far away! Only after some time, after days, after weeks, do I sense a certain weariness.

This is true: whether one believes to the contrary does not matter to me in the least.

On Contemporary Developments, Fashion, and Radio

5.10 Selected Aphorisms and Short Statements, 1926–1930

As is evident from the items below, Schoenberg often set himself apart from the new musical trends of the 1920s and 1930s connected with such composers as Stravinsky, Milhaud, Hindemith, Krenek, and Weill; such slogans as neoclassicism, polytonality, Gebrauchsmusik [music for use], Neue Sachlichkeit [the new objectivity], and Gemeinschaftskunst [art for the community]; and the new technologies of the radio and phonograph that were transforming the audience for music. In "My Blind Alley" (1926) he ironically embraced the frequent charge that he was isolated from the new music: "Measures are needed to stop any more aspiring composer from following me down my blind alley, so I am henceforth shutting off the entry to it with a row of twelve tones."[20]

Schoenberg's claims of isolation from the audience and his attempt, in works like the Three Satires, *to position his school against all other contemporary trends, originate most fundamentally in his conviction that the pure Idea would never be accessible to broad understanding. But there are also important connections between his stance and the formation during these years of what became known as the Second Viennese School, through which Schoenberg, Berg, and Webern associated themselves with the earlier Viennese triumvirate of Mozart, Haydn, and Beethoven, and thus with the one true path of the Austro-German classical tradition. But if the idea of the Second Viennese School necessitated the formation of firm aesthetic, stylistic, political, and national boundaries, Schoenberg's compositional activities and other writings indicate a much deeper and more ambivalent encounter with contemporary developments (see 5.14, 5.15, 5.16). In the essay "My Public," from 1930, he wrote: "But whether I am really so unacceptable to the public as the expert judges always assert, and whether it is really so scared of my music—that often seems to me highly doubtful."[21]*

"Alone at Last," February 4, 1928

Oh, how good it is.

How ashamed I was several years ago; how I nearly sank into the ground; how I would gladly have sought out the darkest corners of the earth, hidden myself in the most remote places—when I thought of the many who had become my admirers overnight.

Innocent, as I believed myself to be, I saw it as a test from heaven, but then almost became mad and began to believe in my guilt.

It was a period of deepest depression as I saw myself suddenly surrounded, hemmed in, besieged, by a circle of admirers I had not earned.

I overcame them, starved them out, remained deadly serious, moralized to the point of suicide—they fell off like rotten fruit—I am rid of them.

What good that does me!

Finally alone again!

"Easily Understood," April 26, 1928

Many who liked my earlier works dislike my current ones. They simply have not understood the earlier ones properly.

"The Tempo of Development," Roquebrune, 1928[22]

A French critic thinks (on the occasion of my Suite for Seven Instruments [Op. 29]) that I would surely by now have overcome purely intellectual counterpoint.

I don't develop so quickly as the gentleman thinks. He is confusing me with Milhaud, Poulenc, Stravinsky, and all these producers of the new fashions, who throw a new garb on the market for every season.

To be quite exact, for about twenty-five years (if not longer) I have always said the same thing, and always better. One can recognize that I am always saying the same thing mainly in the fact that this is still not understood.

"Fashion," Roquebrune (c. 1928–1929)

Senseless as fashion often seems—and leaving aside the excesses of brainless dreamers and Romantics—it has far more sense to it than one would usually assume. One cannot jump on a streetcar with long skirts; sewn-on collars get dirty sooner than the most well-cared-for shirt; one can run faster with knickerbockers than with long pants; but to fasten socks comfortably and reliably remains difficult, and the search will continue for other ways of doing it.

But the color and shape of cars and even typewriters change apparently without reason: their appearance does not fit in, so one changes them, like the color and pattern of material. But is that really the reason? Or is it not that the factories which keep a hundred thousand men occupied would have to be locked up if everyone acquired his car, his typewriter, and his evening clothes for life, and perhaps could even pass them on to the next generation, just as was the case with wedding dresses in earlier times?

There is no objective justification for fashion, but only nonobjective, subjective reasons. And it is this senseless nature of fashion that one would now like to transfer to art.

And it succeeds. Except for one thing: it changes like fashion, but ceases to be art.

In this America dominates. Film and jazz, rejecting long-lasting riches through worldly living, are dedicated—to understate and exaggerate at the same time—to sudden and unfounded change, on the one hand, and to the standardized mass production of successful models on the other. It was easy to foresee that such overexploitation must quickly lead to failure. It would have happened the same way with music, if the true art did not possess the strength to withdraw to a lonely island and, in the shadow of true spirituality, to remain untroubled by the hustle and bustle of the day. One day or many: what role does that play in the eternity of the Idea?

"Radio" (1), May 28, 1927

Previously someone who wanted to broadcast platitudes relied on the fact that he was talentless and the others witless. Today their connection can even be wireless.

"Radio" (2), July 23, 1932

The radio broadcasts no voices lower than the tenors: no basses! The upper half of the music—a woman without any lower parts![23]

"Telegraphic Delivery," April 9, 1929

The Prussian minister of education, (and on his behalf Mr. Kestenberg) have telegraphically ordered music for the community [Gemeinschaftsmusik], and expect now not only that it will come but also that it will be telegraphically delivered.

But lo and behold: now it comes through the radio! The upper half of all music for the lower ten thousand times ten thousand.

"Music for the Community," Berlin, March 15, 1929

It is never too soon to write music for the community, but even more so: music for use [Gebrauchsmusik] (an awful word). By my reckoning, one would have to start fifty to a hundred years in advance.

"Art for the Community," February 28, 1928

Surely I have already said it often enough:

I do not believe that the artist creates for others. If others want to establish a relationship between themselves and the artwork, that is their concern, and the artist cannot be expected to deny this to them.

Although he should!

Although he should deny them the possibility of adorning themselves with a pale reflection of the artwork.

The friend of art always profits by association with the artwork; it always gives, and as a result mostly loses—it is in danger of acquiring use value.

Art for the people: one can also see the danger here.

Art is from the outset naturally not for the people.

But one wants to force it to be. Everyone is supposed to have their say. For the new bliss consists of the right to speak: free speech! Oh God!

Art bound, speech free!

The speech out of every man's mouth may assault art!

Can one expect that an artist creates for others?

And what is one supposed to think of art for the community [*Gemeinschaftskunst*]? (But I don't want to say what that is, for in ten years in any case no one will know anymore, and so why should I introduce the term into music history?)

An imaginative thoughtlessness—an idea without a conception: "Oh how beautiful this world would be if all people were artists (also those without talent)"; that is approximately the world of sentiment and ideas to which it corresponds.

"O word, thou word, that I lack!"

5.11 Moses und Aron, *1928–1932*

Schoenberg's ideas for Moses und Aron *date back at least to 1926 and* The Biblical Way; *he wrote the first draft of the text in September and October 1928 and continued to revise it over the following years. The music for the first two acts was composed from 1930 to 1932; only a few sketches survive for the third act. Adapting material from the book of Exodus, the first act begins with the calling of Moses to lead his people out of Egypt through the intermediation of Aron, who persuades the people with miracles. In the second act Aron creates the Golden Calf to appease the people, who have grown angry about Moses's long absence at the Mount of Revelation. The resulting bloody "orgy of drunkenness and dancing" is interrupted by the sudden return of Moses bearing the Tablets of the Law, depicted below in act 2, scene 5. The third act consists of an extended dialogue between Moses and Aron, ending with Aron's death.*

Although the fragmentary state of the opera has become part of its meaning, as the ultimate embodiment of its central theme of the unimaginable, unrepresentable Idea, Schoenberg did hope to complete it. In a letter dated January 22, 1945, requesting support from the Guggenheim Foundation, he mentioned both Moses und Aron *and* Die Jakobsleiter, *writing: "I feel: my life task would be fulfilled only fragmentarily if I failed to complete at least those two largest of my musi-*

cal [works]."²⁴ Only the "Dance round the Golden Calf" was performed during Schoenberg's life, in a Darmstadt concert conducted by Hermann Scherchen on July 2, 1951.

Although Schoenberg was not consistent in his spelling of the title of the work (see, for example, 1.1 where it reads Moses and Aaron*), he most frequently used the version given here:* Moses und Aron. *As an alternative to the explanation that Schoenberg shortened Aaron to Aron so that the title would have twelve rather than thirteen letters, Allen Forte has argued that, among other numerological and symbolic consequences, with the change the name Aron becomes an anagram of the first four letters of Arnold.²⁵ Such an allusion would be consistent with Schoenberg's complex relationship to the figures of Moses and Aron; while there is no doubt that he identified primarily with Moses, as the keeper of the pure idea, it is also clear that he understood Aron as well. In his "Radio Lecture on the Variations for Orchestra" (excerpted below in 5.16), he prefaced a discussion of the technical features of twelve-tone composition with the remark, "That exceptional difficulties originate from this is very unpleasant for me, and there can be no one for whom it is more painful to be unable to communicate in an understandable way with his contemporaries."²⁶*

Act I

Scene 1: The Calling of Moses

MOSES: One and only, eternal, invisible, ever present, and unimaginable God!

VOICE FROM THE BURNING BUSH: Lay aside your shoes. You have gone far enough. You stand on holy ground. Now be God's prophet!

MOSES: God of my fathers, God of Abraham, Isaac, and Jacob, who has once more awakened their idea in me, my God, force me not to be thy prophet. I am old; let me tend my sheep in peace.

VOICE: You've seen the horror, recognized the truth, so you can do nothing else: you must set your people free!

MOSES: Who am I to oppose the power and force of that blindness?

VOICE: Allied with the one God, joined to him, set against Pharaoh!

MOSES: What will attest to the people my mandate?

VOICE: The name of the One! The Eternal will set them free; they will no longer serve what is transitory.

MOSES: No one will believe me!

VOICE: Before their ears you will do wonders. Their eyes will recognize them. By your rod they will behold you and admire your wisdom! By your hand they will believe in your power. They will feel in the Nile waters what their own blood commands them.

MOSES: But my tongue is stiff: I can think, but not speak.

VOICE: As from this thorn bush, in darkness, ere the light of truth fell upon it, so will you perceive my message in everything. I shall enlighten Aron, he will be your mouth! From him will your own voice then speak, as my voice from you. And your people will now be blessed, for this I promise you: your people are the chosen ones before all others, to be the people of the one God, to recognize him and dedicate themselves to him alone; to survive through millennia all the hardships to which the idea shall be exposed. And this I promise you: I shall conduct you forward to where, one with the eternal; you will be a model to all peoples. Now go! Aron nears you in the desert. He will meet you on your path; by this you will recognize him. Be God's prophet!

Scene 2: Moses meets Aron in the desert

ARON: O son of my fathers, are you sent by mighty God?

MOSES: O son of my father, brother in spirit, through whom the One is to speak, now hear me, and him, and tell me what you perceive.

ARON: My brother, did the Almighty One give me to you as his vessel, to pour forth on our brothers the Infinite's holy grace?

MOSES: Grace is granted through recognition.

ARON: O happy people, to have one single God to belong to, against whose forces no other power prevails.

MOSES: There are others only with men, only in fantasy; but God the Almighty exists apart from men.

ARON: O vision of highest fantasy, how glad it is that you're roused to form it.

MOSES: No image can give you an image of the unimaginable.

ARON: Love will surely not tire of image forming. O happy people to love such a God!

MOSES: A people chosen to know the invisible, to think the unimaginable.

ARON: Chosen is this people, to love one single God eternally, with a thousand times more devotion than all other peoples love their may gods. Invisible, unimaginable. A people chosen by the One; can you love what you dare not even imagine?

MOSES: Dare not? Unimaginable because invisible; because immeasurable, because everlasting, eternal, because ever present, because almighty. Only One is almighty.

ARON: Unimaginable God: Thou punishest the sins of the father on his children and children's children.

MOSES: Punish? Are we able to bring something about that forces Thee to an outcome?

ARON: O righteous God: Thou rewardest those who are faithful to thy commandments!

MOSES: O righteous God: Thou hast directed how everything must befall. Is reward then due to him who wants things to be different, or to him who would want nothing changed?

ARON: Gracious God! Thou hearest the pleas of the beggars, takest up the offerings of the good.

MOSES: O almighty God, the offerings of beggars then buy Thee, who Thyself made them poor! Purify your thinking, free it from worthless things, dedicate it to the true: no other reward is given your offerings.

ARON: Only an almighty God could choose such weak and downtrodden people to show them his might and his wonders, to teach them to believe in him alone.

MOSES: Irresistible law of thought forces fulfillment.

ARON: O Almighty! Be the God of this people! Release them from Pharaoh's bondage.

[. . .]

Act II

Scene 5

MOSES: Aron, what have you done?

ARON: Naught different, just my task as it ever has been: when your idea gave forth no word, my word gave forth no image for them, I worked wonders for ears and eyes to witness.

MOSES: Commanded by whom?

ARON: As always, I heeded the voice from within.

MOSES: But I did not instruct you.

ARON: Nevertheless, I still comprehend.

MOSES (*Threateningly he steps toward Aron*): Silence!

ARON (*Steps back alarmed*): Your . . . mouth . . . you were far away from us . . .

MOSES: . . . there with my idea. That must have been close to you.

ARON: When you remained apart we believed you were dead. And because the people had long expected both law and commandment soon to issue from your mouth, I was compelled to provide an image for them.

MOSES: Your image faded at my word!

ARON: But your word was denied both the image and wonder that you detest. And yet was the wonder no more than an image, when your word destroyed my image.

MOSES: God's eternity opposes the idol's transience! No image this, no wonder! This is the law! The everlasting say it, just as do these tablets so temporal, in the language you are speaking. (*He holds out the tablets to Aron.*)

ARON: Israel's endurance attests to the idea of the Eternal.

MOSES: Grant you now the power of the idea over word and image?

ARON: I understand only this: this people shall remain protected. But a people can only feel. I love this people. I live just for them and want to sustain them!

MOSES: . . . for the idea! I love my idea and live for it!

ARON: You also would have loved this people, had you only seen how they lived when they dared to see and feel and hope. No people can believe what it does not feel.

MOSES: You have shaken me not! They must comprehend the idea! They live only for that!

ARON: What a piteous people, a folk made of martyrs that would then be! No people can comprehend more than just a partial image that expressed the graspable part of the idea. Thus it makes itself understood to the people in their own accustomed way.

MOSES: Am I to debase the idea?

ARON: Let me resolve it for them! Describing without specifying: restrictions, fear-inspiring yet not too harsh, further perseverance; the need thus will be the clearer. Commandments, stern, give rise to new hopes and strengthen the idea. Unbeknown, what you want will be done. Human wavering you'll find your people still have . . . yet worthy of love.

MOSES: I shall not live to see it!

ARON: You must live! You can do nothing else! You are bound to your idea!

MOSES: Bound to my idea, as even do these tablets set it forth . . .

ARON: . . . they're images also, just part of the idea.

MOSES: Then I smash these tablets, and I shall ask God to withdraw the task from me.

(*He smashes the tablets.*)

ARON: Faint-hearted one! You, who have God's word! With or without the tablets, I, your mouth, do rightly guard your idea whenever I utter it.

MOSES: Through images!

ARON: Images of our idea; they are one, as all is that emerges from it. I simply yield before necessity; for it is certain this people will be sustained to give witness of the eternal idea. This is my mission: to speak it more simply than I understand it. Yet, the knowing ones surely will ever again discover it!

CHORUS (*Moving past in the background, led by a pillar of fire*): For he has chosen us before all other peoples to be the people of the one God, Him alone to worship, serving no one else! He will then lead us to the land where milk and honey flow, and we shall enjoy then what he once did promise our fathers. Almighty, Thou art stronger than the Egyptian gods!

ARON: Look there!

MOSES: The fiery pillar!

ARON: To lead us by night—thus through me has God given a sign to the people.

(*In the background day arrives quickly. The pillar of fire fades and is transformed into the pillar of cloud. The foreground remains relatively dark.*)

MOSES: The cloudlike pillar!

ARON: It leads us by day.

MOSES: Idolatrous image!

ARON: God-sent sign, like the burning thorn bush. The Eternal thus shows not Himself, but shows the way to Him and the way to the Promised Land!

CHORUS: He will then lead us to the land where milk and honey flow, and we shall enjoy then what he once did promise our fathers. (*Aron slowly exits in the background.*) Almighty, Thou art stronger than the Egyptian gods!

MOSES: Unimaginable God!

Inexpressible, many-sided idea, do you permit this interpretation? Shall Aron, my mouth, fashion this image? Then I have fashioned an image too, false as an image only can be. Thus am I defeated! Thus, all was but madness that I believed before, and can and must not be given voice. O word, thou word, that I lack!

(*Moses sinks to the ground in despair.*)

Act III

Scene 1

[...]

MOSES: To serve, to serve the idea of God, is the purpose of the freedom for which this people has been chosen. But you subject them to strange gods, subject them to the calf and to the pillars of fire and cloud; for you do as the people do, because you feel and think as they do. And the god that you showed to them is an image of powerlessness, is dependent upon a law beyond itself, must fulfill what it has promised, must do what it is asked, is bound by its word. Just as men act—well or badly—so must it; it must punish their wickedness, reward their virtues. But man is independent and does what pleases him, according to free will. Here images govern the idea, instead of expressing it. The Almighty—and He retains that quality forever—is not obliged to do anything, is bound by nothing. He is bound neither by the transgressor's deeds, nor by the prayers of the good, nor by the offerings of the penitent. Images lead and rule this people that you have freed, and strange wishes are their gods, leading them back to the slavery of godlessness and earthly pleasures.

You have betrayed God to the gods, the idea to images, this chosen folk to others, the extraordinary to the commonplace . . .

SOLDIERS: Shall we kill him?

MOSES: Whensoever you went forth amongst the people and employed those gifts—which you were chosen to possess so that you could fight for the divine idea—whensoever you employed those gifts for false or negative ends, that you might rival and share the lowly pleasures of strange peoples, and whensoever you had abandoned the desert's renunciation and your gifts had led you to the highest summit, then as a result of that misuse you were and ever shall be hurled back into the desert.

(*To the soldiers*) Set him free, and if he can, he shall live. (*Aron, free, stands up and then falls down dead.*)

MOSES: In the desert you shall be invincible and shall achieve the goal: unity with God.

Recommending New Members to the Prussian Academy

5.12 *Letter to Georg Schumann, January 6, 1929*

The composer Georg Schumann served as chairman of the Section for Music of the academy's senate for several years. Despite Schoenberg's harsh criticism of younger composers like Krenek and Weill, it is noteworthy that he sought to acknowledge their achievements by nominating them as honorary members to the music section, which included both composers in Berlin and out-of-town members. Of his nominations, only Berg was elected; although Heinrich Kaminski (1886–1946) did take over a master class the following year, after Pfitzner's departure. The letter was sent from Monte Carlo, where Schoenberg made several visits in the fall and winter of 1928 and 1929.

Dear Professor,

Unfortunately, I shall not be able to appear for the election of the new Berlin and out-of-town members. Allow me with this letter, provided that it is permissible to do so, also to cast my vote for the new members that I am recommending.

Unfortunately, the list of the members is not accessible to me, therefore I can only proceed by memory.

As *Berlin* members I propose:

in the first place: Alexander von Zemlinsky

in the second place: Heinz Tiessen or Kurt Weill[27]

As "out-of-towners" I propose:

Anton von Webern, Alban Berg, Josef Matthias Hauer, Ernst Krenek, and Heinrich Kaminski.

Permit me to explain the strong preference for Austrians, and to request that my reasons be acknowledged:

I. in Austria there is not a single election that provides a corresponding possibility of honoring someone.

II. as a matter of principle, if there were such a thing there, it would never be awarded appropriately (I would certainly not yet be a professor, if it had not been in Prussia, although it would be just as difficult for the most insignificant musician in Vienna to avoid the bestowal of a title).

III. the composers I am recommending are those who would have already found recognition if they lived in Germany, and for whom—due to the general indifference with which they are thought of in Austria—encouragement from generously minded colleagues is particularly necessary.

I would be very thankful to you, dear colleague, if you would lend these points of view your warm support. If it is possible, please send me a word on the outcome.

I remain, with sincere respect,

A Note to Gertrud

5.13 "Since I am unable to speak about matters of feeling," January 8, 1929

Monte Carlo

Since I am unable to speak about matters of feeling, especially when it comes to questions of love, there will be no witness (except for those who have seen it, who must know it, and who should be believable) who will be able to testify how happy I was with my Trude. I can only say: I absolutely did not know that there was such happiness, and would never have hoped to have it for myself.—One never knows if one might not be suddenly called away: so I wanted, my dear, sweet love, to have said this here.

Schoenberg and *Zeitoper*

5.14 "An Introduction to a Broadcast of Von heute auf morgen [From one day to the next]," Op. 32 (1928–1929)

At the same time he was working on the text for Moses und Aron, Schoenberg composed another, and very different, opera, Von heute auf morgen, to a libretto written by Gertrud using the pseudonym Max Blonda. Composed between October 1928 and August 1929, the work marks Schoenberg's entrance into the realm of what was called "Zeitoper" (topical opera), a genre associated with such composers as Krenek (Jonny spielt auf, 1927), Hindemith (Neues vom Tage, 1929), and Weill (Der Zar lässt sich photographeiren, 1928), and marked by up-to-date texts, an emphasis on everyday events and settings, modern technology, and popular musical idioms, especially jazz.[28] Yet despite the similarities to Zeitoper, and in comparable ways to pieces like the Accompaniment to a Film Scene or the Six Pieces for Male Chorus (see 5.15), the work was intended simultaneously to participate in and challenge the genre. Although the orchestra includes saxophone, variants of the row are used to create tonal scalar patterns in some places, and there are allusions to dance rhythms, the music does not for the most part deviate from the style of the other twelve-tone works from these years.

Anticipating that the opera would achieve the same kind of success as the works of Weill and Krenek, and after rejecting an offer of 30,000 marks from the Berlin firm Bote and Bock, Schoenberg published the work at his own expense—which ultimately resulted in a considerable financial loss. Von heute auf morgen was premiered in Frankfurt under Hans Wilhelm Steinberg on February 1, 1930. The following introduction was prepared for a radio broadcast from Berlin on February 27, with Schoenberg conducting. For the broadcast, the text was read by Josef Rufer.

Not many people have an idea how things would be if the slogans on everybody's lips became reality. This reminds me of the anecdote about an Austrian reservist at the beginning of the war. Having enthusiastically rushed from his desk to military service, he finds himself with his unit in a forest. Perched in the trees some Russians are firing at them. Appalled, he shouts at them, "What's going on here? How dare you shoot? Can't you see there are people walking here? This could cause the worst sort of accident!" He had imagined the war to be just like a field drill! He was so enthusiastic about it because he had no idea of reality. How much evil would remain undone in life, in politics, in art, in all private affairs if everyone could imagine the consequences of their actions: for example if a politician could picture those whom he sends to their death, if an employer could see the effect of a dismissal, or the employee, the consequences of an omission.

However harmless, in comparison, the slogans of fashion might seem, however unimportant it is to imagine how you would look with a wide or a narrow tie, in tight-fitting or in baggy trousers, with long or short hair, or with longer or shorter hemlines—for you are covered by the fashion, and the next one will bring something different again—the matter becomes serious when fashionable slogans shake the foundations of private life, the relationship between the sexes, and the institution of marriage: for the next fashion will bring something different again.

And here it is of no use to be covered by others, for when the foundations are destroyed, rebuilding can only be superficial. Nevertheless, there are fools who lack fantasy and are without imagination, who choose to destroy their happiness in life, as lightly as they would choose a wider tie, a baggier pair of trousers, long or short hemlines. No *petit bourgeois,* no citizen can easily ignore the demands of fashion. He may be forgiven, when fashion dictates it, for being a pacifist or a war hero, decadent or gentlemanly, a damned fool or a modest man, because it takes more courage than the average man has to be different. And yet some weak people can be encouraged; perhaps some of them will be satisfied merely by using the modern-sounding phrases but maybe they will take a chance and remain decent. And possibly they are only pretending!

Such are the trains of the thought that the libretto of the opera *Von heute auf morgen* intends to stimulate. Despite the intentionally light and unpretentious form that everything is clothed in, its purpose is to make the audience aware of such aspects of life.

In the following synopsis attention is drawn to some moments that are not perceptible in this rendition as a radio drama, namely, to certain actions of the characters and some stage effects that are not audible.

The husband and wife return home from a party. The husband is in raptures about the wife's school friend, with whom he had spent the evening in conversation, brusquely emphasizing the difference between her elegant appearance and his "steady housewife." The wife hides her annoyance, gently attempting to divert him by pointing out that he is dazzled by "every new appearance that seems fashionable," but she recognizes the danger that threatens her happiness. In order to awaken his jealousy, she tells him about the famous tenor who courted her in an entertaining way that same evening. As the husband mocks her in a wounding manner, she loses her patience and announces that she will show him something that he had not suspected since he lacks imagination: that she can also be modern if she wants to, and in particular how things would go with him if she were a "woman of today."

And it becomes evident that it would be here as in every average marriage: the one who makes it easy for himself but difficult for others possesses the upper hand. And how easy it is, as Strindberg says, for someone to look and behave for an evening so that, in comparison, the spouse, who is at the mercy of the daily routine, must be at a disadvantage.

After one of their duets at the words "That will be over!" (to which moment the listener should pay special attention), she puts on a modern dress that the husband's sister—a dancer, and Aunt Liesl to the child who will appear later—had left with her, puts on modern makeup, and appears before him looking fascinating. Now she demonstrates to her husband, who is transformed at once from the bored married man to the "captivated admirer," all the consequences he would have to deal with. She speaks of her series of future lovers and of wanting nothing to do with the husband she already knows; she seeks new things—"diversion." Saying that she does not want to belong to anyone permanently, she forces him to take her out into the evening drinking and dancing. But as he goes to bring her beer—for which she mocks him: "Do you want me to slum it?"—she takes care as the good housewife that the cushions which she had flamboyantly flung on the floor are not damaged.

The noise of the dancing wakes the child, who appears half asleep in his nightshirt. To the husband's great horror she rebuffs the child: "Leave me alone and go to sleep." He has to heat milk and doing so burns his finger. But the doorbell rings: the gasman presents a bill. No money is in the house. She used the household money for the clothes, which she now shows him and puts on. "But what if the gasman turns off the gas?"—"Then we move to a hotel and live on credit, just like all upstanding people today do." And now she capriciously forces him to pack a suitcase for the move.

At this moment the telephone rings and one hears the voice of the singer, who is still in a bar with the school friend and who would like to complete the conquest, which he believes he has made of the wife. She gladly lets herself be talked into coming to the bar, bringing along her husband, who in any case is already crumbling, for the friend. But the man has no more interest in the friend. With the words: "She's the source of our unhappiness," he confirms the wife's victory and his subjugation. And putting on a well-worn, inconspicuous house dress, she can show herself again without playacting: "Should I be myself again, one who is not prepared to give up husband and child for the dictates of a crazy new fashion?" Half reconciled, they have only one more trial to pass: the famous tenor and the school friend who have waited in vain now appear. Here begins a lively ensemble movement in which the friend and tenor attempt to entice them to a free, up-to-date view of life, inviting them "to live their own lives." But they are rebuffed: "If together we both live our life, then each will live their own." The friend and singer must withdraw and apostrophize the husband and wife in their confidence of victory: "But you're simply faded theater characters."

Husband and wife sit down to breakfast and know that also the question of what is faded and what glimmers, what is today still felt to be "shining and colorful," in life as in art and in opinions is really only a matter of fashion. For it changes "from one day to the next."

Schoenberg Writes for a Workers' Chorus

5.15 The Six Pieces for Male Chorus, Op. 35, 1929–1930

The Six Pieces for Male Chorus originated with a commission from the Deutsche Arbeiter-Sängerbund, the main organization of workers' choruses in Germany, with more than three-quarters of a million members in 1929. Two movements, No. 4, "Glück," and No. 6, "Verbundenheit," were first published by the Deutsche Arbeiter-Sängerzeitung *in 1929 and 1930. The complete set was published in Berlin by Bote and Bock in the summer of 1930. Following earlier performances of individual movements by various workers' choruses beginning in 1929, the complete set was premiered, widely performed, and eventually broadcast by the "13er-Quartett" of the* Arbeitergesangverein Vorwärts *from Hanau in the 1931–1932 season. After extensive rehearsals, this group of thirteen amateur singers performed the works from memory before large and enthusiastic audiences.[29] Such choral compositions occupied the centerpiece of Leo Kestenberg's program for involving the masses in music as a means for building community and for raising* the level of musical education. Schoenberg's folk-song arrangements also date from this period, and they include three pieces for mixed choir and four for voice and piano, written as part of the state-sponsored Volksliederbuch für die Jugend, published by Peters, alongside pieces by Hindemith, Krenek, and others.

In a letter to Schoenberg from February 1931, Berg commented on the relationship between the Six Pieces and contemporary developments: "How wonderfully beautiful and how wonderfully new they are! And yet behind the absolute, eternal values of this opus there seems to be something timely as well: just as in the magnificent texts (especially in II, III, and V and VI) you reflect upon today's communal ideas [Gemeinschaftsideen] (in such a way that they also become those of tomorrow and of all times.) [. . .] it also appears that you (you who have always shown the younger generation the way) for once wished to show something after the fact, thereby demonstrating that the simple forms generally associated with the low 'communal music' can also lay claim to the highest standards of artistry and skill and that their level need not be so debased as to make them suited to be sung only by children or on the street."[30]

Schoenberg's interest in finding a common ground with the intended audience for these pieces is evident in the fact that, while movements 1, 2, 3, and 5 are twelve tone, the final movement is tonal, Schoenberg's first newly composed tonal work in more than two decades (see fig. 5-2). The fourth movement is a tonal and twelve-tone hybrid.

Six Pieces for Male Chorus

I. "Inhibition"

> Do words fail them?
> Or don't they feel it?
> Have they nothing to say?
>
> But they speak all the more freely
> the less an Idea inhibits them!
> How difficult it is to express an Idea!
>
> And they speak ever so freely,
> if they've got a plan in mind!
> So often must one be amazed!

II. "The Law"

> If things turn out the way we expect,
> it's alright: we can understand it.
> But if things turn out differently, it's a miracle.
> And yet, just consider this:

That things always turn out to be the same
is the real miracle;
and what should seem incomprehensible to you:
that there is a law
which all things obey,
just as you obey your Lord,
which commands all things
just as your Lord commands you.
This is what you should recognize as a miracle!
That someone rebels
Is a banal commonplace.

III. "Mode of Expression"

Speaking from within us, in mass instinct,
Some say it's God,
For others it's the original condition.

For some we pass as models of culture,
Others cite us as a deterrent.

What we really are,
we know as little about as what every single one is.
When we are together, everyone feels just like everybody else,
not himself anymore.
When we are separate, each acts like the other
and yet like himself.

Praise or reproach leaves each
and every one of us indifferent.
But when we strike
we all strike as one.

IV. "Happiness"

Happiness is the ability,
to long for it still,
to have not yet enjoyed it,
to see it still beckoning;
so long as it is denied, it is happiness.
Or:
if it could disappear,
if one did not expect it,
if one did not earn it;

so long as you still have it, it is happiness.
Or:
if you can't give it a name,
don't know what it consists of,
don't believe that others know it;
so long as you don't understand it, it is happiness.

V. "Mercenaries"

We all have to die sometime,
but who thinks about it?
And what's that: to die?
So what!

We know how to live in each moment.
Just for that very moment, but things go on.

Tapp, tapp, hopp, hopp!
To the pasture!
Oh, it's raining today; little grass—none good—
Marvelous: I am alone here!
The best spot! No one else will find it.
A luxuriant pasture for us all.
Make peace: there's enough for everyone!

Go away! The women are mine.
Run, or I'll run you through.
Die! Now I'm the master here!
The young are provided for
The young—So what!
Live for the moment!

Oh, there's a smell of blood?
Of our flesh and blood.
So, that's the way it goes?
Will we be slaughtered already?
One ought to flee:
One is paralyzed!
What's the use of that?
Mercenaries' fate!

VI. "Bond"

You are helped into this world, ... Be blessed!
a grave is dug for you, ... Rest in peace!

your wounds are patched up in the hospital, ... *Get well soon!*
the fire in your house is put out, you're pulled from the water,

. . . . *Don't be afraid!*
after all, you yourself have compassion for others!

. . . . *Help is near, you are not alone!*

You don't leave the old man behind,

. . . . *you yourself will fall someday,*
you lift the burden from the weak, ... *without reward,*
you slow the flight of the skittish horse, ... *not sparing yourself,*
fight off the thief, protect your neighbor's life,

. . . . *you bring help without hesitation:*
try denying that you too are part of all this! . . . . . . *you won't stay alone.*

On the Individual and the Majority

5.16 From the "Radio Lecture on the Variations for Orchestra, Op. 31," February 28, 1931

Schoenberg composed the Variations for Orchestra between 1926 and 1928, his first large orchestral work since the Five Pieces for Orchestra. It was premiered on December 2, 1928, by Wilhelm Furtwängler (1886–1954), conducting the Berlin Philharmonic. Perhaps motivated by the hostile response from part of the audience at the first performance, Schoenberg wrote the following radio lecture for a broadcast on March 22, 1931, prior to a Frankfurt performance under Hans Rosbaud (1895–1962). In addition to the extensive and systematic discussion of the theme, the character of each variation, and the basic concepts of twelve-tone composition, Schoenberg also stresses the connections between his work and those of his predecessors, such as Beethoven, Brahms, and especially Bach, whose name is invoked by the B-A-C-H [B♭-A-C-B] theme in the finale.

The innovative presentation combining detailed commentary, more general discussion of aesthetic issues, and musical excerpts performed on piano and by the orchestra, reflects Schoenberg's interest in the medium of the radio for both the performance and promotion of his music and new music in general. In a reply to a questionnaire about the influence of radio he identified it as a foe, singling out the damage done by its poor tone quality and the "boundless surfeit" of music it provided, which could so harden the listener that music would be reduced to background noise. Yet he ends the essay on a more optimistic note, comparing the radio to publishing, which had resulted in the "virtual extinction of illiteracy." He suggests that the easy availability of music similarly had the potential of making music available to "every human being," with the possibility that everyone might be "moved, touched, taken hold of, gripped, by music."[31] A photograph of Schoenberg conducting for the Berlin radio is given at the beginning of this chapter.

Far be it from me to question the rights of the majority. But one thing is certain: somewhere there is a limit to the *power* of the majority; it occurs, in fact, wherever the essential step is one that cannot be taken by all and sundry.

For example, if cave explorers come to a narrow passage, where only one of them can get through, they are all certainly entitled to give their views. All the same, they will have to choose some one person and rely on his judgment.

But such narrow passages lead to all unknown places; we should still be wondering what it is like at the North Pole if we had waited until the majority made up their minds to go and see for themselves. The first railway or motor-car journey, the first flight and the first one over the ocean or in a rocket-powered plane could not have been undertaken by a majority, quite apart from the fact that you wouldn't have been able to find a majority willing to take the risk.

That is something for individuals. And if the majority leave them to face the danger, they must also allow them their rights—must recognize the rights of those who dare to do what is necessary, who know that they must pass on their discoveries, though the majority are not on their side. They know that all the others would refuse to undertake such hazards.

That is my situation: I find myself in a minority, facing not only those who prefer light music, but also those who prefer serious music. It would be inconceivable to attack the heroes who make daring flights over the ocean or to the North Pole, for their achievement is obvious to everyone. But although experience has shown that many a pioneer trod his path with absolute certainty at a time when he was still held to be wandering half-demented, most people invariably turn against those who strike out into unknown regions of the spirit. Here on the radio the majority are given their due. At all hours of the day and night their ears are pampered with tidbits which they seem to need in order to survive. So if they ever have to do without them they are utterly aghast. Against this delirium of entertainment I want to assert the rights of a minority; the essential should have a place as well as the super-fluous. We accept the activities of cave explorers, polar explorers and pilots as essential. So, if I say so in all modesty, are the activities of those who try to achieve something comparable in the spiritual and artistic fields. They, too, have rights: they, too, have a claim to the radio.

New music is never beautiful on first acquaintance. We know that not only did new works by Mozart, Beethoven and Wagner meet with resistance, but that Verdi's *Rigoletto,* Puccini's *Madame Butterfly,* and even Rossini's *Barber of Seville* were booed off the stage, and *Carmen* was a complete failure.

The reason is simply this: one can only like what one remembers; and with all new music that is very difficult.

[. . .]

In my style of composition this is frequently the reason why I am difficult to understand: I employ constant variations, hardly ever repeat anything unaltered, jump quickly to the remoter stages of development, and I take for granted that the educated listener is able to discover the intervening stages for himself. I know this can only let me in for disappointments, but if I am to fulfill the task that I have been set, there appears to be no other way of presenting my thoughts.

Perhaps I can give an example to illustrate why this method of presentation strikes me as justified. If I want to explain to someone a complicated mechanism, such as a motor-car, it will take endless time if I first have to explain to him the basic concepts of physics, mechanics and chemistry. But the more knowledge of that kind he has, the sooner I shall succeed in explaining the subtler distinctions: the quickest communication of all is between one expert and another. In music it is the same: if the composer can take for granted that the listener will at once grasp a musical complex, then he can let another complex follow quickly, even though the transition from one to the other is made without detailed preparation.

But if I now have to write a theme for a set of variations, then I must adopt a slightly different mode of expression. For the theme must not merely be felt as the basis of the ensuing variations; to a certain degree it must also be *heard* as such. I must therefore lay it out so as to help the listener to perceive, remember and recognize it. For this purpose, the theme must be as short, distinct and clearly organized as possible. It must be characteristic, that is to say contain shapes that are rhythmically and melodically striking; not too many, for that would make them hard to remember; repeated a number of times, then, and not varied too much, since that would make them unrecognizable. In a word, the theme must be relatively *simple*, amongst other things because after all the variations are going to become steadily more complicated.

[...]

Now we come to the Finale. I want to explain to you what a finale is, and I looked it up in a number of books, but all to no avail. I found either stock phrases or emotional twaddle. Glad as I should have been to offer you something objective and generally recognized as true, I am thrown back on my own resources, since musicology is no use.

Suppose a painter wants to paint everything that can be taken in at a glance; he faces the question, whether to paint his picture so that it fills out the entire frame, or to paint only what he was able to see all at once. Where and how is he to stop?

For the musician this question is far more difficult. Even though there are pieces in our classical literature which stop without coming to a close, such as Barbarina's little aria in the third act of *The Marriage of Figaro*, it is generally speaking traditional to take particular care in constructing the end of a work, and I find that the great masters' wealth of imagination is nowhere more beautifully apparent than in their final sections. It looks as if the problem were less to prepare for some way of ending than

To draw a conclusion!

To point to a moral.

This need is felt especially strongly in the symphonic works of the great masters.

Doubtless orchestral variations approximate to symphonic construction, though there is one thing about them that pulls the other way: however intimately the individual variations may be connected, they are still merely placed one after another, juxtaposed. Whereas symphonic thought is different; the musical images, the themes, shapes, melodies, episodes follow one another like turns of fate in a life story—diverse but still logical, and always linked: one grows out of another. They are not merely juxtaposed. Perhaps a comparison will make this difference clear. Variations are like an album with views of some place or landscape, showing you particular aspects of it. A symphony, on the other hand, is like a panorama in which one certainly views the pictures separately: but in reality they are closely linked and merge into each other.

Perhaps this comparison makes it almost harder to explain why I add a finale and so switch abruptly from the one mode of presentation to the other. In doing this, I am following the example of the classical masters—think of Beethoven's *Eroica Variations* and of Brahms' *Haydn Variations*. I would willingly own up to having followed these great composers blindly and trustingly, but that is an honor I cannot claim. In fact, I feel I am compelled by necessity, just as they were: let me explain myself.

I could certainly have ended with the final variation, like Bach in the *Goldbergs*. But this work belongs to a style in which juxtaposition is a dominant principle. On the other hand, the symphonic style, whose procedure I have described as one of construction by developing variation, can no longer be content to break off so simply. Otherwise the question would remain unanswered as to how sections of equal length, which are simply juxtaposed, can at one time signify a beginning and at another time an ending. Just as we believe the beginning must have about it something that makes its function clear, and as the middle sections must then look different, so the end, too, must have its special character, and this character can only result if all the formal elements co-operate. Here it is above all the organization and the general outline of the theme that must surrender their original form, since these were designed to express a different purpose. Consequently, in what follows, you will not hear the theme again from beginning to end, but broken down into fragments which are put together in a different way; and we shall take our farewell of the world embodied in this work with a final bird's-eye view of our panorama—a view that will once more impress certain images on us and create new links between the sections, giving a total impression which, as I have already remarked, sums up and points to the moral.

The finale begins with an introduction which again calls to mind the name of BACH, first in the first violins, then in the horns.

[…]

A final word: I know unfortunately that I cannot expect my work to thrill you at this concert, and I must resign myself to that. But if I have succeeded in showing that I may regard my work as well organized, that I gave it much thought and worked on it with diligence; if you have been able to gather that I myself am entitled to believe in it, to believe that it is a good piece: then I have certainly achieved a great deal.

On Nationalism, Racism, and Wagnerians

5.17 To the Editor of the New Viennese Journal *(c. March / April 1932)*

This letter was written from Barcelona, where Schoenberg was spending an extended absence from Berlin of nearly eight months, partly on account of his chronic asthma but also, as he wrote to his friend Joseph Asch on May 24, 1932, to avoid the "swastika-swaggerers and pogromists":

> For some time I have been living in the South for reasons of health, and on these grounds, but also because of political conditions, am very reluctant to go back to Germany at this juncture.
>
> But the currency restrictions make it impossible for me to get money out of Germany. And besides, I should like to finish the third act of my opera *Moses and Aron* (two acts are finished, scored for orchestra).
>
> Now just think: I am surely the only composer of my standing there has been for at least a hundred years who could not live on what he made from his creative work without having to eke out his income by teaching. And when I think how many things rich people find money for, I simply can't understand that there still isn't some rich Jew, or even several, who together or single-handed would give me an annuity so that at long last I needn't do anything but create![32]

In one of his first public addresses after arriving in America, Schoenberg discussed the blows to his self-esteem and self-confidence growing up as an "Austrian-Jewish" artist under the influence of Wagner's music and his Weltanschauung. *"You were no true Wagnerian if you did not believe in his philosophy," with its Teutonism and anti-Semitism, evident, as suggested in the letter below, in the* Ring of the Nibelung, *with its opposition of the gods in Valhalla and the avaricious Nibelungen in their dark caverns. He writes that whereas Wagner still held out the*

hope of redeeming the Jews through assimilation, prominent disciples like Hous-
ton Stewart Chamberlain claimed that the Jews were an inferior race, lacking any
creative capacity.[33] *(See further 5.19.)*

As a Spaniard who has lived for nearly twenty years in Germany, may I permit myself to express an opinion on the letter from the gentleman from East Prussia, which you published on March 27, 1932, under the rubric "The Public Speaks."

I have always been surprised that a great nation believes it necessary to have other nations to disparage in order to establish its own worth; namely, that the Germans—and admittedly not merely the mediocre minds among them but also the most significant—are of the opinion that other peoples who are not blond like they are represent a less estimable race. And at the same time it especially surprises me that they don't say: all peoples are very good, but we are still better; rather that they say: all peoples are bad and only we are good. For there is not really much skill in being better when the others are worse.

But the gentleman from East Prussia presents once again all these arguments that I already heard in my youth in Germany from all the Wagnerians, and which really no one among us would believe: that blond men are worth more than the dark haired. And he goes so far as to observe that those with dark hair are cowardly, while blonds are courageous, but "still quite often become the victims of the dark haired." Now I have to be amazed that even important men in Germany forget that the dark-haired peoples like the Italians, Greeks, Spaniards, etc., also have tales of heroes, and that they honor these heroes not for their cowardice but for their courage.

But that we dark-haired men are always only frauds, while you blond-haired men of light [*Lichtmenschen*] alone are honorable, is attested to not just by your poets. I know that Kleist in his "Hermannsschlacht" lets Hermann commit a deception justified by love of the fatherland, but nevertheless one that is evident and that no dark-haired man could easily surpass. But then the gentleman from East Prussia should not have just spoken about the *Ring of the Nibelung,* where it is Wotan who first deceives the giants, then Alberich, and then again the giants at the end as he wanted to withhold the ring from them. It is also surely a contradiction if Loge, a sort of Lucifer, a bringer-of-light, a Prometheus, is actually the bringer-to-light of the greatest deception of the whole *Ring.*

Perhaps it should not be forgotten that compared with a representation of gods like this one, the idea: "my kingdom is not of this world," which first took root with non-blond-haired men, shows these figures of light in a light other than the East Prussian men of light might wish.

It would please me, if in your esteemed pages you would print my opinion, in which I am not alone in the southern lands, and bring it to public discussion.

[A note at the end of the letter adds, "If you should print my letter I ask that you not include my name for business considerations."]

On Politics and Human Nature

5.18 "About Power, Majority, Democracy, Fascism, Etc., Especially also Mussolini" (August 1932)

This essay was written in response to an article entitled "Dream and Reality," by Erich Krämer, that appeared in the Berlin Vossische Zeitung *on August 20, 1932. Krämer's article is an enthusiastic review of Mussolini's article "Fascism," from the* Enciclopedia Italiana. *In a letter to Thomas Mann of January 15, 1939, Schoenberg commented further on democracy and fascism: "Please don't misunderstand me, I know to value the worth of democracy, although I am not in a position to overlook its weakest points: included in the orthodox exaggeration of its principles is the possibility of overthrowing it. The free expression of opinion allows anyone to make propaganda for a change in the form of government, and as a result democracy everywhere has proven itself unable to deal with opposition. And I in no way overlook the evil of fascism, since the power that is bestowed through it can scarcely do other than to fall into the wrong hands. There is probably up to now no form of government that can make all of human society happy, but at most a number of individuals, insofar as their happiness should be dependent on a form of government."*[34]

The author of the article, K., finds Mussolini's "formulations" to be "brilliant," and Mussolini to be a great writer; he speaks of the "vitality" of the sentences and of the expressions employed, "energy, conquest, vital power, uprising," etc. One could believe that this praise was mere courtesy, or even that it had a stylistic purpose, beginning with praise as a foil for later censure; but in reality it is probably the similarity in nature of the two journalists that makes one admire the style of the other.

—This journalistic style, which can take big words into a constantly opened mouth because it does not know their extent or meaning.

—This conceptionless language would never be capable of producing a sentence like the preceding one, because the hasty "formulations" through which it is violated every day could never come into being if the image in the word used to describe the situation stood inhibiting before the eye of the one who misuses it. Before the spiritual eye.

In Germany we also have these pretentious journalists. And many are regarded as scholars because nothing stops them from assaulting what they

want to assault. I am thinking of those like Spengler, and Riemann, Mersmann, Chamberlain, indeed even, with the appropriate distinction, of Nietzsche.[35] Loos entitled his first book of essays "Spoken into the Void." Quite
correctly: this wholeness spoken into that void; it does not find an echo.[36] But
these journalists blare out into the wide world only the echo of the words and
concepts, (words from which the cream of the conception has been skimmed
off); and see or listen: the echo finds its own echo, it nearly sounds better than
the original echo—in a word, it sounds "more brilliant" (so much so that the
eye must be averted, though only the spiritual eye).

"The peoples' thirst for authority . . . has never been stronger . . . "[37]

What force of figurative language.

One sees: thirsty people and fears they could die of thirst.

But what does the dying one long for, what quenches his thirst, saves his
life?

Authority—not bottled, but poured over him from full basins.

That's all water for his mill: the driving force.

Dying people, driven, compelled by the water of authority, feeling thirst
no more, because their mills are turning again.

A marvelous image!

That says nothing against Fascism.

Even if only because Fascism would first have to say something for itself
before something could be said against it.

But I want to speak for it,

I want to arm it.

I would also like to give it a name, not one by which one can think
something just as you please, something or everything; everything possible
and therefore: nothing, but a name by which one *must think something quite
definite* (!!) But I don't really care that much about a new name in this regard.

Fascism provides therefore the one

necessary,

but inadequate

and also otherwise futile

attempt at resistance against

the probably *inevitable* Communism (more on that later . . .), and thereby
proceeds to combat

the fallacies, mistakes, blunders, and inhumanity of the democratic, and
in particular social-democratic theories, and their tactics, propaganda, and
organization.

Taken purely intellectually, it is no "worldview" with positive qualities,
but rather, in its essence, the negation of another.

In this respect its name must be regarded as fortunately chosen. Every
other name, which is bound up with some essential quality, would contain an

obligation. Fascism means nothing, not even symbolically. One can therefore put everything into the name while deriving nothing from it. Everything pertaining to a "worldview" is foreground scenery, interchangeable, replaceable (and in this sense K. should not be surprised at the pacifistic activity of the current Fascism), and has merely a *tactical* purpose.

The *commitment to a purpose* and therefore that everything is *tactical* are also, as a result, the sole characteristics of Fascism; and it would be conceivable in this sense that it could even change the symbol of its tactics, since the bundle of sticks only remains in existence as an *emblem of power.*

Now the concept of Fascism begins to reveal its true meaning.

If one says:

democracy wields the power (in "the name of the people") that is has received through the consent of the majority, or of the more heavily armed sector of the people; autocracy and aristocracy wields the power (in "the name of the people") that it possesses owing to a skillful jockeying for position by the armed opposing parties within the upper class (and their supporters).

And consider at the same time that whoever granted the power expects that it will be used to their advantage; they always present the threat of demanding the power back or of withdrawing it again forcibly (or by other means).

And consider further that, on the one hand, no monarch, despot, autocrat, no oligarch or otherwise aristocratic rule could rule if not enough of the strong party faithful supported him.

and that, on the other hand,

in democracy the people only seem to rule, whereas in reality the rule is wielded not only by a more or less large number of individuals, but

in particular,

that the "spiritual" leadership of the numbers of people happens to be just these individuals, so that even in the case that they the act as they have promised, they are only leading the state according to *their will.*

If one brings this all together, the question,

"From whom has the government received its commission and power?"

absolutely appears to be no longer so fundamentally essential, as do much more so the questions:

1. *How long does the ruler reign?* (who dismisses him?)

2. *To whom is he responsible?*

(Still to be interjected here now is that, strangely enough, Fascism, in Italy at least, wields power:

a) in the name of the King, {for indeed the king no longer wields it himself!}

b) in the name of the people, {for it was a people's movement against the king that brought Mussolini to rule})

August 29

Since I do not know—after this break—when and if I shall again be able to write about this further, I want to indicate only briefly in catch phrases why I regard Fascism as insufficient and communism as neither desirable or achievable.

Fascism is—although it pretends to be—not modern enough, not truly new. It has nothing of an equal value with which to oppose communism, which looks out from the totality of the present-day situation to a utopian but fantastic future. Its attempt to renovate something old into something new with modern trappings must fail because of the degree to which technology and science have now advanced. It is not that history does not allow itself to be reversed that stands mostly in the way; for one need not reverse it if one seeks an earlier point of origin; but that Fascism uses the new means not to a modification, or more precisely reworking, in the sense of its possibilities, but only serves its slogans without believing them. But communism is not desirable because the *"life of security"* it aspires to would make men into civil servants lacking any ambition; *if it were to succeed in realizing its goal.* But it is neither good to make men into civil servants, nor possible: they are both too good and too bad for that. A greater power must always be placed into someone's hand. And it is not in the nature of man to abstain from using a power he possesses to his own advantage.

August 29, 1932

All such efforts, be they now pacifism, Christianity, communism, the Salvation Army, loving thy neighbor; all these that are based on the assumption that man is good enough must fail because man is, at least in this sense, not good enough.

But if now Fascism is not new, it is no use to it that communism is also not new. For if communism, which was in any case "old," did not *help* (the people), then it could hope for a miracle from something new; but not from something *old* (even if it acted new!)

On Webern, Hauer, and the Origins of Twelve-Tone Composition

5.19 "Priority," September 10–11, 1932

In the spring and summer of 1932, Schoenberg occupied himself with the project of cataloguing the huge corpus of his unpublished writings. He wrote to Webern on August 12: "I'm intensely busy sifting, sorting, and filing the 'little manuscripts' I've been piling up for some 15 years and collecting the printed essays and also my lectures, there are often several days at a time when I don't feel like sitting down at my desk to do anything that requires concentration. The times aren't such that one can always keep one's mind on one's work and let one's thoughts run freely."[38] *A growing concern, evident in this collection of fragmentary notes entitled "Priority," was defending his historical position as the originator of atonal and twelve-tone composition, not only from Hauer but from Webern as well. In a short statement entitled "Peace " [Ruhe], dated July 20, 1932, Schoenberg commented on the process, and his feelings toward Webern in particular:*

> In these pages are many remarks of great vehemence. I would not have been able to answer for many of them even a short time afterward; but I am far less able to do so today. I can be excused before the world on account of the vehemence and pain of the attacks (especially in 1923) that rained down on me. This was also the time of the engagement with anti-Semitism. Now my stance toward the whole complex of questions is entirely different from before, when the ejection from Germanness had provoked me to the utmost. But today I think more leniently about many people (even if they were not without guilt at the time as, for example, my dear W., whom then, despite everything, I still held very dear, and whom today I look upon as my only true friend). With this I am not saying that I am reconsidering the injustices of others. Only that today I know better how easy it is to be unjust oneself—and yet not be bad.[39]

After recently examining the pages of my short manuscripts that sharply criticized Webern, and writing comments that sought to moderate these words that seem so harsh to me now, I was reminded again today by Cowell (the American) of the cause of my anger.[40] Cowell told me about Webern, went into raptures about him, and said that he had seen things from the year 1907 that were supposedly already very interesting. (Why? Webern must have shown these to him specifically, for they are not among what is published; he is therefore still conducting this underground battle of falsehoods against me!) I have long since established that Webern must have simply backdated these compositions. At that time, every person in our circle knew this series of events: how Webern was breathing down my neck, and scarcely after I had written a piece he wrote a similar one; how he carried out ideas, plans, and intentions that I had expressed in order to get ahead of me! I can hardly believe anymore that he can in good faith start up once again with this lie.— I have always suspected that Webern would someday use his chance, the chance of the Aryan against the Jew. It could be a matter of indifference to me: so much has been stolen from me that the small bit of fame for originality also does not matter. But it is hateful. Hauer always does the same.

Arnold Schoenberg

To explain in detail:

Hauer does it continually—and I remember precisely that I had a discussion with Hauer in which the following was still said, and in which it was established: that I had begun some months earlier with 12-tone composition than he. (I showed him technical matters that he did not know.) I think that I demonstrated clearly to Webern that he could not yet have composed "atonally" in 1907, and that he must admit it. Witnesses? Someday I will ask Berg and Stein about it.

Hauer continually does the same. Time and again someone tells me that he claims priority for himself in 12-tone composition (*this name is from me. Up until our discussion Hauer spoke* always exclusively of <u>atonal</u> music—which I had already rejected in my *Harmonielehre* no later than 1920.)

I am astonished at this.

There is nothing to be said against it if he maintains that he arrived at the same thing without being influenced by me (although I can show at any time that *atonal* music and 12-tone composition were completely different up until our discussion.)

But just the same, I have proved to him that I arrived at it independently. I showed him that I had already before worked "with tones" (*Jakobsleiter,* piano piece [Op. 23], the Variations and March from the *Serenade*), and that the step from there to 12 tones arises completely on its own as the farthest-reaching fulfillment of the principle already expressed in my *Harmonielehre* 1910–1911: to allow no tonic to arise. We then established jointly that in September 1921 I wrote the first 12-tone piece (Suite for Piano; witness: Erwin Stein in Traunkirchen), while he first wrote a 12-tone composition in December of the same year.

Whoever compares the two pieces with each other would be able to see without difficulty by which path each of us could have arrived there. It is already clear to me in this first piece that using the row as a basis serves the purpose of increasing the coherence-forming factors by one, since tonal harmony is no longer available: But here *I have* the (and if one may say so, the *exclusive*) *priority.* With Hauer it had to do with the overtones, with the key, the tonality, the independent course of all twelve tones, and with him, at least up until that point, it did not have anything to do with compositional concerns, with musical logic and the forming of ideas, but merely with a new sound.

For this reason I was able to show him many technical matters, toward which I had already been working, which were obviously new to him, and which he accepted and then further processed in his own way. Also as a result of our discussion and as evidence of my influence, I must point in particular to the fact that until then Hauer wanted on principle *to write only for tempered instruments* (piano, Celeste, etc.), and was only brought around by me to writing for others also. In the same way I directed him to the use of classical formal types.

I have the advantage. For my independence from Hauer can be gathered by anyone knowledgeable of the development evident in my works, and from the fact that I at once brought together what was, after all, the almost inevitably occurring event of only allowing the row (which is established once and for all as a motive) to begin again after running through all 12 tones—with one of the artistic means that I had already employed before in the Variations[41] and that had originated out of the same conception: 1. immediately to form projections from the row on three other levels (inversion, retrograde, retrograde-inversion); 2. to use these four forms as motivic material; 3. to employ no other row succession than these; 4. to employ transpositions; 5. to use harmonies [*Zusammenklänge*] of the various projections, and such like—everything that points to the origin of my idea: to introduce a new coherence-building factor.

Hauer, in contrast, has the disadvantage, and already for this reason—because he could not prove his independence from me; for in the first edition of one of his writings he still used, without naming me as the author of this sentence, my sentence about the avoidance of the tonic, and still others, which he then in the second edition deleted without saying a word—I want to emphasize that, to my knowledge, Hauer might have arrived at his "atonal" music independently of me.

But he does not have the priority.

And since now it has been clearly said how things stand, I can say for myself:

It is a matter of complete indifference to me who has the priority, and if I speak of it all, it is because the dishonesty annoys me, which always, and against better knowledge, makes such claims. And because I know that Aryan hypocrisy, which is determined to take away, along with the priority, my status—which one does not in any way want to acknowledge to a Jew. For, as Herr Chamberlain has observed, the Jew lacks in creative ability.

With regard to Hauer and Webern the question of priority is thus completely unimportant to me. For what does it really matter in the mass of smaller and greater inventions if these two were not from me. And wouldn't all that I have invented then still remain *merely in music* of shapes, of themes, of figures, of accompaniments, of rhythms, of sounds, of melodies, of forms, of externals, of expediencies, as sufficient witnesses of my outstanding originality. But what about my completely independent achievements in other areas: theory, painting, poetry, politics, etc.—If I had robbed Webern or Hauer, then I would have to be a kleptomaniac, for I would not have done so out of need.

But how do things stand in this regard with Hauer and Webern.

Why do both deviate from the truth?

Webern could not have written something atonal in 1907, otherwise my first attempts would not have *appeared so new* to him.

And *Hauer* would have given my name in the second edition, instead of omitting the stolen sentence, if he didn't have egg on his face.

September 11, 1932. Arnold Schoenberg

I just saw something I did not know or had forgotten, namely that Hauer dedicated his *Vom Melos zur Pauke* to me—1925!

I just saw that Hauer's book *Vom Wesen des Musikalischen* was sent to me by Waldheim-Eberle Press on September 18, 1920, and that it would certainly follow from this book that Hauer had already then invented "atonal" music, and further that I had read this book just before September 1921 when I wrote the first pure 12-tone piece.

Now I must first [the sentence is incomplete]

1. The description is not such that after it one would have to find the way to the principles of 12-tone composition.

2. In comparison, I had quite definitely already begun at least a year before to work with rows, with tones.

And Webern had later brought to my attention—which I had forgotten—that in 1914 I had already written a pure 12-tone theme: in the Scherzo for that great symphony, the last movement of which was to be *Die Jakobsleiter.*

I do not believe, although I apparently read this book at that time, that there is an influence. For my path is too clear that I would have required coaching. In any case it is annoying.

September 11, 1932. Arnold Schoenberg

Yes, it is annoying. For as sure as I am of the matter: that I myself, and myself alone, have invented all that it concerns, it is now just as hard to prove it.

Above all: my 12-tone composition is

1. Composition with rows (basic shape!! [*Grundgestalt*])

and

2. Composition with *one single* row:

I had already arrived at that earlier; just as I had already invented a 12-tone row earlier.

The greatest step was not to the 12 tones, but *the invention of the countless means:*

to create *from a basic shape the themes* and all remaining material (quite apart from inversions and retrogrades and transpositions).

Here I am indisputably alone.

But then:

Even if I had first been led by Hauer's description of an atonal music (one can perhaps gather only today that he can have meant by it 12-tone composition) to my form of 12-tone composition, the matter would still stand in my favor in the following way:

Hauer spoke the law of the
use of all 12 tones
and the prohibition
of the repetition of a tone.
But in the horizontal lines.

But I first expressed the prohibition of the repetition of tones, but only those in the *vertical lines:* in 1910!!

From both of these now arises (in the end, if also not at once) the law of the *longest possible delay of the repetition of a tone* in the horizontal lines—<u>and so I also arrived at it.</u>

I do not believe that Hauer even only stimulated me. But if that is indeed the case, it was to something that I also would have done *without him sooner or later;* and further, it was to something that he *neither would have found himself* nor was on the path to finding. That would become clear if I would call my method:

Composition with a basic shape consisting of twelve different tones.

That is it in reality; I have been steering toward it since 1908; one thousand individual moves that point to it turn up in these years.

But it was never a concern with me simply to play through the twelve tones again and again without observing a definite row order.

Good or not: I have done that alone

September 11, 1932. Arnold Schoenberg

His Final European Composition

5.20 Foreword to the Concerto for String Quartet and Orchestra (after Handel), c. 1935

The Concerto for String Quartet and Orchestra after the Concerto Grosso, Op. 6, No. 7, by G. F. Handel, was Schoenberg's last work before his emigration to the United States. The concerto is one of a series of adaptations from the 1920s and 1930s that includes the Bach and Brahms arrangements and the Cello Concerto, a recomposition of a keyboard concerto by Handel's contemporary Georg Matthias Monn.[42]

Following Hitler's appointment as chancellor in January 1933, and the March parliamentary elections in which the National Socialists won a sizable majority, Jewish and left-wing intellectuals in the Prussian Academy were increasingly under siege. Schoenberg was in attendance at a March meeting of the academy's senate when the composer Max von Schillings, who had replaced the painter Max Liebermann as president of the academy, officially denounced the Jewish element. With the passage in April of the Law for the Restoration of the Professional Civil Service (Gesetz zur Wiederherstellung des Berufbeamtentums), it became legally possible to void the contracts of those who could not prove Aryan descent.[43]

Schoenberg completed the first two movements of the Concerto for String Quartet on May 10 and 12, 1933; five days later he hastily departed from Berlin to Paris with Gertrud and his daughter Nuria, who had been born in 1932. They remained in France throughout the summer, primarily in the town of Arcachon. In Paris, on July 24, 1933, he reconverted to Judaism (see 6.1). He did not give up the idea that he might return to Berlin until his contract with the academy was finally terminated in September. Schoenberg's only substantial compositional work between his departure from Germany and his emigration was the completion of the final two movements of the concerto in August and September. In response to an offer of a teaching position at the Malkin Conservatory in Boston, Schoenberg and his family boarded ship for the United States on October 25.[44]

I wrote the String Quartet Concerto in mid-1933, right after the Concerto for Violoncello. Written specifically for the Kolisch Quartet, which also performed the premiere in Prague, it fulfills a part of my intention to set new technical tasks for the individual instruments, which I propose to pursue further through a piano and a violin concerto. It was not my concern here to win from the instrument new colors or sounds, though this should scarcely be lacking. But I wanted to use certain unutilized possibilities, fingerings, ways of playing, which by learning to master should allow the instrumentalists to become more accomplished in playing modern themes and melodies.

From the standpoint of composition, I have gone further than Brahms or Mozart in their Handel arrangements. I have not limited myself, as they did, to expunging sequences and uninteresting figure work and to enriching the texture; instead, especially in the third and fourth movements, whose insufficiency with respect to thematic invention and development could satisfy no sincere contemporary of ours, I have acted quite freely and independently, and, while employing what was usable, undertaken an entirely new structure.

I believe that such freedom will be found hardly more disturbing, stylistically, than the cadenzas that modern writers apply to classical concertos. I do not venture much further than they do in matters of harmony. Nor do I believe that I need yield to them as regards solidity of form and intensification of motivic development, and their interrelating.

On Racism and the Idea

5.21 "The Germans' racial pride now driven to its peak," September 25, 1933

The Germans' racial pride now driven to its peak is as groundless as it is recent. No people on Earth has intermingled with others so willingly and easily, and it is well known that as emigrants they always endeavored to assimilate as quickly as possible and to disavow their racial characteristics.

Thus up to now: no pride. And the exaggeration arises from their being so unaccustomed to it. At the same time, racism, except for the specific German exaggerations, is an imitation (every good imitation is a bad imitation) of the Jewish faith in itself. We Jews calls ourselves the chosen people of God and have the Covenant. And we know that we are chosen to think the idea of the unitary, eternal, unimaginable, unrepresentable, and invisible God to its end; to preserve it. Nothing can be compared to this, therefore German racism is stuck in slogans and in the material: in appearances. Therefore they measure noses, ears, legs, and bellies, precisely because the Idea is lacking.

A Farewell to His Critics

5.22 "My Enemies," October 6, 1933

Time and again I have considered the question whether I am attacked so much because I have too little talent, am capable of too little, have not worked seriously enough, or because I am on the wrong track.

But now I place the following facts side by side:

I.   a) Nationalistic musicians regard me as *international*
     b) but abroad my music is regarded as too *German*

II. a) National Socialists regard me as a *cultural Bolshevik*
     b) but the communists reject me as *bourgeois*

III. a) Anti-Semites personify me as a Jew, my direction as Jewish
     b) a) but almost no Jews have followed my direction
        b) in contrast, perhaps the only ones who have continued further in my direction are Aryans:
        Anton von Webern, Alban Berg, Winfried Zillig, Norbert von Hannenheim, Nikos Skalkottas
        c) and the composers (except for my pupils) who stand closest to me are Aryans: Bartok, Hauer, Krenek, and Hindemith

And now I draw the following conclusion:

Everything that is said against me and that is created by my divided enemies appears as the confluence of every kind of stupidity, ignorance, lack of cultivation, cowardice, lack of character, and lack of imagination.

6 "Driven into Paradise":
Boston, New York, and Los Angeles,
1933–1943

Zionism, Democracy, and Jewish Unity

6.1 From "Notes on Jewish Politics," September–November 1933

Schoenberg wrote to Berg on October 16, 1933: "It wasn't until 1 October that my going to America became the kind of certainty I could believe in myself. Everything that appeared in the newspapers both before and since was founded on fantasy, just as are the purported ceremonies and the presence of 'tout Paris' at my so-called return to the Jewish faith. (Tout Paris was, besides the rabbi and myself: my wife and a Dr. Marianoff, with whom all these dreadful tales probably originated.) As you have surely observed, my return to the Jewish faith took place long ago and is even discernible in the published portions of my work ('Du sollst nicht . . . du musst [Op. 27, No. 2]') and in Moses und Aron, which you've known about since 1928, but which goes back at least another five years; most especially in my drama Der biblische Weg, which was also conceived in 1922 or '23 at the latest, though not finished until '26-'27."[1]

The "Notes on Jewish Politics," started in Arcachon and then continued in the United States, lays the groundwork for Schoenberg's most substantial statement on Jewish politics, "A Four-Point Program for Jewry," completed in 1938 (and see 6.3).[2] Almost immediately upon his arrival in France, Schoenberg became actively involved with efforts to establish a Jewish state. He wrote to Webern on August 4 of his desire to sacrifice his art, and "to do nothing in the future but work for the Jewish national cause."[3] He outlined a plan that would occupy him intensively over the next months to travel the world speaking and producing recordings and films to organize assistance for the German Jews.

The items, of which there are many more, are presented in the order Schoenberg established.

We are faced with facts that most of you—not I—would probably have called fantastic only a short while ago. We are faced with fantastic necessities

and that means making decisions that one would normally consider fantastic.

November 3, 1933

Photo previous page: Schoenberg at his home on North Rockingham Avenue, Los Angeles. Arnold Schönberg Center, Vienna.

Schoenberg lived here from May 1936 to his death.

"Jewish Internationalism"

is a product of necessity; arises from the Diaspora; would never have come to be without this; must be fought under all circumstances.

Faith in the power of internationalism is harmful in every respect.

I. It lulls the Jews into a sense of security, although they are in danger.

II. This very security-superstition prevents the Jews from obtaining another security for themselves; the only one that there can be for a people: its own state.

III. Never and nowhere has the Jew been truly regarded as a member of the host people.

Not even when he attempted to give up his Jewishness!

IV. But no one can belong to two nations.

Therefore the Jew must cease being a citizen in the host country.

September 3, 1933

"Homeland"

Why do we Jews love Palestine, and why does the idea of living there fill us with emotion?

Because it is the land that our forefathers have won by fighting for it with their blood and by defending it with their blood in countless wars: therefore it was their land and therefore we desire so ardently for it to become our land again.

But:

a people truly possesses a land only if it has paid for it with its blood, if it has fertilized the soil with its blood.[4]

September 3, 1933

"The Jewish Religion"

The Jewish people are a people through their religion, and can again become, be, and remain a people only as a *Religious People*.

In the Diaspora, the idolatry of the host peoples uprooted us and robbed us of our own faith.

We must again give ourselves over to the faith.

It alone makes us capable of living; worthy of being preserved.

September 2, 1933

"Democracy"[5]

Democracy has always meant one thing for me:

that in it *I* will *never* succeed even so much as to make my will known, let alone to have it prevail.

———

A thought arises from *one* brain; with its merits; with its faults.

If others interfere with it, the mistakes are not improved.

An idea that has arisen from one's brain is only to be used as it presents itself to its creator. It is useful only if the relationship of the merits to the faults is relatively advantageous. Every improvement merely makes the relationship of the merits to the faults worse.

Democracy, however, works on the basis of ideas that no one has had; that have arisen from no single brain; that are not bound to a fixed relationship of merits and faults,

but:

that—supposedly—correspond to the agreed-upon will of the whole,

but in reality correspond only to the accidental majority which decided on them—as a result the many minorities that had voted against them remain ineffectual, even more so those who did not even make the attempt to express themselves.

This will of the whole, however, is nothing real but comes about only through compromises: in striving to belong to a majority the individual corrupts his own will. For no matter *how* advantageous the relationship between mistakes and merits may be, only a relationship originating in nature can last. It would naturally be more advantageous for carbon, which as carbon-monoxide must content itself with one oxygen molecule, and as carbon-dioxide with a second, if there were carbon-trioxide. But it simply cannot retain the third oxygen molecule.

September 3, 1933

"My Plans"

You want to know what I am planning?

You are asking in vain.

I have no intention of telling you that.

That trust can only be gained by one whom I can use for a specific task.

My most intimate friends, my most loyal followers will only know as much of my plans as is useful for them and that they require for the fulfillment of their task.

But I shall tell you something: when I have carried out my intentions and there are enemies of the Jews, who have done something to Jewry or to individual Jews, they will be paid back in kind.

September 2, 1933

"Unity Party"

I want to found it.

Today this is nothing new.

More important for us than for all others. If all the others are divided seven ways, we are divided seventy times seven ways,

because we are still international.

We must become *national.*

We must give up being international.

And the time will come when we shall demand from the Jews in every land that they renounce the emancipation, that they put aside their citizenship, and they be only Jews.

September 2, 1933

"Zionism"

Palestine is our land

That's where we belong

That's where we must go

Magnificent Idea

If Jews do not flourish in another climate—are sick—

physically—psychologically

in their overall constitution

morally—

socially—

religiously—

everything has one cause: Palestine

Palestine

the Goal

but the Way

September 2, 1933

On Program Music, Tradition, and the Public

6.2 "The First American Radio Broadcast: An Interview with William Lundell," November 19, 1933

The Sunday broadcast on NBC Radio in New York took place from 11:00 to 11:30 A.M., preceded by a performance of Verklärte Nacht *by the Kroll Sextet.*

In an open letter to his friends for his sixtieth birthday, on September 13, 1934, Schoenberg described his first year on the East Coast of the United States leading up to his move to Los Angeles: "I have to say that for disappointments, annoyance and illness it was worse than quite a lot I have been through so far. [. . .] the Malkin Conservatory offered me rather less than a quarter of what I had regarded as compensation for my Berlin salary, that is to say as a minimum; by now I had been sufficiently softened up to accept this solitary offer, after a few hours' reflection. The next big disappointment, to mention only the more important things, was discovering that I had carelessly agreed to teach, for the same salary, not only in Boston but also in New York—a demand, made at a late stage, whose insidious nature I failed to detect. These journeys, every week, were the main cause of my illness.[6] Then: on the way from Washington to Boston I asked Malkin what the conservatory orchestra was like, and on my arrival in Boston I found a little school of music with perhaps five to six classrooms."[7] He had a different tone in a speech delivered in Hollywood on October 9, 1934; contrasting his situation to the snake driven out of the Garden of Eden: "I on the contrary, came from one country into another, where neither dust nor better food is rationed and where I am allowed to go on my feet, where my head can be erect, where kindness and cheerfulness is dominating, and where to live is a joy and to be an expatriate of another country is the grace of God. I was driven into paradise!"[8]

LUNDELL: The work of yours, Mr. Schoenberg, we have just heard, is very interesting to me, because it has such a close relationship to the great classical tradition. In that respect it is very different from your more recent compositions. It prompts me to ask if it is true, as some have said, that you demand as an essential requirement that any pupil who wishes to study with you must have a thorough training in the classical tradition?

SCHOENBERG: Well, I prefer to instruct pupils which have learned something before coming to me. The degree of instruction he has before he comes to me is not always significant, for there is much instruction, and many teachers. It is not that I wish to criticize the teachers, or any method they employ, for each teacher is a *good* teacher if he has a good pupil. And he is a *bad* teacher very often if he has a *bad* pupil.

LUNDELL: Mr. Schoenberg, you are a superb diplomat.

SCHOENBERG: (Laughs) I have had *bad* pupils, and I have had *good* pupils. And *I* have always been the same teacher to both.

LUNDELL: But we are getting away from the point. What I mean is this. Do you demand a training in Bach, Beethoven and Brahms? Must any pupil coming to you know these classics?

SCHOENBERG: No, Mr. Lundell, it is not absolutely necessary. But I would prefer if the pupil knew Bach and Beethoven and Brahms, and Mozart. Even if he has *not* this classical training, but has musical ability and talent, I can sense it—*ich kann es bemerken*—yes, how you say it—in English—I can see it.

LUNDELL: Well now, about yourself, Mr. Schoenberg. We have just heard the Kroll String Sextet play this *Verklärte Nacht* Suite. But Mr. Bela Rosza, whom I have heard playing your music all the past week, and who will play some of your piano music following this interview at the close of the program, shows with this piano music a totally different style from the *Verklärte Nacht* Suite. He tells me that there is a great difference between your Opus 10, for instance, with its classical tone, and this later style of Opus 11 and the succeeding works. Why did you make that change?

SCHOENBERG: Why? Well I was forced to.

LUNDELL: What do you mean, forced to?

SCHOENBERG: My fancy, my imagination. The musical pictures I had before me. I have always had *musical* visions before me, all the time I was writing still in the more classical mode, in the earlier days. Then finally, one day, I had the courage to put on paper these pictures I had seen in music. Many times before I have written my music in this new style—what you call a new style—I have seen this music in my mind. And so, for me it was not such a great *Sprung*—as you say in English, jump—for me it was a gradual development.

LUNDELL: But, Mr. Schoenberg, these pictures you saw in your mind, and which you finally had the courage to put down in music on paper, they were not pictures of flowers and brooks and thunderstorms, or landscapes?

SCHOENBERG: No, it was music and tones—It is not a transcription of natural scenery. Musical figures and themes and melodies I call pictures. It is my idea that it is a musical story with musical pictures—Not a real story, and not real pictures—Quasi pictures.

LUNDELL: Would you call it absolute—pure music?

SCHOENBERG: No, I do not prefer to call it that. Fancy is the dominant force which drives the artist, and it is not of great difference to me, whether it is a poetic idea or a musical idea. A musician can always only see music, and the *cause* is of no importance. I am not against what you call "program music."

LUNDELL: If a composer can write music describing a storm at sea or a skyscraper, you would agree that they may be thoroughly good music?

SCHOENBERG: Yes, if a composer can describe a skyscraper, a sunrise, or springtime in the country—that is all right, the cause and the source is irrelevant.[9] It is the *result* that is always important.

LUNDELL: A number of critics and students of music in discussing your music refer to this change from your earlier to your later style as a change from the classical to the *atonal.*

SCHOENBERG: Ah, no, don't say atonal. I do not like the word "atonal."

LUNDELL: But there is a distinct difference in your styles. Have you developed any theory of composition based upon your later style?

SCHOENBERG: Not in this sense. I am <u>never</u> *after* a *theory;* and for the *general* public there is no difference between my *present* manner to compose and my *earlier* manner to compose. I am always writing *that,* what my *fancy* gives me, and always I can only write if I have seen a musical idea.

LUNDELL: When you have seen that musical idea, how do you seek to express it?

SCHOENBERG: Well, it is hard to explain. With the musical idea I get an impression of musical form and extension, and of the whole and of the parts. By and by I am seeing this form more exactly, and I begin to hear themes and sonorities, and then I begin with the writing with the pen. Sometimes with sketches, and sometimes I write the music directly. And then, there the music is.

LUNDELL: About the appreciation and understanding of your music, Mr. Schoenberg. As we know, it took people generally many years to understand and appreciate Wagner and Berlioz, Ravel, Stravinsky—but they are all now so well accepted as to be performed in movie theatres, and in one instance, in a musical comedy. Have you any anticipation as to the length of time that will be needed for an understanding of your compositions?

SCHOENBERG: Ach, I only hope it will not be so long, but I am not sure. The difficulty for the public to understand my music is the *conciseness* and *short-ness.*

LUNDELL: You mean you speak musically in a kind of aphorism, epigrams—I almost said enigmas, Mr. Schoenberg.

SCHOENBERG: Yes, my works are apparently enigmas to many people, but there is an answer to all of them. What I mean is, <u>I never repeat</u>. I say an idea only once.

LUNDELL: But even saying it once, Mr. Schoenberg, was too much for some people 25 years ago. Did these riots among the critics and the audience during that celebrated concert in Vienna when the public was so excited about your music as to let fists fly and shout and scream—did all that uproar discourage you? And does the present-day failure to understand your work trouble you?

SCHOENBERG: Yes, my feelings are always *offended* by trouble and misunderstanding. For I think the public could know that I have worked with the greatest sincerity and I think I have the right to demand the respect of the public for my work.

LUNDELL: Now that you have come to America from Europe, Mr. Schoenberg, to be at the Malkin Conservatory of Music in Boston and New York, and from your knowledge of modern music—what would you say is the greatest need in contemporary music?

SCHOENBERG: I think what we need in music today is not so much new methods of music, as <u>men</u> of <u>character</u>. Not *talents. Talents are here.* What we need are *men* who will have the *courage* to *express* what they *feel* and *think.*

LUNDELL: Are there any men like that on the musical horizon today?

SCHOENBERG: Oh yes, I have seen some of them. For instance, I have some of them among my pupils. Alban Berg, Anton von Webern, and others. For it is my important intention to fortify the morale of my pupils. The chief thing I demand of my pupils, with their basic technical knowledge of music taken for granted, of course, is the courage to express *what they have to say.*[10]

Foreword to a Jewish Unity Party

6.3 "The Jewish Situation," April 29, 1934

Schoenberg worked on this lecture in Boston and New York between December 1, 1933, and April 29, 1934. Also entitled "Foreword to a Jewish Unity Party," it was presented for a meeting of the Mailam Society in New York. The lecture was one of Schoenberg's first extended writings in English. The heavily annotated typescript has been lightly edited for readability, but also to preserve the character of the original as a spoken text and as evidence of Schoenberg coming to terms with his new language.

The outbreak of anti-Semitism—unexpected by many people and considered just as surprising by its unusual violence as by its getting up in a world, which believed of itself, that war could be avoided (*Nie wieder Krieg:* Never war, they cried), that culture was its outstanding characteristic, that crudeness and cruelty should be only leavings of a primitive state, disappearing quickly and entirely—this outbreak has awakened in our people many new ideas and has made many problems arise, which have not been considered very important during the past years.

I don't know whether there are many people who have asked themselves: How was it possible that so many Jews could get a place in the first rank of human activities?

This fact is astonishing in such a manner, that it can only be called a biological fact. Jewry foreseeing the coming fight for its life, scraped together the entire genius of its race and produced in fifty years notable men in such a number as other people could not have produced in a multiple of the same time.

Our religion does not allow an investigation of the ways of our God, of the Unimaginable, of the Unconceivable. But we know His handwriting, we know the size of the letters, which correspond with the destiny He ordered and we could know—if there were Prophets, as in former, more blessed times—we *could* know by the words of such prophets, what our God is willing to communicate to us, what we should know as His Will.

Indeed: if there were prophets!

Indeed: if this would have been a blessed time! But there was nobody to hear what God asked, there was nobody to feel, nobody to foresee what the coming troubles demanded from the Jewish people. In brief, it was indeed just as in biblical times; it was just as if prophets spoke and nobody understood them: this unconceivable silence of intuition, this perfect absence of prophetic gift, this absolute submersion in . . .—this submersion, it is of this submersion, of which I will speak.

As I mentioned before: the Jewish people produced ten times the number of important men than other nations. But at that time, these important Jewish men were perfectly submerged into the feelings and into the ideas of other nations, and therefore they became deaf against the need of their own, of the Jewish people. But perhaps this submergence was the only possibility for such an unfolding of the Genius of our Nation, and without such an economy, without concentrating all forces to only one goal, the success could not have been accomplished: to produce outstanding men in such a number. This success, let us now call it by its true name, this success is: the appearance of leading personalities, who are able to be guides of their people in times of need through their prominent qualities of intelligence, of understanding, judgment, and perception, as well as by their willingness—founded on their character, their personal courage, their temperament, their idealism, on their integrity, unselfishness, and by their self-sacrificing spirit—yes, I spoke of their willingness to make themselves sacrifices for their faith; for only such men, who esteem the honor and the future of their people more than their life, only such men have the right to ask the same sacrifice of other people.

I have the honor to speak in a meeting of outstanding Jewish ladies and gentlemen, amongst whom surely will be found a great number of characters like those described above. This is the first reason that causes me to speak here on this subject. But the second reason is, that *here* I am speaking to *my confreres of art,* whose manner of feeling, their world-impressions, are homogeneous with mine, and especially in the case of this society that I know has a very idealistic purpose and is striving to a holy goal, to a goal, which if accomplished, will form one of the most important steps to a strong national feeling. Yes: to create a national Jewish music is a holy task, and especially interesting for Jews—who in great numbers in former times, as well as in our days, have helped Aryan music to become as perfect as it is today—for we can prove our superiority in spiritual matters in creating this new Jewish music.

The whole Jewish world has acknowledged the fact that the anti-Semitism everywhere arising is a danger of unusual and alarming dimensions. And if they had the courage to envisage this danger without a lot of conventional optimism, without an unanswerable amount of faint-hearted euphemism, they could not do otherwise than recognize that the Jewish situation today is not the same as on other occasions—as, for example, when Jews had been driven out of Spain, but found an exile in Holland; or when they were persecuted in Poland, and found an asylum in America—they could not fail to acknowledge that there could remain no country in the whole world where Jews could flee, if anti-Semitism began to arise into such forms as it has in Germany in countries where it is until now only in its first phase; in this first phase, which I know from Germany and Austria, and which made me foresee already 20 years ago the outbreak we have learned now; this first phase in which I spoke with so many Jews and tried to persuade them of this coming danger, and got no other answer than a scornful and charitable smile: scornful because I seemed stupid, and charitable for they considered me as faint-hearted, whilst I was only clear sighted: please do not believe this to be an arrogance: it was not difficult to see clearly in this case, if you had only the courage and the willingness to acknowledge the truth.

Let me begin again: the Jewish people should acknowledge the coming danger of a world-wide anti-Semitism.

Let me begin again: the Jewish people should not only acknowledge, no, it is *forced to* acknowledge facts, indubitable and indisputable facts and it is indeed forced to draw conclusions, conclusions which must be drawn by every people threatened by war, which must be carried out, which are un-avoidable. But the Jewish people are not willing to see the danger. They have played too long the unworthy play with pacifism, which is entirely out of their interest (for nobody could expect war-like activities of them—until now, but participation in defense of the country cannot be refused by Jews as long as they live in strange countries with strange people).

A people, threatened by a danger of their existence, are not allowed to reflect whether it has to protect a principle, as for example with pacifism. It is the duty of each people to protect at first their existence, but not different principles. But a people such as the Jews, who have a promise, and who call themselves God's elected people, such a people does not only injure biological laws if it neglects the obligation of self-preservation, but it shakes also the religious basis of its national existence; and religion is the only indisputable basis of Jewish claims for its existence as a people.

It is astonishing that the Jewish people always strive to fight against anti-Semitism.

If a man should fall into the water and thinks only how to save his clothes, but does not try to swim: what would you think about this man? Or: if some-body in case of a large fire should try to fight against the heat, but let the fire burn, would you believe this man to be very intelligent? Or: if a patient is suffering from appendicitis, would you like to have a doctor who fights against the fever, but who lets the inflammation break through?

To this very hour Jewry has not understood that anti-Semitism is not the cause of the persecution of the Jews, but only the *effect of the totality* of Jewish *existence*; the result of our faith, of our selection, the *consequence of* all the qualities we possess owing to our destiny, to our task; the *comprehensible reaction* to all the qualities shown everywhere and always where Jews are living.

If hence anti-Semitism is not a cause, but a result: if hence it is not because of their anti-Semitism that people persecute Jews, but that anti-Semitism is joined to Jews, inseparably, like some of their other qualities; if this is so: is it not without intelligence to fight against this result? Is it not just as unintelligent as to fight for his clothes, instead of swimming: to fight against the heat, instead of against the fire: to fight against the fever, than against the inflammation?

Anti-Semitism will exist just as long as there are Jews amongst other peoples, and just as long as they offer a menace to each people who do not possess a high faith, a high trust in their future and in their task, like the Jewish people!

Is it not clear that the fight against anti-Semitism is not worthy of a people, distinguished by a high promise? It is not worthy to fight against the hostility, but it is only honorable *to annihilate the enemy.*

It is disdainful to hope to gain the love, or even less the estimation of the enemy, for an enemy is only to be hated and his estimation can only be an offense: but his disdain can make rise the self-consciousness, the pride, and the courage of people, who possess a promise like Jews. It is not a shame to be surrounded by enemies. I hope you know who is telling you that: I hope you know that it is one who has the right to pretend: it is honorable to have enemies!

———

A proud people like the Jews has the obligation to look danger resolutely in the face. If some people are anti-Semites and wish no longer to live together with us—Well: we don't wish to either: the only answer worthy to be given by a people of our high destiny.

Neither the anti-Semitism, nor the anti-Semitic people, neither the hate, nor the hater have to be the object of our consideration. There is only one enemy which must be annihilated, annihilated at any price.

But who is this enemy? This strongest, most inconsiderate, most unfeeling, most foolish, most unintelligent, and most uncompromising enemy?

I think it is not necessary to say it. Is it possible that there is a Jew, who does not know that this terrible enemy of our people is no other than Jewish discord? That there is no other cause of all the evil in the Jewish world? Each Jew for himself, does he not know, that each Jew is disunited with each Jew in each question? Has not each Jew remarked that, whenever it would be necessary to resolve something of the greatest importance, that in the same instant a lot of different opinions, ideas, principles, formalities, caprices, vanities, and last but not least, personally material interests, self-seeking interests arise: and, that in the same instant there are a lot of theories, one more intelligent than the other, one profounder than the other; and has he not remarked, that in the same instant a heavy battle arises and everybody attacks the theories of all the others— but: of the matter to resolve, and of an action to do . . . no more is spoken?

This is the very tragicomedy of the Jewish democracy: everybody has the right to utter his opinion. Well; but a man of another people may attach himself to the good opinion, to the theory of another man, without a loss of prestige, because the conviction, the loyalty to the chosen party, is sufficient to fix a man's value. On the contrary: within an old people, like the Jews, instruction of spirit and mental culture are advanced to such a high degree that everybody can prove his value only by producing an opinion of his own. These circumstances have produced a mania for originality, useful perhaps in scientific matters, but pernicious in national questions!

Seeking for an object to recognize best the consequence of this mania, I cannot find a better one than the Zionist movement.

All people are indeed divided in many parties. But the Zionist movement shows at first many different parties, only concerning ways, meanings, policies, etc. of the Zionist Idea. But each of these parties for itself is divided into just as many parties, as otherwise, a whole nation is divided. Should, for instance, another people be divided into 7 parties, the Jewish-Zionist-Party must consequently be divided into 7 times 77 parties![11] Well; all these parties strive for the best for the Jewish people, as well as they understand. But there are moreover parties that are not content to establish the luck of the Jews, but that feel also the vocation to correct the social fate of strange nations.

We know the success of these noble-minded reformers: riots broke out to reduce the immigration.

A very fine success!

It is the tragicomedy of the democracy in our people: our aim to freedom in spiritual things has caused a new Babylonian captivity. And the effort to conciliate an enemy, who by his self-preservation is forced to detest us, is a worse serfdom than the Egyptian had been.

It must be said:

As long as we remain in discord, just as long shall anti-Semitism be able to make us suffer and to trouble the security of our life, of our property, or our religious culture, and our national sciences. Everybody, who was yesterday your friend, brother, and admirer—there is no reliance to be placed on him in general: tomorrow he can be your enemy, can deliver you, can detest you. There are exceptions, but they are rare, as we have seen a thousand times: rare, just as every good thing.

Therefore it is clear: the fight against anti-Semitism is of no use, can never change the mind of other people who are accustomed for many centuries to hate the Jews, can never protect us from their hostile actions.

Only a real and incontestable unity can grant a nation the power needed for such decisions as to save the future of a nation. And therefore it is necessary to unify the Jewish people in the same manner in which other peoples have unified themselves: with power, with force, and, if needed, with violence against all those who oppose themselves to this unifying.

I am sure: youth will be found among the Jewish people, who are not willing any further to endure insolence and the disesteem of other peoples; youth who estimate the honor of their nation higher than their lives. But this youth shall be willing to work in favor of the unity of our people with its whole ardor and enthusiasm, with affection and with hate, and with the same defiance of death with which they have until today fought at each front, at fronts where ideals were defended, but also at such fronts where only the advantage of individual self interest was fought for. Jews have sacrificed their blood to all the states where they live and to all political parties, be they monarchical or republican, capitalistic or socialistic, democratic or communistic! And they have for that scarcely been rewarded otherwise than by their conviction: to have worked in favor of an ideal.

But now, our youth is urged to forget all that in the establishment of a NEW JEWISH UNITY PARTY, in which only the *Jewish Interest* is allowed to be regarded: to lay the foundation of a new Jewish life in HONOR and POWER.

Concerning a Music Institute in Russia

6.4 Letter to Hanns Eisler, August 20, 1934

The letter and a plan for a music institute in Russia—evidence for how uncertain Schoenberg felt his situation in the United States to be—were written in Chautauqua, N.Y., where Schoenberg was spending the summer.[12] Eisler (1898–1962) had studied with Schoenberg in Mödling between 1919 and 1923, but they had had a falling-out in 1926 due to Eisler's criticism of twelve-tone composition and Schoenberg's rejection of his Marxist politics.[13] After leaving Germany in 1933, Eisler traveled widely through Europe; this letter was sent to him in Denmark. In a letter of September 12 to his long-time friend Fritz Stiedry, who was then conductor of the Leningrad Philharmonic, Schoenberg wrote that Eisler had been in touch with him through his son Georg to determine his interest in going to Russia to help establish a music institute. Asking Stiedry if he was in a position to help further these plans, Schoenberg complained of his difficult financial situation in the United States, of his inability to find a teaching position, and his planned move to California in September on account of the healthier climate and lower cost of living.[14] Stiedry replied with caution several months later, suggesting that Schoenberg would not like it in Russia. Eisler ended up emigrating to the United States, teaching first at the New School for Social Research before moving to Hollywood in 1942.

Dear Eisler,

I have enclosed a brief outline. I had at first written twenty pages with all sorts of far-reaching special recommendations for every class but have described here merely the main contents; I believe that for a first attempt that would be best. One can certainly believe me, if at all, of being quite capable of having something new and good to say about these matters, which, to a certain degree, is already quite apparent in this sketch.

I believe that for the establishing, founding, building, and development of such a school a director must possess dictatorial power.

So far as my personal material demands are concerned, I can only give you general terms, since I know absolutely nothing about conditions in Russia. If I had to undertake such a grueling task (you know if I am entrusted with it, every task is grueling), I could not do without the accustomed comforts in my lifestyle. Furthermore, every year I would need to have the possibility to restore myself thoroughly and also to compose something. Likewise, I would also occasionally need to travel abroad in order to keep up my foreign connections and to give concerts and lectures. I would need to have a contract of an extended duration to ensure the complete realization of my plans. I would need to have the certainty that if I wanted to, or had to, leave Russia at the end of the contract, I would have enough money to be able to live abroad, or rather that I could take with me what I had saved or earned; or that if I stay in Russia, my old age would be provided for corresponding to my rank and service.

Obviously, I can make detailed special recommendations if it is desired, although I am actually of the opinion that something definitive arising out of the particular experience would certainly look different than the "paper form" of the idea. Nevertheless, one should be able to recognize my ambition.

It would please me very much if I were to be in the position of realizing my old cherished ideas, and I am most certain that it would make you happy to help me in this. I would do even better to compose!

I did not mention in the draft my wish that the institute should be in the south, since I can certainly not judge whether this is advantageous in Russia, and because I don't want to make such an important matter dependent on my health alone. Though, whether I should be able to manage it in my sickness . . . ? In any case, I am feeling very well again in this warm climate, I am even playing a little tennis once more.

Please confirm the receipt of this letter immediately. And make an effort to see to it that where possible all the ministry's questions, demands, answers, decisions are sent to me all at once.

Also let me know sometime how you are. What do you hear from Rankl?[15] Why is he a conductor in the Nazi city Graz?

Many warm regards,

On Life in the United States

6.5 Letter to David Joseph Bach, March 13, 1935

While he was in Chautauqua in July 1934, Schoenberg had written a short text for a birthday canon for his old friend: "He who wants to run with the world must have time: or else he will run too fast. / He who wants to fight like a hero must bear sorrow: or else he will be found too slight. / He who wants to get value for his money must seek afar: or else he will spend too much, spend too much!"[16] The letter below was addressed to the "Fifth Avenue Hotel" in New York.

Dear Friend,

The reason I have not written to you in so long is above all that I have been terribly exhausted and that I am not at all well. Furthermore, I just had a concert in San Francisco (*Pierrot* and the Chamber Symphony) for which I had to prepare, and now have one in Los Angeles, the latter being the first well-paid concert in America.[17] Along the way I have to teach—beginners (!), as almost all are here, most of whom would be better off as quitters. God help us! The golden days are over here (only not for the film people who are still swimming in money), but unfortunately they don't know this in Europe. Nevertheless, I too, am of the opinion that you should stay here as long as possible, even at the risk that you will have to keep yourself above water through small earnings from various jobs until something suitable comes along. I know for myself how hard it is to fit in here. We are all a bit *Boches,* that is, we let people feel how deeply we despise them, so it is difficult for us to smile incessantly (*keep smiling*) when we would like to spit, to spit fire.[18] You have certainly already noticed that on no account may one speak the truth here—even when one knows it; even when the other does not know it; even when the other wants to know it: for that is the game. I have only understood this incompletely, and still have scarcely learned it. But I have already come to appreciate how damaging the opposite is. And even if you want to warn someone of a danger, this is not permitted to take place in a more open way than I am doing here (in which I am already taking into account that I must speak to you more "directly" than they would like in America.) Here in the partly (the greater part) still Wild West, warnings are still given thus, as I recently found written on a house: "If you want to shoot, do it now, or else you will never shoot again!" But otherwise there is, for example, no exclamation mark on my typewriter: *keep smiling,* but don't cry out. Here everything is supposed to be praised: *marvelous, very nice, beautiful.* As if to say: I also won't tolerate criticism, because it bores me and because I believe I can manage everything so it is *all right.* But here, where everything is *all wrong,* it is the insecurity and fear of exposure that will only tolerate praise. Certainly, for example, Frau Ledermann is so repulsive that if needs be I would give preference to the most disgusting spittoon.[19] But unfortunately, though one would like to spit, one must smile; at least to their face!

Do you know Paul Bekker and are you in good standing with him?[20] He is with the *Staatszeitung,* a German newspaper that appears in New York. I have endeavored for a long time to get you in there. But then everyone maintained that it had Nazi sympathies. It's a shame; that would have been a good possibility. Perhaps you could write some articles for him, and perhaps he knows of further possibilities. It seems to me to be a definite possibility for the time being, supposing that you are thinking of staying here permanently. But even if you want to go back to Europe, it should be possible to deliver an article each month to a series of the major newspapers. There are countless big cities here, and if you give them articles that have already been printed they will take them nevertheless. Only you must always *demand* with the first printing that the copyright be registered under *your* name. Cities with more than 500,000 inhabitants are: New York; Chicago; Philadelphia; Detroit, Mich.; Los Angeles, California; Cleveland, Ohio; St. Louis, Mo.; Baltimore, Md.; Boston, Mass.; Pittsburgh, Pa.; San Francisco, Cal.; Milwaukee, Wis.; Buffalo, N.Y.; but then still come: Washington, D.C.; Minneapolis, Minn.; New Orleans, LA.; Cincinnati, Ohio; Seattle, Wash.; Indianapolis, Ind.; Rochester, N.Y. that also have 500,000, and many, many others.—Possibly, if your English is good enough, lectures could also be considered. One earns 50–100 dollars for that. The Americans are very eager to learn, they say, but they would rather learn from lectures than from reading: because that offers no opportunity for handshaking. Mainly one must tell them anecdotes, as you probably have already noticed if you have heard the lectures by Mr. Gilman that are given in the intermission of the Philharmonic Concerts each Sunday (over all American stations).[21] Though till now I personally have only given lectures at Princeton and at the University of Chicago, but have had to decline other lectures.[22] My lectures were too academic for the universities, I believe, although I had to endure a great deal of applause and handshaking.—But I don't want to fall into the European error and only complain. There is very much that is good here (they say) and the country is young (they say) and I assume that there are in fact good possibilities. I have found very many people that I have liked, but, as they say, that proves nothing.—No, in fact it is not easy for us here; but one has to buy into it, even if it is hardly a buy.[23] Unfortunately the golden days are over here. We have chosen a bad time for emigration. But something else positive: really the best people here are the English, while those who have only lived here for thirty or forty years are mostly inferior, although often very good-natured and even helpful.

So now I have given you a short introductory lecture and am certain that it will not discourage you but will encourage you as I intended: for now you know some of the difficulties and can prepare for them. I firmly believe that in time you can achieve something. Even in Hollywood, where it [end of sentence illegible.] I hope that I shall hear from you again soon and that you don't take my silence amiss.

On the Duty of the Listener

6.6 "What Have People to Expect from Music?" November 7, 1935

This lecture, prepared for a radio broadcast ("over KHJ"), reflects Schoenberg's attempts to come to terms with an American public unfamiliar not only with his music but also with new music in general. The typescript is carefully annotated to indicate correct accentuation and words to be emphasized.

When you go to lunch in a restaurant, you choose *yourself* what you *like,* but when you are invited to a dinner party, you do not know in *advance what* you will be given. If you are very hungry you will generally be satisfied by the mere fact that you are *getting* some food. In many cases perhaps you will be satisfied by the quantity alone and will not ask very much about the quality. Certainly even people whose palates possess gastronomic discernment will react in the same manner if they are starving.

There may perhaps be some men who, when they want to buy clothes, will not ask much about good looks, but certainly *no woman* will be indifferent about such matters. In general, everybody knows approximately how he likes to appear and will ask for definite objects. And this is all right, because the more educated a man is, the more he will distinguish between good and bad, between beauty and ugliness, between sense and nonsense, between usefulness and uselessness, between value and worthlessness, because culture *can be called the capacity to distinguish.* And the better a man distinguishes, the better he will know what he wants, and the more precisely he will imagine how things with which he likes to come in contact have to look and function and work upon him.

Is it not the same in matters of art?

When you want to buy a book, or visit an exhibition of paintings, what is it by which you are directed to a decision? To decide which book you will buy is in many cases very easy. You read the advertisements or the criticisms concerning the book, or you even read the blurb where you find not only the most favorable criticisms but also a statement of the contents. Now you can choose. And even if you should *not* be convinced that this book is the best book written in years, as the blurb maintains, you know the contents and you know whether it may be the love story you like, or fiction, adventure, politics, science, the difficult or easy to understand, or the melancholy, the amusing, the tragic, or the exciting story which you prefer. Certainly, these are not decisions from an artistic point of view. And if you should leave it up to similar reasons whether you will visit an exhibition of paintings you would not get better decisions than that. It seems improbable that anybody would go to see the portrait of an ox, unless he was the owner. And especially in *our* days, one might enjoy the portrait of a relative, a friend, or even of a renowned person more in a photograph. And a picture of a part of the country, a building, a ship or any scene of human life, will be *better* shown today in the movies than by a painting.

Nevertheless, when you visit an exhibition of paintings, you will certainly be directed by some reasons, and these reasons seem to be the same which bring you in contact with music. In both cases you are expecting something, and in both cases, that will not be a thing which you can name, as you can with the aforementioned. And perhaps it will be difficult or impossible to express exactly what you are waiting for.

When you are going to listen to music and you know the work to be performed, in that case you will expect to get the same impression that you got when you heard it before, and often that will prove true, although sometimes your reaction may be very different, because of the circumstance that the impressions do not only depend on the sender, that is on the music, but also on the receiver, that is on the listener. Nevertheless, knowing in general how you react, you will hope to be touched in one of the manners which correspond with your general experience. Thus, for instance, you will expect to enjoy beauty, enchanting sounds, charming melodies, exciting rhythms, interesting moods, and you will perhaps hope to find edification, enthusiasm, pleasure, delight, gladness, or even only amusement, diversion, and recreation, and sometimes sensation, excitement, exaltation. Thus far, and with some changes and variations, the expectations connected with music correspond to those connected with paintings.

But it will be quite different when you are going to hear a musical work which you do not know, which you will hear for the first time. Suppose one is a regular visitor, for instance, of symphony concerts. In this case, many people will go there with the accustomed feeling, with an ordinary expectation, and they will not be occupied with the question of the kind of amusement, excitement, or even disappointment to which they are going to be exposed until they have gotten the official program in their hands and have information about the unknown work to be performed. But now, one will become interested. The title of the new work, the name of the new or well-known composer awakes curiosity. And expectations may arise. What will it be like? Will it please you? Or will it excite you? Or will it annoy you? Or will it not touch you at all and only bore you? Will it provoke any of these feelings of edification, enthusiasm, pleasure, delight, gladness, amusement, diversion, sensation, or exaltation, which music in general produces? Certainly one of these effects will be produced. And that is all you know beforehand. You may expect one of the different kinds of effect upon you, but you are perfectly unable to imagine anything about the nature of the work itself. Even if anyone could predict the impression the work will make upon you, you could not imagine any of its details, not to speak of its totality or nature. And if anybody should tell you the work is like Beethoven, or Mozart, or Bach, or Tchaikovsky, or modernistic, you could not imagine one of its themes. And after all, such an attempt seems to be useless because every work is a particular case, and only if a work were perfectly unoriginal would there be a slight possibility of imagining it before hearing it.

Therefore the only correct attitude of a listener has to be: to be ready to listen to that which the author has to tell you.

The correctness of such an attitude is proven when we consider some corresponding cases.

Suppose a man comes back from the moon, or from Mars, or any other planet. Would you expect him to tell you a Hollywood love story, or would you not be without any idea what you were going to learn? Or if a scientist is going to report about a very new discovery, a new chemical, a new physical law, are you right to expect him to tell you, for instance, how such a discovery will be used in the future or for industrial purposes?

Is it not the duty of every artist to tell you what you do not know, what you never have heard before, what you never could find out, or discover, or express yourself? And is it not the duty of the listener to be open to what he has to tell, and not to provoke disappointment by expecting things which the artist does not intend to tell?

Nobody can imagine music which he has not heard before, and therefore nobody could have the right expectations before listening to it.

How much such expectations can lead one astray, shows best when composers are evaluated from expectations based, for instance, on their reputation. Because it is not only his privilege to express what he wants to express and what his talent and his fantasy force him to present; it is on the contrary his duty to produce the unexpected, and to surprise by the newness and originality of his subjects and by the manner in which he treats them. And therefore, everybody is wrong who expects definite accomplishments from a work of an artist; the only correct attitude toward a new or unknown work is to await patiently what the author wants to say.

In this case, you have the opportunity to receive what art can give you: Things which nobody can imagine, but what the artist can express.

On Tonality and the Suite for String Orchestra

6.7 "Analysis by Ear—Draft of a Letter to Olin Downes," October 1935

Starting with the final movement of the Six Pieces for Male Chorus, *and continuing with the recompositions of Handel and Monn in the Concerto for String Quartet and the Cello Concerto, Schoenberg had been increasingly interested in tonal composition in the early 1930s.*[24] *During his final years in Germany he made sketches for several tonal pieces, including a piano concerto in D major. His first work completed in America was the tonal Suite for String Orchestra (September to December 1934); for more on the origins of the work see 6.8.*

The following draft of a letter was a response to an article by Downes[25] *that discussed both the Suite and the Variations for Orchestra, entitled "New Suite by Arnold Schoenberg: Composition in Old Style for String Orchestra to be played by Philharmonic-Symphony—The Atonalist's Progress," published a few days before a performance by Otto Klemperer and the Philharmonic-Symphony on October 17, 1935.*[26] *The article (as marked with Schoenberg's emphases) begins: "Only one thing more fantastical than the thought of Arnold Schönberg in Hollywood is possible, and that thing has happened.* Since arriving *there about a year ago Schönberg has composed in a melodic manner and in* recognizable keys. That is *what Hollywood has done to Schönberg. We may now* expect atonal *fugues by Shirley Temple."*

Attached to the letter draft are several clippings, including a very negative review of the concert by Lawrence Gilman in the New York Herald Tribune, *Saturday, October 19, 1935, where he writes of the "most menacing of the ultramodernist composers" that "the inference is unescapable. Some Hollywood Delilah must have shorn his locks; for this Samson of the twelve-tone scale, this once horrific atonalist who made even the mighty Richard Strauss sound like Ethelbert Nevin—this insuperable champion of the New Era has become a harmless composer of salon music." A review by Downes from the New York* Times, *Friday, October 18, 1935, describes the piece as "a pale monument to lifeless theory"; the opening movement is "an affectation of the old sturdy manner, and thereafter mordant counterpoint. But it is an empty and unbeautiful exhibition."*

Dear Mr. Downes,

a friend sent me your article, "New Suite by Arnold Schoenberg," and I am very glad to have the opportunity to tell you how much I enjoyed it. It is not only very brilliantly written, but shows too an astonishing knowledge about the subjects of my aims. And when I consider that it is already two years since I had the pleasure to meet you and to give you some explanations about this so-called "method," and when I further consider how poor my English was at this time (even in comparison with the little capacity I possess at present), then I can congratulate you very heartily.

I understand very well that you do not mean it in earnest, as your nice little jokes in the beginning of your article make believe, that I am now in the least influenced by the spirit of Hollywood. I came to this city because I was seriously sick and I restored indeed here my health. Also I am convinced you do *not* believe that I intend to leave my former musical creed. But, although I know that to write a work "Im alten Stile" as many of my predecessors did (even Bach wrote his English and French Suites, which are doubtless understandable in a similar meaning) would be sufficient to justify this, my attempt,—confidentially, and please do not publish it, I shall tell you the story of this opus. Mr. Martin Bernstein, a music professor of the New York University whom I met in Chautauqua,[27] told me once in such a nice and interesting manner of his own doings with student orchestras and of the general aims of all the other orchestras of this kind, that I found it a worthwhile thing for the sake of these youths to enlarge their repertoire, and especially to lead them to a better understanding of modern music and the very different tasks which it puts to the player. And so I promised to write something for him and already the next day I noted a number of sketches.

Now, unfortunately, musicians to whom I showed the work when it was finished found it too difficult for pupils, but liked the music very much. (I can not object to this because I did my best, and like it too.) And so it came to be that I agreed with the publisher's wishes to let it at first be a normal concert work and only later to develop its original purpose.

Meanwhile, you listened to it and I hope you find for yourself that this work does not need an excuse, and that if I should have had intentions like Ernst Bloch I did not have to regret it.[28] Because I had indeed much pleasure during the composing; I could see for myself how much my knowledge is based on the masters, and how much I developed it on my own, and how many ways, still unused, I could show to composers who hate "atonality."

Now, speaking of your very interesting analysis of my Variations for Orchestra, I want to tell you that a certain number of aesthetic or compositional concerns which you find problematical, or even baseless or wrong, seem in my opinion not only very well to be resolved and explained, but I myself have already been able to do it.[29] First to the concept of atonality. Already in the first edition (1911) of my *Harmonielehre* is stated: that atonality is a wrong expression, which never could be used for musical matters. A table is atonal, or a ship, or a pair of scissors, etc., but there exists almost always a relationship between tones, at least from one to another. But atonality would indicate the perfect absence of any tonal relation between them, and it is obvious that this is impossible. There-fore: a table is atonal, but tones possess always tonal relations. Therefore: I said in my *Harmonielehre,* it might perhaps be a kind of tonality, not known, not discovered, not described up to the present. I believe this point of view eliminates some of the problems. And it does so especially in connection with your very brilliant statement that the reappearance of the notes of the theme in every variation constitutes a tangible substitu-tion for tonality. Of course, the use of the "basic set" and its transforma-tion is founded on the intention to substitute for the formal and unifying effect of the key. And as this is the foremost principle of this method, you will understand that I am glad to find your explanation perfectly conform-able with my own theories. On the other hand, I do not believe that the simple use of one or more tonal chords can be called tonality, because it can never have its result. The effect of tonality is based on the more or less complicated use of the relations of the different degrees (roots) to the tonal center, to the basic root. (I think my "Suite" gives an example of extended tonality, similar to that of my former works {Kammersym-phonie, etc.}).

Now I arrive at the point where you blame the "unconventional length of the four sections" of the theme of the "Variations." Now, I have at first to state that this irregularity of the length of formal parts is one of the characteristics of all my writing. I would almost suppose that the capacity to write this way is an inborn-one, if I did not *know* that I owe it to two masters: Mozart and Brahms, who were my foremost models during the greatest part of my existence as a musician. By the way, Brahms not only used structures of an irregularity like that himself, but he even asked younger composers to study these forms and referred to Mozart and Haydn. I myself gave once in Germany a lecture about Brahms in which I mentioned many very characteristic examples of that kind, among them the one of Mozart which no pupil of mine during thirty years could escape.[30]

Menuett from Mozart, String Quartet in B-flat Major (K. 458).

Certainly, I myself have developed this kind of phrasing—which by Mozart I called: "barock"—to a degree which corresponds to a concept of *"rhythmical prose,"* or even right away "prose." And you will perhaps agree, that besides the "quasi versified" style of music which approaches dance forms, there could be written a musical prose. And I am certainly not the first who writes it and not the only one. Because the form of an *"introduction,"* if not directly "prose," is at least very related to it.

Now, although this letter is already unduly extended, one more, but fortunately simple question, and a short answer. Although this aspect of my scores seems to be alike: counterpoint, and although the use of vertical and horizontal inversions originates from the contrapuntal methods, I do not believe that my style has to be called a contrapuntal one. First, I find already in the contrapuntal style that inversions have for themselves no contrapuntal meaning but only one of motivic utilization. Therefore, (2ndly), you find them also used in homophonic compositions. 3rdly, it is here too only a manner in which the "basic set" is turned to avoid monotony and to produce, under the suppositions of the unifying interval relations, different themes. But besides these negative facts, I have the positive feeling that there can be stated a new style of structure, vertically and horizontally. I am at present not able to describe this style in a scientific manner and could not even give it a name. Perhaps I shall know it in a few years, but the fact seems to me to be doubtless. Certainly there are places where I write real contrapuntal combinations. But a new style does not mean that no connection is to be found with former styles. By that reason we find in Mozart and Haydn and Beethoven very often parts with a contrapuntal retrospective aspect. By this circumstance we can better realize the manner of the development of the styles.

Now, finally, I want only to express the feeling that it might be very useful if critics and composers would converse and discuss as often as possible such matters. I should have done it very often if it were not so seldom that critics understand as much of these questions as you do, but also utter their judgment in such a respectful manner, as you do too. And now I am very anxious to learn your reaction to my opinions and I will very much appreciate your answer,

With heartfelt greetings, I am yours truly

On Conservatism, Progress, and Pedagogy

6.8 Sketch of a Foreword to the Suite for String Orchestra (Undated)

The composition of this piece was suggested to me by the favorable impressions and perspectives which Prof. Martin Bernstein, New York University, gave me concerning the ambitions, achievements and successes of American college orchestras.[31] I became convinced that every composer—especially every modern composer, and I above all—should be interested in encouraging such efforts. For here, a new spiritual and intellectual basis can be created for art; here, young people can be given the opportunity of learning about the new fields of expression and the means suitable for these.

Thus, my task was set. This is what I had to achieve.

Without harming the students by a premature dose of "Atonality Poison," I had to prepare them, using harmony which leads to modern feelings, for modern performance technique. Fingerings, bowings, phrasing, intonation, dynamics, rhythm—all this should be developed without the introduction of insuperable difficulties. But modern intonation, contrapuntal technique and phrase-formation were also to be emphasized, so that the student might gradually come to realize that "melody" does not consist only of those primitive, unvaried, symmetrical structures which are the delight of mediocrity in all countries and among all peoples. Already here there are higher forms, which belong to a higher order of art not only technically, but also, and especially, *spiritually*.

In doing this, I was guided not only by my personal knowledge of the stringed instruments, but also by the advice of the one who suggested the work to me and who has practical experience in this field.

With the piece, an analysis (perhaps of some individual sections only?) is included.[32] This, too, has a double purpose. Above all, it should enrich the knowledge of the student players; but it should also be informative to their teacher and conductor. Today, so many call themselves "conservative" who have nothing to conserve because they possess nothing that is worth conserving—not even the capacity to write a fugue like the one in this work. Therefore, they maintain and conserve only their own incapacity and ignorance; they want to protect themselves and others from the possibility that new things should ever be said which would call for at least one prerequisite: technical competence. Therefore, this work should give genuine, real teachers and propagators of culture—genuine and authentic leaders, in other words—an opportunity which they have certainly been wishing for: the chance to educate their students to have the deepest respect for artistic capacity, and to make it clear to them that culture can be maintained only through growth. Like everything that lives, it can live only so long as it grows; as soon as it stops developing, it dies and withers away. Therefore, any technical or spiritual achievement is worth conserving (from the artistic point of view) only because it is preliminary to a new step forward, to new life. Only then— and only *therefore*—is it worth conserving. Perhaps after the above it is superfluous to mention that this piece represents *no repudiation* of what I have created up till now.

On Atonality, Modernism, and Counterpoint

6.9 "Fascism is no article of exportation," c. 1935

Schoenberg had previously been on good terms with the Italian composer Alfredo Casella (1883–1947), who had performed together with Ravel the Valses nobles et sentimentales *at a Society for Private Musical Performances concert in October 1920, and who in 1924 had helped to organize an Italian tour of* Pierrot lunaire. *Yet Schoenberg had been provoked by a 1926 article "Harmony, Counterpoint, etc." that characterized him as a "late-Romantic" composer. He was even more strongly provoked by the 1934 article "Modern Music in Italy," in which Casella wrote of the "complete independence of the national spirit" from the "corruption and harmonic decadence" of Wagnerian chromaticism. While not mentioning Schoenberg by name, he described atonality as "the end of an historic cycle," [. . .] "the extreme consequence of the Germanic chromaticism of the last century."³³*

"Fascism is no article of exportation." At the time when Mussolini made this statement he was very correct. Correct not only in so far as he considered Fascism like a particular form of government, only fitting for the Italian people, but also in as far as he showed himself to be a very skilled politician who knows, according to the words of Bismarck, that a politician does not have to take his measures for eternity, but to imagine how the next development of the future would be. And so he understood by this enunciation to calm other countries that were afraid of the possibility offered by the Soviets: the aim of an international Fascism.

When Mr. Casella tells us on the one hand that the Italian public remains jealously independent—anti-European, it sounds like a variation of Mussolini's statement and could also be formulated: Italian music is no article of exportation. But on the other hand, Casella himself exported not only his own music, but besides he does not appear as uninterested in "a universal return to artistic normality" as one could expect by the said anti-European independence of his aim; it seems on the contrary, he would consider just this universal return as an important support, as an aid to an international victory of his national ideas, although they are no article of exportation.

As Mussolini certainly foresaw it, but Casella by mistake did not foresee it, Fascism has in the meantime become an article of exportation, and the return to artistic normality has found in every country the powerful patronage of those people who have lain at the ready for a long time in wait of a crushing defeat of artistic modernism. Of course, as Casella states: "Today, when so many works which seemed audacious and revolutionary and destined to change the face of music are already falling into desuetude and inexorably disappearing from programs, the Italian public may congratulate itself on not having wasted time pretending to love them."³⁴ Of course, what a glorious international victory: A country that does not want its music to be

considered as an article of exportation, has managed it that many other countries—if not every country—put their own music out of commission, although
it still could serve as an article of exportation, and that these countries resolve
also to write only music which is inappropriate for exportation.

What a glorious victory!

But this victory, does it not bring to mind other such victories? For example, the victory over Bach, which made his whole work fall thus perfectly into
desuetude, so that his greatest works were unknown by the musical public already fifty years after his death. And the victory over Schubert's symphonies,
which would scarcely be alive today if not exhumed by Robert Schumann
thirty years after Schubert's death from starvation, or the victory over Wagner,
whose *Lohengrin* was resurrected by Franz Liszt—but in this case political
reasons were decisive.

I am very sorry, but I cannot agree with Mr. Casella in this point, and I
regret it the more, the more I am happy that there is one author of so called
"atonal" music for whom he has "a great admiration": my friend and former
pupil, the author of *Wozzeck,* Alban Berg. I am happy, although I myself am
unable to resolve the contradiction consisting in "the strong opposition to
atonality" and the appreciation of an atonal work, for: if a work can be worthy
of his great admiration though it is an atonal one, atonality cannot be a hindrance; and the only explanation seems to be found in the smart agility of his
mind which made him capable of participating in every artistic movement of
the last thirty years, and which makes me hope to find him perhaps once
again as a partisan of atonality—of course: not without seeing him supported
by the favorable inclination of public circumstances. And perhaps I can personally already enjoy his approach to myself by his use of some important
ideas from my work, as for example the manner of differentiating the character of the movements by only using, in his *Serenata,* a selection of the five
instruments in some movements as I did in my *Pierrot lunaire.* And also I
recognize with pleasure in the thirds of the *Gavotta* of this work a nice compliment to the fourths of my *Kammersymphonie,* and I am very surprised to find
this way of palpably making me offers of peace—a kindly hand in my pockets.

But desires and hopes are deceptive and therefore, alas!, I have to consider
today only the enemy who considers atonality as "the extreme consequence of
the German chromaticism of the last century." Here is made a very subtle
distinction between German chromaticism, of which we have to realize, "how
small was" its "influence in our (Italian) country," and any other chromaticism; and this distinction wants to make us believe that Italy has never been
influenced by any kind of chromaticism. But Mr. Casella is surely an expert in
the knowledge of the musical history of his country, in contrast to my poor
knowledge, which makes me unable to recall more than *one* very renowned
name of the famous *Italian school of chromaticism,* the name of *Gesualdo;* and

unfortunately I cannot state the century, whether the 17th or the 18th, when this composer lived, or the name of his partisans. And also I cannot remember all the very famous names of the contrapuntal Italian school, but I know only the fact that at this time the difference between the musical style of Italian and, for example, Dutch composers, between Orlando di Lasso and Palestrina, was not contradictory, although they certainly showed national distinctions. And in spite of the vehement war between Lully-ists and Piccini-ists, their music seems not to show any difference that justifies a harshness like that. And indeed when you consider Casella's non-chromaticism of the aforementioned *Serenata,* like that

Casella, Serenata. *Philharmonia / Universal Edition, p. 35.*

Casella, Serenata, *p. 26.*

Casella, Serenata, *p. 27, B♭-clarinet.*

and his non-atonality like that:

Casella, Serenata, *p. 25; Schoenberg misread the top voice for a clarinet in A, rather than a clarinet in B♭.*

and his weakness for beauty like that:

Casella, Serenata, *p. 37.*

Casella, Serenata, *p. 4.*

after all you can perhaps remark a significant "independence"—perhaps—but surely in a hundred years they will never find a significant difference. And the more Casella's music seems today to be "brought into line" "*gleichgeschaltet*" with some political principles (which I personally esteem very highly) the more his music will seem to coming generations as having been "brought into line" with my style, so that only creative capacity will define the difference.

I am again a little hopeful!

But I would remember an astonishing fact: the Italian public in "their weakness for beauty and perfection" (as Casella tells us) did not accept Casella's music with much more love than mine, when we made together a tour though a part of Italy with a string quartet of Casella and my *Pierrot lunaire.* They hissed and laughed about my *Pierrot lunaire,* but they hissed also Casella's string quartet. And I have to confess that in this quartet there were some places, and especially a cadenza for the first violin, where my own weakness for beauty corresponded somewhat to that of the Italians. But I am not convinced of the same correspondence between their weakness for perfection and mine, and I am doubtful that they acknowledged errors like that to which I called Casella's attention: not to bring the tonic after the development sooner than with the "reprise" of the first theme. Such errors are not very unimportant to a well-educated weakness for perfection, and though I heard and read this quartet ten times I had firstly to conquer some shyness before giving Casella as a comrade the proposal to correct it, but I was rewarded in seeing eliminated in the printed score this great C of the violoncello; a success which made me hope that I could reach up, if not to the aforementioned weakness for beauty, so at least perhaps to that for perfection.

In the score of Casella's *Serenata* is to be found an analysis which curiously calls the part at number 8 a double fugato. Probably it is only a slip of the pen of the writer and he wanted to call it a "Fugato renversé," for two of the four entrances are answering in contrary motion. But this circumstance gives me the occasion now to consider some questions exclusively from a purely musical and artistic point of view, but also to avoid rendering the truth obscure by sentimental principles like weakness for beauty and the aim of independence.

I confess frankly that the use of a fugato or a even a fugue in a sonata form seems to me, although as a follower of the classics I did it myself sometimes, to be a matter of a very dubious (not taste) but meaning. A fugue is a method of developing a musical picture from a basic construction, and its meaning is a contrapuntal one which does not correspond with the method of sonata forms, which develop their ideas in a perfectly other way. Those [former] methods correspond to past centuries just as that [latter] method [does] to the last century, and to join these two different methods (do not believe me to despise fugues because of this comparison) appears like an attempt to draw a hay cart by an airplane. Just as the one attempt is not very practical, so is the other, the artistic one, not very logical. Although it may be granted that the very contrapuntal manner of manifesting hidden relations between, for instance, two different themes of a sonata movement (as in Beethoven's last string quartet in F major

Beethoven, String Quartet in F Major, Op. 135, first movement, mm. 1–2.

Beethoven, String Quartet in F Major, Op. 135, first movement, mm. 10–14.

where the unexplainable construction of A and B is revealed in the development as a contrapuntal one,)[35]

Beethoven, String Quartet in F Major, Op. 135, first movement, mm. 62–70.

although these very contrapuntal methods of getting new sounding-pictures by changing and shifting the vertical joining of such themes are not quite inappropriate ways of fulfilling the demands of homophonic methods, which I have defined as the "Method of developing by Variation." Indeed: in spite of not being developing, it is a variation. But unfortunately composers today write not only fugatos in sonata forms but also independent fugues solely for a contrast of mood and expression. This is as ridiculous as using a machine gun like a sugar coater. But it has its cause in a very profound misunderstanding of the nature of counterpoint. This difference can here be explained in a few words only by one circumstance. Homophonic music concentrates the whole development in one principal part, making it so the other elements are of subordinate importance, supporting only the development and the under-standability of the principal part. Therefore this principal part is enabled to develop on its own pretty quickly and can produce very different characters, moods, figures, pictures and sounds without losing coherence, without be-coming incomprehensible. On the other hand, the contrapuntal method asks the full attention of the listener not only for one principal part, but simulta-neously for two, three, or more parts of which none is a principal one, for all are principal ones. If the listener's mental capacity has to realize the meaning, the form, the idea of these different parts and besides that: the mutual connec-tion of them, it would be nearly unable to understand them, if at the same time these elements would start to develop in such an extensive manner as is usual in homophonic forms. Therefore contrapuntal themes in contrast with homophonic ones are mostly relatively short. But when I saw modern com-posers today writing a lot of unconnected parts each as meaningless as the other, I got an explanation by a magazine story for this kind of style: An actor is asked by the stage manager to speak very quickly and without emphasis, so as not to leave the public time to think or even to investigate the words for their inner correctness.[36] I am sure contrapuntal writers don't have such intentions, but their writing fortunately has the same effect: quick, incoherent notes in many parts hinder the listener from realizing the lack of basic ideas.—Real contrapuntal parts are connected one with another at least by a mutual harmonic relationship, mostly too by motivic coherence, but in any case their further development shows the purpose of their joining. Regarding such laws, I could sympathetically feel for a "strong opposition against" real counterpoint, for it is very uncomfortable to make an unnecessary fuss.

But the "strong opposition against atonality" asks another kind of research. I have often proved that the objections against atonality are less directed against the lack of tonality, than against the use of unresolved and untreated dissonances. And it seems to be the same case in Mr. Casella's opposition. For if you play simultaneously seven different tones, for instance on a piano the seven successive white notes at the keyboard, your ear will tell you that these are the seven tones of C-Major, but I am doubtful you can state it to be the tonality of C-Major, for the statement of a key depends at least on the use of a certain number of means, of which the most important is: to emphasize the tonic. I will likely concede that only the employment at the start and at the end could satisfy lower claims, but higher arts ask a well-organized skirmish among the different degrees which pretend predomination, and the victory of the tonality is without deeper meaning if not achieved by a defeat of these usurpers. I consent to the function of tonality as a means of unifying, of differentiating, and of organizing the parts and members and therefore also of comprehensibility. And although I do not very much appreciate this method, if you hear a chord like that (A)

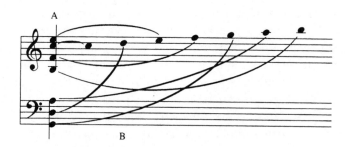

which uses the 7 tones of C-Major (B), you will judge it otherwise than the aforementioned attempt at a piano keyboard, and it would be difficult to define the function of such a chord whether ending a phrase or introducing another or joining only two degrees. On the other hand, we know, that tonality cannot only be expressed by chords composed of a diatonic scale. Who only regards a chorale of Bach must concede that chromaticism is not a hindrance to tonality, if only the strange chords are used in such relations that they remain in subordination as *coherent contrasts.* And if you do not regard chromaticism from a superficial but principal point of view you will be unable to deny the impossibility of a stubborn national independence in artistic matters and a return to artistic normality, which has never been the norm at any historical time. Always people have derived advantages from the inventions of other people. You cannot scorn the weapons your adversary uses, if you will win a war. And you can not interrupt your international telegraphic communications, for you would not realize in time that your adversary is moving his troops against your frontier. And your airplanes have to use the airports of foreign states if they want gasoline, and your ships will use foreign harbors if they want coal or intend to sell merchandise. Your desire for independence can yield your merchandise a trademark, but as dependence has to be mutual, independence would be too, and you could neither sell your merchandise in case of mutual stubbornness; nor would you like, on the other hand, to produce the kind of glittering and trembling moving pictures as twenty years ago, when other people were already producing talkies. Or would you?

On Conservatism in the Arts

6.10 "Some Objective Reasons to Educate Rising Generations to Contemporary Music" (c. 1936)

Ladies and Gentlemen:

I want at first to say thanks to the president and the board of Directors for the invitation to speak and for giving me so the occasion to express some thoughts, which perhaps can bring about some good effect.

The title of the speech I announced informs you, in short, of my intentions:

SOME OBJECTIVE REASONS REQUIRE THE EDUCATION OF THE RISING GENERATIONS FOR CONTEMPORARY MUSIC.

Why do I want to adduce *objective* reasons?

It seems clear: I am a modern composer; a composer whose name is rather well known, also in this country, but whose works are, especially in this country perfectly unknown. It is clear: any reason other than an objective one I would adduce, would have thrown the suspicion on myself that I mention it only in my own interest as a composer who wants to propagate his own works, who wants to procure himself performances of his works or to prepare at least the public in this way: to make it favorably inclined for his works and for the desire to hear them.

Such intentions are far from my thoughts and I could furnish many proofs of my disinterestedness in personal matters. My very different intentions are the following:

I feel the necessity to act as a fighter, as a battering ram for the interest of the development of the art.

I feel the obligation to work for the interest of both contemporary and future artists, who are unable to carry through their works; who are unable to get over the resistance of the so-called conservatism in the sphere of art; who have to suffer owing to that aversion against new art, against any new thought and against any new manner of expressing new ideas; artists who have to stay in the shadow, whilst they are creating new and joy-producing works; in the interest of artists, who, in spite of their incapacity in the struggle for existence, are able to create new artistic beauty, predestined to spread elevation, promotion, excitation, elation, pleasure and delight not only to future generations, but also to a part of their contemporaries whose influence, unfortunately, is much smaller than surely its number.

I feel the duty to support such artists in the same manner as we have been supported by the similar actions of our predecessors; I feel the obligation to pay my debt to those predecessors who facilitated our own combat and made it hopeful by their manliness and steadiness and their unyielding character. I have to keep in mind the stubbornness of a Beethoven, who did not bend himself in front of Grandees: I have to keep in mind the combat of a Mozart against a prince who wanted to consider him like a valet, like a servant; I have to keep in mind Wagner's combats, which led him to create Beckmesser, this incarnation of all this conservatism, enemy number one of any artistic development.

I have to act as a fighter and as a battering ram like these men: in favor of suffering artists.

And that is the reason for my intention to bring about no subjective proofs, but only objective ones.

———

Have you perhaps once asked, what would have been, if teachers, performers and the public had abstained from their duty to accustom their contemporaries to the music of our predecessors?

How, if no teacher had taught his pupils to play the sonatas of Mozart and Beethoven, the piano music of Chopin, Mendelssohn and Schumann: if no singer had performed Schubert and Brahms songs, if no conductor had performed Beethoven symphonies, no theater Wagner's and Mozart's operas? Do you think it was without trouble to perform music like this, when its creators were still contemporaries? Do not forget that when Mozart's *Don Juan* had its "premiere," the Emperor Joseph the Second of Austria said to the composer: "das ist zu schwer für unsere Lieben Wiener" (that is too difficult for our beloved Viennese); that Brahms was hissed, when he conducted personally the first performance of his Serenade, and that his fourth symphony after the first performance could not be repeated in Vienna during ten years and only in the year of his death, when everybody knew that it happened as a last honor conferred to a dying person; do not forget that *Fidelio* had to be overhauled and that the great Austrian poet and outstanding and well-instructed music lover Franz Grillparzer, when he heard the first performance of the Ninth Symphony, called it abstruse and mad. Do not forget that Brahms' Concerto for Violin was at first considered unsuitable for a fiddler. You know surely many more such stories than I do, and you can prove to yourself what I contend: that it was not without trouble to perform the works of the contemporaries.

And now imagine the state of our musical culture if, as before mentioned, the contemporaries of great masters had neglected their duty, had not performed their works, if teachers had not educated the young generation for an understanding of contemporary thinking and expressing. We know one historical fact of this kind: Bach, after his death, disappeared from the musical life so completely that nobody knew his work. And we know, that Mendelssohn, at the beginning of the nineteenth century, about 60 years after Bach's death, made the first performance of the Mattheus Passion and brought Bach's music to the knowledge of both the public and the musicians.

But: can you warrant an accident like this? Can you be assured that always an artist like Mendelssohn will come and awake the dead? Can you assure that always the public then will possess the maturity to understand the resurrected master's ideas, his manner of expression, his language?? You have to remember that this was possible only because in another case public and artists had fulfilled their duty, so that Haydn's, Mozart's, and Beethoven's music were well known. And although the music of these masters was not founded on Bach himself, so it was based partly on another composer of Bach's time, on his contemporary *Handel,* whose music these masters knew and appreciated very much. And only this circumstance: that the public was capable of understanding the music, the language of these masters, only this circumstance made it capable of accepting Bach's music, although it was already the time of Beethoven when Mendelssohn performed it.

But: what would have happened if Haydn, Mozart, and Beethoven as well as Handel had been neglected in the same manner by their contemporaries as Bach.

Let me give the answer:

Mendelssohn would have not only been unable to perform Bach, he would have not only been unable to understand the music himself, he would not at all have paid any attention to a score of Bach, for he would have been as unscrupulous as his predecessors and as uneducated as they were, and he would never have had either the intention or the idea to play an unknown work of an unknown composer.

And now again:

Imagine: Suppose all conductors, all singers had neglected their duty in the same manner and in the same measure as the successors of Bach:

What would they conduct, what would they sing today, what perform, what teach—all the people who make their lives conducting, singing, performing, teaching the works of Haydn, Mozart, Beethoven, Brahms, Schubert, etc.?

Can you imagine this state of our musical life, of our musical culture?

Can you answer this question?

I myself could not answer it.

I do not want to deceive you; I can indeed do both: I can imagine and I can answer.

I know what they would do, for we see it in our time. They would play old melodies and dances, and variations and transcriptions of such things, national melodies first and as long as possible of their own countries, and afterwards little by little, of every other nation, the less cultivated the better; and then they would go as far backward as possible in the history of music—and suddenly they would arrive at a state of musical culture, which would annihilate every progress of higher minded men and every ability to express higher ideas.

And I am afraid: not only performers would do so—let them make their life as they think they have to do it—but I am afraid, teachers also would lose the ambition for higher arts, and would teach only those abilities which would be asked for, which are customary in the market, and which are without any artistic ambition in the meaning of this art in which we are educated by the great thinkers and masters.

Whoever today calls himself a conservative does it exclusively with the intention to suppress every development of mind, to hinder new ideas from coming about, to paralyze the inventive capacity of the spirit, to suffocate every tendency of life—for life is *changing, developing, growing.*

But on the contrary: whoever wants to call himself a conservative in the very meaning of life, has the duty to protect new ideas, has to promote development, has to animate inventive capacity of spirit, has to encourage true tendencies of life—for life has to be conserved—to conserve the possibilities of development means to conserve life, means to protect it against rote-ness, against decay, against decomposition.

Only in this meaning can it be admitted that teachers have to be conservative. They have to educate the young generation for an understanding of the development of mental culture and they have to make them able to comprehend the necessity and the duty to conserve and protect every development in artistic matters. For: as long as a nation is developing itself, as long as it will produce new ideas, then just as long will it possess a new art. But when it ceases creation, when it is becomes content to possess what predecessors have produced, then it is at its end.

And therefore, the young generation has to be educated for an understanding of new music.

On Modernism, Conservatism, and the Passing of the Old Guard

6.11 "The Twenty-Fifth Anniversary of Mahler's Death," August 8, 1936

In a letter to Thomas Mann dated January 15, 1939, concerning the Four Point Program for Jewish Unity, *Schoenberg wrote in similar terms to those he uses below about his political stance: "I don't hesitate to confess that I am not a leftist. Namely, inasmuch as I would in no way grant to everyone the right of freedom of expression, only to those who actually possessed an opinion worthy of expressing. I would also not call myself a rightist, since I do not believe in the equalizing value of stultification. Perhaps I am a progressive conservative, who would like to develop and advance things worthy of preserving."*[37]

The twenty-fifth anniversary of Mahler's death, and a few months later Karl Kraus dies. Not long ago Adolf Loos and Alban Berg passed away (not to forget Franz Schreker). Together with a few others, with Kandinsky, Kokoschka, Webern, I alone am left of the old guard. Of the older ones, I am actually the only one. For my contemporaries, except for Loos, were rather restrained, hesitant, always staying a few steps back, following along only when it was high time. The younger ones from the time of Stravinsky and Hindemith were always unreliable recruits. They flirted with everything that is contrary to the pure idea: with folklore, popularity, objectivity, and suitability for use. [*Volkstum, Volkstumlichkeit, Sachlichkeit, Gebrauchsfähigkeit*]. They flirted, while we were hotly striving to fortify the borders of the artistically-morally acceptable to the most severe and impenetrable degree. Our relationship to folklore was aristocratic: we did not think of adapting ourselves, but rather of setting an example; we expected popularity as little as Kant could have expected it; objectivity means for us not this seeming elimination of the creative individual but the most painstakingly exact restriction to the essential; suitability for use, if we had wanted to think of it at all in connection with art, could not have changed anything in our style of representation, since we would have left it up to the "user" to develop for himself the ability necessary to use something. But we led, or endeavored to lead, our lives as is fitting for national heroes. Purity of motives, incorruptibility of conviction, strength of character, selflessness in attack, chivalrousness in defense. We demonstrated better respect for the past than its traditional guardians, whose conduct was always disrespectful in the present, and who always wanted the past to be such that it would not ever have been worth preserving.[38] We made the teachings of the past our own and possessed them in a form of culture that viewed nothing that had been achieved as an end but rather as a stage that we also honored, even if we were forced to go beyond it. Culture enabled us to think further: we had a heritage to protect and knew, instinctively, that what does not grow dies. Conservatism of any other kind means decline, for it brings it about. But in no other time has conservatism had more corrupting results than in ours. I am not thinking of the political endeavors of the radical parties when I am speaking of the great upheavals of our time. Radicalism attacks the root of the good and the evil in the same measure. I am thinking of the inevitable changes necessitated through the modern technological manner of production. Mass production must somehow find masses that consume. For which these masses, who have been brought to a higher standard of living through the products that have been provided, must have an income corresponding to this standard. This manner of production, however, also forces workers and peasants to achieve a higher level. Not only would they otherwise not understand how to operate or use the machines, they would also not understand how to consume the mass products. Our technology tolerates only mass products, but this in turn demands consuming masses. So in any case there must ensue, if one hopes not also bloody revolutions, drastic changes in comparison with our previous development; these no conservatism would be able to hold back, even if it actually wanted to cause the decline they stand for.

Perhaps we did not know this conclusively, but we felt it. And so our stance against conservatism was justified in many ways. Nevertheless, strangely enough none of these men was linked with radical politics. We were all rather conservative—though conservative in the sense of recognized or suspected necessities.

Notes on the Fourth String Quartet, Op. 37, 1936

6.12 From "Prefaces to the Records of the Four String Quartets" (1937)

This string quartet also has been commissioned by the great patron of chamber music Mrs. Elizabeth Sprague Coolidge.

It was first performed on the occasion of a festival given by Mrs. Coolidge to the students of the University of California at Los Angeles. As there were no speeches made by officials at this occasion, the public perhaps did not realize that Mrs. Coolidge wanted to honor me in choosing the programs of these four concerts performed by the world-renowned Kolisch Quartet. In each of these programs was played one of my four string quartets and one of the last four Beethoven string quartets.[39] Even if I had not known the intention of Mrs. Coolidge, I would certainly have regarded it an honor to appear in such a program in such a neighborhood. But I had meanwhile become a California composer and professor of composition at this University. And while every one of my premieres had caused a great sensation and excitement, so that whole cities were agitated, and visitors and critics came from neighboring towns to attend these events, and while, besides the riots with the first two quartets there were long articles in the papers—this time it was a perfectly commonplace affair.[40] There was no special excitement and at least the anticipation was in no way exaggerated.

Nevertheless, I was very content with the attitude of the public. The whole audience listened with respect and sincerity to the strange sounds with which they were faced and it seems a number of them were really impressed. Of course, the appreciation for the first and second quartets was much more intense, and it could not be expected that a work of my present period would provoke such enthusiasm as does my "Verklärte Nacht," this work of my first period. But I will never forget how long it took until there was an understanding for the works of my first period and I will also not forget that even "Verklärte Nacht" caused riots and real fighting and that the first critics in Vienna wrote, "This Sextet seems like a calf with six (!) feet, such as is often shown at fairs."

This string quartet, if also a calf, has at least only four feet.

On Sacred Music and Tradition

6.13 On the Kol Nidre, Op. 39, c. 1938

Schoenberg's Kol Nidre *was one of a series of explicitly religious works from his last years. Written at the request of Rabbi Jakob Sonderling in Los Angeles, Schoenberg completed the* Kol Nidre *on September 22, 1938, in the hope that it would be appropriate for both the synagogue and the concert hall. In a letter to the composer and conductor Paul Dessau (1894–1979) dated November 22, 1941, he described the task of "vitriolising out the 'cello-sentimentality of the Bruchs, etc. and giving this DECREE the dignity of a law, of an 'edict.' "[41]*

The melody suffers from monotony and sentimentality. This is partly caused by the circumstance that it is composed in a minor-like church mode. At the time the Kol Nidre originated there was seemingly no discrimination between the emotional effect of major and minor. No doubt, Bach would have composed it in major, because to him, as to us, minor expressed mournful and touching emotions. Certainly in the 16th century this melody expressed dignity, seriousness, solemnity, and awe. Today we feel, if not the contrary, so at least the discrepancy between the solemnity of the words and the sentimentality with which they are presented.

This sentimentality unfortunately is enhanced by the cheap embellishments and ornamentations added by the singers (chasans???). They too were seemingly influenced through the mournful sound of this tune and accordingly they were not quite wrong to follow a singer's natural inclination toward sentimentality.

I decided to compose the Kol Nidre at first. Having consulted about seven different versions of this traditional tune I found out that they have not too much in common as regards to a modern concept of musical contents. Some basic features could be recognized but, as it always happens with tradition (which partly could be translated as an imprecise memory) there were far reaching differences to be found. Not every motive appeared in every version. Even the order in which they succeeded each other was not the same. But the most striking fact is that also the words were not used to the same melodies. Besides, the melody, in spite of its very striking beginning, suffers from monotony, principally caused by the minor key in which most of its parts are composed.[42]

Furthermore, there were some objections against the structural appearance of this melody. We are accustomed to melodies that are "built up" into a certain climax. Nothing of this kind can be observed in this melody. It ends without any musical reason. It simply does not continue, but the ending is neither prepared, nor built up, nor emphasized. This is very unsatisfactory.

Another objection concerned the words. It is known that these words have always been an object of argument. Nobody could understand why Jews should be allowed to make oaths and vows and promises which they could consider as null and void. No sincere, no honest man could understand such an attitude.

I assume that at the time when these words were spoken the first time, everybody understood them perfectly: Whenever under pressure of persecution a Jew was forced to make oaths, vows, and promises counter to his inherited belief in our religious principles, he was allowed to repent them and to declare them null and void. Thus he was allowed to pray with the community as a Jew among Jews.

This seems to me the very idea of atonement: purgation through repentance.

Standing Alone

6.14 Letter to Edgard Varèse, May 23, 1939

After spending his early years in Paris and Berlin, Edgard Varèse (1883–1965) came to the United States in 1915, where he helped to found the International Composers' Guild in 1921. His Density 21.5 *from 1936 was his last piece for more than a decade, during which time he taught, lectured, and sought to build interest in new electronic instruments. The composers' association proposed here did not come into being. See further 6.21.*

Dear Mr. Varèse:

I am sorry to have to tell you I cannot be a member of your "TEN." I hope you will understand my reasons—but in any case, my decision is definitive.

I have known already for a long time that my work must wait until there will be a generation of young men who do not consider it as that of just another contemporary composer. This will not happen earlier than in twenty years and even a great number of performances of my works could not change this.

I know I have to go this way and I do not intend to interfere with my destiny.

I appreciate it highly that you were kind enough to include me in your activities.

Wishing you the best success, I am

yours very truly.

On Vienna

6.15 "Vienna, Vienna Only You Alone," November 1939

A parody of the song "Vienna, City of My Dreams" ("Wien, du Stadt meiner Träume"), by Rudolf Siecznski. Schoenberg made two versions, signing one, "November 1939, but I have thought this for a long time."

Vienna, Vienna only you alone,
You should be despised by all.
Others may possibly be forgiven,
You will never be freed from guilt.

You should be destroyed,
Only your shame shall endure.
You are branded for eternity,
For falseness and hypocrisy.

Comments on His Students

6.16 Letter to Robert Emmett Stuart, January 27, 1940

In this letter, Schoenberg is responding to a request from Stuart, director of the St. Louis Institute of Music, whom he had met the previous December at the Music Teachers' National Convention in Kansas City. Stuart's letter of January 13, 1940, listed conditions for the kind of composition teacher they were looking for at the St. Louis Institute of Music, including a record of publication, the ability to teach theory and analysis, a willingness to teach piano, as well as the following: "[. . .]

he must be adaptable, *and possess a personality and attitude that will make for early acceptance in our local social and musical circles. Obviously fluency in the use of the English language is most desirable."*[43] *Schoenberg's surprising categorizations of his pupils (Aryan, Jewish, half-Jewish) may be in response to the implications in Stuart's comment about "local social and musical circles," or else have related to their discussions when they met in Kansas City.*

Dear Mr. Stuart:

I can name a certain number of my students and will do this a little later in the course of this letter. But at first I want to tell you a little more about Mr. Violin:[44]

I assume he must possess some letters from Johannes Brahms and he is, I hope, intelligent enough to send you one of them, which prove that Brahms considered him a great talent as a composer—I hope he did not lose them, when he was forced to flee from Vienna. I heard an Octet of his (or was it a sextet?) in the "Wiener Tonkünstler-Verein" where Brahms was honorary president, in about 1895 or 1896.

I recommended him because he is one of the few living musicians who was educated in the spirit of Brahms (so as I am) and I consider a teaching of composition in this spirit as very effective for beginners up to 24 years of age. This is what I do myself.

I assume all this proves the sincerity of my recommendation: I wanted to do the best for your school and recommended a man whom I considered the most suitable.

As to the other objection Mr. Galston brought about, I can assure you that Mr. Violin will never try to interfere with the field of another teacher. I can guarantee this personally. And I am sure such quarrels as were usual 40 years ago between the pupils of the piano teachers of different styles will not be provoked through Mr. Violin. There are other times, other problems, a different mentality and a new concept of life today.

I recommend Mr. Violin to write you himself and I wish sincerely it should turn to your and his best.

Now to my pupils:

Mr. Rosza is a very brilliant man, extremely brilliant as a composer and as a pianist. His vitality is enchanting and I am sure all his pupils will fall in love with it.[45] There is no doubt that he will be a great acquisition to every musical institution. As a composer he is a follower of the most modern styles, but possesses a sense of form and balance which distinguishes him from many others of this kind.

Among the students who worked with me is also *Mr. Gerald Strang.*[46] He was my assistant at U.C.L.A. during three years and has now an independent teaching position at the Long Beach (Calif) Junior College. His address is: 129 E. Pleasant Street, North Long Beach, Calif. I don't know whether he can teach piano (curiously!), but I know that he knows many wind instruments very well. (Aryan)

He has already got some reputation as a composer of modern music and is at present also editor of "Modern Music." He is American.

The American composer *Mr. Adolph Weiss* [1891–1971], who is a well-known modern composer studied with me in Berlin and Vienna for at least four years. He is a first class bassoon player, plays viola fairly well and is a very good pianist. Though he is occupied now in the movie studios and earns much more money there than he ever will earn with teaching, he is very interested in this position, because he *likes* to teach—which, I think, is already a recommendation for itself. He lives at 1803¹/₂ Bronson Ave, Hollywood, Calif. (Aryan)

My present assistant at U.C.L.A, *Mr. Leonard Stein,* a young musician of an unusual knowledge, has not yet the teaching experience to satisfy me, but if I had a position like yours, I would give it to him.[47] He is an excellent musician, perhaps not a concert pianist, but he plays every score—orchestra or chamber music—at first sight, plays everything (which is a little exaggerated) by memory, has an astounding knowledge of literature for his age (I guess 22 or so) and is very gifted as a composer. He can be reached through me. (Jewish, American)

There live in America also two pupils of Alban Berg: Dr. Wiesengrund-Adorno and Mr. Josef Schmid.[48] If you are interested I will find their addresses. Mr. Wiesengrund is a composer, who has been played internationally. He is also a philosopher and an important theorist (musicologist) and has published interesting essays. Mr. Josef Schmied has been conductor in Prague, Berlin, and other places. He is a very good pianist, has studied theory with Berg. Whether he composes or not, is unknown to me.

The best of my pupils of 1919–1923 are Hanns *Eisler,* Karl *Rankl,* Rudolf *Kolisch,* Eduard *Steuermann.* The best of my "Meisterklasse an der Akademie der Künste zu Berlin" are N. von *Hannenheim,* Peter *Schacht,* Nicolas *Skalkottas* and Winfried *Zillig* (1927–1932).

Let me speak at first of these who can scarcely be in consideration: Hanns *Eisler:* He would be grand as a musician and an intelligence. But I don't want to recommend him because of his political implication. (Jewish)

Rudolf *Kolisch,* the primarius of the Kolisch quartet is no composer, though he has studied it with me.[49] I don't think he wants to abandon his quartet. (Half-Jewish)

Eduard *Steuermann:* composes, but he cannot be asked to teach beginners. (Jewish)

Nicolas *Skalkottas* [1904–1949] is a highly gifted composer, an excellent violinist and good pianist. He was in my "Meisterklasse" but returned to his native country, Greece, in 1932 and I do not know his address. Perhaps Mr. Mitropolis [Dimitri Mitropoulos] (I can not remember the name), who is now conductor in Detroit or a place like this, might know it, because he was introduced to me in Berlin by Mr. Skalkottas. (Aryan)

Norbert von *Hannenheim* [1898–1943] is one of the most interesting personalities I have ever met. He possesses a tremendous originality as a composer. But I do not know whether he plays the piano. Perhaps he does, but he never played for me, when he was in my "Meisterklasse" for at least three years. I think I could find out where he lives. (Aryan)

You will perhaps be astonished that I praise my pupils so much. I must say, I am astonished myself. It seems improbable that there are so many good composers. But if you consider how many excellent pianists and violinists are existing, then one might conclude, composers can also be good if they have learned the right thing.

Now I come to these two men, whom I must consider as my "first choice."

Karl Rankl, the son of an Austrian farmer, only supported through his talent has pursued the following career: born (about) 1900, he came from the trenches to me in 1918, studied until 1923, became assistant conductor Vienna Volksoper; Director, Opera in Reichenberg; Assistant conductor with Otto Klemperer, Krolloper, Berlin; Director of the Operntheater in Graz, Austria; Director and first Kapellmeister of the Deutsches Operntheater in Prague. He had to flee from Prague, because (he is Aryan) he is married to a half-Jewish wife.

Besides he is an extremely gifted composer. His activity as a conductor did not allow him time enough for composing. But I still expect outstanding works of him.

Winfried Zillig: studied at first privately with me in Vienna (1925) and came with me to Berlin as a pupil of my "Meisterklasse." About 1928 he accepted a position as assistant conductor and made hence a very successful career as a conductor in great German opera theaters. Besides he composed several operas which have been successfully performed in many German opera theaters. He is a very good pianist, plays besides viola and French horn. I think he is unusually talented as a composer and possesses a brilliant technique. (Aryan)

Karl Rankl lives at present in London. But he could easily come to America, because his father in law was rich. Zillig still lives in Germany as do some of the following composers.

But I think this war can last thirty years and can cease in thirty days. So one must not exclude Germans from consideration.

Peter Schacht [1901–1945], good pianist, as a composer performed in many German places and also internationally, was also a student of my "Meisterklasse" (about 1927 to 1933), very serious, industrious and dependable. Intelligent, from a well to do Bremen patrician house, behaves as perfectly as a diplomat of the best school. I think he is the born teacher. He will perhaps not make the same impression of brilliance but that of dependableness.

I must now recommend a person whom I would like to get the position which you offer. It is

J o s e f   R u f e r.   [50]

He studied with me from 1919 to 1923, went then to Hamburg where he taught composition and conducted smaller groups. In 1926 he came to Berlin and was then my assistant in my "Meisterklasse." As such he prepared students who failed to know some of the subjects I demanded and taught as my substitute when I was sick or absent on concert tours. I think his piano playing must be sufficient to teach beginners, because I know he was able to accompany my "Pierrot Lunaire"-melodramas. I do not know whether he continued to compose after his time of apprenticeship. But what I know is, that the students he prepared for me became excellent and so he is doubtlessly a teacher, which might be something to consider.

He is really a charming personality and I am sure he would be liked everywhere. (Aryan)

At present he lives in Berlin and is music critic of a Berlin newspaper. I can give you his address.

May I resume: all these whom I mentioned here are pupils of mine, selected from several hundred whom I taught during my more than forty years of teaching. I would have recommended in first line Anton von Webern. But there is no hope that he would leave Vienna, although he is— I assume—not happy.[51]

Please tell me whom you will contact. If you want to know more, I will gladly serve you.

With cordial greetings I am

very sincerely, yours

On Recognition and Royalties

6.17 Two letters to Mr. Gene Buck, President of ASCAP, April 10 and September 5, 1941

These two letters to the American Society of Composers, Authors, and Publishers represent a small example of the considerable energies Schoenberg expended attempting to receive both the financial reward and the respect he felt he was due.

Dear Mr. Buck:

Would you, please, believe me that I write this letter not because of vanity, or because I am in need of publicity: several weeks ago I had enough publicity, when Mr. Deems Taylor[52] talked a half hour about my composition with twelve tones: and shortly ago, when Wallenstein[53] played my *Verklärte Nacht* over KECA with the Toscanini Orchestra, there was a long talk about me, and the same happened when a few weeks ago in rapid succession the Budapest String Quartet broadcast my *Verklärte Nacht,* Dr. Stiedry conducted my second Chamber Symphony and likewise broadcast it, and when I myself conducted the performance and broadcast of my "Pierrot Lunaire"—there was always publicity through talks about me of between 5 to 10 minutes, but also music of mine of between 20 and 30 minutes.

But if this would not have satisfied my hunger for publicity, the first performance of my Violin Concerto with Louis Krasner in Stokowski's Philadelphia Symphony Concerts must have done it,[54] or my Annual Research Lecture at the University of California,[55] which was attended by more than a thousand persons: or the numerous broadcasts of the Victor recordings of my *Verklärte Nacht* (duration 30 minutes) or of my *Gurre-lieder* (duration 2 and $^1/_2$ hours) WOULD HAVE DONE IT.

No, certainly, it was not vanity and it was not hunger for publicity, when I now tell you: I wonder why my name is never mentioned in your publications.

As often as you state which great list of renowned names is that of your membership, my name is omitted.

If I would not know it, because of the royalties I received several times already from ASCAP, I would doubt, whether I am really honored of having become a member of this ASCAP, and whether or not ASCAP is ashamed of having me belonging to them.

May I again implore you not to think that vanity drives me to this letter. And may I be excused for saying that my reason is: I feel a certain discrepancy between the honor bestowed upon me by universities, audiences, the publicity given to me by lecturers and announcers, the success procured by performers and broadcasters, on the one hand—and—may I be excused for being so "direct"—the "classification," the qualification, the way you "rate" me as a composer, as expressed in the amount of dollars which my annual income from ASCAP comprises. I don't believe that I belong to that class of "Untouchables," who should never be mentioned—because publicly I am mentioned, and was, for almost forty years.

May I make a story, which is already much too long, now, at least now, short?

It seems to me, on account of the great number of performances and broadcasts (from coast to coast) of large works (20 to 150 minutes) that I deserve to be rated much better than hitherto.

I know, my position in asking a raise, is not a favorable one. As I must be afraid that you do not consider my belonging to you in the way I was accustomed (I am and was an honorary member of many a high-ranking society)—I have not to offer you more than a mere commercial value, when I rather would prefer to offer you honor.

But don't you find that even from a commercial point of view, every composer is not as often broadcast as I am?

I would appreciate a kind consideration of my suggestion very much, and I am looking forward to that with great anticipation.

> Most respectfully, yours
> Arnold Schoenberg
> Professor of Music at the University of California at Los Angeles

[Written in by hand at the end of the letter:] How about "justice for the Genius?"

Dear Mr. Buck:

Let me at first express my great thankfulness for granting me the advance on royalties of $500.00 for which I had applied and also for the kind words, which accompany this grant.

Enclosed you will find the signed receipt for $500.00 and a program of the Los Angeles Broadcast station KFAC, the "Evening Concert" given six times a week by the Gas Company from 6–8.

As soon as the radio conflict was ended the Gas Company put this work on a program—which, as they informed me, they could not during the eight months this conflict lasted.

I dare to repeat my application for reconsideration of my classification on the basis of the fact that those two recorded works of mine: *Gurrelieder* (120 minutes of playing times) and *Verklärte Nacht* (30 minutes) are in Los Angeles alone played on at least three stations several times every year. And I know that also many other stations throughout the country broadcast them frequently, which is proved to me by many fan letters I received previous to the radio conflict. In a few weeks Columbia will also release the new records (8 sides) of my *Pierrot Lunaire*.[56] This has a playing time of about 30 minutes. Certainly this new set will now be broadcast even oftener than the older records.

Now I beg you to consider the following facts (I do not take in consideration the established value of works which have been composed forty years ago, but have not declined in the appreciation of the music lover, but on the contrary, have progressed in their success the older they become—and they will outlast many a musical day-fly).

The composition and scoring of the *Gurrelieder* took more than eighteen months. I am a fast writer, and I wrote, for instance, many of my best songs in between one and six hours, mostly in one or two days.

If you consider the duration of a song 3–5, in the average 4 minutes, the 120 minutes of the *Gurrelieder* are equivalent to about 30 performances—a full month—of an average successful song or similar composition.

I hope that you do not find it unfair if I mention also how much even popular song writers are in debt to my innovations. See only how dance writers have profited from my new harmonies, from the effects of my orchestration. And: do you know that I introduced forty years ago the "glissando" of the trombones, which afterwards so many orchestrators have applied—without giving me credit—not to speak of royalties. . . .

May I therefore repeat my application for reclassification and, let me hope, for a really adequate one, considering—if not my merits, at least the actual success.

With repeated thanks, I am

most faithfully, yours

Arnold Schoenberg

Reactions to World War II

6.18 "How I Came to Compose the Ode to Napoleon" (Undated)

Schoenberg composed the Ode to Napoleon Buonaparte, *for String Quartet, Piano, and Reciter, Op. 41, from March to June 1942. The work was performed, in a version for string orchestra, on November 23, 1944, by Artur Rodzinski (1892–1958), leading the New York Philharmonic Orchestra, with Steuermann on the piano and Mack Harrell as the speaker.*

Leonard Stein has described the origins of the work and Schoenberg's selection of the bitingly ironic text by Lord Byron: "The events of the previous December [1941]—Pearl Harbor and the Declaration of War—had, of course, stirred up tremendous excitement. I had spent the afternoon of December 7th at Schoenberg's home discussing with him the implications of the bombing of Pearl Harbor. The next day we heard Roosevelt's 'day of infamy' speech, declaring war on Japan, broadcast in Royce Hall at UCLA. Perhaps it was at that moment that Schoenberg conceived the idea for what was to be his first musical statement on the war. The second work, A Survivor from Warsaw, was composed shortly after the termination of the war. [. . .] The association of Byron with the particular expression Schoenberg had in mind was clear: Byron was a leading voice in the support of Greek independence and had even given up his life for the cause. As an English poet (Schoenberg definitely wanted to use an English text) Byron served as a powerful spokesman for his now beleaguered country."[57] Stein suggests as well

*that Schoenberg's admiration for the oratorical skills of Winston Churchill may
have provided models for the declamation of the text. A page of Schoenberg's
annotated text for the* Ode *is given in fig. 6-2. On Schoenberg's next work, the Piano
Concerto, Op. 42, see fig. 6-3.*

The League of Composers had (1942) asked me to write a piece of chamber
music for their concert season. It should employ only a limited number of
instruments. I had at once the idea that this piece must not ignore the agitation aroused in mankind against the crimes that provoke this war. I remembered Mozart's *Marriage of Figaro,* supporting repeal of the *jus primae noctis,*
Schiller's *Wilhelm Tell,* Goethe's *Egmont,* Beethoven's *Eroica,* and *Wellington's
Victory,* and I knew it was the moral duty of the intelligentsia to take a stand
against tyranny.

But this was only my secondary motive. I had long speculated about the
more profound meaning of the Nazi philosophy. There was one element that
puzzled me extremely: the relationship of the valueless individual being's life
in respect to the totality of the community, or its representative: the queen or
the *Führer.* I could not see why a whole generation of bees or of Germans
should live only in order to produce another generation of the same sort,
which on their part should also fulfill only the same task: to keep the race
alive. I even surmised that bees (or ants) instinctively believed their destiny
was to be successors of mankind, when this had destroyed itself in the same
manner in which our predecessors, the Giants, Magicians, Lindworms, Dino-
saurs, and others, had destroyed themselves and their world, so that at first
men knew only a few isolated specimens. Their and the ants' capacity of
forming states and living according to laws—senseless and primitive, as they
might look to us—this capacity, unique among animals, had an attractive
similarity to our own life; and in our imagination, we could imagine a story,
seeing them growing to dominating power, size, and shape, and creating a
world of their own resembling very little the original beehive.

Without such a goal, the life of the bees, with the killing of the drones and
the thousands of offspring of the queen seemed futile. Similarly all the sacrifices of the German *Herrenvolk* [Master Race] would not make sense, without a
goal of world domination—in which the single individual could vest much
interest.

Before I started to write this text, I consulted Maeterlinck's *Life of the Bees.*
I hoped to find there motives supporting my attitude. But the contrary happened: Maeterlinck's poetic philosophy gilds everything, which was not gold
itself. And so wonderful are his explanations that one might decline refuting
them, even if one knew they were mere poetry. I had to abandon this plan.

I had to find another subject fitting my purpose.

On Composers and Music History

6.19 From "Materials for Orchestration" (Undated)

The following list is taken from one of several unfinished projects from the late 1940s concerning a book for the teaching of orchestration. Schoenberg's detailed guidelines for the selection of an anthology of score excerpts provide a concrete measure of his view of the musical canon, as well as his sense of the current musical scene. Among the many notable features is the equal space he allots to both himself and Stravinsky: 8 percent, thirty-six examples.

[⋯]

AS TO *PERIODS* (centuries etc)
Pre-Bachian
Bachian
pre-Classical
Classical
pre-Romantic
Romantic
modernistic Wagnerian,
Mahler; Strauss & Debussy
Schoenberg—Stravinsky—Hindemith
   American
[⋯]

COMPOSERS

A) *GERMAN*

Händel[58]
Bach
Haydn
Mozart
Beethoven
Schubert
Schumann
Mendelssohn
Wagner
Weber
Liszt
Bruckner
Hugo Wolf
Mahler
Strauss
Reger
Schoenberg
Hindemith
Berg
Webern
Krenek

POPULAR, DANCE
Johann Strauss
Johann Strauss
Lanner
Offenbach
Lehar

NORWEGIAN
Grieg

FINNISH
Sibelius

POLISH
Chopin

ITALIAN
Rossini
Bellini
Donizetti
Cherubini
Spontini
Verdi
Puccini
Casella

ENGLISH
Elgar
Vaughan[-Williams]
Walton
Goosens
Bliss
Lambert

RUSSIAN	Boieldieu	Harris
Rimsky	Gounod	Thomson
Glazunow	Halèvy	Piston
Borodin	Bizet	Barber
Tchaikovsky	Saint-Saëns	Gershwin
Stravinsky	Berlioz	Weiss
Shostakovitch	Dukas	Barber
	Debussy	Schumann
CZECH	Massenet	Gould
Smetana	Meyerbeer	Carpenter
Dvorak	Ravel	Hanson
HUNGARIAN	Franck	Still
Bartok	Milhaud	Cadman
Weiner	Honegger	Berezowski
Kodaly		Moore
	AMERICAN	Cowell
FRENCH	Copland	
Auber	Sessions	

If one uses music paper with 30 staves printed on a page, there would be about 7–8 systems of 3 or 4 staves each. Counting 8 measures to the stave would allow on the average at least 4 examples per page.

On 100 pages there could be about 400 examples.

Probably most of the examples will not exceed 8 measures; many will be less.

Thus there might be perhaps 6 examples on a page.

 100 pages might contain then 600 ex.

 150 pages might contain then 900 ex.

At least half of the examples should be taken from Wagnerian and
post-Wagnerian composers that is 50%   450
about 28 percent from Romantic composers, especially opera composers 250
the rest, about 22% should Classic and pre-Classic   200
                                                                          900

pre-Bachian	5%	10 examples
Bach	10%	20 examples
Haydn	12%	24 examples
Mozart	18%	36 examples
Beethoven	20%	40 examples
Schubert	10%	20 examples
Mendelssohn	10%	20 examples
Schumann	5%	10 examples

Cherubini	5%	10 examples
Auber		
Rossini	5%	10 examples
		200 examples

Weber	5%	7 examples
Gounod	5%	8 examples
Bizet	15%	32 examples
Berlioz	20%	50 examples
Franck	5%	7 examples
Massenet	5%	8 examples
Saint-Saëns	10%	25 examples
Rimsky-Korsakov	12%	30 examples
Borodin, Glazunov	5%	8 examples
Verdi	16%	34 examples
		209 examples

Wagner	30%	135 examples
Mahler	15%	67 examples
Strauss	12%	54 examples
Debussy	10%	45 examples
Tchaikovsky	9%	40 examples
Ravel	5%	22 examples
Schoenberg	8%	36 examples
Stravinsky	8%	36 examples
Bartok	3%	14 examples
		451 examples

American (living) composers	150 examples
Copland	Barber
Sessions	Gershwin
Carpenter	Weiss
Hanson	Cowell
Harris	Barber
Thomson	Schuman
Piston	Gould
Still	Berezowski
Cadman	Moore
Carter	Griffes
McDonald	
Villa Lobos	

On Growing Older

6.20 Two Canons for Carl Engel, 1943

Carl Engel (1883–1944) was president of the G. Schirmer publishing house. As part of a birthday offering the musicologist Gustave Reese (1899–1977) was preparing for Engel's sixtieth birthday, Schoenberg wrote new English texts for two canons he had written earlier.

No man can escape; no man yet remained forever twenty.
Suddenly one is sixty, and is surprised and is perplexed, and asks oneself:
"What is the matter now?
Did I do something wrong?
Why can I not dance and jump as formerly?
Even the music is too fast, I am really out of breath—should—perhaps—now I sing only slower voices?"

*   *   *

I, too, was not better off, but I have rapidly consoled myself and enjoyed the dignity of wisdom, that, at forty, I should have possessed, but which drops slowly and gradually down upon me, now, when its benefits come too late!
Scorn it!
That is silly trash, and only those that never have been young, never risked a foolish blunder—they boast now with wisdom.
We who are of different stuff dare still to expose ourselves, for we know for sure:
"Life begins at sixty."

Publications and Recordings Available in 1943

6.21 Letter to Edgard Varèse, October 27, 1943

Dear Mr. Varèse:

I am very pleased that you are giving a lecture about me, especially because I am sure you are one of the few musicians of today, who by his own writings is in the position to understand aims like mine.

As to material about me, there remains still only the biography by Egon Wellesz,[59] which has not been carried forward to the present time.

But there is a book "Schoenberg" by Merle Armitage which consists of contributions of various authors and perhaps includes also 1938.[60]

If you can find these books in the Public Library, you might also find the *Anbruch* (*Blätter des Anbruch*) and *Pult und Taktstock*, both formerly published by Universal Edition. There are many articles about my works.

Besides my son in law, Mr. Felix Greissle, (Symph. Orch. Dept.

G. Schirmer Inc. 3 East 43d Str), Mr. Rudolf Kolisch and Mr. Eduard Steuermann might be able to help you to find more material.

Records. There are only *Verklärte Nacht, Gurrelieder* (both Victor) and Six Little Piano Pieces. Besides *Pierrot Lunaire* (Columbia). I have my four string quartets on records, but I doubt it will be possible to re-record them—and too expensive. I might have in a short time a recording of the two piano version of the second chamber symphony.

I have given a lecture on Composition with Twelve Tones, but I don't like it very much—or I have to change it considerably. Otherwise it would have been printed by the University of California Press. Perhaps I could loan you a copy—if you think it is worthwhile.

I was very glad to have heard from you again. How is your choral society going along?

Many cordial greetings to you and Mrs. Varèse from Mrs. Schoenberg and myself. The children are growing fast, Nuria is in Junior High, Ronny in first grade, and Lawrence is soon three years old and seems to be very intelligent.

Most cordially yours.

Rejecting a Cut in *Transfigured Night*

6.22 Letter to Bruno Walter, December 23, 1943

Verklärte Nacht *was the most frequently programmed of Schoenberg's works, including a very successful choreographed version entitled* Pillar of Fire, *first performed in 1942 at the Metropolitan Opera. This letter was written in response to Bruno Walter's request, in a letter dated December 18, 1943, for permission to make a substantial cut in* Verklärte Nacht: *"I am more anguished than ever over the similarity between bars 338 and 391. That the spiritual development that follows these bars containing the definitive version of the same, flows into the same bars also becomes a performance problem for me apart from anything else."*[61]

Dear Mr. Walter:

I thank you very much for the friendly manner in which you make the unfortunately unacceptable suggestion to me of a cut in *Verklärte Nacht.*

I am not only opposed to cuts in an otherwise acceptable work as a matter of principle—but also because they have never helped, but at best draw attention to an existing weakness in a disagreeable way.

I was certainly the first in our time who had turned away from the "lengthy style." But the new brevity was then just as organic as that previous length.

A cut shifts the balance of all the proportions. I have always found this to be so.

In the case of *Verklärte Nacht* the length is definitely the result of the manner in which the thematic material is treated in the whole piece. And this results from the structural nature of this material.

I learned this for myself in a convincing way when I attempted to rework this piece several years ago, that is, to undertake such changes as to make many things more concise without touching on the fundamentals. I was rather far along in this. But suddenly I got the feeling that I was simply murdering the piece.

I believe, if the lengths are not unbearable, that there are then only two ways out: 1) to perform it as it is. One must in that case hold on to the good. Or 2), as I once wrote, "To omit the *whole* unchanged."

But the cut you suggest would also be unacceptable for still other reasons. Bar 338 to 344 is the end of the third part, and a part like this must have a composed-out conclusion before the coda begins; that is, the tonic must (must) be explicitly present. I grant you that the coda is long, but I believe that, and the explicit close in D major, are particularly necessary here because such a large section of this part was in D♭.

Perhaps the following will interest you in connection with this.

In a sleepness night, in Barcelona 1932, I suddenly discovered what was previously unknown to me, that probably one of the causes why the third part is in D♭ so much is this characteristic of the principal theme:[62]

Three notes are a D-minor triad, the other three are (D♭) C♯ minor; minor indeed, this, however, makes no essential difference with the tonic relationship of major and minor. I was always conscious while composing that the D♭ major is a counterbalance against the E♭ major, but I had not known that the basis for this apparently lies in the principal motive. The manner in which this D♭ major is twice introduced through a chord that points to D major (the diminished chord in bar 276, the augmented seventh chord in 319) and the recurrence of the latter in bars 322 (second quarter) and 324, and its utilization for the modulation back to D major in bars 336/337 pleases me very much. I am very happy that at the age of 25 I was already so assured in my feeling for form that I could do such things unconsciously.

Now to close: I must thus ask you to refrain from making the cut. I also find the piece too long in many sections. But I believe: if its other qualities are not capable of compensating for that, then it is just as bad as most of Schubert—who is always much too long—without wanting to compare myself with him further, or at most in this respect.

When is your concert? I would not want to miss the broadcast, especially since I have recently heard so many bad performances and expect of you a beautiful one.

Respectfully yours,
Arnold Schoenberg

7 Final Years:
Los Angeles, 1944–1951

A Schoenberg Lullaby

7.1 Canon for Richard Rodzinski, 1944

Schoenberg wrote this text for a canon in celebration of the birth of the son of Artur Rodzinski, who had conducted several of Schoenberg's works, including the Ode to Napoleon *and the* Violin Concerto.

> *I am almost sure, when your nurse will change your diapers,*
> > *she will not sing you one of my George Songs,*
> > *nor of my Second String Quartet;*
> > *but perhaps she stills you:*
> *Sleep, Richard, Sleep! Your father loves you!*

On His Character, Contemporary Composers, and Conducting

7.2 From "Notes for an Autobiography" (1944–1945)

Most of the items in the "Notes for an Autobiography" date from 1944 and 1945, following his mandatory retirement from the University of California at Los Angeles, with a pension of $29.60 a month. Included under the section "Rascals" is an entry dated January 4, 1944, entitled "UCLA and Sproul" (referring to Dr. Robert G. Sproul, who was then president of UCLA): "When he engaged me he promised me many things and called my appointment a life position. But now still quite capable, at 70, I must retire. It seems, by not keeping their promises, they hoped to make this in a short time my life position."

"Franz Schreker," January 2, 1944

At the end of this note, which is labeled as belonging to the section "Colleagues," Schoenberg adds: "Schreker performed with his 'Philharmonisches Chor' my Friede auf Erden *and (1913) the* Gurrelieder *for the first time. In about 1922 he performed* Gurrelieder *again with the Hochshule orchestra and chorus when he was director there."*

Photo previous page: Schoenberg at his home, c. 1948. Arnold Schönberg Center, Vienna.

I want at first to mention one of my colleagues who really always had been very friendly and faithful to me, though—from the viewpoint of most other colleagues—he should rather have been jealous of me. Because in spite of his great success with his operas, and though he was not a follower of my developments, he had always shown some true personal appreciation of me.

It is *Franz Schreker.*

He himself was a thorough musician with an excellent background and great technical ability. In fact, I had also much and real appreciation of his art. It was a time when he was perhaps overrated. But afterwards he was certainly underrated. I am sure some of his operas could survive and I hope sometime they will be rehabilitated.

"To all my critics," August 23, 1945

Years ago I became always very angry about the nasty words critics applied to me.

Since then I have found out that a sewer does not stink in order to annoy me. Though, when I pass, it stinks at me, it is not its intention to annoy me. But it stinks because it can only stink.

I am not anymore offended by critics.—They would do better if they could.

"Anton von Webern" (Undated)

I am perfectly convinced that Webern was a passionate admirer and friend of mine.

Admiration was his nature. He was never at medium temperature. He hated or loved, he felt contempt or admired.

Though I know that the objects of his admiration have changed many times, I know also that he never changed his meaning about Karl Kraus, Peter Altenberg, Peter Rosegger, Gustav Mahler and me. These were his *"Fixsterne* [fixed stars]."

"Koussevitzki—Toscanini" (c. August 1944)[1]

I had written the beginning of this *August 11, 1944,* intending to send it to Mr. Kurt List, editor of *Listen* as a protest against his article on Koussevitzki.

I decided: I have enough enemies—I can renounce giving many others a special reason.

————

I have known intimately the four greatest conductors of this time: Mahler, Strauss, Nikisch and Furtwängler.[2] None of these four was a mere *"takt-beater* [time beater]"; they all were perfect musicians in every respect. They all were experts of musical knowledge and ability; they all knew the technical requirements of musical composition; they were composers themselves, they understood artistic values and respected the demands of aesthetics.

Strauss in 1902, after having glanced through the (then unfinished) scores of my *Pelleas* and *Gurrelieder* procured for me the "Liszt-Stiftung" for two years at a thousand marks yearly; acquired a little job at the Stern Konservatorium for me; and tried to have my *Verklärte Nacht* performed at the "Allgemeine Deutsche Musikverein"—he did not succeed at this last.

Mahler who between 1904 and 1907 also became acquainted with my music persuaded Rosé to perform my Ist and IInd string quartet, made the "Bläser-Kammermusik-Vereinigung der Hofoper" play the 1st performance of my Chamber Symphony, Op. 9, and suggested to several singers that they sing in a song recital of my songs.

Nikisch was in 1913 the first German conductor to perform the orchestra version of the Chamber Symphony, Op. 9. He wanted to perform the *Gurre-lieder* and conducted the string orchestra version of *Verklärte Nacht.*

Furtwängler was the first conductor to play one of my orchestra works (I think it was the Five Orchestra pieces op. 16) in *Vienna.*[3] I don't know exactly what else he conducted. Certainly he conducted *Pelleas* in Mannheim and Berlin (probably also elsewhere), and the "Variations [for Orchestra]" and the "Bach-Preludium und Fugue in E♭."

One might find it unfair to apply this yardstick to today's heroes of the baton. But a conductor exerts an almost incontestable power over the life and death of his subjects, the composers; and that: whether or not he performs their works.

Must not the artistic and musical standard, knowledge and ability of a conductor equal at least approximately that of the four masters.

Of course it should—but it does not: there is no other explanation of the failure of those two and many other conductors (among them also Otto Klemperer, whose incompetence became known to me in a surprising manner, when I had to realize that he was unable to harmonize a chorale and to become acquainted with music without playing it on the piano—not by reading it) to see the true merits of my music but: their lack of basic knowledge of music, their incompetence, ignorance and illiteracy.

Imagine: if they were absolutely denying performance to contemporary music: this would be stupid and—what is usually the same—a crime. But at least such an idiot might have one thing to his credit: he would be consistent.— But Koussevitzki has conducted music about whose inferiority to mine he could not have the slightest doubt—in spite of his illiteracy! And so have Toscanini and Klemperer and all the other half-wits!

As often as I hear a performance of these people I feel this lack of education. I have no doubt that these men came to their leading position only by their mechanical ability of takt-beating and by their knowledge of how to deal psychologically with an orchestra.

I imagine in teaching composition to talented pupils like: Webern, Berg, Eisler, Zillig, Hannenheim, Skalkottas, Schacht, etc. I was confronted with a triple task: 1) I had to read (I can not play the piano) the works they had written as long as it took until I heard in my imagination the true sound. 2) I had to find out if and what was wrong and why. 3) I had to find out how it should be corrected.

After having fulfilled these three tasks, it was only (!) necessary to find a way to explain all this to the pupils and (!) to explain how I thought it could be improved.

That was all!

Compare to that the incompetence of these conductors who dare to give judgments about my music and to take the responsibility about the existence of a composer—artistically and financially—after all, also that counts!

Those undignified persons, those impostors on artistic territory, these falsifiers of musical expertise, those masters over death and life: . . . ask them to do one of these things.

Do not forget that in former times a conductor was an expert who even could teach a *young* composer and ask him to change and improve certain sections in a composition when he would not perform it. Such knowledge was possessed by Alexander von Zemlinsky and many others (for instance Johann Nepomuk Fuchs [1832–1899]). And I know that Mahler exerted such criticism; creative criticism.

In contrast to that I will relate two significant events which are well enough witnessed.

The one with Koussevitzki:

Everybody knows that *Kouss.* has two pianists: Jan Romano and Slonim-sky, to play new music 4-hand-piano for him. But besides he has also Richard Burgan, his concertmaster, who rehearses the orchestra for him.

Everybody knows that.

But not everybody knows what I saw when Schnabel, Arthur Schnabel, and I were in a box in the concert hall in Boston (1934) when Burgan re-hearsed a piece of Copland. Silently one of the orchestra players came up to our box and pointing toward a distant box in the dark hall, where Koussevitzki was seated reading the score and conducting—practicing *takt-beating!* (I hope Schnabel will not refuse to testify to that.)

The story of Toscanini deals with his "photographic memory." That it is *only* a photographic memory, something entirely mechanical, which has nothing in common with intelligence (which remembers relations) is proved by the following story whose truth can easily be established. Toscanini performed my transcription for orchestra of Bach's Prelude and Fugue in E flat major. (Besides the only time he played a thing with which my name was connected.)

At the first rehearsal the first viola player (all the others could have done the same) advanced to Toscanini asking whether there was not a misprint in measure 12:[4]

Bach-Schoenberg, Prelude and Fugue in E-flat Major.

The maestro looked into his photographic master mind and unceremoniously shoved him away with a brusque: "No, it is correct."

But the viola player, who needed to know not more than his instrument, knew that this double stop could not be played on the viola and therefore in the next rehearsal he approached Toscanini again with the same question. He did not succeed better this time.

But only in the next rehearsal did Toscanini discover that this must be wrong and should be corrected.

It took the master mind several days to find the truth.

But it pays to analyze this.

A candid camera need not question the peculiarities of subjects—its straightforwardness is satisfactory if it only stores visible facts. So far Toscanini's memory has functioned faultlessly—it had preserved unbiasedly the correct facts and the faults.

But this is not the way a musician would read it. He might overlook that these two clefs are missing. But as one usually reads horns and trumpets—if it is not too complicated—in the right key; even if it is not marked at the margin. Without such subconscious adjustment one could not read a Wagnerian score—where often two or more keys appear in the brass. One would see the "G" in the horns, one would deem it improbable that the "F" of the first violas would be doubled in unison in this manner because it is the 9th to the bass and, if doubled, would probably be resolved into the 8th (E♭) of the bass. One would further at once realize the nonsense of doubling these two Fs (on the D-string)—why *divisi?*—but if that is in alto-clef, that one of the 2 G's is the open string G, the other is the same tone at the 4th finger of the C-string—a very conventional double stop.

Or one would see at once that this must be wrong and correct it—if the photographic memory were not a candid, but a stupid, camera.

This discussion would be incomplete if I would not at least try to describe why I feel that these conductors are illiterate when I hear their performances.

At first about the machine-like manner in which they keep the meter. This certainly stems from *popular dance music*. Especially in the dances of less cultured nations and savages the strict and entirely unchanged duration of the beat is a necessity because differences would cause difficulties to the feet.

Variation is the sign of higher developed brains and therefore it should be active in every vital part of every work of art.

In fact as far as the originators, the creators, the composers are concerned, there is variation in melody, rhythm, harmony, in instrumentation, in orchestration, in accompaniment, in mood and even in form. The higher the artistic standard of a composition, the [less] there will be repetition without variation.

One who has a true sense of form will not understand how within a series of those stiff, mechanical, constantly unchanged metronomic beats a ritardando, an accelerando or a fermata possibly can become "intermixed." Such regularity of beats of equal length cannot be connected with irregularity such as shorter or longer beats and entire stops. One who has the sense of form must find it as uncouth as if an otherwise regular ball would deviate on some places from its measurements to be more concave or more convex than regularity would admit.—This, if a "form" at all, is not the form classic masters up to Brahms would have written.

But these masters used ritardandos, accelerandos, and fermatas, because the beat in their form was—though a unit—of a flexible, adaptable nature, changing its size imperceptibly in conformity with the higher requirements of phrasing, mood, character, expression; and even to facilitate comprehensibility if e.g. a very remote variation of the basic motive or a sudden, unexpected contrast had to be connected.

In contrast to the primitive necessities of dance steps it may suffice to remember the Italian style of singing, still alive in the first two decades of this century. One used to speak in this respect of the Italian temperament, or, in consideration that the same was true in Spain or in Southern France, of the Southern Temperament. This should never have been understood as a kind of violent, irritable character, which rather deserved the name of *"furor teutonicus."* This Italian temperament was in fact only a very refined sensibility, acknowledging and at once expressing the slightest shades of a mood, illustrating the most delicate changes unobserved by tougher nerves.

It is quite evident that music is built by a number of flexible, adaptable, relative elements, as: tempo, measure, dynamic, accentuation, mood (and even character), etc., and a number of static, unchangeable, absolute elements as: pitch, key, harmonic progressions and their structural functions, motivic, thematic and melodic contents, including accompaniment. Between these two extremes might be considered: instrumentation (selection of instruments), octave doubling of tones of the harmony, and orchestration which might admit modification without endangering the true meaning.

In order to understand the problems of a changing size of the beat, it is useful to consider the case of the *Recitative*.[5] Evidently the recitative could not find its place in music if it were not musical. The so-called *"Secco-Recitative"* avoids entirely everything which could become *obligatory,* (or obliging). There is no melody, no theme, even no basic motive, no common rhythm, no other phrasing than that dictated by the text; also the harmonic progressions are different from all musical forms: One could even to a certain degree—and with the exception of the cadences—call them: non-functional. These progressions are always roving and settle down in a key only for an insignificant span of time. But most of all, there is no obligation to keep the beat of equal length. The reciter is free to be faster or slower whenever he deems it better for the characterization of the text. Even more does this become evident, if one thinks about the "accompanied recitative" with its stable segments and its "arioso" sections, both preceded and followed by free declamation of recitative.

This is possible only if the more stable sections, as well as the free sections avoid as much as possible arousing "false expectations": the expectations of a form to be produced by developments of a basic motif, or even a constant length of the beat. It is the fault of most post-Wagnerian composers not to discriminate enough in formulation between those sections, which should not become "pieces" (arias, duets, etc.) of established forms, and those which serve merely to put parts of the text "under music" which do not promote "closed forms." The thus-aroused false expectation (as I proved once to a friend—a successful opera composer) has the effect of unnecessary "lengthenings" which are boring. Let us look at two recitatives from Mozart.

But at first a word about today's manner of performing recitatives.

When Wagner established his own style of dramatic expression in contrast with the then predominant Italian "virtuoso" style, he blamed Italian singers for ignoring dramatic requirements in favor of their own vocal effects. They used *ritardandos* and *accelerandos* where it was flattering for the voice, they exaggerated fermatas in a never ending manner if it helped to expose a high note and to demonstrate a long breath. Curtailing singers was the first step toward restriction of exaggerating "rubato"-conductors and -players. They were predominant in the years after the advent of Wagner and were still "effective" in 1920.—Then, this other exaggeration came into power, which in Germany was called *"Neue Sachlichkeit."* It originated as a natural and justified reaction against those individualistic conductors, singers and instrumentalists, who considered the masterworks as nothing more than their given chance to demonstrate the greatness of their souls, the emotionality of their hearts, the nobility of their temperament and many more of their merits and excellence—it was not so much the work of the master they wanted to render but their own interpretation of it.

There is some justification even in that. Music cannot renounce interpretation because musical notation is still so imperfect that, as every composer knows, many important details remain undefined or even untold. One must excuse a layman for not knowing the circumstances of creation and believing that musical notation can exist without interpretation. This is interpretation: but *mis*interpretation, if you compare it with Busoni's wonderful utterance: "Scription (notation) is transcription." He knew such visions as are granted only to the inspired mind, and he knew how sketchy is the part one can express in our notation.

One example may illustrate the stupidity of "non-interpretation." In the 3rd movement of Beethoven's 5th symphony in the 7th measure is prescribed "poco ritard" the 8th has a fermata. The tempo is ♩. = 96.

Beethoven, Symphony No. 5 in C Minor, third movement.

♩. = 96 means ♩ = 3 times 96 = 288 ♩ in a minute which determines the duration of quarter notes in the preceding measure. The *ritardando* should lead gradually ("so as one opens an umbrella") into the fermata. Let us try a little arithmetic. The ancient rule (which nobody obeys today) for the fermata was: it "prolongs the duration for half its own duration (♩ + ♩ = ♩.) and adds a rest of the size of the prolongation (♩. ¦ = ♪). This would give ms. 8 a length of ♩. ¦ + ¦ that is: meas. 8 is ♩.⌣♩ or in fractions:

♩. = 60/96 = 5/8

♩ = 1/3 of 60/96 = 20/96 = 5/24

♩. + ¦ + ♩ (= 5 ♪) = 5 times 5/24 = 25/24 (100/96)

measure 7 should gradually lead into ms. 8, accordingly

1) it will not last as long as ms. 8, but longer than ms. 6 that is

2) each of its three ♩ notes should be longer than the preceding ♩

    If ms. 6 is (20 ♩ + 20 ♩ + 20 ♪)/96 = 60/96

ms. 7 could be {(23 + 26) ♩ + 31 ♩}/96 = (49 + 31)/96 = 80/96

    ms. 8 would be (60 ♩. + 20 ¦ + 20 ♪)/96 = 100/96

♩. = 60/96

¦ = 20/96

♩ = 20/96

In fact the denominator should be changed (instead of the numerator, but this might make comparison more difficult). There might be constructed a mechanical instrument which can carry this out exactly. But one thing is improbable: that a man can do this; and one thing is certain: that it would be nonsense to aim at it.

The beat is not the master of music, but its servant.

The beat's measure is taken "by the eye" so to speak.

The beat is supposed to help unifying ~~the rhythm by relating~~ [the sentence breaks off]

"My sense of measures and forms" (Undated)

My sense of measures and forms (circle, distances, weights, temperature, forms . . . (least pitch and rhythm).

I believe that the sense of form is based on a sense of measure.

Sense of time, of duration, length, pitch, speed, tempo etc. seem to be the foundation of ordinary musicianship.

But a creator needs a sense of shape, size and proportion more urgently than of pitch and rhythm. But he could scarcely do without a sense of tempo and duration, because they are interdependent.

A good proof is that I personally possess a "first vision" of my composition which is quite distinctly limited in time and size. Of course also key (if any) and rhythm are distinct but not as obligatory. (The themes seem to me only *details* of the *idea.*)

"Hindemith" (Undated)[6]

I should perhaps consider it rather flattering that Hindemith bases so much of his theory in his book *Unterweisung im Tonsatz*[7] on one little detail in my *Harmonielehre,* which certainly was a discovery, but in a real textbook— teaching musical technique—did not require too much importance.

It is my (hypothetical) attempt explaining the difference between a sixth-chord and a four sixth-chord by the difference in the tension of the overtones. This tension is heavier in the 4-6 chord accordingly it is "less" consonant than the 6-chord.[8]

This is certainly a possibility which might be applied to evaluate the degree of discordance of the chords. One might deduce some aesthetic principles from that; and possibly (in the manner in which Richard Strauss uses dissonances to express pains, griefs, satires, travesty by discords, contrasting them with concording sounds) one might arrive at well founded advice for illustrations and expression of moods etc.

But this is not the task of an "Unterweisung in Harmonielehre." I felt obliged not to evaluate the single harmony, but the progression of harmonies in their structural function. I did this in 1910/11, improved it in 1921 and still have developed it in a manner which might be an "Unterweisung" for a "Tonsetzer," though I would not consider the "Tonsatz" as a mere "Setzen" of tones, but as the art and logic of presenting and carrying out of musical ideas.

In my drama *Der biblische Weg* (*The way of the Bible*) one of the basic ideas is expressed in the sentence "Aus einem guten Gedanken fliesst alles von selbst" ("From a good idea everything develops by itself").

It seems to me that, inversely, this sentence is also valid: "Everything deriving from a wrong (or poor, or weak) idea, will never flow by itself" or, in other words: "The derivatives of a poor idea will also be poor (distorted, wrong)."

I have difficulties explaining Hindemith's idea, because I did not read his book myself, but have only been told about how he applies this principle, at first established by me.

Further I do not know whether he applies it logically, correctly and consistently; whether his deductions are straight to the point; whether his abstractive faculty is solid enough to strip a concept of all its non-essential details.

But suppose he does, then it should be possible to draw conclusions backward from his end to his point of issue. That means: departing from his criticism of one of my piano pieces it might be possible to explore his theory.

There is unfortunately already in the beginning an inconsistency: [the document breaks off here]

"My music is supposedly not emotional . . . " (Undated)

My music is supposedly not *emotional.*

Of course, it is not:

"Oh, darling, you are so wonderful; I love you so much"

There are also other kinds of love, for instance Alberich's, Monostatos', Don Juan's, but also Petrarca's (not expecting early reward)

There are also different kinds of emotion.

There is jealousy, hatred, enthusiasm.

There is love of ideals, of virtues, of one's country, town or village and its inhabitants.

There is not only joy, there is also sadness, mourning, pity, and envy.

There is also anger;

There is contempt, pride, devotion, madness, fear, panic, courage, admiration.

Love of justice, honesty, and good manners.

Love of good food and drinks and of the beauty of nature; of animals, flowers, and exotic stones.

Love of a bird's song and of competitive games.

"Schopenhauer," September 24, 1944

Schopenhauer, "Über Bescheidenheit" [Concerning modesty] says, "It is not possible that a man 6 feet 6 inches tall would not once discover that he is bigger than his surrounding." (I *quote* from memory.) Thus a man of higher intelligence must be aware of his superiority. But inferior people hated for him to realize this and therefore they invented the virtue of "*modesty,* which should prevent him from drawing consequences from his superiority. They wanted the important one to be modest, so as not to outshine their own obscure personalities."

Curiously enough, Schopenhauer thinks that an important man should manifest his superiority at the expense of the mediocre.

I feel the opposite of that.

It has often been said and written that I am modest. The contrary is true: I have a distinct and strong feeling of my value compared to that of others. But the more I am convinced of it, the less it seems necessary to me to let other people feel it.

I am sure a boxing champion would rarely have a fight outside of his professional contests in the ring.

It is evident that an elephant does not need to have his superior power constantly exhibited. He will not humiliate inferior animals, it suffices that none dares to attack him.

It is only the small dog who barks when he fears facing attack and always hopes he can frighten away his big adversary by his barking.

"When I was a young man in Vienna . . . " (Undated)

When I was a young man in Vienna there was among my friends and colleagues a very talented musician whom I admired very much.

He was extremely brilliant as a pianist and composer. But he was more than admired for his facility at ironic remarks.

Perhaps it is not too much to say that he was practically dreaded. His sarcastic remarks exposed everything and everybody to the laughter of those not referred to.

His looks too were those of a villain when he was not mocking. But before he would open his mouth a little for a great malice he would distort his face in a manner which frightened even the more intrepid ones.

I was perhaps the only friend he had.

But finally he lost me—I had suffered enough from his treatment and my patience was exhausted.

I had not seen him for a couple of years but then when I met him I did not recognize him.

He greeted me with an open bright smile; he asked cordially about my life and about my compositions; he congratulated me sincerely for some of my early successes—and there was nothing left of his former malice.

And all this was so natural that I suppressed at once the suspicion whether this was not a trap; to beat me after he had lulled me asleep.

He must have noticed how amazed I was, because before I could form a question about the change in his nature, he started to explain:

You are astonished, but you are not the only one who does not recognize me.

I will tell you now what occurred. Do you remember Dr. N. N. the dentist? He has to be credited with the change in my life.

Through carelessness I had lost more than half of my teeth. I knew my mouth looked ugly and my face was distorted. So I tried to hide its appearance behind a grimace which was a compound of presumptuousness, self-conceit, malice, malevolence, and real superiority.

You have no idea how much I regretted all my sarcastic remarks which I had to use to fit my looks.

But since Dr. N. N. helped me to a face which I need not hide anymore, I am free to show my true nature.

My friend became my friend again and remained so in an amiable manner. Why have I told this story?

It was not because of the lack of teeth that I do not use words to express my sympathies and my appreciation for the kindness, compliments, civilities, and even honors with which I have been frequently overwhelmed.

If, in my embarrassment I did not find the words in this language, which I hope to master in 25 years from now, I had no other way to express my feelings of gratitude than through my face—though in a manner contrary to that of my friend.

Please take my smile as my words of thanks.

On a Record-of-the-Month Club

7.3 Letter to Kurt List, February 12, 1945

Kurt List (1913–1970), who had studied composition with Berg and Webern, was the editor of Listen *magazine. Schoenberg had raised the issue of a Record-of-the-Month Club to several others, including Gustave Schirmer (1890–1965), who served as president of G. Schirmer (1919–1921, 1944–1957). The "Notes for an Autobiography" include a letter from Schirmer dated October 6, 1944, turning down Schoenberg's proposal for such a club, commenting that it was not a new idea, and that there were many problems that would have to be overcome.*

Dear Mr. List:

Only these three of my works: *Transfigured Night, Gurrelieder* and *Pierrot Lunaire* have been recorded. I was told that at present they are out of print, accordingly my income from records is about nothing.

Because of the absence of European royalties, my income from published printed works and from performance fees is less than a third of my total income.

My main income derives from teaching. At present only private pupils, since I am retired from the university.

About twenty years ago I elaborated a memorandum for Mr. Emil Hertzka, the owner of Universal Edition, in which I probably anticipated the idea of the book of the month club.

I suggested to organize in as many towns as possible, large or small, societies (or members of a greater society) who agreed to pay a rather small yearly amount in compensation for which the members should have the right to select from a list of published modern music those 5 or 6 works in which they were interested.

It was supposed that in Germany and Austria it might be easy to find several thousand members at the rate of 6, 12, 18, or 24 Marks per year. This would enable Universal Edition to sell works of about 24 pages at a price of one Mark and to print between 30 and 40 works every year.

Mr. Hertzka was very enthusiastic about this idea—but why he did not carry it out, [portion of the sentence missing] soon afterwards and maybe he did not feel well enough to undertake such a large enterprise.

It seems to me such an organization could be created in America. This might reduce the price of records immensely, as there are no dealers involved.

Of course, orchestral works could only be recorded in connection with performances or—and this seems to me important—either in arrangements for piano solo, or piano duo or chamber orchestra. Perhaps the chance of being recorded might stimulate composers to compose also chamber music, abandoning the habit of writing exclusively for large orchestra. They might begin to understand that it is important to expose one's musical ideas, demonstrating what they are worth without the colors of the large orchestra, what they are worth if denuded, stripped of the brilliant apparel of exterior beauty.

I think I should formulate this a little better. But I am very busy. Perhaps you can use it anyway.

I am with cordial greetings,

Yours,

On the String Trio, Op. 45, 1946

7.4 "My Fatality," 1949

Schoenberg composed the String Trio, Op. 45, between August 20 and September 23, 1946. Although he had started to make plans for the work the preceding June, in response to a commission from A. Tillman Merritt of Harvard University, the final character of the piece was very much influenced by the severe illness he suffered on August 2. Thomas Mann, in his account of the origins of Doctor Faustus, *reports that Schoenberg told him the following about programmatic elements in the trio: "He told me about the new trio he had just completed, and about the experiences he had secretly woven into the composition—experiences of which the work was a kind of fruit. He had, he said, represented his illness and medical treatment in the music, including even the male nurses and all the other oddities of American hospitals. The work was extremely difficult to play, he said, in fact almost impossible or at best only for three players of virtuoso rank; but, on the other hand, the music was very rewarding because of its extraordinary tonal effects. I worked the association of 'impossible but rewarding' into the chapter on Leverkühn's chamber music."[9] For more on* Doctor Faustus, *see 7.11, 7.12.*

On August 2 of this year it will be three years since what I jokingly call "my fatality." I want to record the whole story to the best of my ability, not because it would make an interesting chapter in my biography, but because it should give doctors something to think about.

But first: I began the Trio, of which I have told many people that it is a "humorous" representation of my sickness, soon after I was over the worst. But at that time I did not yet know the full reality of my sickness. It was kept a secret from me.

I had been sick ever since I had retired (i.e., $29.60 a month) in March 1944. First I was treated for diabetes for two years, then it was not long before attacks of giddiness and fainting came (along with my asthma) and something was also apparently wrong with my heart (arrhythmia). But in 1946, in March or April, I decided on my own to leave off the insulin injections. At this time I suffered most from the fainting attacks, of which I had many every day in rapid succession.

That was still the case when I went to Chicago for a month as "visiting professor." It was a wonder that I could maintain all my lectures and classes with this sickness. It continued the same way. I was then examined and treated by several doctors: Dr. Bauer, Dr. Waitzfelder, and Dr. Wolf. None could detect the real cause, and thus they thought me clearly hysterical; and Professor Bauer even believed my case was similar to that of women in the "change of life."

On August 2, 1946, Dr. Waitzfelder was here. I had just had Gerald Strang here to work on the composition book. We were at lunch. Dr. Waitzfelder examined me and prescribed a pill, something "new" that had only just come out. I do not recall. I took one immediately, but soon afterward, while still at lunch, suddenly I became extremely tired and sleepy, so that I had to put my head down. Trude put me to bed and I slept until 9:30. Then I awoke with a terrible pain in my chest. I sprang from the bed and sat down in my armchair. (I must correct this, for I just remember that it was different: I awoke with an extremely unpleasant feeling, but without a definite pain, but I hurried in spite of it (!) to my armchair.) I became continually worse. We called doctors, but none was available. Thus I insisted that Leonard Stein be called so that he could provide a doctor. It was not long before he came himself with Dr. Lloyd Jones (who has treated me ever since).

I had believed that I had a heart attack or heart spasm. But Dr. Jones determined that this was not the case and gave me an injection of *Dilaudid* "in order to bring the patient at ease." It worked very quickly. The pain went away. Then I must have lost consciousness. For the last thing that I heard was my wife saying "you take his feet and I will take his shoulders," and apparently they returned me to the bed.

I do not know how long I was unconscious. It must have been several hours, for the first thing I remember was that a man with coal-black hair was bending over me and making every effort to feed me something. My wife said (to keep me from being alarmed!) "This is the doctor!" But I remember having been astonished since Dr. Jones had silver-white hair. It was *Gene,* the male nurse. An enormous person, a former boxer, who could pick me up and put me down again like a sofa cushion.

On the Performance of New Music

7.5 *"For the Radio Broadcast of the String Trio," May 1949*

This may have been written to accompany a broadcast of the trio by members of the Walden Quartet in conjunction with a series of modern-music broadcasts by the Hessian Radio in Frankfurt on Main. The concerts were affiliated with the Darmstadt Summer School, which included a course of twelve-tone composition conducted by René Leibowitz.[10]

A true musician, reading the score during the performance of one of my later works, went to the artists' room and showed the players many errors, faults and other shortcomings he had observed in their rendition. He was given the very strange answer: "Maybe, but nobody noticed that!"

Strange indeed: Strange at first the morality, which is quite comparable to the viewpoint that excuses a crime if it cannot be proven. But strange also the logic to make such a contention when facing a man who *has* noticed those "differences." It seems that these players expected nobody would notice differences, which they themselves probably did not notice.

I am the last to blame the failure of a work of mine on the more or less important shortcomings of a performance. Though they are not entirely without influence, especially if they spoil character and mood by false tempo, dynamics and expression. I know that the obstacle to comprehension lies even more with my musical thoughts than with their presentation, and on my musical language. I know that little niceties repeated over and over without, or with little variation or development are easier to grasp and provide better for temporary success than a language which insists on brevity, and that accordingly would not repeat without exhibiting the new form resulting from the destiny of an idea.

I am acquainted with the preference of many concert goers for easily digestible entertainment. But one should never forget that there is popular music—operettas, shows, and movies—for people who want to be entertained; and that producers of those entertainments are not measured and criticized according to the viewpoints of the initiated, who desire to be elated, "even if it hurts."

The artists who perform the TRIO this time do not need the excuse that "nobody noticed it," because they studied it for an audience which consists exclusively of people who "notice it."

On Those Who Stayed in Germany

7.6 "On Strauss and Furtwängler," 1946

After stepping in at Bayreuth to conduct Parsifal *in 1933, in place of Toscanini, who had resigned in protest at Nazi policies, Strauss was perceived as sympathetic to the Third Reich, leading to his naming as president of the Reichsmusikkammer. But by 1935 his continuing collaboration with the Jewish novelist and librettist Stefan Zweig led to his dismissal. He spent the war years keeping a low profile in Garmisch and Vienna, going to Switzerland after the war. He underwent "denazification" in 1948. Furtwängler was named conductor of the Staatsoper in 1933, in addition to his post at the Berlin Philharmonic, but with the Nazis' suppression of Hindemith's* Mathis der Maler *the following year, he publicly protested with the article "The Hindemith Case," and resigned. He remained in Germany, attempting, not always with success, to continue an active conducting career while avoiding being used for propaganda purposes. He underwent de-nazification in 1946 but continued to face strong opposition in the United States.*[11]

I am not a friend of Richard Strauss, and, though I do not admire all of his work, I believe that he will remain one of the characteristic and outstanding figures in musical history. Works like *Salome, Elektra, Intermezzo,* and others will not perish. But I do not believe that he was a Nazi, just as little as W. Furt-wängler. They were both *Deutsch-Nationale*—Nationalistic Germans, they both loved Germany, German culture, and art, landscape, language and its citizens, their co-nationals. They both will raise their glass if a toast is brought to Germany *"Hoch Deutschland,"* and though they esteemed French and Italian music and paintings highly, they consider everything German as superior. Their enthusiasm—on a higher level of course—is in nature closely related to that of the *"Bierbank"* and of the *"Deutsche Männergesangs-Verein."* May I re-peat: of course on a higher level, because both men, Strauss and Furtwängler, had a higher education. One must, however, not be blinded by this education. We know that scientists, doctors, professors, writers, poets and artists could stand the musical vulgarity of the "Horst Wessel Lied" and sing the horrible text with as much fire and enthusiasm as the simple man in the street. I have no information about St's and F's attitude in this respect; but it seems to me doubtless that they at least despised the music.

But, Nazi or not, that Furtwängler cannot come to America and that he has to live lonely in Switzerland without work is due to the intrigue of one man:[12] this powerful man whose word power is not great enough to explain his ideas understandably to musicians, the man who throws a golden watch to the floor in anger over his verbal impotence—this man is capable of keeping a Furtwängler, who is many times his superior, from conducting in America and in the rest of the world.

But I wanted rather to speak about Strauss.

People who do not agree that the ban on F. is justified will have to admit that there is at least consequence in a perfect ban. But even if there were truth in a ban on Strauss, there would only be consequence if his music would also be banned.

But those who allow his music to be played but refuse to pay what they owe him, act as shamelessly as pirates.

I do not speak because of sentimental reasons. Of course, I regret an old man of eighty-two years, who wrote throughout his entire life and has created things which 90% of the music lovers of the earth enjoy; I regret that this old man now has lost—for the second time in his life—all his fortune; I regret that he lives at present in two rooms in Switzerland on charity which is extended to him by an eminent lover of the arts, Mr. Reinhart of Winterthur.

I do not speak as a friend of Richard Strauss; though he was helpful to me in my youth, he has later changed his attitude toward myself. I am sure that he does not like my music and in this respect I know no mercy: I consider such people as enemies.

I speak from the standpoint of honesty.

"A small anti-Semitic tarnish"

7.7 "A Solemn Declaration about Pfitzner," September 10, 1947

After leaving Berlin in 1930, Pfitzner taught at the Munich Academy until 1933. In the early years of the Third Reich, Pfitzner attempted to accommodate himself to the Nazis, and his works were championed for a time as examples of German art. But he was soon marginalized and lost his post, only being granted a pension in 1937. By the end of the war he was personally and professionally devastated; he underwent denazification in 1947.

I met Dr. Pfitzner at the time of the premiere of *Rose im Liebesgarten* in Vienna, at Gustav Mahler's house.[13]

It was always known to me that he was a nationalistic German in the sense of Richard Wagner, thus with a small anti-Semitic tarnish. I have often spoken with him through all these years. In spite of all the differences that separated us, including artistic ones, I have never had the feeling of aggressivity.

It is no wonder that after the migration of so many musical powers, Pfitzner was among the few who stayed behind who was first class and found recognition as such, recognition, of which unjustly, he had not always had his share before.

If the Nazi system was an advantage for him, I am convinced that he never bowed to it, never would have made a concession, and certainly would have condemned atrocities.

On His Enemies

7.8 Schoenberg's Reply to the National Institute of Arts and Letters, June 1947

In response to a $1,000 "Award of Merit for Distinguished Achievement" from the National Institute of Arts and Letters, Schoenberg submitted the following letter of thanks along with a recording of himself reading the text. The statement was published with a commentary by Virgil Thomson in the New York Herald Tribune *on June 1, 1947. Thomson writes of Schoenberg's "grace and irony," which* *"expresses to perfection those combined feelings of exasperation and respect that make up any artist's attitude toward all institutes and academies [. . . .] He has recalled to the musician members of the institute that it was they and their kind all over the world who fought for fifty years his achievement, who by so fighting made it always clearly an unaided one and who by now capitulating before it award him a victory that has not been and will not be the privilege of any of them. The irony of the composer's final sentence is both courteous and thoroughly tonic."*[14]

To the National Institute of Arts and Letters,

Mr. President, Ladies and Gentlemen:

I am proud about the formulation under which this award has been given to me.

That all I have endeavored to accomplish during these fifty years is now by you evaluated as an achievement seems in some respects to be an overestimation.

At least not before now could I sum it up—that is: while it still looked like a pell-mell of incoherent details—at least then did I fail to understand it as a direction leading toward an accomplishment. Personally I had the feeling as if I had fallen into an ocean of boiling water, and not knowing how to swim or to get out in another manner, I tried with my legs and arms as best as I could.

I do not know what saved me; why I was not drowned or cooked alive—

I have perhaps only one merit: I never gave up.

But how could I give up in the middle of an ocean?

Whether my wriggling was very economical or entirely senseless, whether it helped me to survive or counteracted it—there was nobody to help me, nor were there many who would not have liked to see me succumb.

I do not contend it was envy—of what was there to be envious?

I doubt also that it was absence of good will—or worse—presence of ill wishing.

It might have been their desire to get rid of this nightmare, of this unharmonious torture, of these unintelligible ideas, of this methodical madness—and I must admit: these were not bad men who felt this way—though, of course, I never understood what I had done to them to make them as malicious, as furious, as cursing, as aggressive—I am still certain that I had never taken away from them something they owned; I had never interfered with their rights; with their prerogatives; I never did trespass on their property; I even did not know where it was located, which were the boundaries of their lots, and who had given them title to these possessions.

Maybe I did not care enough about such problems; maybe I myself failed to understand their viewpoints, was not considerate enough, was rough when I should have been soft, was impatient when they were worried by time and pressure, ridiculed them when indulgence was advisable, laughed when they were distressed.

I see only that I was always in the red—

But I have one excuse: I had fallen into an ocean, into an ocean of overheated water and it burned not only my skin, it burned also internally.

And I could not swim.

At least I could not swim with the tide. All I could do was to swim against the tide—whether it saved me or not.

I see that I was always in the red. And when you call this an achievement, so—forgive me—I do not understand of what it might consist.

That I never gave up?

I could not—I would have liked to.

I am proud to receive this award under the assumption that I have achieved something.

Please do not call it false modesty if I say:

Maybe something has been achieved but it was not I who deserves the credit for that.

The credit must be given to my opponents.

They were the ones who really helped me.

Thank you.

On the Holocaust

7.9 A Survivor from Warsaw, *Op. 46, 1947*

Schoenberg wrote this text and the setting for narrator, male chorus, and orchestra in August 1947 in reaction to accounts he received "directly or indirectly" of the Warsaw Ghetto uprising in 1943.[15] A sketch page is given in fig. 7-1.

NARRATOR: I cannot remember ev'rything. I must have been unconscious most of the time.—I remember only the grandiose moment when they all started to sing, as if prearranged, the old prayer they had neglected for so many years—the forgotten creed! But I have no recollection how I got underground to live in the sewers of Warsaw for so long a time.—

The day began as usual: Reveille when it still was dark. Get out! Whether you slept or whether worries kept you awake the whole night. You had been separated from your children, from your wife, from your parents; you don't know what happened to them—how could you sleep?

The trumpets again—Get out! The sergeant will be furious! They came out; some very slow: the old ones, the sick ones; some with nervous agility. They fear the sergeant. They hurry as much as they can. In vain! Much too much noise, much too much commotion—and not fast enough! The Feld-webel shouts: "Achtung! Stillsjestanden! Na wirds mal? Oder soll ich mit dem Jewehrkolben nachhelfen? Na jutt; wenn ihrs durchaus haben wollt!" ["Stand at attention! Hurry up! Or do you want to feel the butt of my gun? Okay, you've asked for it!"] The sergeant and his subordinates hit everybody: young or old, quiet or nervous, guilty or innocent.—It was painful to hear them groaning and moaning. I heard it though I had been hit very hard, so hard that I could not help falling down. We all on the ground who could not stand up were then beaten over the head.—

I must have been unconscious. The next thing I knew was a soldier say-ing: "They are all dead," whereupon the sergeant ordered to do away with us. There I lay aside—half-conscious. It had become very still—fear and pain.

Then I heard the sergeant shouting: "Abzählen!" ["Number off!"] They started slowly and irregularly: one, two, three, four—"Achtung!" the sergeant shouted again, "Rascher! Nochmal von vorn anfangen! In einer Minute will ich wissen, wieviele ich zur Gaskammer abliefere! Abzählen!" ["Quicker! Start again! In one minute I want to know how many I'm going to deliver to the gas chamber! Number off!"] They began again, first slowly: one, two, three, four, became faster and faster, so fast that it finally sounded like a stampede of wild horses, and all of sudden, in the middle of it, they began singing the *Shema Yisrael*.

MALE CHOIR (sung in Hebrew): Hear Israel:
The Lord our God is one Lord,
And you should love the Lord, your God,
With all your heart and with all your soul
And with all your might.
And these words, which I command you today,
Shall be in all your heart;
And you shall teach them diligently to your children and talk of them
When you sit in your house
And when you walk along your way,
When you lie down and when you rise.
(*Deuteronomy* 6: 4–7)

On the Premiere of A *Survivor from Warsaw*

7.10 Letter to Mrs. Jay Grear, November 13, 1948

The first performance of A Survivor from Warsaw *took place with the Albuquer-que Civic Symphony Orchestra under the direction of Kurt Frederick on November*

4, 1948. An account from the Albuquerque Journal *the next day reports: "It is a short, extremely difficult descriptive work, accompanied by a narration and climaxing with a surging chorus. The first performance left the audience a little breathless and bewildered, but they loyally and loudly applauded until the conductor, and Sherman Smith, who lent his tremendous bass voice to the narration, returned to the platform and inquired if the audience would like to hear it again. The applause immediately doubled in volume and enthusiasm, and the entire work was repeated."*[16] *This letter was sent to Mrs. Jay Grear [Isabel Grear], of the Albuquerque Civic Symphony Orchestra.*

Dear Mrs. Grear:

I am very thrilled by the great success of my "Survivor from Warsaw" in Albuquerque. It must have been a wonderful performance; but it must be a wonderful audience who responded in this manner. Everybody whom I told about this success and that an audience in Albuquerque demanded a repetition of a work of mine played for the first time is very astonished and thrilled by it, almost as much as I am.

It seems to me that this fact should be known by many people. Because it's a wonderful attitude toward a new work.

This should become a model to many, many other places.

A friend of mine has sent a report of the whole affair, especially the review of it, to New York and he expects that it will be published now in magazines and newspapers.

I would like to ask you to show this letter to all people concerned. In the first place, of course, to Mr. Kurt Frederick whose enthusiasm must have contributed much to the achievement of this miracle. Then of course all the performers and particularly the narrator Mr. Smith. I know it is always very difficult to find a narrator who can do a task as difficult as this. And as Mr. Smith has contributed so much to the success, he must have been excellent. The same is true with Mr. Firlie who conducted the men's chorus. A very difficult part to study. Of course, the task of the orchestra was a very difficult one and it is astonishing that people who have probably not yet played a work of this difficulty could achieve such an excellent performance. This concerns of course the orchestra but a special word seems to me to be deserved by the chorus and especially the Estancia Chorus. Such a devotion to a work of art is very unusual and should be noted as a significant moment in the history of performances.

If I regret only one thing, it is that I could not be present. My thanks are as great as is possible; but I am sure my enthusiasm would have inspired me to even warmer words of thanks. But believe me, I am really happy about this performance. Thank you very much.

You would oblige me if you would bring the contents of this letter to be known by all participants of this performance. This is why I send you a number of photostatic copies of it, perhaps it is simpler and easier in this way.

I am most cordially yours,

Very sincerely,

A Controversy with Thomas Mann

7.11 "A Text from the Third Millennium," February 1948

Thomas Mann had left Germany in February 1933, settling first in Zurich and then immigrating to the United States in 1938. After two years in Princeton, Mann joined the émigré community in Los Angeles. The previously friendly relationship between Mann and Schoenberg was severely strained by the publication of Doctor Faustus *in 1947 (English translation in 1948), due to its attribution of the invention of the twelve-tone method to the character Adrian Leverkühn. To express his concerns about the possible historical repercussions of this act, Schoenberg sent Mann the following hypothetical encyclopedia entry from the distant future. The article is signed "Hugo Triebsamen," who as Schoenberg later explained, was a combination of Hugo Riemann and Walter Rubsamen.[17] In the text below, Schoenberg also took the opportunity to cast aspersions in the direction of the Parisian neoclassical circles around Nadia Boulanger, who appears here as "Budia Nalanger."*

Mann responded to the "Text" in a letter of February 17, describing it as "a curious document," and writing, "It touched me, showing as it does the zeal with which your disciples stand guard over your glory and honor. But so much strained malice, which at the same time so completely misses the mark, also has its comic aspect."[18] See further 7.12. It was not until 1950 that the argument was finally smoothed over.[19]

The name of Arnold Schoenberg is mentioned in one of the few letters by Anton v. (does that mean von or van?) Webern. In the letter which he wrote a few weeks before he was killed fighting against the Russians (1938) he spoke enthusiastically about this Schoenberg, and called him the greatest living composer, whose services to art would never be forgotten. How wrong he was in this prophecy! I read through six ten-yearly volumes of the *Encyclopaedia Americana* without finding a mention of his name. It was not till I came to the edition of 1968 that I found this name and a short biographical notice.

He must have played a part forty or fifty years before this volume, that is to say almost a hundred years ago, because although not a single one of his compositions are mentioned, two facts are of interest to me. First that he also wrote theoretical works, and clearly had a large number of pupils. However, none of his theoretical writings have survived him. The biography says that they were already out of date at the time they were written. They dealt with traditional methods of composition, functions of harmony, variations, musical logic, and referred to composers of the romantic era of chromaticism. Secondly, he must have had a kind of battle with the well-known German writer Thomas Mann, who was clearly the inventor of the method of composing with twelve tones, based on the emancipation of the dissonance, i.e. the equality of the presentation of dissonances with the presentation of consonances. Webern mentions the invention of this theory and the terminology which belongs to it as an achievement of Schoenberg's, but this seems to be wrong, for Schoenberg was an unscrupulous exploiter of other people's ideas.

It has been said that in his youth Mann urgently wanted to become a musician, but turned to writing in his 20s.

Probably Mann was in contact with Schoenberg about this time; Schoenberg was living in Vienna, only a few minutes' flight from Munich, where Mann lived. He probably invented the twelve-tone theory at that time (1933), and as he had given up composing himself, he allowed Schoenberg to use it and publish it under his own name. Mann's liberal nature never mentioned this violation of his rights. But it seems that they became enemies in the last years of their lives, and now Mann took his property back and attributed its origin to a person whom he had created himself (Homunculus). So the great American music came into the position of being able to profit from Mann's theoretical invention, and this led to all the progress in American music from the fusion of this with Budia Nalanger's model methods of producing real old music which works like new music.

If this accusation of the forgotten "theoretician" Schoenberg and his hateful crime as well as his disregard of the rights of cultural property are aggravating, the way in which Mann has presented this, his own idea, is all the more grandiose. Only a real inventor is in a position to give such an illuminating presentation. Schoenberg would never have had the *capacity for work of this kind.*

Hugo Triebsamen.

More on the *Doctor Faustus* Controversy

7.12 *Letter to René Leibowitz and Josef Rufer, October 20, 1948*

In response to Schoenberg's concerns, Mann included the following "Author's Note" in subsequent editions of Doctor Faustus: *"It does not seem superfluous to inform the reader that the method of composition presented in Chapter XXII, known as the twelve-tone or row technique, is in truth the intellectual property of a contemporary composer and theoretician, Arnold Schoenberg, and that I have transferred it within a certain imaginary context to the person of an entirely fictitious musician, the tragic hero of my novel. And in general, those parts of my book dealing with music theory are indebted in many details to Schoenberg's* Theory of Harmony."[20]

Dear Friend:

You asked me some time ago whether the presentation of my twelve-tone method in Dr. Mann's book, *Doctor Faustus* was carried out on the basis of information that I had given him. I believed until recently that Dr. Mann would furnish the necessary declaration in his book. At least he answered accordingly to an attack in a Swiss newspaper, so that one could believe that we had reached an understanding about it. But that is not so.

Thomas Mann received this information behind my back from Wiesengrund-Adorno, concealing it from me until I learned about it from a newspaper article.

Then Alma Mahler Werfel took the matter in hand and brought Mann to the conviction that it was a literary theft. But then it required a long back and forth to make clear to Mann that he must somehow make good on his injustice.

First I sent him attachment 1), this satirical excerpt from a music history from the year 1960 (or so) in which I drew his attention to the possible consequences of his deed.[21] To this he answered in attachment 2), acting as though he did not understand what it was about. Attachment 3) explained it to him in my letter. Then finally after repeated interventions by Frau Mahler (attachment 4) he consented to include a declaration in all subsequent printings of his book. I wrote him an enthusiastic letter of thanks, attachment 5). But since then I had heard nothing; I had actually expected that he would present this declaration to me, and never suspected that he had not presented it to me for a definite reason.

Only recently an employee of the *New York Times Magazine* called me and wanted an interview on account of the soon to be appearing *Doctor Faustus* of Thomas Mann, which was to include his declaration about the use of the twelve-tone technique. Thereupon I wrote a letter to his publisher, Bermann-Fischer, in which I asked whether that had happened. Mann himself answered me that Bermann-Fischer had called him and wrote, how could I believe that he would not fulfill such a promise. That is the next attachment.

He was sending me the book, he wrote, but that did not ensue in the next few days, whereupon I wrote him myself a very enthusiastic letter happy that the matter was settled. But then the book arrived and I found that I was a contemporary, a certain Arnold Schoenberg, whom scarcely anyone knew, just as Triebsamen had foreseen.

I would like for you now to make this shameful, treacherous deed of Thomas Mann known.

I would very much like that you yourself or some of your friends make the necessary excerpts from Mann's letters and reprint my letters to place the matter in the proper light. I believe he really deserves a beating for this shameful deed.

This letter is going at the same time to Leibowitz/Rufer, and I hope that both will act in the same spirit.

The originals of Mann's letters, from which photostatic reproductions are attached, are available at any time to give witness to the accuracy of my presentation.

I would also very much like that the Swiss newspaper, which attacked him on its own behalf—without my intervention, I knew nothing about it, but learned it from a newspaper clipping that was sent—I would like very much that this newspaper be notified of this whole matter. Accordingly I have attached a second copy for this purpose. Perhaps one could write the article and the other translate it so that the same version could come out in the Swiss newspaper and perhaps also in other papers and magazines. I believe one should distribute it widely.

On Inspiration and Construction

7.13 Formalism, *February 13, 1949*

Schoenberg is responding here in part to the long-standing accusations that he was a "constructor." In a letter about twelve-tone composition to the music critic Julius Korngold, who had also settled in Southern California, he wrote: "I know, as I said, that such theories don't help my work, but harm me greatly. I am a mathematician, an engineer, I lack immediacy, feeling, expression, etc., etc. All right, in spite of that I am not willing to pretend to be an idiot, as many would like to see me do. Like I once said about someone who claimed he was a 'master fallen from heaven' (Josef Hauer!!), 'yes, but on to his head.' Everything was fine with him, if one would only accept his genius."[22] It is also likely that Schoenberg had in mind the public censure of Prokofiev on the basis of "formalism," and the composer's subsequent apology in February 1948 to the General Assembly of Soviet Composers, which included the following: "As far as I am concerned, elements of formalism were peculiar to my music as long as fifteen or twenty years ago. Apparently the infection caught from contact with some Western ideas."[23]

Formalism is a term, which wants to degrade the care an artist has to take in profound organization. It presupposes erroneously that such occupation reduces spontaneity and inspiration thus resulting in a mere cerebral artifact, which is not produced out of human interest and emotions and therefore is not capable of provoking such interest and feelings.

I have never heard or read such accusation made by one of the great composers, but, on the contrary, I read Mozart's: *"Lernts'was, Buben damit ihr 'was könnt,"* (study, boys in order to know something); or Beethoven, who signed *"Hirnbesitzer"* (owner of a brain") in a letter to his *"Gutsbesitzer"* (owner of a ranch) brother, and who said *"Musik muss einem Manne Feuer aus dem Geiste schlagen"* (a man's brain must spit fire if music hits it).[24] A wonderful word. It equates the brain of a man to flint and to being as hard as that; and fire means to him both "human warmth of feeling" as well as "enthusiasm"; and do not ignore the qualities he ascribes to the manly mind!

I don't know what was Brahms' response. Maybe he was silent, he who was one of those who, as formalists, were made the scapegoat of the emotionalists. But a *pathetique* symphony like Tchaikowsky's sixth bears perhaps no less the indications of intensive brain work—or its substitute: subconsciously produced. Almost all of its themes consist of this part of a scale and some extensions thereof with which the first theme begins. Thus if formalism means cerebrally, it combines quite well here with emotion, with pathos.

Perhaps also this could much easier be described if one were to state its contrary, that is: what is non-Formalism? Considering that apperception is excluded if memorability is missing. Memorability requests coherence: at least no piece longer than a small number of measures can impress the memory if its limbs are not connected by coherence, by a certain relationship.

to be continued

Art, Science, and the Idea

7.14 *"My Subject: Beauty and Logic in Music" (Undated)*

My subject: beauty and logic in music, shall deal with the mutual relation between beauty and logic in music. Its main purpose shall be to dethrone beauty as much as possible as a serious factor in the creation of music. It shall be assumed that it is neither the aim of a composer to produce beauty nor is a feeling of beauty a producing "agent" in his imagination. It might and often does occur that, in spite of an occupation with a different direction, the complete work produces a feeling of beauty in a listener.

But the main problem of a composer is: expression and presentation of musical ideas; the right organization, which is based on musical logic and what one calls form in music, is not a preconceived shape in which music has to be filled and fitted in.

Musical ideas are such combinations of tones, rhythms, and harmonies, which require a treatment like the main theses of a philosophical or—[space was left for another word] subject. It poses a question, sets up a problem, which in the course of the piece has to be answered, resolved, carried through. It has to be carried through many contradictory situations, it has to be developed by drawing consequences from what it postulates, it has to be checked in many cases and all this might lead to a conclusion, a *pronunciamento.*

But of course, art is not science and while science cannot avoid passing systematically through every possible problem, art will only bring about those situations which are characteristic—and will leave it to the imagination of its audience to continue to dream about more.

The problem of a musical idea consists of the tension between the overtones if 2 or more tones appear simultaneously and [sentence breaks off]

People often excuse children, saying it is not their fault that they are born, but the fault of the parents.

I believe: love is the demand of the children to be born. Their desire to become men forces the man and wife to love each other, forces them into reproduction.[25]

No doubt a similar desire for reproduction works in a musical idea, once one row of overtones has met its contrasting companion.

On Abstract Art, Politics, and the Audience

7.15 *"To the San Francisco Round-Table on Modern Art," April 8, 1949*

The following remarks were prepared for a roundtable lead by Alfred Frankenstein (1906–1981), who at the time was music critic for the San Francisco Chronicle. *Schoenberg did not personally take part.*

I would like to see the question discussed whether there existed reasons or causes which forced artists to abandon the imitation of nature and to stylize or conventionalize their works. In our own time, it seems to me that there are some circumstances which have forced painting to abandon nature. It was photography which never could deliver artistic works, but in every other respect satisfied the buyer, the purchaser, the audience, the public, in a manner which corresponded to their wishes, as a support to their memory, to see things which they wanted to remember, and to see things which they otherwise would never have seen.

Painting could differ from the achievements of photography only by deviations and, of course, by artistic virtues. These artistic virtues might easily have been understood as a mannerism rather than as art. This might be wrong, but it might have some influence on many artists. No such cause existed for sculpture. Sculpture still satisfies the purchaser who wants to see the resemblance of a portrait, of a model and therefore, at least this branch of art does not need to deviate from nature.

The question is now: why did sculpture also deviate?

I always wondered when I saw a picture gallery in the castle of Sans Souci near Berlin—in Potsdam—which all had one thing in common, one peculiarity: portraits of Hohenzollern, or perhaps Kurfürste of Brandenburg, with very narrow and long heads, such as one would hardly ever see among men. It seems to me doubtless that also these painters, or this painter, have stylized or conventionalized their works. Here there was no reason which forced them to abandon nature. It might be that in some Asiatic nations there existed religious laws which forbade true imitation of the image of man. We all know that, for instance, Jews were not allowed to reproduce the image of man. This might be partially an explanation for some of the Indian images of man and of many other East-Asiatic nations' products. One might doubt whether they did not do it because of the difficulty of imitating nature in such a perfect manner that the resemblance is satisfying. But it seems to me that this idea is quite wrong. If one compares the skill with which their goldsmiths worked and their other metal works, and if one compares the wonderful buildings they understood how to erect, then one must give up such an accusation. There must have been the idea of stylizing, of conventionalizing, in Egypt and Asiatic countries, especially in India. Whether for religious reason or simply for artistic reason: about this I would like to hear your opinions.

It seems to me that the right of the artist to deviate from nature cannot be contested. It was not only in our time, but it was also probably in all times, that there was a tendency of artists to produce a work of art independently of realism, independently of what one really sees. To use his imagination, his fantasy, is certainly the right of an artist, and, admitting this, one must not forget, for instance, that Breughel's paintings are also not nature—they are real imagination.

But on the other hand, I would not be so strict as to forbid painters to paint what their imagination dictates them, if they cannot prove that they can also paint something else, that they also can imitate nature. I know paintings of Kandinsky before he turned to his abstract painting. I know that Kokoschka can draw a wonderful picture, a wonderful portrait, in the knick of time, and I knew also other painters who had the same ability and nobody can say that they turned away from nature because of lack of ability. Doubtlessly the same is true with Picasso, Matisse and many others of these great artists. And it is very agreeable for the lover of art to see that the man who deviates from nature is not forced to do it by lack of ability.

Perhaps there are also some other qualities which make the work of one master convincing and fail to do this with others. If one looks at Matisse's

"Goldfish and Sculpture," one cannot deny the artistry of this work. The same seems to me true with Rouault's "Three Judges." This is really very far from nature. Nevertheless, it has such a great expression, especially the central figure looks in such a manner at the criminal that it is very convincing.

There is certainly nothing in such works of the *épater le bourgeois* which might be observable in some others of the modernistic painters and sculptors. I would not deny the right to *épater le bourgeois* to a young artist. It is a matter of temperament and he might sometimes even do something which he would later perhaps not defend any longer. I have to admit that I applied these viewpoints, because I also applied them in music. In fact, I believe in stating all the technical requirements of musical art thoroughly before turning to modernistic forms. And I believe that there will always be a difference between those who went through these studies and learned everything which one can learn from preceding masters. The minimum is that they always learn at least a certain feeling of balance and of the limits of expression, not to forget the elaboration.

An idea in art must be presented in every section and segment of it. I would not go so far as the judgment of Mr. Huxley who finds that it is a unifying means to use only one face for all females. Why only the face? Why only the women? Is the rest not also included in this unity? Besides, this idea is very materialistic in producing unity by such a mechanical means. The face of a person in motion is not in a painting a very decisive fact. You will rather observe the motion than the face. I also would not call this a formal relationship, I would rather say it is a material relationship.

I personally believe in *l'art pour l'art*. In the creation of a work of art, nothing should interfere with the real idea. A work of art must elaborate on its own idea and follow the conditions which this idea establishes. This does not mean that an artist must have principles which he obeys and which he carries out under all circumstances. Such principles would probably be, in general, external and their application would certainly deprive a work of art from its natural conditions. There is perhaps only one principle which every artist should obey, that is: never to bow to the taste of the mediocre, to the taste of minor people who prefer that which an artist never would do. This does not mean that there does not exist a popular art which has its own viewpoints and its own code of honor even. I would say that the Viennese composer, Johann Strauss and the Viennese satiric poet, Johann Nestroy, and for instance the American, Gershwin, and Jacques Offenbach, had the capacity of expressing exactly what people think and feel. Their ideas would be on a direct level with the feelings and the ideas of the masses. There is nothing wrong in such creations, but it is wrong of a serious composer to write or include in his works such parts which he feels would please the audience or that would have a general effect. There is one great composer of whom one contended that he said—I don't believe it—"In every one of my works there must be a melody which the most stupid listener can understand." I don't believe it, as I have said. But I am sure that if it were true, there would only be idiotic listeners for his work—which was not the case.

The idea to combine serious writing with popular writing is entirely out of the way. Thus the idea of the communistic musicians to write music which is for everybody, and in which people can hear their old songs which they can understand entirely, is a crime on art. Besides, what I cannot understand is: that there exists such a necessity. Why should there not be music for the ordinary man, for the mediocre, for the un-understanding, for the uninitiated on the one hand, and on the other hand, such music for the few who understand? Is it necessary that a composer who can write for the few, just this same composer must also write for all? Is it not better if they are specialists, one writes for all, and the other writes for the few.

And the same seems true to me in art. At least the same standpoint.

Undeniably art has served frequently political purposes. One must not forget to mention the many poets who wrote political poems or dramas like fighters for liberty, and also those who wanted society changed. This goes on for a long time and has probably always been done. In music one should not forget Mozart with his *Marriage of Figaro* and his *Magic Flute* and Beethoven with his *Fidelio,* and doubtlessly caricaturists contributed much to political movements. It is curious that such works of art often have greatness even if they do not belong to the immortals. This shows how inadequate principles are, in general, because all depends on the inspiration. Probably one would have to admit such an idea can be the result of an inspiration of a politically convinced artist. I myself have written some pieces which are undeniably political. For instance, my *Ode to Napoleon* and perhaps one will find the same of my opera *Moses und Aaron.* I must admit in my inspiration I did not feel that I deviated from any artistic principle in this case.

I am not quite convinced that everybody is capable—this is to your question No. 10—of grasping the artistic values of Michelangelo and other artists whom you quote. But to a certain degree he sees something in them. He is certainly moved by some of its qualities. There is nothing surprising in it. Schopenhauer says that the appreciation of works of art and literature by the great is based, as he says, in *auctoritas*—we would say authority—and he means that so many responsible men had established the glory of this work, that nobody is in the position to deny it.

But it seems, also, to be the factor of the time which has passed since the creation which facilitates grasping its values. I myself have had so many experiences even in my short life, or call it long life, that works which at their first performances have been hissed and laughed-at are now very successful. For instance, my *Transfigured Night* and also others of my works are now accessible to almost everybody, while they had great misfortune in the beginning.

I, personally do not like the term "Modern" very much. It has too much the meaning of fashion, something which does not survive its time. I, personally, would rather say that Richard Wagner was right when he called his music "the art of the future." I mean, an artist should write so that the future will still appreciate what he did. Not only the present. This means for me—writing for the present—to write modern. Thus the word "contemporary" is in many cases more adequate. Many works of art are really only the work of people who lived at the same time and who will die at the same time.

To your question No. 12: The proposition of offering an alternative to modern art, seems to me quite out of the question. I wonder how serious men can make such a proposition. How would it be if you would make the same proposition to a scientist? That he should look for an alternate discovery in chemistry or physics. I mean one which has already been made, or to ask a chess player to make exactly the same moves as another master has done a hundred years ago. To me art is: new art. That which has never been said or done before—only that can be art, though it need not yet be art because there are still a number of other qualities which have to be present at the same time; but this is the minimum requirement—to be new in every respect.

To your question No. 15: I am quite convinced that the thinking and feeling of painters and sculptors and other artists is exactly the same as that of musicians. I mean the basic feeling, this that asks for creation, this urge to produce. This consideration might entitle me to answer as a musician that I do not believe that the possession of the fastest airplane, or the biggest atombomb, or of the cheapest refrigerator, has any influence on the quality of the creative work.

To your question No. 8: That so many great painters as Delacroix, Courbet, and composers as Debussy and poets like Victor Hugo and Flaubert have been attacked by hostile criticism, shows, in my opinion only how wrong critics always are. Please, would the critics who are present excuse this and not consider it as an attack. I myself, though I was never a critic in the newspaper, have given very many criticisms which I later considered very regrettably poor. Therefore I have concluded that I am very happy never to have been forced to publicly criticize works of art and have escaped the guilt which is connected with it.

To your question No. 5: Whether the art which corresponds to the complex society of ours would be of a definite excellence cannot be predicted. I believe it has nothing to do with it; it depends only if there is a genius who is capable of producing this excellence or not.

On the Founding of the State of Israel

7.16 "Israel Exists Again!" June 10, 1949

Text for an unfinished work for mixed chorus and orchestra. In addition to "Israel Exists Again!" Schoenberg completed two other choral works in honor of the 1948 founding of the State of Israel: Dreimal Tausend Jahre *[Three times a thousand years], Op. 50a (April 1949), and* Psalm 130, De Profundis, *Op. 50b (July 1950), both for mixed chorus.*

> *Israel exists again!*
> *It has always existed*
> *though invisibly.*
> *And since the beginning of time,*
> *since the creation of the world*
> *we have always seen the Lord,*
> *and have never ceased to see Him.*
> *Adam saw Him.*
> *Noah saw Him.*
> *Abraham saw Him.*
> *Jakob saw him.*
> *But Moses*
> *saw He was our God*
> *and we His elected people:*
> *elected to testify*
> *that there is only one eternal God.*
> *Israel has returned*
> *and will see the Lord again.*

Open Letter on His Seventy-Fifth Birthday

7.17 "To become recognized only after one's death—!" September 1949

Among the many recipients of this letter were Helene Berg, Edward Clark, Elizabeth Sprague Coolidge, Alma Mahler, Hans Nachod, Josef Rufer, Leonard Stein, Eduard Steuermann, and the Italian composer Luigi Dallapiccolla (1904–1975).

I have been given during these days much personal appreciation, which I have enjoyed immensely, because this showed me that my friends and other well-meaning people respect my aims and endeavors.

On the other hand, I have for many years closed my account with the world, in bowing to the fact that I may not hope for plain and loving understanding of my work, that is: of all I have to express in music, as long as I am alive. However, I know that many friends have familiarized themselves thoroughly with my manner of expression, and have acquired an intimate understanding of my ideas. They then might be such who carry out what I have predicted 37 years ago in an aphorism.

"The second half of this century will spoil by overestimation, all the good of me that the first half, by underestimation, has left intact."

I am somewhat embarrassed by so much eulogy. But, in spite of this, I find in it also some encouragement. Is it readily understandable, that one does not give up, though facing the opposition of a whole world?

I do not know how the Great felt in similar situations. Mozart and Schubert were too young to be forced to occupy themselves with these problems. But Beethoven, when Grillparzer called the Ninth abstruse, or Wagner, when his Bayreuth plans seemed to fail, Mahler, when everybody named him trivial—how could these men continue to write?

I know only one answer: to say what man must know.

Once, when serving in the Austrian Army, I was asked whether I was really "that composer," A. S.

"One had to be it," I said, "nobody wanted to be, so I volunteered."

———

And now, may I pray that you, all of you who procured for me real joy by honoring me and wishing me luck, accept this as an attempt at expression of my deeply felt gratitude.

Many cordial thanks.

On the Non-Performance of His Works

7.18 "To Twelve American Conductors," September 13, 1949

There is no record of this letter having been sent.

On the occasion of my seventy-fifth birthday I most cordially thank you for the numerous performances of my works from which you have refrained in the last fifteen years. You have thereby assured yourselves of a place of honor in the history of music, in my autobiography, and in my gallery of talentless cowards.

This letter will be sent to the following eleven of your peers and to twelve specially chosen international newspapers.

Arnold Schoenberg

P.S. My attorney tells me that you don't have to put up with this. But I say: you are much too cowardly to attack me. And I stand by my opinion by affixing my personal signature to it.

Arnold Schoenberg.

On Schenker's Theories

7.19 Letter to Roger Sessions, November 7, 1949

American composer Roger Sessions (1896–1985) was then at the Department of Music of the University of California at Berkeley. Their correspondence had started after the publication of Sessions's article "Schoenberg in the United States," in Tempo 9 *(1944).*[26]

Dear Friend:

You would do me a great favor if you would give Mr. Moritz Violin, a very old friend of mine with whom I have had a connection of friendship for at least fifty years, I mean, if you could give him a chance to talk to you about the manner in which he would like to give classes in piano playing at the University of California.

I wonder whether you know the Viennese theorist, Dr. Heinrich Schenker, who has published quite a number of books on harmony and counterpoint and especially on this theory of his—the *Urlinie*—if you have heard of it. Frankly, I was opposed to most of his conclusions, but on the other hand I have to admit that he has also made some very valuable analyses, (of the Beethoven Ninth for example), and has some new ideas in respect to understanding the thoughts of composers.

Mr. Moritz Violin was a friend and pupil of Dr. Schenker, and he believes in his theories and he has shown and explained to me some of the things which he does with his pupils, I don't know whether you will believe in these theories more than I do. To me they seem a little exaggerated at least, but I would not say they are untrue. There are things which it might be an advantage to know. I think I know everything about music without knowing this. But, if you see the effect which it makes when he has explained what he does, first playing how it is usually performed and how it can be played according to his theories, then you will perhaps admit, as I have had to admit, that this is very impressive. Mr. Violin is, of course, an excellent piano player. I must say, the difference is striking.

I would like now, if you could give him a chance to show you these things, and if it would really be possible to give him the chance to teach, I am certain something would come out of this, and certainly some who would take the thing seriously enough and learn something from Mr. Violin will have profited very much from this. I am sure of this, because Mr. Violin is a very serious man and a man of deep thinking and profound knowledge.

He calls this system, Applied Theory for Piano Playing. By this he means something which I would rather describe in this manner: recognition of some aesthetic features of a composition makes you see the piece in a different light; not only in many details, but also in total. I think this is what he will show you.

I would like it if you would inform me whether you can do this, and afterwards what was the result of your interview with Mr. Violin. I would be very glad if this very valuable man could get a position for which he has fought for many years, and you would do something good to a very serious man.

How is everything with you? When will you come again to Los Angeles? We will be glad to see you soon again.

With cordial greetings,

I am yours sincerely,

On Adorno's *Philosophy of Modern Music*

7.20 Letter to Kurt List, December 10, 1949

Theodor Wiesengrund Adorno was in Los Angeles between 1940 and 1949, as part of the Institut für Sozialforschung. His Philosophie der neuen Musik *was first published in 1949 (English translation as the* Philosophy of Modern Music *in 1973). List was not alone in receiving critical letters from Schoenberg about the book. Stuckenschmidt cites a December 5 letter he received that included the following: "So modern music has a philosophy—it would be enough if it had a philosopher. He attacks me quite vehemently in it. Another disloyal person . . . I have never been able to bear the fellow . . . now I know that he has clearly never liked my music . . . it is disgusting, by the way, how he treats Stravinsky. I am certainly no admirer of Stravinsky, although I like a piece of his here and there very much—but one should not write like that."[27]*

Dear Mr. List:

It surprises me that you so overestimate Wiesengrund. I believe you have not known him long enough. Over twenty years ago he published an enthusiastic article about me in *Anbruch*, which disgusted me with its hackwork style. I demonstrated in an example at the time that I could express a seven- or eight-line-long sentence in two lines with complete clarity. He already then used this blathering jargon, which so warms the hearts of philosophy professors when they introduce a new awkward expression. It looks so learned and profound but is actually only a mannerism to conceal the complete absence of an idea or insight. It is just such an "esoteric" style that Schopenhauer had in mind when he said, one must "express the most extraordinary ideas with the most ordinary words."

Wiesengrund's attack is an act of vengeance. Once when he was getting on my nerves, I made him look ridiculous, and although I thoroughly excused myself on account of nervousness, sickness, etc., he has apparently not forgiven me for this. He has found a clever solution to the dilemma that earlier he was a supporter of mine and especially of his teacher Alban Berg. He carves me up into two pieces—into which I certainly do not crumble, but out of which I am developmentally composed. Just like every other man, I am at one time younger and at another time older. But he intended to avoid the Nietzsche-Wagner model. Therefore he plays my middle period against my, presumably, last period. I have not read the book, but only parts of scattered pages—I can't choke down any more.

But he can't get past some difficulties. There he helps himself with lies. He claims to have written the book much, much earlier. But that is, at least so far as the attack is concerned, not true, for I know quite precisely that he made use of me highly enthusiastically in 1942 after the Second Chamber Symphony. I also believe that after the Piano Concerto he praised the piece in the highest tones (he speaks only in the highest tones). It must therefore be at least from after 1942, and that would be quite right; I insulted him around '44 or '45. I really believe that one should respond to him. Everything he says looks as if it were so very correct, but it actually proves nothing even if my music had the errors for which he reproaches me, for it could still be good music. But it is indeed not proven, only asserted.

One thing is very characteristic. One reproach is that when I repeat a theme I retain only the rhythm, not the intervals. This shows that he either really does not understand what is happening, or that he at least acts that way when it seems necessary for his attack, for he must know that the constant iteration of the row has the single goal of achieving logic through unity. And that if the rhythm were to be used (actually the rhythm is also not used precisely, but rather very freely) and the tones were different, the relationships of the tones would always stay the same through the whole piece. That is its only purpose. I believe it would be very easy to disprove him in many of these matters. Let me hear more precisely what you think about it.

I must close now. With best wishes,

Yours,

On Adorno and Composition with Twelve Tones

7.21 "Wiesengrund" (December 1950)

I could never really stand him. When he engulfed me with his piercing eyes, advancing on me ever nearer until a wall prevented further escape, I had to think, "Do you not breathe the sweet scents with me?"[28]—(like Nestroy's high priest Kalchas in *Orpheus* said when a roasted calf's tongue was brought to him: "How can one eat what another has already had in their mouth?")—and say to ward him off: "How can one want to breathe what another has already exhaled," if we are not Lohengrin and Elsa. And into the bargain: the "grandioso" of his statements, his oily pathos, his bombast, and the affected passion of his admiration.

But the worst took place in two episodes. Not without Rudi's [Rudolf Kolisch] fault, he was regarded in our circle as a great scholar. It cannot be disputed that he possesses certain estimable abilities. He is very musical, plays piano well, and possesses a great knowledge of the musical literature, from which he can play many pieces by heart due to his good memory. He has looked into musical-theoretical problems a great deal and with success, and he knows the history of our art most thoroughly.

These were the reasons I asked him if he would be willing to write a book with me, a lexicon of "compositional-theory concepts." I expected that he would contribute the historical, aesthetic, and philosophical fundamentals, while I (possibly in consultation with him) would have contributed formulations acquired through my compositional and teaching practice. He rejected this recommendation in an arrogant way: he is no musician, but a philosopher.

I couldn't say anything against that.

But when we all had to leave Germany, and I labored hard giving theory lessons to insufficiently prepared beginners (for very low pay) in order to earn a living for myself and my family, every Sunday afternoon—in these few hours of rest—I had a few friends over for conversation: in order to live a little at my previous level.

Then along came Mr. Wiesengrund. Instead of feeling sorry for me, however, about the will required to bring unprepared or talentless compositions in order, he played his own for me, desiring opinions, recommendations, improvements—in a word, work, just what I had been doing for the pay during the work week—for the pay! But he, the well-off one, did not give a thought if he should ask whether I, the penniless one, wanted to teach him for nothing.

I would have given lessons for nothing to any penniless professional musician of his ability (he had studied with Alban Berg).

But he had declared he was *no musician* when I wanted to write a book with him.

Now here he was suddenly a musician?[29]

But I must now return to the subject, unpleasant as it is to refute or elucidate someone who already through the formulation of the title of his book has lost the claim to be taken seriously. Grammar would have to ask: "whose philosophy?"—answer: "that of the new music," or: "what does the new music do?"—answer: "it philosophizes." Only a nonsensical formulation of a question can provoke such a nonsensical answer. That recalls the title of a famous book that foresaw the decline of a considerable continent, something I could expose as at least a linguistic impossibility.[30]

How often has the "decline" of our art been prophesied? I'm certain that it happens many times in every century that spiritual impotence rises up against the powers the new can produce. It is sad to be forced to admit that it was not always the most incapable who had lost all trust in the productive powers. These at least would have had the obligation of inferring the future from the past.

To the matter itself: the first thing to be established is the following: Wiesengrund's knowledge about composition with twelve tones is *not founded on the knowledge of my own explanations.*

When a few years after the First World War I invited my friends and acquaintances to take note of my recently developed new technique, I first explained what led me to it. Then I illustrated the use of the rows with examples from my most recent works. At the end I formulated my most important thesis: one follows the row, but otherwise composes as before.

Already then and ever afterward, I have made clear that this, my method—my method—is not the only way to a solution of the new problems but just one of the possibilities. The strict rules that were established, come—at least in this strict, restrictive form—only in the smallest part from me. Under the pressure of the apostles they have become harsher than is necessary. I neither intended to deter anybody from this method, nor did I want to invite them to the grounding of a school. I found it necessary to show the way that, over the course of around ten or twelve years, had led me to this method. It was my own way that guided me because of my feat: to write music without tonality.

In the fall of 1921, when I completed the first compositions based on this new method, I called Erwin Stein (today's Britten propagandist)[31] to come to Traunkirchen and asked him to guard as my secret for as long as I found it necessary what I thought to share with him. He gave me this promise and kept it loyally. When, however, I returned to Vienna some time later, I heard rumors about Josef Hauer's *Tropenlehre,* which would have made me appear as a plagiarist of Hauer. That wounded and disturbed me, and I had to resolve to comment on it. From the very beginning, I had recognized that the difference between me and Hauer presented itself as that between a (more or less good) composer and a highly interesting philosophical fabulist. To whom in the Vienna of those days would one have wanted to explain this? My friends would not have wanted to withdraw their trust from me, and I myself don't give a damn about such originality. *What* I have to say is important to me. But whether I say it with seven, twelve, or twenty-one tones is of very little importance.

I have indeed always said why I have felt pressed to introduce a method of composition with twelve tones. First: not as a method of composition but rather as a—as my—method of *composition with twelve tones*. It aims at replacing the form-building effect of functional harmony through another central force: through a row of unchanging tone relationships. It was, secondly, intended to regulate in *non-tonal music* the appearance of dissonant harmonies (but it would be superfluous in tonal harmony). I have, thirdly, emphasized countless times that one could certainly also employ *other* methods. I have fought against its being called a "system." Through a definition of both concepts, which are viewed as identical in America, I have made their difference clear: "Curiously and wrongly, most people speak of the 'system' of the chromatic scale. Mine is no system but only a method, which means a modus of applying regularly a preconceived formula. A method can, but need not be, one of the consequences of a system. I am also not the inventor of the chromatic scale; somebody else must have occupied himself with this task long ago."

On a Jewish National Music

7.22 "Four Statements," January 28, 1950

The challenges of creating a national music and determining how this would relate to European art music—especially modern music, Eastern European Jewish folk music, traditional liturgical music, and the many musics of the Middle East—were hotly debated in the new state of Israel.[32] *Schoenberg's compositional responses to the problem in* Dreimal Tausend Jahre, *and in* Psalm 130, De Profundis, *commissioned for the* Anthology of Jewish Music (1953), *reflect many of the same convictions evident in these four statements, which were in turn already prefigured in the letter to his cousin from sixty years before (see 1.8). For his appointment as honorary president of the Israel Academy of Music, see 7.30.*

I.) *Tradition:* What happens to a sentence, if along a line of men it is passed on only by whispering to one's neighbor, illustrates what tradition can have done to its originals.

II.) If only elements of the *biblical cantillation* should be used, why not also exclude all modern musical instruments and use only those of Bible-times. And how about Parisian-Pitch? How about well-tempered tonality?

III.) *Music has its own laws* and develops in accordance with them. If in spite of that, a national flavor is desired and possible—let it have it.
But why keep people away from *progress in music,* when they are allowed to profit from products of all technical, scientific, legal, social, medical, and philosophical progress?

IV.) It is curious that Jews are always the last ones to accept my achievements, whether in Israel or in the rest of the world. They perform everything: Debussy, Ravel, Hindemith, Stravinsky, Shostakovich, Bartok etc.—but not me! In spite of my contributions, they are my greatest enemies!

A Controversy with Copland

7.23 "For My Broadcast," August 22, 1949

Schoenberg became increasingly concerned about his own status in the United States as several members of the German émigré community in Los Angeles were brought before the Committee on Un-American Activities, most notably Hanns Eisler, who was questioned in 1947 and extradited the following year, eventually settling in East Berlin. In a letter of August 9, 1950, Schoenberg wrote to his attorney Milton Koblitz asking if he should sever ties with the conductor Hermann Scherchen (1891–1966) after hearing that he was a communist: "It would be a terrible loss for me if I had to break up communication with him. He is one of the most understanding musicians I know, and he has a great appreciation of my music and is an excellent performer of it. He has made great projects to perform parts of my Jakobsleiter *and* Moses and Aaron, *and wants to publish these scores and also books of mine. My loss would be very great. I want now your advice and if possible an official opinion about this problem. You know, I am anti-communism. I was never a communist and hate to be suspected of any wrong action in this respect."[33]*

Schoenberg's remarks below were broadcast in Los Angeles and then published in an article by Virgil Thomson in the New York Herald Tribune *that appeared on September 11, 1949, in conjunction with a concert of the Five Orchestral Pieces. While Schoenberg's statement focused on the opposition his music had faced, it was the concluding sentence linking Copland (1900–1990) and Stalin that precipitated the controversy, due in part to Copland's having met with Shostakovich in March 1949 at the Cultural and Scientific Conference for World Peace in New York.[34]*

Olin Downes in the *New York Times* expresses astonishment over a report that Twelve-Tone-Music is spreading out in all of Western Europe while "here one considered it to be a dying art." Let me correct this: one did not only *"consider"* it a dying art; one understood to *"corriger la fortune"* by *"making"* it a dying art.

When in 1933 I came to America I was a very renowned composer, even so that Mr. Goebbels himself in his "Der Angriff" reprimanded me for leaving Germany. Thanks to the attitude of most American conductors and under the leadership of Toscanini, Koussevitzki, and Walter, suppression of my works soon began with the effect that the number of performances of my works sunk to an extremely low point. A year ago I had counted in Europe alone about a hundred performances of my works. There was also opposition and violent propaganda against my music in Europe. But musical education was high enough to meet the opposition of the illiterate. Therefore there existed a satisfactory number of first class musicians who at once were able to recognize that logic, order and organization will be greatly promoted by application of the method of composing with twelve tones.

Even under Hitler, twelve-tone music was not suppressed as I have learned. On the contrary, it was compared to the idea of *Der Führer* by the German composer Paul von Klenau, who composed operas in this style.[35] In order to try to make this art a dying art, some agitators had to use a method, which I will baptize "the prefabricated history." Namely, assuming that history repeats itself, they compared our period to that of Bach, or rather of Telemann, Kaiser, and Mattheson. Even if this comparison is correct I can be very happy. Because we see how Bach has died, and how hale and hearty Telemann's, Keiser's and Mattheson's music is alive.

It should be discouraging to my suppressors to recognize the failure of their attempts. You cannot change the natural evolution of the arts by a command; you may make a New Year's resolution to write what everybody likes, but you cannot force real artists to descend to the lowest possible standard, to give up morals, character, and sincerity, to avoid presentation of new ideas. Even Stalin can not succeed and Aaron Copland even less.

A Political Affair

7.24 *"In Answer to Aaron Copland's Reply, December 23, 1949"*

Copland, who had become concerned about his own reputation in connection with communism, published a reply to Schoenberg in the New York Herald Tribune *on September 25, writing: "In America it is still possible (I hope) to share a forum platform with a man whose musical and political ideas are not one's own without being judged guilty by association. What Dmitri Shostakovich said during that visit, condemning the music of Stravinsky, Hindemith and Schoenberg, may make some sense as the statement of a citizen of the Soviet Union; but it certainly makes no sense over here. I dissociate myself from such an attitude absolutely."[36] Thomson did not publish Schoenberg's "answer," but sent it directly to Copland.*

I did not see a picture of Aaron Copland and Dmitri Shostakovich and I did not know about their discussion. But some of Mr. Copland's malicious remarks about my dwindling attractiveness to audiences had been reported to me. That, of course was mere propaganda and could be ignored.

But as a teacher who for about fifty years has worked hard to provide young people with the tools of our art, with the technical, esthetic and moral basis of true artistry, I could not stand it to learn that Mr. Copland had given young students who asked for it, the advice to use "simple" intervals and to study the masters. Much damage had been done to an entire generation of highly talented American composers, who, when they, in the same fashion were taught to write a certain style. It will certainly take a generation of sincere teaching until this damage can be repaired.

And only in this respect did I couple Mr. Copland with Stalin: they both do not consider musical composition as an art to present musical ideas in a dignified manner, but they want their followers to write a certain style, that is to create an external appearance, without asking about the inside.

This I must condemn.

But otherwise, if my words could be understood as an attempt to involve Mr. Copland in a political affair, I am ready to apologize—This was not my intention.

A Peace Offering

7.25 Letter to Aaron Copland, February 21, 1950

Copland wrote Schoenberg a conciliatory letter on February 13, to which Schoenberg replied in the letter below. In the spring of 1950, Copland adopted the twelve-tone method for his Quartet for Piano and Strings.[37]

Dear Mr. Copland:

Your letter from February 13 pleases me very much. True, I am a fighter, but not an attacker. I "backfire" only, when I have been attacked. But otherwise it is very easy to live in peace with me. I am always inclined to do justice to every merit and to sincerity. And I am sure that the Hungarian pianist who played your music (and Bartok's) for me about a year ago in my home (I cannot remember his name) will have told you that I appreciated your music without any restriction.

But there is at least one man here in Los Angeles who goes around forbidding people to "make propaganda" for Schoenberg, when they only speak about facts. And CBS has evidently intended to hit *me*, when they ordered "no controversial music" to be broadcast—while they broadcast quite a number of controversial music from other composers. And you might know also about the attitude of "MY" publisher G. Schirmer, who if possible tries to counteract performances of my music . . . and many other similar facts.

You will perhaps understand then that I become inclined to believe people, who told me that you uttered surprise about the difference of attention paid to me here by audiences—in contrast to New York. How am I to know that this might be only gossip to sow discord? I believe that there are people who aim for production of enmity between public figures, but, considering the facts I know, I have no way of discrimination.

When I said at the beginning of this letter that your letter pleases me very much, I can repeat this now, adding that I am always ready to live in peace, because I strongly believe that at least my sincerity deserves recognition and respect, so I am in the position to consider merits of other composers with kindness.

I don't want to conclude this letter without mentioning the great danger which the American nationalism might provoke. Will it not finally degenerate into anti-Semitism? We have seen such things.

I am with best greetings,

Yours,

On Twelve-Tone Composition and Various Activities in 1950

7.26 Letter to Josef Rufer, April 8, 1950

Rufer had written to Schoenberg concerning his preparations for the book Die Komposition mit zwölf Tönen, *which was published in 1952.*[38] *Some excerpts of Schoenberg's letter were directly quoted in the book (see* Composition with Twelve Tones, *pp. 94–95).*

Dear Friend:

I have assembled all your questions and now want to endeavor to answer them. Perhaps in the future you could do as you did in 1920 when you always sent me questionnaires to Holland in two copies with the questions on the right and room for my answers on the left. That would save me a lot of time, for I have to leave a great many letters unanswered because I don't have enough time.

The *Violin Phantasy* has not yet appeared; a photocopy of it would cost $5. Should I order it?[39]

It couldn't hurt to ask Scherchen about the *Violin Phantasy* and a German edition of *Style and Idea*. But since I must live on these earnings, a royalty and percentages come very much into the question.

I would rather hand over *Style and Idea* and a book containing poetry, texts, aphorisms, and sayings to the Atlantis publishing house, if they could pay a good advance on royalties. What is their reputation? Don't you want to request them to write to me directly about whether they would be interested? The quartet analyses will appear in my second book.[40] Both books, in English, would first have to be translated into German.

Leibowitz's athematic music: that goes back forty years to when I maintained the same thing for a short time. But I soon recanted, for coherence in music can be founded on nothing other than motives and their transformation and development. Haba also then took it up as his own idea, naturally without knowing that I was the first who raised this question.[41] I am also completely of your opinion that Leibowitz, intelligent as he is, frequently exaggerates: not all that doesn't glitter isn't gold, and something can be thematic that does not at all appear to be. The additional half of a row he mentioned is also incorrect. In the Third String Quartet I merely used, out of fear of monotony, the row succession of the consequent in two forms, while the antecedent, the first six tones, remained unchanged. It does not seem right to me to use more than one row, but the main thing is certainly whether the music is good. From which principles it is produced is a question of the second or third order.

I can only answer your question about Krenek's being housebroken with the most discretion: I believe he is respectable, although he is one of those who would gladly "buy their own revolver" in order to be more self-assured.

So now to questions from your older letters. January 29: my health is better for the moment. I had misplaced your letter of December 16. We received the *Pierrot* and trio recordings. I recently heard the trio, it is technically not as good as Koldofsky, but musically is presented much more fluently. I hope to hear *Pierrot* next.[42] In the last months I haven't composed anything, but I have written a great deal. Whether Bomart will indeed write to you, I do not know.[43] They are bloody amateurs.

It pleases me that Robert Heger has approached us.[44] It would be fine if he would take you to Munich.

I am glad that Zillig has again secured his position. The *Pelleas* disc (Capitol-Telefunken) is really very good. In the Pieces for Orchestra he frequently took tempi that were much too slow. It would be best if he could do them again, since Peters is bringing out a new revised score.[45]

I would be very thankful to Fricsay, RIAS, if he would raise a scandal with Schirmer and demand that they send him decent parts for the suite.[46] But vigorously.

I have received *Stimmen*, nos. 16–19. But not the book from Roh. I can send you an article for *Stimmen* any time. Why can't Stuckenschmidt translate it? His English is good.

It will not often happen that one gets all at once, as the first inspiration, a complete and usable row. A little touching up is usually necessary. But the character of the piece is already present in the first form of the row. This touching up is based primarily on constructive considerations. For example, out of fear of monotony I try to avoid having it that one of the forms ends with the same tones that another begins with and inverts. I personally try to make the row so that the inversion of the first six tones a fifth lower yields the remaining six tones. The consequent, the seventh through twelfth tones, is another ordering of the second six tones. That has the advantage that one can accompany melodic parts of the first six tones with harmonies from the second six tones without getting doublings. As you know, I don't think much of these canons. The canon in itself is a representative of a primitive form which could not yet develop through variation and which could only produce coherence through canonic repetition. The only merit of canon is that it is able to escape from the old laws of consonance and dissonance. But here it is has merely to escape from a single consonance, that is not enough thereby to earn merit. But as I said, the main thing is: whether the music says something. Then one can gladly excuse one or more faults. Only don't be pedantic. Invention and expression, logic and the flow of the presentation are real values.

What you write about Boris Blacher is very gratifying. I hope to hear from him soon. Likewise Varga is very gratifying.[47]

Furtwängler is a great ass. He is a good musician, and I have made a lot of propaganda for him here, in particular because Toscanini, the ape, is so incredibly overrated. This one is a good musical sergeant, like Zit for the Komzak, 84th Infantry Regiment in Vienna was. But the way he performs German music is ridiculous, and I have always advised people to listen to Furtwängler recordings. And this is now my thanks from this ass, for whom I have even written a letter to Kurt List: not merely a rejection, but taking up a directly hostile position against me.

As far as the translation of my article "A Self-Analysis" is concerned, I unfortunately cannot help you. I have read a bit of it and have seen that in one regard one is better, and another time the other is. Couldn't Stuckenschmidt help?

I believe that now I have answered everything and would only still like to thank you for your kind greetings to me and my family, and to return them just as warmly to you and yours from all of us,

Most warmly yours,

Concerning a Performance of *A Survivor from Warsaw*

7.27 *Two Letters to Dimitri Mitropoulos, April 26 and July 4, 1950*

Dimitri Mitropoulos (1896–1960), who had studied piano with Busoni, conducted the Minneapolis Symphony Orchestra (1937–1949), and then the New York Philharmonic, starting in 1949 following the resignation of Stokowski.

Dear Mr. Mitropoulos:

I was very disappointed that you, whose speech upon your belief in contemporary music I had heard, did not broadcast my *Survivor from Warsaw*. Frankly, I would not have allowed a performance without a broadcast.

Furthermore, I would like to learn whether Mr. Olin Downes was right when he wrote about an action—I say action in a cantata—according to which the singers took off their coats.

It seems to me that you should have seen that I did not compose such an action, not only because of higher taste, but also because the concert stage is not a theatre.

I am looking forward to your explanations.

Yours truly,

Dear Mr. Mitropoulos;

Believe me, it was not my intention to hurt you. I appreciate your friendship toward me too highly to do this. It was an unfortunate circumstance which made me write in so sharp a manner. When I read Olin Downes' malicious report about your "choreographic" addition to the *Survivor,* I was still furiously excited about Mr. Leibowitz's violation of my artistic intention, who recorded the *Ode* with a woman, the part which I wrote in the bass clef.[48] This record has since been sold in France in spite of my protest. I am very precise in my expression. If I want other than a musical motion, it would certainly show up in the whole style of the work. Whether I write chamber music, or something with a text, makes a great difference in my conception. You cannot change anything without reducing the effect which should be derived from the work.

You are right, at my age I should not be anymore as temperamental as I was—very much to my disadvantage—during my whole life. True, I lost many friends and won only their respect. Thus nothing has been left to me except to hope that people who understand me will continue to perform my music, even if they dislike my behavior.

On His Health from Childhood to 1950

7.28 *"Gentlemen: My case differs in some respects from the average,"* August 2, 1950

Gentlemen:

My case differs in some respects from the average. This is why I think it might be valuable if I augment your very conclusive questionnaire by some facts of my life.

As a child I was often very sick. I remember that I used to hold up my arms because it facilitated my breathing. Several times in my life I suffered from an inflammation of the eardrum, supposedly a consequence of scarlet fever. My hearing capacity was often reduced by that for short periods.

In 1890 there was a tremendous influenza epidemic in Europe, which caused many deaths. My father, who was a heavy drinker and smoker, and suffered from asthma, died also in this epidemic. The cause of death was stated as edema and emphysema. I myself, then 16, suffered three attacks of influenza. Subsequently, during about 12–15 years I had every spring and fall a heavy attack of influenza (I called them recidives) which gradually became less severe.

Thereafter, I don't remember any severe asthma. I was breathless after exercises or climbing stairs, but I cannot remember any attack. 1915, serving in the Austrian army, I was discharged from front service, on account of asthma, whose symptoms were: heavy coughing and breathlessness. I was also a very strong drinker and smoker. After the first world war I acquired again an influenza, which was then a world-wide epidemic, called the Spanish Grippe. A consequence of that was probably that I now was awakened many a night by breathlessness and coughing. I was then examined by the renowned Viennese, Professor Chvostek, who could not determine any constitutional disease and also denied that smoking and drinking of alcohol could cause my trouble.

I gave up smoking and drinking and that really helped me considerably. At this time I was assured that I was well. A few days after I had taken to abstinence, I stopped coughing and did not become breathless.— Unfortunately, less than two years later I had returned to the two vices, with the result that all the evil consequences reappeared.

In all this time I had not used any drugs. My only attempt to fight asthma consisted in inhaling the smoke of a French Asthma Powder, which helped.—But in all these years I have never ceased to exercise my body by swimming, rowing, jumping, playing tennis, Ping-Pong, and other games.

In 1923/24 before I married my second wife, I was drinking again and inhaling 60 cigarettes every day. In order to conquer the evil consequences, I acted foolishly. I drank, besides liquor, every day 3 liters of strong coffee, took codeine and pantopon. It helped me a little, though basically it became worse. But during my honeymoon in Venice I possessed the willpower to give up all my aforementioned vices, in consequence of which I gained again a "respirium" of about two years.

In 1926 I had an appendicitis operation which had no influence on my health.

In all the following years I had always periods of two years, when I did not smoke or drink, but only in 1944 I abandoned smoking for good, but not yet drinking, which only now I have restricted to an occasional glass of whisky or cognac.

I should mention that I continued playing tennis until 1942—I was 68 years of age. I feel I should not yet have stopped it then. Because of the need to breathe very deeply after running for a ball or hitting it hard, I ascribed the better stage of my asthma. I had in these years only a little trouble therefrom.

I have now to report the peculiar case of what I call my *"Todesfall"* (decease). On August 2, 1946, our family doctor tried against my asthma a new drug "Benzydrin." An hour or two thereafter, during lunch, I became suddenly sleepy, went to bed—which was quite unusual for me. About ten o'clock in the evening, I awoke, jumped out of bed and hurried to sit in a *fauteuil* (used in asthma attacks). A very heavy pain started at once in my whole body, especially in the chest and around the heart. After attempting for half an hour to get a doctor, a friend sent Dr. Lloyd Jones, our present family physician, who then saved my life. I thought I had had a heart attack, but he did not find my heart to be the cause. He gave me an injection of Dilaudid, in order to ease my pain. This helped instantly; but after ten minutes I lost consciousness, had no heart beat or pulse and stopped breathing. In other words, I was practically dead. It has never been revealed to me how long his lasted. The only thing I was told is that Dr. Jones had given me an injection straight into the heart.

It took three weeks ere I recovered. I got about 160 injections of penicillin; heart and lungs were checked, X-ray pictures were taken and there were sometimes 3 or 4 doctors present, consulting and discussing my case. But most of all I am obliged to the great care and deep intuition of Dr. Lloyd Jones.

I have now to state that at no time a weakness of my heart was established. My asthma has undergone some little changes: I have seldom a severe attack, but rather the state of breathlessness is more or less chronic. Only for 4 or 5 hours in the day time I feel free and almost every night I awake because of being short of breath. I then often cough for 2 or 3 hours and only when I am exhausted enough I can sleep again—only to go through the same ordeal in the morning.

For several months I do not dare to sleep in my bed, but only in a chair. Various treatments have been administered to me. I was treated for diabetes, angina pectoris, pneumonia, kidney, hernia, dropsy. I suffer from fainting spells and dizziness and my eyes, formerly extremely good, make reading for me difficult.

Draft for a Preface to *Style and Idea*

7.29 *"To My Dead Friends," c. 1950*

This preface was ultimately not used when Style and Idea *was published in 1950.*

To my dead friends,
to my spiritual kindred,
to my
> Anton von Webern
> Alban Berg
> Heinrich Jalowetz
> Alexander von Zemlinsky
> Franz Schreker
> Adolf Loos
> Karl Kraus

to all those men to whom I could talk in the manner I speak in some parts of this book.

They belong to those with whom principles of music, art, artistic morality and civic morality need not be discussed. There was a silent and sound mutual understanding in all these matters. Except that every one of us was constantly occupied with deepening and holding more strictly[49] those principles and refining them to the last point.

On His Appointment as Honorary President of the Israel Academy of Music

7.30 *Letter to Oedoen Partos, April 26, 1951*

Israeli composer and string player Oedoen Partos (1907–1977) became the director of the Israel Academy of Music in 1951.

Mr. O. Partos,

I accept my appointment as Honorary President of the Israel Academy of Music with pride and satisfaction but feel, by the same token, that I should explain why I consider it so important that you chose me in particular for that distinction.

I told your friends, who visited me recently here in Los Angeles, as I told you, esteemed Director Partos, how for over four decades it was my most ardent wish to witness the creation of an independent Israeli state. And more than that: to become a resident citizen of that state.

Whether my health will grant me fulfillment of this second wish, I cannot say at the moment. I do hope to be able, at any rate, to arrange it so that the greatest possible number of my many compositions, literary works and articles, which I produced with an eye on the artistic propagation of my plans, will get into your hands for the Israel National Library. How much I would like to contribute personally to the institution's direction and instruction I cannot express in words. I was always an impassioned teacher. I have always felt the urge to find out what is most helpful to beginners, how to imbue them with a sense of the technical, intellectual, and ethical prerequisites of our art; how to convey to them that there is such a thing as artistic morality and why one must never cease to cultivate it and, conversely, to oppose as forcefully as possible anyone who commits an offence against it.

Unfortunately, I must give up any further thought of such wishes. But it seems to me that the half century by which my experience antedates that of many of my colleagues authorizes me to explain what I would have attempted to make of this institution, had I the good fortune and the strength as yet to do something along these lines.

And here I address myself with my warmest good wishes to the Director, Mr. O. Partos.

I would have tried to give this Academy universal significance so as to place it in a position to serve as an alternative for a mankind that caters in so many ways to an amoral, business-inspired materialism. A materialism behind which any ethical assumptions of our art are rapidly disappearing. A universal model cannot condone half-knowledge. It cannot train instrumentalists whose greatest skill is their ability to comply to perfection with the universal demand for entertainment.

From such an institution must go forth true priests of art who confront art with the same sense of consecration that the priest brings to God's altar. For, just as God chose Israel whose task it is to preserve, in spite of all suffering, the pure, true, mosaic monotheism, so it behooves Israeli musicians to offer the world a model possessed of the unique capacity to make our souls function once more in ways apt to further the development of humanity toward ever higher goals.

These are my wishes, and if I should be able to serve you with additional comments or explanations regarding certain details, I can only hope that you'll call on me.

Arnold Schoenberg

On Prayer, Superstition, and the Child's Faith

7.31 From the Modern Psalms, 1950–1951

Originally envisioned as a large collection to be entitled "Psalms, Prayers, and Other Conversations with and about God," Schoenberg worked on the Modern Psalms *in 1950 and 1951, with the last of the sixteen written on July 3, 1951, ten days before his death on July 13. An eighty-six-measure setting for Sprechstimme, chorus, and orchestra exists of the* Modern Psalm, No. 1, *breaking off after the words, "For all that, I pray . . . " (the beginning of this draft is given in fig. 7-2). Schoenberg first numbered this poem "151," to signal the relation of the set to the Biblical Psalms.*

Modern Psalm, No. 1, September 29, 1950

> *O Thou my God, all peoples praise Thee*
> *and assure Thee of their devotion.*
> *But what can it mean to Thee, if I also do that or not?*
> *Who am I that I should believe my prayer is a necessity?*
> *When I say God, I know that I speak of the Unitary, Eternal, All-Powerful,*
> *Omniscient, and Unrepresentable, of whom I neither can nor may make*
> *an image. On whom I neither may nor can make a demand, who shall*
> *fulfill my most fervent prayer or not notice it.*
> *And for all that, I pray, as all that lives prays; for all that, I beg for mercies*
> *and miracles: fulfillments.*
> *For all that, I pray, for I don't want to lose the blissful feeling of unity, of*
> *union with Thee.*
> *O Thou my God, Thy mercy has left us prayer as a connection, as a blissful*
> *connection with Thee. As a supreme bliss which gives us more than*
> *would every fulfillment.*

Modern Psalm, No. 6, December 31, 1950

It is the arrogance of the Philistine scientific atheists, which brings them to look down with such great contempt on the superstitious. They hate above all the faith of the superstitious, and don't perceive that in it there always exists a kernel of a more profound truth, even if such underlying knowledge transformed through veiling additions appears as mystery.
Admittedly, that the cards or stars never lie is a false interpretation at the least. Of course, in the event they reflect something really prophetic that pertains to us, they say such mysteries in a language we don't understand. Their mode of expression is just as mysterious as their constellations' predictions of future fortunes.

What truly moves us in superstition is the faith of the superstitious, his faith
in mysteries. His is a true and profound faith, and it is so closely related
to faith in all that is true and profound that one is often accompanied by
the other.

The learned Philistine abhors mysteries, because they reveal that which can
never be proven.

Modern Psalm *(Unnumbered)*, *"Why for Children?" March 28 to July 2, 1951*

Children don't question the unquestionable, if they are not specially trained
to do so. The child's faith is a fragment of the consciousness of eternity
and infinity which they should protect if they descend into the world of
our problems and doubts. It is the adults whose imagination's capacity
fails to understand the fact of eternity and infinity. They are the ones
who require the assistance, to whom one would have to provide the
spiritual power through stirring examples and tales to make their
imagination's capacity productive.

In their own language, in the language of the Enlightenment of which they
are so proud, one must show them the insufficiency of such
Enlightenment; Enlightenment that only darkens what in itself is full of
light enough.

Notes

Introduction

1. This seeming overabundance of interpretation has led Allen Shawn to preface his recent study with the remark, "It is not entirely in a spirit of facetiousness that I have said to friends that I feel perhaps Schoenberg's work deserves a more superficial treatment than it has hitherto received." *Arnold Schoenberg's Journey* (New York: Farrar, Straus, and Giroux, 2002), p. xx.
2. *SI*, pp. 214–245, 79–92.
3. E.o. ASC T31.16 (undated).
4. *SI*, p. 469.
5. It is noteworthy that even this essay on Mahler is known in a version from 1948 that differs significantly from its first incarnation in 1912. For a study of another essay that went through many versions before its final publication, Schoenberg's influential "Brahms the Progressive" (*SI*, pp. 398–441), see Thomas McGeary, "Schoenberg's Brahms Lecture of 1933," *JASI* 15/2 (1992): 5–21.
6. *SI*, pp. 482–483.
7. *H*, p. 1.
8. See *SP* and *GS*.
9. Schoenberg's *Nachlaß*, along with newly acquired materials, and a collection of secondary sources was housed at the Arnold Schoenberg Institute in Los Angeles (ASI) from 1977 to 1997, and then at the Arnold Schönberg Center in Vienna (ASC), starting in 1998.
10. *C*, pp. 109–110. And see Walter Bailey, "Filling in the Gaps: Jean and Jesper Christensen's *From Arnold Schoenberg's Literary Legacy, a Catalog of Neglected Items,*" *JASI* 12/1 (1989): 91–97.
11. See Thomas McGeary, "The Publishing History of *Style and Idea,*" *JASI* 9/2 (1986): 181–209.
12. E.o. LC.
13. The bulk of Schoenberg's letters are held at the Library of Congress (LC). For a detailed catalogue of the correspondence with much additional useful bibliographic material, see Paul Zukofsky, R. Wayne Shoaf, Stephen Davison, Marilyn McCoy, Camille Crittenden, Jacob Vonk, "A Preliminary Inventory

of Correspondence to and from Arnold Schoenberg," *JASI* 18/1-2; 19/1-2 (1995–1996): 9-752.

14. *ASL*, p. 110.
15. *SK*, p. 89.
16. *BSC*, p. 445.
17. *SI*, p. 144.
18. E.o. LC. The American pianist, composer, and author Dika Newlin (1923–) studied with Schoenberg at UCLA, edited and translated *SI* (1950), and has written many books and articles about Schoenberg.
19. E.o. LC and ASC T66.12.
20. Additional information on many of the sources can be found in *SI, GS,* C, Rufer, and *SW*; facsimiles of some items are published in *LB*. The web page of the Arnold Schönberg Center ⟨www.schoenberg.at⟩ also includes detailed catalogues of the *Nachlaß* as well as many facsimiles. For further information on all of Schoenberg's works see Gerold Gruber, ed., *Arnold Schönberg: Interpretationen seiner Werke* (Laaber: Laaber, 2002).

Chapter 1: Early Years in Vienna and Berlin

1. Omitted in the list of works are the *Cabaret Songs,* or *Brettl-Lieder,* from 1901, which Schoenberg wrote at the time of his involvement with the first German cabaret, Ernst von Wolzogen's Buntes Theater [Motley Theater]. Also known as the "Überbrettl," a Nietzschean play on the word *Brettl,* or "stage boards," the theater opened in Berlin in January 1901, closing May 1902. Schoenberg's contract is given in Stuckenschmidt, pp. 537–538. The song texts were taken from the collection *Deutsche Chansons,* published in 1900 and edited by Otto Julius Bierbaum, containing verses by Richard Dehmel, Gustav Falke, Frank Wedekind, Wolzogen, and others. Of the *Cabaret Songs,* only "Nachtwandler," for soprano, trumpet, piano, and snare drum, was performed at the Buntes Theater. See Peter Jelavich, *Berlin Cabaret* (Cambridge, Mass., and London: Harvard University Press, 1993), pp. 36–61.
2. Alban Berg (1885–1935) had little formal musical training before beginning his studies with Schoenberg in 1904; Webern (1883–1945) began his composition lessons on the advice of Guido Adler from the University of Vienna, where Webern wrote a dissertation on the Renaissance composer Heinrich Isaac.
3. For more details on the publication history of the *Theory of Harmony,* see 2.16.
4. *Preliminary Exercises in Counterpoint,* ed. Leonard Stein, was published in 1963.
5. Published in 1967, ed. Gerald Strang and Leonard Stein.
6. Mostly composed 1900 to 1901, completed 1911.
7. *Begleitungsmusik zu einer Lichtspielszene,* Op. 34.
8. Started in 1906 and worked on at several points before its completion in 1939; see 3.18.

9. Also omitted, *Variations on a Recitative,* for organ, Op. 40 (1941).

10. See 6.19.

11. Irish folk song later set by Beethoven and used as the basis of a piano fantasia by Mendelssohn.

12. Schoenberg's grades for his last full semester in school, class 5, from the 1889/1890 school year, were as follows: "German, Praiseworthy; French, Praiseworthy; English, Satisfactory; History, Praiseworthy; Mathematics, Praiseworthy; Natural History (Zoology), Sufficient; Chemistry, Satisfactory; Practical Geometry, Satisfactory; Free Drawing, Satisfactory; Stenography, Praiseworthy; Work in Chemical Lab, Satisfactory; Outward Appearance of Written Work, Commendable; General Progress Class, First; Moral Behavior, Satisfactory; Industry, Satisfactory; Number of Lessons Missed, Excused 13; Received a Report, 5.7.1890; School Fees, Exempt." Cited in Stuckenschmidt, p. 536.

13. Cited and discussed in C, pp. 9–10. G.o. ASC T 04.07.

14. G.o.

15. Steven J. Cahn, "Variations in Manifold Time: Historical Consciousness in the Music and Writings of Arnold Schoenberg" (Ph.D. dissertation, State University of New York at Stony Brook, 1996), pp. 125–128.

16. A handwritten note in the margin adds that this uncle Fritz Nachod had taught Schoenberg French while he was in school. Stuckenschmidt reports that Nachod "loved poetry, especially Schiller's and he wrote some poems himself." Of the Nachod family in general, Stuckenschmidt writes: "The Nachods were an old Jewish Prague family, whose male members for many generations had been cantors of the Altneuschul, Prague's chief synagogue. They inherited vocal and musical talent. Pauline had two sisters and three brothers. All six children seemed to have come with their parents to Vienna when they were young. Pauline's brother Gottlieb had two sons of whom the elder Walter Josef Nachod, became an operatic singer. Another brother of hers, Friedrich Nachod, also had two sons of whom Hans had a notable career as an operatic tenor. The newly married couple opened a shoe shop which more or less supported the family. A first baby boy died immediately after his birth." Stuckenschmidt, p. 16, 18.

17. Of Samuel Schoenberg, Ringer writes, "His father, a native of Szécheny in Hungary, had lived and worked in Preßburg, the later Slovak capital of Bratislava, before moving on to Vienna. . . . it was [Arnold Schoenberg's] Czech background which at the moment of gravest danger [in 1933] enabled the composer and his family to reach safety abroad, thanks to a cooperative Czechoslovakian consul willing to issue urgently needed passports." Ringer, p. 161. Schoenberg's father's Hungarian roots, however, also played a role in his release from active service in the Austrian Army in the First World War, with the intervention of the Society of Hungarian Musicians, whose secretary was Béla Bartók. Stuckenschmidt, p. 240.

18. Stuckenschmidt describes both Schoenberg's father and his uncle, Fritz Nachod, as being "idealistic free thinkers," in contrast to which, "Pauline

Schoenberg maintained the conservative principle in the family." Stuckenschmidt, p. 18. The term *freethinker* [*Freisinniger*] referred to an adherent of Reform Judaism, which viewed Judaism as subject to historical development and change and thus as adaptable to present-day circumstances (see further 1.8). Cahn, "Variations in Manifold Time," pp. 127–128.

19. For further information on Schoenberg's earliest works see Frisch, *The Early Works of Arnold Schoenberg, 1893–1908* (Berkeley and Los Angeles: University of California Press, 1993), pp. 20–75.

20. Oskar Adler (1875–1955), physician, philosopher, violinist, performed at the Society for Private Musical Performances; later wrote *The Testament of Astrology*.

21. David Joseph Bach (1874–1947), worked as music critic for the Viennese socialist newspaper the *Arbeiterzeitung*. He was founder in 1905 of the Workers' Symphony Concerts (conducted in the 1920s by Webern). After WWI, he served as cultural adviser to the Social Democratic Party in Vienna. Emigrated to London in 1938; also traveled to the U.S., see 6.5.

22. Alexander von Zemlinsky (1871–1942). Composer and conductor; studied at the Vienna Conservatory; from 1899 conductor of Carlstheater in Vienna; 1911–1928 conductor of the Deutsches Landestheater in Prague; 1927–1930 at the Kroll Opera in Berlin; emigrated to the U.S. in 1938. In 1900 and 1901 he had a romantic relationship with Alma Schindler, ending when she became involved with Gustav Mahler. Schoenberg married Zemlinsky's sister Mathilde in 1901.

23. Letter to Ferenc Molnar, October 4, 1943. E.o. LC.

24. With Zemlinsky's help, the D-major quartet (summer 1897) was premiered at a private performance of the Wiener Tonkünstlerverein on March 17, 1898. It was then revised following Zemlinsky's suggestions. The Fitzner Quartet gave the first public performance of the revised version at the Bösendorfersaal of the Gesellschaft der Musikfreunde on December 20, 1898. Frisch, *The Early Works of Arnold Schoenberg*, pp. 32–33.

25. Stuckenschmidt, p. 25.

26. From an excerpt of a letter given in *LB*, p. 17.

27. Cahn, "Variations in Manifold Time," pp. 128–129.

28. See R. John Specht, "Schoenberg Among the Workers: Choral Conducting in Pre-1900 Vienna," *JASI* 10/1 (1987): 28–37.

29. Schoenberg, "My Attitude Toward Politics" (1950), in *SI*, p. 505.

30. See Bryan R. Simms, "Schoenberg's Early Fragmentary Operas" (forthcoming). As Simms points out, there are many parallels between *Odoakar* and Schoenberg's later texts for *Die glückliche Hand* (2.13) and *The Biblical Way* (5.8).

31. In 1906 he made sketches for an opera on Gerhart Hauptmann's *Und Pippa tanzt*. Stuckenschmidt, p. 86.

32. Schoenberg used various spellings for the main character: "Odoacker" in the libretto itself, and "Odoakar" on the title page.

33. Gaiseric led the Vandal invaders of Italy until Odoacer took over the territory.

34. From this point on the manuscript is heavily revised, with several illegible passages.
35. Schoenberg would avoid the number 13 where possible, including numbering measures in his manuscripts: 11, 12, 12a, 14. On his numerological interests, see "Faith and Symbol," in Ringer, pp. 176–191.
36. Cross, "Schoenberg's Earliest Thoughts on the Theory of Composition: A Fragment from c. 1900," *Theoria: Historical Aspects of Music Theory* 8 (1994), p. 129 (with slight modifications).
37. Possibly Nietzsche, though a later reference reads "N. N."
38. A marginal note here reads: "departure—father wants to marry her off—confidence in conversation—appointment and confirmation."
39. The precise coordination of the musical sketch given in the example with the action is not indicated in the text.
40. Cited in Frisch, *The Early Works of Arnold Schoenberg*, 66.
41. November 16, 1913. Joachim Birke, "Richard Dehmel und Arnold Schönberg: Ein Briefwechsel," *Die Musikforschung* 2 (1958), p. 285.
42. Examples are identified by rehearsal number or letter; thus R2, 1–3 indicates the first three measures of rehearsal number 2; R+3, 1–2 indicates the two measures starting three measures after rehearsal number 2. R2-5 indicates five measures before rehearsal number 2.
43. Before composing *Verklärte Nacht,* Schoenberg started three other programmatic works, *Hans im Glück* (based on the German fairy tale), *Frühlings Tod* (Nicholas Lenau), and *Toter Winkel* (Gustav Falke).
44. Translation from Mark Benson, "Arnold Schoenberg and the Crisis of Modernism" (Ph.D. dissertation, University of California Los Angeles, 1988), p. 74.

I.   I. Melisande, Fate
   II. Golaud, timid Melisande   Fate: large
   III. Golaud, Melisande   Fate: large warning
II.   I. Melisande dreamy, Pelleas youthful:
      King Arkel, Premonition, Restrained
      Love motive and Fate motive (I.)
   II. Ring lost, Golaud . . . Ring sought.
      Love motive and Fate motive II. greater force
   III. Golaud suspicious, Jealousy, Menace and Mistrust:
      Golaud and Yniold, Grotto, Atmosphere of disaster . . .
      change toward Melisande
   IV. Love scene (large and broad) Fate motive
      Jealousy—Golaud kills Pelleas and wounds Melisande
III.   I. Atmosphere of disaster
   II. Golaud and Melisande, Entrance of the servants
   III. Melisande's expiring

45. Oskar Fried (1871–1941) conducted the work with the Blüthner Orchestra in Berlin, October 31, 1910. Stuckenschmidt, p. 134.

46. Henry-Louis de La Grange, *Gustav Mahler: Volume 2, Vienna: The Years of Challenge (1897–1904)* (Oxford and New York: Oxford University Press, 1995), pp. 687–688.

47. Wolfgang Behrens, "Der Komponist Oskar C. Posa, 1873–1951" (M.A. thesis, Free University Berlin, 1996).

48. Cross, "Schoenberg's Earliest Thoughts on the Theory of Composition: A Fragment from c. 1900," pp. 129–131.

49. The Austrian composer and conductor Gustav Mahler (1860–1911) studied at the Vienna Conservatory. After several different conducting posts, including Kassel, Prague, Budapest, and Hamburg, he returned to Vienna in 1897 as conductor of the Court Opera (a position made possible by his conversion to Catholicism that same year); the following year he became conductor of the Vienna Philharmonic. In the face of anti-Semitic opposition, he resigned both posts in 1907, accepting an offer from the Metropolitan Opera and two years later from the New York Philharmonic Orchestra. Austrian composer and author Alma Mahler Werfel (1879–1964) was daughter of the painter Emil Schindler, and later step-daughter of painter Carl Moll. She studied composition with Josef Labor and Zemlinsky. In 1902 she married Gustav Mahler; after his death she was married to Bauhaus architect Walter Gropius, 1915–1929, and to novelist Franz Werfel, 1929–1945. She emigrated to the U.S. in 1940. Fourteen lieder, composed c. 1900–1901, were published in 1910, 1915, and 1924.

50. Alma Mahler, *Gustav Mahler: Memories and Letters,* ed. Donald Mitchell, trans. Basil Creighton (New York: Viking Press, 1969), p. 78.

51. See Fred Steiner, "A History of the First Complete Recording of the Schoenberg String Quartets," *JASI* 2/2 (1978): 122–137. The recordings have been re-released by Archiphon, ARC-103/4 (1992).

52. Stuckenschmidt, p. 420.

53. *SI,* p. 42.

54. He goes on to demonstrate the purely musical organization of the work, stressing its connection to Beethoven's Third Symphony: "The great expansion of this work required careful organization. It might perhaps interest an analyst to learn that I received and took advantage of the tremendous amount of advice suggested to me by a model I had chosen for this task: the first movement of the 'Eroica' Symphony. Alexander von Zemlinsky told me that Brahms had said that every time he faced difficult problems he would consult a significant work of Bach and one of Beethoven, both of which he always used to keep near his standing-desk (*Stehpult*). How did they handle a similar problem? Of course the model was not copied mechanically, but its mental essence was applied accommodatingly. In the same manner I learned, from the 'Eroica,' solutions to my problems: how to avoid monotony and emptiness; how to create variety out of unity; how to create new forms out of basic material; how much can be achieved by slight modifications, if not by developing variation, out of often rather insignificant

little formulations. From this masterpiece I learned also much of the creation of harmonic contrasts and their application.

"Brahms' advice was excellent and I wish this story would persuade young composers that they must not forget what our musical forefathers have done for us."

55. Cited in Mark Benson, "Schoenberg's Private Program for the String Quartet in D Minor, Op. 7," *Journal of Musicology* 11 (1993): 377–378.

56. See Benson for a discussion of the program and its relationship to the formal design of the quartet. *Ibid.*, pp. 374–395.

Chapter 2: "Air from Another Planet"

1. Schoenberg, "How One Becomes Lonely," *SI*, p. 49.

2. Note in original: These numbers refer to the "Philharmonia" edition of the Universal Edition, Vienna.

3. See Stuckenschmidt, pp. 93–97, and Jane Kallir, *Arnold Schoenberg's Vienna* (New York: Galerie St. Etienne and Rizzoli, 1984), pp. 23–28.

4. See Bryan Simms, *The Atonal Music of Arnold Schoenberg, 1908–1923* (Oxford and New York: Oxford University Press, 2000), pp. 39–41.

5. In the song "Am Strande," c. 1908 or 1909, and in first movement of the Three Piano Pieces, Op. 11 (1909), Schoenberg uses piano harmonics by silently playing a chord to lift the dampers and then striking the same pitches in a lower octave.

6. From "Preface to the Four String Quartets," see 1.6.

7. Schoenberg's rejection of the word *atonal* was closely bound up with his disputes with Hauer about the origins of twelve-tone composition; see 4.14 and 5.19. In an essay from November 1923 responding to a Hauer article in *Die Musik,* he wrote, "I find above all that the expression 'atonal music,' is most unfortunate—it is on par with calling flying 'the art of not falling,' or swimming 'the art of not drowning.' Only in the language of publicity is it thought adequate to emphasize in this way a negative quality of whatever is being advertised." *SI*, p. 210. See also 6.7.

8. *SI*, p. 86.

9. Marie Gutheil-Schoder (1874–1935), a soprano at the Vienna Opera, performed many works by members of the Second Viennese School, including the Prague premiere of *Erwartung* in 1924. The Rosé Quartet was led by Arnold Rosé (1863–1946), concertmaster of the Vienna Philharmonic.

10. "About Music Criticism" is published in *SI*, pp. 191–197. For a related exchange with the critic Leopold Schmidt, see Walter B. Bailey, "Composer Versus Critic: The Schoenberg-Schmidt Polemic," *JASI* 4/2 (1980): 119–138.

11. In a letter to Karl Kraus written shortly after the interview was published (see 2.5), Schoenberg pointed out several places where he was misquoted in the interview: instead of "harmony of expression" [*Harmonie des Ausdrucks*] he said "harmony as expression" [*Harmonie als Ausdruck*]. Rather than

"symbolization of technique" [*Versinnbildlichung der Technik*] he meant "a simplification of technique" [*Versimpelung der Technik*].

12. Joan Allen Smith, *Schoenberg and His Circle: A Viennese Portrait* (New York and London: Schirmer, 1986), pp. 33–34.

13. The first volume of August Strindberg's *Ein Blaubuch* was written in 1906 and was published in a German translation by Emil Schering in 1908. The book consists of short commentaries presented as a dialogue between a teacher and a pupil. The three items Schoenberg mentions all concern various degrees of people who depend on, borrow from, or steal and claim as their own someone else's ideas. August Strindberg, *Ein Blaubuch: Die Synthese Meines Lebens,* trans. Emil Schering. *August Strindbergs Werke: Deutsche Gesamtausgabe* (Munich: Georg Müller, 1919), pp. 129–131.

14. Translation adapted from an excerpt in Nicolas Slonimsky, *Lexicon of Musical Invective: Critical Assaults on Composers Since Beethoven's Time* (Seattle and London: University of Washington Press, 1965), pp. 148–149.

15. All were important figures in harmony, counterpoint, and composition at the Vienna Conservatory.

16. Schoenberg's catalogue of his aphorisms is included in C, pp. 66–92.

17. See William M. Johnston, "The Vienna School of Aphorists 1880–1930: Reflections on a Neglected Genre," in *The Turn of the Century: German Literature and Art, 1890–1915,* ed. Gerald Chapple and Hans Schulte (Bonn: Bouvier Verlag, 1983), pp. 275–290.

18. *SI,* pp. 414–415.

19. "A Self Analysis," *SI,* p. 78.

20. "Gustav Mahler," *SI,* p. 468.

21. Translation adapted from the version by Leo Black, in Reich, *Schoenberg,* pp. 56–57. In the original manuscript and typescript the last sentence continues with a passage that was later crossed out: "what bursts out is merely the echo: the work of art, which finds the doors closed by the Society 'Against Poverty and Begging' through which charity pays off its obligations." It is noteworthy that, in contrast to the inward trajectory of the final version, the original form circles back to the social sphere in which the artist operates.

22. A play on words, opposing *Vorgefühl,* literally "feeling before," with the neologism *Vorgedanken,* "thinking before." Schoenberg's use of the word *Gedanke* in this and the preceding aphorism should be distinguished from his later usage in the 1920s and 1930s. Here he is making an opposition between conscious thought and feeling (see further, 2.10).

23. A play on the words *Selbstzucht* and *Selbstsucht.*

24. In the open letter to his friends from 1949 responding to greeting on his 75th birthday, Schoenberg recalled this aphorism, for which he supplied his own translation: "The second half of this century will spoil by overestimation, all the good of me that the first half, by underestimation, has left intact" (see 7.17).

25. Kallir, *Schoenberg's Vienna,* p. 32, nn. 35 and 36.

26. Stuckenschmidt, p. 130.

27. The stylish American Bar was designed by Adolf Loos.
28. In a February 10, 1912, entry in his diary, Schoenberg commented: "Afternoon walk to Zehlendorf with Mathilde. She goes out so rarely that I find it worth mentioning." Schoenberg, "Attempt at a Diary," trans. Anita Luginbühl, *JASI* 9/1 (1986): 27.
29. E.o. LC. Steuermann (1892–1964) studied piano with Busoni, and composition with Schoenberg starting in 1912. He premiered most of Schoenberg's works for the piano, as well as works by Berg and Webern.
30. Heinrich Jalowetz (1882–1946), who became an active conductor, and Erwin Stein (1885–1958), conductor, critic, and scholar, were among Schoenberg's earliest pupils. Both remained closely involved with Schoenberg throughout his life.
31. In 1912 the American pianist Richard Buhlig (1880–1952) gave the first performance of Op. 11 in Berlin (Stuckenschmidt, p. 464), but Marietta Werndorf gave the January 14, 1910, premiere performance in Vienna (see 2.11).
32. The chronology of works from this very productive period is given below. Unless noted, dates, which are taken from M, 1:63–76, refer to the date of completion.

Op. 11, No. 1	February 19, 1909
Op. 11, No. 2	February 22 (started)
Op. 15, No. 15	February 28
Op. 16, No. 1	May 23, short score; June 9, full score
Op. 16, No. 2	June 15, full score
Op. 16, No. 3	July 1, full score
Op. 16, No. 4	July 17, short score; July 18, full score
Op. 11, No. 3	August 7
Op. 16, No. 5	August 11
Op. 17	August 27–September 12, short score.

33. Stuckenschmidt, pp. 222–223.
34. Footnote in Beaumont: "Orig. Sie soll Ausdruck der Empfindung sein. Allusion to Beethoven's comment about his 'Pastoral' Symphony, 'Mehr Ausdruck der Empfindung als Malerei' = more an expression of feeling than painting." Beaumont, *Busoni: Selected Letters,* p. 390, n. 3.
35. Busoni had mentioned in his letter of August 20 that Schoenberg had neglected to ask to see his "paraphrase." *Busoni: Selected Letters,* p. 391.
36. Footnote in Beaumont: "Intended as a quotation from Beethoven's Symphony No. 9. The actual words are: 'O Freunde, nicht diese Töne! Sondern laßt uns angenehmere anstimmen . . . ' Schoenberg's words mean: now let us strike up other sounds." Beaumont, p. 397, n. 1.
37. Schoenberg is referring here to Busoni's *Outline of a New Aesthetic of Music* (first published in 1907). A version of the text with Schoenberg's extensive annotations from 1917 was published in 1974.
38. "In the *Outline of a New Aesthetic of Music* Busoni writes: 'All composers have

drawn nearest the true nature of music in preparatory and intermediary passages . . . where they felt at liberty to disregard symmetrical proportions, and unconsciously drew free breath. Even a Schumann (of so much lower stature [than Beethoven]) is seized, in such passages, by some feeling of boundlessness of this pan-art (recall the transition to the last movement of the D Minor Symphony); and the same may be asserted of Brahms in the introduction to the Finale of his First Symphony.' (Trans. Theodore Baker.)" Beaumont, p. 397, n. 2.

39. Footnote in Beaumont: "This was the philosopher Dr. Robert Neumann, who studied with Schoenberg from 1907–1909." Beaumont, p. 397, n. 3.

40. Footnote in Beaumont: "In the *Outline of a New Aesthetic* Busoni writes: 'I have made an attempt to exhaust the possibilities of the arrangement of degrees within the scale; and succeeded, by raising and lowering the intervals, in establishing *one hundred and thirteen different scales.*' (Trans. Theodore Baker.)" Beaumont, p. 397, n. 4.

41. Schoenberg is here responding to Busoni's question in a letter of August 20, " . . . to what extent do you realize these intentions? And how much is *instinctive,* how much is *'deliberate.'* " Beaumont, p. 390.

42. Translation altered here to follow the original: "Nichts da hinein geraten zu lassen, was durch Intelligenz oder durch das Bewußtsein hervorgerufen ist."

43. In his letter of August 20, 1909, Busoni wrote, "The third piece, which you sent me in such good faith, supplements the two preceding ones without presenting any new facet; so it seems to me. Particularly from a harmonic standpoint, it does not overstep the established boundaries. . . . Laconicism becomes a mannerism." Beaumont, pp. 390–391.

44. There is no record of Busoni having performed the pieces in public. See Beaumont, p. 403, n. 2.

45. Schoenberg, "How One Becomes Lonely," *SI,* p. 49.

46. Neighbour, "Schoenberg," *The New Grove Second Viennese School* (New York and London: W. W. Norton, 1983), p. 38.

47. *ASL,* pp. 25–26.

48. Thomas Zaunschirm, ed. *Arnold Schoenberg Paintings and Drawings* (Klagenfurt: Ritter Verlag, 1991).

49. Arnold Schoenberg, "Painting Influences (Los Angeles, February 11, 1938)," trans. Gertrud Zeisl, *JASI* 2/3 (1978): 237–238.

50. In a 1949 interview with Halsey Stevens, Schoenberg spoke in related terms: "I must answer that as a painter I was absolutely an amateur; I had no theoretical training and only a little aesthetic training, and this only from general education, but not from an education which pertained to painting." Halsey Stevens, "A Conversation with Schoenberg about Painting," *JASI* 2/3 (1978): 179.

51. Schoenberg, "Breslau Lecture on *Die glückliche Hand,*" in *SK,* p. 107.

52. See Elizabeth Keathley, "Revisioning Musical Modernism: Arnold Schoenberg, Marie Pappenheim, and *Erwartung*'s New Woman" (Ph.D. dissertation, State University of New York at Stony Brook, 1999), pp. 102–118.

53. Schoenberg, "Breslau Lecture on *Die glückliche Hand,*" in *SK,* pp. 106–107.
54. These are reproduced in *SK* and in Zaunschirm, ed. *Arnold Schoenberg: Paintings and Drawings.*
55. See Auner, "The Evolution of Form in *Die glückliche Hand,*" *JASI* 12/2 (1989): 103–128.
56. *SK,* p. 100.
57. The exhibition at Hugo Heller's bookshop opened on October 8. It consisted of forty-four paintings listed in the catalogue as: Portraits and Studies (identified as L. H., Dr. Mizzi Pappenheim, Alban Berg, Dr. Werndorf, Ing H., book merchant, H. H., Dr. B., Frau W., two portraits of his wife, and one self-portrait); Drawings (two self-portraits); Impressions and Fantasies (fourteen paintings); Caricatures (two paintings); four portraits of Gustav Mahler; Night-pieces (three paintings, one identified as a self-portrait); and Studies and Figures for the Drama with Music, *Die glückliche Hand* (five paintings). A facsimile of the announcement is given in *LB,* p. 73.
58. The October 12, 1910, concert, which was for invited guests only, included the Rosé Quartet performances of the First Quartet, Op. 7, and the Second String Quartet, Op. 10, the latter with Marie Gutheil-Schoder. Stuckenschmidt reports that Mahler attended the final rehearsal and saw the exhibition, about which he was enthusiastic. Three paintings were sold at the exhibition—as Schoenberg later learned in a letter from Webern (September 10, 1912)—purchased by Gustav Mahler: "Dear Herr Schoenberg, I am very glad to be able to tell you the following. Since yesterday evening I know who the buyer of your pictures was. He did not want you to know it. Now he has gone to eternal rest. I do not think that he wants you not to know it. If so, I hope he pardons me, for telling you now. But to know it, and not do this, is impossible for me. Your pictures were bought by GUSTAV MAHLER." Stuckenschmidt, pp. 134, 143.
59. Presumably the Three Piano Pieces, Op. 11.
60. The connection between the January 2, 1911, concert and the Kandinsky paintings is discussed in Peg Weiss, "Evolving Perceptions of Kandinsky and Schoenberg: Toward the Ethnic Roots of the 'Outsider,' " in *Constructive Dissonance: Arnold Schoenberg and the Transformations of Twentieth-Century Culture,* ed. Juliane Brand and Christopher Hailey (Berkeley and Los Angeles: University of California Press, 1997), pp. 35–57.
61. *SK,* p. 21.
62. For a range of approaches to the question of Freudian influence on Schoenberg and the origins of his conception of the unconscious, see Bryan Simms, "Whose Idea Was *Erwartung?*" in *Constructive Dissonance,* pp. 100–111; Lewis Wickes, "Schoenberg, *Erwartung,* and the Reception of Psychoanalysis in Musical Circles in Vienna until 1910/11," *Studies in Music* 23 (1989): 88–106; Keathley, *Revisioning Musical Modernism,* pp. 200–255; Alfred Cramer, "Music for the Future: Sounds of Psychology and Language in Works of Schoenberg, Webern, and Berg, 1909 to the First World War" (Ph.D. dissertation, University of Pennsylvania, 1997).

364   Notes to Pages 89–91

63. *Arnold Schönberg* (Munich: R. Piper Verlag, 1912). The entire collection of essays has been published in a translation by Barbara Z. Schoenberg in *Schoenberg and His World,* ed. Walter Frisch (Princeton: Princeton University Press, 1999); Kandinsky's essay appears on pp. 238–241.

64. In his letter of January 18, Kandinsky had asked about some excerpts from the still unpublished *Harmonielehre* that were included on the poster for the concert. These were taken from an excerpt on "Parallel Octaves and Fifths," from chapter 4, which was published in *Die Musik* 10/37 (October 1910): 97–105. These passages appeared with some alterations in the first edition of the *Harmonielehre,* pp. 81–82. The sentences as they appeared on the poster are as follows (translation adapted from *SK,* pp. 24–25, and *H,* pp. 70–71:

> In one sense one should never be untimely—in a backward direction!
> Dissonances are only different from consonances in degree; they are nothing more than remoter consonances. Today we have already reached the point where we no longer make the distinction between consonances and dissonances. Or at most, we make the distinction that we are less willing to use consonances.
> I believe that it will eventually be possible to recognize the same laws in the harmony of those of us who are the most modern as in the harmony of the classics; but suitably expanded, more generally understood.
> Our teaching persuades us to regard even the productions of the young, which the ears of their elders despise, as necessary steps in the development of beauty. However, they should never wish to write things for which one can take responsibility only by staking a fully developed personality; things which artists have written almost against their will, compelled by their development, but not out of the unrestrained wantonness of an absolutism unsure of form.

65. *ASL,* p. 29. Schoenberg did conduct the lectures during the 1910–1911 academic year. Reich, *Schoenberg,* p. 60.

66. *SI,* p. 50. After completing the *Harmonielehre* he wrote to Hertzka at Universal on July 23, 1911, proposing a number of other theoretical works, including studies of counterpoint, instrumentation, form, and an investigation of the origins of the influence of modern composition. Stuckenschmidt, pp. 125, 133, 140. Of the other proposed theoretical writings, Schoenberg worked only on the counterpoint treatise, for which he prepared a detailed outline, dated June 29, 1911. For a transcription and discussion of the draft, see Rudolf Stephan, "Schönbergs Entwurf über 'Das Komponieren mit selbstständigen Stimmen,'" *Archiv für Musikwissenschaft* 29 (1972): 239–256.

67. *SI,* p. 366.

68. For general information on these and later revisions, see Carter's "Translator's Preface" to *H,* p. xvi.

69. Carter identifies many of the most substantial changes in the two editions in his preface and in editorial notes throughout the translation. Carter, "Translator's Preface," *H*, p. xvi.

70. Alma Mahler, *Gustav Mahler: Memories and Letters*, pp. 197–198. Through her help a committee was created, including Busoni, Strauss, and Bruno Walter, that raised funds for a stipend that was awarded to Schoenberg in 1913, 1914, and 1918. *BSC*, p. 35, n. 3.

71. *H*, pp. 4–5.

72. Her "Five Songs" were published by Universal in 1910.

73. "Gustav Mahler: In Memoriam" (1912), *SI*, pp. 447–448, and "Gustav Mahler" (1948), *SI*, pp. 449–472.

74. Letter of December 21, 1911. *BSC*, p. 60.

Chapter 3: "War Clouds"

1. Reich, *Schoenberg*, p. 60.

2. *BSC*, pp. 21–22; for more details on the reasons for the move, see pp. 7–12.

3. *ASL*, p. 31.

4. ASC. G.o. Schoenberg satirized just this kind of publicity in his opera parody, *Pfitzner* (4.3).

5. The First Chamber Symphony, Op. 9, was published by Universal in 1913.

6. *The Book of the Hanging Gardens*, Fifteen Songs on texts of Stefan George, Op. 15, was published by Universal in 1914.

7. Possibly referring to the two songs published as Op. 14, composed in 1907 and 1908 but not published until 1920, by Universal Edition. The posthumously published song "Am Strande," at one time identified as Op. 14, No. 3, may have also been included with the set at this time. See Reinhold Brinkmann, *Arnold Schönberg: Drei Klavierstücke, Op. 11. Studien zur frühen Atonalität bei Schönberg*. Beihefte zum Archiv für Musikwissenschaft 7 (Wiesbaden: Franz Steiner Verlag, 1969), pp. 3–4.

8. The Two Ballades, Op. 12, published by Universal Edition in 1920.

9. The *Six Little Piano Pieces*, Op. 19, published by Universal Edition in 1913.

10. In his reply of October 23, 1911, Hinrichsen responded that Schoenberg could wait until the early spring to send in his works, adding: "It is well known to me that for now a large number of our musicians are 'afraid' of your music and cross themselves (but not musically) before it, but I'm not frightened." Eberhardt Klemm, "Der Briefwechsel zwischen Arnold Schönberg und dem Verlag C. F. Peters," *Deutsches Jahrbuch der Musikwissenschaft* 15 (1970): 13.

11. *BSC*, p. 38, n. 2.

12. *BSC*, p. 51.

13. *SK*, p. 48.

14. Kandinsky sent Schoenberg a copy of his book *On the Spiritual in Art* (*Über die Geistige in der Kunst*), which was first published in December, 1911 (with a

publication date of 1912). See Wassily Kandinsky, *Complete Writings on Art,* ed. Kenneth C. Lindsay and Peter Vergo (Boston: G. K. Hall, 1982), pp. 114–116.

15. Four of Kandinsky's paintings were included in the 1912 Neue Sezession Berlin exhibit.

16. Kandinsky's painting "Composition IV," which was shown in the Berlin exhibit, measured more than 5′ × 8′. Magdalena Dabrowski, *Kandinsky's Compositions* (New York: Museum of Modern Art, 1995), p. 79.

17. Franz Marc (1880–1916) collaborated with Kandinsky on the *Blaue Reiter* exhibitions and almanac; Emil Nolde (1867–1956) had been a member of Die Brücke and was co-founder of the Neue Sezession Berlin; Bohumil Kubista (1884–1918).

18. Hahl-Koch suggests that this refers to Picasso's circus pictures from 1905. *SK,* p. 190, n. 19.

19. For more on the Budapest exhibition, see Janos Breuer, "Schoenberg's Paintings: 'Visions, Impressions and Fantasies,' a 1912 Exhibition in Budapest," *New Hungarian Quarterly* 39/111 (1988): 215–221.

20. Albert Paris von Gütersloh (1887–1973), Austrian writer and painter; he contributed an essay on "Schoenberg the Painter" to *Arnold Schönberg* (1912).

21. The topic of sexual violence was widely discussed in connection with German Expressionist art; see Maria Tatar, *Lustmord: Sexual Murder in Weimar Germany* (Princeton: Princeton University Press, 1995).

22. This play on the expression "many are called, few are chosen" also anticipates Schoenberg's image of himself as the "chosen one" in *Die Jakobsleiter* (see 3.22).

23. Both this aphorism and the next play on the word *Nachahmungstalent.*

24. *"Elemia"* is a veiled reference to the acronym "L.m.i.A." (*Leck mich im Arsch*), linked to Goethe's *Götz von Berlichingen,* Act III, Scene 17.

25. *SK,* p. 48. The two articles referred to are: "Sleepwalker," *Pan* (Berlin 1912), *SI,* pp. 197–198, dated February 22, 1912, and "The Music Critic," *Pan, SI,* pp. 198–201, dated February 29, 1912.

26. Reinhold Brinkmann, "What the Sources Tell Us: A Chapter of *Pierrot* Philology," *JASI* 10/1 (1987): 12.

27. Max Marschalk, critic and publisher, co-founder of Dreililien-Verlag, which published Schoenberg's Opp. 1–4.

28. Referring to Richard Gerstl.

29. The piece was performed by Eduard Steuermann, two other pupils of Busoni—Louis Closson and Louis Grünberg—and Webern.

30. Referring to the lectures at the Stern Conservatory.

31. The title he gave to the last movement of the Five Pieces for Orchestra.

32. Emil Gutmann (1877–1934), a concert promoter in Berlin and Munich, was active in arranging conducting opportunities, performances, lectures, and commissions for Schoenberg, including the commission and tour for *Pierrot lunaire.*

33. See 3.6.

34. *Arnold Schönberg* (1912); in Frisch, *Schoenberg and His World*, pp. 195–261.

35. "Gebet an Pierrot," No. 9 in the completed work.

36. Letter of June 29, 1912, *ASL*, p. 33.

37. Egbert M. Ennulat, ed., *Arnold Schoenberg Correspondence: A Collection of Translated and Annotated Letters Exchanged with Guido Adler, Pablo Casals, Emanuel Feuermann, and Olin Downes* (Metuchen, N.J., and London: Scarecrow Press, 1991), p. 91.

38. The Austrian composer and conductor Franz Schreker (1878–1934), conducted the 1913 premiere of *Gurrelieder* in Vienna. He later taught at the Musikhochschule in Berlin and was instrumental in Schoenberg's being offered the position at the Prussian Academy of the Arts. Czech composer Vítězslav Novák (1870–1949).

39. Portion of the page with the second half of the sentence is torn off.

40. A one-page fragment of the beginning of a setting of *Seraphita* for voices and orchestra dates from December 27, 1912. Marie Pappenheim prepared a libretto for the work, though this has not survived. In a letter to Alma Mahler dated November 11, 1913, he wrote: "Now I am doing the final pages of the *Glückliche Hand* score, then I will compose Balzac's *Seraphita* as a work for the theater. Do you know it? It is one of the most wonderful books there is. It will be a labor for some years and will require its own theater. I will need for the 'Ascent to heaven' alone a choir of at least two thousand singers." See further 3.13. Alma Mahler Collection. University of Pennsylvania.

41. In his essay that preceded *Der gelbe Klang*, "On Stage Composition," Kandinsky wrote, "All the *forms* mentioned, which I call forms of substance (drama—word, opera—sound, ballet—movement), and the combination of various methods, which I call methods for effect, were constructed to form an *external unity. All these forms originated from the principle of external necessity."* Wassily Kandinsky and Franz Marc, *The "Blaue Reiter" Almanac. New Documentary Edition*, ed. Klaus Lankheit (New York: Viking Press, 1974), 198.

42. These included the *Sinfonia a quattro* in A major and concertos in D major and D minor by Georg Matthias Monn, as well as a *divertimento* in D major by Johann Christoph Monn, published in *DTÖ*, no. 19, vol. 39. For further materials see the *Arnold Schoenberg Correspondence*, 152–186; 278–308.

43. Footnote in *BSC:* "Mahler's *Das Lied von der Erde* was given its first Berlin performance on 18 October with the Berlin Philharmonic Orchestra under Oscar Fried."

44. Julia Culp (1880–1970). Footnote in *BSC:* "In February 1912 Schoenberg had orchestrated Beethoven's 'Adelaide' for her. His arrangements of Schubert songs ('Suleika,' 'Suleika's zweiter Gesang,' 'Ständchen,' as well as a fourth unidentified song) were completed in September. Culp had sole performance rights for two years, after which Schoenberg intended to publish the arrangements. Nothing came of that plan and the manuscripts of the arrangements have now been lost."

45. Footnote in *BSC:* "Following the 16 October premiere of *Pierrot lunaire,* the tour took place as scheduled, with the exception of Stettin and Leipzig. The subsequent performances took place in Munich (5 November), Stuttgart (11 November), Mannheim (15 November), Frankfurt (17 November), with repeat performances in Berlin (1 and 8 December). Performances in Danzig, Karlsruhe, and Graz did not take place." Stuckenschmidt reports that Stravinsky was in the audience for the December 8 performance: "We know his judgement: Aestheticism, return to the Beardsley culture which was long out of date. However, the perfection of the instrumentation was unquestioned. And in a letter to the St. Petersburg critic V. G. Karatygin of 13 December 1912, he said that in *Pierrot lunaire* by Schoenberg 'the whole unusual stamp of his creative genius comes to light at its most intensive.'" Stuckenschmidt, p. 207.

46. Conductor Artur Bodanzky (1877–1939), Mahler's assistant at the Vienna Opera; principal conductor of the Mannheim Court Theater, 1909–1915; later years at the Metropolitan Opera in New York. Willem Mengelberg (1871–1951), conductor of the Amsterdam Concertgebouw, 1895–1945.

47. Richard Specht (1870–1932), editor of the Viennese music journal *Der Merker.*

48. Schoenberg is here referring to patrons of the Gustav Mahler Trust Fund, see 2.17, a frequent topic in his letters to Berg from this period.

49. Rudolf Stephan, "Zur jüngsten Geschichte des Melodrams," *Archiv für Musikwissenschaft* 17 (1960): 184.

50. In the sketches and draft of *Die glückliche Hand* Schoenberg began to make a transition from the earlier form of *Sprechstimme* notation, with a cross on the notehead, used in the *Gurrelieder* and *Pierrot lunaire* manuscripts, to the later notation, with a cross on the stem, that first appeared in the published score of *Pierrot* in 1914.

51. Schoenberg, "This Is My Fault," *SI,* pp. 145–146.

52. Schoenberg conducted a Hamburg performance of *Pierrot lunaire* on October 19, 1912.

53. Ernst Hilmar, "Arnold Schönberg's Briefe an den Akademischen Verband für Literatur und Musik in Wien." *Österreichische Musik Zeitschrift* 31 / 6 (1976): 273–292.

54. Footnote in *BSC:* "Josef Reitler, who studied with Schoenberg in 1903, joined the *Neue Freie Presse* in 1907." Julius Korngold (1860–1945), influential critic, and father of the child-prodigy composer Erich Wolfgang Korngold (1897–1957).

55. Brand, *BSC,* p. 170; for further repercussions of this event on a growing estrangement between Berg and Schoenberg, see pp. 166–172.

56. See Hilmar, "Arnold Schönbergs Briefe an den Akademischen Verband," pp. 274–275, and *BSC,* p. 168, n. 6.

57. *Maeterlinck Lieder,* orchestral version, songs 1, 2, 3, and 5.

58. Simms, "New Documents in the Schoenberg-Schenker Polemic," *PNM* 16 (1977): 113–114.

59. Schoenberg, "Composition with Twelve Tones" (2), *SI*, p. 247. For discussions of the Symphony sketches, see Walter B. Bailey, *Programmatic Elements in the Works of Arnold Schoenberg* (Ann Arbor: UMI Research Press, 1984), pp. 79–118; Jennifer Shaw, "Schoenberg's Choral Symphony, *Die Jakobsleiter,* and other Wartime Fragments" (Ph.D. dissertation, State University of New York at Stony Brook, 2002); and see Ethan Haimo, *Schoenberg's Serial Odyssey: The Evolution of His Twelve-Tone Method, 1914–1928* (Oxford: Clarendon Press, 1990), pp. 42–68.

60. British conductor Henry Wood (1869–1944) had conducted the premiere of the Five Pieces for Orchestra in a Promenade Concert in London on September 3, 1912.

61. Based on sketch materials, Bailey has determined that Schoenberg had considered the following biblical passages for this movement: "Jeremiah" (10:14–15; 17: 1, 5; 23:23–24), "Romans" (2: 1–3, 19–23; 3:20; 8: 10, 18–25, 29–30, 38–39; 9:17; 10:20), and Psalms, Nos. 22 and 88. Bailey, *Programmatic Elements,* p. 96.

62. The inconsistent numbering scheme for the last movement in this plan reflects Schoenberg's changing conception of the work as it evolved (see Shaw, "Schoenberg's Choral Symphony," pp. 74–107). For example, in a letter to Zemlinsky of January 9, 1915 (3.16), he speaks of writing the texts for the third and fifth movements, while in a letter to Zemlinsky of July 29, 1915, he identified the *Death Dance* and *Die Jakobsleiter* as the final two movements of a four-movement work. See Bailey, *Programmatic Elements,* p. 86.

63. From "My War Psychosis (1914) and That of the Others," G.o. ASC.

64. *BSC,* 247.

65. Horst Weber, ed., *Briefwechsel der Wiener Schule: Band 1, Alexander Zemlinsky, Briefwechsel mit Arnold Schönberg, Anton Webern, Alban Berg und Franz Schreker* (Darmstadt: Wissenschaftliche Buchgesellschaft, 1995), p. 128.

66. Karl Linke (1884–1938) was among the group of Schoenberg's earliest pupils.

67. Footnote in Weber, p. 131, n. 338: "The first two songs of the *Maeterlinck Songs,* are a whole tone higher in the orchestral version that Schoenberg had first gotten to know."

68. ["als sie noch so (!!) klein war . . .]. *Die Fackel* 404 (December 5, 1914): 1. See *In These Great Times: A Karl Kraus Reader,* ed. Harry Zohn (Manchester: Carcanet Press, 1984), p. 70.

69. Carl E. Schorske, *Fin-de-siècle Vienna: Politics and Culture* (New York: Vintage Books, 1981), p. 358.

70. M, pp. 48–49.

71. Op. 22, No. 1, "Seraphita," completed October 6, 1913 (orchestral score November 9, 1913); No. 2, "Alle, welche dich suchen," December 3, 1914 (orchestral score January 8, 1915); No. 3, "Mach mich zum Wächter deiner Weiten," January 1, 1915 (orchestral score January 14, 1915); "Vorgefühl," July 28, 1916 (orchestral score November 1, 1916).

72. Here Schoenberg is developing a formulation from his 1924 Breslau lecture

on *Die glückliche Hand,* where he writes that instead of Expressionism he preferred the phrase "the art of the representation of *inner* processes." *SK* p. 105.

73. Stuckenschmidt, *Arnold Schoenberg,* p. 249. For more on Schwarzwald, see Smith, *Schoenberg and His Circle,* pp. 159–170.

74. Stuckenschmidt, *Arnold Schoenberg,* p. 253.

75. Dated April 21, 1917.

76. Schoenberg here omitted number VI and changed the numbering scheme to Arabic numerals.

77. A performing version of the first half was prepared after Schoenberg's death by his pupil Winfried Zillig (1905–1963).

78. Jennifer Shaw, "New Performance Sources and Old Modernist Productions: *Die Jakobsleiter* in the Age of Mechanical Reproduction," *Journal of Musicology* 19/3 (2002): 434–460.

79. Christensen indicates that the "it" here refers to a preceding phrase, "the unspoken, unwritten law," which was deleted in the final version. Jean Christensen, "Arnold Schoenberg's Oratorio *Die Jakobsleiter*" (Ph.D. dissertation, University of California at Los Angeles, 1979), vol. 2, p. 36, n. b.

Chapter 4: "The Path to the New Music"

1. Karl Theodor Körner (1718–1813), German poet of patriotic verse. The town of Lützen was the site of an important battle during the Napoleonic wars.

2. Cited in Reich, *Schoenberg,* p. 114.

3. For first-person accounts by many who were involved with the society and much other useful information, see Smith, *Schoenberg and His Circle.* Ringer discusses the reasons for the end of the society's activities in Vienna as well as the continuation of a branch of the society in Prague, see Ringer, pp. 161–175.

4. Cited in Simms, "The Society for Private Musical Performances: Resources and Documents in Schoenberg's Legacy," *JASI* 3/2 (1979): 148.

5. Cited in Messing, p. 146.

6. Both here and below, "1919" is written over the original "1918."

7. Presumably referring to one of the Modern Masters. Compare these press notices to those discussed in 3.1 and 4.12.

8. Original "Gähnius," a play on words combining "Genius" and "gähnen" (to yawn).

9. A clear reference to Julius Korngold and his son Erich Wolfgang Korngold.

10. Steininger Collection, Geheimes Staatsarchiv Preussischer Kulturbesitz, Berlin.

11. Ringer, p. 153.

12. Referring to a later formulation of the material from *Coherence, Counterpoint, Instrumentation, Instruction in Form;* see 3.21.

13. Berg was working on *Wozzeck* from 1917 to 1922.

14. Reich, p. 130. For Schoenberg's account of this event, see 7.21.

15. Among Igor Stravinsky's (1882–1971) works from this period are Symphonies of Wind Instruments (1920), *Pulcinella* (1920), and the Octet (1923); works by Darius Milhaud (1892–1974) include *Le Boeuf sur le toit* (1919) and *La Création du monde* (1923).

16. *SI*, pp. 173–174. "National Music" also remained unpublished in Schoenberg's lifetime.

17. Note in margin: "Shall I send you the book? I'd like to know what you think of it."

18. Felix Greissle (1899–1982), a pupil of Schoenberg's in Mödling and active in the Society for Private Musical Performances, he married Schoenberg's daughter in 1921.

19. See "Composition with Twelve Tones" (2), in *SI*, p. 247; and "My Evolution," *SI*, p. 89.

20. Nicolas Slonimsky, ed. *Music Since 1900* (New York: Schirmer, 1971), pp. 1315–1316.

21. *SI*, pp. 88–90.

22. Quoted in Reich, p. 140.

23. Quoted in Reich, p. 147.

24. "Kunst und Revolution," G.o. ASC.

25. Schoenberg, *H*, p. 400.

26. *ASL*, p. 83, and see Weber, *Briefwechsel der Wiener Schule*, pp. 245–247.

27. *SK*, p. 75.

28. Stuckenschmidt, p. 290; Hahl-Koch, "Stages of Their Friendship," *SK*, pp. 138–139.

29. *SK*, pp. 77–78.

30. Although this was to be the end of their regular correspondence, Schoenberg and Kandinsky did reestablish some contact in 1927. *SK*, pp. 139–140.

31. Anton Webern, *The Path to the New Music*, ed. Willi Reich (Bryn Mawr, Penn.: Theodore Presser, 1963), p. 44.

32. Josef Hauer (1883–1959) trained as a teacher and employed in elementary schools until 1919, also worked as a musician and conductor. Self-taught in theory and composition, he began in 1919 to develop a twelve-tone system using unordered hexachords. He composed prolifically and wrote several theoretical treatises on his methods, including *Vom Wesen des Musikalischen* (1920), *Deutung des Melos* (1923), *Vom Melos zur Pauke* (1925), and *Zwölfton-technik* (1926). His music was performed at the Society for Private Musical Performances, Donaueschingen, and other new music festivals. See Bryan Simms, "Who First Composed Twelve-Tone Music, Schoenberg or Hauer?" *JASI* 10/2 (1987): 109–133.

33. Erwin Stein (1885–1958), conductor and scholar, was among Schoenberg's earliest pupils; he was active in the Society for Private Musical Performances and was an adviser for Universal Edition. Emigrating to England in 1938, he joined Boosey and Hawkes. On the attribution to Stein see Shaw, "Schoenberg's Choral Symphony, *Die Jakobsleiter,* and other Wartime Fragments," pp. 582–583. The document has also been discussed by Arved Ashby in

"Schoenberg, Boulez, and Twelve-Tone Composition as Ideal Type," *Journal of the American Musicological Society* 54/3 (2001): 593; it was first published by Rudolf Stephan, "Ein frühes Dokument der Zwölftonkomposition," in *Festschrift Arno Forchert zum 60. Geburtstag am 29. Dezember 1985,* ed. Gerhard Allroggen and Detlef Altenburg (Basel, London, New York: Bärenreiter Kassel, 1986), pp. 296–302.

34. This essay grew out of a lecture delivered at Princeton in 1934; see Arnold Schoenberg "Vortrag/12 TK/Princeton," ed. and trans. Claudio Spies, *PNM* 13 (1974): 58–136.

35. The techniques described here coincide most closely with Schoenberg's approach in the Suite for Piano, Op. 25. See Haimo, *Schoenberg's Serial Odyssey,* pp. 85–90.

36. *SI,* p. 207.

37. For a translation of many of these documents and an extensive discussion, see Arnold Schoenberg, *The Musical Idea and the Logic, Technique, and Art of Its Presentation,* ed., trans., and commentary by Patricia Carpenter and Severine Neff (New York: Columbia University Press, 1995).

38. *SI,* pp. 122–123.

39. Cited in *LB,* p. 216. On the manuscript for the first part is the indication "1920?? or 1921?" M, p. 111.

40. Weber, ed., *Briefwechsel der Wiener Schule,* p. 259.

41. *LB,* p. 216.

42. In the next entry for December 9, 1923, Schoenberg reports that while playing through Beethoven's Seventh at the piano with Steuermann and Greissle, they heard a mysterious noise in the other room that they traced to the sound of the sugar tongs striking the rim of the bowl. He writes, "Of course, I have not mentioned a word to either Steuermann or Greissle, neither before nor after the event of 11/28." Arnold Schoenberg, "1923 Diary," trans. Jerry McBride and Anita Luginbühl, *JASI* 9/1 (1986): 81–83.

43. For further information on the festival, see Martin Thrun, *Neue Musik im Deutschen Musikleben bis 1933* (Bonn: Orpheus, 1995), pp. 368–395.

44. *ASL,* p. 109.

45. The performance took place in Vienna at the home of the music patron Norbert Schwarzmann; the performers included Alfred Jerger, who sang the Petrarch Sonnet, Rudolf Kolisch, and Marcel Dick. Stuckenschmidt, p. 294.

46. *LB,* p. 228.

47. Leonard Stein, "From Inception to Realization in the Sketches of Schoenberg," *Bericht über den 1. Kongress der Internationalen Schönberg-Gesellschaft, Wien: 4–9 Juni, 1974* (Vienna: Verlag Elizabeth Lafite, 1978), pp. 225–227.

48. Busoni died on July 27, 1924.

49. Fritz Stiedry conducted the premiere of *Die glückliche Hand* on October 14, 1924, at the Volksoper in Vienna.

50. Ringer suggests Schoenberg's poems were in part a response to the anti-

Semitic attacks that greeted the announcement of his appointment to the Prussian Academy of the Arts. Ringer, pp. 56–66.

51 *BSC*, p. 446.

52. *ASL*, pp. 271–272.

53. Schoenberg, "The Current Situation of Music," G.o. ASC MS 20. Adapted from a translation by Maja Reid, ASI.

54. Schoenberg is referring here and in the preceding sentences to Krenek's 1925 essay "Musik in der Gegenwart," with the phrase "wie der Medio*kre neck*isch sagt," a response to the wordplay hidden in the opening line of Krenek's opera *Jonny spielt auf*: "Du schöner Berg! der mich anzieht, der mich antreibt, zu gehn fort von der Heimat, fort von der Arbeit." [Lovely mountain! You attract me, you urge me to leave my native country, my work.] See 5.3.

55. Viennese dialect for "ham" and "edelweiss."

56. Schoenberg described the second movement to Filippi, "The title 'Manysided' ['Versatility'], means only that it can be used by turning around the paper and reading it from the end to the beginning and the same music (if you call it music) would come out. This piece was never intended by myself to be sung or performed." *ASL*, p. 272.

57. Music theorist Hugo Riemann (1849–1919).

Chapter 5: Prussian Academy of the Arts

1. For letters and documents concerning Schoenberg's appointment, see *ASL*, pp. 117–173, and Josef Wulf, *Musik im Dritten Reich: Eine Dokumentation* (Gütersloh: Sigbert Mohn Verlag, 1963), pp. 39–44.

2. See Peter Gradenwitz, *Arnold Schönberg und seine Meisterschüler: Berlin, 1925–1933* (Vienna: Paul Zsolnay Verlag, 1998).

3. Stuckenschmidt, p. 316.

4. "Krenek's *Sprung über den Schatten*," *SI*, pp. 480–481.

5. See Auner, "Soulless Machines and Steppenwolves: Renegotiating Masculinity in Krenek's *Jonny spielt auf*," *Siren Songs*, ed. Mary Ann Smart (Princeton: Princeton University Press, 2000), pp. 222–236. Starting around 1930, and despite his earlier strong criticism of Schoenberg, Krenek adopted the twelve-tone method in such works as *Karl V* (1933). He emigrated in 1938 to the U.S., where he continued actively composing and teaching at various colleges and universities.

6. As translated in Susan C. Cook, *Opera for a New Republic: The Zeitopern of Krenek, Weill, and Hindemith* (Ann Arbor: U.M.I. Research Press, 1988), p. 196; the complete essay is printed on pp. 193–203.

7. A pun on the name of Bach (= stream, brook).

8. In the margin of the manuscript Schoenberg added another play on Krenek's name (as in the *Three Satires*), "thus they are Krenek-cornerstones, [Kren-Ecksteine]," referring to a dog's habit of marking street corners or the corners of buildings.

9. "Art and the Moving Pictures," *SI*, pp. 153–157. See Sabine Feisst, "Arnold Schoenberg and the Cinematic Art," *Musical Quarterly* 83/1 (1999): 93–113.

10. In addition to her many commissions, Elizabeth Sprague Coolidge (1864–1953) was a major patron for the music division of the Library of Congress, the Berkshire Festival of chamber music, and Yale University.

11. W. H. Haddon Squire, "Schönberg in London,'" *Christian Science Monitor*, February 23, 1928. Steininger Sammlung. Geheimes Staatsarchiv Preussischer Kulturbesitz, Berlin.

12. The Zionist movement was initiated in 1896 with the publication of Theodor Herzl's *The Jewish State*. As in Schoenberg's play, Herzl had proposed that a Jewish state could be established in Africa or South America. The Fourteenth Zionist Congress took place in Vienna in 1925. See Ringer, pp. 116–149, and E. Randol Schoenberg, "Arnold Schoenberg and Albert Einstein: Their Relationship and Views on Zionism," *JASI* 10/2 (1987): 134–191.

13. Cited and discussed in Moshe Lazar, "Arnold Schoenberg and His Doubles: A Psychodramatic Journey to His Roots," *JASI* 17/1–2 (1994): 54. See also Ringer, pp. 56–66.

14. Ibid., p. 84.

15. In a letter to Hans Rosbaud of May 12, 1947, Schoenberg wrote in similar terms, "There is nothing I long for more intensely (if for anything) than to be taken for a better sort of Tchaikovsky—for heaven's sake: a bit better, but really that's all. Or if anything more, then, that people should know my tunes and whistle them." *ASL*, p. 243.

16. Referring to a secret weapon Aruns had commissioned, with the code name "trumpets of Jericho," which he justified as a visible manifestation of God to deter enemies and to quell internal dissension.

17. Adolf Weissmann, *The Problems of Modern Music*, trans. M. M. Bozman (1925, reprinted Westport, Conn.: Hyperion Press, 1979), pp. 176, 182–183.

18. See, for example, "Heart and Brain in Music" (1946), *SI*, pp. 53–75. For an extended discussion from 1931 of his creative process, see "Self-Analysis," Reich, *Schoenberg*, pp. 236–242.

19. Next to this paragraph Schoenberg made the annotation, "I could extend this list considerably. But it is only intended to identify works from various times and various stylistic epochs."

20. *SI*, p. 95.

21. *SI*, p. 99. And see Auner, "Schoenberg and His Public in 1930: The Six Pieces for Male Chorus, Op. 35," in *Schoenberg and His World*, ed. Walter Frisch (Princeton: Princeton University Press, 1999), pp. 85–125.

22. Schoenberg spent several months in the French town of Roquebrune from the summer of 1928 through the new year of 1929.

23. Referring to the limited frequency range of the radio, a topic that was much discussed by composers and critics. See Christopher Hailey, "Rethinking Sound: Music and Radio in Weimar Germany," in *Music and Performance During the Weimar Republic*, ed. Bryan Gilliam (Cambridge: Cambridge University Press, 1994), pp. 13–36.

24. *ASL,* p. 232.

25. Allen Forte, in a submission to the AMS-List (ams-1@Virginia.edu), April 30, 1999.

26. *GS,* p. 263. This passage does not appear in the English translation, as printed in *SP,* pp. 41–53.

27. Heinz Tiessen (1887–1971), German composer and critic; conductor and composer for the Berlin Volksbühne; active in the workers' music movement, co-founder of the German division of the International Society for Contemporary Music in 1922. After being silenced during the Nazi period, he returned to a prominent role in German musical life after the war. Kurt Weill (1900–1950) studied composition with Busoni; among his many works, he collaborated with Brecht on *Die Dreigroschenoper* (1928) and the radio cantata *Der Lindberghflug* (1929). After leaving Germany in 1933, Weill traveled to Paris and London before arriving in 1935 in the U.S., where he launched a successful Broadway career.

28. See Cook, *Opera for a New Republic: The* Zeitopern *of Krenek, Weill, and Hindemith;* and see Juliane Brand, "A Short History of *Von heute auf morgen* with Letters and Documents," *JASI* 14/2 (1991): 241–270, and Stephen Davison, "Of its time, or out of step? Schoenberg's *Zeitoper, Von heute auf morgen,*" *JASI* 14/2 (1991): 271–298.

29. Joan Evans, "New Light on the First Performances of Arnold Schoenberg's *Opera* 34 and 35," *JASI* 11/2 (1988): 163–173.

30. *BSC,* pp. 412–413.

31. "The Radio: Reply to a Questionnaire" (1930), *SI,* pp. 147–148.

32. *ASL,* p. 163.

33. *SI,* pp. 502–505.

34. G.o. LC.

35. Oswald Spengler (1880–1936) published *The Decline of the West* in 1918. See Schoenberg, "Those who complain about the decline" (1923), *SI,* pp. 203–204. Hans Mersmann (1891–1971), musicologist and editor of the journal *Melos,* 1924–1934, published *Die Moderne Musik seit der Romantik* (Potsdam: Akademiche Verlag, 1928).

36. This initiates an extended pun on the word *widerhall,* literally, to echo, but also figuratively "a response."

37. Referring to a statement by Mussolini quoted in the article, "The people's thirst for authority, for directives, and for order has never been stronger than at this moment."

38. *ASL,* p. 166.

39. "Ruhe." G.o. ASC T 04.02, Bio 50. Transcribed by Anita Luginbühl; translation adapted from Susan Sloan, ASI.

40. Henry Cowell (1897–1965) had played for Schoenberg's master class in 1932.

41. The third movement of the Serenade is a theme and variations based on a fourteen-tone row with eleven different pitches.

42. The Cello Concerto (November 1932 to January 1933) is based on Monn's

1746 *Concerto per Clavicembalo* in D major, one of the works for which Schoenberg prepared a basso-continuo realization for the *DTÖ* (see 3.6).

43. Schoenberg's letter to the academy responding to this meeting and other documents are given in Wulf, *Musik im Dritten Reich: Eine Dokumentation*, pp. 40–41.

44. See R. Wayne Shoaf, "The Schoenberg-Malkin Correspondence," *JASI* 13/2 (1990): 164–257; and Auner, "Schoenberg's Handel Concerto and the Ruins of Tradition," *Journal of the American Musicological Society* 49/2 (1996): 264–313.

Chapter 6: "Driven into Paradise"

1. *BSC*, p. 446.
2. Ringer, "Unity and Strength: The Politics of Jewish Survival," in Ringer, pp. 116–149; the complete "Four-Point Program" is printed on pp. 230–244.
3. Ibid., p. 116.
4. In the margin he adds: "*Buying a country*/owning it by being able to defend it. Pioneer work. To buy: for what purpose has God endowed us with the peculiar characteristic of earning money?"
5. In the margin this section is identified as: "Democracy, Liberalism, Pacifism."
6. Referring to the severe asthma attacks he suffered during his time on the East Coast. See 7.28.
7. *SI*, pp. 25–26.
8. *SI*, p. 502. And see Reinhold Brinkmann and Christoph Wolff, *Driven into Paradise: The Musical Migration from Nazi Germany to the United States* (Berkeley and Los Angeles: University of California Press, 1999), pp. 172–193.
9. Originally this clause read: "because the inspiration is not important."
10. At the bottom of the page is typed the question from Lundell: "Would you care to tell us something about your new work—*Moses and Aaron*"? But no response was included.
11. For Schoenberg's graphic representations of the subdivisions of the Jewish people, see *LB*, p. 352.
12. Stuckenschmidt, pp. 390–391.
13. For correspondence documenting their rupture, see *ASL*, pp. 119–121.
14. LC.
15. Karl Rankl (1898–1968) studied with Schoenberg in Mödling; he later conducted at the Kroll Opera in Berlin, in Graz, and at the German Theater in Prague; he emigrated to England in 1946 to become conductor at Covent Garden.
16. G.o. Based on the translation in *Arnold Schönberg: 30 Kanons*, ed. Josef Rufer (Kassel: Bärenreiter, 1963), p. 48.
17. The San Francisco concert on March 7, 1935, was given under the auspices of the New Music Society. On March 21 and 22, 1935, Schoenberg was guest conductor for the Philharmonic Orchestra, normally conducted by Otto Klemperer, in a program consisting of Brahms's Third Symphony, the string

orchestra version of *Verklärte Nachte,* and the three Bach arrangements. See *LB,* pp. 314, 318.

18. "Boches" is a derogatory French term for Germans. Here and below, the italicized phrases were originally in English.

19. Minna Ledermann (1898–1995), editor of *Modern Music,* founding member of the League of Composers.

20. Author of numerous books, Paul Bekker (1882–1937) was an influential music critic in Berlin and Frankfurt; 1925–1926 Intendant in Kassel, 1927–1933 Intendant in Wiesbaden. Emigrated to the U.S. in 1934.

21. Lawrence Gilman (1878–1939), from 1923 music critic for the New York *Herald Tribune;* 1933–1935 radio commentator for Toscanini's broadcasts.

22. "My Method of Composing with Twelve Tones Which are Related with One Another," early version of "Composition with Twelve Tones" (*SI,* pp. 214–215). Given on February 3, 1934, in Chicago, and March 6, 1934, in Princeton. See *LB,* p. 308. And see Arnold Schoenberg, "Vortrag/12 TK/Princeton," 58–136.

23. Free translation of the wordplay on "Kauf": "aber man muss es in Kauf nehmen, wenn es nur ein Kauf wird."

24. Jan Maegaard, "Schoenberg's Late Tonal Works," in *The Arnold Schoenberg Companion,* ed. Walter B. Bailey (Westport, Conn.: Greenwood Press, 1998), p. 177.

25. Olin Downes (1886–1955) was the music critic for the *New York Times,* 1924–1955. According to Stuckenschmidt it was Downes who put Joseph Malkin, of the Malkin Conservatory, in contact with Schoenberg. Stuckenschmidt, p. 371.

26. Otto Klemperer (1885–1973) had conducted performances of *Erwartung, Die glückliche Hand,* and *The Accompaniment to a Film Scene* at the Kroll Opera in Berlin. He emigrated to the U.S. in 1933, becoming conductor of the Los Angeles Philharmonic Orchestra, 1933–1939. He also studied composition with Schoenberg in Los Angeles.

27. See 6.8.

28. Downes had compared the suite to Bloch's Concerto Grosso (1925), describing it as a "momentary excursion into classic forms," rather than a rejection of Schoenberg's past.

29. The second half of the article turns to the Variations for Orchestra, Op. 31. Downes (again showing Schoenberg's emphases) describes the unconventional phrase length of the theme and the "wholly *arbitrary* arrangement of tones" in the series and various transformations of the row, which he compares to a "*Chinese puzzle of contrapuntal calculation.*" But he disputes the idea that this piece is atonal, because, "*in every variation, the theme, inverted or otherwise, is kept rigidly upon the same notes of the scale . . .* constituting at least a *tangible substitution for tonality.*" He compares the function of the row to the theme of Bach's C-minor passacaglia, which provides a "tonal centre for the counterpoint."

30. Schoenberg is no doubt writing the excerpt from memory, and there are

some rhythmic differences from the original. He uses the same excerpt, though differently annotated, as example 16 in the essay "Brahms the Progressive" (1947), *SI*, p. 410. In that essay Schoenberg also develops many of the same points about "musical prose."

31. For additional details on how the work came about, see Martin Bernstein, "On the Genesis of Schoenberg's Suite for School Orchestra," *JASI* 11/2 (1988): 158–162.

32. No analytical section was included with the draft.

33. Casella, "Modern Music in Italy," *Modern Music* 12/1 (1934): 19–20.

34. This passage continues: "They were, for the most part, the works of musicians who, with the tranquil diligence of zealous clerks, for twenty years insisted upon keeping *avant-garde* positions." Ibid., p. 21.

35. Schoenberg's transcription, no doubt written from memory, varies significantly from the original in the last two measures.

36. In the margin is written: "*Rhabarber-Polyphonie.*" Schoenberg uses a similar explanation in "New Music, Outmoded Music, Style and Idea" for "a kind of polyphony, substituting for counterpoint, which, because of its inexact imitations, in former times would have been held in contempt as 'Kapellmeistermusik,' or what I called 'Rhabarber counterpoint.' The word 'Rhabarber,' spoken behind the scenes by only five or six people, sounds to the audience in the theater like a rioting mob. Thus the counterpoint, thematically meaningless, like the word 'rhubarb,' sounded as if it had real meaning." *SI*, p. 120.

37. LC. G.o.

38. Originally: "would not have been worth their hat," a play on words between "Hüter," or guardians, and "Hut," or hat.

39. The concerts were given on January 4, 6, 7, and 8, 1937, and included Schoenberg's Op. 7, Beethoven's Op. 127; Op. 10, and Op. 130/133; Op. 30, and Op. 131; Op. 37, and Op. 132.

40. In a letter to Elizabeth Sprague Coolidge of February 5, 1937, Schoenberg wrote angrily of the lack of recognition he felt from the university. *ASL*, pp. 200–202.

41. *ASL*, pp. 212–213.

42. Omitted here is a varied repetition of a previous passage: "Minor has become during the last century an expression for sad and touching feelings. At the time from which this melody comes, church modes were in use, which were preferably minor-like. In this century the musical feeling in this respect was not so distinct as in our time and probably the effect on the listeners was that of dignity, seriousness, solemnity. No living musician feels this way today. One can substitute a self suggestion as an immediate effect."

43. E.o. LC.

44. Schoenberg's childhood friend, the pianist and theorist Moritz Violin (1879–1956) had contacted him for help leaving Austria. On Violin's behalf Schoenberg also wrote to Alfred Hertz, the conductor of the San Francisco

Symphony Orchestra, to determine if there was an opening. Stuckenschmidt, pp. 427–428. See further 7.19.

45. Bela Rosza had earlier performed Schoenberg's piano pieces for the 1933 broadcast discussed in 6.2.

46. Gerald Strang (1908–1983) was managing editor of New Music Edition, founded by Henry Cowell. He lated edited, with Leonard Stein, Schoenberg's *Fundamentals of Musical Composition.*

47. Leonard Stein (1916–), American scholar and pianist. Studied with Schoenberg at USC and UCLA, soon becoming his assistant. Edited many books and articles by and about Schoenberg; edited *SI.* Director of the Arnold Schoenberg Institute, 1974–1991.

48. Philosopher Theodor Wiesengrund Adorno (1903–1969), see further 7.20, 7.21. Josef Schmid (1890–1969) studied with Berg before WWI.

49. Austrian violinist Rudolf Kolisch (1896–1978), studied with Schoenberg in Mödling from 1919 to 1922. After being active in the Society for Private Musical Performances, he in 1922 founded the Kolisch Quartet (originally the Wiener Streichquartett): Rudolf Kolisch, Eugene Lehner, Felix Khuner, Benar Heifetz. He immigrated to the U.S. in 1935.

50. Josef Rufer (1893–1985), also worked as music critic for the Berlin newspapers *Morgenpost* and *Die Welt;* after the war published the periodical *Stimmen.* His *Die Komposition mit zwölf Tönen* (1952) was the first major study of the method (see 7.26). Published the first catalogue of Schoenberg's works, was first editor in chief of the *Complete Works.*

51. Schoenberg had become concerned as early as 1937 that Webern had developed Nazi sympathies. In a letter of June 20, 1937, he wrote to Webern that he planned to dedicate his Violin Concerto to him but first had to ask if he had become a member of the Nazi party. In a response of July 15, 1937, Webern sharply denied the allegation. See *LB,* p. 339. On Webern's ambivalent relationship to National Socialism, see Kathryn Bailey, *The Life of Webern* (Cambridge: Cambridge University Press, 1998), p. 170, and Anne Shreffler, "Anton Webern," in Bryan Simms, ed., *Schoenberg, Berg, and Webern: A Companion to the Second Viennese School* (Westport, Conn.: Greenwood Press, 1999), p. 302.

52. Deems Taylor (1885–1966), music critic and editor of many publications, including *Musical America* and the *New York World;* at this time director, later president, of ASCAP; broadcast commentator for the New York Philharmonic.

53. Alfred Wallenstein (1898–1983), principal cellist of the New York Philharmonic under Toscanini, began conducting in the 1930s; 1943–1956 music director of the Los Angeles Philharmonic.

54. The Concerto for Violin and Orchestra, Op. 36, was completed in September 1936; the premiere took place on December 6, 1940. Louis Krasner (1903–1995) commissioned and premiered Berg's Violin Concerto, along with works by Casella, Sessions, and others. See Louis Krasner, "A Performance History of Schoenberg's Violin Concerto, Op. 36," *JASI* 2/2 (1978): 84–98.

55. This was "Composition with Twelve Tones," delivered on March 26, 1941. *SI,* pp. 214–245.

56. This 78 rpm recording features Erika Stiedry-Wagner, reciter; Leonard Posella, flute and piccolo; Kalman Bloch, clarinet and bass clarinet; Rudolf Kolisch, violin and viola; Stefan Auber, cello; Edward Steuermann, piano; with Schoenberg conducting. Columbia M 461.

57. Leonard Stein, "A Note on the Genesis of the *Ode to Napoleon,*" *JASI* 2/1 (1977): 52–53.

58. The name of Händel was added later, after the list was typed.

59. Egon Wellesz, *Arnold Schönberg* (Vienna, 1921; English trans. 1925). In an otherwise critical commentary on Wellesz from the "Notes for an Autobiography" (1944–1945) Schoenberg wrote of the book, "*Wellesz* who had written perhaps a year before a biography (1923??) of mine at this time still acted as a friend and admirer of my music. The biography is excellent, firstly because of the cooperation of my friends Webern, Berg and Stein who were extremely eager to have all the dates correct and helped also with the analysis and description of the works. Secondly because I told *Wellesz* from the very first beginning: 'Avoid all adulation and extravagant praise. Describe the facts and let them speak.'" E.o. ASC.

60. Merle Armitage, ed., *Schoenberg* (New York, 1937; reprinted Freeport, N.Y.: Books for Libraries Press, 1971). The collection includes contributions by Leopold Stokowski, Roger Sessions, Ernst Krenek, Boris de Schloezer, Eduard Steuermann, Otto Klemperer, Franz Werfel, Nicolas Slonimsky, and many others.

61. Cited in Steven Cahn, "Variations in Manifold Time," p. 164. And see Frisch, *The Early Works of Arnold Schoenberg,* pp. 129–139.

62. In a document entitled "Konstruktives in der *Verklärten Nacht,*" Schoenberg explores this analysis in more detail. See Frisch, *The Early Works of Arnold Schoenberg,* pp. 123–129.

Chapter 7: Final Years

1. Sergey Koussevitzky (1874–1951) was conductor of the Boston Symphony Orchestra from 1924 to 1949. Arturo Toscanini (1867–1957) at this time was the conductor of the NBC Orchestra. Also included in the "Notes for an Autobiography" is a draft of a letter (August 27, 1944) to Olin Downes concerning Toscanini. "Dear Mr. Downes, I would like to have this suggestion printed in the *New York Times:* 'As lovers of serious music seemingly are not capable of liking symphonic programs in the summertime would it not be a good idea to allow the serving of beer, frankfurters, and cigarettes during Toscanini's popular concerts over NBC? Too bad that such service can not be extended to listeners of the broadcast.'" Schoenberg indicates that the letter was not sent.

2. Arthur Nikisch (1855–1922), conductor of the Leipzig Gewandhaus Orchestra and the Berlin Philharmonic.

3. Furtwängler conducted the Berlin premiere of the revised version of the Five Pieces for Orchestra in 1922.

4. As Schoenberg explains below, there is a missing alto clef in m. 12 and a missing treble clef in m. 13.

5. In the margin is added, "beats measured by '*Augenmass* [by eye]', *Takt* is not the master but the servant of music," a topic to which he returns at the end of the essay.

6. Paul Hindemith (1895–1963) had been a major force in new music from the time of the premiere in 1921 of his opera *Mörder, Hoffnung der Frauen*, based on the Kokoschka play. He became co-director of the Donaueschingen Festival in 1923; in 1927 was named professor of composition at the Hochschule für Musik in Berlin. His opera *Mathis der Maler* was banned by the Nazis in 1934. He immigrated to Switzerland in 1937 and then in 1940 to the U.S., where he taught at Yale until 1953. See David Neumeyer and Giselher Schubert, "Arnold Schoenberg and Paul Hindemith," *JASI* 13/1 (1990): 3–46.

7. *The Craft of Musical Composition*, first published 1937; English translation 1942.

8. See "Inversions of the Triads," in *H*, pp. 52–58.

9. This and the preceding information about the trio are taken from Bailey, *Programmatic Elements*, p. 155.

10. Stuckenschmidt, p. 503. The French musicologist, composer, and conductor René Leibowitz (1913–1972) founded the International Festival of Chamber Music in 1947. His publications include *Schoenberg and His School: The Contemporary Stage of the Language of Music* (1946, English trans. 1949) and *Introduction to Twelve-Tone Music* (1949).

11. See Sam Shirakawa, *The Devil's Music Master: The Controversial Life and Career of Wilhelm Furtwängler* (New York and Oxford: Oxford University Press, 1992).

12. A note in Stuckenschmidt (p. 545) indicates that this refers to Toscanini.

13. Pfitzner's opera was first performed in 1901; in 1905 it was performed in Vienna, conducted by Gustav Mahler, in a production designed by Alfred Roller.

14. Facsimile of the article in *LB*, p. 406.

15. For a discussion of the origins of the work, see Camille Crittenden, "Texts and Contexts of *A Survivor from Warsaw*, Op. 46," in Charlotte Cross and Russell Berman, eds., *Political and Religious Ideas in the Works of Arnold Schoenberg* (New York and London: Garland, 2000), pp. 231–258.

16. Facsimile in *LB*, p. 411.

17. Stuckenschmidt, p. 492; for an overview of the controversy, see pp. 494–496. Included in the "Notes for an Autobiography," under the category "Rascals," is a statement on Rubsamen, who was Schoenberg's colleague at UCLA: "He is a very small personality and he is just as big as a rascal. I was perhaps a little too much infuriated, when I learned what he had said about me in his classes."

18. Richard and Clara Winston, ed. and trans., *Letters of Thomas Mann—1889–1955* (Berkeley and Los Angeles: University of California Press, 1990), p. 396.

19. See *ASL*, p. 278. And see Jo-Ann Reif, "Adrian Leverkühn, Arnold Schoenberg, Theodor Adorno: Theorists Real and Fictitious in Thomas Mann's *Doctor Faustus*," *JASI* 7/1 (1983): 102–112.

20. Thomas Mann, *Dr. Faustus: The Life of the German Composer as Told by a Friend,* trans. John E. Woods (New York: Alfred A. Knopf, 1997), p. 535.

21. Schoenberg probably intended to write 2060 for the year.

22. Letter of October 12, 1944. G.o. LC.

23. Reprinted in Piero Weiss and Richard Taruskin, eds., *Music in the Western World: A History in Documents* (New York: Schirmer, 1984), p. 500.

24. Schoenberg discussed the same anecdote about Beethoven in "New Music, Outmoded Music, Style and Idea" (1946), in *SI,* p. 122.

25. Schoenberg developed this idea further in the tenth of the *Modern Psalms* from February 9, 1951. See *Moderne Psalmen von Arnold Schoenberg,* ed. Rudolf Kolisch (Mainz: B. Schott's Söhne, 1956).

26. Andrea Olmstead, "The Correspondence Between Arnold Schoenberg and Roger Sessions," *JASI* 13/1 (1990): 47–62. For more on his stance toward Schenker's theories, see Jonathan Dunsby, "Schoenberg and the Writings of Schenker," *JASI* 2/1 (1977): 26–33.

27. Stuckenschmidt, p. 508.

28. A quotation from Wagner's *Lohengrin,* act 3, scene 2, where Lohengrin and Elsa are alone on their bridal night looking out of an open window to a flower garden.

29. Originally the manuscript ended here and was dated and signed by Schoenberg.

30. Oswald Spengler's *The Decline of the West.*

31. Stein wrote several articles about Benjamin Britten in the late 1940s and early 1950s.

32. See "Jewish Music and a Jew's Music," in Ringer, pp. 192–205.

33. Letter to Mr. Milton S. Koblitz, August 9, 1950. E.o. LC; for facsimiles of this and related letters, see *LB,* pp. 428–429. And see Hans Mayer, "Ein Briefwechsel zwischen Arnold Schönberg und Hermann Scherchen, 1950," in *Hermann Scherchen Musiker, 1891–1966,* ed. Hansjörg Pauli and Dagmar Wünsche (Berlin: Akademie der Künste, 1986), pp. 62–67.

34. See the discussion in Jennifer L. DeLapp, "Copland in the Fifties: Music and Ideology in the McCarthy Era" (Ph.D. dissertation, University of Michigan, 1997), pp. 100–104.

35. Danish composer Paul Klenau (1883–1946) had been a student of Max Bruch and Max von Schillings, already establishing an active composing and conducting career prior to WWI. After the war he studied with Schoenberg in Mödling and settled in Vienna, where he remained an active composer until he returned to Denmark in 1940.

36. DeLapp, "Copland in the Fifties," pp. 101–102.

37. Ibid., p. 104. And see Ennulat, *Arnold Schoenberg Correspondence,* p. 272, for another version of this letter Schoenberg prepared for publication.

38. Josef Rufer, *Die Komposition mit zwölf Tönen* (Berlin: Max Hesses Verlag, 1952); and as *Composition with Twelve Tones,* trans. Humphrey Searle (New York: Macmillan, 1954).

39. The *Phantasy for Violin,* Op. 47, was completed in March 1949. It was premiered on the occasion of Schoenberg's seventy-fifth birthday on September 13, 1949, by Adolf Koldofsky and Leonard Stein.

40. The proposed "second book" did not materialize. See McGeary, "The Publishing History of *Style and Idea,*" pp. 181–209.

41. Czech composer and professor of composition at the Prague Conservatory, Alois Hába (1893–1973) explored athematic, serial, and microtonal composition.

42. The Koldofsky Trio had recorded the String Trio in 1950, Dial DLP 3. The *Pierrot* recording may be that conducted by Leibowitz, with Ellen Adler, Dial DLP 16 (1951?).

43. Boelke-Bomart published *Kol Nidre,* the String Trio, *A Survivor from Warsaw,* and the Three Songs, Op. 48.

44. German conductor and composer Robert Heger (1886–1978) had conducted at the Städtische Oper in Berlin (1945–1950); in 1950 he went to Munich as president of the Musikhochschule.

45. Zillig conducted the Radio Symphony Orchestra of Frankfurt, Capitol P 8069 (1949). On the revised score for the Five Pieces for Orchestra, see Robert Craft, "Schoenberg's Five Pieces for Orchestra," in *Perspectives on Schoenberg and Stravinsky,* pp. 3–24.

46. Ferenc Fricsay (1914–1963), Hungarian conductor.

47. German composer Boris Blacher (1903–1975), who adopted the twelve-tone method, had contributed an appreciation of Schoenberg to *Stimmen.* Tibor Varga (1921–) had performed Schoenberg's Violin Concerto at the summer Darmstadt courses.

48. In a letter of January 16, 1950, Schoenberg wrote to Leibowitz: " . . . you do the *Survivor* and the *Ode* with a woman's voice, although both are quite clearly for a man's voice, indeed in the *Ode* I even used the bass clef [. . .] you don't accept that I have always heard this as a low voice, if I placed higher notes above, or if I have placed lower notes below, then that naturally cannot be a woman's voice. I also can't think that *Pierrot* can be spoken by a man; it was sometimes possible to perform the Speaker from *Gurrelieder* with a woman, but how it was then done by a man was a thousand times better." G.o. LC.

49. Schoenberg wrote "deepening and strictening."

Bibliography of Sources

Archival items from the Arnold Schönberg Center (ASC) are identified by the ASC catalogue number followed, where available, by Schoenberg's categorization.

Chapter 1: 1874–1906

1.1 "Arnold Schoenberg, composer, teacher of musical composition" (c. 1944). E.o. ASC T43.05, BIO V 4.1-2.

1.2 Notes Toward a Biography (c. 1949). E.o. ASC T43.09, BIO V/7.

1.3 From "Notes for an Autobiography" (1944–1945). E.o. and G.o. ASC T42.03. While the layout of the original has not been preserved, line breaks and Schoenberg's annotations are indicated. Facsimiles of several pages are given in *LB*.

1.4 Letter to Leopold Moll, November 28, 1931. G.o. LC.

1.5 From "My Evolution," 1949. *SI*, pp. 79–80. This essay was first written in English, completed August 2, 1949, and then revised for a lecture at UCLA on November 29, 1949.

1.6 From "Preface to the Four String Quartets," c. 1949. E.o. ASC T70.02, and from the Wisconsin Music Archive, Mills Music Library, University of Wisconsin—Madison. As printed in the program book for a series of five concerts (1959–1960) at the University of Wisconsin—Madison School of Music by the Pro Arte Quartet (first violinist Rudolf Kolisch) that paired Schoenberg's quartets and String Trio with Mozart quartets. These notes may have been written for a planned new recording of the quartets in 1949 (see GS, pp. 502–503).

1.7 "If upon your life's journey," c. 1891. G.o. *LB*, p. 14.

1.8 From a Letter to Malvina Goldschmied, May 25, 1891. Cited in Stuckenschmidt, pp. 25–26.

1.9 Letter to David Joseph Bach, July 25, 1895. G.o. PML. Transcribed in Dümling, Albrecht. " 'Im Zeichen der Erkenntnis der sozialen Verhältnisse,' Der junge Schönberg und die Arbeitersängerbewegung." *Zeitschrift für Musiktheorie* 6 (1975): 11–14.

1.10 "Some Ideas for the Establishment of a Modern Theory of

Composition." G.o. ASC T27.11. Translation adapted from Cross, Charlotte M., "Schoenberg's Earliest Thoughts on the Theory of Composition: A Fragment from c. 1900." *Theoria: Historical Aspects of Music Theory* 8 (1994): 127.

1.11 From *Odoakar,* c. 1900. G.o. ASC T06.07, Dich 4. Translation adapted from a version by Nora Henry, ASI.

1.12 From *Superstition,* c. 1901. *Aberglaube* G.o. ASC, T06.06, Dich 3. Translation adapted from a version by Nora Henry, ASI. The libretto, comprising a prose draft of two acts and the beginning of a third, includes two musical sketches and a number of drawings for the staging. Simms dates the libretto to c. 1901 on the basis of the paper and handwriting, and the style of the musical sketches. Simms, Bryan. "Schoenberg's Early Fragmentary Operas" (forthcoming).

1.13 From the "Program Notes to *Verklärte Nacht,*" Op. 4 (August 26, 1950). E.o. ASC T77.06G. Written for *Schoenberg's Verklärte Nacht, Op. 4.* Capitol L-8118 (1950). Also published in *The Music of Arnold Schoenberg,* vol. 2. Columbia M2S 694 (1963). Edited after the manuscript, ASC.

1.14 "Foreword to a Broadcast of *Pelleas and Melisande,*" February 17, 1950. E.o. ASC T69.05. *SP,* p. 116. Program Notes to *Pelleas und Melisande,* Op. 5 (December 1949). E.o. *SP,* pp. 110–112. Written for Capitol P 8069 (1950). Also published in *The Music of Arnold Schoenberg,* vol. 2. Columbia M2S 694 (1963). The version presented here has a few additional passages from the typescript (ASC), indicated by brackets.

1.15 Prospectus for the Society of Creative Musicians, March 1904. Translation adapted from Reich, *Schoenberg,* pp. 16–19.

1.16 Letter to Gustav Mahler, December 12, 1904. Published in Mahler, Alma. *Gustav Mahler: Memories and Letters.* Edited by Donald Mitchell. Translated by Basil Creighton. New York: Viking Press, 1969, pp. 256–257. Mitchell suggests that this letter refers to one of the performances of Mahler's Third Symphony in Vienna on December 14 and 22, 1904, concluding on the basis of this that the date must have been incorrectly transcribed.

1.17 "Bells over the Thury," July 21, 1932. G.o. ASC T04.16, BIO III 16 "Glocken am Thury," 21. VII. 1932. Translation adapted from Lebrecht, Norman. *Mahler Remembered.* New York: Norton, 1988, pp. 170–171. Format and emphases following original ms (ASC).

1.18 From "Prefaces to the Records of the Four String Quartets" (1937). E.o. ASC T70.01, from the edited typescript.

1.19 Schoenberg's "Private Program" for the First String Quartet (c. 1904). Translation from Benson, Mark. "Schoenberg's Private Program for the String Quartet in D Minor, Op. 7." *Journal of Musicology* 11 (1993): 379.

Chapter 2: 1906–1911

2.1   From "Program Notes for the First Chamber Symphony," Op. 9 (1906), 1949. E.o. ASC T31.13G. Written for a Dial Records recording DLP 2 (1950); also published in *The Music of Arnold Schoenberg,* vol. 3. Columbia M2S 709 (1965). The version here follows Schoenberg's typescript (ASC), with small changes for readability.

2.2   Draft of a Will ("Testaments-Entwurf"), c. 1908. G.o. ASC T06.08. Transcription by Anita Luginbühl, ASI; translation includes passages from a translation by Thomas Wallner, ASI.

2.3   From "Prefaces to the Records of the Four String Quartets," 1937.

2.4   "With Arnold Schoenberg: An Interview by Paul Wilhelm." G.o. Published in the *Neues Wiener Journal,* January 10, 1909. Reprinted in *GS,* pp. 157–159. The opening section of the article in the introductory notes is given in *GS,* pp. 488–489.

2.5   Letter to Karl Kraus (c. January–February, 1909). G.o. LC. Addressed: IX. Liechtensteinstrasse 68/70.

2.6   "Open Letter to Mr. Ludwig Karpath," *Die Fackel* 10, nos. 272–273 (February 15, 1909): 34–35. G.o.

2.7   Aphorisms from *Die Musik* 9/4, no. 21 (1909): 159–163. G.o. ASC T03.63G and T27.12.

2.8   From a Letter to Mathilde Schoenberg, June 23, 1909. G.o. From an excerpt printed in *LB,* p. 60.

2.9   Introduction to the Three Pieces for Piano, Op. 11, July 27, 1949. E.o. ASC T31.17. Written for Steuermann's recording of the piano music, Columbia ML 5216 (1957).

2.10 From Two Letters to Ferruccio Busoni, c. August 18 and August 24, 1909. Beaumont, *Busoni: Selected Letters,* pp. 388–389; 391–397. The first, undated letter was started sometime before the completion of Op. 11, No. 3, on August 7, 1909; the final section was added shortly after. According to Beaumont the partly illegible postmark is dated either August 13 or 18, 1909. Ibid., p. 390, n. 1.

2.11 Program and Foreword to a Concert, January 14, 1910. G.o. ASC T14.05. Facsimile in *LB,* p. 70. Translation adapted from Reich, *Schoenberg,* pp. 48–49.

2.12 Letter to Carl Moll, June 16, 1910. G.o. PML. Transcribed by Isabella Goldschmidt. An excerpt was printed in translation in Kallir, Jane. *Arnold Schoenberg's Vienna.* New York: Galerie St. Etienne, 1984, p. 44. Addressed: Hietzinger Hauptstrasse 113.

2.13 From *Die glückliche Hand,* Op. 18 (libretto completed June 1910, music composed 1910–1913). Translation, with small modifications, by David

Johnson, published in the liner notes to *The Music of Arnold Schoenberg,* vol. 1, Columbia M2S 679 (1963), and in *SK,* pp. 91–98.

2.14 Letter to Alma Mahler, October 7, 1910. G.o. Correspondence of Alma Mahler Werfel, University of Pennsylvania Library. Translation of the first paragraph adapted from Crawford, John. *"Die glückliche Hand: Further Notes."* *JASI* 4/1 (1980): 73.

2.15 Letter to Wassily Kandinsky, January 24, 1911. *SK,* pp. 22–24. German originals in Hahl-Koch, Jelena, ed. *Arnold Schönberg–Wassily Kandinsky: Briefe, Bilder und Dokumente einer außergewöhnlichen Begegnung.* Salzburg and Vienna: Residenz Verlag, 1980, pp. 21–22. Addressed: Hietzinger Hauptstrasse 113.

2.16 From the *Theory of Harmony* [*Harmonielehre*]. First edition, Vienna: Universal Edition, 1911, pp. 30–33; third edition, 1922, *Theory of Harmony.* Translated by Roy E. Carter. Berkeley and Los Angeles: University of California Press, 1978, pp. 29–31.

2.17 From a Letter to Alma Mahler, March 27, 1911. G.o. From an excerpt published in *LB,* p. 77.

2.18 Letter to Kraus (c. summer 1911). G.o. LC. Addressed: Hietzinger Hauptstrasse 113.

Chapter 3: 1911–1917

3.1 Letter to C. F. Peters Publishing House, October 19, 1911. G.o. Klemm, Eberhardt. "Der Briefwechsel zwischen Arnold Schönberg und dem Verlag C. F. Peters." *Deutsches Jahrbuch der Musikwissenschaft* 15 (1970): 12–13. Addressed: Berlin-Zehlendorf, Wannseebahn, Machnower Chaussee, Villa Lepcke.

3.2 Letter to Kandinsky, December 14, 1911. *SK,* pp. 38–40. Addressed: Berlin-Zehlendorf.

3.3 Aphorisms, 1911–1912, published in the *Gutmann Concert Calendar* for the 1911–1912 season, Aphorisms VII 2 9 L. 9; and in *Der Ruf,* February 1912, pp. 46–47. G.o. ASC T14.13 and T14.14. Aphorism VII 3 10. Translations of "A poor devil . . ." and "Dramatic music . . ." adapted from *BSC,* p. 73, n. 9.

3.4 From the *Berlin Diary.* Translation adapted from Schoenberg, "Attempt at a Diary." Translated by Anita Luginbühl. *JASI* 9/1 (1986): 9–16, 21–22, 29–30, 35–36, 39–41. German original in Schönberg, Arnold. *Berliner Tagebuch.* Edited by Josef Rufer. Frankfurt am Main: Verlag Ullstein, 1974. Annotations adapted from these two sources.

3.5 Letter to Kandinsky, August 19, 1912. *SK,* pp. 53–55 (translation modified).

3.6 Letter to Guido Adler, September 7, 1912. Ennulat, Egbert M., ed.,

Arnold Schoenberg Correspondence: A Collection of Translated and Annotated Letters Exchanged with Guido Adler, Pablo Casals, Emanuel Feuermann, and Olin Downes. Metuchen, N.J., and London: Scarecrow Press, 1991, pp. 92–95. Addressed: Berlin-Zehlendorf-Wannseebahn, Machnower Chausee, Villa Lepcke.

3.7 Letter to Berg, October 3, 1912. *BSC,* pp. 115–116. Annotations adapted from this source.

3.8 Preface to the Score of *Pierrot lunaire,* Op. 21. G.o. ASC T22.04G, and from the first publication of the score in 1914 by Universal Edition, translation in *SP,* p. 14.

3.9 Letter to Richard Dehmel, December 13, 1912. *ASL,* pp. 35–36. Addressed: Berlin-Zehlendorf.

3.10 Letter to the Academic Society for Literature and Music in Vienna, March 10, 1913. G.o. Hilmar, Ernst. "Arnold Schönbergs Briefe an den Akademischen Verband für Literatur und Musik in Wien." *Österreichische Musik Zeitschrift* 31/6 (1976): pp. 286–288. Addressed: Berlin-Zehlendorf-Wannseebahn, Machnower Chaussee, Villa Lepcke.

3.11 "Why New Melodies Are Difficult to Understand," October 10, 1913. G.o. ASC T14.19. First published in *Die Konzertwoche.* Vienna: Universal Edition, 1914; translated in Bryan Simms, "New Documents in the Schoenberg-Schenker Polemic," *PNM* 16 (1977): 115–116.

3.12 From a Letter to Alma Mahler, April 1, 1914. G.o. Alma Mahler Collection. University of Pennsylvania.

3.13 Plan for a Symphony (1914–1915). G.o. ASC. Translation and all textual identifications from Bailey, *Programmatic Elements,* p. 85.

3.14 From a Letter to Alma Mahler, August 28, 1914. G.o. From an excerpt of the letter printed in *LB,* pp. 132–133.

3.15 From the *War-Clouds Diary,* 1914–1915. G.o. Translation by Paul Pisk from *JASI* 9/1 (1986): 61, 63, 75, 77, with small modifications. This transcription includes facsimiles of several of the drawings.

3.16 From a Letter to Zemlinsky, January 9, 1915. G.o. Weber, Horst, ed. *Briefwechsel der Wiener Schule: Band 1, Alexander Zemlinsky, Briefwechsel mit Arnold Schönberg, Anton Webern, Alban Berg und Franz Schreker.* Darmstadt: Wissenschaftliche Buchgesellschaft, 1995, pp. 129–133. Translation adapted from a version by Jennifer Shaw.

3.17 "Death Dance of Principles," January 15, 1915. G.o. ASC T07.06. Translation from Bailey, *Programmatic Elements,* pp. 97–100.

3.18 "Turning Point," Text for a Melodrama for the Second Chamber Symphony (c. 1916). *SW* Orchesterwerke IV. Edited by Christian Martin Schmidt: B, 11, vol. 2 (1979), p. 202. Adapted from a translation by Severine Neff in "Cadence after Thirty-Three Years of Revolution: Tonal Form in Schoenberg's Second Chamber Symphony, Op. 38" (forthcoming), and from a translation by Steiner, Ena. "The 'Happy' Hand: Genesis and Interpretation of Schoenberg's *Monumentalkunstwerk.*" *Music Review* 51 (1959): 210–211.

3.19 From the "Analysis of the Four Orchestral Songs, Op. 22." G.o. ASC T17.01. Translated by Claudio Spies, *Perspectives on Schoenberg and Stravinsky.* Edited by Benjamin Boretz and Edward T. Cone. New York: Norton, 1972, pp. 26–27, 31–32, 39.

3.20 Seminar for Composition, September 1, 1917. G.o. ASC T39.01. *LB,* p. 152. Translation adapted from Reich, *Schoenberg,* 110–111, and Smith, Joan Allen. *Schoenberg and His Circle: A Viennese Portrait.* New York: Schirmer, 1986, pp. 161–162.

3.21 From the treatise *Coherence, Counterpoint, Instrumentation, Instruction in Form,* 1917. Translation (with modifications) from Schoenberg, *Coherence, Counterpoint, Instrumentation, Instruction in Form.* Edited by Severine Neff. Translated by Severine Neff and Charlotte Cross. Lincoln and London: University of Nebraska Press, 1994, pp. 3, 5, 7, 9, 11, 13, 15. ©1994 by the University of Nebraska Press. The presentation of the text has been simplified.

3.22 *Jacob's Ladder,* from the Opening Scene, 1915–1917. Translation from Christensen, Jean. "Arnold Schoenberg's Oratorio *Die Jakobsleiter.*" Ph.D. dissertation, University of California at Los Angeles, 1979, vol. 2, pp. 33, 35–38.

3.23 "We knew we didn't live in Paradise . . . " (undated). G.o. ASC T52.15, Fragment V 2.

Chapter 4: 1918–1925

4.1 From "What Is the Influence of the War on Composition?" (undated). E.o. ASC T67.03.

4.2 From the "Prospectus of the Society for Private Musical Performances," 1918. Translated by Stephen Somervell, in Slonimsky, Nicolas. *Music Since 1900.* 3rd ed. New York: Coleman-Ross, 1949, pp. 1307–1308. As cited in Smith, *Schoenberg and His Circle,* pp. 245–247.

4.3 From "Pfitzner: *Three Acts of the Revenge of Palestrina*" (c. 1919). G.o. ASC T06.09, Dich 6. Based on a translation by Nora Henry, ASI.

4.4 "Certainty," June 20, 1919. Translation from Rufer, pp. 148–149. The article was first printed in the *Musikblätter des Anbruch* 4/1–2 (1922): 2–3.

4.5 Letter to Berg, July 16, 1921. *BSC,* p. 308. Addressed: Traunkirchen.

4.6 "When I think of music . . . " Published in *Faithful Eckart* [*Der getreue Eckart*] 2/11 (1921): 512–513. Translation adapted from Maja Reid, ASI.

4.7   "Ostinato," May 13, 1922. G.o. ASC T34.05. Translation adapted from
      Messing, p. 146.

4.8   Letter to Kandinsky, July 22, 1922. *SK*, pp. 73–75. Addressed:
      Traunkirchen.

4.9   "Art Golem," August 15, 1922. G.o. ASC T34.01. From Leonard Stein,
      "Schoenberg: Five Statements," *PNM* 14 (1975): 165.

4.10 From a Letter to Josef Stransky, August 23, 1922. *ASL*, pp. 74–75.

4.11 From the *Theory of Harmony*, third edition, 1922, pp. 400–401.

4.12 Letter to Emil Hertzka, Universal Edition, March 13, 1923. G.o. LC.
      Addressed: Mödling, Bernhardgasse 6.

4.13 Two Letters to Kandinsky, April 19 and May 4, 1923. *SK*, p. 76, pp. 78–
      82. Addressed: Mödling, Bernhardgasse 6.

4.14 From "Composition with Twelve Tones," c. 1923. Translated (with
      modifications) from Shaw, Jennifer. "Schoenberg's Choral Symphony,
      Die Jakobsleiter, and Other Wartime Fragments." Ph.D. dissertation, State
      University of New York at Stony Brook, 2002, pp. 596–606. I have also
      consulted the translation by Arved Ashby in "The Development of
      Berg's Twelve-Tone Aesthetic as Seen in the 'Lyric Suite' and Its
      Sources." Ph.D dissertation, Yale University, 1995, pp. 229–233.

4.15 From the *Gedanke* manuscripts. G.o. ASC, August 19, 1923, T34.29,
      November 12, 1925, T35.02. Translation from Schoenberg, Arnold. *The
      Musical Idea and the Logic, Technique, and Art of Its Presentation.* Edited,
      translated, and with commentary by Patricia Carpenter and Severine
      Neff. New York: Columbia University Press, 1995, pp. 18–19, 395.

4.16 From the *Requiem* (1923). G.o. ASC T07.08. Translation adapted from
      Reich, *Schoenberg*, pp. 142–143, and a translation of the complete text by
      Nora Henry, ASI.

4.17 From a Diary, November 28 and 29, 1923. Arnold Schoenberg, "1923
      Diary." Translated by Jerry McBride and Anita Luginbühl. *JASI* 9/1
      (1986): 79, 81.

4.18 Letter to Prince Egon Fürstenberg, undated, c. April 1924. *ASL*, pp. 108–
      109.

4.19 Foreword to Webern's *Six Bagatelles for String Quartet*, Op. 9, June 1924.
      SI, pp. 483–484.

4.20 From a Letter to Gertrud Kolisch, July 28, 1924. G.o. *LB*, p. 229.

4.21 From the Four Pieces for Mixed Chorus, Op. 27. Universal Edition, 1926.
      Copyright renewed 1953 Gertrud Schoenberg. Translation of No. 1, "No
      Escape," from Ringer, p. 66. Translation of No. 2, adapted from Reich,
      Schoenberg, p. 97.

4.22 Foreword to *Three Satires for Mixed Chorus*, Op. 28 (1925–1926).
      Universal Edition, 1926. Copyright renewed 1953 by Gertrud

Schoenberg. Adapted from the translation in *SP,* pp. 25–26, and Messing, *Neoclassicism,* p. 144.

4.23 *Three Satires for Mixed Chorus,* Op. 28 (1925–1926). Universal Edition, 1926. Translation of I and III adapted from Martin Thrun-Mithoff in Schönberg, *Das Chorwerk,* Sony Classical 1990. S2k 44571. Translation of "Versatility" from White, Eric Walter. *Stravinsky: The Composer and His Works.* Berkeley and Los Angeles: University of California Press, 1966, p. 282.

4.24 Letter to Alexander Weprik, May 11, 1925. G.o. LC. *LB,* p. 247. Addressed: Mödling bei Wien, Bernhardgasse 6.

Chapter 5: 1926–1933.

5.1 "Requirements for Admission to the Master Class at the Prussian Academy of the Arts" (1925). G.o. ASC T21.09, C 1 8 1925.

5.2 "Is There an Opera Crisis?" 1926. G.o. Published in the *Musikblätter des Anbruch* 8/5 (1926): 209.

5.3 "Krenek for Light Music: With Regard to Krenek's Article 'Music in the Present,'" February 26, 1926. G.o. ASC T35.16, D Mus 62.

5.4 "Draft for a Speech on the Theme of the Talking Film," February 1927. G.o. ASC T01.13.

5.5 From "Prefaces to the Records of the Four String Quartets," (1937). E.o. ASC. From "Preface to the Four String Quartets, c. 1949. E.o.

5.6 Letter to Edward Clark, February 24, 1927. G.o. LC. Addressed: Charlottenburg 2, Steinplatz 2, Pension Bavaria.

5.7 "Suggestion for the Foundation of an International School of Style," March 1927. G.o. ASC T39.14. *LB,* p. 254.

5.8 *The Biblical Way,* 1926–1927. G.o. ASC T12.01. Translation by Moshe Lazar, *JASI* 17/1–2 (1994): 229–235; 303–307, 319.

5.9 "Creative Agony," April 7, 1928. G.o. ASC T35.18, BIO 161.

5.10 Selected Aphorisms and Short Statements, 1926–1930. "Alone at Last," February 4, 1928. G.o. ASC T04.15, BIO 124, *LB,* p. 270. "The Tempo of Development," Roquebrune, 1928, ASC T04.17, BIO 135. "Fashion," Roquebrune (c. 1928–1929) ASC T03.57, 58, Aph 403, "Radio" (1) and (2) and "Telegraphic Delivery," ASC T03.25, Aph 228; "Music for the Community," ASC T01.01, Aph 153. "Art for the Community," February 28, 1928. G.o. ASC, T01.04, Ku 127, translation adapted from Anita Luginbühl, ASI. Other aphorisms, G.o. ASC T03.25, Aph 1 25.

5.11 *Moses und Aron,* September–October 1928. Portions of the translation adapted from a translation by Allen Forte, as reprinted in the liner notes for *Moses und Aron,* Pierre Boulez, cond. Deutsche Grammophon 449 174-2 (1996).

5.12 Letter to Georg Schumann, January 6, 1929. G.o. LC. Addressed: Monte Carlo.

5.13 "Since I am unable to speak about matters of feeling," January 8, 1929. G.o. ASC T05.08, Denk 185.

5.14 "An Introduction to a Broadcast of *Von heute auf morgen* [From one day to the next]" (1928–1929). G.o. First section translated in *SP,* p. 38. Complete text in Schönberg, *Berliner Tagebuch,* pp. 43–46. Excerpts from the libretto as translated in Brand, Juliane. "Of Authorship and Partnership: The Libretto of *Von heute auf morgen.*" JASI 14/2 (1991): 167–229.

5.15 The Six Pieces for Male Chorus, Op. 35, 1929–1930. Portions of the translation adapted from Martin Thurn-Mithoff. *Schönberg: Das Chorwerk,* Sony 1990 S2K 44 571, and from the translation by D. Millar Craig and Adolph Weiss in *Sechs Stücke für Männerchor,* Berlin: Bote and Bock, 1930.

5.16 From the "Radio Lecture on the Variations for Orchestra, Op. 31," February 28, 1931. G.o. ASC T16.06. Translation from *The Score—A Music Magazine,* ed. W. Glock, London, July 1960, as printed in *SP,* pp. 41–53.

5.17 To the editor of the *New Viennese Journal,* c. March/April 1932. G.o. LC. Addressed: Juan Marti, Barcelona, Ronda Universidad 132.

5.18 "About Power, Majority, Democracy, Fascism, Etc., Especially also Mussolini" (August 1932). G.o. ASC T33.23, Deut 395.

5.19 "Priority," September 10–11, 1932. G.o. ASC T04.41. Based on the transcription by Michael Beiche, as printed in *Terminologische Aspekte der "Zwölftonmusik."* Munich: Katzbichler, 1984, pp. 159–162.

5.20 Foreword to the Concerto for String Quartet and Orchestra (after Handel), c. 1935. G.o. ASC T20.06, Vermischtes 70. The document is on the verso of a letter dated February 2, 1935. A partial English translation appeared on Columbia Records ML 4066 (1951).

5.21 "The Germans' racial pride now driven to its peak," Arcachon, September 25, 1933. G.o. ASC T39.35, Vermischtes 357 b.

5.22 "My Enemies," October 6, 1933. G.o. ASC T04.30, BIO 355. The first page is dated October 5, 1932.

Chapter 6: 1933–1943

6.1 From "Notes on Jewish Politics," September–November, 1933. G.o. ASC T15.07, Jew 5. Portions of the translations adapted from Maja Reid, ASI.

6.2 "The First American Radio Broadcast: An Interview with William Lundell." E.o. ASC T17.04. Emphasis shown is from the typescript. Also published in Feisst, Sabine. "Schoenberg and America." In *Schoenberg and His World,* edited by Walter Frisch, pp. 293–296. Princeton: Princeton University Press, 1999.

6.3 "The Jewish Situation," April 29, 1934. E.o. ASC T17.09.

6.4 Letter to Hanns Eisler, August 20, 1934. G.o. *LB,* p. 311.

6.5 Letter to David Joseph Bach, March 13, 1935. G.o. LC. An excerpt is printed in Stuckenschmidt, pp. 405–406.

6.6 "What Have People to Expect from Music?" November 7, 1935. E.o. ASC T18.07.

6.7 "Analysis by Ear—Draft of a Letter to Olin Downes, October, 1935." E.o. ASC T36.27, Mus 420. Also printed, with additional materials, in *Arnold Schoenberg Correspondence,* pp. 217–230.

6.8 Sketch of a Foreword to the Suite for String Orchestra, Composed for College Orchestras by Arnold Schoenberg. Undated. G.o. ASC T20.05. Translation by Dika Newlin, in Rufer, p. 81.

6.9 "Fascism is no article for exportation," c. 1935. E.o. ASC T38.12G. Published in a German translation in *GS,* pp. 313–319.

6.10 "Some Objective Reasons to Educate Rising Generations to Contemporary Music," c. 1936. E.o. ASC T19.01. According to *GS,* p. 497, it was given the date 1934 in Schoenberg's catalogue of his writings. Rufer assigned it the date 1936, remarking, "Probably spoken at a meeting of teachers."

6.11 "The Twenty-Fifth Anniversary of Mahler's Death," August 8, 1936. G.o. ASC T24.14. Translation adapted in part from Nora Henry, ASI.

6.12 From "Prefaces to the Records of the Four String Quartets" (1937).

6.13 On the *Kol Nidre,* Op. 39, c. 1938. E.o. ASC T24.04.

6.14 Letter to Edgard Varèse, May 23, 1939. E.o. LC. The letter was addressed to Edgar Varèse, Chairman, The Ten, c/o Mr. Adolf Weiss, 1803½ Bronson Avenue, Hollywood, Calif.

6.15 "Vienna, Vienna, Only You Alone," November 1939. G.o. ASC T24.13. Facsimiles of both versions are given in Feisst, "Schoenberg and America," in *Schoenberg and His World,* pp. 303–305. Translation adapted from Feisst.

6.16 Letter to Robert Emmett Stuart, January 27, 1940. E.o. LC.

6.17 Two letters to Mr. Gene Buck, President of ASCAP, April 10 and September 5, 1941. E.o. LC. The letter is addressed to: Mr. Gene Buck, President, American Society of Composers, Authors, and Publishers, 30, Rockefeller Plaza, New York, N.Y.

6.18 "How I Came to Compose the Ode to Napoleon" (undated). E.o. ASC T68.05. Facsimile published in *JASI* 2/1 (1977): 55–57.

6.19 From "Materials for Orchestration" (undated). E.o. ASC T68.13, Orch 1 7.

6.20 Two Canons for Carl Engel, 1943. G.o. Translation from *Arnold Schönberg: 30 Kanons,* ed. Josef Rufer. Kassel: Bärenreiter, 1963, p. 27.

6.21 Letter to Edgard Varèse, October 27, 1943. E.o. LC. The letter is addressed to: Mr. Edgar Varèse, 188 Sullivan Street, N.Y.C.

6.22 Letter to Bruno Walter, December 23, 1943. G.o. LC. Translation adapted from Cahn, Steven. "Variations in Manifold Time: Historical Consciousness in the Music and Writings of Arnold Schoenberg." Ph.D. dissertation, State University of New York at Stony Brook, 1996, pp. 167–168. The letter is addressed to: Mr. Bruno Walter, 965 Fifth Avenue, New York, N.Y.

Chapter 7: 1944–1951

7.1 Canon for Richard Rodzinski, 1944. E.o., except for final sentence, G.o. *Arnold Schönberg: 30 Kanons,* p. 63.

7.2 From "Notes for an Autobiography" (1944–1945). E.o. and G.o. ASC T42.03. "Franz Schreker," January 2, 1944; "To all my critics," August 23, 1945; "Anton von Webern" (undated); "Koussevitzki—Toscanini" (c. August 1944); "My sense of measures and forms" (undated); "Hindemith" (undated); "My music is supposedly not *emotional . . .* " (undated); "Schopenhauer," September 24, 1944; "When I was a young man in Vienna . . . " (undated).

7.3 Letter to Kurt List, February 12, 1945. E.o. LC. The letter is addressed to: Mr. Kurt List, Editor, *Listen,* 274 Madison Avenue, New York 16 N.Y.

7.4 "My Fatality," 1949. Translated in Bailey, *Programmatic Elements,* pp. 152–154.

7.5 "For the Radio Broadcast of the String Trio," May 1949. E.o. ASC T52.05.

7.6 "On Strauss and Furtwängler," 1946. Printed in Stuckenschmidt, pp. 544–545.

7.7 "A Solemn Declaration about Pfitzner," September 10, 1947. G.o. LC.

7.8 Schoenberg's Reply to the National Institute of Arts and Letters, June 1947. E.o. ASC T66.01. *LB,* p. 406.

7.9 *A Survivor from Warsaw,* Op. 46, 1947. E.o. As printed in *SW.* Abteilung V: Chorwerke, Reihe B, Band 19. Chorwerke II, edited by Christian Martin Schmidt, pp. 72–73. Mainz and Vienna: B. Schott's Söhne and Universal Edition, 1977. Translation of German passages and the closing *Sch'ma Israel* by Martin Thurn-Mithoff. *Arnold Schoenberg, Music For Chorus.* Sony Classical: S2K 44571 (1990).

7.10 Letter to Mrs. Jay Grear, November 13, 1948. E.o. LC. The letter is addressed to: Mrs. Jay Grear, Albuquerque Civic Symphony Orchestra, P.O. Box 605, Albuquerque, New Mexico.

7.11 "A Text from the Third Millennium," February 1948. Cited in Stuckenschmidt, pp. 547–548.

7.12 Letter to René Leibowitz and Josef Rufer, October 20, 1948. G.o. LC.

7.13 *Formalism,* February 13, 1949. E.o. ASC T51.15.

7.14 "My Subject: Beauty and Logic in Music" (undated). E.o. ASC T67.02, Notebook III.

7.15 "To the San Francisco Round-Table on Modern Art," April 8, 1949. E.o. ASC T72.01. German translation in *GS,* pp. 392–396.

7.16 "Israel Exists Again!" June 10, 1949. E.o. ASC T32.20, as printed in *SW.* Abteilung V: Chorwerke, Reihe B, Band 19. Chorwerke II, p. 138.

7.17 "To become recognized only after one's death—!" September, 1949. G.o. ASC T44.07. Translation by Schoenberg, LC. An edited version of the English text is published in *ASL,* p. 290.

7.18 "To Twelve American Conductors," September 13, 1949. E.o. ASC T52.15, Fragment V 6.

7.19 Letter to Roger Sessions, November 7, 1949. E.o. LC. The letter is addressed to: Professor Roger Sessions, Music Department, University of California, Berkeley, California.

7.20 Letter to Kurt List, December 10, 1949. G.o. LC. The letter is addressed to: Mr. Kurt List, 120 Riverside Drive, New York, 25, NY.

7.21 "Wiesengrund," December, 1950. G.o. ASC T32.12.

7.22 Four Statements, January 28, 1950. E.o. LC.

7.23 "For My Broadcast," August 22, 1949. E.o. LC and ASC T31.14.

7.24 "In Answer to Aaron Copland's Reply, December 23, 1949." E.o. LC and ASC T56.07.

7.25 Letter to Aaron Copland, February 21, 1950. E.o. LC. The letter is addressed to: Mr. Aaron Copland, River Road Palisades, New York, N.Y.

7.26 Letter to Josef Rufer, April 8, 1950. G.o. LC. The letter is addressed to: Mr. Josef Rufer, Juttastrasse 16, Berlin-Zehlendorf, Germany.

7.27 Two Letters to Dimitri Mitropoulos, April 26 and July 4, 1950. E.o. LC. The first letter is addressed to: Mr. Dimitri Mitropoulos, Director, New York Philharmonic, New York, N.Y.; the second letter is addressed to: Mr. Dimitri Mitropoulos, 118 West 57th Street, New York 19, N.Y.

7.28 "Gentlemen: My case differs in some respects from the average," August 2, 1950. E.o. ASC T43.10, BIO V 8.

7.29 "To My Dead Friends" (c. 1950). E.o. ASC T75.10; a German translation is published in *GS,* p. xix.

7.30 Letter to Oedoen Partos, April 26, 1951. E.o. ASC T32.07. Published in Ringer, pp. 245–246. The letter was addressed to Frank Pelleg, who was director of the Music Section of the Israeli Ministry of Culture.

7.31 From the *Modern Psalms,* 1950–1951. G.o. ASC T32.13 and T69.13. Facsimile edition of sketches and texts, *Moderne Psalmen von Arnold Schoenberg.* Edited by Rudolf Kolisch. Mainz: B. Schott's Söhne, 1956. Translation of No. 1 adapted from Reich, *Schoenberg,* pp. 232–233. Translation of the last two paragraphs of No. 6 from Ringer, p. 180.

Selected Bibliography

Armitage, Merle, ed. *Schoenberg*. New York, 1937; reprint, Freeport, N.Y.: Books for Libraries Press, 1971.

Arnold Schönberg. Publikation des Archivs der Akademie der Künste zu Arnold Schönberg-Veranstaltung innerhalb der Berliner Festwochen. Berlin: Berlin Festspiele, 1974.

Arnold Schönberg in höchster Verehrung von Schülern und Freunden. Munich: R. Piper Verlag, 1912; reprint, Wels, Austria: Duckerei Welsermühl, 1980.

Arnold Schönberg zum fünfzigsten Geburtstage, 13. September 1924. Vienna: Sonderheft der *Musikblätter des Anbruch,* 1924.

Auner, Joseph. "The Evolution of Form in *Die glückliche Hand.*" *JASI* 12/2 (1989): 103–128.

——." 'Heart and Brain in Music': The Genesis of *Die glückliche Hand.*" In Brand, *Constructive Dissonance,* pp. 112–130.

——. "On the Emotional Character of Schoenberg's Music." In *Schönberg & Nono: A Birthday Offering to Nuria on May 7, 2002.* Edited by Anna Maria Morazzoni. Florence: Leo S. Olschki, 2002.

——. "Schoenberg and His Public in 1930: The Six Pieces for Male Chorus, Op. 35." In Frisch, *Schoenberg and His World,* pp. 85–125.

——. "Schoenberg's Handel Concerto and the Ruins of Tradition." *Journal of the American Musicological Society* 49/2 (1996): 264–313.

——. "Soulless Machines and Steppenwolves: Renegotiating Masculinity in Krenek's *Jonny spielt auf.*" In *Siren Songs.* Edited by Mary Ann Smart. Princeton: Princeton University Press, 2000, pp. 222–236.

Ashby, Arved. "The Development of Berg's Twelve-Tone Aesthetic as Seen in the 'Lyric Suite' and Its Sources." Ph.D. dissertation, Yale University, 1995.

——. "Schoenberg, Boulez, and Twelve-Tone Composition as Ideal Type." *Journal of the American Musicological Society* 54/3 (2001): 585–625.

Bailey, Kathryn. *The Life of Webern.* Cambridge: Cambridge University Press, 1998.

Bailey, Walter Boyce. *The Arnold Schoenberg Companion.* Westport, Conn.: Greenwood Press, 1998.

——. "Composer Versus Critic: The Schoenberg-Schmidt Polemic." *JASI* 4/2 (1980): 119–137.

——. "Filling in the Gaps: Jean and Jesper Christensen's *From Arnold Schoenberg's Literary Legacy, a Catalog of Neglected Items.*" *JASI* 12/1 (1989): 91–97.

——. *Programmatic Elements in the Works of Arnold Schoenberg.* Studies in Musicology, No. 74. Ann Arbor: UMI Research Press, 1984.

——. "Schoenberg's Published Articles: A List of Titles, Sources, and Translations." *JASI* 4/2 (1980): 156–191.

Beaumont, Antony, ed. and trans. *Ferruccio Busoni: Selected Letters.* New York: Columbia University Press, 1987.

Behrens, Wolfgang. "Der Komponist Oskar C. Posa, 1873–1951." M.A. thesis, Free University Berlin, 1996.

Benson, Mark. "Arnold Schoenberg and the Crisis of Modernism." Ph.D. dissertation, University of California at Los Angeles, 1988.

——. "Schoenberg's Private Program for the String Quartet in D Minor, Op. 7." *Journal of Musicology* 11 (1993): 374–395.

Birke, Joachim. "Richard Dehmel und Arnold Schönberg, ein Briefwechsel." *Die Musikforschung* 11 (1958): 279–285.

Boss, Jack. "Schoenberg's Op. 22 Radio Talk and Developing Variation in Atonal Music." *Music Theory Spectrum* 14/2 (1992): 125–149.

Brand, Juliane. "A Short History of *Von heute auf morgen* with Letters and Documents." *JASI* 14/2 (1991): 241–270.

Brand, Juliane, Christopher Hailey, and Donald Harris, eds. *The Berg-Schoenberg Correspondence: Selected Letters.* New York: Norton, 1988.

——. "Catalog of the Correspondence Between Alban Berg and Arnold Schoenberg." *JASI* 11/1 (1988): 70–97.

Brinkmann, Reinhold. *Arnold Schönberg: Drei Klavierstücke, Op. 11. Studien zur frühen Atonalität bei Schönberg.* Beihefte zum *Archiv für Musikwissenschaft* 7. Wiesbaden: Franz Steiner Verlag, 1969.

——. "What the Sources Tell Us: A Chapter of *Pierrot Philology.*" *JASI* 10/1 (1987): 11–27.

Brinkmann, Reinhold, and Christoph Wolff, eds. *Driven into Paradise: The Musical Migration from Nazi Germany to the United States.* Berkeley and Los Angeles: University of California Press, 1999.

Breuer, János. "Schoenberg's Paintings: 'Visions, Impressions and Fantasies,' a 1912 Exhibition in Budapest." *New Hungarian Quarterly* 29/111 (1988): 215–221.

Brown, Julie. "Schoenberg's *Das Buch der hängenden Garten:* Analytical, Cultural, and Ideological Perspectives." Ph.D. dissertation, London University, 1993.

Cahn, Steven J. "Variations in Manifold Time: Historical Consciousness in the Music and Writings of Arnold Schoenberg." Ph.D. dissertation, State University of New York at Stony Brook, 1996.

Carter, Roy E. "On Translating Schoenberg's *Harmonielehre.*" *College Music Symposium* 23/2 (1983): 164–176.

Cherlin, Michael. "Dialectical Opposition in Schoenberg's Music and Thought." *Music Theory Spectrum* 22/2 (2000): 157–176.

Christensen, Jean. "Arnold Schoenberg's Oratorio *Die Jakobsleiter.*" Ph.D. dissertation, University of California at Los Angeles, 1979.

——. "Schoenberg's Sketches for *Die Jakobsleiter:* A Study of a Special Case." *JASI* 2/2 (1978): 112–121.

Christensen, Jean, and Jesper Christensen. *From Arnold Schoenberg's Literary Legacy: A Catalog of Neglected Items.* Warren, Mich.: Harmonie Press, 1988.

Comini, Alessandra. "Through a Viennese Looking-Glass Darkly: Images of Arnold Schoenberg and His Circle." *Arts Magazine* 58/9 (1984): 107–119.

Cook, Susan. C. *Opera for a New Republic: The* Zeitopern *of Krenek, Weill, and Hindemith.* Ann Arbor: UMI Research Press, 1988.

Covach, John. "Schoenberg and the Occult: Some Reflections on the History of an Idea." *Theory and Practice* 17 (1992): 103–118.

——. "Schoenberg's 'Poetics of Music,' the Twelve-Tone Method, and the Musical Idea." In Cross, *Schoenberg and Words: The Modernist Years,* pp. 309–346.

——. "The Sources of Schoenberg's 'Aesthetic Theology.'" *19th-Century Music* 19/3 (1996): 252–262.

Cramer, Alfred. "Music for the Future: Sounds of Psychology and Language in Works of Schoenberg, Webern, and Berg, 1909 to the First World War." Ph.D. dissertation, University of Pennsylvania, 1997.

Crawford, John. "*Die glückliche Hand:* Further Notes." *JASI* 4/1 (1980): 68–76.

——. "Schoenberg's Artistic Development to 1911." In Hahl-Koch, *Arnold Schoenberg–Wassily Kandinsky,* pp. 171–186.

Crawford, John and Dorothy. *Expressionism in Twentieth-Century Music.* Bloomington: Indiana University Press, 1993.

Crittenden, Camille. "Texts and Contexts of *A Survivor from Warsaw,* Op. 46." In Cross, *Political and Religious Ideas in the Works of Arnold Schoenberg,* pp. 231–258.

Cross, Charlotte. "Schoenberg's Earliest Thoughts on the Theory of Composition: A Fragment from c. 1900." *Theoria: Historical Aspects of Music Theory* 8 (1994): 113–133.

Cross, Charlotte, and Russell A. Berman. *Political and Religious Ideas in the Works of Arnold Schoenberg.* New York and London: Garland, 2000.

——. *Schoenberg and Words: The Modernist Years.* New York and London: Garland, 2000.

Dabrowski, Magdalena. *Kandinsky's Compositions.* New York: Museum of Modern Art, 1995.

Dahlhaus, Carl. *Schoenberg and the New Music.* Translated by Derrick Puffett and Alfred Clayton. Cambridge: Cambridge University Press, 1987.

Davison, Stephen. "Of Its Time, or Out of Step? Schoenberg's *Zeitoper Von heute auf morgen." JASI* 14/2 (1991): 271–298.

DeLapp, Jennifer L. "Copland in the Fifties: Music and Ideology in the McCarthy Era." Ph.D. dissertation, University of Michigan, 1997.

Dümling, Albrecht. " 'Im Zeichen der Erkenntnis der socialen Verhältnisse,' Der junge Schönberg und die Arbeitersängerbewegung." *Zeitschrift für Musiktheorie* 6 (1975): 11–14.

Dunsby, Jonathan. *Schoenberg: Pierrot lunaire.* Cambridge Music Handbooks. General editor Julian Rushton. Cambridge: Cambridge University Press, 1992.

Ennulat, Egbert M., ed. *Arnold Schoenberg Correspondence: A Collection of Translated and Annotated Letters Exchanged with Guido Adler, Pablo Casals, Emanuel Feuermann, and Olin Downes.* Metuchen, N.J., and London: Scarecrow Press, 1991.

Erwin, Charlotte E., and Bryan R. Simms, "Schoenberg's Correspondence with Heinrich Schenker." *JASI* 5/1 (1981): 23–45.

Evans, Joan. "New Light on the First Performances of Arnold Schoenberg's *Opera* 34 and 35." *JASI* 11/2 (1988): 163–173.

Feisst, Sabine. "Arnold Schoenberg and the Cinematic Art." *Musical Quarterly* 83/1 (1999): 93–113.

——. "Schoenberg and America." In Frisch, *Schoenberg and His World,* pp. 288–311.

Forte, Allen. "Schoenberg's Creative Evolution: The Path to Atonality." *Musical Quarterly* 59/2 (1978): 133–176.

——. Posting concerning *Moses und Aron* to the AMS-List (ams-1@ Virginia.edu), April 30, 1999.

Frisch, Walter. *The Early Works of Arnold Schoenberg, 1893–1908.* Berkeley and Los Angeles: University of California Press, 1993.

——, ed. *Schoenberg and His World.* Princeton: Princeton University Press, 1999.

Glennan, Kathryn, et al. *A Preliminary Catalogue of the Archives of the Arnold Schoenberg Institute.* Los Angeles: Arnold Schoenberg Institute, 1986.

Goehr, Alexander. "Schoenberg and Karl Kraus: The Idea Behind the Music." *Music Analysis* 4 (1985): 59–71.

Goehr, Alexander. "The Theoretical Writings of Arnold Schoenberg." *PNM* 13/2 (1975): 3–16.

Gradenwitz, Peter. *Arnold Schönberg und seine Meisterschüler: Berlin, 1925–1933.* Vienna: Paul Zsolnay Verlag, 1998.

Gruber, Gerold, ed. *Arnold Schönberg: Interpretationen seiner Werke.* Laaber: Laaber, 2002.

Hahl-Koch, Jelena, ed. *Arnold Schoenberg, Wassily Kandinsky: Letters, Pictures, and Documents.* Translated by John C. Crawford. London and Boston: Faber and Faber, 1984.

Hailey, Christopher. "Rethinking Sound: Music and Radio in Weimar Germany." In *Music and Performance During the Weimar Republic.* Edited by Bryan Gilliam, pp. 13–36. Cambridge: Cambridge University Press, 1994.

——. "Webern's Letters to David Josef Bach." *Mitteilungen der Paul Sacher Stiftung* 9 (1996): 35–40.

Haimo, Ethan. "Atonality, Analysis, and the Intentional Fallacy." *Music Theory Spectrum* 18/2 (1996): 167–199.

——. *Schoenberg's Serial Odyssey: The Evolution of His Twelve-Tone Method, 1914–1928.* Oxford: Clarendon Press, 1990.

Hansen, Mathias, and Christa Müller, eds. *Arnold Schönberg—1874 bis 1951; Zum 25 Todestag des Komponisten.* Berlin: Akademie der Künste der Deutschen Demokratischen Republik, 1976.

Heller, Friedrich C., ed. *Arnold Schönberg–Franz Schreker Briefwechsel.* Tutzing: Hans Schneider, 1974.

Hilmar, Ernst. "Arnold Schönbergs Briefe an den Akademischen Verband für Literatur und Musik in Wien." *Österreichische Musik Zeitschrift* 31/6 (1976): 273–292.

——. "Zemlinsky und Schoenberg." In *Alexander Zemlinsky: Tradition im umkreis der Wiener Schule.* Edited by Otto Kollertisch. Studien zur Wertungsforschung, No. 7. Graz: Universal Edition für Institut für Wertungsforschung, 1976.

Hilmar, Ernst, ed. *Arnold Schönberg, Gedenkausstellung 1974.* Vienna: Universal Edition, 1974.

Hough, Bonny Ellen. "Schoenberg's 'Herzgewächse' and the *Blaue Reiter Alamanac.*" *JASI* 7/2 (1983): 197–221.

Hyde, Martha. "The Format and Function of Schoenberg's Twelve-Tone Sketches." *Journal of the American Musicological Society* 34/3 (1983): 453–480.

Janik, Allan, and Stephen, Toulmin. *Wittgenstein's Vienna.* New York: Simon and Schuster, 1973.

Jelavich, Peter. *Berlin Cabaret.* Cambridge, Mass., and London: Harvard University Press, 1993.

Johnston, William M. *The Austrian Mind: An Intellectual and Social History, 1848–1938.* Berkeley and Los Angeles: University of California Press, 1972.

——. "The Vienna School of Aphorists, 1880–1930: Reflections on a Neglected

Genre." In *The Turn of the Century: German Literature and Art, 1890–1915*. Edited by Gerald Chapple and Hans Schulte, pp. 275–290. Bonn: Bouvier Verlag, 1983.

Kallir, Jane. *Arnold Schoenberg's Vienna*. New York: Galerie St. Etienne and Rizzoli, 1984.

Kandinsky, Wassily. *The Blaue Reiter Almanac: New Documentary Edition*. Edited and with an introduction by Klaus Lankheit. New York: Viking Press, 1974.

——. *Kandinsky: The Complete Writings on Art*. Edited by Kenneth C. Lindsay and Peter Vergo. 2 vols. Boston: G. K. Hall, 1982.

——. "The Paintings of Schoenberg." *JASI* 2/3 (1978): 181–184.

Kater, Michael H. *The Twisted Muse: Musicians and Their Music in the Third Reich*. New York and Oxford: Oxford University Press, 1997.

Keathley, Elizabeth. "'*Die Frauenfrage*' in *Erwartung*: Schoenberg's Collaboration with Marie Pappenheim." In Cross, *Schoenberg and Words: The Modernist Years*, pp. 139–178.

——. "Revisioning Musical Modernism: Arnold Schoenberg, Marie Pappenheim, and *Erwartung*'s New Woman." Ph.D. dissertation, State University of New York at Stony Brook, 1999.

Klemm, Eberhardt. "Der Briefwechsel zwischen Arnold Schönberg und dem Verlag C. F. Peters." *Deutsches Jahrbuch der Musikwissenschaft* 15 (1970): 5–66.

Kraus, Karl. *In These Great Times: A Karl Kraus Reader*. Edited by Harry Zohn. Manchester: Carcanet Press, 1984.

Kropfinger, Klaus. "Latent Structural Power versus the Dissolution of Artistic Material." In *Schoenberg and Kandinsky: An Historic Encounter*. Edited by Konrad Boehmer, pp. 9–65. Amsterdam: Harwood, 1997.

La Grange, Henry-Louis de. *Gustav Mahler: Volume. 2, Vienna: The Years of Challenge (1897–1904)*. Oxford and New York: Oxford University Press, 1995.

Lazar, Moshe. "Arnold Schoenberg and His Doubles: A Psychodramatic Journey to His Roots." *JASI* 17/1-2 (1994): 8–161.

Lebrecht, Norman. *Mahler Remembered*. New York: Norton, 1988.

Leibowitz, René. *Schoenberg and His School: The Contemporary Stage of the Language of Music*. Translated by Dika Newlin. New York: Da Capo Press, 1979.

Lesure, François. *Dossier de Presse de* Pierrot Lunaire *d'Arnold Schoenberg*. Geneva: Minkoff, 1985.

MacDonald, Malcolm. *Schoenberg*. London: Dent, 1976.

Maegaard, Jan. "Schönberg: The Texts He Used." *Dansk aarbog for musikforskning* 25 (1997): 15–42.

——. "Schoenberg's Incomplete Works and Fragments." In Brand, *Constructive Dissonance,* pp. 131–145.

——. "Schoenberg's Late Tonal Works." In Bailey, *The Arnold Schoenberg Companion,* pp. 177–206.

——. "Schoenberg's Manuscripts, What Do They Tell Us?" *JASI* 1/2 (1977): 68–74.

——. *Studien zur Entwicklung des dodekaphonen Satzes bei Arnold Schönberg.* 2 vols. and supplement. Copenhagen: Wilhelm Hansen, 1972.

Mahler, Alma. *Gustav Mahler: Memories and Letters.* Edited by Donald Mitchell. Translated by B. Creighton. Seattle: University of Washington Press, 1975.

Mann, Thomas. *Dr. Faustus: The Life of the German Composer as Told by a Friend.* Translated by John E. Woods. New York: Alfred A. Knopf, 1997.

——. *Letters of Thomas Mann—1889–1955.* Edited and translated by Richard and Clara Winston. Berkeley and Los Angeles: University of California Press, 1990.

Mayer, Hans. "Ein Briefwechsel zwischen Arnold Schönberg und Hermann Scherchen, 1950." In *Hermann Scherchen Musiker, 1891–1966.* Edited by Hansjörg Pauli and Dagmar Wünsche, pp. 62–67. Berlin: Akademie der Künste, 1986.

McGeary, Thomas. "The Publishing History of *Style and Idea.*" *JASI* 9/2 (1986): 181–209.

——. "Schoenberg's Brahms Lecture of 1933." *JASI* 15/2 (1992): 5–21.

Mersmann, Hans. *Die Moderne Musik seit der Romantik.* Potsdam: Akademiche Verlag, 1928.

Messing, Scott. *Neoclassicism in Music: From the Genesis of the Concept Through the Schoenberg-Stravinsky Polemic.* Studies in Musicology, No. 101. Ann Arbor: UMI Research Press, 1988.

Metzger, Heinz-Klaus, and Rainer Riehn, eds. *Musik-Konzepte Sonderband: Arnold Schoenberg.* Munich: edition text + kritik, 1980.

Meyer, Andreas, and Ullrich Scheideler, eds. *Arnold Schönberg (1874–1951): Autorschaft als historische Konstruktion Vorgänger, Zeitgenossen, Nachfolger und Interpreten.* Stuttgart: J. B. Metzter Verlag, 2001.

Morgan, Robert P. "Secret Languages: The Roots of Musical Modernism." *Critical Inquiry* 10/3 (1984): 442–461.

——. *Twentieth-Century Music: A History of Musical Style in Modern Europe and America.* New York and London: Norton, 1991.

Neff, Severine. "Cadence after Thirty-Three Years of Revolution: Tonal Form in Schoenberg's Second Chamber Symphony, Op. 38" (forthcoming).

Neighbour, Oliver W., et al. *The New Grove Second Viennese School.* London: Macmillan, 1983.

Neumeyer, David, and Giselher Schubert. "Arnold Schoenberg and Paul Hindemith." *JASI* 13/1 (1990): 3–46.

Newlin, Dika. *Bruckner-Mahler-Schoenberg.* 2nd rev. ed. New York: Norton, 1978.

Nono-Schoenberg, Nuria. "The Role of Extra-Musical Pursuits in Arnold Schoenberg's Creative Life." *JASI* 5/1 (1981): 51–58.

——, ed. *Arnold Schönberg, 1874–1951: Lebensgeschichte in Begegnungen.* Klagenfurt: Ritter, 1992.

Olmstead, Andrea. "The Correspondence Between Arnold Schoenberg and Roger Sessions." *JASI* 13/1 (1990): 47–62.

Raessler, Daniel M. "Schoenberg and Busoni: Aspects of Their Relationship." *JASI* 7/1 (1983): 7–23.

Rauchhaupt, Ursula. *Schoenberg/Berg/Webern: The String Quartets: A Documentary Study.* Hamburg: Deutsche Grammophon, 1971.

Reich, Willi. *Schoenberg: A Critical Biography.* Translated by Leo Black. New York and Washington: Praeger, 1971.

Reif, Jo-Ann. "Adrian Leverkühn, Arnold Schoenberg, Theodor Adorno: Theorists Real and Fictitious in Thomas Mann's *Doctor Faustus.*" *JASI* 7/1 (1983): 102–112.

Rognoni, Luigi. *The Second Vienna School.* Translated by Robert W. Mann. London: Calder, 1977.

Rosen, Charles. *Arnold Schoenberg.* Princeton: Princeton University Press, 1981.

Rufer, Josef. *Die Komposition mit zwölf Tönen.* Berlin: Max Hesses Verlag, 1952. English edition: *Composition with Twelve Tones.* Translated by Humphrey Searle. New York: Macmillan, 1954.

——. *The Works of Arnold Schoenberg: A Catalogue of His Compositions, Writings, and Paintings.* Translated by Dika Newlin. London: Faber and Faber, 1962.

Schoenberg, Arnold. "Analysis of the Four Orchestral Songs, Op. 22." Translated by Claudio Spies. *Perspectives on Schoenberg and Stravinsky.* Edited by Benjamin Boretz and Edward T. Cone, pp. 25–46. New York: Norton, 1972.

——. *Arnold Schönberg: 30 Kanons.* Edited by Josef Rufer. Kassel: Bärenreiter, 1963.

——. *Arnold Schoenberg Letters.* Edited by Erwin Stein. Translated by Eithne Wilkins and Ernst Kaiser. Berkeley and Los Angeles: University of California Press, 1987.

——. "Attempt at a Diary." Translated by Anita Luginbühl. *JASI* 9/1 (1986): 7–51.

——. *Berliner Tagebuch.* Edited by Josef Rufer. Frankfurt am Main: Propyläen Verlag, 1974.

——. *The Biblical Way.* Translated by Moshe Lazar. *JASI* 17/1–2 (1994): 162–330.

——. *Coherence, Counterpoint, Instrumentation, Instruction in Form.* Edited by Severine Neff. Translated by Charlotte Cross and Severine Neff. Lincoln, Neb.: University of Nebraska Press, 1993.

——. *Fundamentals of Musical Composition.* Edited by Gerald Strang and Leonard Stein. London and Boston: Faber and Faber, 1967.

——. *Moderne Psalmen von Arnold Schoenberg.* Edited by Rudolf Kolisch. Mainz: B. Schott's Söhne, 1956.

——. *The Musical Idea and the Logic, Technique, and Art of Its Presentation.* Edited, translated, and with commentary by Patricia Carpenter and Severine Neff. New York: Columbia University Press, 1995.

——. "1923 Diary." Translated by Jerry McBride and Anita Luginbühl. *JASI* 9/1 (1986): 78–83.

——. "Painting Influences." Translated by Gertrud Zeisl. *JASI* 2 (1978): 237–238.

——. *Preliminary Exercises in Counterpoint.* Edited by Leonard Stein. London: Faber and Faber, 1963.

——. "Die Priorität." Transcribed by Michael Beiche. In *Terminologische Aspekte der "Zwölftonmusik,"* pp. 159–162. Munich: Katzbichler, 1984.

——. *Schöpferische Konfessionen.* Edited by Willi Reich. Zurich: Verlag der Arche, 1964.

——. *Stil und Gedanke: Aufsätze zur Musik, Gesammelte Schriften 1.* Edited by Ivan Vojtech. Frankfurt am Main: Propyläen Verlag, 1976.

——. *Structural Functions of Harmony.* Rev. ed. New York: Norton, 1968.

——. *Style and Idea: Selected Writings of Arnold Schoenberg.* Edited by Leonard Stein. Translated by Leo Black. Berkeley and Los Angeles: University of California Press, 1984.

——. *Theory of Harmony.* Translated by Roy E. Carter. Berkeley and Los Angeles: University of California Press, 1978.

——. "Vortrag/12 TK/Princeton." Edited and translated by Claudio Spies. *PNM* 13 (1974): 58–136.

Schoenberg, E. Randol. "Arnold Schoenberg and Albert Einstein: Their Relationship and Views on Zionism." *JASI* 10/2 (1987): 134–191.

Schoenberg, Lawrence, and Ellen Kravitz. "Catalog of Arnold Schoenberg's Paintings, Drawings, and Sketches." *JASI* 2/3 (1978): 185–231.

Schoenberg-Nono, Nuria, ed. *Arnold Schoenberg: Self-Portrait.* Pacific Palisades: Belmont, 1988.

Schorske, Carl E. *Fin-de-siècle Vienna: Politics and Culture.* New York: Vintage Books, 1981.

Schroeder, David. "Arnold Schoenberg as Poet and Librettist: Dualism,

Epiphany, and *Die Jakobsleiter.*" In Cross, *Political and Religious Ideas in the Works of Arnold Schoenberg,* pp. 41–59.

Schweiger, Werner J. *Der Junge Kokoschka: Leben und Werk, 1904–1914.* Vienna and Munich: Edition Christian Brandstätter, 1983.

Shaw, Jennifer. "Androgyny and the Eternal Feminine in Schoenberg's Oratorio *Die Jakobsleiter.*" In Cross, *Political and Religious Ideas in the Works of Arnold Schoenberg,* pp. 61–83.

——. "New Performance Sources and Old Modernist Productions: *Die Jakobsleiter* in the Age of Mechanical Reproduction." *Journal of Musicology* 19/3 (2002): 434–460.

——. "Schoenberg's Choral Symphony, *Die Jakobsleiter,* and Other Wartime Fragments." Ph.D. dissertation, State University of New York at Stony Brook, 2002.

Shawn, Allen. *Arnold Schoenberg's Journey.* New York: Farrar, Straus, and Giroux, 2002.

Shirakawa, Sam. *The Devil's Music Master: The Controversial Life and Career of Wilhelm Furtwängler.* New York and Oxford: Oxford University Press, 1992.

Shoaf, R. Wayne. *The Schoenberg Discography.* Berkeley: Fallen Leaf Press, 1986.

——. "The Schoenberg-Malkin Correspondence." *JASI* 13/2 (1990): 164–257.

Simms, Bryan. *The Atonal Music of Arnold Schoenberg, 1908–1923.* Oxford and New York: Oxford University Press, 2000.

——. "New Documents in the Schoenberg-Schenker Polemic." *PNM* 16 (1977): 110–124.

——. *Schoenberg, Berg, and Webern: A Companion to the Second Viennese School.* Westport, Conn.: Greenwood Press, 1999.

——. "Schoenberg's Early Fragmentary Operas" (forthcoming).

——. "The Society for Private Musical Performances: Resources and Documents in Schoenberg's Legacy." *JASI* 3/2 (1979): 127–150.

——. "Who First Composed Twelve-Tone Music, Schoenberg or Hauer?" *JASI* 10/2 (1987): 109–133.

——. "Whose Idea Was *Erwartung?*" In Brand, *Constructive Dissonance,* pp. 100–111.

Slonimsky, Nicolas. *Lexicon of Musical Invective: Critical Assaults on Composers Since Beethoven's Time.* Seattle and London: University of Washington Press, 1965.

——, ed. *Music Since 1900.* New York: Schirmer, 1971.

Smith, Joan Allen. *Schoenberg and His Circle: A Viennese Portrait.* New York: Schirmer, 1986.

Specht, Robert John. "Relationships Between Text and Music in the Choral Works of Arnold Schoenberg." Ph.D. dissertation, Case Western Reserve University, 1976.

——. "Schoenberg Among the Workers: Choral Conducting in Pre-1900 Vienna." *JASI* 10/1 (1987): 28–37.

Spratt, John. "The Speculative Content of Schoenberg's *Harmonielehre*." *Current Musicology* 11 (1971): 83–88.

Squire, W. H. Haddon. "Schönberg in London." *Christian Science Monitor.* February 23, 1928.

Stein, Leonard. "A Note on the Genesis of the *Ode to Napoleon*." *JASI* 2/1 (1977): 52–53.

——. "From Inception to Realization in the Sketches of Schoenberg." *Bericht über den 1. Kongress der Internationalen Schönberg-Gesellschaft, Wien: 4–9 Juni, 1974,* pp. 213–227. Vienna: Verlag Elizabeth Lafite, 1978.

——. "Schoenberg and 'Kleine Modernsky.'" In *Confronting Stravinsky.* Edited by Jann Pasler. Berkeley and Los Angeles: University of California Press, 1986.

——. "Schoenberg: Five Statements." *PNM* 14 (1975): 168–171.

——. "Schoenberg's Jewish Identity: A Chronology of Source Materials." *JASI* 3/1 (1979): 3–10.

Steiner, Fred. "A History of the First Complete Recording of the Schoenberg String Quartets." *JASI* 2/2 (1978): 122–137.

Steiner, Ena. "The 'Happy' Hand: Genesis and Interpretation of Schoenberg's *Monumentalkunstwerk*." *Music Review* 51 (1959): 207–222.

Stephan, Rudolf. "Der musikalische Gedanke bei Schönberg." *Österreichische Musik Zeitschrift* 37/10 (1982): 530–540.

——. "Ein frühes Dokument der Zwölftonkomposition." In *Festschrift Arno Forchert zum 60. Geburtstag am 29. Dezember 1985.* Edited by Gerhard Allroggen and Detlef Altenburg, pp. 296–302. Basel, London, New York: Bärenreiter Kassel, 1986.

——. "Schönbergs Entwurf über 'Das Komponieren mit selbständige Stimmen.'" *Archiv für Musikwissenshaft* 29 (1972): 239–256.

——. "Über Schönbergs Arbeitsweise." In *Arnold Schönberg, Gedenkausstellung 1974.* Edited by Ernst Hilmar, pp. 119–124. Vienna: Universal Edition, 1974.

——, ed. *Bericht über den 1. Kongress der Internationalen Schönberg-Gesellschaft, Wien: 4–9 Juni, 1974.* Vienna: Verlag Elizabeth Lafite, 1978.

——, ed. *Bericht über den 2. Kongress der Internationalen Schönberg-Gesellschaft, Die Wiener Schule in der Musikgeschichte des 20. Jahrhunderts.* Vienna: Verlag Elizabeth Lafite, 1986.

Steuermann, Clara. "Schoenberg's Library Catalog." *JASI* 3/2 (1979): 203–218.

Steuermann, Edward. *The Not Quite Innocent Bystander: Writings of Edward Steuermann.* Edited by Clara Steuermann et al. Translated by Richard Cantwell and Charles Messner. Lincoln: University of Nebraska Press, 1989.

Stevens, Halsey. "A Conversation with Schoenberg about Painting." *JASI* 2/3 (1978): 178–180.

Strindberg, August. *Ein Blaubuch: Die Synthese Meines Lebens.* Translated by Emil Schering. *August Strindbergs Werke: Deutsche Gesamtausgabe.* Munich: Georg Müller, 1919.

Stuckenschmidt, H. H. *Arnold Schoenberg: His Life, World, and Work.* Translated by Humphrey Searle. New York: Schirmer, 1978.

Taruskin, Richard. "Back to Whom? Neoclassicism as Ideology." *19th-Century Music* 16/3 (1993): 286–302.

Tatar, Maria. *Lustmord: Sexual Murder in Weimar Germany.* Princeton: Princeton University Press, 1995.

Theurich, Jetta. "Briefwechsel zwischen Arnold Schönberg und Ferrucio Busoni." *Beiträge zur Musikwissenschaft* 19/3 (1977): 163–211.

Thrun, Martin. *Neue Musik im Deutschen Musikleben bis 1933.* Bonn: Orpheus, 1995.

Türcke, Berthold. "The Schoenberg-Mengelberg Correspondence." *JASI* 6/2 (1982): 181–237.

Vergo, Peter. *Art in Vienna, 1898–1918: Klimt, Kokoschka, Schiele, and Their Contemporaries.* Ithaca: Cornell University Press, 1975.

Weber, Horst, ed. *Briefwechsel der Wiener Schule: Volume 1, Alexander Zemlinsky, Briefwechsel mit Arnold Schönberg, Anton Webern, Alban Berg und Franz Schreker.* Darmstadt: Wissenschaftliche Buchgesellschaft, 1995.

Webern, Anton. *The Path to the New Music.* Edited by Willi Reich. Translated by Leo Black. Bryn Mawr, Penn.: Theodore Presser, 1963.

Weiss, Peg. "Evolving Perceptions of Kandinsky and Schoenberg: Toward the Ethnic Roots of the 'Outsider.'" In Brand, *Constructive Dissonance,* pp. 35–57.

Weiss, Piero, and Richard Taruskin, eds. *Music in the Western World: A History in Documents.* New York: Schirmer, 1984.

Weissmann, Adolf. *The Problems of Modern Music.* Translated by M. M. Bozman. Westport, Conn.: Hyperion Press, 1979.

Wellesz, Egon. *Arnold Schoenberg.* Translated by W. H. Kerridge. London: J. M. Dent and Sons, 1925; reprint, New York: Da Capo Press, 1969.

White, Eric Walter. *Stravinsky: The Composer and His Works.* Berkeley and Los Angeles: University of California Press, 1966.

Wickes, Lewis. "Schoenberg, *Erwartung,* and the Reception of Psychoanalysis in Musical Circles in Vienna until 1910/11." *Studies in Music* 23 (1989): 88–106.

Wulf, Josef. *Musik im Dritten Reich: Eine Dokumentation.* Gütersloh: Sigbert Mohn Verlag, 1963.

Zaunschirm, Thomas, ed. *Arnold Schönberg: Das bildnerische Werk / Arnold Schoenberg: Paintings and Drawings.* Klagenfurt: Ritter, 1991.

Zukofsky, Paul, R. Wayne Shoaf, Stephen Davison, Marilyn McCoy, Camille Crittenden, and Jacob Vonk. "A Preliminary Inventory of Correspondence to and from Arnold Schoenberg." *JASI* 18/1–2; 19/1–2 (1995–1996): 9–752.

Index